From a photo by   Beken & Son, Cowes, I. of W.

Sailing Boats

from Around the World

The Classic 1906 Treatise

Henry Coleman Folkard

DOVER PUBLICATIONS, INC.
Mineola, New York

Published in Canada by General Publishing Company, Ltd., 30 Lesmill Road, Don Mills, Toronto, Ontario.

Bibliographical Note

This Dover edition, first published in 2000, is an unabridged republication of the Sixth Edition of the work originally published in 1906 under the title *The Sailing Boat: A Treatise on Sailing Boats and Small Yachts* by Chapman and Hall, Ltd., London.

Library of Congress Cataloging-in-Publication Data

Folkard, Henry Coleman, 1827–1914.
 Sailing boats from around the world : the classic 1906 treatise / Henry Coleman Folkard.
   p. cm.
 Originally published: The sailing boat. London : Chapman and Hall, 1906.
 Includes bibliographical references and index.
 ISBN 0-486-41099-4 (pbk.)
  1. Sailboats. 2. Sailing ships. 3. Sailing. I. Folkard, Henry Coleman, 1827–1914. Sailing boat. II. Title.

VM321 .F663 2000
623.8'203—dc21

00-025778

Manufactured in the United States of America
Dover Publications, Inc., 31 East 2nd Street, Mineola, N.Y. 11501

PREFACE

TO

THE SIXTH EDITION.

In the previous edition of this work the Author remarked, in Part IV, on the changeable and unsatisfactory mode of measurement and rating of small yachts for racing purposes, and on the elasticity of the rules of measurement promulgated by the Yacht Racing Association, which culminated in the load-water-line being made the basis of the rule of measurement for classification and rating for match-sailing.

The objections to that mode of measurement and the inevitable results are reiterated in the text of the present edition.

Since the publication of the previous edition a Conference has been held for the purpose of considering and adopting an international mode of measurement for racing-yachts; the result of which will be found stated at page 166 of this edition.

As to the Illustrations (other than photogravures) contained in this work, the majority of the drawings from which they have been produced are pen-and-ink sketches by the Author himself, in which the one object throughout has been simply that of accurate delineation of the type or form of the craft below as well as above the water-line, with sails, rig and other details : though, as an inevitable result, pretty effect in the pen-and-ink sketches has thus been sacrificed to strict detail.

Preface to the Sixth Edition.

As to many of the Illustrations in Part VIII., 'Foreign and Colonial Boats,' they are from sketches made by the Author from time to time when on voyage and tour in foreign parts : others he made from models in the United Service and other Museums ; and some are from paintings, models and drawings in his own and other private collections ; a few only having been copied from well-authenticated works of voyage and travel.

The Author regrets that space would not admit of his including in this volume fuller details as to the larger classes of yachts. At the outset he intended doing so, having for many years past been collecting materials for the purpose, more particularly with reference to some of the most famous of the racing-fleet of the last century ; but as the subject would have extended these pages beyond the ordinary limits of a single volume, and would thereby have further delayed its publication, he felt compelled to abandon that intention.

Throughout the present work care has been taken to give accurate descriptions as well as illustrations not only of the different classes of small yachts and sailing-boats of the British Islands, but also of the most curious and remarkable boats, canoes and sailing-vessels of the various countries of the world.

TEMPLE,
    LONDON.

CONTENTS.

PART I.

PAGE

BOATS OF THE ANCIENTS . . . . 1 to 14

PART II.

SAILING BOATS OF THE BRITISH ISLANDS . . . . 15 to 96

PART III.

PRACTICAL: MANAGEMENT, &c., &c. . . . . 97 to 161

PART IV.

SMALL RACING-YACHTS AND YARAFTS . . . . 162 to 232

PART V.

THE ONE-DESIGN AND RESTRICTED CLASSES . . . . 233 to 326

PART VI.

FISHING AND SHOOTING BOATS . . . . 327 to 349

PART VII.

SAILING CHARIOTS AND ICE YACHTS . . . . 350 to 361

PART VIII.

FOREIGN AND COLONIAL BOATS, CANOES, &c. . . . . . . 362 to 539

PART IX.

NAUTICAL VOCABULARY . . . . 540 to 547

INDEX . . . . 549 to 555

LIST OF ILLUSTRATIONS.

FRONTISPIECE—A SAILING BOAT.

PART I.

BOATS OF THE ANCIENTS.

PAGE	DESCRIPTION.	DRAWING BY
2.	A Trireme	The Author.
4.	An ancient Pleasure Boat	,,
7.	Roman Galley (section, &c.)	,,
9.	Coracle	,,
13.	Modern Irish Curragh	,,

PART II.

SAILING BOATS OF THE BRITISH ISLANDS.

PAGE	DESCRIPTION.	DRAWING BY
16.	Sea Lugger	J. R. Kirby.
17.	Half-decked boat	The Author.
18.	Combination row and sail boat	J. H. Rushton.
18.	Plan of Combination row and sail boat	,,
20.	Pilot Lugger	J. R. Kirby.
22.	Sprit-sail and foresail rig	The Author.
24.	Three-masted Sprit-sail	,,
25.	Anglo-Bermudian rig	,,
27.	The Settee rig	T. Sulman.
28.	Settee with mizzen	The Author.
28.	Sliding-gunter rig	,,

ix

List of Illustrations.

PAGE	DESCRIPTION.	DRAWING BY
29.	Sliding-gunter rig with mizzen	The Author.
31.	The Una rig	,,
32.	The Sloop rig	,,
34.	The Cutter rig	Photogravure.
35.	Old type of Cutter rig.	The Author.
36.	Cutter rig (tail piece)	Photogravure.
37.	Schooner rig	,,
38.	Square-rigged Schooner.	,,
39.	Captain's gig (tail piece)	J. R. Kirby.
40.	The Ketch rig	Photogravure.
42.	The Yawl rig	,,
43.	The Yawl rig (tail piece)	,,
44.	The 'Wenda' Canoe yacht.	Albert Strange.
45.	The 'Wenda' Canoe yacht (sail plan)	,,
46.	The Lugger rig	J. R. Kirby.
49.	The Lugger rig (another form)	,,
50.	The Split-lug rig	The Author.
51.	The 'Querida' (split-lug type)	Photogravure.
52.	Yarmouth Salvage Yawl	J. R. Kirby.
54.	Yarmouth Beach boat	Photogravure.
55.	Yorkshire Coble	The Author.
57.	Yorkshire Coble (under sail)	,,
58.	Yorkshire Pilot Coble.	J. R. Kirby.
60.	The Latine rig	The Author.
62.	The Latine rig (sails goose-winged)	,,
63.	Norfolk Latine	The Author.
65.	The Strangford Latine	Lord de Ros.
66.	Norfolk Wherry	T. Sulman.
67.	A Quant (Norfolk)	The Author.
68.	The Solent rig (two sails)	Photogravure.
69.	The Solent rig (three sails)	,,
70.	The 'Fairy'	J. R. Kirby.
71.	Bembridge Club boat (profile and section)	Capt. E. du Boulay.
73.	Sailing Canoe, with Radix folding-plate	The Author.
74.	Cruising Canoe rig	J. H. Rushton.
75.	New style of Canoe rig	,,
76.	The Mohican rig.	,,
77.	Canoe Cruising-Yawl 'Lapwing'	Max Howard.
80.	Canoe Yacht 'Otter'	Albert Strange.
81.	Canoe Yacht 'Otter' (sail plan)	,,
82.	The Revolving rig	Capt. M. Shuldham.
84.	The Revolving rig (scudding).	,,
86.	Single-masted Revolver	The Author.
89.	The Revolver close refeed	Capt. M. Shuldham.
90.	Centre-board keel	The Author.
90.	Sliding-keel	,,

List of Illustrations.

PAGE	DESCRIPTION.	DRAWING BY
91.	Revolving-keel	The Author.
91.	Revolving-keel (example of)	,,
92.	The 'Truant' (sloop-rigged American boat)	,,
94.	The 'Vigilant' (American) Profile	,,
95.	Revolving or Drop-rudder	J. H. Rushton.

PART III.

PRACTICAL.

——◆——

102.	Boat-sailing	Photogravure.
103.	A Lady's Sailing-boat	,,
104.	Becalmed	,,
105.	At Anchor on the Medina	,,
107.	Stability under sail	,,
108.	Tail piece	,,
109.	Sailing-boat 'Cobalt'	,,
110.	Sailing-boat 'Spell"	,,
111.	The 'Semibreve'	Capt. E du Boulay.
112.	Profile, showing fin and bulb keel	T. Sulman.
113.	Profile, American	The Author.
113.	Profile, another type	,,
114.	Profile (Sibbick type)	,,
114.	Profile, a British design	,,
115.	Profile, another type	,,
115.	Sailing-boat 'Speedwell'	Photogravure.
117.	The Angulated Jib . . , ...	Matthew Orr.
119.	Sailing-boat with Battens in mainsail	Photogravure.
120.	Sailing-boat (tail piece)	,,
122.	Setting sail	,,
123.	Cutter yacht 'Ermin' under reefed mainsail	,,
124.	Cutter yacht 'Zerlina' under reefed mainsail . . .	,,
125.	Sailing-boat with roller foresail	,,
127.	A Lady of the West steering her Yacht to victory . . .	,,
128.	Sailing to windward	,,
129.	Sailing-boat 'Thetis' (no heads above deck)	,,
130.	Sailing-boat 'Edie' (close-hauled)	,,
131.	Reaching and sailing on a bowline	,,
133.	Sailing-boat 'Grafin' scudding	,,

List of Illustrations.

PAGE	DESCRIPTION.	DRAWING BY
134.	Sailing-boat 'Will o' th' Wisp' scudding	Photogravure.
136.	Boats at moorings	,,
138.	Boat with sails furled	,,
140.	Match-sailing, Start of Yachts at Cowes	,,
141.	Racing-cutter 'Caress'	,,
142.	Racing-cutter 'Koorangah'	,,
143.	Racing-cutter of 1850	The Author.
145.	Blanketing an opponent	Photogravure.
146.	Boat-racing by Ladies	,,
148.	Sailing-boats in a squall	,,
149.	Sailing-boat 'Sheelah' in a squall	,,
151.	Sailing-boat capsized	,,
152.	Just before the capsize	,,
156.	A Drogue	The Author.
157.	Sailing-boat in a gale	J. R. Kirby.
158.	Sea boat with balance-reef	The Author.
161.	Boat-lowering apparatus	,,

PART IV.

SMALL RACING YACHTS.

———

162.	Group of small racing yachts	Photogravure.
163.	The Yaraft	The Author.
166.	The 'Plover,' Solent One-Design boat	Photogravure.
168.	Profile and section of Skimming-dish type	The Author.
168.	Profile and section of Skimming-dish type, deck plan	,,
169.	Tail piece	Photogravure.
170.	Upper Thames Sailing-boat	The Author.
171.	Upper Thames Racing-yaraft 'Tiger Cat'	Photogravure.
172.	Like tailors on a shop-board	,,
173.	Group of small yachts and yarafts off Ryde	,,
174.	Profile showing Dagger-blade type of centre-plate	The Author.
175.	The Solent sea	Photogravure.
177.	Start of Half-raters (yarafts)	,,
178.	Profile of an 18-ft. linear rater	The Author.
180.	Profile of 'Diamond,' 18-feet linear rater	,,
182.	Profile of 'Spruce IV.' with deep narrow fin-plate and bulb	,,

List of Illustrations.

PAGE	DESCRIPTION.	DRAWING BY
183.	Profile of American boat 'Wee Win'	The Author.
184.	Profile of 'Kismet,' with sails and rig	,,
185.	Sailing-craft 'Viva' and 'Pique' half-raters	Photogravure.
187.	A Flag for every victory	,,
188.	Start of one-raters	,,
189.	Sailing-boat 'Fay II.' (young lady steering)	,,
190.	Profile of 'Gaiety Girl' (successful prize-winner)	The Author.
190.	Sailing-boat 'Gallia' (one-rater)	Photogravure.
191.	Sailing-boat 'Tartar VII.'	,,
192.	Sailing-boat 'Triangle' (24-footer)	,,
193.	Sailing-boat 'Bandicoot' (24-footer)	,,
194.	Sailing-boat 'Eione' (one-rater)	,,
195.	Group of $2\frac{1}{2}$ raters	,,
196.	Profile of famous boat 'Gareth'	The Author.
197.	Sailing-boat 'Corolla' ($2\frac{1}{2}$ rater)	Photogravure.
198.	Profile of 'Corolla' showing fin and bulb keel	The Author.
198.	'Vaquero' (American design)	Photogravure.
199.	'Nanta,' $2\frac{1}{2}$ rater (1895)	,,
200.	'Strathendrick' and 'Petrel' racing	,,
201.	Profile of American boat 'Swanhild'	The Author.
202.	Profile of 30-rating Cruiser (body plans and section)	J. S. Helyer.
203.	Profile of 30-rating Cruiser (sail plan)	,,
204.	'Emerald' and 'Forella' racing	Photogravure.
205.	Profile of 'Dacia' (body plan)	The Author.
206.	'Fenella,' body and sail plan	,,
207.	'Norman,' body and sail plan	,,
208.	'Sea shell' (broad and shallow type)	Photogravure.
209.	'Heartsease' racing cutter	,,
210.	'Westra' under reefed mainsail and foresail	,,
210.	Profile of 'Hermes,' 36-footer (body plan)	The Author.
211.	'Koorangah,' 36-footer	Photogravure.
212.	'Forella,' racing cutter	,,
213.	'Eileen,' racing cutter	,,
214.	'Sakuntala,' racing cutter	,,
215.	Profile showing old type of racing yacht	The Author.
216.	Profile of 'Tiny,' 8 ton Cruising yacht	,,
216.	Profile of 'Yseult' (1892)	,,
216.	Profile of 'Trial' (1889)	,,
217.	Profile of 'Janetta' (1890)	,,
217.	Profile of 'Typical winning boat' (1890)	,,
217.	Profile of 'Beatrix' (1892)	,,
218.	Profile of 'Manx Cat' (1893)	,,
218.	Profile of 'Squall' (1893)	,,
219.	Profile of 'Kelpie'	,,
219.	Profile of 'Helen'	,,
219.	Profile of 'Sarnia'	,,

PAGE	DESCRIPTION.	DRAWING BY
221.	Profile of Model Yacht showing novel arrangement of fin and bulb keel	The Author.
222.	Profile of ' Heathen Chinee ' (curious type)	,,
223.	' Fan Tan,' curious bat's-wing sails	Photogravure.
224.	Profile body plan of ' Fan Tan '	Landseer MacKenzie.
225.	Triangular keel-yacht ' Problem '	H. Dempster.
226.	Plans of Hull, Deck, &c., of ' Problem '	The Author.
227.	Swan boats.	,,
230.	The Umbrella boat-rig	Photogravure.
231.	' Nautilus ' rig	The Author.
232.	' Nautilus ' close reefed	,,

PART V.

THE ONE DESIGN AND RESTRICTED CLASSES.

233.	Start of Solent One-Design Boats at Cowes	Photogravure.
234.	Solent O.-D. Boats racing	,,
235.	A Solent O.-D. Boat	,,
237.	A Belfast Lough O.-D. Boat	,,
239.	Solent O.-D. Class, body and deck plans	H. W. White.
240.	' Eilun ' Solent O.-D. Class	Photogravure.
241.	' Philippine ' Solent O.-D. Class	,,
242.	Redwing Class, ' Paroquet ' and ' Jeanie '.	,,
242.	Profile, body plan, Redwing Class	The Author.
243.	Profile, midship section, Redwing Class	,,
243.	' Jeanie,' Redwing Class	Photogravure.
245.	Solent ' Sea Bird ' Class, body, deck and sail plans . . .	H. Gale.
247.	' Western ' 25 ft., l. r., O.-D. Class, body plan and section . .	A. F. G. Brown.
248.	' Western ' 25 ft., l. r., O.-D. Class, sail plan	,,
250.	Raleigh Class, sail and body plan and section	G. N. Philip.
252.	Teignmouth Dinghy Class, body plan and section . . .	G. F. Flemmick.
252.	Teignmouth Dinghy Class, sail plan	,,
253.	Bristol Channel O.-D. Class, body plans and section . . .	Harold Clayton.
254.	Bristol Channel O.-D. Class, sail plan	,,
255.	Trent Valley O.-D. Class, body plans and sections . . .	C. Bathurst.
256.	Trent Valley O.-D. Class, sail plan	,,
258.	Orford White Wings O.-D. Class, body and sail plans and section	H. W. Ridsdale.
259.	Yorkshire and Hull O.-D. Class, body plans and section . .	J. S. Helyer.
260.	Yorkshire and Hull O.-D. Class, sail plan	J. S. Helyer.

List of Illustrations.

PAGE	DESCRIPTION.	DRAWING BY
261.	Southport Corinthian O.-D. Class, body plan and section	W. Scott Hayward.
262.	West Lancashire Y. C. O.-D. Class 'Imp'	Photogravure.
264.	West Lancashire Sea-bird Class, body plans.	W. Scott Hayward.
264.	West Lancashire Sea-bird Class, midship section	,,
265.	West Lancashire Sea-bird Class, sail plan	,,
266.	West Lancashire O.-D., Class III., profile, body plan and section	,,
266.	Southport Corinthian O.-D. Class, profile, body plan and section	,,
267.	'Ma Mie,' Southport Corinthian O.-D. Class	Photogravure.
267.	Hoylake Sailing Club, Restricted Class, 'Slut,' body plan and section	W. Scott Hayward.
268.	Hoylake Sailing Club, Restricted Class, 'Slut,' sail plan	,,
270.	'Mischief,' New Brighton Restricted Class, sail plan	M. T. Reade.
271.	'Mischief,' body plans and midship section	,,
273.	Yachts becalmed on Lake Windermere	Photogravure.
274.	Sailing-yachts on Lake Windermere	,,
275.	Windermere Y. C. modern type of yacht	,,
276.	'Sirius,' Lake Windermere Yacht	,,
277.	'Turtle,' Lake Windermere Yacht	,,
278.	Lake Windermere Yachts : a close finish	,,
280.	Clyde Yachts racing	,,
281.	Clyde Yacht 'Alruda'	,,
282.	Clyde Class, Yacht 'Vida I.,' body and deck plan	G. L. Watson.
283.	Clyde Class, Yacht 'Vida I.,' midship section	,,
284.	Clyde Class, Yacht 'Vida I.,' sail plan	,,
285.	'Vida II.,' Clyde Restricted Class	Photogravure.
285.	'Klysma,' Clyde Restricted Class	,,
286.	Clyde Restricted Class, 'Lola' and others racing	,,
287.	'Hatasoo,' Clyde 17 ft. Class	,,
288.	'Ceres,' Clyde 19 ft. Class	,,
289.	Diagram, showing mode of measurement	From Club Rules.
291.	Clyde 20 ton O.-D. Class, midship section	Alfred Mylne.
292.	Clyde 20 ton O.-D. Class, body and deck plans	,,
293.	Clyde 20 ton O.-D. Class, sail plan	,,
294.	Yacht 'Noyra,' Clyde 20 ton Class	Photogravure.
295.	Clyde Innellan Corinthian Class, Start of	,,
295.	'Lola,' Clyde Innellan Corinthian Class	,,
296.	Innellan Corinthian Class, body plan	J. & H. M. Paterson.
296.	Innellan Corinthian Class, midship section	,,
297.	Innellan Corinthian Class, sail plan	,,
298.	Tay Sea-bird, 18 ft. O.-D. Class, body and deck plans	Alfred Mylne.
299.	Tay Sea-bird, 18 ft. O.-D. Class, midship section	,,
299.	Tay Sea-bird, 18 ft. O.-D. Class, sail plan	,,
300.	Sailing Boat of the Tay, O.-D. Class	Photogravure.
300.	Holy Loch Sailing Club, O.-D. Class, body and deck plans	Alfred Mylne.
301.	Holy Loch Sailing Club, O.-D. Class, sail plan and midship section	,,

List of Illustrations.

PAGE	DESCRIPTION.	DRAWING BY
302.	Belfast Lough Sea-bird, O.-D. Class, Start of Class I.	Photogravure.
303.	Belfast Lough Sea-bird, O.-D. Class, 'Flamingo' and 'Widgeon' racing	,,
304.	Belfast Lough Sea-bird, O.-D. Class, 'Merle,' Class I.	,,
305.	Belfast Lough Sea-bird Class, body and deck plans	W. Fife, junr.
306.	Belfast Lough Sea-bird Class, midship section and sail plan	,,
307.	Belfast Lough O.-D., Class II., Group of Yachts	Photogravure.
308.	Belfast Lough O.-D., Class II., body and deck plans	W. Fife, junr.
309.	Belfast Lough O.-D., Class II., midship section and sail plan	,,
310.	Belfast Lough Jewel Class, yacht 'Opal'.	Photogravure.
311.	Belfast Lough Jewel Class, yacht 'Opal,' sail and body plan, and midship section	Linton Hope.
312.	Belfast Lough New O.-D. Class, body and deck plans	Alfred Mylne.
313.	Belfast Lough New O.-D. Class, midship section	,,
314.	Belfast Lough New O.-D. Class, sail plan	,,
315.	Ulster Insect Class, 'Moth' and 'Hornet'	Photogravure.
318.	Water Wags, New Class, body and deck plans, midship and other sections	J. E. Doyle.
319.	Water Wags, New Class, sail plan	,,
321.	Droleen O.-D. Class, body, deck and sail plans.	W. Ogilvy.
322.	Droleen O.-D. Class, boat under sail	Photogravure.
323.	Cork Harbour O.-D. Class, sail plan .	W. Fife, junr.
324.	Cork Harbour O.-D. Class boat	Photogravure.
326.	Tail piece .	,,

PART VI.

FISHING AND SHOOTING BOATS.

———

328.	Profile, Fishing Smack showing perforated Well for live fish	The Author.
330.	South Coast Fishing-boat.	,,
331.	Cornish Fishing Lugger	,,
332.	Yorkshire Fishing Coble .	,,
333.	Brixham Trawler .	,,
334.	Scottish (Zulu) Fishing-boat	,,
336.	Orkney and Shetland Isles, Fishing-boat	,,
339.	The Peter boat .	,,
341.	Shooting Yacht 'Wildfowler'	,,
342.	Gunning Punt .	,,

List of Illustrations.

PAGE	DESCRIPTION.	DRAWING BY
344.	Sailing Punt	The Author.
346.	'Hooper,' Sloop-rigged Shooting-boat	,,
348.	The Beacon Light	,,

PART VII.

SAILING CHARIOTS AND ICE YACHTS.

352.	The Shuldham Land Sailing-boats	Capt. M. Shuldham.
356.	The Shuldham Ice boat	,,
358.	American Ice Yacht, runner plank	The Author.
359.	American Ice Yacht with sails, side view	,,
360.	American Ice Yacht, rudder skate	,,

PART VIII.

FOREIGN AND COLONIAL BOATS.

366.	Boat of the Ancient Egyptians	The Author.
368.	Dahabéëh and other Boats of the Nile	,,
371.	Egyptian Funambuli furling the sail	,,
373.	American Yacht 'America'	,,
376.	The American Cat rig	,,
377.	American Sharpey, midship section	,,
378.	Rig of Sharpey (two-masted)	,,
379.	Rig of Sharpey (single-masted)	,,
381.	'Glencairn,' Canadian racing-boat	,,
383.	'Glencairn,' sail plan	G. H. Duggan.
385.	Canadian Birch-bark Canoe	The Author.
388.	Birch-bark Canoes of Nova Scotia	,,
390.	Canoe of Oregon Indians	,,
392.	Bermudian Sailing-boats	F. Fowke.

List of Illustrations.

PAGE	DESCRIPTION.	DRAWING BY
394.	Bermudian rig, showing boom fittings, &c.	The Author.
396.	Tail-piece	,,
397.	Portuguese Sailing-boat.	,,
398.	Madeira Boat	,,
399.	Maltese Galley, under sail	,,
400.	Maltese Galley, deck plan	,,
400.	Maltese Galley, mid-section	,,
403.	Modern Sailing-boats of the Mediterranean.	,,
405.	Venetian Gondola	T. Sulman.
408.	Boat of the Italian Riviera	The Author.
410.	Native Sailing-boat of the Lake of Geneva	,,
412.	Cargo boat of Lake Zurich	,,
412.	Boat of Lake Thun	,,
415.	Norway Yawl	,,
416.	Sondmore Yawl	,,
418.	Norway Praäm	,,
422.	Dutch Boëyer rig	The Author.
423.	Dutch Spiegel rig	,,
424.	Dutch Fishing Schuyt	R. T. Pritchett.
426.	Turkish State Caïque	The Author.
429.	Arab Batelle	,,
430.	Arab Pirate Boat	R. T. Pritchett.
431.	The Bugala	,,
435.	Indian Pleasure Boat	The Author.
436.	A famous yacht of the Bombay Yacht Club	,,
439.	Bombay Dinghy	J. R. Kirby.
441.	Ganges Sailing-Boat	The Author.
443.	Ganges Rowing-Boat	,,
444.	Pattamar, sailing with a free wind	,,
446.	Mohr Punkee	,,
447.	Massoolah Surf Boat	,,
450.	Madras Fishing Catamaran	,,
451.	Madras Sailing Catamaran and section	,,
452.	The Dhoney and section	,,
455.	Sailing Canoe of Ceylon	,,
456.	Sailing Canoe of Ceylon	,,
458.	Burmese Pleasure Boat	,,
460.	Canoe of Andaman Islanders	,,
461.	Tail-piece, Indian boat	,,
463.	Flying Proa of the Ladrone Islands	Anson's Voyages.
467.	Sailing-boat of Borneo and Celebes	Marryat's Borneo.
469.	Sooloo Canoe and section	The Author.
471.	Tartar Galley	,,
472.	Paduakans of Celebes	,,
475.	The Corocora	,,
477.	Kei Islanders' Canoe	,,

List of Illustrations.

PAGE	DESCRIPTION.	DRAWING BY
480.	Malay Jellore	The Author.
484.	Manilla Banca	,,
485.	Tambangan	,,
486.	Sandwich Islands Canoes	,,
488.	Fiji Islands Sailing Canoe	,,
491.	Friendly Islands Double Canoe	,,
494.	Canoe of Salòmon Islands	,,
495.	Savage Island Canoe	,,
497.	Samoan Canoe	,,
498.	Union Group Islands Canoe	,,
499.	Kingsmill Island Canoe	,,
501.	Section of Pahie	,,
501.	Tahiti Sailing Canoes	,,
502.	Common Tahitian Canoe	,,
503.	Double Canoe of the Paumotu Group	,,
504.	Wytoohee Canoe	,,
505.	South American Sailing Balza	,,
509.	Bahia Market Boat	,,
510.	Bahia Fruit Boat	,,
511.	Zangada of Pernambuco	,,
512.	Zangada of Pernambuco	,,
513.	Fuegian Canoe	,,
514.	Chinese Boats	,,
516.	The Sampan	,,
517.	Chinese River Junk	,,
518.	Chinese Sailing-boat	J. R. Kirby.
523.	Hoppos' Boat	The Author.
526.	Chinese Duck Boat	,,
529.	Japanese Cargo Boat	,,
530.	Japanese Pleasure Boat	,,
531.	Japanese Fishing Boat	,,
535.	Greenlander's Kaiak	,,
536.	Esquimaux Canoe and section	,,
537.	Tchuktchi Skin Canoe	,,
539.	Tail-piece	,,

THE SAILING-BOAT.

PART I.

BOATS OF THE ANCIENTS.

'Illi robur et æs triplex
Circa pectus erat, qui fragilem truci
Commisit pelago ratem
Primus.'—Hor. *Od.* I. iii. 9.

THE boats or vessels of the Ancients were of a very diminutive size in comparison with those of later date. Few of them exceeded the ordinary dimensions of a modern ship's launch. But as civilization advanced boats and vessels of larger size were constructed, though in a rude and primitive style; and when provided with vessels of burthen, it was a long time before the boldest mariners ventured to trust themselves and their vessels far from land.

The earliest mode of navigation was by rafts constructed of balks or planks of wood, to which were afterwards added borders of wicker-work, covered with the skins of animals. Of this kind were the Coracle of Ancient Britain, and the *Cymba sutilis* of Virgil.

It is mentioned by Homer that the boat built by Ulysses was put together with wooden pegs instead of bolts;[1] and that the gunwale was raised by hurdles of osiers to keep off the waves of the sea.[2]

The Egyptians had boats of *terra cotta*, and some of the leaves of the papyrus; the Indians made rafts and boats of bamboo cane. The skins of animals were used by the Romans and others for the outer covering of boats; and the Roman boatmen were called *Utricularii*.

The invention of ships was not known to the Romans until after the first Punic war, A.U.C. 490.[3]

[1] Od. v. 249. [2] Ib. 256. [3] Fosb. Encyclo. Antiq.

1

The Sailing-Boat.

To be represented in a boat was the Egyptian symbol of *apotheosis*; and many Emperors (as our Kings in a ship on their coins) are thus distinguished.[1]

The early Greeks are mentioned in history as the first who devoted attention to boat-building; the Trireme, Bireme, and other galleys were of their invention. The Trireme, which had three ranks or benches of rowers, was preceded by the Bireme with two such ranks; and the latter was a modification of the simple galley or long-ship, with only one rank on each side.[2] The bows of some of the war-galleys were ornamented with carved heads of boars and other ferocious animals, projecting four or five feet; beneath which was a sharp iron pike or *rostrum*. It was in boats of this

A Trireme, after Bafius, Schæffer, and others.

kind that the first naval action recorded in history was fought between the Greeks and their colonists, the inhabitants of Corfu.

The Romans afterwards improved upon the trireme, and built a faster class of vessels, called the Liburni: these were more manageable than the others, and better adapted for sailing. The Liburnian galleys were in use at the beginning of the Roman Empire; and the naval engagement at Actium, in which Augustus Cæsar was victorious over Antony, was fought and won in Liburnian galleys.

An Etruscan boat has the prow turned up, but the stern flat and concave, with a hole in the side for the rudder. The latter is merely a long oar for steering.[3]

In most of the vessels of the ancients it appears that the prow was made in the form of a fish, a dolphin, or the head of some animal, with the eyes very distinctly marked on both sides.

Vessels with oars long preceded those with sails. But whatever kind of sail was used, it was never relied on as the only means of propulsion: all ancient vessels were provided with oars, but the use of thowls in which to work them was apparently unknown, as the bulwarks or sides of the vessel were pierced with round holes, through which the oars were thrust and worked; and in vessels of the larger size, such as the

[1] Fosb. Encyclo. Antiq., Charnock's Marine Architecture, &c.
[2] See Ships and Sailors, Ancient and Modern, by C. C. Cotterill, B.A. and E. D. Little, B.A., 1868.
[3] Kirke, pl. 18.

Boats of the Ancients.

Liburni, in which the rowers sat in tiers one above the other, the oars were worked in the same manner : the boat being termed a *bireme* if there were two tiers of rowers, and *trireme* if three.   Homer mentions masts, but not fixed, only put up as wanted.

As to rudders, some vessels had two, others four, two at the prow and two at the stern.

The ancient practice of rowing was as follows :—a boatman-director, called *Celeustes*, gave the signal for the rowers to pull, and encouraged them by his song.   This song, termed the *celeusma*, was either sung by the rowers, played upon instruments, or effected by striking a gong, after the manner of the Chinese, Japanese, and others at the present day.   Ossian and others mention the rowing song :—

> ' And all the way to guide their chime,
> With falling oars they kept the time.'

The commander of the rowers, called *Hortator remigum*, *Pausarius*, and *Portisculus*, was placed among them in the middle of the boat.   He carried a staff, with which he signalled by waving or otherwise when his voice could not be heard.   The Anglo-Saxon *batswan* (boatswain) also used a staff wherewith to direct the rowers.

The Greeks had boats called *ampheres ;* these were long and narrow, and were rowed by a single boatman only, with one pair of sculls.   Rowing with the face to the prow is mentioned as customary with the ancients ; but this may have been paddling, or pushing ahead with a paddle or sweep.

The oar upon the Etruscan vases is in the form of a narrow pyramid from top to bottom.

Baldarius was the inventor of oars, as applied to large fighting vessels. [1]

Masts and sails are said to have been invented by Dædalus.   Varro says they were invented by Isis, who, with an affection bolder than usually falls to the lot of women, sailed in quest of her son Harpocrates : so that while her maternal fondness urged her to the completion of her wishes, she appears to have displayed to the world arts till then unknown to it.[2]

In Stosch and the Florentine Museum is a small vessel with oars, the prow of which ends in a *cheniscus* of the form of a swan's neck.   Precisely in the place of a mast and mizzen sail are two large extended wings, proper to catch the wind, as if for flying. This would seem to explain the fable of Dædalus.

---

[1] Aristoph. Ran. iv. 2.   Rutil. Itin. i. 367.   Pedian. ad Cicer. p. 37.   Xenoph. l. 5.   Polyb. i. 21.   Strutt's Horda, 70.   Kirke's Hamil. Vases, pl. 18.   Evelyn's Mem. i. 196.

[2] ' Vela Isis rata primum suspendit, cum per mare Harpocratem filium audaci fœminea pietate perquireret : ita dum materna charitas suum desiderium festinat explere, mundi visa est ignota reserare.'—Lib. v.

The Sailing-Boat.

The cheniscus, or swan's neck, was also, it appears, an ornament of the stern, but bent downwards towards the sea.[1]

The hull of the ancient galleys, as improved by the classical ancients, was made in conformation of the body of a duck, which was said to furnish the best model.[2]

The materials of which sails were anciently made were rushes, broom stuff, skins of animals, and the dried skins of the intestines of animals and fish; linen and hemp were afterwards used; indeed, from the time of Homer, linen was in use.

The forms of ancient sails were various—square, circular, crescent-shaped, and triangular, and the colours white, blue, purple, and sometimes curiously painted.

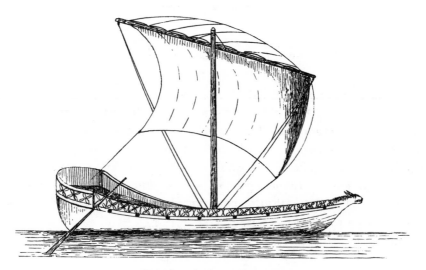

Navigiolum ad animum oblectandum.

According to Pliny, they were at first set one above another on the same mast; and afterwards on two masts, at the stern and prow.

The sails set on the stern or mizzen-mast were called *epidromus;* those on the fore-mast at the prow *dolones;* at the top of the mast *thoracium;* stun sails, called *orthiax,* were also used occasionally in very light winds. Sometimes, when two or more masts were used, the sail of the main-mast was called *artemon.*

The topsails were of a triangular or *latine* shape, and were sometimes set with the apex downwards.[3]

It is clear that both sails and oars were employed in many of the vessels of the

[1] Fosb. Ency. Ant.
[2] See Pownall's Provincia Romana, pl. 3, f. 7.
[3] Cotterill's Ships and Sailors, Ancient and Modern, p. 10.

ancients. Winckelman, however, observes that ships disposed for battle had neither sails nor yards.[1]

The boats and vessels of the classical ancients were of many kinds; with ten, twenty, thirty, and up to 100 oars. Those distinct from war service were as under :—[2]

Actuariæ naves—Long and light vessels, propelled both by oars and sails : never manned by less than twenty rowers.

Annotinæ Frumentariæ—Provision vessels.

Busse—A ship made like a wine-cask.

Calones—Boats for carrying wood.

Cercuri—Ships of burthen, both with sails and oars.

Celoces, or the Greek *Celetes*—Light vessels, used chiefly for piracy, with only two sets of oars, without deck or *rostra*.

Catascopia—Small despatch vessels, for carrying letters and reconnoitring.

Constratæ—Those which were entirely decked.

Cubiculatæ—Those with cabins and the conveniences of a house.

Dromones—Long boats, first used in rowing matches.

Fluviatiles—Boats of the river, as distinguished from those of the sea.

Gauli—Phœnician, and round for carriage.

Hippagines, or *Hippagogæ*—Transports for carrying horses and cavalry after the fleet.

Horiolæ—Small fishing boats.

Hornotinæ—Those built in a year.

Lenunculi—Small fishing boats.

Lentriæ.   Pontones fluviatiles—Those employed exclusively upon rivers.

Lembus—Light and undecked, used chiefly on rivers, and on the sea by pirates.

Liburna, Liburnica—Light galliots, used both with sails and oars; from one to five ranks of rowers.

Lintres—Canoes made out of the trunk of a tree, and capable of carrying three persons.

Lintrarii—Boatmen.

Leves—Very light boats without decks.

Longæ Militares—Built to carry a large number of men, all with oars.

Lusoriæ—Pleasure boats and vessels, used by the guards of the boundaries of the empire in large rivers.

---

[1] See also Stosch, Mus. Flor. t. ii. pl. lx. lxi. 5.   Enc. Mon. Ined. ii. 280.   Pliny, L. ii. 48.
[2] Vide Pollux. Aulus Gellius, x. 25.   Liv. xliv. 28.   Plaut. Fulgent. Enc.   Plaut. Rud. iv. 2. 5. Nonn. xiii. 8.

The Sailing-Boat.

Myopara—A fly boat; a corsair's vessel.

Moneres Monocratæ—Modern galleys, and vessels with only one rank of oars.

Naves tabellariæ—Advice boats.

Navigiolum ad animum oblectandum—A pleasure boat.

Onerariæ—Ships of burthen, both with sails and oars.

Orariæ, Littorariæ, Trabales—Coasting vessels.

Oriæ—Wherries, and very small fishing boats.

Parunculus—A small bark.

Phaselus—A small vessel, with sails and oars.

Prosumia—A small watch boat.

Piscatoriæ—Fisher boats.

Pontones—Ferry boats of a square form for carrying horses and carriages.

Plicatiles—Portable boats, built of wood and leather in such a manner as to be capable of being taken to pieces and carried over land.

Præcursoriæ—Boats which preceded the fleets.

Piraticæ, Prædatoriæ, Prædaticæ.—Long, swift, and light boats, used by pirates or picaroons.

Serilla—Boats or barges stuffed in the chinks with tow.

Sagitta, Saguntia—A kind of galley.

Scapha—A long boat.

Solutiles—Boats which fell to pieces of themselves, such as that in which Nero exposed Agrippina.

Stationariæ—Those which were moored or remained fixed at anchor.

Sutiles—Made of strong staves, and covered with leather.

Stlatæ—Broader than high; used by pirates.

Trabariæ—Canoes (same as *Lintres*).

Thalamegus—A yacht or vessel of parade and pleasure.

To the above list a few others might be added from Rosinus; but as the definitions are doubtful and various, the author has extended it no farther.

Although it is abundantly clear from this list that sails, as well as oars, were employed on some of the vessels of the ancients, it is doubtful if they practised the art of sailing to windward, with its accompanying tactics. There is, however, evidence that the Romans were acquainted with the art.

But whatever knowledge the ancients possessed of the use of sails as a moving power to the vessel, there is no doubt that they relied mainly on the oars as a means of propulsion, particularly in adverse winds; and that the sails were used only as an auxiliary in a fair wind.

The engraving represents the elevations, head and stern, of a Roman galley, with

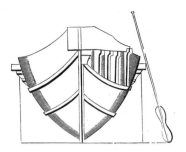

oar or paddle; it is taken from a model presented many years ago to Greenwich Hospital by Admiral Lord Anson.

This model is one of the most reliable authorities that can be referred to; it is made from one in marble, which was found in the Villa Mathei during the sixteenth century, and now stands before the Church of Santa Maria in Rome.

The model is not a war-galley, but was probably used for commercial purposes, or for the transportation of warlike stores, provisions, and troops.

BOATS OF THE ANGLO-SAXONS.

THE Anglo-Saxons appear to have had *pleasure vessels*, if such be the proper meaning of *pleg-scip*, *i.e.*, 'play-ship.' Some of these are described as having ovens, fireplaces, and other domestic conveniences: and boats covered with hides accompanied them.

The large sailing ships of the Anglo-Saxons were called *Carikes*.[1]

There were also *gallyetis*,[2] which were probably a small sort of galley.

They had also *Crayers*, or small fishing boats; and *Balingers*, small sailing vessels.

The Saxon ships of the eighth century were not much larger than the open pleasure boats of the present day; such as are used at seaside places for taking pleasure parties out to sea for a sail. Their prows and sterns were very erect, and stood high out of the water; and they were ornamented at the top with the rudely-carved head of some animal. They had but one mast, the top or head of which was also decorated with a bird, or some such device. To the mast was made fast a large sail, which from its nature and construction could only be available for the purpose of driving the vessel before the wind.[3]

The Saxons were very magnificent in the appearances of their royal vessels. King Athelstan had one (which was presented to him by Harold, King of Norway), the head of which was wrought with gold, the sails were purple, and the deck was elegantly gilt all round with gold.[4]

Both sails and oars were sometimes used in the galleys of the Normans.

An ancient author, who wrote a history of King Richard the First, in rhyme, says of the King :—

> ' Were the Maryners glad or wrothe,
> He made them seyle and rowe bothe,
> That the galley gede so swyfte,
> So doth the fowle by the lyfte.'[5]

---

[1] Grafton's Chron., p. 571. [2] Caxton in Polychronicon, p. 409, cap. 14. [3] See Strutt's Horda.
[4] Strutt's Horda. [5] MS. Harleian, No. 4690.

The Sailing-Boat.

Persons skilled in climbing the shrouds and rigging and furling the sails, were styled *funambuli*, as they were in the classical æra.

CANOES OF THE ANCIENT BRITONS.

THERE is overwhelming evidence that canoes made out of the solid trunks of trees, by rounding them on the outside and hollowing them on the inside, were in general use by the Ancient Britons. Several of these have been dug out of the fens and beds of rivers in various parts of England and Scotland within the last century; some of them perfect in form, and in an excellent state of preservation.

Sir Chas. Lyell[1] mentions that Mr. John Buchanan, a zealous antiquary, writing in 1855, states that in the course of the eighty years preceding that date no less than seventeen canoes had been dug out of the estuarine silt on the margin of the Clyde at Glasgow; and that he had personally inspected a large number of them before they were exhumed. Five of them lay buried in silt under the streets of Glasgow. Twelve others were found about a hundred yards back from the river at an average depth of about nineteen feet from the surface of the soil. And that within the then last few years (1869) three other canoes were found in the silts of the Clyde between Bowling and Dumbarton, which were preserved for inspection in the adjacent grounds of Auchentorlie.

Almost everyone of these ancient boats was formed out of a single oak stem, hollowed out by blunt tools, probably stone axes, aided by the action of fire. A few were cut beautifully smooth, evidently with metallic tools. Hence a gradation could be traced from a pattern of extreme rudeness to one showing great mechanical ingenuity. In one of the canoes a beautifully polished celt or axe of greenstone was found.

Two of the canoes were built of planks, one of which, dug up on the property of Bankton in 1853, was eighteen feet in length and very elaborately constructed. Its prow was not unlike the beak of an antique galley; its stern, formed of a triangular-shaped piece of oak, fitted in exactly like those of our day. The planks were fastened to the ribs, partly by singularly shaped oaken pins and partly by what must have been square nails of some kind of metal; these had entirely disappeared, but some of the oaken pins remained.

It is further observed that there can be no doubt that some of these buried canoes are of far more ancient date than others. Those most roughly hewn may be relics of the Stone period; those more smoothly cut, of the Bronze age; and the regularly built boat of Bankton may perhaps come within the age of Iron.[2]

It is stated in King's 'Munimenta Antiqua,' that in a morass called Lockermoss, a very little distance from the Castle of Wardlaw, in Dumfries, an ancient canoe was dug up in the year 1736. This canoe was seven feet long, and dilated to a considerable breadth at one end: its paddle was found at the same time in the morass near to it.

---

[1] The Antiquity of Man, by Sir Charles Lyell, Bart., M.A., F.R.S., 4th edition, 1873.　　　[2] Ibid.

The Coracle.

A canoe was also found near Kiblain, eight feet eight inches in length, and two feet in breadth; having a cavity of six feet seven inches in length, and of eleven inches in depth, the hollow of which had plainly been formed originally by means of fire.[1]

In the year 1720 several canoes were dug up in the marshes of the river Medway, above Maidstone; they were made of the trunks of trees hollowed on the inside: one of which was so perfectly preserved that it was afterwards used as a boat for some time.[2]

On the draining of Martine Mere, or Marton Lake, in Lancashire, not many years ago, there were found sunk at the bottom eight canoes, each made of a single tree, which there is every reason to believe had been used by the ancient Britons in fishing upon that lake, and which in size and shape were much like the American (Virginian) canoes.[3]

So also in the early part of the present century, on the draining of Whittlesea Mere, and in other parts of the Fen districts, canoes in a very good state of preservation have been excavated at a considerable depth from the surface.

THE CORACLE.

'We dared to think, we dared to say, that he could frame a boat,
And many others said the same, but questioned—" would it float?"'—ELIZA COOK.

APART from the canoes of the ancient Britons, the Coracle is one of the earliest forms of boat ever constructed in Great Britain.

Some of the coracles of the ancient Britons, composed of two hides and a

---

[1] Pennant's Voyage to the Hebrides.   [2] King's Munimenta Antiqua, vol. i. p. 20.
[3] King's Munimenta Antiqua, vol. i. p. 29.

half, were large enough to contain three men, with a week's provisions; others were of sufficient capacity only for an armed man and a rower.

As coracles of this construction are mentioned by Herodotus, the pattern was probably derived from the Phœnicians, particularly as Sidonian and Phœnician vessels were almost round in form.[1]

It is evident that coracles were known and used by the Saxons, for Sidonius Apollinaris (a Gaulish bishop of the fifth century) writes—'The Saxon corsair, whose pastime it is to plough the British sea in a boat made of skins and stitched together.'

In the time of Henry V., light boats framed with wicker or thin timber and covered outside with leather, were carried by ship to the wars to enable the soldiers to pass the waters which might be in their way on their marches. Such were also the *Naisselles* carried over to France in the wars by Edward III.[2] These were artfully made with prepared or boiled leather,[3] and would each hold three men therein to fish or take their pleasure.

Hollinshed also alludes to Henry V. making great preparations for the war, on his second expedition into France, by providing 'boats covered with leather to pass over rivers.'

Lucan, in describing the boats of the ancient Britons, says they were made of osiers twisted and interwoven with each other, which were covered over with strong hides.[4]

> 'With twisted osiers the first boats were made,
> O'er which the skins of slaughter'd beasts were laid:
> With these the Britons on the oceans row,
> And the Venetians on the swelling Po.'

Pliny speaks of voyages of six days' sailing being performed in 'vessels covered with leather round about, and well sewed.'[5]

And he also speaks of certain wicker boats being met with on the 'British Ocean,' made of twigs covered with leather, and stitched round about.[6]

Strabo mentions a kind of boat called *pécton*, apparently similar to the coracle; he describes it as 'made of thongs, so as to resemble wicker-work.'[7]

One of the most curious circumstances connected with the art of British boat-building is that at the present day, boats (*i.e.* coracles) are carefully made and

---

[1] Gauli, p. 318.

[2] Froissart's Chron. vol. ii.

[3] 'Faittees et ordonnees sy soubtillement de cuir boully.'

[4] Vide also Strutt's Horda, vol. i. Also Cæsar de Bello Civ. lib. i. s. 54.

[5] 'Ad eam Britannos vitilibus navigiis corio circumsutis navigare.' Plin. Nat. Hist., Lib. iv. cap. 14.

[6] 'Etiam nunc in Britannico oceano vitiles corio circumsutæ fiunt.' Plin., Book vii. cap. 56, sec. 57.

[7] Strabo, xvii. p. 562.

constantly used in parts of England, Wales, and Ireland, almost identical in size, form, construction and materials, with those in use nearly nineteen centuries ago. And, however mean and insignificant the contrivance of the coracle may appear in the yards of British boat-builders, and on the wide world of waters, it is a stubborn fact that the coracle is now, as then, fully adequate to the purpose for which it was intended.

Coracles are as much in use as ever in South Wales, on the rivers Wye, Usk, Towey, and other favourite resorts of anglers and fishers, and so also on the western coast and inland waters of Ireland; and they are just the same sort of vessels as those in which the ancient Britons used to cross the seas and brave the storms of the Irish and English Channels more than eighteen hundred years ago. The native fishermen and boatmen of the north and western coasts of Ireland still express their entire confidence in the sea-going qualities of their coracles (*curraghs*), and prefer them in bad weather to any other kind of boat, on account of their remarkable buoyancy.

The English peasants term these interesting little boats 'cruckles.' In Hereford and Monmouth they are called 'thoracles,' and 'truckles;' and on the western coast of Ireland, 'curraghs,' 'corraghs,' or 'corachs.' The original term is supposed to have been coriacle; and if so, was probably derived from the Latin *corium*, a skin or hide, or *coriago*, hidebound.

The engraving at page 9 represents a modern coracle of the river Wye, in South Wales, and explains the manner in which they are carried by the fishers and others in that locality.

In shape the Welsh coracle resembles the half of a gigantic walnut-shell, but varies a little in form in different counties; and so also as to the material of which they are composed. But the framework, or main fabric of the coracle, is now (as it has always been) composed of wicker or basket-work: inside the wicker-work is a thin trellis-like framework of wood, and the outside of the wicker-work is covered with canvas.

In Cardiganshire the framework is covered with flannel, and dressed with tar. In the neighbourhood of Shrewsbury they are covered with canvas, oiled and painted. Some of the most fragile are merely covered with white linen, and dressed over with resin, varnish, or other like compound. The most durable are coated with hides or skins, and such is the material of which the ancient ones were made. Tarpaulin, and other waterproof material, is now the more general article used; and the interior is usually dressed over with hot pitch, so as to make them perfectly water-tight.

There is no lighter nor more portable and inexpensive kind of boat than the coracle: their average weight is about twelve pounds. The fishermen of the Wye, and of the west and north of Ireland, usually make their own; but the cost of a small coracle of the best construction in the neighbourhood of the Wye is only about twenty-five or thirty shillings.

The common size of the coracle is from three and a half to four feet wide, by two feet deep, and less than six feet in length.

If the coracle gets pierced or injured, it may be quickly repaired with a bit of cloth or canvas, and a daub of warm pitch.

The coracle is a great acquisition to the salmon-fisher, who desires to pass from river to river, and pool to pool: as he is enabled to carry his boat on his back by means of a leather strap slung across his shoulders, and so to pass from place to place, though miles apart, thereby placing himself in a perfectly independent position as regards horse, ferryman, and even umbrella.

When fishing from the coracle at mid-stream, if a large fish be hooked, the coracle is sometimes spun round as if on a pivot, and dragged a considerable distance, unless checked by the fisherman with his paddle.

The position in which the occupant of the coracle sits is facing the bow or fore part; when, by means of a single paddle (though sometimes a double one, called a *sweep*, having a blade at each end), the coracle is propelled through the water. When a sweep is used it is held firmly in the middle with both hands, each about one foot apart, as in a Rob Roy canoe, and flourished after the manner of a see-saw movement; dipping each blade in the water alternately, and thereby drawing or 'sweeping' the coracle ahead. When well practised, it is astonishing with what rapidity the coracle may be made to skim the surface of smooth waters. This, however, is more generally the mode of propelling the larger ones. The smaller ones are usually navigated with a single-bladed paddle, the top of the handle of which the coracler places against his shoulder, and works the paddle with his left hand, whilst holding his fishing-rod with the right. Slow progress only can be made with the single-bladed paddle; the sweep is the instrument wherewith to drive them ahead rapidly.

At the annual regatta at Monmouth, the coracle race is usually one of the most amusing and attractive of the day; and before it is concluded, at least half of the competitors are capsized in the scramble for pride of place.

Within the last sixty or seventy years the modern Irish Curragh has, to a certain extent, superseded the ancient Celtic coracle. The difference, however, is chiefly in the material of which the outer covering is composed: strained canvas, coated with tardressing used in preference to horse-hide, as less liable to stretch when exposed to sea-water, and also as a far less costly material than leather.

The modern Irish curragh is of local construction and of an improved shape, being considerably longer, and of a form better adapted for the open coast than the English coracle; but in all other respects the curragh is much the same as the coracle of the ancient Britons.

Irish curraghs are from fifteen to twenty feet in length, by two and a half and three in breadth; they are so light that they are carried to and fro by the fishermen, from the coast to their cottages, almost daily. But notwithstanding their lightness, against a heavy sea and wind they are said to possess great superiority over boats built of wood. They are, however, best adapted for fishing with hook and line, as their light and fragile nature is not adapted to the working and manipulation of fishing nets.

These curraghs are used for line fishing in the Atlantic on the rock-bound coasts of the west and north of Ireland, more particularly co. Kerry; they are neatly and beautifully made, light and buoyant as of cork, and are a credit to the native industry and ingenuity of the Irish people. In shape, on the inside, they are like a long light galley; but they have a bold, high bow, which, on the outside and under part, resembles the bow of a Norway praam. They have a flat rounded floor, but no keel.

Modern Irish Curragh.[1]

The upper part of the curragh, from the thwarts to the gunwale, on the inside, is composed of wood: but all the bilge and bottom parts are of wicker-work lined with a light trellis framework of wood. The outside of the curragh is entirely covered with canvas, strained tightly over the wicker-work and then served with a dressing of tar.

Curraghs are each fitted with four thwarts at equal distances apart; but there is no thwart of any kind either in the stern or the bow, it being important in a sea-way to keep both ends of the curragh light, and free of any dead weight. There is also a fifth thwart, which is placed just forward of the fore-thwart, and is pierced for a small mast: this thwart is fixed lower than the others, and is in fact but a few inches above the bottom of the boat.

With a free wind, a light lug-sail is sometimes used, but only in fine weather. These curraghs, when managed skilfully under oars, are said to be capable of living in a heavier sea than other open boats of their size, by reason of their extraordinary buoyancy.

They are usually manned by four persons; in fact, the curraghs above described

[1] The engraving is from a drawing by the author, of a full-sized modern Irish curragh, exhibited at the Fisheries Exhibition at the Imperial Institute, 1897.

are constructed to carry that number as their complement, each of whom plies a pair of short oars (or sculls), as occasion requires.

The *Tory Island* (Co. Donegal) *Canoe* is of more antiquated contrivance than the curragh, and of more rustic construction; it is also shorter, and broader in proportion to length than the other.

This primitive craft, though resembling in some respects both the ancient British coracle and the Irish curragh, has none of the modern improvements of either: its use is confined to the fishermen of that remote island off the north-west coast of the county Donegal. It is usually manned by a crew of two only, and is perhaps, with its spillets and lines, the most ancient form of fishing-boat and gear in use at the present day in any part of the United Kingdom.

END OF PART I.

PART II.

—◆—

SAILING BOATS OF THE BRITISH ISLANDS.

THERE is considerable variety in the sailing-boats of the British Islands, both as regards type or form, and rig; and although some possess fewer general advantages than others, it is often found that the nature of the coast, the harbour, river, or other circumstances, render it necessary that a boat of special—and in some places peculiar—form and rig should be provided for the purposes of safe and useful navigation. And a sailing boat, to be safe and serviceable, must be adapted to the waters and locality in which it is to be employed; the most reliable being that in general use by the resident boatmen, the form and rig of which will usually be found to possess some special advantages with reference to the nature of the coast or the waters to which it belongs; and generally such advantages, or peculiarities, are the result of years of practical experience by those familiar with the navigation and locality of the waters.

A boat constructed and rigged for sailing on the smooth surface of narrow inland waters would be ill suited to the broad expanse of water on a sea-coast, and *vice versâ* ; and as some parts of the coast are much more dangerous than others, it is found that the ingenuity of the native boatmen has enabled them, from long experience, to design a form of boat admirably suited to the locality and purposes required. For instance, the north-country cobles, employed off the perilous north-east coast at Flamborough Head and such-like exposed parts, are ingeniously contrived to meet the dangers of the navigation of that bold and stormy coast, but they would be ill adapted to the shallow waters of an inland bay or a narrow river. So also as to the long, shallow, open yawls employed on and off the coast of Yarmouth and the neighbourhood, which abounds with shoals, shallows, and sands. The feats of seamanship and daring performed in boats such as these, by the native boatmen in gales of wind and heavy seas, are truly astonishing, whilst in boats of an ordinary form it would be certain destruction to attempt such.

Sailing-boats for sea-going purposes should have high bows, and the ballast should be trimmed rather farther aft than in such as are employed in smooth water. It is also better for sea-going boats to be so rigged as to carry a mizzen-sail, which is of great assistance on ' coming about ' in a sea-way.

15

The Sailing-Boat.

Boats employed in the pilot service, which have constantly to be run under sail, alongside of vessels at sea, for the purpose of putting a pilot aboard, are rigged with a view to the convenience and facilities of that service, and generally carry all their sail inboard; some however have a mizzen, the clew of which is run out on an outrigger at the stern; but they seldom carry any sail extending beyond the stem of the boat, nor indeed any bowsprit, because of the peril of snapping it off, or other mishap when alongside a vessel in a rolling sea.

The main-mast of a pilot lugger is therefore placed forward, in the bows of the boat. With boats so rigged, pilots fearlessly luff up to leeward alongside ships at sea,

Sea Lugger.

deliver a pilot, and bear away again without striking sail or lowering any of their canvas.

Pilot boats, however, are not all rigged as luggers; there are various other rigs for pilot boats, as schooners, cutters, sloops, &c. But of late years steamboats are employed considerably in the pilot service.

River boats for sailing on broad tidal rivers should not be less than fifteen feet in length, by at least five in breadth: they should be sharp and fine at the bows, broad amidships, and by no means narrow at the stern.

Inexperienced persons are warned against the danger of setting sail in small boats of a narrow form of hull; such boats, though well suited to the oar, are unsafe with a sail.

Boats with narrow sterns are not desirable for sailing; those with tolerably broad sterns and good breadth of beam are enabled to carry sail with far greater safety than those with wedge-like bottoms and narrow beam.

Short, wide boats, with good depth of keel, are the safest and swiftest for beating to windward in tortuous rivers and narrow channels.

Half-decked and Open Boats.

Long boats are best adapted for wide waters, 'sailing on a bowline,' and 'running free'; and generally, in places where long 'tacks' may be made.

HALF-DECKED BOATS.

Boats decked fore and aft, and with a narrow deck, or water-way on each side within the gunwales, are called 'half-decked boats'; the object of the deck being to render them safer under sail when listing over in a breeze. All open boats with large sails should be so constructed. The half-deck is a great safeguard when careening to the breeze, particularly in squally weather; it also makes the sailing-boat more complete—but nevertheless, if too much sail be set, and the sailor too

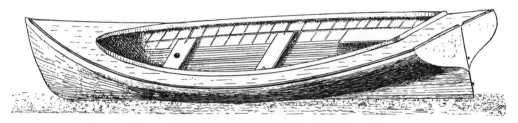

Half-decked Boat.

venturesome in strong winds and a rough sea, the half-decked boat is not infallible, and in the hands of a reckless boat-sailer may be capsized, notwithstanding the half-deck.

SMALL OPEN SAILING-BOATS.

Although every yacht is a boat, it is not every boat that is a yacht.

It is in the small open sailing-boat that most amateurs learn the rudiments of boat and yacht sailing; and generally in a boat with one sail only, or two at the most. If with one sail, it is usually a lug-sail; if two, then a sprit-sail and fore-sail; or the settee rig: the latter is perhaps the preferable, because the simplest, and it is besides an exceedingly handy one for a small open boat—it requires only a very short mast, shorter and lower than that of any other rig, and the fore-sail is smaller, has less hoist, and stands lower than that of other rigs with higher mast. It is, moreover, a rig that may be readily managed by one person.

In rigging a boat to be sailed with one sail only, it will be found that if the mast be stepped too far forward the boat will not steer properly in a breeze, unless it be a short, broad type of boat. The illustration on next page of a combination row and sail

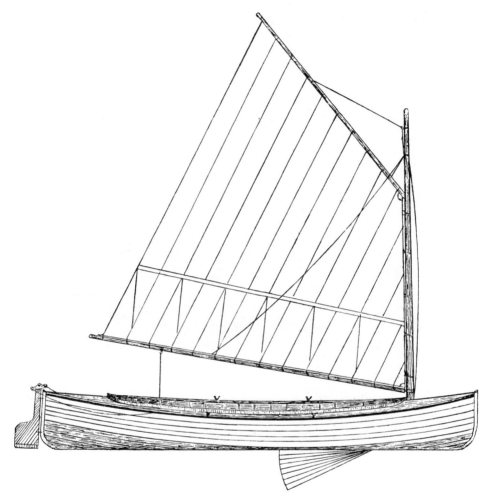

Combination Row and Sail Boat.

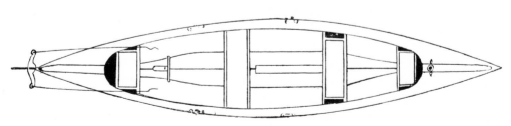

Plan of Combination Row and Sail Boat.

boat, with Radix patent folding centre-plate, is an American design by Mr. J. H. Rushton, boat builder, of Canton, New York.

The Una style of boat, with its one sail, once so popular among the boating fraternity at Cowes and elsewhere, is now a type of the past. It is, in fact, almost entirely supplanted by a less shallow form of boat and a handier kind of rig.

There are, however, modern boats of the match-sailing classes that are even shallower than the Una class: a description of these will be found in subsequent pages of this work.

But whatever the rig, there is always one important consideration that cannot be lost sight of in regard to the boat itself, and that is the depth of water in the locality in which the boat will be used.

In shallow waters, bar harbours, and many parts of tidal rivers, a boat of deep draught would be out of place. A shallow boat with a drop keel would be well suited to such waters; but a fixed centre-plate and bulb-keel would be dangerous, and probably bring both boat and occupant to disaster.

Locality has always to be kept in view by the designer of a sailing-boat or a small yacht; and this accounts for the many varieties of design in the local boats of different parts of the British Islands, as it also does for the curious and interesting types of boats and canoes of the inhabitants of remote islands in various parts of the world. And it is found, too, that boats designed and built for use in a certain locality perform best in that locality.

At most of the seaside resorts where there is no inside harbour, and consequently the boats have all to be beached, those belonging to amateurs are fitted with a centre-plate for sailing to windward, which is unshipped on coming ashore. Small open boat-sailing is freely indulged in at most of such places; and some of the boats of members of the local Sailing Clubs are of excellent type and construction. Small sailing boats of various sizes, from 10 to 15 or 20 feet, are numerous on and about the beach at various places on the South Coast. Most of them have a centre-plate of some kind, which can be either drawn up or taken out before beaching. The position of the centre-plate varies considerably: in some it is fitted to the fore part of the boat, in others a little less forward, and in some farther astern. In the larger boats it is usually placed in or near about midships; but in some of the smaller craft which are sailed with one sail only, when the mast is stepped in the fore part of the bows, the centre-plate-case is fixed close abaft the mast. On coming ashore the centre-plate is always drawn up and taken out before beaching.

The Sailing-Boat.

SEA-GOING SAILING-BOATS.

Pilot Lugger.

WITH regard to the best form of sailing-boat for cruising in a sea-way, there are various models, adapted more or less to the purposes for which they are required, and the nature of the sea, or rather the locality of the waters, in which they are intended to be sailed; but speaking generally of sailing-boats, whether entirely open or half-decked, if intended absolutely for sea-going purposes, there is much to be said in favour of a boat with bow and stern alike, as a life-boat, or a modern North-east Coast fishing-lugger, or a Norway yawl. A broad, square-sterned boat, though perhaps stiffer under sail, and equally safe in a sea-way, is not always so reliable when running through broken water in a heavy sea as a boat with a life-boat form of stern, and higher at both ends than amidships.

A sea-going sailing-boat, to be safe and reliable, must have the weight, power, and buoyancy to meet heavy seas. Such a boat cannot be made stiffer under sail by loading her with ballast to such an extent as to bring her down in the water below her proper bearings. A boat so laden is like an overburdened ship, dangerous in a sea-way and liable to founder, through her want of buoyancy and ability to meet heavy seas.

A boat intended for sea-sailing must be buoyant; particularly at the bows and stern. Such a boat should be designed and built with a view to the heavy seas she assuredly will encounter; and if of true scientific design, will rise to, and go over heavy seas and not through them.

The Sprit-sail and Fore-sail.

If it is desired that the boat should be able to keep to the sea in rough and boisterous weather, the nearer she approaches in form to the modern Scotch fishing-lugger before mentioned the greater perhaps will be her capability of so doing. The advantages of such a model have been abundantly proved, and are of world-wide adoption. Such boats have the power, at both ends, of dividing and throwing off high seas, whether meeting them at the bows or following them up astern.

It is not, however, to be supposed that every or any boat with such a bow and stern will be safe in a heavy sea; the boat must also be broad, with a tendency to flatness in the floor, and with plenty of beam. She must also be judiciously ballasted, and rigged with a suitable sea-going suit of sails; and besides, must be under the management of an experienced boat-sailer and an efficient crew.

As to the best kind of rig for a sea sailing-boat, there are several to choose from, but the size and capacity of the boat must always indicate the basis of choice.

If the boat be an open one, the lugger rig will perhaps be found the safest and most useful, by reason of the readiness with which the sail, or sails, may be set, and the facility with which they may be lowered.

THE SPRIT-SAIL AND FORE-SAIL RIG.

ONE of the most primitive, and at the same time handiest and most useful rigs for a small open sailing-boat, is the sprit-sail (or spreet-sail) and fore-sail. A boat so rigged has been the cradle-boat of many an afterwards distinguished boat-sailer. There is no sail that stands flatter than a well set sprit-sail; and it has the merit, when old and somewhat stretched, of standing as flat as ever. To a tyro boat-sailer it is recommended as superior to many others for an open boat under sixteen feet in length; when longer some other rig is preferable, as the spreet required to set the sail will be found too long and heavy to be conveniently managed—at all events by one person.

The sprit-sail, in shape, resembles a cutter's mainsail, but has a sharper peak, which is raised by means of a small spar called a *spreet*, the heel of which is set in a selvagee-strop, or a grommet formed into a snouter, which encircles the lower part of the mast; the top end of the spreet is set in the peak-eye of the sail, and so the whole is spread.

A spreet heel-rope will be found of great assistance in peaking and setting up the sail. The heel-rope should be rove through a small block fitted to the upper part of the mast, and the eye at the lower end of the heel-rope should be slipped over the lower end of the spreet as it stands in the snouter; a pull or two on the fall of the heel-rope will then peak the sail as much as may be required.

The usual sized boat suitable for the sprit-sail rig is one about fifteen or sixteen feet in length ; such a boat should have an iron boomkin, about a foot long, or a short wooden bowsprit, fitted to the stem.

As to the mast, a very short one will suffice, as the spreet relieves it of most of the

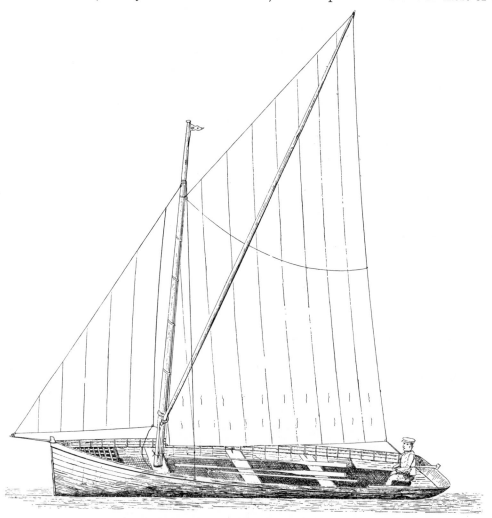

Sprit-sail and Fore-sail.

upper pressure, which is thereby thrown upon the lower part of the mast.   No boom is required for the sprit-sail.

As to the shrouds, a single small-sized rope on each side of the mast will be sufficient ; but a small boat will sail better and be safer without shrouds.

The sprit-sail must be fitted with brails, wherewith to furl it at any moment and on any emergency ; the brails should be attached to the outer leech of the sail, as shown in the illustration, so that, when the main sheet is let go and the brail-rope is hauled taut, it brails the sail up close to the mast at the very throat of the sail, and the boat is thereby immediately relieved of the pressure of the mainsail. The brails should at all times be kept clear and ready for use, in order that the sail may be frapped or brailed up quickly when required. By way of caution, it should be pointed out that a dangerous error prevails with careless persons who use the sprit-sail : it is in setting the spreet ; the error being, in shipping it *between* the sail and the brails, so that spreet and sail are both brailed up together close to the mast when the brail-rope is hauled taut—but such is erroneous, and sometimes dangerous. The spreet should always be set *outside* the brails, by which means the sail may be drawn closer to the mast, and much more readily ; the flapping and sagging of the sail at the upper part is also avoided ; whilst the spreet, instead of being drawn up, as it would be if within the brails, remains in its proper position.

On reefing the sprit-sail the heel-rope halliards must be slackened, the snouter can then be slipped lower down the mast, which will bring the spreet lower, and generally admit of one reef ; but when two reefs are necessary, and the heel of the spreet cannot be got down low enough, the spreet must be unshipped, the top-end taken out of the peak, and the eye thereof lashed securely to the spreet, about a foot or so from the top ; this is termed ' reefing the spreet.' It is advisable, however, to carry an extra spreet, of shorter length, when reefing is anticipated ; but the sprit-sail should always be so made as to allow of the sail being close-reefed with one and the same spreet standing, and without unshipping, or taking it out of the snouter.

Another method of reefing the sprit-sail consists in providing a spreet in two parts ; the lower part having a shoe of brass or copper-tube, with a short sprit-end, so that the latter may be shipped on or taken off from the spreet without lowering or disarranging the peak. By this plan, when the sail is reefed, the upper part only of the spreet is required, which is in fact a complete short spreet ; but when the reefs are shaken out, and the whole of the sail is required to be spread, then the lower or tubular end of the spreet is shipped on, and you have a full-length spreet at once.

On setting the sprit-sail, the boat should always lay *head to wind*, and the same on shortening or taking in sail. It will be found a difficult task (in fact, almost impossible with a tolerably large sail) to set the spreet with a fresh breeze *abaft*.

The following are suitable *dimensions for a suit of sails* (*sprit-sail and fore-sail*) for a small open sailing-boat, or skiff, fifteen feet in length, by five feet six inches in breadth.

	ft.	ins.		ft.	ins.
Hoist of mainsail	7	6	Length of spreet	16	0
Head	8	3	Fore-sail luff	10	6
Aft leech	12	0	,, aft leech	7	10
Flap (or foot) of mainsail	9	0	,, foot	5	9

23

The Sailing-Boat.

Three-masted Sprit-sail.

THE three-masted sprit-sail rig is a very pretty and useful one for a small boat, about eighteen or twenty feet in length, by five feet beam.

The rig consists of four sails, viz. three sprit-sails and a jib; or it may be two sprit-sails, jib, and Bermudian mizzen (as shown in the above engraving).

The main-mast should be stepped amidships, the fore-mast well forward, and the mizzen-mast at the extreme end of the stern.

Open boats, so rigged, are very handy under sail; and they may be sailed under various changes as regards shortening and dispensing with one or more of the sails in strong winds. The rig is also useful for a boat used for mackerel and other kinds of sea fishing; it stays well in a sea-way, and has besides, many advantages as a safe and handy rig for a small sailing boat.

Tyro boat-sailers are cautioned against narrow boats for sailing purposes. The narrow form of hull may be well adapted for rowing, but is not a safe and reliable one for sailing. Large fore-sails in small open boats are also attended with danger, and are more frequently the cause of accidents than the main-sail. It should always be borne in mind that the boat, to be safe under sail, must carry a 'weather-helm;' and such will not be the case if the fore-sail be too large Short wide boats of suitable depth, rigged as sloops or cutters, or with sprit-sail and fore-sail, are best adapted for turning to windward in narrow channels. Long boats are fastest for long reaches, sailing on a bow-line, and running before the wind.

For small open boats it is not considered a safe plan for the fore-sail to work on an iron hawse; a fore-sail hawse should only be fitted to decked boats, and those where a jib is used as well as a fore-sail.

Anglo-Bermudian Rig.

The danger lies in the sails being struck by a squall when, if the fore-sail is worked on a hawse, the pressure of the sail cannot be quickly taken off in emergency; and many a small sailing-boat has been upset by the fore-sail. But if the sheet be rove through a free-running block attached to the hawse the danger is removed, as it may be readily eased to the pressure of the wind, if the fall of the sheet be ready at hand, or be otherwise free to let go or ease off.

THE ANGLO-BERMUDIAN RIG.

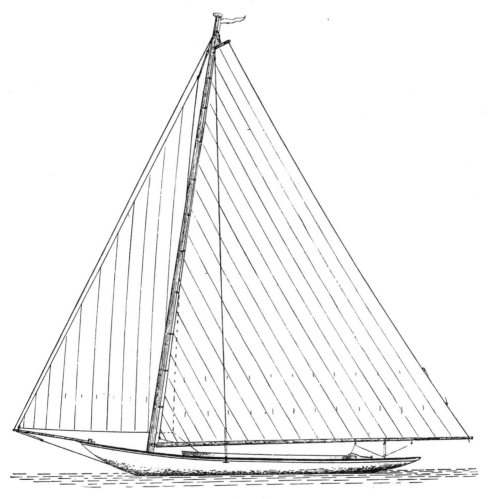

Anglo-Bermudian.

THE Anglo-Bermudian rig has come into fashion of late years as a safe and handy one for small yachts and sailing-boats. It differs from the native Bermudian rig chiefly in this, that the boom is attached to the mast by a goose-neck in the same manner as for the Cutter rig; whereas in the native Bermudian boats the fore-end of the boom is set in an eyelet formed in the tack of the main-sail, like the peak end of a sprit-sail, and projects a foot or more in front of the mast according to the size of the boat—the boom being held close to the mast by a strong grommet, and the clew of the sail is then hauled taut to the outer end of the boom.[1]

The Anglo-Bermudian is a rig best suited for smooth inland waters. The main-sail, when properly shaped, is neat and pretty; whilst the tapering peak is useful under high cliffs, when the lower part of the sail is sheltered from the wind.

The sail requires neither spreet nor yard; but a tall tapering mast, placed well forward in the bows of the boat with considerable aft-rake. The halliards need only be of small size, much smaller than for square-headed sails, and should be rove through a small block at the mast head; no other halliards will be necessary for the main-sail of a small boat of this rig. The sail may be bent to the mast by a lacing, or by small hoops or rope grommets; but neither hoops nor grommets must extend higher up than the fore-halliard block, which should be seized to the mast at about three-fourths of its height from the deck. A boom is required for the main-sail, which is held to the mast by a goose-neck; and the fore-sail, which is necessarily lofty, must be narrow, unless the boat is very broad and stiff under sail, in which case a larger and more powerful fore-sail may be used.

The advantages derived from this rig are, that the heavy sway of spreet or yard is avoided; that, on reefing the sail the widest and heaviest part is taken off the boat at once, whilst the lighter and more tapering part is still maintained.

Boats under this rig sail well in smooth water, are easily worked, and quickly reefed; brails may be fitted to the main-sail in the same manner as for the sprit-sail.

---

[1] *Vide infra*—'Bermudian Boats.'

The Settee Rig.

Settee Rig.

THE settee rig, though formerly but little used in English waters, has of late years become quite a favourite for small open boats ; and it is one of the safest and handiest of rigs for a tyro boat-sailer with which to learn boat-sailing. It is still the most general form of rig that is used for the native sailing-boats of India ; it has in fact the appearance of a latine sail with the fore angle cut off.

In some respects, and for some purposes, it is to be preferred to a latine sail, because of the facilities afforded for reefing, which cannot so readily be accomplished in a tall latine sail, and by reason also that a settee sail may be set with a shorter yard than a latine.

The settee main-sail when close-reefed forms a triangle, and has then the appearance of a true latine.

Another very important consideration in favour of this rig for small sailing-boats is that it requires only a very low mast. And therefore, although the settee sail has a lofty peak, the hoist is low, and consequently the fore-sail is short in the aft-leech. If a mizzen be used it may be of the same shape as the main-sail, but much smaller.

The settee is a safe and pretty rig for a skiff, or any small open boat. It also

27

answers well for boats of a somewhat narrow form, in which it is important, for safety's sake, to keep the broadest part of the sails as low down as possible.

It is also well adapted for any other small open boat fit for carrying sail; no higher peak need be made to the main-sail than necessary, but for a stiff and powerful boat the lofty peak is very effective in smooth water.

Settee with Mizzen.

THE SLIDING-GUNTER.

THE sliding-gunter is a pretty and ingenious form of rig for a pleasure boat; it is also one that was formerly much in use for the sailing-boats attached to large yachts and merchant ships, but has in that respect been superseded by the modern steam-

Sliding-Gunter Rig.

launch. It consists (as regards a *single-masted* sliding-gunter) as a rig for a pleasure boat of two sails only, viz. main-sail and fore-sail. The main-sail of the sliding-gunter is of similar shape to a latine sail, but is set differently, the lower part of the main-sail of a sliding-gunter being laced to the mast, whereas the whole of a latine sail, from peak to tack, is laced to a long yard. The sliding-gunter has a short mast, but a long pointed yard, the upper part of which stands high above the mast, though parallel with it, and is contrived so as to slide up and down the mast by means of two iron travellers, called gunter-irons.

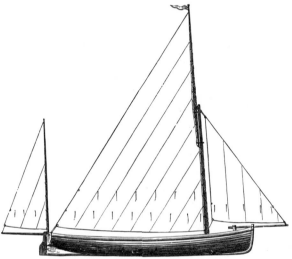

Sliding-Gunter with Small Mizzen.

Either one, two, or three masts and sails of this rig, may be fitted to a boat. The sliding-gunter is one of the safest of rigs for open boats, and it is besides, one by which the sails may be quickly set and as quickly furled; the masts being low they are very convenient for unshipping in case of using the boat for rowing. Reefing this sail is also easily and effectively accomplished, the widest part, or that having the greatest pressure on the boat, being shortened to such an extent, that two reefs will generally take up nearly half the sail; and this, too, at its broadest part. No better rig can be used for open boats in bad weather; and in fine weather, no rig looks prettier for a pleasure-boat than a two-masted sliding-gunter. The sail should be well peaked up, and the luff laced close to the mast and yard.

The bowsprit may be run through a gammon at the bows of the boat, in the usual way, and the heel secured as in other boats.

The fore-sail and main-sail should be secured to the yards by a small marline, which answers better than grommets; but from the lower iron of the yard downwards to the tack-clew, a running lacing is best, and will be found most convenient for casting off when about to trice up the tack. Small metal thimbles must be worked into the luff of these sails, to facilitate the working of the ratline in the process of lacing.

The brails, which catch the sail under the throat, in the same manner as for a sprit-sail, should lead through a small block, or a bull's-eye strapped to the lower side of the lower gunter-iron; the brails will also answer the purpose of down-haulers if required, and trice rope for tricing up the main-tack.

The best plan of setting the main-boom for this rig is, by pointing the aft end so as to fit into the clew of the main-sail, in the same way as a spreet fits into the peak-eye of a sprit-sail; the inner end of the boom is then secured by means of a lanyard rove through a half sheave in the boom end. By this method the goose-neck is dispensed with, and the foot of the sail may be stretched taut, and will stand as flat as possible without lacing to the boom. It should be observed, however, that in setting the sail care must be taken to keep the foot of the sail taut, or the shaking when the boat is in stays, may cause the clew to slip off the boom end; but a little practice soon renders this easy.

With regard to the gunter-irons, whether for a single or two-masted rig, the upper traveller may be made so as to be readily detachable when the yard is lowered; the advantage of which is, that the yard may then be stowed with the sail on the top of the boom (where one is used), in the same way as the gaff of a cutter's main-sail.

THE UNA RIG.

The term 'Una rig' implies a boat with one sail only. The Una rig (as here illustrated) is of American origin, and is nearly identical with the well-known Cat rig of the United States of America; it was first introduced into this country by the Earl Mount Charles (afterwards Marquis of Conyngham) who brought one of the Una boats over from America in the year 1853. The boat was very broad and shallow, and had a revolving drop-keel. The rig became very popular for a time, as a handy form of rig for small half-decked boats; but its popularity has long since waned considerably, though it still finds favour on some parts of our coast and inland waters where their surroundings are adaptable to a shallow form of boat.

The striking characteristics of the Una rig are, the position of the mast, which is stepped in the bows of the boat, as far forward as possible; and the one sail only— a gaff sail—narrow at the upper part, but very broad at the foot, which consequently requires a long boom extending considerably over the stern.

The rig is best suited for turning to windward in a narrow channel, with short half-decked boats of a broad and shallow type, fitted with a centre-plate or a revolving keel.

The Una Rig.

It is a type of boat and rig that answers best in smooth waters. In a sea-way, the mast standing so far forward in the bows, is a source of discomfort and danger, more or less, causing the boat to steer wildly, pound heavily, and to wet all on

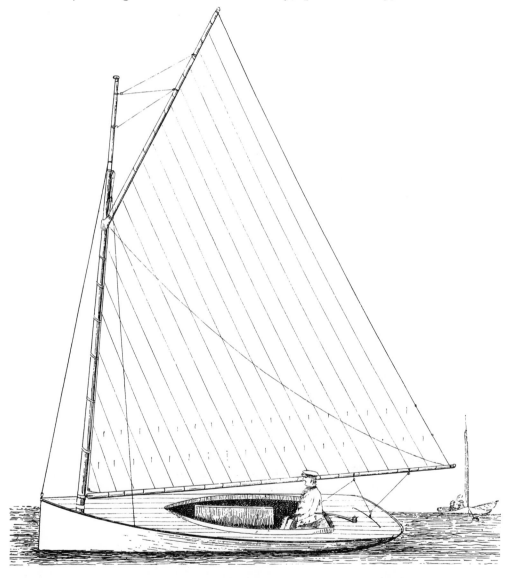

The Una Rig.

board; as the boat after mounting a wave bounces down into the trough of the sea, with her mast and sail pressing her bows down, somewhat dangerously, drenching the crew with spray, and sometimes making more leeway than headway.

The Sailing-Boat.

The chief objection to the Una rig is, the stout heavy mast (in proportion to the size of the boat), and its position so far forward in the bows. The rig is all very well for sailing in smooth water, but is not suitable for rough water, as the boat cannot be hove-to with either certainty or safety in a heavy wind, and is very liable to broach-to in a seaway.

THE SLOOP RIG.

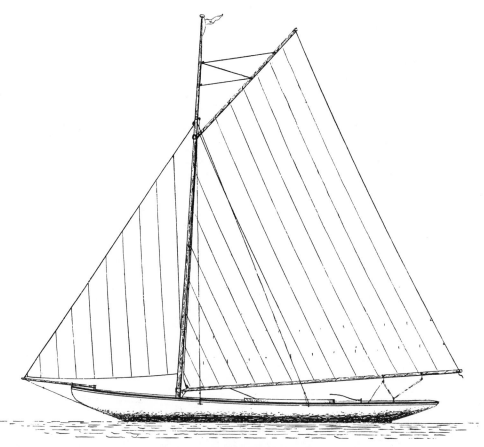

Sloop Rig.

THE sloop (anciently shaloop), a somewhat old-fashioned but most useful rig, resembles the cutter in several respects. The main-sail is in fact precisely the same, being fitted with gaff and boom; but the fore-sail is set on a fore-stay attached to the outer end of a standing bowsprit—and therefore, if a jib be used, a jib-boom becomes necessary.

The sloop rig, as used in British waters, was formerly confined chiefly to fishing boats and small trading vessels; but after the Americans improved upon it, and turned out several very decided clippers rigged as sloops, it became a popular rig for pleasure boats in other countries. A boat with a long sharp bow is desirable for the sloop rig.

Some of the New York sloops were among the fastest boats in America, beating even their famous schooner-rigged pilot boats. The chief difference between the rig of the English cutter and the New York sloop is, that the mast of the latter is stepped farther forward, and has consequently a larger main-sail, which is laced to the boom; and a fore stay-sail (also laced to a boom) in the place of the cutter's fore-sail and jib. The smaller of the American boats rigged as sloops are usually very broad and shallow, and they are fitted with a centre-board or revolving keel.

In the American sloop-yachts the main-sail is cut in a scientific manner, so as to make it stand very flat; and the fore-sail, instead of being reefed in the ordinary way is made with a bonnet, and so cut as to stand quite flat when laced to a small boom, whether with or without the bonnet.

The sloop is generally considered one of the handiest and most powerful of rigs for a small yacht or large open sailing-boat, and as simple in management as any; no top-sail should be used, unless the boat is sufficiently stiff to bear one; and more or less peak can be given to the main-sail by simply pulling on or easing the peak-halliards.

THE CUTTER RIG.

THE illustration is from a photograph by Beken and Son, of Cowes, of a full-rigged modern Cutter Yacht of repute, *The Hermes*, a five-rater (or thirty-six-footer).

No form of rig is better known nor more in favour among the boating and yachting fraternity than the Cutter. For sailing boats, small yachts, and small vessels generally, the Cutter rig is decidedly the favourite.

Cutter yachts are more numerous, and have achieved more victories in sailing matches than any other class of vessels. Formerly Cutter-rigged vessels were much employed by the English Government in the revenue service, as the most useful and convenient for the navigation of the English and Irish Channels, where short seas and broken waters prevail; and as the swiftest kind of vessel for chasing smugglers, and preventing the landing of contraband goods; but now small steam vessels are more frequently employed for the purpose.

The Cutter possesses many and great advantages: the rig ordinarily comprises four sails—main-sail, fore-sail, jib, and top-sail. The main-sail is spread by means of a gaff and boom; the outer end of the latter generally extends more or less over the stern; the fore-leech of the fore-sail is ordinarily attached to the fore-stay by means of small brass thimbles or a lacing of ratline; the jib is hauled out upon the bowsprit clear of the fore-sail.

Cutters of the old type carried a very long bowsprit, but by reason of the deep fore-gripe of the old form of hull having long been superseded, and the bows considerably extended, the length of bowsprit of the modern Cutter is very much

Cutter Yacht "Hermes."

shorter. The bowsprit is fitted with a bobstay and can be reefed by hauling it inboard so as to suit the size of the jib that is used, or it may be hauled in entirely in a heavy sea, and the vessel may then be sailed under main-sail and foresail.

The illustration on next page is that of one of the Author's yachts, Cutter-rigged, which he had in use about forty years since: it is introduced here merely to show the old-fashioned type of Cutter yacht, with a view to comparison with the modern type, which is a vast improvement in every respect.

Cutters of the old type carried a gaff-topsail in fine weather, when reaching, running, or sailing free, but a gaff-topsail was seldom of any use to the boat when on a wind.

Gaff-topsails are now rarely, if ever, seen on a Cutter yacht of the modern type:

they carry instead either a jib-headed top sail or a jack-yard top-sail, either of which may be set without a top-mast. And cutter-rigged yachts of the smaller class are

The "Gauntlet" (Old type of Cutter Yacht).

usually rigged as *pole-masted boats;* that is, without a top-mast; or rather the pole mast forms, in itself, top-mast as well as main-mast.

The Cutter rig is suitable for boats of any size, and for small vessels up to sixty or eighty tons; beyond that tonnage either the yawl rig or the schooner rig is preferable as being lighter, and capable of easier manipulation in a sea-way; the boom and other spars required for a large Cutter being found very heavy, and sometimes dangerous, and the sails difficult to reef and manage in strong winds and heavy seas.

The Sailing-Boat.

There are, however, among the pleasure squadron, cutter yachts up to, and even above, one hundred tons. But when at sea in bad weather the crew usually haul in the bowsprit, unship the boom, and set a try-sail, in place of the main-sail.

Cutter Rig.

THE SCHOONER RIG.

THE Schooner rig is best adapted to a large cruising yacht, because so much easier in a sea-way, and requiring fewer hands to manage than large yachts of the Cutter and Sloop rigs.

It is besides a rig that finds favour with the native boatmen and pilots on exposed parts of the coast, as a safer and handier rig than that of either cutter or sloop: and it is also much in favour with some yacht owners for small cruising yachts of a long and narrow type.

Its advantages are, that a Schooner-rigged craft is under better control in strong winds and heavy seas, because the principal, or most pressing sail, is in two parts, and the masts and top-hamper are much smaller and lighter than in a one-masted or Cutter-rigged vessel; and consequently the sails are more easily manipulated; and when it is necessary to shorten sail, one or more of the Schooner's sails may be dispensed with, and the vessel sailed under one or two sails only.

Some years ago the Author tried the experiment of the Schooner-rig on a half-decked boat, about three tons measurement, of long and rather narrow dimensions. He was much pleased with the rig, it was very pretty, and he found it remarkably handy in bad weather; but in fine weather and light winds he was not so satisfied, as he found the Cutter and Sloop-rigged boats easily outsailed him.

From a photo by   *West & Son, Southsea.*

" Rainbow," Schooner Yacht.

The beautiful yacht *Rainbow*, the subject of the above illustration, is the largest of the modern class of Schooner-yachts, and the property of Mr. C. L. Orr-Ewing, M.P. The *Rainbow* was built by Messrs. Henderson at Meadowside on the Clyde in 1898, from designs by Mr. G. L. Watson.   Her dimensions are :—

> Length over all, 164 feet.
> Length on load-water line, 116 feet.
> Breadth of beam, 24 feet.
> Draft of water, 17 feet.
> Tonnage about 270 tons.
> And she has a lead keel weighing about 108 tons.

The Sailing-Boat.

The fore and aft Schooner rig consists of two masts, with top-masts, and three principal sails: the larger of the two masts is termed the main-mast and stands usually just abaft the midship-part of the vessel, whilst the fore-mast stands just abaft the bows. The three principal sails are, main-sail, spencer (by some called fore-sail, by others try-sail), and stay-fore-sail. In addition to these, Schooners of the fore and aft class carry top-sails, jibs, and flying-jibs; and when match-sailing large balloon-sails as well.

Schooners are fitted with a short standing bowsprit pointing slightly upwards from

Square-rigged Schooner.

the bows; and when a jib is used, a jib-boom is run out so as to extend several feet beyond the outer end of the standing bowsprit.

Both main-sail and spencer are gaff-sails: the main-sail is always fitted with a boom; but the spencer not always; at least not when cruising or on a long voyage; but when match sailing, a boom is now generally fitted to both spencer and fore-stay-sail, as well as to the main-sail.

The two principal masts are connected at the top by a jumper stay; and the peak of the spencer should swing clear of that stay.

When running before the wind the main-sail and spencer are boomed out, one to starboard, the other to port—termed 'goose-winged': the vessel then runs upon an even keel without list on either side.

Schooners of a larger class are fitted with square-rigged top-sails; in some vessels on the fore-mast only, in others on both masts. Such are termed square-rigged schooners, and square-top-sail schooners, and sometimes square-headed schooners: this rig is chiefly confined to trading vessels.

After the victories gained in English waters by the famous schooner yacht *America*, in 1851, various improvements were made in the form, design, and rig of schooners; and schooner-rigged yachts of a superior class became numerous both as racing and cruising yachts.

But during the last twenty-five years or more, there have been but few matches sailed exclusively by schooners though they have often been classed in handicap sailing matches with yawls, ketches, and cutters.

There are many magnificent schooner-yachts belonging to members of the Royal Yacht Squadron and other British yacht clubs, some of which are of beautiful form and construction. Such vessels are truly an ornament to our seas and the pride of the pleasure squadron. Of late years, however, steam yachts have been much in vogue, and many of the larger class of schooner-yachts are now fitted with steam engines, shaft, and screw-propeller as auxiliary to their sails.

The Sailing-Boat.

THE KETCH RIG.

"Cariad," Ketch Rig.

THE Ketch, like the schooner, carries two masts, but the rig differs from that of the schooner in one very important feature, viz., that in the Ketch the larger mast and sail stand foremost in the vessel, and the smaller, or mizzen mast and sail, aftmost: whereas in the schooner the reverse is the case, the larger mast and sail standing aft, and the smaller foremost; and such is the chief distinction between the two rigs; but both of the principal sails in each rig are gaff-sails. The head-sails of the Ketch are fore-stay-sail and jib; a top-sail and flying jib are also used in light winds.

The beautiful yacht *Cariad*, the subject of the above illustration, is the property of

The Yawl Rig.

the Earl of Dunraven, and is Ketch-rigged. The *Cariad* was built by the firm Summers and Payne, of Southampton, in 1895-6, is of a hundred and twenty tons burden; a cruising yacht of considerable reputation, and winner, among other trophies, of the Vasco de Gama Challenge Cup, at Lisbon, in the month of May, 1899.

The Ketch is a very old form of rig, used chiefly for small trading-vessels and fishing trawlers, with the crews of which it has always been much in favour. Its advantages have, however, of late years been recognised by experienced yacht owners as a handy form of rig for a sea-going yacht; particularly by those who keep large yachts for cruising purposes. A Ketch-rigged cruising yacht can be efficiently managed with fewer hands than yachts of the Cutter rig, and is, besides, a safe, easy-going, comfortable kind of rig for a vessel in a sea-way.

THE YAWL RIG.

THE Yawl is another form of rig in which two masts are employed: but it differs from both Schooner and Ketch in this, that the mizzen-mast of the Yawl is stepped farther aft, near the stern-post, and is much shorter and smaller in proportion to the main-mast; and the mizzen-sail is not necessarily a gaff-sail, but in the smaller class of Yawls a lug-sail takes the place of the mizzen-gaff-sail; the clew of the Yawl's mizzen is hauled out abaft the stern on an outrigger.

The illustration is from a photograph of the famous racing Yawl *Satanita*, one hundred and twelve tons, Sir M. Fitzgerald, owner. She has a splendid record of victories in the sailing matches of the larger class of racing yachts.

There is a great variety in the size of boats and yachts rigged as Yawls; the larger are decked yachts, and the smaller half-decked, whilst others are open sailing-boats. The rig is a very convenient one, and the larger or decked boats of the Yawl-rig are considered handy and reliable in a sea-way; and they do not require so numerous a crew as a Cutter-rigged boat.

Occasionally large-sized yachts built and rigged as Cutters, have, on being converted into Yawls, proved faster under that rig than under their original Cutter's rig. As modern instances confirmatory of this, may be mentioned the German Emperor's famous yacht *Meteor;* the *Ailsa,* and some others.

The term *yawl,* as distinguished from the Yawl-*rig,* signifies a boat with stem and stern alike; both ends being sharp, like a lifeboat or a Norway yawl.

A Yawl is also a term applied to a man-of-war's boat, resembling the pinnace, but smaller; carvel built, and generally rowed with twelve oars.

The *Yawl-rig* is a distinct term applied to the special form of rig above described; so that any sailing-boat that is Yawl-rigged is termed a Yawl.

The Sailing-Boat.

For comfort and convenience, the Yawl-rig is one of the best and handiest that is known, whether for a yacht or pleasure boat, large or small. The main-sail being all inboard, and much narrower than that of a Cutter, is less difficult to manage, and

From a photo by   *West & Son, Southsea.*

"Satanita," Yawl Rig.

can be the more readily reefed; and a mast of smaller proportion suffices. The boom being also sometimes dispensed with is another advantage, as it considerably lightens the rig and enables the boat to ride easier in a sea-way; and the annoyance of a heavy boom swinging overhead from side to side when tacking is avoided.

The Yawl Rig.

The Yawl-rig is admirably adapted for a shooting or fishing yacht; in fact, no better rig is known for either purpose.

THE DANDY RIG.

THE Dandy-rig bears a striking resemblance to the Yawl-rig, the only difference being in the mizzen-sail; which, in the Dandy-rig, is of Bermudian, or jib-like form, and set on the mast without yard or gaff.

The advantages belonging to the Dandy-rig are precisely the same as those of the Yawl-rig; the main-sail swings clear of the mizzen, and may be worked without a boom, whereby the danger and inconvenience of that heavy contrivance swaying overhead is avoided—a matter of considerable importance in a boat laden with passengers.

SOUTH COAST YAWLS.

SOME of the open pleasure boats employed at Hastings, Brighton, and other places on the south coast of England, for taking excursionists and others out for a sail, are rigged as Yawls, and are fine, powerful vessels. Some of the larger ones are nearly fifty feet in length, by thirteen and a half or fourteen feet in width, and of the burthen of twenty tons and upwards; perfectly open boats, capable of carrying twenty or thirty persons, without crowding.

Although large and capacious, these boats are safely managed at sea in ordinary weather by a crew of two or three experienced boatmen.

The most laborious work belonging to them is, the beaching and launching; but with the facilities of capstans, rollers and other contrivances the toil is considerably lightened.

From a photo by　　　　　　　　　*Mr. Harold Fraser.*

Yawl.

THE WENDA, CANOE YACHT.

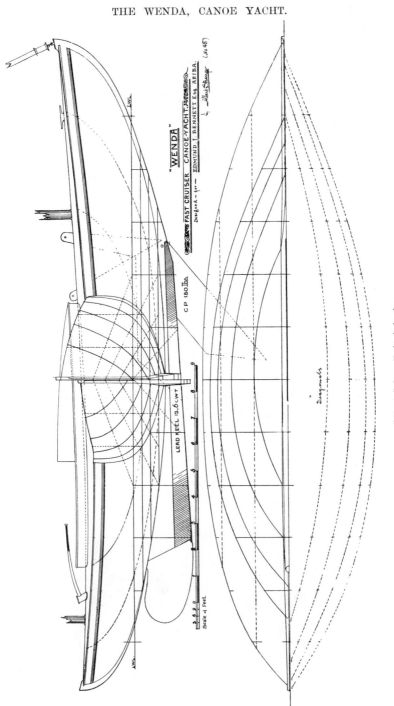

"Wenda," Canoe Yacht, body plans.

Canoe Yawl.

This beautiful little cruising-yacht was designed by Mr. Alfred Strange, of Scarborough, the designer of several other canoe-yachts well known to fame: among which may be mentioned *Cherub II.* and *Tavie II.*, of the Humber Yawl Club, the latter the property of Mr. John D. Hayward, M.C.C., B.C.A.

The *Wenda*, which is Yawl-rigged, was designed as a cruiser for Mr. Edmund

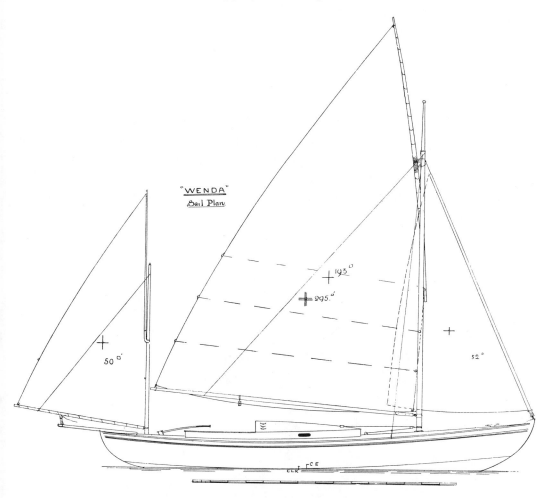

"Wenda," Canoe Yacht, sail plan.

J. Bennett, the leading requirements of which were that the yacht should be constructed with as light a displacement as possible consistent with immunity from capsizing: with fair accommodation for a crew of two persons, but as regards management, to be within the power of one to work a passage single-handed, or to enjoy an afternoon's sail: speed was to be kept in view, but at the same time the extent of sail-area was to be very moderate. In fact the instructions were that the boat should, as far as consistent with other special requirements, be " a good all-round cruiser, capable of making coast passages and yet be a good performer on the river." The necessity of light displacement was imperative, as the boat was to be capable of being shipped to foreign ports as inexpensively as was compatible with the length.

The chief dimensions of the *Wenda* are—

	ft.	ins.		ft.	ins.
Length over all	24	9	Draft with centre-plate down...	5	0
Length on L. W. L.	19	3	Least freeboard	1	6
Beam, extreme	6	5	Head room in cabin	3	9
Beam at L. W. L.	5	10½	Displacement ... ... 3360 lbs. (30 cwt.)		
Draft	2	3	Sail area ... ... 295 sq. ft.		

The extra length over all of the *Wenda* as compared with the two other boats above mentioned, will, it is conceived, be found of advantage when cruising off the coast at sea, in giving extra buoyancy and dryness, with steadier movements in broken water. The Well is small, so as to be the more readily covered when necessary.

The illustrations show the leading details of the hull and body plan, with the midship section and sail plan.

LUGGERS.

Three-masted Lugger.

A LUGGER is a boat or vessel rigged with lug-sails; some with one sail only, others with two or three; and boats of a large size, as sea-going and coasting luggers, in fine weather carry top-sails as well.

Anciently the lug-sail, if not the only form of rig used for sailing-boats and small vessels, was certainly the most general one. The *ancient* lug-sail was of square-like form, with a yard at the top slung at the middle part, and a sheet or guy at each of the lower corners.

There are several forms of lug-sails, the more general of which are the standing lug and the balance lug. A boat rigged with a standing lug may be put about and sailed on either tack without lowering the sail or easing the halliards; but a balance lug requires to be shifted to the other side of the mast on tacking the boat; so that the yard is always on the lee side of the mast when the boat is under way.

The lug is a handy form of rig for boats and small vessels, whether decked or open. Lug sails are cut, with more or less peak, according to fancy and the form of the boat for which it is intended, but all have a yard at the top, which is slung at one-third or one-fourth from the fore end—if a dipping lug at one-third, and if a standing lug at one-fourth.

The lugger rig has been from time immemorial a favourite one with beachmen, pilots, fishermen, and indeed boatmen of all classes, for open sailing-boats: and, as such men have great experience in boat-sailing, and would naturally select that which they consider the safest, most effective, and handy, it may be fairly concluded that the lugger is the most general and convenient rig of all for an open coasting boat. Besides, too, the lug-sail may be set and lowered more readily than any other, and requires less ropes and rigging. In small open boats, the single halliard serves as a stay (when such is necessary) to the mast, the only other rope required being the main sheet.

Some of the sea-going luggers employed on various parts of the coast rank among the finest and most powerful open boats within British waters; particularly the large open three-masted luggers, an illustration of one of which is shown on the previous page.

One of the chief advantages in the lugger rig is the facility with which sail may be shortened: and a lugger which in fine weather carries three lug-sails, besides jib and topsail—in all, five sails—may be sailed in heavy weather under one or two only of the lug-sails, selected from the larger or smaller, according to the weather. Another advantage is the lightness of the spars, and the facility with which one or more of the masts may be struck, and the boat relieved of the heavy pressure of top-hamper; a great advantage in bad weather.

A large and well-appointed lugger, with two or three masts, is probably as safe, handy, and powerful a form of rig for an open sailing-boat, for knocking about at sea in " all weathers," as any that has been contrived; and there are, undoubtedly, among the fishing, piloting and coasting class, more boats fitted as luggers than of any other form of rig; from which it may be inferred that the lugger rig is, for general purposes, the handiest and safest that is known.

A properly rigged lugger has besides, great power as a sailing-boat; and the masts being small and light in proportion to the large area of canvas that is spread, the boat rides easily under her spars, and sails with less labouring in a sea-way than one with a single heavy mast, boom and gaff sail.

Pilots, on approaching ships at sea, are enabled to lower a lug-sail in an instant, and strike the mast, to avoid collision with any part of the ship's rigging. A rope is then thrown them from the ship; with this they make the boat fast, and then quickly board the vessel. But in very rough weather and heavy seas, there would be great danger in running a boat alongside a vessel; so the pilot takes a couple of turns round his waist with the rope thrown him from the ship, and casts himself into the sea; he is then cautiously drawn aboard the vessel.

The Balance Lug.—This old-fashioned rig is a good and useful one for small boats: the lug-mainsail and fore-sail being both in one, the tack is hooked in the bows of the boat, and the yard is slung about one-third from the fore end.

The Standing Lug.—For a standing lug the yard should be slung at about one-fourth of its length from the fore end, and the tack made fast at the lower part of the mast: a separate fore-sail is generally used with a standing lug.

Dipping the lug is a smart active performance, although simply that of swinging the yard to the other side of the mast at the instant of coming about, for the purpose of placing the yard on the leeward side of the mast. In dipping the lug the sail need only be partially lowered. It requires two persons to dip the lug, one to slack the halliards a few inches, another to attend the tack, the main-sheet being also eased off; then, at the moment the boat is in stays, one of the crew steps upon the thwart, and dexterously swings the fore-part of the yard to the other side of the mast; the halliards are then set taut, the tack secured, the main-sheet hauled in, and the boat is quickly on a fresh tack with the sail fairly set. When actively done, dipping the lug is a smart sailor-like performance.

The original method of shifting the lug-sail, when putting about on change of tack, is to lower the sail, unhook the yard from the traveller, and shift it whilst down; this, although a primitive performance and one to which many objections may be raised, is still a good deal practised by fishermen and others in small open boats on various parts of the coast, particularly in bad weather.

Some of the north country cobles which are fitted with standing lug-sail and fore-sail are ingeniously rigged, so that the sails may be managed with the same facilities as the sprit-sail and fore-sail; they sail on either tack without dipping the lug or lowering the sail, the yard remaining on the same side of the mast as when first hoisted. Where this plan is adopted, brails are generally fitted to the sail, so that it is seldom necessary to lower the yard of the main-lug when bringing up in harbour.

The Lugger Rig.

An excellent mode of rigging a lugger as a pleasure-boat, or for general purposes, was suggested to the Author many years ago by a yacht owner of great experience in boat-sailing, and who for a long time had a boat in constant use rigged upon this plan. As the Author had many opportunities of testing the merits of the rig, and of seeing the boat alluded to under sail, he is enabled to recommend it with confidence as a safe and handy rig for a small boat.

The engraving is from a drawing by the inventor himself, showing his two-masted lugger so rigged and under full sail.

The method consists in a lug-sail of ordinary cut being laced to the yard, slung at

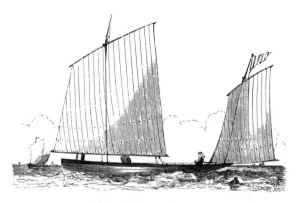

Useful Design for a Lugger.

the middle, and hoisted with a mast-traveller and halliards; but the foot or flap of the sail is laced to a boom, and bowsed down quite flat and taut, by means of a small tackle in front of and at the foot of the mast; as shown in the engraving. With a boat under this rig, there is no necessity for dipping the lug, or lowering it in any way, on coming about; the sail stands flat on either side of the mast, and the man at the helm can alone do all that is necessary in manipulating the sail by means of the main-sheet. This mode of rig is, of course, applicable to a single-masted lugger with one sail only, as well as to one with two masts. The rig is, in fact, almost equal, as regards convenience for tacking and manœuvring, to that of a revolving or sheer-masted boat, as the sail may be turned in any direction with rapidity and precision on coming about in a narrow tide-way: and so, too, on reaching or running before the wind.

The Sailing-Boat.

Split Lug Rig.

THE peculiarity of this rig consists in the head of the fore-sail (which is square at the top) being laced to the fore part of the main-sail yard, as shown in the illustration. The rig has therefore the appearance of being contrived out of a lug-sail split from top to bottom in line with the mast, so that the fore part of the sail, although suspended from the same yard, forms a fore-sail, and is trimmed and managed with independent sheets just the same as any other fore-sail; the singularity being that both sails are laced to the same yard, and neither can be hoisted or lowered without the other; therefore one pair of halliards suffices for both sails. The tack of the main-sail is made fast at or near the lower part of the mast; whilst the tack of the piece which forms the fore-sail is secured in the bows of the boat, or to the outer end of the bowsprit or boomkin; and the clew is worked with fore-sheets, just as an ordinary fore-sail. One

50

The Split Lug.

of the advantages of this rig is that in tacking the yard need not be dipped or lowered, but the boat may be worked to windward with the facility of a fore-and-aft rigged boat, and without once lowering the yard or slacking the halliards

It is an old-fashioned rig, seldom used at the present day.

From a photo by   Beken & Son, Cowes, I. of W.

The "Querida."

The *Querida*, though of the split-lug type of rig, differs in several respects from the ordinary split-lug already described.

The most striking peculiarity in the rig of the *Querida* is the outstanding fore-sail, the head of which is slung from the outer fore-end of the yard, which extends about one-third of its length in front of the mast; but the luff of the main-sail, being in line with the mast, the fore part of the yard is bare from the mast to the extreme fore-end from which the fore-sail is slung. One of the advantages of this rig is that the fore-sail always stands at the same angle as the main-sail, being guided, moved, and adjusted by the yard itself; so that when running before the wind the head of the fore-sail is held out by the yard so as to catch the full benefit of the wind: the foot of the fore-sail, although not laced to the boom, yet is fitted with a boom, the inner end of which works in a goose-neck attached to the fore part of the mast, and the outer end of the fore-sail-

51

boom stands about two feet above the stem, and is fitted with guy-ropes so as to regulate the position of the outer end of the fore-sail-boom, particularly when running before the wind.   The fore-sail is also fitted with a batten, which extends across it in an oblique direction, as shown in the illustration.   The main-sail is narrow at the head, but broad at the foot; and is laced to a boom which extends the sail over the stern and a little beyond it, the fore-end of the boom being fitted to the mast with a goose-neck : the boat also carries a triangular-shaped top-sail, as shown in the illustration.

The *Querida* is owned by Dr. P. W. Hughes, of Ryde, is one of the boats of the *Redwing* class, and has proved a highly successful and capable boat—the winner of many cups and other prizes in the various matches she has contested in the Solent and neighbouring waters.

YARMOUTH SALVAGE YAWLS.

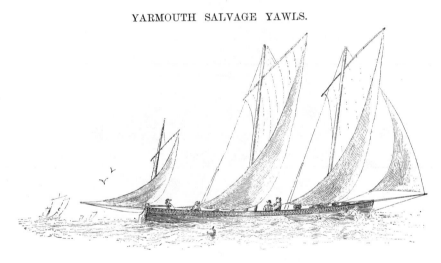

Yarmouth Salvage Yawl.

THESE splendid boats, formerly the admiration of all who visited Yarmouth, Cromer, Lowestoft, Aldborough, and some other watering places on the eastern coast, are now a relic of the past, having been superseded by steam boats : a matter of regret to all who remember them.

They were the longest and swiftest open sailing-boats in the world.   Some of them being upwards of sixty feet in length,[1] and from ten to twelve feet in breadth, with a remarkably sharp and gracefully formed bow, rising gradually from amidships ; the stern was also somewhat elevated, so that they were much lower amidships than at bow and stern.   They were propelled with oars in calm weather or adverse winds.

[1] The yawl *Reindeer*, of Yarmouth, was 69 feet.

Yarmouth Salvage Yawls.

When sailed, they were ballasted simply with bags of shingle, an inexhaustible supply of which was always at hand on the beach. The advantages of being so ballasted, were that as the crew frequently had to throw all their ballast overboard on beaching through a heavy surf, they had only to untie and open the bags and shoot it out, which was merely the work of a few moments. The boat was then light and buoyant; and on touching the beach, the crew quickly jumped out and hauled her up out of danger. They were always well-manned and cleverly handled; and in strong winds and heavy seas, all, except those who had the actual management of the sails, squatted down in the bottom of the boat, to preserve its stability.

With a stiff breeze on their quarter, these Yarmouth yawls have been known to sail *sixteen* knots in an hour, a pace unequalled by any other kind of open sailing-boat in the world. Their beautiful proportions, large sails, lightness, and buoyancy, added to which, the exquisite seamanship of their crews, gave them a reputation among the boating class such as will never be forgotten by those who remember them.

When under sail, the Yarmouth yawls were rigged with three masts, on each of which they carried a lug-sail, the largest, or main-sail, being amidships; the next size forward, and called the fore-sail or fore-lug; and the smallest aft, called the mizzen. They were also provided with a bowsprit, and in fine weather they set a fairly large jib. In a strong wind or gale, the jib and bowsprit were dispensed with; and the lug-sails close-reefed; sometimes, on such occasions, the two smallest only were used, viz., fore-sail and mizzen, in which case the main-mast was lowered, thereby enabling the boat to ride easier in a heavy sea.

These yawls were employed not only for the purpose of taking out pilots to passing merchantmen, but also as salvage boats. They generally belonged to companies or crews, each man being entitled to a share in the earnings of the boat. The brave fellows who manned them were a hardy, fearless class, who ventured to sea in perilous gales to ships in distress. Hundreds of lives and valuable cargoes have been saved by their daring exertions. It was no uncommon thing in a heavy sea for two or three of the crew to be constantly employed in baling out the water that was shipped from the surf breaking over the bows of the boat when in the perilous surroundings of the sands on which the wreck was lying.

Nothing daunted by wind or weather, when they espied a ship at sea with a signal of distress flying, or a signal for a pilot, they launched one of their famous boats from the beach and at all risks proceeded towards the ship, sometimes a distance of ten or fifteen miles. It was truly wonderful to witness the buoyancy and capabilities of these boats in a heavy sea.

One great precaution which the crew adopted in the management of them was never if possible to allow a heavy sea to strike the boat *a-broadside*, but always *stem on*. In turning the boat, when the waves were running high, they watched for ' *a*

The Sailing-Boat.

smooth'; then, if rowing, all oars on one side pulled one way, whilst the others backed water, and the boat, although of such a great length, was quickly round.

Certain parts of the eastern coast, off Norfolk and Suffolk, abound with sands and shoals, some of which are many miles out at sea; the value, therefore, in those parts, of the services of such boats and crews could not be over-estimated by the shipping and mercantile community in the days preceding the steam boats which have now superseded them.

YARMOUTH BEACH BOATS.

Yarmouth Beach Boat "Britannia."

THE modern type of boat employed by the beach boatmen at Yarmouth at the present day, though very different to the yawls above described, are a fine, capable and powerful class of open sea-boat.

They are used chiefly in the summer season for taking visitors and pleasure-parties out for a sail on the open sea in the Yarmouth roads and neighbourhood of the Scroby sands; and, although boats of a similar class are employed at other popular sea-side resorts, there are no finer or more able sea-boats than those at Yarmouth, of which the illustration above given is that of the *Britannia*, one of the largest, most modern, and best type; a powerful and splendid sea-boat.

The Yorkshire Coble.

The *Britannia* was built by the Messrs. Beeching Brothers, of Great Yarmouth, the well-known and highly-reputed designers and builders of many of the most famous yawls and other boats in that neighbourhood.

The dimensions and other particulars of the *Britannia* are:—Length, 42½ feet; breadth, 12 feet; depth, 4 feet 9 inches; Cutter-rigged; clench built, entirely of oak, and copper fastened. The spars are—mast, hoist, 30 feet; boom (length), 35 feet; gaff, 27 feet; bowsprit (outside stem), 14 feet. This boat is managed by a crew of four; and in fine weather by three.

The most difficult and laborious work in relation to these large beach boats is that of launching and hauling up. For this purpose, however, every modern facility is at hand on the beach; such as capstans, cradles fitted with rollers, turn-tables, warps, chain cables, and such-like: so that they are quickly hauled up out of the surf, high and dry on the beach, where they are turned round and got ready for launching again with as little delay as possible.

It will be remembered that the late Mr. James Beeching (now Beeching Brothers), of Great Yarmouth, ship and boat builder, was in the year 1850 the successful competitor, amongst two hundred and eighty others, for the prize offered by the then Duke of Northumberland for the best model of a life-boat combining certain standard qualities specified by a carefully selected Committee formed for the purpose, and to examine and decide on the two hundred and eighty models afterwards exhibited at Somerset House in that year. The model of the Beeching prize life-boat was afterwards deposited at the United Service Museum, where it still remains.[1]

THE YORKSHIRE COBLE.

Coble.

THE Cobles of the north-east coast of England are, probably, the most perfect form of open sailing-boat for putting out to sea in rough weather of any yet invented (life-boats alone excepted). Cobles are of Yorkshire origin, and from time immemorial have been renowned for superior qualities as safe sea-boats, when under experienced management; but in unskilful hands they are as liable to disaster as other boats.

---

[1] In the previous edition of this work a full description was given, with an illustration, of the Northumberland or Beeching Prize Life-Boat; but the whole chapter on Life-Boats, occupying about 20 pages in the previous edition of this work, has been, to the Author's regret, unavoidably crowded out for want of space in this edition.

The Sailing-Boat.

Cobles are the favourite and prevailing form of boat all along the north-east coast of England. At Flamborough Head, that stormy and dangerous part of the Yorkshire coast, no other description of open boat (unless a life-boat) is considered safe to put to sea in when the weather is bad; and it is seldom that any other is used there in rough weather; but that is a very perilous rock-bound coast, upon which a north-east wind causes a tremendous sea.

Cobles have several very distinct features: in the first place, they have a high, flaring, but beautiful, bow, sharp and hollow; and a graceful wave-like form of rim from stem to stern; at the latter point the graceful proportions of the coble cease, for the stern presents a flat, raking surface. The rudder is deep and narrow; reaching four feet or more below the bottom of the boat, in a slanting direction, and acting both as rudder and keel (or aft-gripe) it is of infinite service in a heavy sea, the deep hold of the rudder enabling the steersman to keep the boat from broaching-to.

These boats have no actual keel aft, but the sharpness of the bow gives them a good fore-gripe. All along the other part of the bottom they have a very flat floor; indeed, *quite* flat towards the stern, where the form of the boat is much narrower than amidships. The sides are bulged out in form, abaft the bow, but 'tumble home,' or incline inwards, at the top and gunwale.

The coble is generally sailed under a single fore-and-aft lug-sail, a small fore-sail being occasionally used, and, in fine weather, a jib. The lug-sail is, in modern-rigged cobles, fitted upon the most approved plan, so that it need not be dipped or lowered on coming about.

To the floor of the coble, near the bows, are fitted three separate heel-steps or sockets for receiving the heel of the mast, so that in light winds the mast is stepped in an upright position; in a fair breeze it is stepped in the middle step, which inclines it aft, in a raking attitude; and when blowing heavily, the sail is reefed and the mast stepped in the third position, which is very raking. The aft rake of the mast tends to ease the bows of the boat in a heavy sea, and to assist it in rising to the waves.

The larger class of Cobles generally carry two masts, though one only is used at a time, the tall one in fine weather and the short one, with a smaller sail, in stormy weather and heavy seas. In fine weather the short mast is sometimes utilised as a bowsprit for a jib-sail.

When a jib is used, the bowsprit is not placed in a horizontal position as in other open boats, but with the outer end tipped up like the jib-boom of a schooner, the advantage of which is obvious. If the bowsprit were run out horizontally the boat, when pitching in a heavy sea, would plunge it under water and soon carry it away, and the pressure of the sail, acting on the bows, would assist in burying the head of the boat under the waves; but by inclining the bowsprit upwards, such an evil is avoided, and the sail acts as a lifting, as well as a powerful drawing sail.

The Yorkshire Coble.

The safety of the coble under sail depends in a great measure on the proper adjustment of the main-sheet: in a strong wind it is never made fast, but has

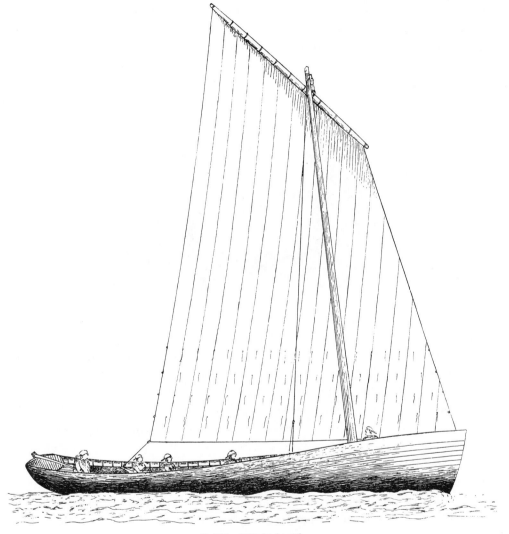

Yorkshire Coble (under sail).

frequently to be eased and humoured to the wind and waves, particularly when the sea is running high.

When ballasted, the coble has a great hold of the water forward, but very little aft; the deep-diving rudder has therefore to be shipped before anything can be done with the boat under sail. This rudder is then a powerful lever for preventing the boat from broaching-to in a heavy sea, which a coble would be very liable to do in the absence of such a rudder, by reason of the sharp fore-gripe of the bow.

In order further to guard against such an evil, in some instances revolving keels, or centre-boards, have been introduced among the north-country boatmen, and found to answer fairly well; for when the centre-board is down, the coble has all the properties of a keel-boat, both in working to windward and reaching or running in a heavy sea.

Cobles are used by all classes of boatmen on the north-east coast: for instance, there are pleasure-boat cobles, fishing cobles, pilot cobles (the engraving represents a pilot

Pilot Coble.

coble with its sail struck, and about to approach a ship for the purpose of putting a pilot on board), and there used to be salvage cobles, but the latter are now superseded by steam-tugs. The largest sized cobles are those employed in the herring fishery; some of these are from ten to fifteen tons burthen, and have a cabin, either in the bows or just abaft the mast. A middle-sized coble is about twenty-four feet in length, by five feet two inches in breadth, and two feet two inches in depth; the rudder in a coble of this size projects four feet below the stern.

A few hours before dusk on a summer's evening during the herring season a very interesting scene frequently may be witnessed, as several hundreds of these boats leave the different ports and harbours on the coast. Not a white sail is to be seen among the whole fleet—all are tanned for preservation from wet and mildew, to make them more durable.

The coble fishermen often go many miles from the coast, and drift their nets in company with the Scotch luggers, Dutch, and other fishing boats, from all of which the English and foreign markets are supplied with fish.

The North of England boatmen manage these cobles with remarkable skill and dexterity; and though often exposed to gales at sea on that perilous coast, they seldom come to grief.

The Yorkshire Coble.

As an open sea-boat, the coble is unequalled by those of any other form, with the exception only, perhaps, of the old Yarmouth yawls, before described (but now extinct); and the latter, be it remembered, were adapted to meet the requirements of a shallow coast, whilst the coble is for the deep seas of a bold and rocky headland.

It is astonishing the heavy seas these cobles will live in, under skilful handling; the chief danger to guard against, as in all sea-going boats, is broaching-to in a heavy sea: and when they scud before a gale they are so quick and lively that it is a very rare occurrence for a breaker to curl over the stern and 'poop' them, as would be the case in a heavy sea with many other boats of a different form.

Among other good points, they are handy to beach, easy to row, and good on a wind. On approaching the beach, or going into shallow water, the rudder is unshipped, and the coble backed in, stern first; the stern being of less draught of water than the forepart: and when the coble, thus backed, grounds on the beach, it keeps its upright position, instead of falling over on its side as boats with more or less dead wood aft do. When rowing these boats in smooth water, whether before the wind or otherwise, they are generally propelled stern first, because they row easier and better in that position; and the same when being towed.

The *coble oars* are different to those of other boats. They consist of two separate parts, the loom of the oar being a square or flat-sided piece, and the blade, with a short portion of the loom, is usually joined to the other by two iron bands, which secure and hold the two parts firmly together; the flat part of the loom rests on the gunwale, and in that position will not admit of being *feathered* in a similar manner to that of an oar with a round loom. An iron ring is firmly attached to the coble oar at its proper equipoise, which fits loosely over a standard iron thowl-pin, so that there is no danger of the oars going adrift, although left suspended over the sides of the boat; and they may be turned close in, either towards stem or stern, without unshipping.

In small rivers and shallow waters the coble would prove inferior as a sailing-boat, on account of the deep rudder and high, flaring bow. Some persons have, however, occasionally taken so great a fancy to these boats as to insist on trying experiments with them in smooth-water rivers, for which purpose they have been fitted with a revolving keel or centre-board, and all the lower part of the rudder extending below the boat has to be cut off and added to the aft part, making it of the same shape as the rudder of a flat-bottomed sailing barge; but, independently of the want of a keel, the very high bow is an impediment to fast sailing in smooth water, from its catching the wind, and causing the boat to blow to leeward.

The Sailing-Boat.

Latine Rig.

THE Latine rig is of Eastern origin, but has long been used and adopted, with modifications, in European countries. It is a pretty and graceful-looking rig for a pleasure boat, and one that never fails to win admirers amongst those who are fond of the picturesque, if the sails be true latines, well cut, and fairly set. But there is no rig in which the pretty effect so much depends on the shape and make of the sails.

Latine sails never look better than when gliding along on a summer's evening under the shadow of lofty hills, or beneath the frown of high basaltic cliffs; their tall, slender peaks and white triangles contrasting favourably with the dark features of mountain scenery.

In shape the latine sail is triangular, with a slender, pointed peak; or precisely that of a large jib-sail; it requires a long, stiff tapering yard to spread it with effect.

The Latine Rig.

The mast for the latine rig is placed in the boat in a position raking forwards, or towards the bows of the boat; it is very short, but requires a back-stay.

Boats sail fast under this rig, particularly when close-hauled; the one objection is, the very long yard that is required to set the sail fairly, often considerably longer than the boat, therefore somewhat cumbersome and inconvenient for stowing away if let down on deck, which, however, is seldom necessary. The inconvenience only arises when the boat is rigged with a single latine sail; when two or more are used, the yards are not so long as to be inconvenient.

For latine-rigged boats of broadish build, carrying only one mast and sail, the yard required would be nearly twice the length of the boat. If rigged with two masts and latine sails, then each yard would be at least the full length of the boat.

The yards for small latine-rigged sailing-boats are usually of bamboo, which is not one-tenth the weight of solid pine spars; but as bamboo is more or less brittle when dry, the yards of the larger craft are sometimes made of several pieces of light, tapering spars spliced together, the thickest part being in the middle.

Good sound bamboo spars suitable for latine sails were, until recently, very difficult to procure in England, though found in abundance in far Eastern lands.

The latine rig is best suited to smooth water and light winds, but perilous in heavy seas and strong winds, because of the loftiness of the peaks of the sails and the difficulty of satisfactorily reefing them. The peak of a latine sail cannot be dropped or lowered with the facility of a gaff-sail, though brails are usually fitted for frapping the sail close to the yard; but even then the swaying to and fro of the lofty yards in a heavy sea is sometimes attended with danger.

But in smooth water the rig is safe enough, for although the peak of the sail stands very high, the principal breadth and body of the canvas is low—a great consideration in rigging all open boats. It is also worthy of remark that when running before the wind, if the boat be rigged with two latines they may be 'goose-winged,' that is, boomed out over the gunwale, one on each side of the boat, as shown in the illustration on the next page, which is that of a latine-rigged boat thirty-five feet long by nine feet beam, and having a ton of lead on her keel outside.

In the Mediterranean, latine-rigged vessels of various sizes may be seen, and among them are many fast-sailing and beautiful boats. Everyone who has cruised in Mediterranean waters, and along the coasts of Spain and Portugal, is familiar with the latine-rigged vessels and their lofty-peaked and graceful-looking sails, and has, probably, witnessed the activity of the crews who man them, the nimble manner in which they climb the slender yard, frap the sail, and perform other feats of seamanship interesting and amusing to British sailors.

These vessels, when seen off the coast of Spain in fine weather, are seldom without two or three of the crew clinging to some part of the yard, or at the top of the

61

The Sailing-Boat.

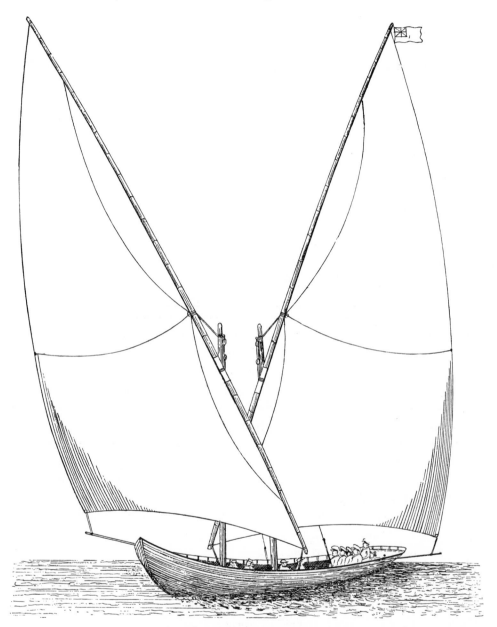

Latine. Sails goose-winged.

stumpy-headed mast, where they sometimes remain for an hour or more at a time, but for what purpose it would be difficult to say.

The latine rig is found in various parts of the world. It is used on most of the navigable rivers of India, also in and about the Mediterranean Sea, on the River Nile, and the Lake of Geneva. It is an excellent rig for a sailing-boat in the neighbourhood of land-locked waters, and where light airs prevail; but for strong winds and rough seas other rigs are to be preferred.

SAILING-BOATS OF THE NORFOLK RIVERS AND BROADS.

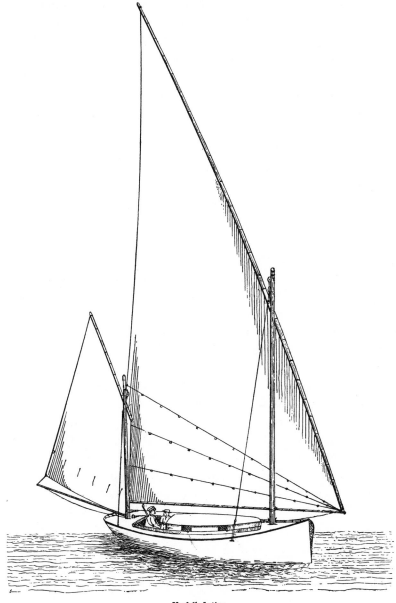

Norfolk Latine,

The Sailing-Boat.

THE extensive and interesting locality of the Norfolk Broads and inland rivers is well adapted for boating; but it is of a kind totally different to that of the coast, or of large tidal rivers: consequently the form of boat and the rig for sailing on the Norfolk rivers differ in many respects from those of the sea-going and coasting class.

The power of 'coming about' with rapidity and precision is indispensable in a sailing-boat destined to navigate the narrow, tortuous rivers which intersect the fens and meadows of Norfolk. The form of hull of the inland small yachts is therefore very broad in proportion to length; some of them so broad as to resemble, on deck, the back of a turbot. They have usually a leaden keel running the whole length of the bottom; and the draft of water varies according to the size of the boat; but it is never very deep, as in some of the broads they navigate the water is shallow.

The latine rig, as shown by the illustration, consists of a latine main-sail and lug-mizzen; and is one that was formerly much in vogue on the River Yare, in Norfolk, for the pleasure-boats of that locality. It is admirably suited for narrow waters and tortuous rivers, where short tacking is unavoidable; but quite unsuited to the open sea off the coast of Norfolk.

Boats for turning to windward in narrow rivers must be short and wide; a long, rakish craft would be unmanageable in such waters: consequently the rig is well chosen for the locality.

Among the Norfolk latines are some fast-sailing and attractive boats after this rig; the largest are twenty-six feet on the ram (*i.e.* from stem to stern-post), and ten feet beam; the smaller size are sixteen feet on deck, whilst the breadth of beam is eight feet six inches. They have good interior accommodation, and a broad, open cockpit or well.

The latine fore-sail, which is, in fact, the main-sail, is much the larger sail of the two, and is peaked up by a yard of almost incredible length in the larger-sized boats. The customary length of yard for the *smaller* size is from *forty-nine to fifty feet!* thus enabling them to set a very large sail with lofty peak; but notwithstanding this, the sail, when well made, stands nicely flat, and the boat is extremely handy under such a rig in tacking, staying, or any other manœuvre requiring quick movements.

The safe management of a boat rigged in this manner may be performed by one person alone. After the latine fore-sail is once set, it is entirely under the control of the person attending the main-sheet, and may be turned about in any direction with ease and precision. An iron traveller is connected with the boom at the lower part of the mast; and as this is the only fastening by which the sail is held down, the Norfolk latine may be worked with almost equal facility to that of a revolving-rigged boat.[1] The boom is elevated a little above deck, so that nothing may incommode the crew; the mizzen works of itself with little or no trouble.

The Norfolk latine is altogether a most useful and ingenious rig for short tacking in

---

[1] Infra, p. 82 *et seq.*

smooth water, in fact, none can compare with it for beating up against wind in very narrow waters ; but for wide waters and sea-going purposes, the Norfolk latines were never intended.

It is matter of regret that this graceful and interesting form of rig is not nearly so much in favour as it used to be on the Norfolk rivers ; the objection being, the enormous length of the yard required for spreading the sail, and the inconvenience of stowing a spar on board which is three times the length of the boat. Consequently, the majority of the small yachts and pleasure-boats of the Norfolk inland waters are now rigged after the fashion of the Upper Thames boats and the more popular Solent rig.

THE STRANGFORD LATINE.

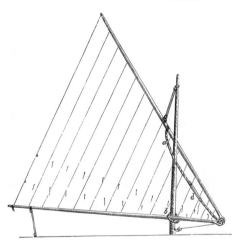

The Strangford Latine Rig.

This is a modern form of latine rig, upon a plan adopted by the late Lord de Ros, who kindly sent the Author a description of it with a drawing, from which the above engraving has been made. His lordship's well-known skill and experience in yachting and boat-sailing are alone sufficient to recommend it ; and it appears to be a handy and weatherly rig for a small boat.

It will be seen that the boom is parrelled to the mast at *b*, but the yard is kept to the mast by a jack-rope, *a*, which is hauled taut by a small tackle, *d*, composed of two small blocks, or of metal thimbles, and ratline ; thus enabling the yard to be lowered, either partially for reefing, or wholly for striking sail, without disengaging the tack from the fore end of the boom, which would have to be done if the yard were hoisted and held to the mast by a traveller.

The boom and gaff thus close like a pair of compasses ; and the reef-points being run from the apex at the tack, to the usual distance on the aft-leech, the sail, when reefed is brought down lower, but the aft-power of it is not diminished.[1]

NORFOLK WHERRIES.

Norfolk Wherry.

THESE vessels may properly be described as the inland cargo boats of the rivers and broads of Norfolk: they are used chiefly for the conveyance of heavy merchandise, such as corn, flour, meal, &c., and bricks, lime, and other building materials, to and from the various towns and business places on those water ways. Of late years enterprising boat owners on the Broads have fitted up some of these vessels as pleasure-wherries, and provided them with centre-boards to enable them to navigate under sail the waterways of the locality; and, it appears, with considerable success; the whole of the cargo-carrying portion of the wherry being thus utilised and fitted with saloon sleeping cabins, and other accommodation, and so converting them into house-boats for small boating parties, who, it seems, avail themselves in summer of the opportunity of a few weeks' inexpensive

[1] The Author has called this the 'Strangford Latine,' as the inventor, the late Lord de Ros, first tried and brought it into use at Strangford.

and thoroughly enjoyable boating and fishing excursions on those interesting and picturesque waters the Norfolk Broads.

The Norfolk wherry is a flat, shallow, barge-like form of vessel, unsuited to sea-going purposes, or indeed any other than the navigation of those inland waters. They vary in size from 20 to 30 tons; and in length from 50 to 60 feet, by 10 to 12 feet beam; they have a very large and broad rudder, and when laden, draw only $2\frac{1}{2}$ to 3 feet of water.

The wherry is rigged with one sail only, a heavy gaff-sail or main-sail which is hoisted with the aid of a windlass, and the gaff is fitted with chain slings, but there is no boom. The mast is a heavy contrivance, standing well forward in the bows, and is pivoted just above deck to a 'tabernacle,' whereby the mast can be raised or lowered at pleasure, for the convenience of passing to and fro under the numerous bridges that span the inland rivers and canals of the locality. The raising and lowering of the mast is accomplished with facility by means of iron weights of several cwts., which are placed in a case affixed to the heel of the mast; and, assisted by a windlass, the whole contrivance of mast, sail, and gaff is quickly raised or lowered as occasion requires. There are no shrouds on either side the mast; but a stout fore-stay is made fast at the stem of the wherry, being set up by means of the windlass and double-sheaved blocks and tackle.

The main-sail is usually fitted with a bonnet, laced to the foot of the sail; this is used only in light winds, but taken off when the wind is heavy.

At the mast-head these wherries carry a small vane, attached to a slender iron staff with a metal revolving tube, to which a little flag is attached, to indicate the true direction in which the wind is blowing: this contrivance is indispensable in navigating, under sail, the narrow winding rivers of the Broads; as, contrary to large open waters, where the direction of the wind can be seen at a glance by the ripples on the surface, in these land-locked canals there are no such indications.

A Quant (Norfolk).

In a calm or head wind, recourse is had to a Quant, or Quanting-pole, similar to an ordinary barge-pole; the quant is shod at its lower end with a stout iron ferule, and with a wooden fin or shoulder just above the ferule, to prevent it from going deep into the mud or the banks of the river; and at the upper end with a knob or shoulder-piece, against which the wherry-man presses his shoulder when propelling the wherry. Quanting the wherry against a strong wind is a somewhat laborious task.

The Sailing-Boat.

In the summer season much pleasure may be derived by a small party with a taste for fishing and boating on fresh water, by a few weeks' sojourn and cruising in a modern well-equipped wherry on the Norfolk Broads.

THE SOLENT RIG.

From a photo by
"Bandicoot" (Solent Rig).
Beken & Son, Cowes, I. of W.

THE chief characteristic of the Solent rig (erroneously called a 'lugger rig') consists in the sail-plan of the main-sail, which, as will be seen by the above illustration, is cut

The Solent Rig.

with a very pointed peak, thereby combining top-sail and main-sail in one. It differs in that respect from a gaff-sail, and also in the fact that, instead of a gaff, it is laced to a yard; and when fairly set the yard stands nearly parallel with the mast, and thereby answers the purpose of main-sail and top-sail combined. The fore-leech of the sail may be laced to the mast, though it seldom is; nor is it necessarily held to the mast by hoops or rings, as in some other modes of rig. The tack of the Solent main-sail is

From a photo by   *Beken & Son, Cowes, I. of W.*

" Adie " (Solent Rig).

bowsed down to a cleat at the lower part of the mast, just below the goose-neck of the boom. So rigged the boat will stay, on being put about, as readily as a cutter-rigged boat: the foot of the sail in the Solent rig is laced to the boom.

A fore-sail is also carried, and, on the larger class of boat, a jib as well; but no top-sail.

It is not at all surprising that the rig has become very popular in our small-class racing and pleasure fleet. It is pretty and attractive : is a powerful and effective one on a small yacht or a half-decked sailing-boat ; is handy and safe under ordinary management, and may be used with a shorter mast than that required for a gaff-sail.

The Solent rig first came into general use amongst the small racing-yachts on the Solent, in the year 1889. It was introduced by Mr. Tom Ratsey, of the firm of Lapthorne and Ratsey, the eminent sail-makers of Cowes, Isle of Wight; and has been a favourite rig for the smaller class of racing yachts ever since.

It was not, however, a new invention, as boats so rigged have occasionally been in

The "Fairy."

use on the rivers of the East Coast for many years past ; and the Author himself had two boats of very similar rig more than forty years ago, one of which is shown by the illustration from the pencil of the late Mr. J. R. Kirby, when he lived at Stour Lodge, Essex, on the banks of the River Stour. But now that the rig has become generally popular on the Solent, the Author calls it 'the Solent rig' as the more appropriate. It certainly is not a lug, and it is a misnomer to call it a 'lug,' as it also is to call a boat so rigged a 'lugger.' No sail cut with such a peak, and standing nearly parallel with the mast, can either properly or correctly be termed a 'lug-sail.' Neither does the fact that a yard is used instead of a gaff make it a lug-sail, the latter being a square-headed sail, so cut that a top-sail may be set above it.[1]

THE BEMBRIDGE CLUB BOATS.

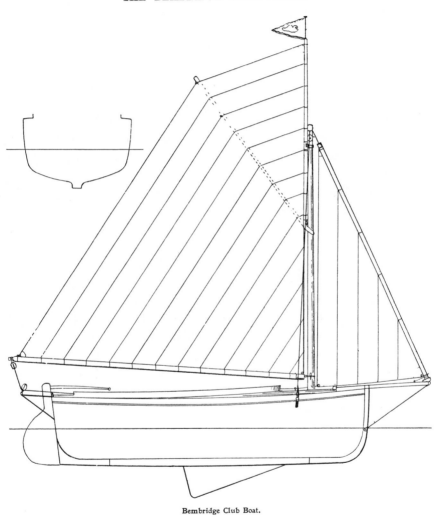

Bembridge Club Boat.

THESE boats, with the now well-known Bembridge rig,[2] were designed by Captain E. du Boulay, of the Royal Victoria Yacht Club, in the year 1889, for the 'Bembridge

[1] See engravings of luggers, supra, pages 16, 20 and 46.

[2] The drawing from which the illustration was made, and the details as to dimensions, &c., were kindly sent to the Author by Captain du Boulay.

The Sailing-Boat.

Sailing Club,' Isle of Wight. The boats are the property of the Bembridge Club, and intended chiefly for the use of the members of that Club to practise boat-sailing in. They are open boats with drop keels and flat rounded floor, square stern, and a scantling or deck-way, leaving an open well with plenty of room for manipulation of the sheets and halliards. Their dimensions are 16 feet over all, by 5-feet-4-inch beam; they are ballasted with 7 cwt. of inside ballast and an iron keel weighing 3 cwt.; the drop keel is made of galvanized boiler plate. With the keel up, they draw only 1 foot of water; the object being to enable them to navigate the shallows off the east coast of the Isle of Wight.

The rig of the Bembridge Club boats consists of main-sail and top-sail combined in one sail, with a batten on one side representing gaff and main-sail peak, as shown in the illustration, and a separate fore-sail. The combined main-sail and top-sail are hoisted by one halliard, the yard being hooked to a traveller which holds it close to the upper part of the mast. The mast is stepped forward in the bows of the boat, and the main-sail has a revolving boom reaching to the extreme end of the stern and extending about 2 feet beyond it. Reefing may be expeditiously performed by slacking the halliard, and then rolling the flap of the sail round the boom (to which it is already laced). The boom can revolve only when pulled away about a couple of inches from the mast. As soon, therefore, as the requisite extent of canvas has thus been rolled up, the boom is pushed back to the mast, and is immediately locked in its original position by the halliard being set up again. The tack of the fore-sail is secured at the outer end of the bowsprit, which extends about three feet beyond the stem, the luff of this sail being seized to a light hollow pine-wood roller, with a brass reel at the lower end. The fore-stay leads from the mast head through the hollow roller to the outer end of the bowsprit, and the fore-sail may thus be readily rolled up, reefed, or furled, as may be required, by a pull on the ratline attached to the reel. The Island Sailing Club at Cowes and the Hythe Yacht Club on the Southampton river, have each two or three of these boats for the use of members of their Club in which to practise boat-sailing.

Sailing-Canoes.

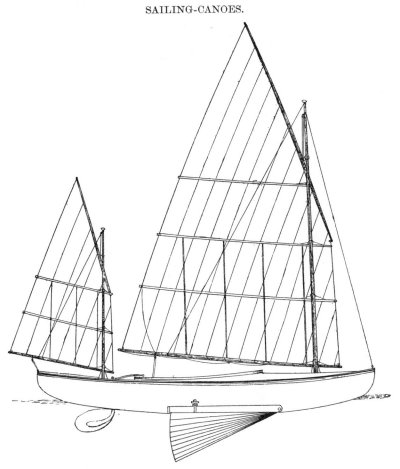

Sailing-Canoe, with Radix patent folding centre-plate.

THE illustration shows the contour of a sailing-canoe of modern type, fitted with a Radix patent folding centre-plate. It will be observed that the rudder, instead of being fitted to the stern of the canoe, as usual, is forward of the mizzen-mast, the object being to enable the canoeist to have complete control of the rudder from the well of the canoe. The rig is that known as the ordinary yawl rig for canoes, with battened lug-sail, fitted with the modern self-reefing fittings.

The smaller class of sailing-canoes at the present day are, many of them, very attractive and charming little boats; some are fitted with one mast, some with two: most of them have a revolving centre-board, and occasionally one may be seen with two. The rig varies, but the favourite is the battened gunter-sail, with self-reefing fittings, light bamboo spars, and a balance rudder.

The Sailing-Boat.

Those competing for prizes in the sailing matches of the Royal Canoe Yacht Club, or in the matches of some other canoe sailing clubs, must be constructed according to the requirements of the club as to length, breadth, depth, sail area, and other details : they are also required to be fitted with bulkheads, and to be unsinkable if capsizable ; or to be of a heavier class and non-capsizable.

Sailing-canoes are of various sizes, and are classed accordingly when competing in sailing matches. The chief advantages of a small sailing-canoe are that, if the wind

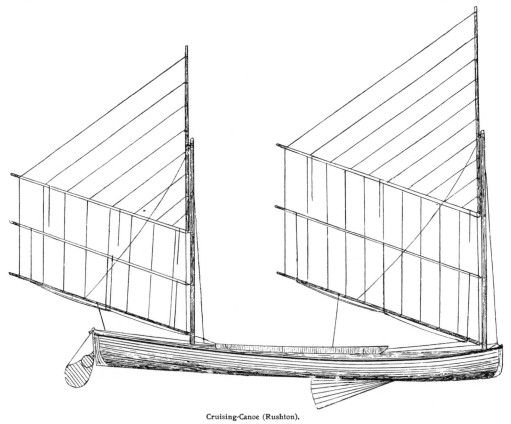

Cruising-Canoe (Rushton).

fails, the canoe may be propelled by a pair of light sculls, or by a double-bladed hand-paddle : and, being of easy draft, may be navigated in shallow water ; and the whole structure is so light and handy that the canoeist can readily lift it out of the water and haul it up on going ashore.

The sail-carrying power of a canoe of this class depends mainly on the live ballast, or that of the position in the canoe of the canoeist, who sits or reclines more or less to windward, according to the strength or power of the wind upon the sails : and in a strong wind he may sometimes be seen leaning over the gunwale, with the object of throwing his whole weight out to windward to counterpoise the canoe and keep her on her keel.

In some of the small American sailing-canoes, and so also in some of the British, a sliding-seat is used, which may be slid out to windward so that the canoeist may sit out over and beyond the gunwale, as if on an outrigger—no doubt very effective as a means of counterpoising the power of the wind upon the sail, but a somewhat perilous and comfortless position, worthy of the South Sea Islanders and other natives of the

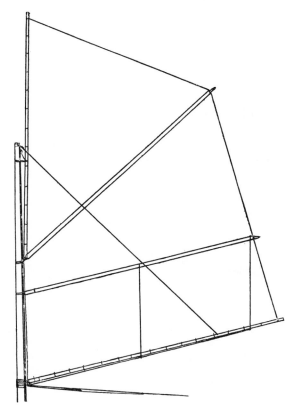

New Canoe Rig (Rushton).

Indian Archipelago ; where, at whatever season of the year the inevitable capsize occurs, the venturesome athlete finds the water nicely warm, and himself, probably, none the worse for his ducking : not so, however, in the chilly waters of the British Islands, where the result of the capsize is usually anything but agreeable.

Under the rules of the Thames Sailing-boat Association, 'appliances for enabling the crew to hang outside the boat' are not permitted.

The Sailing-Boat.

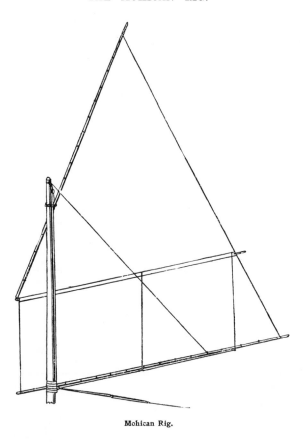

Mohican Rig.

THIS is a rig of American origin, and is one of the best for a small sailing-canoe : it is adapted for a single-handed canoe ; the sail may be set or lowered with facility, and may be reefed in a few moments by the single occupant of the canoe. It is one of Mr. Rushton's admirable contrivances for small sailing-boats.

THE HUMBER YAWL CLUB SAILING-BOATS.

THE sailing boats of this enterprising and popular Club are well worthy of note and description in the pages of any work devoted to the subject of boats and boat-sailing.

To the Humber Yawl Club belongs the credit of the introduction of a modern type of canoe cruising-yawl, possessing advantages and capabilities unsurpassed by those of any other canoe club in the United Kingdom.

The chief merits of the type are, its ample internal accommodation, consistent with

Sailing-Canoes.

length, breadth, and depth, power derived from large displacement, moderate draft, yet possessing fast sailing powers; and it is a safe and capable craft in a sea-way.

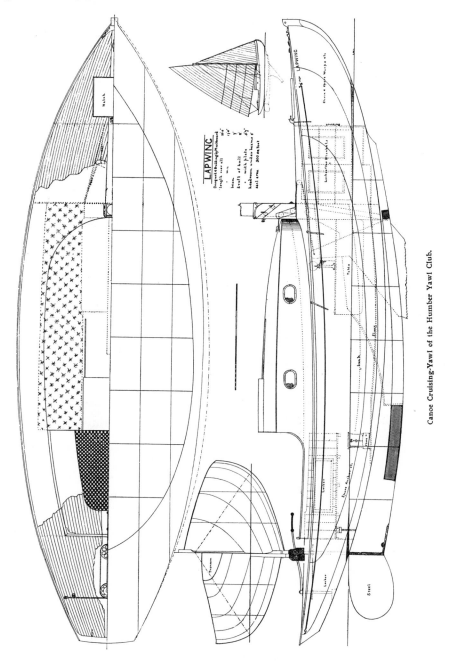

Canoe Cruising-Yawl of the Humber Yawl Club.

The Sailing-Boat.

The cruising-yawls of the Humber Yawl Club are not all of this modern type: some of the older ones vary considerably, but internal accommodation has always been kept in view as an indispensable adjunct to those destined for cruising purposes.

Nor are the boats of this Club all of the same class and rig; some that are destined mainly for the Humber, Hornsea Mere, and other home waters, are only half-decked, whilst others are open boats: some are rigged as Sloops, and some as Cutters; besides which there are House Boats, Sailing Dinghies, &c.; but by far the greater majority are Centre-board Canoe-yawls; and recently a One-Design Class has been started, but at present a few only of the class have been constructed.

In the modern type, the overhang fore and aft has been introduced, but only to a limited extent, and that chiefly in the yawl-rigged boats, whereby the aft-overhang has been utilised for the purpose of stepping the mizzen-mast abaft the rudder-head, and thereby the loop-tiller of the older style, which encircled the mizzen-mast, has been superseded.

The modern design is adaptable to a single-masted and single-handed cruiser as well as to those of the larger class of yawl-rigged cruisers; but always reserving a fairly reasonable extent of accommodation for two persons, in a permanent cabin, at all times dry and cosy, the middle part of which is left entirely clear, thereby greatly increasing the extent of cabin room.

The dimensions of one of the boats of the modern type, as stated in the Year-book of the Club, are:—Length over all, 21 feet 9 inches; length on L.W.L., 18 feet; overhang—bow, 2 feet; stern, 1 foot 9 inches; beam (extreme), 5 feet 9 inches; at L.W.L., 5 feet 3 inches; draft (extreme), 3 feet; displacement, 2,800 pounds, or 1·25 tons; ballast—iron keel, 1,184 pounds.

The construction is essentially that of a canoe, with flat bent keel, the fin being added after the hull is completed. The iron keel is bolted up through the dead wood of the fin and the main keel and floors.

In the cruising-yawls of this Club the members do not confine themselves to the cruising waters of the British Islands; some of them venture year by year on cruises in foreign waters, the favourite locality for their excursions being the inland seas, rivers, and dykes of Holland and Belgium; and the year 1897 saw, for the first time, the flag of the H.Y.C. in German waters; than which no finer canoe cruising ground could, perhaps, have been chosen. The upper reaches of the Elbe and the picturesque lakes of Mecklenburg offer pleasant and interesting varieties to the canoeist; and the new Kaiser Wilhelm Canal affords a ready and accessible route to the broad and tideless waters of the Baltic.

The illustration of the canoe cruising-yawl *Lapwing* is that of one of the most recent acquisitions to the Humber Yawl Club.

The *Lapwing* was intended to be adaptable as far as possible to the various purposes of inland cruising both at home and abroad: a boat alike suitable for navigating the waters of Hornsea Mere, the Humber, Bridlington, and other home localities, as well as for the land-locked waters of Holland, Belgium, Denmark, and Germany.

The *Lapwing* is from a design by Mr. Max Howard, who is a Member of the H.Y.C. Her dimensions are:—Length over all, 23 feet 6 inches; length on L.W.L., 17 feet 6 inches; beam, 7 feet; draft of hull, 2 feet; with centre-plate down, 5 feet 7 inches; sail area, 300 square feet; the steel centre-plate weighing about two hundredweight; and a steel rudder, sharpened on the lower edge.

The *Lapwing* is rigged with one mast only, and has three battens extending across the main-sail from fore-leech to aft-leech; the complete rig being baften main-sail, and roller jib.

The steering gear is worthy of special note. In order to get the advantage of a long tiller, two chain wheels are used, connected by an endless chain kept taut by a turn-buckle; the arrangement does away with the necessity of having the tiller projecting far into the cock-pit. The cock-pit is self-baling, with waste pipe and valve. The mast does not come below, but works in its tabernacle above deck, thus avoiding the difficulty of manipulating the centre-plate arm, which works through the mast-step as shown in the illustration.[1]

In the Year-books of the Humber Yawl Club are some excellent notes on cruising, not only in the Wash and other home waters, but also in the inland waters of Holland, Belgium, Northern Germany, and Denmark. The notes are written for the purpose of affording information to others who may be contemplating similar trips, and they contain, besides, much useful information as to cost, Customs' charges and other details, of which many a cruising canoeist would be glad to avail himself.

For comfort, handiness, and convenience as a Cruising Canoe-Yacht, probably no better type could be adopted than one of those designed by the master hand of Mr. Albert Strange, the designer of some of the most approved boats of the Humber Yawl Club.

The design of the *Otter* Canoe-Yacht (of which illustrations are here given) is from the board of Mr. Albert Strange. The *Otter* was designed for Mr. R. J. Durley, of the H.Y.C. and of the Canadian Royal St. Lawrence Yacht Club, and was intended chiefly for the Lower St. Lawrence River.

The illustrations of the *Otter* are so complete as to details, &c., that it would

---

[1] Through the courtesy of the Captain and Members of the Humber Yawl Club the Author has been enabled to reproduce the illustrations of the *Lapwing* from the Year Books of that Club. From the same source he desires to acknowledge the assistance he has derived as to details, &c., in the narrative above given of the leading features and objects of the sailing-boats of the Club.

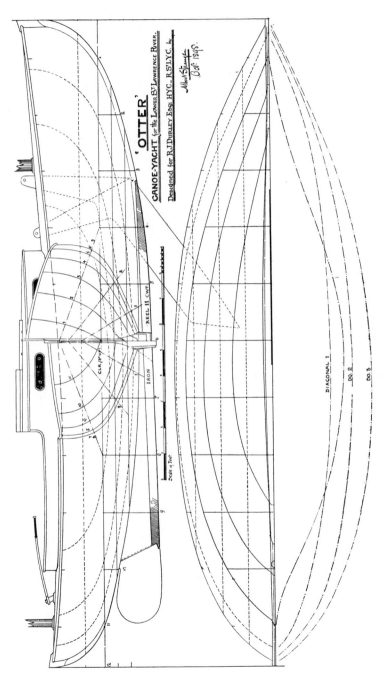

"Otter," Canoe-Yacht.

be superfluous to add to the description what can be better ascertained by reference to them.

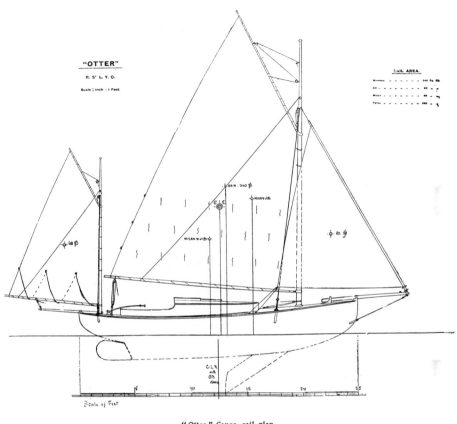

"Otter," Canoe, sail plan.

SHULDHAM'S REVOLVING RIG.

THIS singular but ingenious mode of rig is the invention of the late Captain Molyneux Shuldham, R.N., who kindly sent the Author drawings, sketches, and other original information, together with a brief history of the invention, showing its originality and success under repeated trials at Woolwich and elsewhere; besides which, the Author is enabled from his own personal observation of one of the boats, when under the able management of its inventor, in Harwich Harbour, and on the rivers Stour, Deben, and Orwell, to testify to its power, handiness, and weatherly qualities on a wind.

Many years ago, the revolving rig was frequently submitted to public and practical tests, and was entirely successful under various trials, which called forth letters and reports from some of the then most eminent officers in the Navy, all acknowledging the remarkable capabilities of boats rigged on the revolving plan.

The invention of the revolving mast and rig appears to have originated entirely

Revolving Rig.

with Captain Shuldham. The Navy Board were at fault in their endeavours to find out the non-originality of it; the Chinese boats bore the nearest resemblance, some of which have a shear-mast which revolves on *part* of a circle.[1] Captain Shuldham's first notion

---

[1] Vessels fitted with tripod masts, which revolve on part of a circle, are common in the Indian Archipelago. (*Vide infra*, Foreign Boats.) The Sooloo Pirate Boats are also rigged with a shear-mast. The Ancient Egyptians also used a shear-mast.

was to contrive the rig of a boat so as not only to sail well, but to be easiest handled. He conceived the idea that the most perfect sail would be that which would stand as flat as a board, and be a moveable plane with its axis on a line with it, and which could be placed in any position so as to receive the fullest or the least effect of the wind's power.

It was supposed, when the yacht *America* entered our waters in the year 1851, that no Englishman had ever thought of lacing sails to booms, and making them stand as flat as boards; but it is a plan which Captain Shuldham seems to have adopted from his earliest experiences, which date from the commencement of the present century, when he rigged a sloop with only two working sails, main-sail and fore-sail; the fore-sail was laced to a boom, which was found very convenient, enabling the inventor to work to windward without any help, merely by leading two fore-guys within reach at the helm. Captain Shuldham says he discontinued the rig on account only of his having found it very troublesome in a heavy squall.

One gentleman, a captain in the Navy, in his report upon trials of the revolving rig, says, that 'for squalls, for convenience in reefing and readiness in lowering the sail, I declare it to be the handiest rig I ever witnessed.' Another, also a Captain in the Navy, on reporting a trial which took place at Brighton adds: 'I saw the plan tried here; and although the vessel it was tried upon was built for stowage and not for speed, and she was leaky and very objectionable as a trial vessel, yet under these disadvantages, she went clear to windward of all the fast-sailing craft which were opposed to her, and fully established the superiority of the plan, as presenting a means of effecting a windward passage with greater speed and certainty than any vessel of the rigs hitherto in use.'

The principle of the invention consists of two or more spars affixed to a base turning upon a strong iron pivot, the upper end of the spars being secured by a cap, so that the whole machinery of mast and sail depends for support on an iron spindle, stepped in an iron socket on the keelson. The original invention was confined to two spars only for the mast, which is all that are necessary for small boats; but for those of six tons and upwards, three or more spars, fixed as a tripod, will answer better and add stability and safety to the working of the boat, as the mast then supports itself and takes all the strain off the boom.

For larger or decked boats, a top-mast may be fitted and a jib-headed top-sail used to great advantage in light winds; also a ring-tail boom and stern-sails, for running before light winds.

The boom and bowsprit must be contrived of two separate spars, and may extend as far over the stem and stern of the boat as a cutter's boom and bowsprit, but with considerable spring at each end; the main-sail, fore-sail and jib are maintained as one sail of triangular shape, laced all the way along the boom and spread by a tough yard.

The Sailing-Boat.

The sail, when properly made, should stand just as flat as a board, and without a wrinkle; and as it moves *with* the mast and not around it, is never deranged from its drum-like surface.

At right angles with the sheer and on the revolving base, are fixed two iron rests in which the boom lies; these serve to keep the outer ends of the boom up. The aft rest

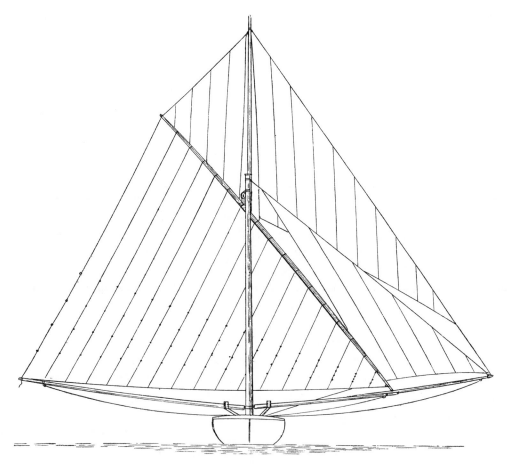

Revolver Scudding.

should be much higher than the fore one, so as to keep the boom from dipping in the water when lying over in a breeze. The fore end of the yard is hinged to the fore end of the bowsprit by means of an iron joint or goose-neck; the reefs are formed in radiating lines along the sail, from the fore end of the boom to the aft-leech of the sail.

With regard to the due proportion of spars for the triangular sail, the boom should be three-fifths of the whole, and the bowsprit two-fifths; but for a lug-sail the bowsprit should be a trifle more than one-third of the whole length. If there be less area of canvas forward, then the strain on the sheet, in sailing before the wind would be greater, which it would be well to avoid.

The slings should be placed on the main yard about two-thirds of its length from the fore end, leaving only one-third to extend abaft the mast, by which means it is impossible for the peak of the sail to sway to leeward, as the peak of a cutter's main-sail; it being kept in a direct angle with the boom, thereby defying any bend of the yard or belly to the sail. The length of the yard must be exactly three-fourths the length of the boom and bowsprit, so as to preserve a central pressure under every increase or reduction of sail.

The bowsprit should be loaded at the outer end with lead, run into it to counterpoise the weight of spars and sails to leeward. This may appear at first sight an injudicious plan; but when carefully considered it is not only practicable but ingenious.

The masts are supported in various ways, according to the tonnage of the vessel. In open boats, a flat-shaped revolving mast without rigging will answer. For decked boats or small vessels a wooden or iron pivot supports the whole strain. In larger vessels, rollers are affixed to the circumference of the revolving base, which work between two circular sweeps or rings, firmly secured to the gunwales and deck, supporting the whole strain in every direction.

A very strong double or treble block is required for hoisting the revolver's sails; and this may be readily inferred, when it is remembered that the revolver's halliards are in lieu of the main, gaff, fore-sail, and jib halliards of a cutter. The purchase should therefore be strong, and one that will overhaul easily. The shears should be let into the mast-head with great nicety, riveted to it and well secured with hoops.

In the illustration, the revolving base is shown above the bulwarks; this has been done for the purpose of explanation. The revolving base is not of necessity fixed so high in the boat; on the contrary, in several of Captain Shuldham's boats the revolving base was hidden below the bulwarks, and the shears only were seen above the gunwale.

In rigging and fitting a revolver, the novice is advised not to deviate in any essential particular from the instructions here given, as Captain Shuldham tried every conceivable plan, before perfecting the invention; and his best and most approved notions with regard to the rig are here stated.

It is one of the *main features in the revolving rig* that *both bowsprit and boom should incline upwards at the outer ends*, as shown in the engravings.

The inventor once tried the experiment of a revolving sail made to *fit a yard of the same length as the boom*. The consequence was, that with one reef down the boat carried an unpleasant weather helm; with two reefs an increased one; and with three she could hardly be kept from luffing into the wind's eye; but by making the yard about four-fifths the length of the boom, the centre of the wind's pressure upon the sail was the

The Sailing-Boat.

same in a longitudinal direction under all reduction of canvas. This experiment at once convinced the inventor of the absolute necessity of maintaining a due proportion in the revolver's yard and boom.

One-masted Revolver.—The illustration shows a revolving-rigged boat with a *single* mast, instead of a tripod : this was the contrivance of a friend of the Author's, who, after studying and experimenting upon the Shuldham revolving rig, contrived to produce

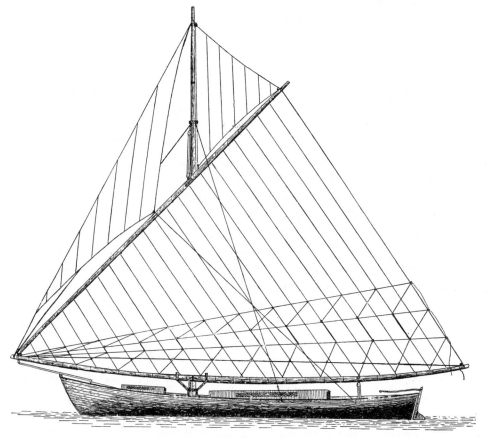

Single-masted Revolver.

a rig with which every manœuvre capable of being performed with the shear-masted revolver could be done with his single-masted revolver. To state the principle of the contrivance in the fewest possible words—it was by turning Captain Shuldham's tripod topsy-turvy, thus making the base revolve around the single mast, instead of the tripod mast revolving around the base. In all other respects he followed the Shuldham rig.

Shuldham's Revolving Rig.

AS TO THE MANAGEMENT OF REVOLVING-RIGGED BOATS.[1]

A revolving-rigged boat, when understood, is easily handled, but it requires another kind of seamanship, constant attendance at the halliards and sheet; for when the latter is let go the sail points itself head to the wind. What sailor would suppose that the quickest way of putting a revolver about would be by easing off the main-sheet? And what sailor would dream of sailing or laying a vessel to—*stern foremost?* Again, what sailor would suppose a vessel could be 'hove to' with all her flying kites set, with the wind abeam on the quarter or nearly right aft? And what sailor would imagine that it was a good plan to place some of the vessel's ballast at the end of the bowsprit? And again, what sailor would suppose that a vessel having *no way* upon her could be put about? However, all the above have been tried and proved over and over again—the inventor not having discovered them all at once but by much experience. As the power is at will to carry as little sail as possible, and also much more than any other rig can possibly carry, a great deal of revolving seamanship must depend upon judging what amount of sail should be carried with prudence.

Many of the peculiarities of the revolving rig, at first sight, will strike the novice as curiously at variance with all other methods. One singular evolution belonging to the rig is that the vessel may actually be hove-to with all sail set and the wind abeam or on the quarter, and kept in that position during pleasure; which is a great convenience when wishing to stop the vessel suddenly to avoid collision, or to allow of a boat coming alongside to shift a passenger or goods from one to the other. This may be done and way given again to the revolver in a few seconds.

The vessel may be laid-to with her stern to windward, or may be sailed stern foremost. A two-masted revolver when close hauled might, in case of emergency, be guided or put about without the aid of a rudder, merely by a slight sway of the sail.

By the revolving method the dangerous practice of jybing the sail is optional, and may be entirely avoided, the whole being worked by means of a bridle, both ends of which are made fast to the fore end of the boom; thus the sail can be twisted on its axis, bringing it fore and aft or at right angles with the keel with great velocity.

The revolving rig will answer for almost any description of sail. The shape is not limited to any one particular form more than another: the lug or any other sail can be worked on the revolving principle with equal facility.

For vessels navigating intricate channels or crowded waters, the revolving rig is peculiarly adapted, as the vessel may be almost instantaneously stopped by all sail being reversed.

[1] The whole of this is *verbatim* from the pen of the late Captain Shuldham.

The Sailing-Boat.

In the event of getting aground, the revolver's sails may all be thrown aback in an instant to help her off; it may therefore, on such occasions, be found very convenient to sail a vessel stern foremost.

Another important feature is that the shear-mast may be easily and quickly lowered, without the necessity of unrigging or deranging a single rope or unbending the sails—a great consideration and convenience for passing under bridges.

A large spread of canvas can be set in running before the wind, and may be reduced with less labour, more simply and expeditiously than by any other mode.

Again, the nicety of its balance renders it impossible to be taken aback, and the worst apparently that can happen is, that the sail may fly fore and aft, or point itself to the wind. To the many advantages before stated may be added the quickness and certainty of staying, either in a sea-way or in smooth water, the facility in wearing and the small compass in which the evolution is performed.

The working of the revolving sails by means of the long sheet or bridle requires some little experience, but when once learnt is simple and perfect. One end of the sheet should be made fast to the extreme end of the bowsprit, and rove through a single block at any convenient distance from the aft end of the boom; the other end of the sheet should be passed to the end of the bowsprit and made fast there, leaving as much slack in the sheet as to belay the bight when the boom is squared or at right angles with the boat's hull. In waring without jybing the sail, the sheet must be eased off or let go when the boat is nearly right before the wind; whilst the boom is swinging overhead the man at the helm must lay hold on the other part of the sheet and haul through quickly, which gives a bridle on the *other* side of the boom, forming both a fore-guy and a sheet, which may be belayed or not.

In addition to the bridle a short main-sheet might be used for working to windward, the standing part made fast amidships; and the fall, leading through a single block affixed to the boom, can be instantly unrove in bearing up to run before the wind. The short sheet will be found convenient, although unnecessary, the bridle being sufficient to answer every purpose.

When sailing close-hauled, in a shear-masted revolver, the top-sail only can be set in addition to her large sail, because the others cannot be made to stand equally flat with them. It is in sailing with the wind on the quarter or abaft that the advantage of additional sails will be felt.

Reefing the Revolving Sails.—There are one or two modes of reefing revolving sails, to which it may be well to call attention.

The first and best is by lacing the foot of the sail to a flat board, painted white to correspond in colour with the sail. This board is pivoted at both ends, and works in two iron stanchions at the extremities of boom and bowsprit, so as to be turned easily; it is provided with self-acting catches at each end so that a reef can be taken by merely a half-turn of the board, and by several turns the sail may be speedily furled.[1]   By turning the board the reverse way, the reefs may be shaken out : the halliards must be slacked

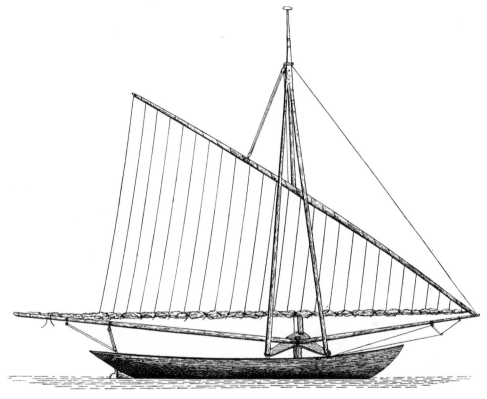

Revolver close-reefed.

during the performance.   If a sail of triangular shape is to be reefed in this manner, the reef-board must also be triangular.

Another method of reefing quadrangular and triangular revolving sails is without any reef-board or roller, but by lacing the reefs with an endless rope, a pull of which will reef the sail on a small scale, and a few pulls on a large one.

The greatest objection to the revolving rig seems to be the room which the revolving base occupies in the boat.

The invention of the revolving rig was for many years patented ; the patent, however, expired in the year 1839.

[1] This mode of reefing sails appears to be similar to that adopted by the islanders of the Indian Archipelago (See *post*, 'Malay Jellores,' &c.)

CENTRE BOARDS, SLIDING KEELS, AND REVOLVING KEELS.

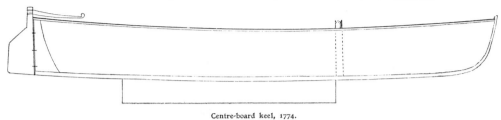

Centre-board keel, 1774.

Centre-boards, as a means of holding a sailing-vessel to windward and for preventing leeway when sailing 'on a wind,' are of ancient contrivance, derived from the catamarans of South America.

In the year 1774 a boat with a centre-board extending about two-thirds of the length of the keel was built for Lord Percy at Boston, and afterwards brought over to England, which, as far as is known at the present day, was the first of the kind brought into use in British waters.

Captain (afterwards Admiral) Schank is said to have been the inventor of what are termed *sliding keels*, and there are several models of them in the United Service Museum.

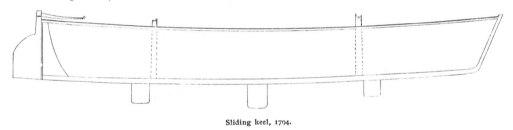

Sliding keel, 1794.

The 'invention,' if such it may be termed, consists merely in that of sliding one or more short planks of wood through a slit, or slits, cut through the keelson so as to permit of the planks being dropped through to the extent required, below the keel, with the object of preventing lee-way when the ship is close hauled, in precisely the same manner as that in use for centuries previously by the natives of Pernambuco in their catamarans.[1]

Captain Schank's invention was publicly tested so long ago as the year 1791, on the cutter *Trial*, and highly laudatory reports thereon were made to the Admiralty. Captain Schank also about that time published a short treatise on the subject.

The Revolving Keel, which is a totally different contrivance to either the centre-board or the sliding keel, was invented by the late Captain Shuldham, R.N., when prisoner of

---

[1] *Vide infra*, South American Sailing Rafts.

Revolving Keels.

war at Verdun, in the year 1809; the original model then made by him is deposited in the Museum at Ipswich, Suffolk; a model was also exhibited in London at the Adelaide Gallery, about the year 1829.

Revolving keels have since been in common use, both in England and America,

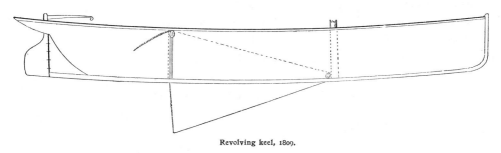

Revolving keel, 1809.

under the name of *Centre-boards.* The probability is, that the idea of the revolving keel was taken from Captain Shuldham's model in the Adelaide Gallery, and about that time found its way across the Atlantic, and was introduced under the name of a 'Centre-board.' It is, however, precisely that of Captain Shuldham's revolving keel. Totally different to the sliding keel, as also to the centre-board, it revolves upon a single pivot or bolt through the fore part of the keelson, whereby it may be raised or lowered at pleasure. The revolving keel itself, in Captain Shuldham's invention, is of *lead*, and thereby serves the purpose of ballast to a certain extent. The keel works in a water-tight wooden case, lined or ribbed with copper or zinc, for the purpose

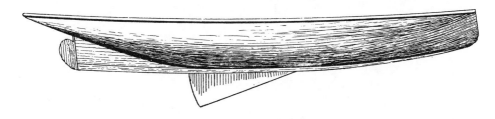

of adding strength to the case, keeping the keel clear of the woodwork, decreasing the friction, and avoiding the liability, otherwise, of getting jammed.

Revolving keels are of different forms, that most generally adopted is (when let down) of triangular shape, as shown in the illustration above.

Another form is that in which the revolving keel assumes a semi-circular form when let down. There are various other types of revolving or 'drop keels,' some of wood, others of metal; but of whatever material, if turning on a pivot when raised and lowered, they follow Captain Shuldham's invention above described.

There are also different ways of raising and lowering the revolving keel: the most

The Sailing-Boat.

primitive and simplest is by means of a keel-rope passed round a sheave fixed to the
upper part of the keel, which gives a double power; to the keel-rope a tackle is
affixed, consisting of a very small four-fold and a treble block, which will increase the
power to twelve. By this means a keel weighing 5 cwt. and upwards may be raised
and lowered with facility by the man at the helm, the utmost extent of raising
being up to the deck beams, which just brings its lower edge even with the keel of the
boat. The centre of gravity is thus vertically moveable at pleasure. An equally
simple but readier mode is by means of a small wheel or ratchet.

SAILING BOATS WITH REVOLVING KEELS.

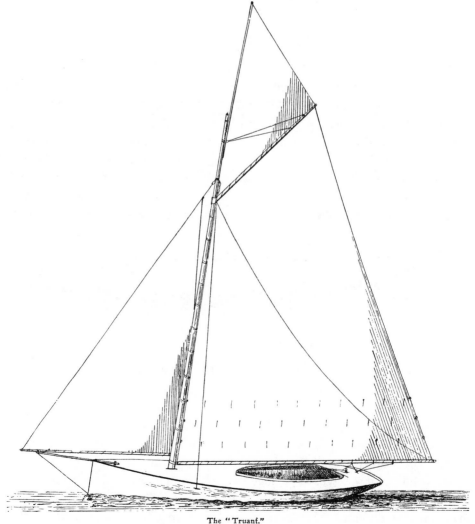

The "Truant."

Sailing Boats with Revolving Keels.

A YEAR or two after the great revolution in yacht building caused by the surprising performances of the schooner-yacht *America* in British waters in 1851, there came another craft from New York, but of diminutive size in comparison with the *America* yacht. It was a sailing-boat of different form and design to anything previously seen in England, being very broad and very shallow, measuring only twenty feet on the water line, but of three and a-half tons burden, and rigged as a Sloop, with fore-sail and main-sail both laced to booms.

This little boat was called the *Truant*, and was constructed with a centre-board (or rather revolving keel), which was pivoted so as to be capable of being drawn up or let down at pleasure, after the manner of the late Captain Shuldham's invention.

The performances of this little vessel in beating to windward and scudding before the wind were astonishing: no English boat of her size could sail so close to the wind, nor run so swiftly before the wind; and the result was, that the *Truant* completely vanquished on the river (as her larger sister the *America* had done on the sea) every boat that competed with her.

Another boat of similar type, called the *Una*, followed shortly afterwards with similar success; but the rig of the *Una* was different to that of the *Truant*. The *Una* was rigged with a single gaff-sail, but without any fore-sail,[1] after the Cat rig of the United States. This boat was also fitted with a revolving keel. The *Una*, like the *Truant*, outsailed all the British boats that competed with her, and thus a sort of *second* revolution in racing boats was brought about.

These two boats, *Truant* and *Una*, were constructed upon the then most approved lines of the New York boat builders, and were in many respects different to those of any kind of boat which had previously been seen in the waters of the British Islands.

It is events such as these that have stimulated the British yacht and boat racing fraternity to a closer study of the art of yacht and boat designing, and fed and fostered the spirit of enterprise so largely shared among them.

The advantages of a centre-board (or revolving keel) are, that it may be drawn up to enable the boat to be sailed in shallow water; and, when in deep water, by letting the revolving keel down, it materially assists the boat in holding its course when working to windward, or when reaching or sailing on a bow-line.

A wooden centre-board does not make the boat any stiffer under sail, only more weatherly; but an iron or other heavy metal revolving keel, if sufficiently deep and heavy, assists (when let down) in making the boat somewhat stiffer, but is not alone sufficient ballast to enable her to carry a large spread of sail in a strong wind.

The Author has seen (though not recently) shallow sailing boats, in shape just like a tablespoon without the handle, but fitted with a revolving keel. Such boats bear a

---

[1] *Supra*, p. 31.

striking resemblance (with the exception of the revolving keel) to some of the smaller class of Sampans seen in Chinese waters, which however are never sailed.

Boats of such a type are not fit to carry sail, because of the danger of capsizing from the force of the wind and sea striking them underneath, when listing to the breeze, and so forcing the hull over and bringing the revolving keel close up to the surface.

A shallow boat with a revolving keel or centre-board should never be allowed to list much under sail. Such boats are meant to sail on their bottoms, not on their bilges; and so of any shallow form of sailing boat with a high centre of gravity. The only means by which boats of such a type may be rendered safe under pressure of sail, without ballast, is by fitting them with a fin and bulb keel after the manner described and illustrated in subsequent pages of this work.

Centre-boards and centre-plates, whether revolving or fixed, are undoubtedly best adapted to boats of a shallow form; they are not suitable for a deep-bodied boat, or for any but small shallow yachts and sailing boats. Our enterprising cousins, the Americans, seem to rely upon them for yachts of any and every size, as they fit them to some of their larger sized racing yachts: for instance, the American yacht *Vigilant*, which sailed the match with *Valkyrie II.* in 1893, was fitted with a bronze revolving centre-board made of two plates set apart with ribs between; the space of two and a-half inches being filled with cement.

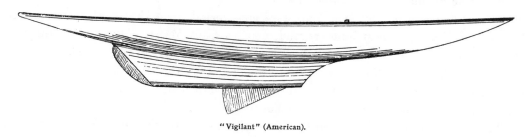

"*Vigilant*" (American).

It is, however, considered very questionable if such an adjunct is of any material assistance to a large, deep-bodied vessel. At the period before alluded to, 1852, down to some ten or twenty years later, small yachts with revolving keels were more or less popular in British waters; but the popularity of that type of yacht has long since ceased, although revolving keels and centre-boards of various shapes are still common enough wherever small sailing boats are used.

Revolving Keels and Rudders.

RADIATING AND FOLDING KEELS.[1]

FOLDING Centre plates, or Drop folding Keels, have occasionally been tried and experimented upon in this country, but with indifferent success. They are, however, used with approval in various parts of America, their application and use being chiefly confined to Sailing Canoes. The most approved are the 'Radix Patent folding centre-board,' and 'Brough's radiating centre-boards,' both American inventions. The latter are made either of plain steel, galvanised steel, iron, brass or bronze, and of any size, weight or thickness, as may be required.

The advantages of the folding centre-plate are that when sailing in shallow water, on drawing up the drop-plate, it folds up into its slot, or case, in the keelson, so that there is no projection above the floor-boards of the boat.

REVOLVING OR DROP RUDDER.

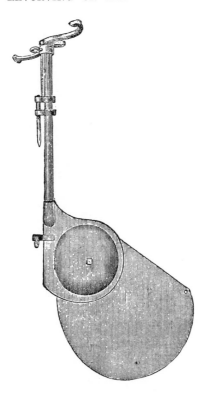

Revolving or Drop Rudder.

[1] For illustrations of boats fitted with radiating and folding keels see pages 73 and 74.

The Sailing-Boat.

THE revolving or drop rudder, shown by the illustration, is used chiefly for sailing canoes. Its advantages are, that when the revolving plate is down it is of material assistance in preventing lee-way, and on going into shallow water it may be pulled up to the level of the boat's keel, and yet retain its guiding power to the boat.

The illustration is from one of Rushton's best and strongest form of drop rudders. Mr. Rushton also has an improved form of drop rudder, designed specially for racing Canoes.

END OF PART II.

PART III.

PRACTICAL.

RUDIMENTARY.

'D'ye mind me, a sailor should be every inch,
    All as one as a piece of the ship,
And with her brave the world, without offering to flinch,
    From the moment the anchor's a-trip.'—DIBDIN.

AS to the practical performance of the art of Boat-sailing, it is not indispensably necessary for the *amateur* Boat-sailor to be what is termed 'an able seaman,' capable of laying out on a yard-arm in a tumbling sea, skilled in the use of the marlinspike and the art of making long and short splices in a rope, turning in a dead-eye, stropping a block, passing seizings and making all the ordinary knots in a neat sailor-like manner; though knowledge and experience of the kind may sometimes be of service to him when in difficulties at sea, yet it *is* necessary that he should know the rudimentary and practical part of the art of boat-sailing before he aspires to undertake the control and management of a sailing-boat.[1]

A *Rope* is composed of three or more strands; each strand consists of a number of yarns twisted together. Yarns in small ropes are sometimes called threads. Bolt-rope is the strongest and most tightly twisted, and the best rope of all for working freely through blocks; it is also used in the rigging for shrouds and stays; being heavier than other rope, it is the most expensive. Manilla rope is made of white flax, and is generally cheaper than hempen rope; it is clean looking, and much used in yachts and pleasure-boats, particularly for halliards—it requires to be well stretched when new, or it is very liable to kink. Wire rope has, however, for many years past superseded hempen rope for shrouds, stays, and standing-rigging.

---

[1] The Rudimentary part of this work is of necessity considerably abridged in this edition, as the space was required for other matter, rendered necessary by the greatly increased variety of sailing-boats and small yachts. And the Author had less hesitation in abridging it, from the fact that since the previous editions several rudimentary Treatises dealing exclusively with those subjects have been published, notably, Sir George Nares' well-known and comprehensive work on Seamanship, which deals exhaustively with all the minor details of rudimentary seamanship, blocks, knots, splices, &c., &c., which treatise has passed through several editions, and is a thoroughly reliable work on the subject.

The Sailing-Boat.

Standing Rigging are those ropes which are stationary, and seldom require alteration, as shrouds and stays.

Running Rigging are ropes which reeve or work through blocks and sheave-holes, as halliards, braces, &c.

The main-sheet.—This rope is so often mistaken for the main-*sail*, by inexperienced persons, that explanation cannot be too clearly given. The main-sheet is *not a sail*, but a *rope* by which the main-sail is hauled in or eased off; it is that *rope* which is made fast to the clew of the sail or the outer end of the mainsail-boom, and is one of the most important when the boat is under way. It should always be kept clear from all entanglement, so as to be ready to be let go in an instant, and so to release the boat from the pressure of the main-sail in case of a squall or sudden gust of wind.

Fore-sheets are ropes of similar use as applied to the fore-sail; they are attached to the aft clew of the fore-sail. It is by means of the fore-sheets that the fore-sail is trimmed, eased off or close-hauled, as occasion requires. When the fore-sail works on an iron hawse and the fore-sheets are led aft to shift the sail from side to side, they are called bow-lines.

Sails.—A sail extended by a yard and slung from the middle is called a square-sail; a sail set upon a gaff, or a stay, is called a fore-and-aft sail.

A *fore-sail* is the sail standing in the bows of the boat in front of the mast, or between the mast and the stem of the boat.

A *jib* is a sail set in front of the fore-sail on the bowsprit.

Parts of a sail.—The upper part of every sail is the head; the lower part the foot and flap; the fore part the luff and fore-leech; the aft part the aft-leech; the top aft corner the peak; the lower fore corner the tack; the lower aft corner the clew.

To *luff* is to bring the boat's head closer to the point from which the wind is blowing; luffing is performed by putting the helm down or towards the lee side.

To *jybe* or *wear* (the reverse of to luff) is to sway the sail over from one side of the boat to the other, when running free or before the wind. It is performed by putting the helm up or towards the windward side. And it is the most risky performance of all in boat-sailing, and therefore requires caution in execution; the sudden jerk of the whole weight of the main-sail falling heavily from one side to the other being likely to upset the boat, or carry away some part of the rigging, or the mast. The most judicious manner of jybing when under a heavy press of canvas in a strong wind is by hauling in the main-sheet gradually; then, when the sudden jerk comes allow the sail to feel the main-sheet, and of its own power, to draw out the slack of it. The precaution is sometimes adopted when jybing in a very strong wind of lowering the peak, and sometimes that of tricing up the main-tack, both of which are good and wise precautions when manipulating a large and heavy gaff-mainsail. If the sail be fitted with brails, it should be brailed up close to the mast, and then all may be jybed in safety.

By carrying a weather helm is implied that in steering the boat on a straight course (close-hauled) the helm has to be kept a little towards the windward side; and on putting the helm down the boat should instantly obey her helm, and shake the sail in the eye of the wind, termed "scantilising" the sail. If a boat refuses this in a breeze she cannot be said to carry a weather helm, and, as a moral certainty, it is because too much head-sail is set; and until such is reduced the boat will not be under safe command.

The *weather side* is that side of the sail against which the wind blows.

The *lee side* is the opposite side to the weather side.

The *port side* is the left-hand side of the boat or vessel, looking forward from the stern.

The *starboard side* is the right-hand side of the boat or vessel, looking forward from the stern.

The port tack.—A boat or vessel is on the port tack when sailing with the wind blowing on the port side.

The starboard tack.—A boat or vessel is on the starboard tack when sailing with the wind blowing on the starboard side.

To *port* the helm is to put it over to the port side.

To *starboard* the helm is to put it over to the starboard side.

To *tack*, to *put about*, or to *stay*, signifies turning the boat (head to wind) so that the wind blows on the other side of the sails; all three are terms applied when beating to windward.

To sail close-hauled, on a wind or *by the wind.*—These are terms which signify sailing as close to the wind as possible.

Sailing large, going free, or *off the wind.*—These imply sailing with the wind on the beam or the quarter.

To *bear up*, or to *keep her away*, is to alter the boat's course by turning her head a little from the wind.

To *weather* any vessel, point or object, is to sail to windward of it.

Wind abeam.—The wind is abeam when blowing full on one side of the boat or at right angles with the keel.

Sailing—beating—or *working to windward* are all applicable to working the boat as closely to the wind as possible, and by tacking from side to side to work a passage ahead, though the wind be against you.

Lying-to or *Laying-to.*—Keeping the head of the vessel to the wind with very little sail, and so arresting progress.

Hove-to.—Keeping the vessel as nearly stationary as possible by hauling one of the sails aweather so that it acts against another.

To *box off* is to haul a head-sail aweather so as to 'pay the boat's head off,' or turn her head if through bad steering or otherwise she has come too near the wind.

The Sailing-Boat.

The *buoy watches* when it may be seen floating on the surface. It *does not watch* when by the force of the current or otherwise it is held down under water.

To *set up the rigging* is to haul it taut by means of the lanyards and dead-eyes, or by the modern rigging screws.

To weigh the anchor, is to pull it up or lift it from the ground or bottom.

Under way (sometimes erroneously termed 'under weigh.')—A boat or vessel is under way when moving ahead with the sails or any one of them set.

In reefing, tie the points without rolling the sail.

Never allow any person to stand on the thwarts or sit on the gunwale of an open sailing-boat when under way.

In lowering or taking in a sail, let go the halliards and haul down on the fore-leech or luff of the sail.

One man should always stay by the helm until the sails are down. Collisions and other mishaps frequently occur with open boats through the helmsman leaving his place before the sails are lowered.

Blocks, Tackles, Purchases, &c.—A boat's block is composed of three parts—the shell, the sheave and the pin. The shell is the outer part or case containing the sheave; the sheave is the circular roller on which the rope runs; and the pin is the bolt which holds the sheave inside the shell. The best sheaves are made of brass or gun-metal, and such are the most durable; hollow brass sheaves, being so much lighter than solid ones, are to be preferred for boats. Blocks are of various denominations according to the purpose for which required; they are very important essentials in all sailing vessels.

For sailing-boats, blocks should be no larger than consistent with strength and convenience; when too large they look heavy and clumsy, and encumber the boat unnecessarily.

Blocks are single, double, treble, or fourfold—according to the number of sheaves.

A *running block* is one attached to the spar or other object to be raised or lowered.

A *standing block* is affixed to some permanent support.

A *snatch block* is a block with one sheave, having an iron hook at one end and a clasp at the side to admit the bight of a rope, without the delay of reeving or unreeving the whole.

A *tail block* has a single sheave, and is strapped with an eye-splice and tail-piece for making fast temporarily to the mast or rigging.

A *long tackle block* has two sheaves one above another; these are sometimes called sister-blocks.

A *fiddle block* consists of two single blocks one above the other but both in one shell, the upper one being the larger; the object being, for the upper rope to have play clear of the under one.

A *morticed block* is made by morticing out a block of wood or spar and fixing a sheave in the aperture.

Double, treble, and fourfold blocks are used where extra power is required, and to ease the working of the rope: thus, a weight may be lifted by *one* man with the aid of a fourfold block which *four* men could scarcely do with the aid of a single block. The main-sheet of an ordinary sailing-boat generally runs through one double block and one single, thereby enabling a fairly large sail to be trimmed by one person.

A *whip-purchase* is merely a rope rove through a block with one sheave. It is the smallest purchase of all.

A *tackle* is a purchase formed of two or more blocks, with a rope rove through each for hoisting or other purpose.

A *gun-tackle purchase* consists of two single blocks with a rope rove through both, one end of which is fast to the strop of the upper block.

A *luff tackle purchase* is formed by a rope leading through a single and a double block, the end of the rope being fast to the top of the single block and the fall leading from the double block.

All tackles have standing and running parts, the *standing part* is so much of the rope as remains between the sheave and the part secured; the *running part* so much as works between the sheaves. The *fall* is the part laid hold of in hoisting or hauling.

Dead-eye.—A circular piece of wood, with three holes in it, and a groove cut round the outer edge for the shroud to lie in. It is used for turning in the ends of shrouds and backstays; the three holes are used for reeving the lanyard through when setting up the shroud or backstay. Dead-eyes are now superseded in yachts and sailing-boats by rigging screws.

A *bull's-eye* is a thick piece of wood of circular shape with a hole through the middle and a groove round the outer edge.

The trunk step.—This is used for the purpose of avoiding the inconvenience that often exists in short open boats carrying a lofty mast. When the mast is lowered and the boat has to be rowed, it is sometimes found inconvenient for the mast to protrude over the bow or stern of the boat; and from its great length it often incommodes the sitters. For boats of this description the *trunk-step* is intended; and if the boat be fitted with a shifting spring-thwart it will tend further to shorten the length of mast, as the trunk-step may be carried several inches higher on account of the extra support derived from the elevated thwart.

The *mast-clamp* is considered a superior contrivance to the trunk-step. It is one by which the mast may be raised and lowered in the boat by one person with great facility —the heel of the mast working on a pivot, and secured, when raised, by an iron pin — the whole performance being only the work of a few moments.

The Sailing-Boat.

BOAT-SAILING.

'The breeze fills my sails, so adieu to the land!
My ensign 's unfurl'd, I 've the helm at my hand.
What sport is more pure, what pleasure more sweet,
Than the sail and the breeze when kindly they meet.'—THE AUTHOR.

From a photo by   *West & Son, Southsea.*

THERE is no more charming and delightful recreation than boat-sailing; and there never was a time within memory of man, when it stood so high in the ranks of popular outdoor pastimes as now.

The good taste of those who indulge in it was never bestowed on a purer or more healthful amusement, nor on one more useful and patriotic. The growing popularity of amateur boat-sailing is undeniable. Who has not experienced such at our regattas, the *rendezvous* of our racing fleet, where yachts and boats from every club, and ladies fair from every part of the surrounding country grace our aquatic festivals with their presence and participation, sharing the triumphs of the victors and administering sweet solace to the defeated.

From a photo by   "*Corolla.*"   *Beken & Son, Cowes, I. of W.*

It is the sailing-boat that gives the charm, as it does also the finish, to many a beautiful picture of lake or river scenery, as artists the most gifted will readily acknowledge.

Yachting, although a princely recreation when conducted on the larger and luxurious style, is one that may be enjoyed with most of its charms and delights upon a smaller and less costly scale, by men of moderate means and humbler aspirations.

Boat-racing, as a sport, requires skill and experience, with promptitude in difficulty. Hesitation and indecision almost invariably lead to trouble and disaster. And when we come to close contest in a sailing-match with some of the fastest boats of the fleet, sailing becomes an art. Then it is that the skill of the sailing-master is put to the severest test; and combined with that skill is the further requisite of sound and unerring judgment.

There is also another occasion when boat sailing becomes an art; and that is when overtaken by sudden squalls and strong winds in a heavy sea.

103

The Sailing-Boat.

On such occasions the sailor-skill of the helmsman is called into requisition. His experience enables him to anticipate the squall and to shorten sail with due deliberation; so that when the gust swoops down upon him he is prepared for it, and meets the sudden impulse with promptitude and intrepidity, as he eases the helm and slacks the main sheet, yet keeps 'good way' on the boat, and so safely weathers the squall.

From a photo by   *Beken & Son, Cowes, I. of W.*

" Eione " becalmed.

It is not always, however, that strong winds and heavy seas try the skill and patience most; the tedious disagreeables of a calm cause sailing to become irksome, because next to impossible; and distances, the performance of which would occupy but a few minutes in a breeze, require hours in a calm.

It is, too, always advisable in these days of bulb-keels and deep fins that the amateur boat sailor should (if his boat be one of deep draft) be well acquainted with the shoals and sandbanks in and about the locality of the waters in which he indulges his pastime, particularly on a falling tide; and the more so if he has a party of friends with him on board, because of the risk of being left grounded on the shallows in that ludicrous predicament in which the poet Moore found a sailing-boat and crew, when he penned the beautiful couplet :—

'I saw from the beach, when the morning was shining,
  A bark o'er the waters move gloriously on,
I came when the sun o'er that beach was declining,
  The bark was still there, but the waters were gone.'

Boat-Sailing.

Boat-sailing Clubs.—Yacht clubs have existed for upwards of a century; but boat-sailing clubs are of more modern enterprise. So popular is the pastime of boat-sailing, and so numerous the sailing-boats and small yachts, that boat-sailing clubs bid fair to outnumber the yacht clubs.

The class of members for whom these clubs were established are those who, for financial or other reasons, prefer to indulge their love of sailing in a less costly and pretentious manner than that involved in the building, fitting, and keeping up of a large yacht.

Enrolled among the members of the boat-sailing clubs are, however, some of the

From a photo by   **At anchor on the Medina.**   *Beken & Son, Cowes, I. of W.*

keenest and most prominent yachtsmen of the day; members of some of the principal yacht clubs in the kingdom, but who nevertheless join a boat-sailing club because of the encouragement they give to, and interest they take in, the humbler pastime, in which the competition is every whit as keen, and the pleasure and excitement nowise less, than in the matches between yachts of the larger type.

There is, moreover, the greater satisfaction that the owner of a small racing-yacht or sailing-boat is generally expected to steer and sail her himself; and, indeed, such is a *sine quâ non* in the Corinthian and some other sailing clubs. So that it often happens that besides the advantage of being far less costly, there is more sport in the boat-sailing matches than in those of the larger class of racing-yachts.

Model Yacht Clubs.—Besides our Royal Yacht Squadron, Royal and other Yacht Clubs, Boat-Sailing and Canoe Clubs, there are in various parts of the British Islands, Model Yacht Clubs, among the members of which are some of the most eminent yacht designers in the kingdom, and others who design and build little model yachts, from 3 to 5 or 6 feet in length, which are sailed by members on the lakes and ornamental waters of the public parks, to the endless diversion of the onlookers, particularly those of the juvenile class.

The members of these clubs have their miniature regattas and sailing-matches for challenge cups and other prizes, matches which are as keenly and earnestly contested as those of the larger class of sailing-boats.

Some of the tiny fleet of these clubs are of exquisite model, ingeniously designed and beautifully constructed, their rig, sails, and fittings being in every respect in accordance with the most modern type of hull, and the newest and most improved equipment ; and they are a credit to the ingenuity and skill of those who design and build them.

And who among the frequenters of the London Parks has not witnessed with pleasure on a fine summer's day a fleet of these miniature vessels careening to the breeze under pressure of their snow-white sails, furrowing the surface of the lakes, throwing up here and there a feathery foam, and gliding to and fro among the ducks and geese, all conscious of their harmlessness and familiarity ? And so they speed from shore to shore, like veritable yachts on a veritable sea-board, to the amusement and delight of throngs of spectators of every class.

STABILITY.

The *stability* of the sailing-boat implies its power to withstand the pressure of the wind upon the sails in a breeze without heeling over to such an extent as to incur the risk of a capsize.

A sailing boat which has good stability is said to be 'stiff' under sail; but a boat of poor stability is said to be 'crank' under sail, which implies a tendency to capsize.

Boats that are rigged in any form that enables them to carry the broadest part of their sails low, have a greater advantage in preserving their stability under a heavy pressure of wind than those which are rigged with lofty sails and wide-spreading gaff.

The stability of the sailing-boat must be derived (*a*) from the form of the hull ; and (*b*) from a proper, or scientific, adjustment of the ballast.

These are the two essentials whereby the boat is enabled to maintain its stability under pressure of sail in a strong wind.

With regard to (*a*)—'the form of the hull'—it is not the mere depth of the vessel that gives it stability, but rather the beam (or breadth) in proportion to length ;

although beam is not alone sufficient to enable a boat to carry a pressure of sail, without some artificial assistance, such as that derived from a counterpoise, provided by placing a certain weight of ballast as low down in the boat as possible; so low indeed that, if it can be placed outside at the bottom of the keel, it will be the more effective.

And as to (*b*)—'the scientific adjustment of the ballast.' This is a matter of skill, particularly in a boat of the racing fleet; for, unless the ballast be placed in proper position, the best sailing powers of the boat will not be ascertained.

An ordinary open sailing-boat intended for cruising in home waters on broad estuaries, tidal rivers, and such-like, may be ballasted with a few hundredweights of

From a photo by   *Beken & Son, Cowes, I. of W.*

lead or iron, securely placed on each side of the keelson beneath the floor of the boat; but when it is intended to 'carry on' her as a racing boat, it will be necessary to ballast her upon modern scientific principles. And as to this, it has been known for more than a century past, that 'a pound of lead on the outside of the keel is worth two pounds carried inside the boat'; and this trite old maxim is as true now as it was then, but it is only within the last thirty years that its general application to the racing yachts of the pleasure fleet has been adopted.[1]

Still the fact remains, that in racing yachts of the smaller class the outside mode of ballasting has at most yachting centres recently become quite general.

[1] When a youthful boat-sailer, the Author was often reminded by old boatmen and river pilots of the advantage of lead or iron bolted to the keel on the *outside*: and accordingly he tried the experiment on an open sailing-boat, with great success; but found it inconvenient on account of the difficulty it occasioned (through the additional weight) in hauling up and launching the boat from the soft sloping banks of the river where he then indulged his pastime, consequently he discontinued its use.

The Sailing-Boat.

With regard to the contrivances that have been resorted to from time to time for the purpose of preserving stability, and procuring the greatest resistance to the leverage caused by pressure of the wind upon the sails, many of them are, undoubtedly, ingenious. In some of the larger of our racing fleet a deep and broad keel is formed by running molten lead into an iron frame or casing, so formed that the heaviest part is at the point of greatest lateral resistance.

In yachts of the smaller class there is considerable variety in the arrangement of the outside ballast; one of the most successful being that of a deep wooden keel heavily weighted with longitudinal castings of lead, bolted to the lower part of the keel. Another is that of a steel centre-plate weighted with bulbs of lead, termed the 'fin and bulb' mode of ballasting.

Each of these will be more fully explained in subsequent pages of this work.

From a photo by   *Mr. Harold Fraser.*

TRIMMING AND BALLASTING.

The trim of a sailing-boat, as of a racing yacht, is a matter of primary importance, and cannot be disregarded without incurring the risk of disappointment and defeat.

Trim depends on the accurate adjustment of the ballast, whether inside the boat or outside. Although a boat be ever so perfect in form and symmetry, and though her sails stand ever so well, unless the boat be in good trim her best qualities cannot be got out of her. Many a race has been lost by the best and swiftest boat of the fleet through being out of trim, such as being 'too much by the head,' or, *vice versâ*, 'too much by the stern.'

To trim a sailing-boat is to arrange the ballast so that the boat may sit upon the water in that position in which she will, when under way, do her best in point of speed. It is therefore an important preliminary to good sailing in every boat that the

Trimming and Ballasting.

proper load water-line should be correctly ascertained; and then, under no circumstances, should there be any deviation from it, nor should the boat be put out of trim in any degree whatsoever.

A boat is supposed to be in trim as regards the sails when, with a moderate wind, she carries her helm amidships, or with a slight inclination to windward; that is to say, will sail a straight course without any or but little steering. In order to be in safe trim, the boat should carry *a weather helm*, should come about quickly, and obey every movement of the helm, however slight.

The heaviest and greatest quantity of ballast should be placed in the aft part of the

From a photo by   *Beken & Son, Cowes, I. of W.*

"Cobalt."

boat and amidships; whilst little or none should be laid before the mast (if rigged with one mast only), and none in the extreme end of the stern. In sea-going boats it is important that this rule be strictly adhered to : a boat rises to the waves so much more buoyantly when her bows are not depressed with ballast. In smooth water, a small portion of the ballast may be stowed in front of the mast in some boats—*i.e.*, supposing the mast to be stepped not less than a third of the boat's length from the stem; in long narrow sailing-boats it is generally necessary to place some of the ballast before the mast, but ballast should never be placed in the bows of the boat.

The Sailing-Boat.

The boat should not be laden too heavily with ballast, but merely weighted down to the true bearings or proper load water-line.

It is a very necessary precaution that, when the boat lists over, the ballast may not slip or move. Should it fall suddenly into the lee-bilge of an open boat a capsize is almost inevitable. Strictly speaking, the ballast should all be secured beneath the platform of a sailing-boat; but in very small boats and those launched from the beach this cannot always be done. It should, however, be lashed or secured, so that it cannot slip when the boat lurches or pitches.

Errors of trim are of common occurrence so long as the centre of gravity remains undetermined; and in boats of the smaller class such is the more difficult to ascertain when the weight of the helmsman and his crew put the boat out of trim, unless such weight be judiciously distributed.

From a photo by   *"Spell."*   *Beken & Son, Cowes, I. of W.*

In ballasting a boat for sailing in a sea-way it is essential that the centre of buoyancy be not too high. If it is, the boat will not only be unable to do her best, but the motion of the surface water will cause her to plunge, roll, and strain in a manner she would not do if the centre of buoyancy were lower; for whatever the sail-carrying power of the boat may be in smooth water, if her displacement is not equal to the strain, she cannot carry her sail with effect in rough water.

In ballasting small open sailing-boats, that kind of ballast which takes up least room in the boat is always to be preferred.

Centre-plates and Bulb-keels.

The best ballast for small boats is lead, but of all kinds the most expensive; it sometimes costs more than the hull of the boat. Lead is, however, preferable where expense is no material object, as it may be stowed away in a very small compass, giving more room for accommodation, and rendering the boat stiffer under sail than by any other kind of ballast. Lead creates neither rust nor dirt; and when done with, like silver and gold, it will always realise its intrinsic worth in whatever shape or quantity.

CENTRE-PLATES AND BULB KEELS.

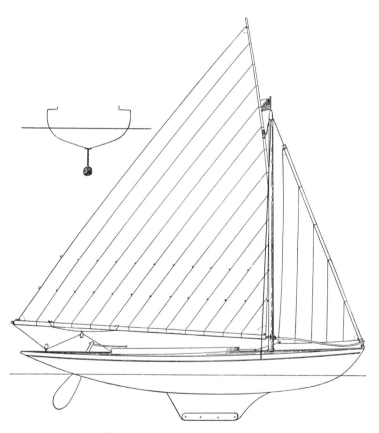

"Semibreve," designed by Captain du Boulay.

A MODERN mode of ballasting small yachts and sailing-boats is by a fixed fin-keel of gun-metal, or lead, more or less thick according to the size of the boat, bolted to the under part of the keelson on the outside, and extending the whole length of the keel. This was introduced in the Solent racing fleet in the year 1888, with remarkable success. Boats so ballasted proved very fast under sail, and stood up well to their canvas in a fresh breeze. The deep form of hull of the former period was, about that time, or shortly afterwards, discarded for the shallower type with the fixed centre-plate; to which was afterwards added the leaden bulb.

The Semibreve.—The illustration (from a drawing by the designer) represents a sailing-boat called the *Semibreve*, designed in 1892 by Captain E. du Boulay, of Bembridge, Isle of Wight, for Mr. F. W. Leybourne Popham, and built by Jacobs of Bembridge. Her dimensions were 22 feet over all; beam 5 feet 6 inches; draft 3 feet. An interesting feature in relation to this boat is, that she appears to have been one of the first boats built on this side the Atlantic with a bulb-keel, having 5 cwt. of lead bolted on to her keel on the outside.

In the same year (1892) boats were designed and built with bulb-keels by Nicholson of Gosport, Sibbick of Cowes, and by others.

The *Semibreve* proved a great success as a prize winner in her first year. She was rigged with two sails only—mainsail and foresail; a peculiarity with regard to the latter being, that she had as a sort of spinnaker boom, a curved brass pipe pivoted to the front part of the mast (as shown in the illustration) for booming out the foresail on either side when running before the wind.

Fin-and-Bulb Keels.—The modern centre-plate and bulb-keel (termed fin-and-bulb keel) consists of a broad and deep centre-plate of wood, iron, steel, or other metal, of a thickness consistent with the size of the boat, firmly bolted to the under part of the

Fin-and-bulb keel.

keelson; the lead ballast consisting of two longitudinal castings usually in the shape of a split cigar (or torpedo), each weighing several hundred weights more or less, according to the size of the boat for which intended. The two sections forming the bulb are bolted to the metal plate at the lower edge, one on each side; a very powerful lever is thus formed, which acts as a counterpoise against the pressure of the wind upon the sails, and makes the boat remarkably stiff under sail—and such is, undoubtedly, an ingenious and very effective mode of ballasting a boat and enabling her to carry larger sails than she could by any other mode of ballasting. And for a racing-yacht of the smaller class, probably no better mode of ballasting, with a view to stability and sail-carrying power, could well be devised. But the cigar-shaped bulb-keel, projecting as it does beyond the plate both fore and aft, in some of the boats, has its disadvantages, as it is liable to picking up under-water-floatage—as sea-weed, &c., and if the bulb should happen to come in contact with a hawser on entering or leaving a harbour, the boat would be very liable to disaster. There are, however, other modes of contriving the bulb-keel in which there is no projection from the plate either fore or aft: many of which are described and illustrated in subsequent pages of this work.

The great advantage of outside ballast, particularly that of lead affixed to the keel, was the primary initiation of bulb-keels, which began with lead castings in longitudinal form bolted to the outer sides of deep wooden keels (as in the *Semibreve*); the enormous advantage of which in enabling a boat to carry a pressure of sail in a strong breeze was at once apparent.

In 1892 a half-rater, American boat, from a design by Herresboff, with fin and bulb-keel of the type indicated by the profile illustration, was introduced and proved a

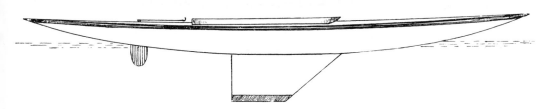

remarkable success. In 1893 British yacht and boat builders introduced a similar type with steel plate and leaden bulb, which, for a time, took the place of the wooden keel and lead bulb before mentioned.

The introduction of this form of keel by British designers was the result of many experiments as to the best mode of preserving the stability of sailing-boats by means of outside ballast, and had the great advantage of dispensing with all kinds of inside ballast; and thereby, if fairly designed, affording more space for internal and cabin accommodation in the larger boats; but, with a view to racing, displacement was disregarded, and in time, advantage was taken of the elasticity of the rules of rating and measurement, with the result that racing boats of the skimming-dish type became the prevailing class.

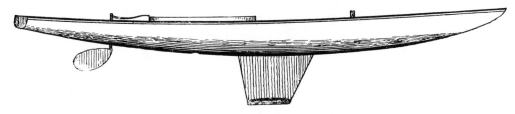

The profile shows a close imitation of the Herreshoff type of fin-and-bulb keel by a British designer.

The Sailing-Boat.

Boats of extreme breadth and shallowness with fin-and-bulb keels were constructed; some of them the merest skimming-dishes; but they nevertheless sailed very fast in smooth water under strong winds, and proved great prize winners.

Undoubtedly, the leverage of outside ballast is so great, that many of the fin and bulb type are, practically, uncapsizable under sail. But boats with fixed centre-plates and bulb keels must keep to deep water, or they come to grief: for, if the bulb touches the bottom, the boat's power of maintaining stability is gone for the time; she cannot so much as maintain an upright position; and if her sails be standing, any wind will capsize her.

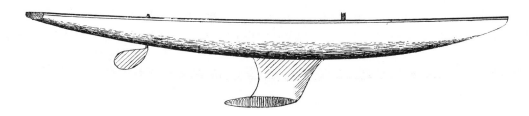

The profile shows the Sibbick type of steel fin and cigar-shaped leaden bulb. The *Silva*, a famous boat and highly successful prize winner of the 36-foot L.R. class, was a boat of this type.

Every alteration in the mode and conditions of measurement has, apparently, developed new exaggerations or departures in the form of the boat; the worst feature of which is the diminution of displacement.

Under the rules of the Y.R.A. in the fin-bulb type of boat of the smaller class, this departure has from time to time become more and more glaring; but it is claimed for boats of this class, that what is sacrificed in space between deck and keelson, is abundantly amplified in power, speed, and safety; and that they are, besides, an inexpensive boat to build, by reason of their rounded form and the absence of any keel, excepting the centre-plate and bulb.

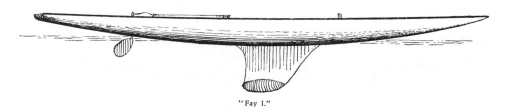

"Fay I."

The profile illustration is that of a very successful boat by a British designer, showing a different arrangement of the fin-and-bulb keel to those of the Sibbick type.

Since the year 1894, among the smaller class of racing-yachts the broad, shallow boat with fin-and-bulb keel and spoon bow (or rather Praam-bow, for such it is) has been much in vogue.

"Tartar V."

The profile shows the contour of another boat of the Sibbick type with steel fin and lead bulb keel, which proved one of the fastest of her class.

For sailing-boats of the racing class known as half-raters, one-raters, and two-and-a-half raters, the fin and bulb type of boat proved faster than any others; consequently it became the fashion of the day in the Solent and some other localities where there is always water sufficient for them to ride afloat. They are, however, typical racing-boats, and as such are not intended for cruising yachts; the displacement is small, and the accommodation on board them is too limited to permit of their being used for any other purpose than that of match-sailing.

Whatever the advantages of the steel fin, or plate, may be over the wooden keel with lead bulb, it would appear that many prefer the latter even for racing purposes.

From a photo by   *Beken & Son, Cowes, I. of W.*
"Speedwell."

The *Speedwell*, 24 feet, designed by Mr. Arthur Payne, and built by the firm Summers and Payne in 1896, is a boat with a wooden keel and leaden bulb: this boat

The Sailing-Boat.

figured conspicuously in the Solent and neighbouring waters in many sailing matches in that and subsequent seasons, winning a great number of prizes. And recently the same firm have built a 36-footer for Mr. A. E. Orr-Ewing, with a wooden fin and leaden bulbs bolted to it.

Boats of the fin and bulb type, having steel fins and cigar-shaped bulbs, are, at the close of the season, lifted out of the water by means of a derrick; their leaden bulbs are then unbolted and removed from the steel plates; then the plates themselves are unbolted and taken off, and the boats, minus their fin and bulb keels, are then stowed away on shelves one above another in boat-sheds, almost with the same facility that long rowing-boats are so stowed.

Experiments have from time to time been tried with *liftable bulb keels*, but apparently with indifferent success; such are not, therefore, very likely to come into general use. The inventors of one or more of them have, however, considerable confidence in them, seeing that they have patented their inventions. The ' Fairbrass lifting bulb keel' is one of these; and several boats have recently been constructed with the patent lifting bulb keel.

SAILS AND SAIL-FITTING.

The sails of a boat, as of a yacht, when viewed at a distance, form its most conspicuous and picturesque feature, as the little vessel glides along in a lively breeze, upon the surface of the waters. And he who is proud of his boat will take care that she is fitted with an appropriate and becoming suit of sails, such as will show her off to the best advantage, and bring out her best sailing powers.

The sails of a boat, whatever the rig, are of primary consideration; for however ingeniously contrived may be the boat itself, and its mode of ballasting, unless the sails are of proper proportions, the best sailing qualities of the boat cannot be brought out.

And unless the sails are cut and made with true sail-maker's skill, they will not stand with that flat and drum-like surface so conducive to holding a good course to windward, and will not be of that propelling force and assistance to the boat they otherwise would be.

An ill-fitting sail is out of place on a good boat, is an eyesore to a nautical onlooker, and usually more or less a hindrance to the display of the best sailing powers of the boat.

The Angulated Jib.—It must be obvious to those who have given attention to the making and standing of sails, that jibs, when made according to the common method, do not retain, when set, so *flat* a *surface* as fore-sails, boom-mainsails, and gaff top-sails; and it has been generally admitted, that if jibs and other trilateral sails could be made on a principle that would ensure their standing flat, many advantages would be gained.

The late Mr. Matthew Orr (of the firm Orr, Hunter, and Co., of Greenock) was the inventor of the angulated jib, which, from its construction, avoids the defect of the knuckle, and makes a stronger and flatter sail than any previously produced.

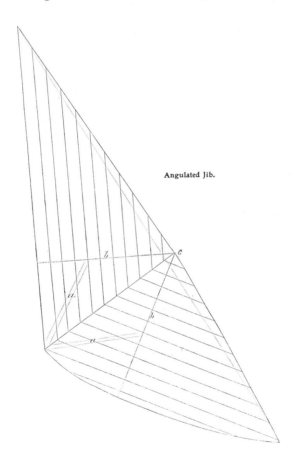

Angulated Jib.

Every seaman is aware that the sailing qualities of a vessel materially depend on the cut of the sails, and particularly on jibs that will trim to the same angle as the other sails. In regard to boom-mainsails and fore-sails, they are made to stand flat without difficulty, and are now generally laced at the foot to booms; but a difficulty long existed in getting large jibs to stand equally flat with the other sails, particularly after much usage, by which the bagging or bulging is increased to such an extent as to render them almost useless when close-hauled.

The Sailing-Boat.

From a consideration of these facts, Mr. Orr, in or about the year 1851, was led to a different method of making all sails the foot of which formed an obtuse angle with the aft-leech, and termed by him the 'angulated method'; the principle of which consists in a (then) new arrangement or combination of the materials used, in a manner calculated to produce a more favourable effect of the power acting on them, and consequently their more advantageous impulse to the vessel; and although the plan deviated from long established custom, its utility and superiority have been abundantly confirmed by subsequent tests and long experience.

The principle of the angulated method is to place the cloths in such a manner as to do away with the knuckle, by binding the warp threads so that they are all acted upon by the strain from the sheet. (See engraving.) The strain bands, a a, are carried from the clew to meet the straight threads b b, running from the point c. Angulated sails are also made with less cloth, as they do not require so much roach on the fore-leech; and the angulated jib can be made to trim to the same angle as the other sails, as it stretches equally, presenting a flat and comparatively even surface to the wind; it also lasts much longer, and requires less trimming of the sheets than the common jib, the strain of which is from the clew to the stay, whereby it forms a bag in the upper and lower part of the sail; and when half-worn is, in consequence, particularly difficult and troublesome to keep properly trimmed when close-hauled.

The angulated jib has a further advantage over the ordinary one in being less liable to shake; and when the vessel is in stays with the sheet to windward, the angulated jib takes effect sooner than the other.[1]

[1] This description of the angulated jib, together with the engraving, was published in the first edition of this work (1853), and in each of the subsequent editions. The (so-called) 'recent invention' of the angulated method (1898) is therefore not new.

Sails and Sail-fitting.

BATTENED SAILS.

From a photo by   *Beken & Son, Cowes, I. of W.*

A BATTENED sail signifies a sail fitted with strips of flat wood, like laths, athwart the sail horizontally; the object being to keep the sail flat and prevent any flicker at the outer, or aft leech of the sail.

Battens are not applied to the sails of yachts of the larger class; they are used chiefly for the main-sails of small yachts, sailing canoes, and small sails made of duck or other light material.

Mode of fitting the Battens to the Sail.—Among the many contrivances of boating-men of recent years to obtain a flat-standing main-sail and to avoid any flicker at the outer leech, recourse has been had to the Chinese mode of battens and reefs. These were first applied to the main-sails of sailing canoes by members of the Royal Canoe Club; and are now in common use on the main-sails of small sailing-boats in every part of the British Islands. The battens are simply narrow strips of pine, of lath-like form, and of a width, length, and thickness in proportion to the size or breadth of the sail, but tapering in thickness at each end. When applied to the main-sail of a sailing canoe they are about one and three-eighth inch in breadth by an inch in thickness at the middle part, where the greatest strain will be, but tapering at each end to about two-eighths of an inch. The battens are slipped into sheaths or pockets formed across the

The Sailing-Boat.

sail from the fore to the aft-leech, by sewing a reef-band along it. In boats of a larger size and carrying larger sails than a sailing canoe, three battens are sometimes attached to the main-sail, but they do not usually extend entirely across the sail, only partly so, and always commencing at the outer leech.

The battens are not always sheathed in a pocket in the manner above described: in some sails, fitted with knittles for the purpose, the battens are laced to the sail, one on each side of the canvas. In others, the battens are utilised for reefing, in a similar manner to that of the Chinese, who reef by hauling the sail down to the extent of one or more battens as may be required.

This mode of shortening sail is now generally adopted in small sailing-boats and sailing-canoes on account of the facility it affords for expeditious reefing; as a reef may be taken in the sail single-handed by means of a ratline readily rove and fitted to the sail; when, by hauling the ratline taut, the batten, and with it the sail, is drawn down to the boom, and the two are thus securely laced together, and the sail thereby reefed in less than a minute of time.

Rigging.

RIGGING.

WIRE rope has now almost entirely superseded hempen and bolt rope for the standing rigging of yachts and sailing-boats. It is so much more slender, and stronger in proportion to size (or rather diameter): the breaking strength of each wire of which the rope is composed being considerable; and the finest wire rope, made expressly for yachts and sailing-boats, is manufactured of a special quality of steel, so that it is thoroughly reliable.

The most important considerations in regard to the use of wire rope for the rigging of yachts, are its much neater and more slender appearance, its greater strength and durability, its non-liability to shrink, stretch, or yield after wetting, and the very much smaller sheaves, &c., through which to reeve it, than those required for hempen rope.

For instance, the fore top-mast stay of a ten ton racing-yacht is invisible at a very short distance to persons ashore, though the yacht may be riding at anchor in the harbour only a few hundred yards or so from the land. And even under the searching power of the camera, the picture sometimes fails to depict the slender wire-rigging of the yacht.

Wire rope, for many years after its invention, so far as its use is concerned on board yachts, was used only for the standing rigging; but of late years, a strong, tough and flexible kind has been manufactured expressly for use in the running rigging of yachts; and such is now generally used for top-sail and jib top-sail halliards, as also for runners and running tackles, out-hauls, bobstay-falls, topping-lifts, and almost every other purpose for which hempen and manilla rope were formerly used in the running tackle of a yacht.

Rigging Screws.—Dead-eyes are now wholly discarded for setting up the standing rigging of a yacht: all such bulky contrivances being superseded by the modern invention of right and left-handed rigging screws, which are now made of a white metal called 'marine silver': and no racing-yacht, whether large or small, now has her standing rigging set taut by means of dead-eyes and lanyards.

The Sailing-Boat.

From a photo by   *Beken & Son, Cowes, I. of W.*

THE illustration is from a photograph by Beken & Son, of Cowes, showing some boats of the two-and-a-half rating class, setting sail and getting ready for the start in a sailing match on the Solent.

On setting sail—say in a small yacht rigged with three sails, main-sail, fore-sail and jib—first see that the bobstay is secure, and the bowsprit bowsed down at the outer end; then cast off the main-sail lashing, and make clear the main-sheet and halliards; unfurl the fore-sail, and lay it out ready to hoist; haul out the jib on the bowsprit, and run the jib-sheets to their berths. Having thus got all three sails ready, hoist the main-sail before you set the head-sails; make the main-halliards fast on one side the mast, and the peak-halliards on the other; the peak should not be entirely set up until the main is well set; then hoist the fore-sail, and slip from the moorings. Having got away clear, set the fore-sail fairly, and hoist the peak of the main-sail. Whilst under way run the jib up and trim the sheets; then coil the halliards neatly and separately, so that they are each clear and ready for use: lay them on deck, the fall end undermost. If the course is to windward, or on a reach, bowse down the main-tack; if before the wind, the main-tack may be cast off and the sheet given freely.

If on slipping from the moorings among crowded shipping, it is necessary to turn the boat quickly and there is but very small space in which to do it, having set one of the head-sails haul it aweather, drop the peak of the main-sail, ease off the main-sheet and put up the helm; the boat will then turn as if on a pivot if she be in proper trim.

122

Reefing.

REEFING.

From a photo by   *Beken & Son, Cowes, I. of W.*

' One night, as we drove with two reefs in the main-sail,
  And the scud came on low'ring upon a lee shore,
Jack went up aloft for to hand the top-ga'nt sail,
  A spray washed him off, and we ne'er saw him more.'—DIBDIN.

THE illustration is from a photograph by Beken and Son, of Cowes, of the cutter-yacht *Ermin*, of the 36-foot racing class; a highly successful boat and the winner of numerous prizes.

Reefing, or shortening sail, is a necessary precaution that should be well understood and capable of practical expeditious performance by every one who ventures to set sail in a boat; whether it be an open boat or a decked one. It is not so from any difficulty in reefing *before* setting sail, nor when under way in smooth-water: the test is, in a strong wind, a heavy sea, a threatening gale, or squall. Such are occasions when the skill and experience of the amateur boat-sailor are called into requisition for reefing the sails as expeditiously as possible.

Every person who ventures to leave the shore and take the command of a sailing-boat, should therefore be capable of hauling down a reef-earing in a tumbling sea; for it is impossible to tell how soon he may be compelled to reef in order to ensure a safe return to himself, his crew, and his boat.

Small sailing-boats have usually one or two reefs to the main-sail, whatever the rig; larger boats and yachts have, generally, three reefs and sometimes four.

Reefing should be done in anticipation of a strong wind or heavy sea; it should always be commenced in time, performed skilfully, and with as little delay as possible; for lost moments in fair weather are difficult to regain in foul.

In a sailing match the boat is kept on her course without reefing as long as she can stagger under her canvas; but on such occasions there are always plenty of hands aboard to assist in the prompt management of the sails.

Under ordinary circumstances, when about to reef the sails, luff the boat up close to the wind, though not so close as to allow her to come about; ease off the jib-sheet, or, if you intend to set a smaller jib, first take in the other; then haul the fore-sail aweather and make it fast; haul in the main-sheet as close as possible, and the boat will be 'laid-to.' Now lower the peak, then the main sufficiently for the intended reef; cast off the main-tack, and begin at the earings or outer end by hauling down the reef and securing it with the reef-earings to the boom; then tie up the points with reef knots all along the sail and make the main-tack fast: do not roll the sail. The reefing being so far completed, set up the peak, ease off the main-sheet, trim the fore-sheets, and the boat will then be under a single-reefed main-sail. Another reef may be hauled down in a similar manner, and the boat will then be under a double or two-reefed main-sail; and so of a third reef.

From a photo by   *Mr. Harold Fraser.*

Reefing.

The illustration at the foot of the previous page, is from a photograph of the yacht *Zerlina*, a seven-ton cruiser, under close-reefed main-sail, in heavy weather, the fore-sail being lowered, but her No. 1 jib left standing, which, however, is not good seamanship ; instead of her No. 1 jib, a storm-jib, 'spit-fire,' or the very smallest jib on board, ought to have been set.

Never tie the points of a second or third reef until the first or lower ones have been secured ; you may then shake out the reefs one at a time, as the wind decreases.

Always look to your reef-tackle before setting sail, and see that the earings are sound and strong ; for it is seldom necessary to reef except in heavy winds, which try the strength of ropes and tackle as well as the stiffness and power of the boat under pressure of sail.

Boat with roller fore-sail.

The illustration is from a photograph of one of the Bembridge Club boats mentioned and described at p. 71. It is introduced here as showing the working of the roller fore-sail.

Reefing by rolling the Sails—a simple, but not novel, contrivance for reefing the sails of a boat by means of a revolving, or roller-spar, after the manner of an ordinary window roll-blind, is sometimes found very convenient for small single-handed boats, whereby the fore-sail can be reefed by means of a ratline attached to a reel affixed to the bottom part of the roller-spar, and led aft to the stern sheets or cockpit of the boat.

The Roller-boom.—The mainsail, too, if fitted with a revolving boom, or ratchet reefing-tackle, may be reefed and furled in a similar manner: but it answers best for small-sized sails. Although it is only of late years that it has come into general use for small yachts and sailing-boats in the Solent and neighbourhood, it is a very ancient contrivance, and has been used in a more primitive form in the boats and vessels of the Malay Archipelago for centuries past,[1] where it is to this day the common mode of reefing and furling the sails of the larger class of outrigger sailing-vessels. It was also in use more than fifty years ago by the late Captain Shuldham for reefing the sails of his revolving-rigged boats.[2] There are several other modes of reefing the sails of small vessels by rolling them, which have been in common use for many years past; notably in the Southampton pilot boats, the Channel Islands fishing-smacks, and others. And an improved mechanical contrivance by Mr. Roger Turner, of Beccles, Suffolk, was recently patented.

SAILING TO WINDWARD.

· Thus tars at sea, like swabs at home,
By tack and tack are biass'd,
The furthest way about we roam,
To bring us home the nighest.'—DIBDIN.

SAILING to windward is one of the highest accomplishments in the art of yacht and boat-sailing. The precision of the eye and the delicate touch of the hand at the helm in keeping the boat close to the wind without sacrificing one iota of the power of the sails in pressing the boat onwards, is the truest test of good and skilful boat-sailing. And the narrower the channel in the beat to windward the greater is the skill and discretion required of the ' man at the helm.'

Sailing to windward being, therefore, one of the most interesting and exciting performances connected with the art of boat-sailing, the tyro should spare no pains to make himself master of it; and with that view he must thoroughly accustom himself to the use of the tiller, and practise sailing in all the varieties of light airs, gentle breezes and strong winds.

The art of sailing a boat against the wind by sundry zig-zag performances is one that requires considerable attention, a watchful eye, and frequent practice; for although the rudiments of the art may be learnt in a few lessons, the art itself, which is the perfection of boat-sailing, can only be acquired by long experience.

[1] *Vide infra*, ' Boats of the Malay Archipelago.'
[2] *Supra*, ' Revolving-rigged boats,' page 88.

Sailing to Windward.

One of the principal things for the young helmsman to attend to in sailing to windward with effect is to watch the fore-leech of the main-sail or that part nearest the mast. The boat should be sailed as close to the wind as possible without shaking this part of the sail, which is always the first to quiver to the breeze, and thereby to warn the helmsman of too close a luff. Some sailors steer by a vane at the mast-head, and some cannot sail a vessel properly without one; but such is an uncertain guide in boat-sailing, and it

From a photo by   *West & Son, Southsea.*

A Lady of the West steering her yacht to victory.

is a bad practice to steer by it. Some steer by the ripple on the water, which may be all very well when the wind is light, but at best an uncertain guide. The young boat-sailor who wishes to become skilful in the art of sailing to windward will practise his eye upon the fore-leech of the main-sail, which is always the most faithful and unerring indicator; the instant the slightest waver is perceptible in this part of the sail he should bear up a little; the least motion of the tiller will suffice if the boat be in proper trim.

The Sailing-Boat.

It often happens that the wind is unsteady, blowing sometimes in a continued strong breeze for two or three minutes or more, and immediately afterwards a light wind follows; but this occurs chiefly with easterly winds, which are generally irregular. On such occasions great advantages may be gained by watching the effect of the wind upon the luff of the main-sail, for the boat can be sailed two points nearer the wind in some of the gusts than in others; then is the time for the skilled helmsman to wedge his way to windward of his opponents.

But it is only by practical experience that the amateur boat-sailor can acquire the art of keeping the boat at the best angle to the wind, and all the while ' keeping her full.'

From a photo by   *Beken & Son, Cowes, I. of W.*

Another point of great importance is the trimming of the jib-sheets. A well-cut jib is a very powerful sail on a good boat, but the jib-sheet must be trimmed to a nicety, so that the sail fills and draws with all its power. The jib-sheets require skilful manipulation; an inch or two more or less, either in hauling them too taut or in easing them too freely, will add to or diminish the progress of the boat.

The amateur boat-sailor should also make a practice of sitting as low down in the boat as possible when under-way, and inculcate the same practice with his crew, making them all keep down as low as possible, as it assists the boat more than many persons would suppose, upon the principle that the lower down in the boat the ballast is, the stiffer she will be and the better she will sail. Therefore, in half-decked boats more particularly, no part of the shoulders nor even the head of either of the crew (below their

From a photo by   "Thetis," no heads above deck.   *Beken & Son, Cowes, I. of W.*

eyes) should be seen above deck during the critical moments of a closely-contested sailing-match.

See the illustration above of a well-trained crew in this respect.

The greater the force of the wind the closer the boat may be sailed to it when in smooth water; and in racing, or match-sailing, an experienced helmsman will so narrowly watch the wind, that should the slightest variation occur, he will take advantage by sailing his boat up to it with all possible precision, but never so as to allow any part of the sail to quiver or hinder the boat's progress. It is a well-known maxim in sailing to windward to 'keep her full,' that is, to keep the sails full of wind and not allow any part of them to quiver, for a shaking or quivering sail is, at the time, of but little assistance to the boat.

In beating to windward in a very narrow channel it is best to take in the jib and work the boat under main-sail and fore-sail; the jib is the sail that puts the boat ashore in channels which are so narrow that a vessel is no sooner round and on a fresh tack than it becomes necessary to put her about again.

On putting the helm down, 'to come about,' it should not be put over too suddenly but gradually, that the boat may obey it quicker. Some people are so impatient in getting the boat round, that the helm is jammed over all at once and oftentimes the boat misses stays in consequence, which not only causes delay and vexation but danger as well. Another practice equally erroneous is putting the helm up before the boat is fairly round, by which means she loses way or lays head-to-wind without going ahead;

From a photo by   *Beken & Son, Cowes, I. of W.*
"Edie."

and it then becomes necessary to haul the fore-sail aweather, to pay her head off, or the main sheet must be eased to allow her to veer off into the wind.

In crossing a tide-way there is always a tendency, more or less according to the strength of the tide, to cause the boat to make lee-way, particularly when close-hauled. Nothing but experience and good judgment, combined with a knowledge of the locality, can enable the helmsman to estimate the extent of lee-way and to lay his course accordingly. But when crossing a tide-way in which the set of the tide is favourable to the

Reaching and Sailing on a Bowline.

course of the boat it acts in a contrary way, and enables the boat to hold a better course and the helmsman to point her closer to the wind.

In sailing to windward a good deal of discretion is required as to the proper sized jib to set. As a general rule a boat will go to windward better with a small jib than with a large one. Many a race has been lost through carrying too large a jib when working to windward. The effect of a large jib is to sag the boat to leeward, particularly when she has but little way on her; this may be seen when the boat is put about. It is a good rule that although the jib-sheet is the first to be eased off on coming about, it should never be trimmed until the boat is fairly going ahead on a fresh tack.

Topsails are seldom of much assistance to a boat when working to windward, except in very light airs and under high cliffs; they are, however, of great service in reaching and running with a free wind.

But, withal, it is impossible to bring out the utmost speed of which a boat is capable unless a number of preliminary points be first carefully attended to—such as ballasting, rigging, setting and shifting sails, trimming the sheets, &c., &c., each of which is almost an art in itself, and cannot possibly be learnt without considerable attention and experience; but with these combined a good sailor with a good boat will frequently have the satisfaction of finding himself foremost in the race. And experience, with skill, may make many an old-fashioned vessel beat a new one.

REACHING AND SAILING ON A BOWLINE.

From a photo by   Mr. Harold Fraser.

Reaching and sailing on a bowline.

The Sailing-Boat.

By *reaching* is meant sailing with a side wind. The boat is said to be on a reach when the main-sheet is not quite close-hauled; and on a bowline, when the wind is free and the sheets are eased off so that all the sails draw powerfully.

The principal points to attend to when sailing on a bowline are, to trim the main and jib-sheets so that the boat feels all their power; not so that they stand too slack or cause any part of the sail to flap or quiver, but so that every inch of sail helps the boat to go ahead. The greatest speed at which a boat can sail is brought out when sailing on a bowline.

Long boats are fastest for this branch of sailing. A boat of narrow form of hull, if judiciously ballasted, will pass many a good sea-going boat in smooth water, with a reaching or bowline wind.

Should a heavy squall strike the sails when reaching in a strong wind, the helm should be put down and the boat brought up head to wind; but if the squall be very sudden and there is not sufficient sea-room for luffing, the main-sheet should be slacked as quickly as possible, by which means the pressure of the sail will be eased and the boat will quickly recover itself.

In bearing up or wearing when on a reach, if the wind is strong or squally the main-peak should be lowered and the main-sheet slacked, or there may be danger of carrying away the mast. If the boat has running tackle or back-stays, they will be a great support to the mast on such occasions.

When a boat is capsized in bearing up or wearing, the water first comes in over the lee bow, which, in hazardous sailing, is sometimes nearly driven under water.

A pressure of sail in a strong breeze, burying the lee scuppers of the boat and dragging her along on her beam ends, is perilous sailing, and, in a heavy sea, the risk is thereby considerably augmented.

SCUDDING, OR RUNNING BEFORE THE WIND.

> ' A wet sheet and a flowing sea,
> A wind that follows fast
> And fills the white and rustling sails,
> And bends the gallant mast.'—CUNNINGHAM.

THIS branch of our pastime is one that should be performed with caution, particularly during a strong wind, or in squally weather: although to the inexperienced it may appear the most simple and easiest mode of sailing as the boat travels more upon an even keel, and without lying over on her side as she does in sailing to windward; yet experience has shown that scudding in a strong wind is often attended with danger because of the risk of the main-sail suddenly jybing.

132

Scudding, or Running Before the Wind.

A back-stay is necessary when running before a strong wind, in order to protect the mast from being carried away. The shrouds are no protection to the mast when sailing with the wind abaft.

When running before the wind the main-sheet should be given out freely, the running tackle cast off to leeward but set up to windward. The main-sail should be allowed to blow out as much as possible, but not so as to chafe against the lee-shrouds; the main-tack should be cast off in order that the main-sail may hold a better wind. A

From a photo by   *Beken & Son, Cowes, I. of W.*
"Grafin" running before the wind.

watchful eye must be kept upon the sail and attention paid to the wind; for should the sail be suddenly jybed, *i.e.* blown over to the other side of the boat, when the main-sheet is all run out, the boat is almost certain to be capsized, or the mast carried away, if there be much wind and sea. But in order to avoid this when running directly before the wind, should the sail exhibit the slightest symptoms of being taken aback—as by wavering to leeward—the helm should instantly be put down a little so as to avoid a jybe if possible.

Should a squall suddenly strike the main-sail when running before the wind, and appear too heavy for the boat, by putting the helm down immediately, the force of the gust may be eased considerably as the boat comes up into the wind, and probably the mast is thereby saved from being carried away.

The boat should be steered as straight a course as possible when scudding. The fore-sail will be of little or no use when going directly before the wind, unless boomed out; the jib-sheets should be slacked, and the jib allowed to draw as freely as the other sails.

When the wind is fresh and squally it may sometimes be advisable to lower the peak of the main-sail on a sudden emergency, or to trice up the main-tack, either of

"Will o' th' Wisp" scudding.

which will take some of the strain off the mast; but the safest precaution is to reef the main-sail and take in the jib.

The danger of scudding or running before the wind is much greater in a heavy sea than in smooth water, and a boat is generally hard to steer when she pitches. The safety of the boat and crew, when scudding in a heavy sea or strong wind, depends almost entirely on the watchfulness and skill of the helmsman, who, on observing the least inclination of the sail to jybe, should instantly ease down the helm.

If the main-sail has no boom, it will be the more liable to jybe suddenly, therefore extra precaution must be used with such a sail when running before the wind.

The amateur sailor should always bear in mind when a squall strikes the sail and the boat is in danger, that he must put the *helm down*, that is, push it towards the same side as the sail is (to put the helm *up*, is to push it from the sail); and this precaution should be distinctly impressed upon his mind.

Boat in Stays.

BOAT IN STAYS.

A BOAT or vessel is ' in stays' immediately after the helm is put down to bring her about, and when the sails are all shaking in the eye of the wind ; but directly the fore-sail has ' payed off' the head, and brought the boat round, she is no longer in stays, but on a fresh tack or reach—the port or starboard tack, or port or starboard reach, as the case may be.

When a boat is in stays in squally weather, it is a critical moment, for should the wind take the sails aback, or a squall strike them, there is danger of upsetting the boat, which has, at the moment, no way on ; *i.e.* is not going through the water, therefore will not when thrown suddenly on her side, answer to the helm. The sheets should be clear and free, lying in coils, when the boat is ' put about,' so as to be ready to let go instantly in case of peril. The jib-sheet especially should be kept slack and in hand, until the boat is fairly round and has recovered way.

Long boats are always more sluggish in stays than short ones ; the short beamy little craft is quickly round, generally before danger can touch her, whilst the long rakish craft makes a more extensive circuit in ' coming about,' sometimes shooting ahead considerably in the performance, and so fore-reaching upon her shorter antagonist.

Missing Stays.—This term implies a failure on the part of the boat to ' come about,' or to answer her helm when it is put down for the purpose of bringing the boat round, head to windward.

Should the boat miss stays in a squall, the main-sheet and jib-sheet must be let go or slackened, and the fore-sail hauled to windward ; after which, if the squall throw the boat so flat on her side as to leave her in momentary danger, let go the halliards of the sail that is pressing upon her, if possible in time to save the boat from capsizing.

When a boat misses stays in a light wind, there is seldom any danger attending it ; but when it occurs in a strong wind or squall, or in a heavy sea, there is always more or less risk ; for the boat when in stays has no way on her, consequently she is very liable to be capsized should a gust of wind suddenly strike the sails. It is necessary therefore on ' coming about,' to attend to the sheets, and see that they are all clear and not made fast until the boat is fairly on her way again.

It is a matter of prudence on the part of the helmsman of a sailing-boat to avoid putting about in a squall, as it is also in a heavy sea, for fear of the risk incurred, and the danger attending the boat if she misses stays. If a boat be judiciously ballasted, and in good trim, she will never miss stays in smooth water. But in a heavy sea there is sometimes considerable risk in ' putting about,' because the stern is alternately out of the water, and the rudder powerless when the boat is on the crest of a wave.

The Sailing-Boat.

TO BRING-UP AT MOORINGS.

From a photo by   *Beken & Son, Cowes, I. of W.*

Boats at moorings.

> ' " I've heard," cried out one, " that you tars tack and tack,
>   And at sea what strange dangers befel you ;
> But I don't know what's moorings " —" What ! don't you ? " cries Jack—
>   " Man your ear-tackle then, and I'll tell you." '—DIBDIN.

A VESSEL riding by two or more anchors in different directions is said to be moored. A boat's moorings consist of a strong mooring-chain, the two ends of which are anchored in different directions ; a smaller chain, called a bridle, is secured to the mooring-chain about midway from each anchor, and a buoy is attached to the upper part of the bridle, to mark or watch the spot where the moorings lie.

Nothing looks more like mis-management than getting into a muddle with the sailing-boat when it is required to be 'brought up' at a particular spot, or 'dropped alongside' a large yacht or a landing place. Bungling hands when endeavouring to effect these elementary performances, sometimes run foul of neighbouring boats, and in their ineffectual attempts to 'bring-up at moorings' keep hoisting and lowering the fore-sail and peak of the main-sail, hauling the boom over, dropping anchor, jamming their fingers, working themselves up into a state of perspiration and excitement, getting their legs entangled in the ropes, and toppling over, head foremost in the boat, and sometimes overboard, to the amusement and ridicule of bystanders, whose hearty laughs at such lubberly seamanship increase the difficulties and add to the perplexities of the unskilful amateur.

An experienced sailing-master, however, is enabled to 'bring-up at moorings,' or drop his boat alongside another, with as much ease as a practised coachman drives along the street and stops the carriage at any particular door.

Bringing-up at moorings in a crowded harbour, though an elementary performance, is one that should be done with skill and precision. A skilled and confident sailor comes boldly up to his berth with head sails down and main-sail standing, and performs the task almost to an inch, and without making a scratch upon the surface of his own or any other boat.

It should be borne in mind in 'bringing-up at moorings' that the greater the length of the boat, the more sweep it requires in 'coming about.' A light sailing skiff requires but little room, and may easily be laid alongside with precision after practice; but a boat heavily ballasted, and of a larger size than an ordinary skiff, cannot always be stopped in a moment when a fresh breeze is blowing or a strong tide running. On coming up to moorings, the distance required for the sweep round must be measured with the eye; and, if in a tide-way, allowance made for strength of current. The boat should be luffed boldly alongside in a good sweep; and after a little experience, it will be an easy matter, in a light wind, to lay her alongside even with all sail standing, but of course, shaking in the eye of the wind. It is usual however, first to take in the jib, that the boat may have less way on her. It is sometimes necessary to keep the fore-sail standing until the moment before the moorings are hooked, so as to be ready to haul aweather and pay her head off, in case of a failure in the performance.

Never attempt to lay a boat on, or too near, a lee shore in a heavy swell or a strong wind; and on going up to a berth at moorings, never do so *before* the wind (except in a strong tide-way), but always to windward. If it happens that there is but short turning-room, and the moorings cannot be approached in any other way than by running before the wind, lower all the sails except the fore-sail, and run the boat up as slowly as possible, hook the buoy with a boat-hook, and make fast quickly with the bridle.

To steer the boat when going through the water stern first, the helm must be put in the same direction as that in which the head of the boat is required to be turned. When drifting with the current in a tide-way, the aft part of the boat being deeper than the fore part, the stern will have a tendency to drive faster than the head; in which case, and in order to retain a proper control over the boat, less aft sail must be set, and more head sail.

The Sailing-Boat.

From a photo by   *Beken & Son, Cowes, I. of W.*

Sails furled.

FURLING the sails—also termed 'stowing the sails'—merely implies rolling them up neatly and in a sailor-like manner, after the boat is moored, or at anchor.

The *main-sail* is furled as follows:—The sail being lowered down into the boat, place the gaff and boom close together, one on top of the other; then lift the flap of the sail over the boom, and lay the aft-leech over the flap, hauling it taut from the gaff end; keep all taut whilst another hand rolls up the loose sail neatly and close to the gaff. The sail should not be rolled *round* the boom nor *round* the gaff, but *close up to* the latter. Then pass three or four small lashings round the sail and over the gaff, and having secured them the main-sail will be furled.

The *fore-sail* may be furled in the following manner:—When the sail is fixed to, and traverses the fore-stay up and down by means of brass thimbles (the most usual way), it should be let down to the stem of the boat, rolled up neatly, and an oilskin spread over it. In small boats, when the fore-sail is not attached to, or does not traverse the fore-stay, but the rope on the fore-leech of the sail forms the fore-stay, then the fore-tack may be unhooked and the fore-sail rolled up in the main-sail or stowed away separately in the locker.

Jibs and top-sails are generally kept in the forecastle, or in the cabin, or whichever is driest and most convenient. In small sailing boats having neither cabin nor forecastle, they are sometimes rolled up in the main-sail.

After the main-sail is furled, a water-proof coating should be put over it, extending from the mast to the boom end; but it is not a good plan to leave the sails coated and furled for any length of time. A few days will sometimes incur the risk of mildew; therefore they should be exposed to the air as often as possible.

The *sprit-sail* is generally furled by rolling it up close to the mast—not round it—after taking out the spreet, and without lowering the main-halliards; the fore-sail should be rolled up inside the sprit-sail. It is a neat method, but an oilskin coating cannot conveniently be fitted over a sail furled in this manner.

When the sails are wet they should be loosely furled, unless they can be spread out to dry. New sails should be well and frequently wetted with salt-water, when the boat is under way, to preserve them from mildew. In damp or wet weather sails require much attention, and must be frequently spread and exposed to the air during the driest part of the day; if neglected for any length of time (although under an oilskin coat) they are very liable to be disfigured and otherwise injured by mildew.

MATCH SAILING (SMALL YACHTS).

' The mast may be bending, and threatening the gale,
The gun'l borne down deep a' lee;
But the stoutest of hearts, and most daring of men,
Win the perilous race on the sea.'—THE AUTHOR.

The Start.—At the present day, where there is sufficient sea-room, the usual mode of starting the competing yachts is that known as 'The Flying Start': in which all the yachts come to the starting line under way with their sails set. They are not allowed to anchor nor to cross the line until the starting gun is fired; consequently if any of the yachts arrive at the line too soon they are required to retreat. The starting line is not defined otherwise than as lying straight between two conspicuous marks, usually flag-buoys. It is obvious that a start of this kind requires sea-room, or a tolerably wide expanse of water.

Another mode of arranging the start is that adopted in narrow waters where there is less sea-room, and in rivers where there are strong currents: in this mode the competing yachts are either anchored or moored in line; sometimes with aft sails set and head sails down, and sometimes with all sails down, as may be previously arranged

The Sailing-Boat.

by the sailing committee. At starts of this kind lots are drawn for stations, which are numbered: the weathermost being, usually, the most desirable.

Other modes of starting are regulated by special rules of sailing clubs, to meet the requirements of particular localities, by reason of the limited space of open water.

As soon as the signal is given for the start, the sheets trimmed, and the spare ropes of the halliards coiled and laid in their proper places, every man on board the racing boat should squat or lie down and so remain until required by the sailing-master to perform some duty. The crew should not congregate altogether in one part of the boat, but judiciously distribute themselves about the vessel, so as not to disturb her trim or depress her bow or stern. In small yachts and open boats this is an important

From a photo by   Start of 2½-raters at Cowes.   *Beken & Son, Cowes, I. of W.*

consideration; the weight of one man in the wrong place may make a material difference in the trim, and consequently in the sailing of the vessel.

The Race.—Those only who have taken part in a spirited sailing match, and joined in the bold efforts that have led the way to victory, can truly appreciate the pleasure and excitement of a public contest on the watery race-course, when every inch of the rippling surface is as closely contested as if life and death were pending the result.

The daring efforts that are made in strong winds and heavy seas by an undaunted crew, and their earnest struggles for pride of place in the race have often and justly been the subject of public admiration.

There is no truer test of skill and daring in a sailor, and of skilful seamanship in a skipper than the fact of his sailing and winning, among a fleet of the fastest boats of the day, a hard-fought sailing-match in a strong wind; and many such matches have been sailed and won by British yacht owners.

Match Sailing.

There must always, in a sailing match, be activity and readiness among every member of the crew; and skill and sound judgment are indispensable at the helm, particularly if 'carrying on' when the wind is strong and the sea heavy.

The boat that can be sailed fastest to windward is considered the best boat, and is generally the winner of the race-cup. Although very much of the success is justly attributable to the form of the hull below the water-line, a good deal depends on the skill of the helmsman; and when it is considered how slight a touch of the helm will

From a photo by   *Beken & Son, Cowes, I. of W.*

Modern racing cutter " Caress."

put a well-trimmed boat out of its course, and turn it a point or more off the wind, it is easy to understand how sailing matches may be won or lost through superior skill on the one hand, and the least inattention or lack of skill on the other. The same test may account for the fact of a famous racing-cutter being signally defeated, time after time, when in the possession of one owner, but, on changing hands, turning out a frequent winner.

In sailing-matches the race is sometimes lost by the fastest yacht because the sailing-master is unable to obtain the lead, or, having obtained it, is out-manœuvred by another, and therefore unable to keep it.

At the present day, when most of the small yacht sailing-matches (particularly those of the one-design classes) are sailed by the owners—or, rather, the owner acts as his own sailing-master—it is necessary that he be able to 'hold his own' without being out-manœuvred by his antagonist. With a good boat, success depends mainly on how she is handled. Many a yacht of the winning type loses the match when capable of winning it had she been handled to the best advantage. The proof comes afterwards when, in other hands, in subsequent matches, she is steered to victory.

Take also the converse of this: without mentioning names, for it is an oft-

From a photo by

"Koorangah."

Beken & Son, Cowes, I. of W.

occurring fact that there are, nearly every year, racing yachts of great repute, with long strings of victories appended to their names, which, on changing hands, fail to retain that pride of place they previously occupied, and the rivals they had vanquished again and again in former races now outsail them with apparent ease.

The failure lies, not with the boat, but chiefly in the handling: sometimes in the trim, the set of the sails, and perhaps half-a-dozen other small matters, not the least of which is, opportunity lost through the lack of sound judgment on one or more occasions during the race.

The importance to be attached to the trimming and ballasting of racing-boats has already been referred to. These, however, as well as some other important considerations, are preliminary steps, to which due attention must be paid before coming to the starting point with any chance of success in a sailing match.

Many years ago a highly discreditable practice prevailed in match-sailing with the smaller class of racing-yachts—that of *ballast trimming*—but which has now long since very properly been discountenanced by all British yacht clubs. The sanction of such an unsportsmanlike and dangerous practice led to the introduction of a class of vessels unworthy the name of British yachts, and which were, not inappropriately, termed *sailing machines*. Those vessels, to all appearances, when under sail, were enabled to carry a tremendous spread of canvas and to bear a great pressure of sail, although of a narrow form of hull; and they were rigged with spars wholly out of proportion to their tonnage. Strangers used to look on with wonder as to how boats of such a rakish form could hold themselves up under such an amazing pressure of spars and canvas, whilst the more sturdy and stiff-looking cutter of the same tonnage, found about half as much sail a sufficient quantum. A peep into the interior of the vessel however, revealed the whole secret; for there, unseen by all above deck, were four or more men trimming heavy bags of shot—real shot, such as sportsmen use to wing the feathered tribe—and those they shifted from the leeward side to the weather side— or rather from lee-bilge to weather-bilge, according to the tack on which the vessel was sailing—to 'hold her up,' or to 'keep her stiff,' as they termed it. In the absence of bags of shot, were long bars of lead or iron which they lugged from side to side in the same manner, and then secured them from slipping by putting up slides or shifting-boards. The four men then cringed over to windward, or laid down upon the shot-bags until they heard the order 'bout!' when the shifting ballast was trimmed to the other side as quickly as possible, and again they coiled themselves up on the

Racing cutter of 1850.

143

shot-bags as before. When there was much turning to windward ballast-trimming was hard work; in fact the hardest work aboard the vessel. As much as a ton was but an ordinary quantum of shifting-ballast for a ten-ton racing cutter of that period, and so in proportion as to larger vessels.

The illustration at foot of previous page, is that of a racing cutter of the year 1850; it is introduced here to show the type of yacht and rig of that period, for the purpose of comparison with the racing cutter of the present day.

Boats for racing purposes require to be very strongly built, or the great strain caused by extra pressure of sail soon tells with effect upon some part of the hull.

When racing in small open boats, the crew should sit as low down in the boat as possible; if on the floor so much the better for the boat.

When putting the boat about, the helm should not be put down too sharply, but slowly and steadily; by which means the boat will shoot farther ahead in turning, come about quicker and be less likely to miss stays.

Every man should be more or less master of the art of boat-sailing, before he aspires to the helm in a sailing-match; therefore all preliminaries as to setting sail smartly, canting round for windward berth, &c., should be first well learnt and practised. Many a race has been lost by carrying too large a jib *on* a wind, and as many more by too large topsails, when, with a jib-headed topsail and a smaller jib, the boat would have sailed faster and made less lee-way. But in reaching, running, or sailing with the wind free, the boat should be allowed all the sail she can carry; set your spinnakers and topsails as large as the weather will allow, always acting with a judicious regard to the safety of the spars and vessel. But be the wind ever so light, those butterfly sails will not answer *on a wind;* on the contrary, they retard the progress of the boat, and deny her a fair chance.

In tacking to windward in a race, great advantages may sometimes be gained by manœuvring; but nautical manœuvres can only be well learnt by practice and experience, and are scarcely a fit subject for book-teaching.

The illustration on next page gives an exhibition of what is termed 'blanketing' in yacht-racing; *i.e.*, one yacht gliding to windward close alongside another, with the object of taking the wind out of her sails and so obtaining an advantage.

When on a wind, the sailing-master who watches the wind and the luff of the main-sail closest obtains the greatest advantage; for it often happens that there are slight variations in the wind in the course of an hour or less, and at some moments he is enabled to lay a much better course than at others. He should take advantage of all these and wedge his way to windward; constantly creeping as close to the wind as possible, so long as he can do so without shaking its power out of the sails. The fault in those unaccustomed to match-sailing, generally lies in their too great fear of not keeping the sails full; and so, having once placed the vessel close to the wind they are careful to keep a straight course, and, regardless of any variation, they steer as straight as an arrow for some object ahead or on shore.   Now, this is undoubtedly an excellent plan when ' running free '; but the man who so steers a racing vessel when *on a wind*, will very seldom succeed in bringing her in first at the winning goal.   The man at the helm should watch constantly for variations in the wind, by keeping his eye on the luff of the main-sail; and by the most delicate touch of the helm he will be enabled occasionally to squeeze the yacht a point nearer to the wind.   It is only by strict atten-

From a photo by   *Beken & Son, Cowes, I. of W.*
Yacht racing. Blanketing her opponent.

tion to such opportunities, and instantly embracing them, that they can be turned to so good advantage ; but, be it remembered, that in a sailing match they are assuredly golden chances when attentively and opportunely seized.

In trimming the sheets in a sailing match, a good deal of discretion is required : a pull of an inch too much on the jib-sheet when on a wind, may render the sail far less effective, and instead of acting as a powerful drawing-sail, half its power may be lost and it then becomes a ' lee driver.'

When sailing on a bowline, care should be taken that the sheets are trimmed so that every inch of the canvas draws and assists the boat in the most effective manner.

The Sailing-Boat.

When running before the wind in a race, the main-sheet should be paid out freely, the jib and fore-sheets eased off, and all the sails allowed to draw powerfully and assist the boat to their utmost.

It is a mistaken notion to set up the shrouds of the mast too taut in a racing vessel when on a wind; the mast should have a little play. If too confined the vessel will appear as if benumbed when close-hauled; whereas, by easing the weather-shrouds and giving the mast more play, the boat will be released as it were from its bonds, and appear as lively under sail as a bird on wing.

BOAT-RACING BY LADIES.

From a photo by   *West & Son, Southsea.*

Boat-racing by ladies.

At the present day when lady-sailors are conspicuous at our sailing matches, and participate *con amore* in the pastime, it is no uncommon occurrence to find a lady at the

146

helm in a sailing-boat on the Solent, any more than it is at other boating places on our coasts. And indeed, boat races by ladies have become frequent at many of the regattas on and about the English coast. And lady-sailors are often to be seen at the helm in their small cruising-yachts on a fine summer's day.

Some ladies have such a love for the sea and aptitude for boat-sailing, and take such a prominent part in aquatic recreations (some as members of yacht and boat-sailing clubs), that they actually have small racing-yachts built and equipped expressly for racing : and thus, occasionally a fair charmer may be found taking her place at the helm and maintaining it throughout a spirited and exciting sailing match ; upon the principle, perhaps, that every yachting lady should be her own sailing-mistress.

Be this as it may, there are undoubtedly some very skilful lady amateur yacht and boat-sailers in and about the yachting stations of the Solent ; some of whom have often steered their yachts to victory in keenly contested sailing matches.

The Sailing-Boat.

From a photo by   *West & Son, Southsea.*

Boats in a squall.

But again we pressed on her, the gale still increasing;
Not a squall now and then, but a squall without ceasing.—THE AUTHOR.

THE amateur boat-sailer who ventures to set sail in squally weather must have ' an eye to windward,' particularly if in an open boat. Squalls of wind require watching, and attention to the helm and the main and fore-sheets. The danger lies in the boat being suddenly thrown upon her beam-ends whilst the main-sheet is fast, and thus over-powered at a moment of incaution on the part of the helmsman. If the main-sheet be free, and the boat carries a good weather-helm, and the helmsman be on his guard, there

148

is nothing to fear on a squall suddenly striking the sails; he should put the helm down and ease off the main-sheet.

On a wide expanse of water, signs of a squall may generally be seen on the surface some few moments before it reaches and strikes the sails of the boat; and at sea a squall may sometimes be seen at a distance of many miles; in which case there is usually time for shortening sail before its effects are felt; but in narrow rivers, and when sailing close under the land, squalls often come down upon the boat with all the suddenness imaginable: such are the most dangerous of all squalls: and it is, besides, difficult to

From a photo by   *Mr. Hill Charley.*

"Sheelah" in a squall.

suggest a means of avoiding their dangerous effects on an open boat; except, that double caution should be taken that the main-sheet is always ready to be let go in an instant, whenever sailing anywhere near high land; for squalls sometimes come sweeping down the valleys with great force, and often catch the boat in a calm, as it emerges from the shelter of some high cliff or mound; and many and sad are the accidents that have arisen from such squalls.

When sailing in an open boat, if a heavy squall is observed approaching, the peak of the main-sail should (as a precaution) be lowered, if a gaff-sail; or, if a sprit-sail, the sail should be brailed up. If only a light or little squall it may be allowed to strike the sails; but then the boat should be immediately luffed up to it, but not so as to lose all way; keep the boat going, or she will not answer the helm. If a very heavy squall, douse the fore-sail and drop the peak, ease the sheets, and 'stand by' the helm.

It is easy to distinguish a light squall from a heavy one. The light one flits over the water like a dark cloud; but a heavy one, or 'white squall,' brings with it a fierce-looking white crest of foam upon the tops of the waves—

> ' " Luff ! luff ! " was the shout, " a white squall to wind'ard ! "
> Then we eas'd her a moment, tho' her progress was hinder'd.'

When threatened with a white squall, if in an open boat, it is safest to let the fore-sail run down, and to drop the peak of the main-sail; and, as a further precaution, to take in the jib.

In an ordinary squall, if the sails be reefed, and the boat a safe and powerful one, there is nothing to fear under judicious management. The boat may be conducted through it with safety, by 'sailing her narrow,' *i.e.* so close to the wind that the fore-leeches of the sails are just on the shake; but great caution is necessary by the man at the helm, lest the sails be taken aback.

In all cases of heavy squalls, it is of the highest importance to *keep good way on the boat;* for if she loses way, or is stationary, the squall will tell upon her with double force and treble danger to what it would if moving rapidly ahead: and a boat with no way on her will not answer to her helm, and is in such event unmanageable.

If a squall should strike the sails whilst the boat is running free, the helm should be *put down*; and this is a very important precaution to take in such cases, for if a mistake be made, and the helm *put up*, the squall will, if a heavy one, almost inevitably capsize the boat.

CAUSES OF BOATS CAPSIZING.

NOTWITHSTANDING the numerous and melancholy accidents that occur, year after year, through the mismanagement and upsetting of sailing-boats, there are persons who will not take warning therefrom, but persist in rushing headlong into dangers which, with ordinary prudence, they might certainly avoid.

The casualties that occur to sailing-boats whereby they are upset, are not always occasioned by stress of weather, but are mainly attributable to causes within control.

Boats are not so frequently capsized on account of large sails, strong winds, and heavy seas, as they are from mismanagement or carelessness; accidents of the kind sometimes occur in fine or moderate weather. Among the principal *causes of boats capsizing* are—inattention to the main and jib-sheets; wrong adjustment of the sails, particularly the head-sails, or those before the mast; large and disproportionate spars; improper trim of hull, whereby the boat carries a lee-helm instead of a weather-helm;

missing-stays ; sluggishness on coming about ; insufficient ballast ; the ballast shifting and rolling over to leeward ; the jamming of a rope, whereby it is checked in running through the blocks or sheaves ; the sail not coming down freely ; ill-fitting blocks ; reckless pressure of sail ; overcrowding the boat with people ; intoxication ; standing up in the boat ; leaning over the gunwale ; and various other causes, some of which are hereinafter explained.

From a photo by   *Beken & Son, Cowes, I. of W.*

" Eos " capsized.

The illustration is from a photograph of the *Eos*, half-rater, capsized off Cowes Harbour, and the steam launch of the Liquid Fuel Company rendering prompt assistance. The *Eos* was the winner in the year 1897 of the £100 West Challenge Cup at Ryde.

Probably one of the most glaring indiscretions of those above mentioned is that of allowing the boat to carry a *lee-helm ;* as such is a *certain* precursor to disaster, sooner or later : the first squall, or even a strong breeze, will inevitably capsize a boat under such circumstances.

There are two principal causes for a boat carrying a lee-helm ; one of which is, that the boat's ballast is too far forward : and the other (or more usual one) that she has too much head-sail in proportion to her aft canvas.

The illustration on the next page is from a photograph of the *Eos* taken a few moments before she was capsized. It will be seen that although the main-sail is close-reefed, she was carrying a fore-sail nearly as large as the reefed main-sail ! a great mistake, and probably the cause of the mishap ; as it seems impossible that the boat could carry a weather-helm with such a disproportionate spread of head-sail.

Every person who ventures on the water in an open sailing-boat ought to know that the most important rope, and that on which the safety of the boat often depends, is the *main-sheet;* next in importance to which are the *fore-sheets,* or, if two head-sails, the *jib-sheets* also. All the halliards, and indeed every rope belonging to the sails, should be laid in a separate coil, so as to be ready to be run out without obstruction, in case of sudden emergency; but more particularly the *main-sheet,* which should never be made fast, except in the slightest and most simple manner. Care should be taken that it be not entangled, or in any way hidden from view; and this whether the boat is sailing before the wind, on the wind, reaching, or otherwise. In many cases, when

From a photo by   *Beken & Son, Cowes, I. of W.*

"Eos" just before capsize.

boats are capsized, the reason is, simply, that the person attending the sheets, in his confusion at the moment of danger—from fright, inattention, or some other unpardonable cause—fails to slack the main-sheet until too late, and at a period when his own weight, and probably that of other inmates of the boat, suddenly jerked over to the leeward side, actually accelerate the upsetting and deny the boat a chance of righting.

It sometimes occurs that the coil or fall of the sheet becomes entangled or twisted about something in the boat, so as to render it impossible to be let go suddenly. Many persons may consider this as very unlikely to occur, but there are others who know it has unfortunately happened too many times to need any comment to prove its probability. *E.g.* suppose the fall, or end of the sheet, to be lying in a neat coil at the bottom of the boat, the part leading from the clew of the sail being uppermost, and apparently all clear and ready for running out in an instant. Now the chances are, that after sailing about a short time, this rope becomes slightly deranged, particularly if there is much of a rolling motion, or several persons in the boat, or any circumstance occurring to call the attention of the person attending the sheet to some other object; the neatly coiled main-sheet is then forgotten, becomes entangled or foul of something, and if required to be slacked meets with some impediment to check its course through the main-sheet block, and thereby the boat is capsized. A rope, when drawn rapidly through a block, assumes a meandering or corkscrew form, and is very liable to catch round something or other in the boat, such as an oar, a boat-hook, a cleat, or person's foot; any slight check from either of which may cause an obstruction, and consequently a capsize.

That expert swimming is not always to be relied on in the event of a capsize has often been proved; and recently confirmed by the lamentable accident which occurred on the 11th August, 1898, whereby an expert swimmer (Mr. O'Connor Glynn) and a friend of his, were both drowned through the capsizing of a boat of the Dublin Bay Colleen class, in Killiney Bay; not during a sailing match, but when returning home from the Bray Regatta to Kingstown. The sunken boat, when brought to the surface revealed, at once, the cause of the melancholy catastrophe; the bodies of both occupants of the boat being found entangled in the spare part of the main-sheet, which was wound tightly round their bodies: and thus it appears they were inextricably entangled and drawn down with the sinking boat. Mr. Glynn was the son of the Hon. Sec. of the Dublin Bay Sailing Club, and was, as already stated, an expert swimmer.

It is not unfrequently the case that a rope, although neatly coiled, becomes kinked on getting wet, particularly if new; a wet rope is also liable to swell and become stiff, and so in either case, the sheave of the block may be choked, or the rope jammed between the parts of the shell. New rope if not well stretched and the turns taken out before reeving through the blocks, will be liable to twist in such a manner as to stop its running freely; therefore, simple as those precautions may appear, they are very important to be observed in fitting new ropes to a sailing-boat, particularly those used for *sheets*, where a temporary obstruction may occasion the most disastrous consequences; for if the sheet be not instantaneously cleared, when the sail is struck by a squall, the boat must inevitably be capsized. Perhaps the most effectual manner of clearing away the obstruction, in such a case, would be to out with a pocket-knife and cut away the sheet; an experiment which has, ere now, saved boat and crew from destruction, even after being thrown flat on beam ends, and the water pouring in over the gunwale.

Small sailing-boats passing under the lee of large vessels, in squally weather, are very liable to be upset on the instant after passing the vessel. The boat having lost the wind out of her sails, has little if any way on her; and if a squall then strikes her, there is great danger of a capsize unless the sheets be slack and clear.

In moderate weather, or during a steady breeze, with a clear sky, and when not likely to be squally, boatmen are frequently inclined to take what is termed a 'slippery hitch' in the sheet: this is done by twisting the bight of the rope once round its own part. A careful sailor, however, will never, under any circumstances, allow the main-sheet of an open boat to be belayed: he either holds, or orders, the slack to be held in the hand.

It sometimes becomes necessary, in light winds, to row and sail at the same time, either on account of a foul tide or from lack of wind; but such a proceeding is highly incautious, if the sheet has to be made fast, and no one be left in charge at the helm. The more prudent course would be either to lower the sails and depend entirely on the oars, or to dispense with the use of oars and trust to the sails. If oars are used whilst sailing, they should be employed on the windward side of the boat: there is consider-able risk of upsetting the boat, through catching the oar under water, with the flat side of the blade uppermost, if the boat lays over or suddenly catches a breeze when the oars are employed on the lee side.

Among other causes of boats capsizing, and one as likely to occur as any, is, when the ballast is placed upon the floor without any platform over it, or other means of keeping it secure from shifting; when, if the boat lists over in a seaway, a slight puff may cause a more than ordinary lurch, and the ballast slips from the windward-bilge to the leeward, and then no effort can prevent the inevitable result.

When running with the wind fair abaft, the sail is more liable to jybe without the boom than with it; a watchful eye should therefore be kept upon the sail, and the main-sheet must not be made fast; for should the sail jybe with the sheet belayed to leeward, it will assuredly upset the boat, though only in a moderate wind. There is no more effectual way of capsizing a boat under sail.

Boats may also be upset by having too large and heavy a mast, which gives too much leeward pressure, and materially weakens the stability of the boat. A mast for a sailing-boat should not be too stiff and unyielding, nor a shade stouter than necessary to sustain the pressure of the sails in a stiff breeze.

Causes of Boats Capsizing.

THE action of the sea upon a boat running into a heavy surf may be thus described. When on the top of a heavy wave or roller, the bows are lifted high out of the water; then, as the sea recedes, the boat is hurled forward, and the bows are buried under water, when the sea acting powerfully on her head and fore-gripe, twists her round broadside to the waves—called 'broaching-to,' and the sea then runs over the gunwale into the boat. The next motion that inevitably follows is a heavy lurch on the other side, and another sea breaks completely over and fills or capsizes the boat. This may happen either under sail or oars. There is considerable difficulty in preventing a boat from broaching-to, when stem and stern are alternately lifted out of the water by the waves; and should the boat broach-to and meet a heavy roller broadside-on, the chances are fifty to one that she will be swamped. Experience teaches, that when a heavy breaker follows the boat up astern, it is useless to attempt running away from it. Then a question naturally arises, What must be done on the impulse of the moment? 'For your lives, men! back her astern; hard at it every one of you! and let the man in the stern-sheets creep forward a moment to lighten the boat's stern!' By this effort the breaker strikes the boat more kindly and passes on; but if allowed to follow her up astern, so surely as such an experiment is tried the sea will either curl over the stern, or the boat will broach-to and take it over the gunwale.

It is much to be regretted that the crews of wrecked vessels, who take to their boats in moments bordering on despair, should recklessly endeavour to gain the shore amidst the fury of the gale, driving their boat through heavy surfs, ignorant of the risk they incur; and, as a dead certainty in such a case, the boat must be swamped. Now, if they could only command sufficient presence of mind to back their boat when heavy seas threaten them astern, and keep her bows on when pulling in the teeth of the gale, they might often land in safety. It is, however, more advisable to keep out at sea during a gale, provided the boat be kept stem on, than to incur the risk of forcing her through breakers. A boat will not rise so buoyantly over surf as over an unbroken wave.

Short boats with high sides are not equal in a heavy sea to long ones with rising bow and stern and low sides. The short boat would be tossed end over end, whilst the long one, under skilful management, might be taken through the surges in safety.

Many sailors though of long experience in sea-going vessels, are unacquainted with the necessary acquirements for managing an open boat in a heavy sea; and when the hour of danger arrives, no wonder at their courage forsaking them, as they abandon the wreck and hasten to their certain doom in an open boat.

No class of men, either at sea or ashore in our maritime islands, or in nations far and distant, understand the management of boats in a sea-way so well as those fishermen and boatmen who pursue their daily avocations on the most exposed parts of our coast. These men learn from daily experience the safest mode of conducting a boat through the difficulties and dangers before mentioned; and they have found, and well proved, that the safest plan when a wave threatens them astern is, to face the danger boldly and drive the stern of the boat at the very crest of the wave, with all the impetus the oars can give. And they are always careful in heavy seas to keep the bows and stern as buoyant as possible, not suffering any one to sit there, nor any ballast to be stowed in either of the ends.

THE DROGUE.

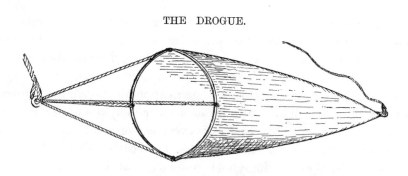

A DROGUE is a conical-shaped collapsible bag, made of stout canvas bound with small rope; it is about two feet in diameter at the mouth, and four feet six inches in length, gradually tapering to a point at the lower end. When towed by the mouth, the Drogue fills with water and draws heavily; thereby checking the progress of the boat. A tripping-line is made fast to the apex or pointed end, and, by slacking the towing-rope and hauling on the tripping-line, the Drogue collapses and may be readily drawn on board again. Drogues are a valuable acquisition to a boat's gear when in a rough sea. They serve to check the boat's way and keep her *end on* to the waves; they are, therefore, of great assistance to the crew in preventing the boat from broaching-to.

Every boat, whether sailing or rowing, which goes to sea in stormy weather, should be provided with a Drogue: the precaution has saved many a small fishing-boat from disaster, by assisting the crew in keeping her head to the wind, and so enabling her to ride out the gale at sea.

Management of Sailing-Boats in a Gale.

AS TO THE MANAGEMENT OF SAILING-BOATS IN A GALE.

'It blew great guns, when gallant Tom
    Was taking in a sail,
And squalls came on in sight of home,
    That strengthened to a gale.'—DIBDIN.

IN order to manage an open sailing-boat or a small yacht with safety in a gale, the sailing-master must have had considerable experience in boat-sailing. There is always more or less danger to be apprehended; and those to whom the control of the boat is entrusted should possess considerable nautical skill, combined with good judgment and discretion. But with these, and years of experience as well, it is sometimes beyond the power of the most skilful to prevent accidents, under such trying circumstances of wind and waves.

No experienced boat-sailer would, under ordinary circumstances, venture to set sail in a gale; but there are occasions when unexpected gales overtake sailing-boats as well as ships; and at such times it would be well to know how to manage the boat with the greatest chance of safety. It is always of great importance that the crew should have confidence in their boat, and also in the man at the helm. Firmness of nerve, decision and good judgment, are highly essential qualifications in a sailing-master at such a time; many boat accidents occur through timidity, hesitation, indiscretion and consequent mismanagement. The man at the helm should be courageous, but wary;

if his courage forsakes him the danger increases; the moment he gets unnerved he becomes more or less bewildered, and on the approach of danger, before he can do what is really necessary, perhaps the boat is capsized or the mast carried away.

When signs of an approaching gale are detected, attention should be immediately turned to the sails; it is always best to shorten sail in time and so prepare for the

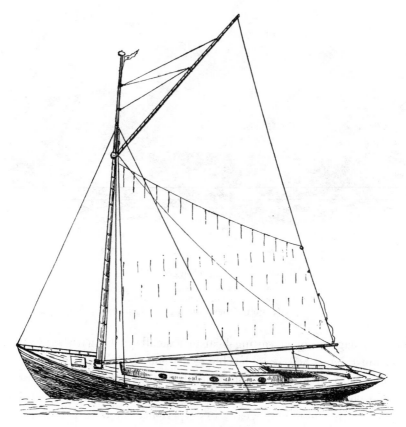

Sea boat with balance-reef.

worst; the sails should therefore be reefed as closely and promptly as possible, and all head-sails that can be dispensed with should be lowered and taken in; all the canvas must be inboard; and if the boat will obey her helm without a jib, it will be advisable to reef the bowsprit by drawing it inboard, to save it from being carried away when the boat plunges in a heavy sea. If the little craft will not 'wend' without a jib, a spit-fire should be set, or the very stoutest and smallest little head-sail that is at hand. If the boat be a two or three-masted lugger, or if it have a mizzen, the main-sail should be lowered and entirely dispensed with, and the boat sailed under a fore-sail and mizzen;

or, if practicable, these may both be lowered, and the boat sailed under a close-reefed main-sail, or a trysail, if furnished with one.

In a very heavy wind, if after close reefing you find you have still too much sail, let the throat of the main-sail run down and lash the jaws of the gaff to the boom. Some sea-going boats have a line of reef-points leading from the throat of the main-sail to the cringle of the upper reef at the outer leech. When so fitted, and these reef-points are all tied down, it is the snuggest reef that can be made in the main-sail, and is termed ' a balance-reef.'

The balance-reef, which extends diagonally across the main-sail from the throat to the upper reef-earing of the sail, is seldom fitted to a pleasure boat ; but usually to fishermen's boats of the larger class, to revenue cutters, pilot vessels, trading craft, and such as are unavoidably at sea in heavy weather, when a small sail only can be set with safety.

To make use of the balance-reef, each reef has first to be hauled down and the reef points securely tied, the throat and peak halliards being lowered accordingly, the throat of the sail is then lowered so that the jaws of the gaff come down to the boom, to which they are then made fast and the reef-points of the balance-reef are then tied all along the sail ; after which the peak may be set up again and the boat is then under sail with the balance-reef down.

Preliminary precautions in anticipation of a gale.—Let us now suppose a crew of three persons in a boat, overtaken by a gale, the boat being cutter-rigged and having three sails set—main-sail, fore-sail and jib, and no harbour is nearer than ten miles, and that dead to windward. There is every prospect of an increasing gale, so let the fore-sail run down, roll it up and lash it securely, take one reef in the main-sail, run the bowsprit in and set a very small jib, take a second reef in the main-sail, and try her to windward. The mast bends like a twig, and the little bowsprit threatens every instant to snap off ; luff the boat up, and set the very smallest jib you have, but in all these movements let the man at the helm keep the main-sheet clear, and ready to ease off at any moment ; he must not leave the helm an instant—let the two other hands attend the sails ; haul the jib-sheet aweather, whilst a third or fourth (if there are so many) and last reef is hauled down in the main-sail. The waves are now running high, and the boat is pitching heavily ; try her cautiously to windward. She flies through it madly, and must be eased or luffed a little, as the approaching waves meet her. Let one hand stand by (¹) the main sheet and one at the jib-sheet, whilst the other remains at the helm, cautiously watching the threatening waves. In luffing to the heaviest, the least motion of the tiller

---

¹ To ' stand by ' does not strictly imply that the man should be on his legs ; it is far better that he should be sitting or kneeling. A man may 'stand by' a rope in any position—that is, be ready to haul in or let go.

will generally suffice; be careful not to allow the boat to lose all way, or she will not answer to her helm; take advantage of every smooth sea, which usually follows three or more bouncing waves, to get good way on; keep her full and keep her at it, and only ease the helm on the approach of a heavy wave that is likely to drive the bows of the boat under; then luff, as it were, into the very crest of the wave, which will impede the boat's progress for a second or more; and such must be regained by bearing up instantly, but slightly, to get the sails full again, that the boat may not roll over into the trough of the seas. Be not frightened at the boat's rising and falling with the waves, so long as she answers to her helm; if she can be kept from broaching-to, there is nothing to fear—on that hangs the chief danger.

When the sea is abeam and the boat in the trough formed by the waves, it is the most perilous position of all; and until she can be got round head to wind, the danger continues.

Never attempt to carry too much sail in a heavy sea; as such increases the risk of broaching to, as well as that of running her bows under water; it also, when before the wind, makes the boat wild and difficult to steer.

No one should give orders but the man at the helm, and he should bawl out so that his voice may not be lost in the wind; his orders should be instantly obeyed, as in his position he can see best what the boat can bear, and when she can bear it no longer. The crew should cringe down as low as possible in the bottom of the boat; every rope should lie in coils, clear and free from kinks; and every movement of the crew should, if possible, be performed without standing up.

The boat should not be sailed so near the wind as in smooth water, but the sails must be kept full; and it will be found that the faster the boat goes, the quicker she will obey her helm. Many boats are upset by large fore-sails; therefore it is advisable to do without them in a gale, and to set a storm-jib instead; but if no jib, set a very small fore-sail. Should the sea increase so much as to render it impossible to prevent the waves from breaking over into the boat, it will no longer be judicious to attempt turning to windward.

Avoid putting the boat about, unless it can be done safely; the most perilous time for open boats in a heavy sea is when in stays. It will, therefore, be more prudent to bear up, and if a port can be reached with the wind abeam, it will be a safer mode of sailing than running directly before the wind. If, in scudding, it should be found that the boat has too much sail, lower the peak of the sail a little, according to your judgment. Get into smooth water as quickly as possible to get out of danger.

Boats and vessels are often wrecked through the rudder being unshipped or carried away by a heavy sea. All sea-going boats should, therefore, have their rudders hung and secured in the safest manner possible.

To Ride out a Gale at Sea.—This may appear a bold undertaking in an open

160

boat or small sailing vessel; it is, however, sometimes not only practicable, but the only means of saving the boat from being swamped, and consequently the crew from drowning. When any attempt to reach the land or force the boat ahead would be certain destruction, then is the time to consider the best mode of keeping her afloat and averting the surrounding dangers; and these may be successfully performed (if there be sea-room) by lashing a few spars together, and casting them overboard, allowing the boat to ride by them from a rope at the bows, made fast to the middle part of the spars. In this manner the boat's head may be kept to the wind, and she may be prevented from broaching-to. With good sea-room, an open boat may so ride out a heavy gale of several days' duration. It is astonishing how a raft of the kind (*i.e.* made of a few spars lashed together) breaks the force of the sea, and so fights the battle of the waves for the boat; and the contrivance may be used whether the boat be laid-to under a small sail or without one. In the absence of spars, or anything wherewith to form a raft, a loosened sail attached to a yard, a Drogue, ([1]) or an oar, will answer the same purpose; and if a sail be used, a weight may be suspended from the clew, which will the better impede the drift of the boat. If the water is not very deep, and you have a small anchor, with sufficient rope, the raft may be anchored, and the boat will still ride in safety; but not in broken water, or among breakers on a lee shore.

Boat-lowering apparatus.—The illustration below shows the mode of hoisting and lowering a boat from the side of a large yacht with the greatest facility. The apparatus should be occasionally overhauled, and always kept in readiness for any emergency.

[1] *Supra*, page 156.

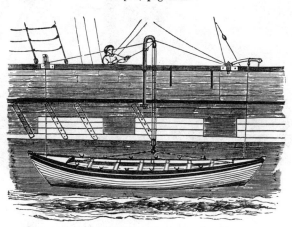

END OF PART III.

PART IV.

SMALL RACING YACHTS AND YARAFTS.

THE numerous fleet of racing-yachts of the smaller class, and Yarafts, that spangle the waters in and around the coasts of the British Islands afford by far the greater extent of sport and amusement to those who take delight in keenly-contested sailing matches.

From a photo by   West & Son, Southsea.

The type of yacht for fast sailing is, and probably always will be, more or less controlled by the rules of measurement prevailing at the time of its construction.

The success of the racing-yacht constructed on the rudimentary principles of yacht and boat-building, depends mainly on the 'lines' (or form) below the water-line; all

Small Racing Yachts and Yarafts.

which are as hidden secrets to the onlooker, as he views with admiration the graceful movements of the fairy fleet, with their tall slender spars and snow-white sails. And, indeed, how few among the spectators and admirers of that picturesque scene, are aware that the secret of success in the champion of that fleet, is not alone in the skilful handling of her helmsman, nor in her sails and other visible features, but in her invisible proportions beneath the surface of the waters she furrows.

That the modern type of racing-yacht of the smaller class, the result of the sail-area rule of rating and the load-water-line basis of measurement of the hull, is a form to be encouraged and permanently adopted, few will admit.

Some of the small racing-yachts (so called) of the present day are very attractive in appearance, with their shallow form of hull, outreaching stem and overhanging stern, the result of the rules of rating and measurement before referred to. That boats of such a type, if of sufficient stability to carry the Y.R.A. allowance of sail-spread, sail very fast, is unquestionable. But that such will eventually prove to be

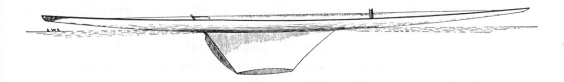

but an ephemeral type of craft has long been predicted by some, at least, of those who are capable of forming a sound judgment on the subject.

Racing craft of such a type are costly to build, as they are also to rig and fit out; and expensive to keep up. The cubical capacity aboard is cramped and limited; all such being sacrificed to speed: the consequence is, that when the craft's racing career is ended, it is seldom that she can, with advantage, be adapted either to the purposes of a cruising yacht or to the more humble occupations of the native boatmen and fishermen.

The time was (and not so very long ago) when the owner and crew of a racing yacht of eight or ten tons only, could go round the coast, take part in the regattas, winning cups here and there; and owner and crew all sleep comfortably aboard: and when the career of the yacht was ended as a racer, she did good service for many years afterwards to the local fishermen and boatmen. Not so now, however, the (so called) accommodation aboard a modern 'rater' of that tonnage, is mere higgledy piggledy and the termination of her racing career also terminates her ephemeral existence; so far at least as any useful purpose is concerned.

The Sailing-Boat.

THE Yaraft is a bastard form of sailing yacht, designed for the purpose of carrying an excessive spread of sail on a crank form of hull; the pressure of the sail, in a breeze, being counterpoised by a bulbous lump of lead, secured to the outside of the keel at its lowermost extremity.

The design and object of the Yaraft is twofold (viz.):—

1. That of evading the rules of measurement as to cubical capacity; and—

2. That of giving extra stability, by means of counterpoise, to an extensive spread of sail, with a view to the winning of prizes in sailing matches.

The peculiarities of the Yaraft are—the shallow and buoyant form of its hull, an undue extent of overhang at bow and stern, its cramped interior space and lack of cabin accommodation; a heavy lump, or bulb, of lead attached to the lower part of a fin, or thin, metal kind of keel, formed of sheet-iron or steel, extending deep down below the bottom of the craft, and acting as a counterpoise to an otherwise crank form of hull. In the larger kind of Yaraft, instead of a fin and bulb, the lead is spread over and secured to a deep form of keel, so as to disguise its nature and make it appear as an integral part of the hull.

In the construction of the Yaraft the elementary principles of boat-building are not followed; and load-water-line measurement forms the basis of rating for match sailing, instead of cubical capacity.

EFFECT OF MODERN RULES OF MEASUREMENT.

UNDER the modern rules of measurement whereby an artificial load-water-line is made the basis for length, with a linear rating for sail-spread, what is termed a 'five-rater' is nearly as large as a 'ten-tonner' of fifty years ago; and the five-rater requires a crew of as many hands as the 'ten-tonner' before mentioned did in her day.

The adoption for the smaller classes of racing craft of the load-water-line-length rule of measurement, has proved disastrous in its effect; as every year since, the aim has been that of taking advantage of the elasticity of the rule, by an extension of the dimensions of the craft above and beyond the load-water-line, to such an extreme that in some of the latest productions, the apex of the angle, as it emerges from the load-water-line mark towards stem and stern is scarcely perceptible; and when the craft careens to the breeze under pressure of sail, her (so called) load-water-line is immediately submerged beneath the surface of the water.

On the introduction of the rule it was, unfortunately, at once adopted for the smaller classes of racing-craft, and advantage was taken of every loophole in the rules

164

of measurement to produce a sailing-craft of the *ne plus ultra* type that should outsail the prize winners of the previous year. Meanwhile the popularity of boat racing was increasing day by day, and the necessity for safety and seaworthiness was seldom kept in view, in the structure of a craft intended for cup winning.

In the design and conformation of small racing-craft of this class the comforts of cabin accommodation are wanting : the one object being to turn out a craft that shall eclipse in speed the latest champion of the season ; and with that object, buoyancy and lightness of construction have been carried to extremes ; everything except that which is used as ballast being lightened. For experience teaches that the lighter the material of which the boat is constructed the more buoyant she will be ; consequently, whilst the load-water-line (as marked upon the hull) forms the basis of length in the measurement for rating, buoyancy and lightness of construction are important considerations : and accordingly, planking as thin as possible has been used, and scantlings thinner still, whereby a band box style of craft has been produced, such as in a short time, under the pressure of racing canvas, is almost certain to be more or less strained, and some of the upper strakes either torn asunder or the seams opened when 'carrying on her' in the struggle for victory in a strong wind and lumpy sea. The bulwarks too, are so reduced in height as to be only two or three inches above deck. In those of the smaller class, bulwarks are sometimes discarded altogether ; in others a mere rail of wire is the substitute. And even in racing-cutters of the larger class the rail is sometimes found to stand only eight or ten inches above the deck.

In some of the racing-craft of this type the fin and bulb are ingeniously concealed, by the latter being spread upon the plate in a flatter form, as will be seen by illustrations in subsequent pages, showing the forms of hull of some of the fastest of the racing fleet ; but in others there is no such disguise, the lead bulb, in two longitudinal halves, being bolted to the fin one half on each side.

Sailing craft of such a type are undoubtedly the fastest of the day in smooth water and moderate weather ; they are also quick in stays, and remarkably stiff under canvas.

The long reaching bow and overhang at the stern, enable them to carry all, or nearly all, their sail inboard, and dispenses with a long outstanding bowsprit. They must however be kept afloat in deep water, even when lying at anchor ; for they cannot, with impunity, be allowed to touch the ground.

The majority of the racing-craft of this class have given ample proof of their sailing qualities, added to which their speed in smooth water, with a good breeze, is simply marvellous ; as also their remarkable agility in coming about ; some of them spinning round in answer to the helm, as if upon a pivot. Standing up to their canvas in a breeze, furrowing the surface of the waters, and presenting a picture such as would assuredly captivate the most imaginative spectator.

The Sailing-Boat.

It is qualities such as these that have engendered the favour and popularity of the Yaraft class among amateurs. But after all, they are not a desirable class of craft, being fit only for summer-day racing; and as soon as the racing season ends, they are dismantled of their sails and spars, hoisted out of water, their bulb-keel and fin-plate unbolted and removed, and the hulls are then stowed away on cross shelves in the laying-up sheds, after the manner of rowing boats, in tiers, one above another; and there they remain until the boat-racing season comes round again.

From a photo by *Beken & Son, Cowes, I. of W.*
"Plover"; Solent one-Design Yacht.

INTERNATIONAL RULE OF MEASUREMENT.

In face of such objections an International Conference was called together, not by the Royal Yacht Squadron, nor by the English Yacht Clubs, but by their representatives—the Yacht Racing Association; for the purpose of discussing the question of a "universal rule for the measurement of yachts," with the object of enabling yachts built in any country to race on fair terms in any part of the world.

A difficult but praiseworthy scheme if carried out on sound and practical lines. The result of the Conference, which met in London in January, 1906, has been the framing of rules for rating and measurement based on the load-water-line system; rules which come into operation on the 1st of January, 1908, and are to continue in force until the year 1918.

The rule for the measurement of yachts for "International" yacht racing agreed upon at the Conference, concisely stated, is, according to algebraical computation, as under (viz.):—

$$\frac{L + B + \tfrac{1}{2}G + 3\,d + \tfrac{1}{3}\sqrt{S} - F}{2}.$$

In the above formula, L = length; B = beam; G = girth; d = girth difference; S = sail area; F = freeboard.

Explanation.—Add together the length, breadth, half the girth, three times the difference between the chain girth and the skin girth, one-third of the square root of the sail area: from the sum of these measures deduct the freeboard, divide the remainder by 2, and the result is the rating.

The measurements are all to be made in accordance with the *metric* system: so that instead of being made in English *feet* as hitherto, they are to be taken in *metres*, and the cubical capacity of the vessel is to be estimated in *kilograms*.

ESSENTIALS OF SAFETY AND SEAWORTHINESS.

In every yacht whether destined for racing or for cruising on open waters, the first essentials of the designer are usually those of safety and seaworthiness. A frail and unseaworthy boat is a curse to the designer, a coffin to the sailor.

It is doubtful however, if the essentials of safety and seaworthiness can always be kept strictly in view in these days of keen competition; particularly in the designs for the smaller class of racing-craft: not through any want of skill on the part of the designer, but because of the emulation of yacht owners in the races of the day, to possess a faster craft than others; an emulation that nothing can quell and such as neither time nor years can exterminate, because it is inherent in the spirit of man.

Effect of too frequent Changes in Rules of Measurement.—The chief cause of so many different designs in racing-craft has been the frequent changes in recent years of the rules of measurement, whereby speculative and experimental boats have from time to time been built; many of which, however meritorious, have had but an ephemeral career before them.

It is very doubtful if such frequent changes, affecting as they do the design, form and construction of yachts, are any permanent gain or advantage either to yacht racing in its original conception or to the science of yacht architecture; for it is, unfortunately, the measurement rules which influence, from time to time, the type and design of the small, as well as the large, racing-yacht.

The chief merit of these frequent changes is, the patronage and encouragement they bring to designers, yacht-wrights, boat-wrights, and sail-makers.

The time will come, and perhaps it is not far distant, when tonnage (or cubical capacity by some other name) will be revived, as the only sound basis on which to formulate and establish a reliable and lasting rule of measurement; and when all excrescences such as fin and bulb-keels and overhangs fore and aft, will be the subject of extra rating; and fuller powers will be given to sailing committees to exclude measurement-evaders of every type from taking part in the sailing matches of any of the yacht clubs.

SAILING BOATS OF THE BROAD AND SHALLOW TYPE.

Boats of great breadth of beam in proportion to length, combined with low free-board and shallow form of hull, are not by any means a desirable type of sailing boat; as they involve the danger of capsizing unless under very experienced management.

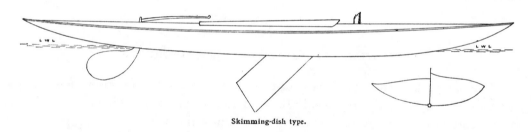

Skimming-dish type.

Boats of this type, as a rule, carry no ballast; but some have a revolving centre-plate of heavy metal. They are not ineptly termed 'the limited draft class,' fit only for sailing in smooth shallow water and over tidal flats, where it would be impracticable to venture with boats of ordinary draft.

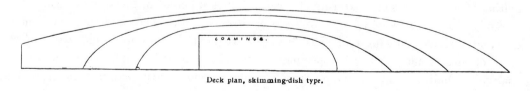

Deck plan, skimming-dish type.

Broad and shallow boats sail fast with light winds, they skim the surface instead of furrowing it; and they are mainly dependent on 'live ballast' (*i.e.*, a numerous crew or party) for their sail-carrying power in a breeze.

The Broad and Shallow Type.

The effect of a rough sea upon a shallow boat is, to cripple the craft in its most reliable powers, such as are conspicuous in smooth water: a rough sea causes such a boat to pitch and toss and make considerable lee-way; she rises and mounts high-crested waves and then down she bounces into the trough of the next, thumping the water with such force as (apparently) to make every plank in her structure quiver, and at the same time scattering showers of spray at every thump, and all the while making unsatisfactory headway.

As to the best proportion of beam to length in a sailing-boat, it is a problem not easy to solve: a certain extent of beam may be entirely successful in one form of boat, which would be a failure in another of a different type: it is believed however that the controlling proportion must be sought, not in regard to the length, but in that of the displacement.

The Sailing-Boat.

THE UPPER THAMES SAILING-BOATS.

The Upper Thames, so famous for its rowing matches, has also its small class of sailing boats; and probably in no inland river in Europe is there to be found a greater variety of pleasure boats (chiefly of the rowing class) than on the River Thames: to classify them would be tedious, to give a description of each class a task beyond the

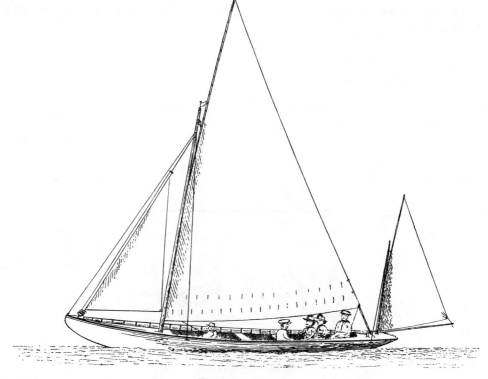

Upper Thames Sailing-boat.

purpose and intention of this work: suffice it to say that there are many of exquisite design and beautiful proportions, particularly among those of the rowing class; but as to the sailing fleet, they are not so numerous nor so various in form and design as the rowing boats.

The Boating Clubs on the Upper Thames are many, but the Boat-sailing Clubs are fewer; both are however well patronised, and the pastime of boat-sailing is freely indulged in nearly all the year round, though to a far greater extent in the summer months; but then it is, too often, impracticable because of the prevailing calms and lack of feeblest zephyr wherewith to aid the fairy fleet and enliven the scene by enabling them to flit to and fro from bank to bank and reach to reach on the glassy surface of the river. But when favoured with a gentle stirring wind, there is no prettier sight to the lover of inland scenery than a lively fleet of Upper Thames Sailing-boats wending their course up and down the tortuous reaches of that beautiful river, amidst the picturesque surroundings of tall oak and elm trees, luxuriant foliage, wooded banks, fertile meadows and green sloping uplands; studded here and there with many a noble mansion and extensive park with cattle, deer, and sheep grazing and fattening on the luscious herbage which the rich soil of the Thames Valley everywhere produces.

The inland boat-sailers enjoy a calm and happy time so long as they are equipped with a suitable boat; but it should always be borne in mind that in lively breezes and strong winds, a boat with too great a spread of sail is just as liable to be upset on the upper reaches of the river as on the lower, or even on the broader waters of the coast.

One of the most successful of the modern racing fleet on the Upper Thames is the *Tiger Cat*, built in the year 1895, from a design by Mr. Linton Hope. The career of this boat has been one of continued success down to the present time.

" Tiger Cat."

In her first season, out of thirty-three starts, she won twenty-five prizes: eighteen of which were firsts, six second and one third; and every year since, she has figured conspicuously among the prize winners on the upper river; and so recently as the year 1899 was at the head of her class at the Bourne End sailing-matches; and in the season of 1900 she has proved a formidable opponent to most of the more modern productions.

The Sailing-Boat.

The dimensions of the *Tiger Cat* are :—Length over all, 22 ft. 6 inches; length on load-water-line, 16 ft. 3 inches; beam, 5 ft. 7 inches; and her draft (with centre-plate down), 4 ft.

She is owned by Messrs. Watney and Ricardo of the 'Upper Thames Sailing Club': and through the courtesy of the latter gentleman I am enabled to give an illustration of the *Tiger Cat* from an excellent photograph by Mr. C. Ingham Reeves.

It is unfortunate that some men, chiefly those who are more or less venturesome in the management of open sailing-boats, will persist in rigging their boats with larger spars and sails than they can carry with safety in a strong breeze. Those large butterfly sails, pretty and pleasing to the eye as they are, can only be carried with impunity in light airs and gentle breezes; for directly they are greeted with a strong wind, it seems to intoxicate their slender forms and set them staggering and reeling beneath the blast, to such an extent as to incur danger to themselves and their crew, as the latter try in vain to keep their boat in an upright position on an even keel.

Boat-sailing on the Upper Thames is, unfortunately, brought somewhat into disrepute by the modern type of racing-craft now so conspicuous at most of the up-river sailing matches. Many of the boats of the racing fleet are of the very shallowest type; so shallow that it is only by a stretch of the imagination that they can properly be called 'Boats,' some of them being as shallow as a Butcher's tray: in such there is no boat (properly speaking) to get into, scarcely room even for the crew to hang down their legs inside them; consequently the occupants sit upon the

From a photo by   *Beken & Son, Cowes, I. of W.*

scantling like tailors on a shop-board, with their legs either doubled under them or sprawled out in an uncomfortable and unbecoming attitude. And yet these tray-shaped boats are among the chief prize-winners in the sailing matches on the Upper Thames.

Happily there are however at most of the principal boating stations on the river, sailing-boats of a different type, safe, roomy and reliable, with ample interior capacity, and capable of carrying their sails and occupants, in ordinary weather, without risk of upsetting. An illustration of one of these has already been given at page 170.

At the Bourne End sailing-matches in the latter part of the month of June, 1899, the weather was very suitable for up-river boat-sailing and the matches were well contested, and proved very popular: the Thames Valley Sailing Club was represented by Mr. T. Foster Knowles' very successful boat *Ulva*, in the match for the Thames Champion Cup, which she won. And again in the season of 1900, the *Ulva* retained her position as one of the fastest of the fleet, winning among other trophies, the Queen's Cup for the second year in succession; besides which she won the Duke of Connaught's Cup of the Upper Thames Sailing Club, and the Champion Cup for the Thames Valley Sailing Club, the latter also for the second year in succession.

SMALL RATERS AND THEIR DANGERS.

From a photo by   Beken & Son, Cowes, I. of W.
Group of Small Yachts off Ryde.

AMONG the class of small raters so popular with the boat-sailing fraternity, and which figure conspicuously at the regattas and sailing-matches on the South Coast, are some that are absolutely dangerous in certain circumstances of wind and water.

The avidity with which any point of advantage is seized upon in order to win a race, has led to extremes in the form and construction of boats of this class, and in the length and size of spars and spread of sail; so that risks of upsetting are run almost daily in season.

Some of these boats are said to be uncapsizable; others, if capsizable, are said to be unsinkable; the first are certainly the more desirable of the two; and the other, if actually unsinkable, may not perhaps lead to loss of life on being capsized; but the experiment had best not be put to the test too often.

The more dangerous boat is that which is both capsizable and sinkable, not so much by reason of any defect in the form of hull, but because of being over canvased. Often, the reason why they are capsizable is, because they are insufficiently ballasted in proportion to the extent of sail they spread. Sometimes the reason lies in the crank form of hull, which shows the boat to be unfit to carry sail at all in a good breeze.

It is to be feared, however, that there are some very successful prize-winners which would prove mere death-traps in inexperienced hands. Of this class are some of the shallow type of centre-plate racing-boats whose only ballast is a metal centre-plate or revolving-keel. The famous *Kismet* is a boat of this type, but nevertheless, the winner of scores of prizes.

The illustration is that of a sailing-boat of British design (1896), of extreme type, with a dagger-blade form of centre-plate. The *Daireen*, a boat with a similar dagger-blade centre-plate, which was her only ballast, was also of this type. Probably in the experienced hands of her designer the *Daireen* would be safe under sail. In other hands, however, in a sailing-match in Dublin Bay on 13th April, 1895, the *Daireen* was capsized; she heeled right over, filled and sank.

The danger of a capsizable boat is increased if, when thrown upon her beam ends, the main-sail gets under water; as the result then is, that the boat cannot right, and assuredly turns over and fills unless assistance be promptly at hand.

It is but a poor justification to the designer that if the boat should capsize she will not sink, though she may turn bottom upwards.

Other racing-boats are rendered unsinkable by water-tight bulkheads, air-tight cases, air-bags and other contrivances. But these bulkheads sometimes burst when put to the test, unless very strongly made; and such strength would seem to be inconsistent with the thin scantling and light material of which they are constructed.

Another and great source of danger in these unballasted and over-canvased boats is in carrying a spinnaker in a race: the danger of so doing has often been realised; and in some of the boat-sailing clubs the use of spinnakers in a race has, in consequence, been prohibited.

Small Raters.

THE SOLENT.

THE Solent sea which separates the Isle of Wight from the main land is the *rendezvous* of the *élite* of fashionable Yachting, and the headquarters of the Royal Yacht Squadron, whose Club House is Cowes Castle, delightfully situated on the banks of the Solent at the entrance to the Harbour forming the estuary of the Medina.

The locality of the Solent and its neighbouring waters with their extensive cruising grounds, bays, harbours, and estuaries, is admirably adapted to the requirements of the pleasure fleet, and the numerous regattas and sailing-matches that are annually held upon its waters. In no part of the British Islands is there to be found a fairer course for our racing-fleet, nor a finer display of yachts and sailing-boats than that which in summer season graces the waters of the Solent.

And when we find that there are now no less than seventeen Yacht and Boat-Sailing Clubs within the vicinity of the Solent, such is tolerably conclusive testimony to the popularity of Yachting and Boat-Sailing in that favoured locality. With so many clubs within the confines of its waters, it is not by any means a matter of surprise that there is a great variety of yachts and sailing-boats; more particularly of the smaller classes of racing-yachts; and amongst them are some of the fairest flowers of the racing fleet.

175

The Sailing-Boat.

THE SOLENT CLASSES RACING ASSOCIATION.

THIS Association was founded in the year 1898. The Earl of Dunraven, K.P., is President, Col. O. A. Grimston is Vice-President; and in addition to the elected members, delegates are appointed to the Council every year, one from each of the several Yacht and Sailing Clubs in the neighbourhood of the Solent.

The principal functions of this Association are, to promote uniformity in the ranks of the Yacht and Boat-Sailing Clubs, more particularly for regulating the sailing-matches of the smaller classes of racing-yachts in accordance with the spirit and intention of the Yacht Racing Association.

It was assumed at first, on the formation of the Solent Classes Association, that it would clash with and operate prejudicially to the Yacht Racing Association, but there was in fact no foundation for such an assumption, nor was such ever in contemplation; on the contrary, its object was that of co-operation with the Y.R.A.

The duties of the S.C.R.A. have thus far, been ably carried out; and the Association has proved not only a most useful and successful one, but has supplied a want felt for some long time past in the arrangement of the courses, and regulation of the sailing-matches, now so numerous in and about the Solent and its adjacent waters.

One of its earliest functions was that of directing the attention of the affiliated Yacht Clubs to the dangers of the larger classes of yachts in races on the same day, rounding the same marks as those of the smaller classes, which had been the cause of several lamentable accidents, in addition to numerous hair-breadth escapes.

The Solent Classes (as defined by the Rules of the S.C.R.A.) consist of yachts of 36, 30, 24 and 18 feet 'linear rating,' and of the Solent One-Design Classes.

And all yachts racing under the regulations of the S.C.R.A. must observe the sailing rules of the Y.R.A., except the One-Design Classes, for which special regulations are provided.

THE DIFFERENT CLASSES OF SMALL RATERS.

THE different classes of small raters, which have become numerous of late years, are of more than ordinary interest to those who take pleasure in boat-sailing; and although the frequent changes in the mode of measurement and rating have proved discouraging to small yacht-owners, because many an owner of the champion boat of the season has found to his dismay in the following year, that his boat has become

Small Raters.

outclassed or disqualified from taking part in the races of her class, by reason of some new rules of rating and measurement. This, however, will not preclude the Author from describing and illustrating in these pages boats that were famous in their day, and such as were a great attraction on the waters of the various boat-racing localities, the scenes of their bygone triumphs.

And it should be observed that the object of the Author of this work is not that of describing and illustrating merely the principal winning yachts of the smaller or other classes, nor of recording their victories (except incidentally): all which details are to be found in periodical publications of the day, devoted specially to such matters. Space here only permits of a selection from some of the most famous, and from others having some striking peculiarity of design, class signification, originality of type, with advantages not possessed by others, novelty of rig or other remarkable quality, with the view of showing by illustration and description the changes and advancement made in recent years in the design, type and rig of small racing-yachts and sailing-boats.

THE CLASS TERMED HALF-RATERS, AND THE 18-FEET LINEAR RATERS.

From a photo by　　　　　　　　　　　　　　　　　　　　　　　*Beken & Son, Cowes, I. of W.*

Start of Half-raters.

THESE are a very popular class, the smallest of the racing fleet of decked boats in the neighbourhood of the Solent, but probably the most numerous.

177

The Sailing-Boat.

Boats of this class are seen to best advantage in light winds and smooth waters. They are not adapted for strong winds and heavy seas.

18-foot Linear Rater.

The illustration is from a pen-and-ink sketch of one of the class known as an 18-feet linear rater.

A beautiful boat of this class, designed by Mr. A. E. Payne and built by Summers and Payne, of Southampton, in 1897, for Mr. Ogden Goëlet, was exhibited at the Yachting Exhibition at the Imperial Institute at Kensington in that year, with all her sails, rigging and full equipment, where she was one of the attractions of the Exhibition.

The hull was apparently that of a powerful-looking boat of the bulb-fin-keel type, 18 feet on the L.W.L. The keel or fin being so constructed that the bulb had the appearance of being all of a piece with the plate; differing in that respect from the bulb-keels of the Sibbick type. The boat was decked all over, with the exception of the cock-pit, or well, which was encircled with an oval coaming.

The rig was that already described as 'the Solent rig'; the main-sail being nearly triangular in shape, and laced to boom and yard; the latter being very prettily peaked, so that at the mast-head, it stood only about six or eight inches from the mast, and the lower end about five feet from the deck. There were three battens in the outer leech of the main-sail, the lower one extending about three or four feet along the sail in horizontal position, the two others higher up the sail and somewhat shorter: the object of the battens being, to keep the sail flat, and prevent the outer leech shivering in the wind. The main-sail had three reefs, the upper one crossing the sail just below the lower end of the main-sail yard. The fore-sail was attached to a roller yard, the upper end of which was hoisted to the upper part of the mast, and the lower end had a galvanised reel, upon which a reefing-line was wound, or unwound as might be required, so that by a pull or two of the line the fore-sail was wound round the yard like a roller window-blind, and so reefed to any required extent.

The boat was rigged with two sails only (main-sail and fore-sail), and there being no bowsprit, and the boom of the main-sail not extending beyond the outer end of the stern, all the sail was inboard.

The standing rigging consisted of two slender wire-rope shrouds on each side, leading from the mast-head to the outer side of the gunwale, just abaft the mast. The aft-shroud was shiftable, working on a white metal hawse, to which it was attached by a small shackle and thimble, and might thus be shifted fore and aft, within the extent of the hawse, as might be required. The halyards were rove through small marine silver blocks, each with double sheaves, at the mast-head; and similar single-sheaved blocks were fastened to the deck on each side of the mast, to receive the fall of the halliards, which then passed through small "fair-leads" (brass pipes, or thimbles) in the coamings at the fore part, and were belayed to cleats affixed to the under part of the deck inside; and the fore-sheets were treated in a similar manner, so that when under way, none of the crew need leave the well of the boat; every rope being under the control of the man or men in the well.

The Sailing-Boat.

DIAMOND.—The illustration is from a pen-and-ink sketch of a small racing-yacht named the *Diamond*, a Solent-rigged 18-feet linear rater, designed and built in 1897, by C. Sibbick and Co., of Cowes.

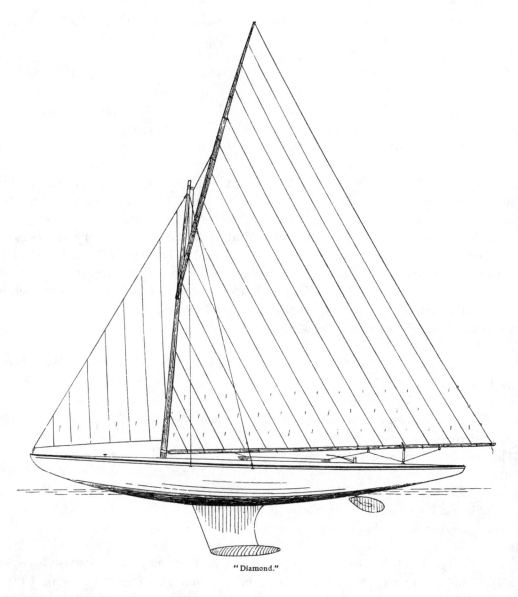

"Diamond."

The boat has a fin-bulb-keel of the 'Sibbick type,' and is a beautiful and powerful looking boat. She was exhibited, fully-rigged with her sails set, at the International Yachting Exhibition at the Imperial Institute, Kensington, in the summer of 1897, where she was an object of considerable attraction, and was afterwards sold and taken to the Mediterranean and then to Russia.

The *Diamond* is decked all over excepting the well or cock-pit. She is broad and full amidships with fiddle-pattern bow, clean run aft, and has a full, flat rounded bottom. Her fin-plate is of steel, to which the lead bulbs are bolted, one half on each side at the bottom of the plate, and extend aft beyond the plate as shown in the illustration. The rudder is of oblong shape, large and deep, and of the same metal as the fin-plate. She is rigged with two sails only, main-sail and fore-sail, the latter all inboard, but the main-sail extends about a foot beyond the stern. The main-sail is of the Solent rig, very pointed and nearly triangular, has a long yard, the peak standing high above the mast and nearly in line with it. The mast is by no means tall, and the fore-sail-hoist is therefore not so high as in some boats of the same rating. The fore-stay is of steel wire-rope of slender proportions; the fore-sail being attached to it by six small marine silver snatch-hooks, so that on being let down, it can be taken off and shifted for a smaller or larger one in a few seconds without casting off the stay. There are also two small wire-rope shrouds on each side the mast, as shown in the illustration. The main boom is attached to the mast by a goose-neck in the usual way, and the same marine silver hoop-band, which receives the spike of the goose-neck, has a shoulder and socket in which to receive the spike of a goose-neck in front of the mast for a boom to spread a spinnaker when required.

The main-sail is laced to the boom as well as to the yard, the tack being held down by a brass shackle. From tack to peak the main-sail measures nearly about the same in height as the length over all of the boat itself: the main-sheet is rove through three blocks on the boom and one on the hawse; the hawse is of brass about sixteen or eighteen inches in length, secured to the deck at about six feet from the outer end of the stern. The falls of the halliards are rove through brass leader-pipes in the deck, and are made fast to marine silver cleats inside the cock-pit; and so also the fore and main-sheets; there are no outside cleats, all are inside the cock-pit; so that there is no necessity for anyone of the crew to go on deck, and so put the boat out of trim when sailing a match: halliards and sheets can be readily hauled taut, eased and slackened by the hands in the cock-pit without putting a foot on deck.

The descriptive details here given of this and the preceding boat are, both of them, full and minute, the boats and rigging of each being in all respects of the most complete and modern style: not that they differ in any material particular from many other boats of the same class, of like build and type: but because that in mentioning or describing others in subsequent pages it may be unnecessary to go so fully into such small details.

It should be further observed that the boat (*Diamond*) last above described is of the small class known as 18-footers, and is not the 36-foot linear rating boat named the

The Sailing-Boat.

Diamond (also designed and built by Sibbick and Co.) which was racing in the Solent in 1897 : the latter was cutter-rigged, and carried a top-sail, jib, and flying-jib besides main-sail and fore-sail.

SPRUCE IV.—An exquisite model of this remarkable little boat was exhibited at the Yachting Exhibition at the Imperial Institute in 1897, from which the illustration below was made. Mr. Brand (the owner) also kindly sent the Author some interesting particulars of the yacht's career as a racing boat.

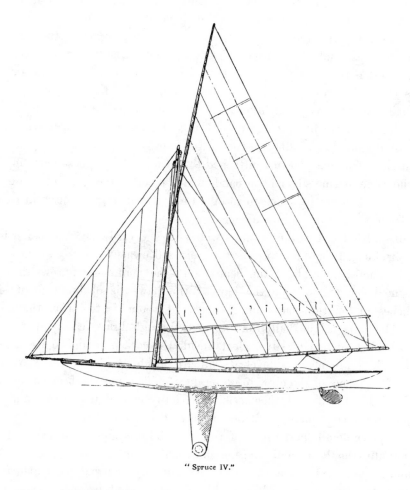

" Spruce IV."

Spruce IV. is of the half-rater class ; was designed and built by Mr. H. C. Smith (then of Oxford, now of Burnham), and made her *debut* as a racing yacht in the year 1895 ; when she was owned and sailed by Mr. John Arthur Brand, then of Dartmouth and Gresham Street, London, under the Burgee of the Minima Yacht Club. She is a boat of shallow form of hull, but very broad amidships ; her chief peculiarity being her deep, narrow fin-plate extending 6 ft. 3 in. below the bottom of the boat, with leaden bulb-keel attached ; the latter weighing 100 lbs., and being of saucer-like shape, bolted in two halves, one on each side of the fin-plate.

Spruce IV. is a Solent-rigged boat, and carries a short bowsprit, so that her fore-sail (or rather jib and fore-sail combined) stands out about two feet beyond the stem : her main-sail also extends about a foot beyond her over-hang at the stern : the main-sail is fitted at the lower part with a batten which extends across the sail from outer-leech to fore-leech, and serves the double purpose of keeping the sail flat and facilitating the reefing, which can be readily performed with the four tackles (shown in the illustration) and lashed down to the boom.

During her racing career in the early part of the season of 1895, after a series of victories, she was unexpectedly defeated four times in succession : her owner suspecting something amiss with her fin-plate, had her hauled up and examined, when it was found that the plate was badly bent, probably through having touched the ground in water too shallow for the deep draft of her fin. A new fin-plate was then substituted and the boat was afterwards taken over to America, where she sailed a series of races in Oyster Bay, Long Island, with the *Ethel Wynn*, the latter beating her in running and reaching, but in the race to windward *Spruce IV.* had the advantage, and was declared winner of the International Cup, September 1895.

Spruce V., an 18-foot boat built by Sibbick and Co. in 1896 for the same owner (Mr. J. A. Brand), was a fin and bulb-keel boat, but not of the same type as the former ; she was however a highly successful prize-winner.

It is with great regret that the author records the fact that, since the above was written, Mr. J. A. Brand has died ; and the yachting fraternity deplore the loss of an able boat-sailer and enthusiastic yacht owner.

THE WEE WIN.—Among other boats of this class may be mentioned the American boat *Wee Win*, a very successful prize-winner during the years 1892—5. The *Wee Win* though measuring only 15 ft. 6 in. on her L.W.L., measures 23 ft. 9 in. L.O.A. ;

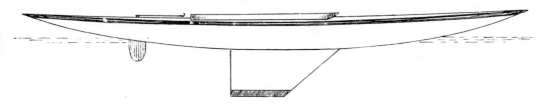

she is therefore a long boat with considerable over-hang, which in fact conceals her short L.W.L. ; she has a bulb-keel weighing 3 cwt. ; and her draft is just under three feet. The *Wee Win* is a shallow type of boat of small displacement, designed and built for small-class racing by the American designer Mr. Nat. Herreshoff, for Miss Sutton.

The Sailing-Boat.

THE KISMET, which has had a highly successful career, was designed by Mr. Linton Hope, who, in most of the earlier matches she sailed, was generally at the helm and steered her to victory. She is a broad and shallow boat with a fine sharp bow and shallow tapering stern : she has a small open cock-pit and a cambered deck. The *Kismet* had originally a centre-plate of dagger-like shape ; but in order to adapt his design to the rating rule of the period, Mr. Linton Hope altered the form of the

"Kismet" (from a drawing).

plate to the rudder-like shape shown in the engraving. The plate which is 150 lbs. in weight, is of Bull's metal ; and is the only ballast (excepting the crew) carried by the boat. The rudder is of the same metal, and of the shape indicated by the engraving. The boat is steered by a forked or double-headed tiller ; the advantage of which is that when the steersman is sitting out to windward in a strong breeze, the helm may be put down without moving from his position. The rig of the *Kismet* is somewhat different to that of other boats of her class : the main-sail which is fitted with bamboo spars, is very broad at the bottom, and extends a little beyond the stern of the boat; but the upper part of the main-sail narrows more rapidly upwards than in the majority of boats of this class : the sail is nicely pointed at the peak by means of a short bamboo gaff. Across the main-sail, above the boom, there are five bamboo battens, each sheathed in the sail at about equal distances one from the other, and extending from outer to inner leech of the sail ; the three lower battens and the boom are each attached to the mast by light metal crescent-shaped gaff-jaws; the sail itself being laced to the boom and gaff ; the main-sail, so fitted and contrived, stands as flat as possible ; indeed it would be difficult to contrive and fit a sail to stand flatter ; the foresail is attached to a roller-yard similar to that already mentioned and described.

From a photo by   Beken & Son, Cowes, I. of W.

" Viva " and " Pique " (half-raters).

The *Kismet* is a boat of elegant and graceful design, and her rig is perhaps very suitable for a small, shallow racing-boat of her type ; but bearing in mind that her drop-keel constitutes her only dead-weight ballast, it is obvious that with her large spread of sail she requires very careful and skilful handling in a strong breeze.

The boat itself was on view at the Yachting Exhibition at the Imperial Institute in the summer of 1897, and as the heroine of so many spirited contests, was an object of interest and attraction.

Besides the *Kismet*, Mr. Linton Hope is the designer of many other small winning boats of similar type, among which may be mentioned the *Coronis, Sorceress, Eos,* and others, all of which are, undoubtedly, very fast-sailing craft, and have proved very successful prize-winners, but are nevertheless an undesirable type for any other purpose than that of match-sailing, being so very shallow and carrying no ballast excepting the drop-keel ; and they have absolutely no accommodation aboard, and are a dangerous type of craft in a breeze under the management of any but the most experienced hands, such as the designer himself, who has so frequently steered them to the front in most of the matches they have sailed.

Sailing-boats of this type usually rely on their ' live ballast,' *i.e.*, a crew of two or three persons who sit to windward on the covered part of the boat as she careens to the breeze, and they shift from side to side on every tack.

The VIVA.—Among the half-rater class the *Viva*, a fin and bulb-keel boat, figured conspicuously in the years 1895 and 1896 as the winner of 85 prizes in those two seasons.

The illustration on page 185 shows *Viva* and *Pique* in close contest off Calshot Castle.

The *Viva* was designed and built by Sibbick & Co., of Cowes, for Mr. A. H. E. Wood. She was, however, subsequently defeated by a boat of a totally different type, the *Lotus*, designed by Mr. Linton Hope, which instead of a fin and bulb-keel had a drop centre-plate of dagger-like shape, but no other ballast excepting her crew. The *Lotus* seems to have outsailed all the bulb-keel boats in running and reaching ; but close-hauled on a wind the others had the advantage. A boat of the *Lotus* type appears to require a special kind of seamanship in the handling, and would probably be somewhat unsafe (in a strong wind), in the hands of anyone unaccustomed to that sort of boat.

When it was found that boats of the ' turn-turtle,' or capsizable type were really dominating the class of the 18-foot linear raters, the Yacht Racing Association at the commencement of the year 1898 passed a resolution to the effect that no certificate of rating be given to any yacht which has less than 15 cwt. displacement without her crew, and that any yacht having a previous certificate of rating and being of less than 15 cwt. displacement, should be disqualified.

This well-timed resolution successfully eliminated the skimming-dish and capsizable craft from taking part in the races with the legitimate type of half-raters and 18-footers.

Small Raters.

From a photo by   Beken & Son, Cowes, I. of W.

"Sayonara" (A flag for every victory).

SAYONARA.—The *Sayonara* is of the half-rater or 18-feet class; was designed by Mr. A. E. Payne, and built by the firm Summers & Payne in 1898, for her owner, Mrs. Lucas, and proved the most successful boat of her class in that, her first season.

The *Sayonara* is a remarkably attractive looking and capable little boat.

The *Inyati*, an 18-foot linear rater, designed by Mr. H. C. Smith, of Burnham, for Mr. J. W. Leuchars, has been a very successful boat, winning in the season of 1898 no less than thirty-two prizes from thirty-nine races, seventeen of which were first prizes and fifteen second; and she has since kept up her reputation in the subsequent seasons of 1899 and 1900.

The *Inyati* is a boat of the 'Restricted Classes' of the London Sailing Club.

The Sailing-Boat.

From a photo by

Start of One-raters.

Beken & Son, Cowes, I. of W.

THE ordinary dimensions of the one-rater class are as under:—Length on L.W.L., 18 feet 6 inches to 21 feet; length over all, 24 feet; beam, 6 feet 6 inches to 7 feet; draft, 2 feet 7 inches to 3 feet.

Though essentially a boat for light weather, this was a class that became more and more popular every year, and was one of the most successful following the introduction of the sail-area rule; notwithstanding the changes in design, whereby there was a slight increase in beam as well as in sail-area, but (perhaps unfortunately) a decrease in displacement.

'FAY I.'—This boat, known as a one-rater, was designed by Mr. J. M. Soper and built by Fay & Co., in 1894, she was a boat of foremost rank as a racer in that her first season, heading the roll of winners with a long list of prizes.

A profile, showing the form of hull of this boat, has already been given at page 114 (*supra*).

Small Raters.

Most of the boats of this class are of the weighted fin-keel type ; and, like those of the half-rater class, they perform best in light winds and smooth water.

The Boat-sailing Clubs usually limit the number of hands to three in sailing matches by the boats of this class.

A one-rater is a much less expensive boat to build in proportion to size, &c., than one of a larger class ; the cost of a one-rater, sails and all complete, being from £100 to £150 ; whilst a two and a-half rater costs from £300 to £400 ; and a five-rater from £500 to £600.

After the change in the rules of rating and measurement by the Y. R. Association, the one-raters were left out altogether ; and so far as racing was concerned, owners found them left on their hands as out-classed boats. Under a subsequent rule, however, some of them were enabled to be classed among what are now termed the ' 24-footers.'

From a photo by   *Beken & Son, Cowes, I. of W.*

" Fay II."

The illustration is from a photograph of the boat *Fay II.*, built in 1895. Her owner, Miss Lord, steering.

The GAIETY GIRL, one-rater, was designed by Mr. C. P. Clayton, for Mr. F. Norman,

The Sailing-Boat.

Darbyshire, of Liverpool, and built by Sibbick & Co., in 1894; she was one of the most successful boats of her class, and so continued for several years afterwards.

"Gaiety Girl."

The dimensions of *Gaiety Girl* were : length over all, 26 ft. 11 in.; length on L.W.L., 20 ft. 2 in.; beam, 6 ft. 6 in.; draft, 2 ft. (with centre-plate up). Lead keel (with centre-plate) weighing 12 cwt.

This boat was of a broad and somewhat shallow type, though not so shallow as some others of her class; and she had a square overhanging stern.

From a photo by   Beken & Son, Cowes, I. of W.

"Gallia."

The GALLIA, one-rater, built by Sibbick & Co., of Cowes, in 1895, for Lord Ashburton, was a very successful boat of her class, remarkably fast in strong winds, and standing up well to her canvas. In her first season she won 25 prizes, 13 of which

Small Raters.

were firsts and 12 second, and in subsequent seasons she scored numerous other victories.

The SPEEDWELL.—Of the 1896 boats of the 24-feet class, the *Speedwell*, designed by Mr. A. E. Payne for Miss Cox, proved remarkably successful, heading the list of winners of her class in the seasons of 1896 and 1897, and she has ever since retained her reputation as one of the fastest of the 24-feet class, being frequently the leading boat of her class in many of the matches she has sailed in the subsequent seasons of 1898, 1899 and 1900.

The *Speedwell* differs from most others of the same class, inasmuch as she has a wooden fin and leaden bulb; and during the first three years of her racing career won no fewer than 145 prizes; thus bearing testimony to the advantages of the wooden fin over the steel plate.

An illustration of the *Speedwell* has already been given at page 115.

From a photo by   **"Tartar VII."**   *Beken & Son, Cowes, I. of W.*

TARTAR VII., a 24-foot linear rater, is the property of Mr. Alfred Hewett, one of the best known racing yacht owners on the South Coast. Mr. Hewett has from time to

191

The Sailing-Boat.

time been the owner of a numerous fleet of *Tartars*, all of which have been racing boats, and, with one exception, very successful prize winners.

Tartar V. (of the fleet) was, perhaps, one of the best, she was designed and built by Sibbick & Co., of Cowes, and was a long shallow boat with a fin and bulb-keel; she made a great reputation in the season of 1896, though perhaps not greater than some others of Mr. Hewett's boats.

The illustration on previous page is of *Tartar VII.*, but Mr. Hewett has a subsequent boat known as *Tartar VIII.*

From a photo by   *Beken & Son, Cowes, I. of W.*
"Triangle."

The TRIANGLE is also one of the class known as 24-footers, was designed and built by Sibbick & Co., in 1897, for the Earl of Harrington, and has the reputation of being a sturdy and powerful boat, winning no less than 24 prizes in her first year, of which seven were firsts.

The BANDICOOT, built in 1898 (the third boat of that name), sailed her first race on the 18th June in that year, and heads the list of winners of the 24-feet class in the season of 1899, with 55 winning flags.

Bandicoot III., as in the case of the two previous boats of that name, is from a design by Mr. Arthur Payne, and was built by Summers & Payne, who have recently constructed a fourth boat, also named *Bandicoot*; all four boats having been built for Capt. R. Dixon, an able and enthusiastic yacht sailer and owner.

From a photo by   *Beken & Son, Cowes, I. of W.*

"Bandicoot."

Amongst *Bandicoot's* competitors in the season 1899 was the *Madge*, a new boat, designed and built by Sibbick & Co. These two boats were frequent competitors, not only in the neighbourhood of the Solent, but at the West of England Regattas; and although the *Mudge* was a powerful opponent, the *Bandicoot* seems to have proved the better boat of the two.

From a photo by   *Beken & Son, Cowes, I. of W.*

"Eione."

THE EIONE, a one-rater, was designed and built by Sibbick & Co., in 1895, for Capt. Fenwick; she is an attractive looking boat of good proportions, and in the first year of her racing career proved one of the best of her class.

Small Raters.

From a photo by   West & Son, Southsea.

THE dimensions of these boats are:—Length over all, 30 ft.; length on load-water-line, 26 ft.; beam, 7 ft. 6 in.; draft, 4 ft. 6 in. to 5 ft.

Amongst the Solent racing-fleet this class is very popular; the size being such as to constitute a fairly comfortable boat whether for racing or day cruising; they are, therefore, a numerous fleet, and are probably the best productions (apart from some of the One-Design Classes) since the adoption of the sail area rule of rating. They are, too, of very suitable size for amateur racing and summer day sailing.

Their chief defect is the very limited displacement, and consequent curtailment of cabin space.

THE GARETH.—One of the most famous boats of this class—one which year after year continued to outsail all her newly constructed rivals—was the *Gareth*.

The *Gareth* (Mr. A. Henderson, owner) was designed by Mr. C. E. Nicholson, of the firm of Camper and Nicholson, of Gosport, and was built by that firm in the year 1892. She was therefore one of the earliest of the fin and bulb-keel type which appeared on the waters of the Solent.

The *Gareth*, though a long and somewhat shallow form of boat, is of a full-bodied section, and has a fine graceful bow and long counter, showing great power and clean run. She is of the Solent rig, and carries a rather longer yard, and consequently

"Gareth."

higher peak, to her main-sail than some of the more modern boats of that rig. Her sails are all inboard, and the main-sail is laced to the boom.

Small Raters.

It will be observed on reference to the illustration, that the form and design of the fin and bulb differ in several respects from those of subsequent designs of the fin and bulb type.

No boat of her class has ever made a greater reputation than the *Gareth*. In 1892, the year when she first made her appearance, she was foremost in every match she sailed ; and in the next and every subsequent year we find her still competing with remarkable success among the very *élite* of her class, in the Solent, the Mediterranean and other waters. In the year 1894, she heads the list with fifty winning flags ; and even so recently as the years 1897 and 1898, despite the recent changes and alterations in the rules of measurement and rating, she figures conspicuously amongst the winning yachts of her class.

From a photo by   "Corolla."   *Beken & Son, Cowes, I. of W.*

THE COROLLA is another two and a-half linear rater designed by Mr. Charles Nicholson, and built by the firm Camper and Nicholson, in 1894-5, for Mrs. Schenley. The *Corolla* is a powerful and attractive looking boat of broad and shallow type, but with a graceful cut-water stem and bow, and a fin and bulb-keel.

This boat was first tried with a novel arrangement of the fin bulb-keel, whereby the cigar-shaped bulb was held by two plates, one at the fore part of the keelson, the other at the aft. The arrangement did not prove satisfactory, and was discarded after her trial race.

In her altered form the *Corolla* proved a great success, in fact one of the fastest of her class; particularly in a fresh breeze, when she displayed powers but little inferior to those of the famous yacht *Gareth*.

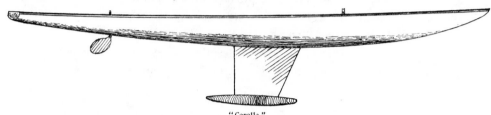

" Corolla."

The *Corolla* has rather less beam than the majority of her class, but is a remarkably well-built boat, and has strong and durable narrow-planked decks.

The *Corolla*, in 1895 (her first year), won fourteen first prizes out of fifty-five starts; but her rival *Zivola* (Hon. Mrs. Oliphant) won fourteen firsts out of forty-eight starts.

Again in 1896, the *Corolla* proved a formidable antagonist to the new boats of that year. And in 1897 she won seventeen prizes, five of them being firsts.

From a photo by   *Beken & Son, Cowes, I. of W.*

" Vaquero."

THE VAQUERO, two and a-half rater, is an American boat designed by Mr.

Small Raters.

Herreshoff, and was a distinguished racer in the Solent and neighbourhood under the old rating rule in the sailing-matches of 1895.

It will be observed that this boat has a gaff main-sail, the chief peculiarity of which, as also of the fore-sail, is that both sails are made with the seams crosswise (an American style); the object being, probably, to ensure their standing flatter than if made in the usual way; but it is very doubtful if any satisfactory advantage is thereby gained. The *Meneen*, also an American boat by the same designer, was similarly rigged. And more recently the *Swanhild* thirty-footer, also American; all three of which proved very capable and successful boats in British waters.

THE LORETTE, of the two and a-half rater class, was built by Sibbick and Co., and made an excellent record in 1895, winning twenty-eight prizes, twenty-two of which were firsts. This boat met the American *Vaquero* in five matches, defeated her in four of them, and was some distance ahead of her in the fifth, when she took the ground. And at the West of England regattas the *Lorette* was again very successful, never once being beaten.

From a photo by   *Beken & Son, Cowes, I. of W.*

" Nanta."

THE NANTA, of the two and a-half rater class, was designed by Mr. W. Fife, Junior, and built in 1895 (Mr. T. C. Burroughes, owner).

The illustration is from a photograph taken of this boat when winning the first prize of the Island Sailing Club at Cowes, and showing the steam yacht *Rona* in the distance.

The Sailing-Boat.

VALERIA I., a two and a-half rater, was another very successful boat, designed by Mr. A. E. Payne, and built by Summers and Payne, for the Earl of Albemarle. The *Valeria* was raced in the Solent in the year 1896, and was afterwards sold and sent out to Australia, where she sailed in the matches of the Royal South Australian Yacht Squadron, but was heavily handicapped, and had to give time to boats twice her size; notwithstanding which she appears to have more than 'held her own' with them.

From a photo by   *West & Son, Southsea.*
" Strathendrick " and " Petrel " racing.

STRATHENDRICK and PETREL.—The illustration is of two of the most famous boats of the thirty-foot class, viz., *Strathendrick* and *Petrel*, which, in the seasons of 1898 and 1899, were in frequent contest at the regattas and sailing matches on the South Coast, with *Mayfly* and other boats of high repute. *Strathendrick* (formerly *Valeria II.*)

was one of Mr. A. E. Orr-Ewing's boats, and has made a high reputation as a racing-yacht of the thirty-footer class.

The *Petrel* was also one of the most successful boats of the class in the same seasons, including that of 1900.

THE SWANHILD.—Amongst the thirty-footers of the season of 1899 was a new American boat, a Herreshoff production, named *Swanhild II.* (Mr. C. E. Bichel), a graceful and attractive-looking boat, sloop-rigged in the usual American style, with gaff main-sail, short bowsprit, and single head-sail; the seams of both sails being crosswise, similar to the *Vaquero*, already described and illustrated.

Swanhild II. proved a fast and powerful boat in smooth water, and she had good weatherly qualities; but when the water was much ruffled or loppy, she was no

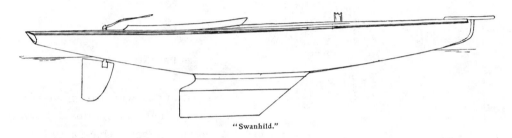

"Swanhild."

match for her more sturdy opponents. At the close of the season (1899) she was, however, credited with nineteen winning flags, comprising ten firsts in her races in the Solent, and five firsts in German waters.

It will be seen by the illustration of contour and body-plan of the *Swanhild*, that she is of a type differing in several respects from those of any boat of British design: the end view of the fin-bulb keel (if such it may be termed) reveals, at the bottom part, a sort of fan-tail form; but there is apparently great power in her hull, and less overhang fore and aft than in many of the Solent racing-yachts of her class.

The dimensions of the *Swanhild* are:—L.O.A., 34·08 ft.; L.W.L., 25·89 ft.; beam (extreme), 7·64 ft.; sail area, 850 sq. ft., of which the main-sail takes 559 sq. ft., and the head-sail 291 sq. ft.

During the season of 1899, two remarkable productions of the thirty-footer class made their appearance among the racing fleet in and about the waters of the Solent. These were the *Marjory* (Mr. G. H. Ward-Humphreys), and the *Flying Fish* (Mr. Harley Mead); the latter being the designer and builder of both boats, which were of similar type, shallow and very flat-floored, with fin and bulb-keels; but their most striking peculiarity was their extraordinary extent of overhang fore and aft. The *Marjory* was tolerably successful at first, but latterly was not so. The *Petrel* and *Mayfly*, both boats of two or three years earlier date, defeating the *Marjory* in several contests during the season of 1900.

It is doubtful if racing-boats of the thirty-footer class will retain the popularity they enjoyed a few years since. They are an attractive size for a small racing-yacht, but they are nevertheless costly playthings when kept exclusively for racing; and the cost of building is nearly equal to that of a five-rater or thirty-six-footer; but the accommodation on board is very cramped and limited as now constructed.

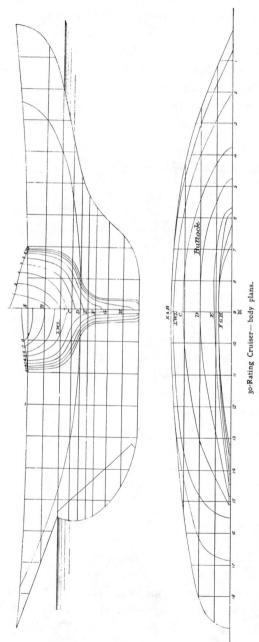

30-RATING CRUISER.

THE illustrations, which are from original drawings, represent a design for a 30-rating cruiser, intended for a One-Design Class. They are from the board of Mr. John S. Helyer, of the yacht-building firm of Field & Co., of Southampton, the designers and builders of some of the most famous cruising yachts of the day; as also of the Solent One-Design Class, and some others of the O. D. Classes.

It will be observed that the design illustrated is that of an excellent type of Cruising Yacht, combining, amongst other desirable qualities, those of good cabin accommodation with safety and power as a cruiser.

The dimensions are:—Length over all, 38 ft.; length, load-water line, 27 ft.; beam (extreme), 7 ft. 6 in.; tonnage (Thames), $7\frac{57}{94}$; rating, Y.R.A., 30 ft.; displacement, 6 tons 1 cwt.; lead keel, 3 tons 12 cwt.; displacement, 1 in. L.W.L., $7\frac{1}{4}$ cwt.

30-Rating Cruiser.

It is a great recommendation in these days of scanty displacement to find a 30-rater with all the requirements of a cruiser, including, more particularly, *six feet head-room* in the cabin, with couches, sleeping berths, and other comforts and conveniences seldom

30-Rating Cruiser—sail plan.

found so complete in a modern cruiser of that size ; and the whole so well arranged as apparently to leave nothing to be desired.

The plans, sections and dimensions also seem to indicate a type of boat in which the qualities of sea-worthiness and fast sailing have been kept in view, without sacrificing any of the comforts that may be reasonably expected on board a yacht of such limited rating.

The yacht is cutter-rigged, and under ordinary cruising canvas carries main-sail, fore-sail, jib and top-sail.   The sail area being :—

Main-sail ...	... 589·94 sq. feet.	
Top-sail ...	... 108·22	,,
Head-sails ...	... 231·34	,,
	—————	
Total sail area ...	929·50 sq. feet.	

THE CLASS TERMED 5-RATERS, AND THE 36-FOOT LINEAR RATERS.

From a photo by   " Emerald " and " Forella " racing.   *West & Son, Southsea.*

THE 5-raters and 36-footers are the largest of those known as the small-class racing-yachts.

Small Raters.

In this class we have a larger and more attractive size for a racing-boat; one that requires a crew of five or six hands in a sailing-match. Boats of this class ought, therefore, to have fairly good accommodation below deck.

The stipulated dimensions are—length over all, 36 ft.; length on load-water line, 31 ft.; beam, 9 ft. 6 in.; draft, 5 ft. 9 in. to 6 ft.; sail area, 1,250 to 1,300 square feet.

In a boat of the 5-rating class something more than a mere skimming-dish is expected. The size of a 5-rater is sufficient to justify her affording comfortable cabin accommodation, with sleeping berths, &c.; such, however, is not the case with those designed and built for match-sailing; the depth from deck to keelson being seldom more than $3\frac{1}{2}$ to 4 feet; everything is thus sacrificed to racing. They have undoubtedly plenty of room on deck, and their power and speed under sail are very great, but comfortable accommodation below deck is not to be found.

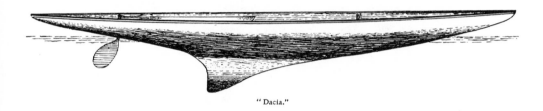

"Dacia."

THE DACIA, a 5-rater of 1892, was designed by Mr. C. E. Nicholson, jun., and was built at Gosport for Mr. R. H. Langrishe, who afterwards sold her to the Earl of Dudley.

The *Dacia* is of peculiar type, with a deep fin-bulb keel of different construction in some respects to other fin-bulb keels (as will be seen on reference to the profile above).

The *Dacia* is nevertheless a powerful and weatherly boat, and has been a remarkable success as a racing-yacht of her class; good in all weathers and on all points of sailing.

In 1892 she won thirty-three first prizes and three others out of thirty-nine starts, and was generally steered by Lord Dudley himself.

THE FENELLA is a boat of graceful proportions, designed by Mr. W. Fife, jun., and in 1894 and subsequent seasons made a high reputation as a racing-yacht.

The *Fenella* is a handsome and powerful looking boat with a broad full-bodied section, but long and shallow with a wide fin-plate and bulb-keel, as shown in the illustration on next page; and a large rudder fitted to her fin-plate; she has a long, sharp bow, and shallow, rounded stern.

The *Fenella* is rigged with two sails only, of the Solent type; she has a short-

The Sailing-Boat.

standing bowsprit, and her fore-sail is laced to a boom. The *Fenella* is altogether a splendid and powerful looking boat, and has proved a very successful prize-winner.

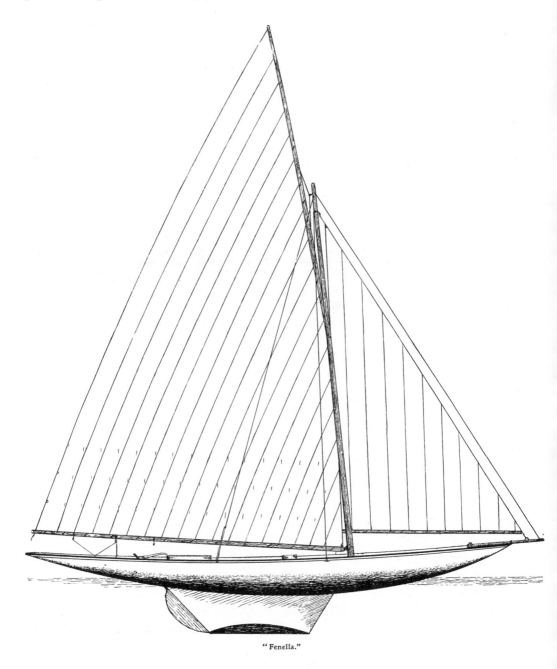

"Fenella."

206

Small Raters.

THE NORMAN, a 5-rater, designed and built by Sibbick & Co., of Cowes, in 1895, for Captain J. Orr-Ewing, is a buoyant and powerful looking boat, and proved the best of

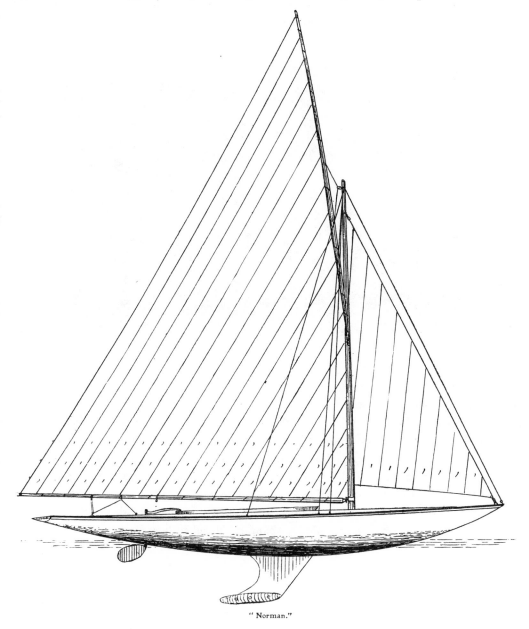

" Norman."

her class in that, her first season, winning no fewer than fifty-two first and two second prizes out of fifty-six starts. The *Norman* is broad and full amidships, with a fin and bulb-keel; she has a fine, graceful bow, and very clean run, with considerable overhang fore and aft. The *Norman* is probably one of the fastest of her class ever turned out by Sibbick & Co. Her success continued year after year under the able handling of Captain J. Orr-Ewing's skipper—Shawyer.

From a photo by   *Beken & Son, Cowes, I. of W.*
"Sea Shell."

THE SEA SHELL is from a design by Mr. G. L. Watson, of Glasgow, for Captain J. Orr-Ewing, but was built at Cowes by Sibbick & Co. She is the broadest and shallowest of her class in the neighbourhood of the Solent, and belongs to the "skimming dish" type; she has a deep fin-plate with heavy leaden cigar-shaped bulb bolted on to the plate, half on each side, at the lower extremity of the fin.

In her first year (1895) she won twenty-three prizes, and occasionally proved a formidable rival to the *Norman*. She usually sailed best in a strong wind, but, as she had no bulwarks and but very low coamings, was a wet boat in rough weather. She has recently (1898) had bulwarks and higher coamings fitted to her.

Small Raters.

THE HEARTSEASE, 5-rater (or 36-foot linear rater), was designed and built by Sibbick & Co., in 1896, for Mr. C. L. Orr-Ewing, and proved one of Sibbick's best productions; the champion of her class among twelve others, and the winner in almost every race she sailed. She was afterwards sold to Prince Colloredo Mansfield, who is an Austrian.

From a photo by   *Beken & Son, Cowes, I. of W.*

" Heartsease."

In the Riviera the *Heartsease* raced as a 10-tonner, where she won a long string of flags; and at the Genoa Regatta, 1898, was the most successful boat there. On that occasion she achieved the honour of winning her 100th prize since her *début* in May, 1896; and at the end of the season of 1899 was able to display no less than 134 winning flags!

The illustration is from a photograph shewing the yacht *Heartsease* when displaying her *first* winning flag in May, 1896.

The Sailing-Boat.

THE WESTRA, 5-rater (or 36-footer), was also designed and built by Sibbick & Co., in 1896; her rig was altered in 1897 from that of a sloop to a cutter, a bowsprit and jib being fitted to her.

" Westra" under reefed mainsail and foresail.

The *Westra* proved one of the best of her class; in her first season out of thirty-four starts she appears to have won twenty-four first prizes and seven second.

The illustration is from a photograph of the *Westra* under reefed mainsail and foresail.

THE HERMES, 5-rater (or 36-footer), was designed and built by Sibbick & Co., in 1897,

"Hermes" (36-ft. rater).

for Capt. John Orr-Ewing. She is a powerful-looking boat, and one of the ablest of the 36-footers. In her first season she won twenty-five prizes, eleven of which were firsts.

It will be seen from the profile of this boat that her bulb-keel is of a different form to that of the *Norman* and most of the other earlier racing-boats by this firm of builders. The fin of the *Hermes* is of a much broader shape, and the rudder is attached to the aft-end of the fin; whilst the lead bulb, instead of being of torpedo-shape projecting beyond the fin, extends the whole length of the lower end of the fin without any projection, and is rounded at the bottom.

An illustration, from a photo of the *Hermes*, has already been given at page 34, shewing the yacht under sail in her full cutter rig.

THE KOORANGAH, 36-foot linear rater, was designed and built by Sibbick & Co., in 1897 (a fin-plate and bulb-keel boat), for Capt. J. Orr-Ewing. In the early part of the

From a photo by   " Koorangah "   *Beken & Son, Cowes, I. of W.*

season of 1898 she was one of the most successful of the class. Her owner usually steered her, and she wound up the season with twenty-seven first prizes out of forty-nine starts, and a long string of forty-one flags. The *Koorangah* was also the winner of the Royal Southampton Yacht Club Medal for best average of her class in the season of 1898.

The Sailing-Boat.

THE FORELLA, 36-foot linear rater, was designed and built by Fife & Son, for Mr. E. S. Parker, in 1897, in which year she was the winner of twenty-one prizes, nine of which were firsts.

The *Forella* is a long, narrow, and deep-bodied boat, and was a keen and successful

From a photo by   *Beken & Son, Cowes, I. of W.*

"Forella."

contestant throughout the seasons of 1898 and 1899, having for her rivals some of the most famous racing-yachts of the Solent, including *Koorangah*, *Eileen* and *Emerald*, with all of which she was in frequent contest, and at the close of the season of 1898 had a record of twenty-five prizes, twelve being firsts and thirteen second.

THE EMERALD,[1] 36-foot linear rater (cutter rigged), was designed by Mr. Arthur Payne and built by Summers & Payne, for Mr. C. D. Rose, and sold by him to Mr. J. Gretton, M.P., in 1897, in which season she was the champion of her class; she has since changed hands twice.

In the season of 1897 she had frequent contests with *Hermes* and *Heartsease*, of the

[1] See illustration of *Emerald* and *Forella* racing, *supra*, p. 204.

same class, Mr. Gretton himself being usually at the helm, steering his beautiful boat to victory.

The *Emerald* was greatly admired as one of the prettiest yachts of her class, with her graceful lines and shapely run.

This yacht was also a frequent competitor in the season of 1898 with the yachts *Eileen*, *Forella*, and *Koorangah*.

THE EILEEN, 36-foot linear rater, was designed by W. Fife, junr., and built by Fife & Son, of Fairlee, for Mr. S. Mason ; she is Solent rigged, and was in frequent contest,

From a photo by   "Eileen."   *Beken & Son, Cowes, I. of W.*

in the season of 1898, with the most celebrated cutters of her class, including *Koorangah*, *Emerald*, and *Forella*. The *Eileen* is one of the best of her class ; she won twenty prizes in 1898, eight being firsts and twelve second.

THE ENDRICK.—Among the Solent 36-footers of the season of 1899 were two new boats, the *Endrick*, designed by Mr. A. E. Payne, for Mr. A. E. Orr-Ewing ; and the *Kestrel*, designed and built by Sibbick & Co., for Capt. F. C. Bridgman.

The *Endrick* had a wooden fin and bulb keel, the *Kestrel* a metal fin and bulb keel : both were very capable boats and were in frequent contest together.

The Sailing-Boat.

The *Endrick* appears to have sailed in fifty-three matches that season, and won forty-four flags, thirty-three of which were firsts.

In the season of 1900 there were no less than five new boats in this class, all constructed within the adjacent waters of the Solent, viz. :—

"Sakuntala."

The SAKUNTALA, which was designed and built by Sibbick & Co., for Capt. J. Orr-Ewing.

The DORIS, from a design by Mr. Chas. Nicholson, for Mr. J. Oscar Clark. This boat was at first slightly over her rating, and her canvas had to be reduced; in her altered form she proved a very powerful boat.

Varieties of Type.

THE POLYNIA, designed by Mr. Arthur Payne, and built by Summers & Payne, for Mr. W. S. Armitage.

THE CUCKOO, another Sibbick boat, designed and built by that firm for Miss Cust.

THE MOONFLOWER, also a Sibbick boat, for Mr. C. L. Orr-Ewing.

These five new boats, together with the *Endrick*, a last year's Payne boat, were in frequent contest together all through the season, at the regattas and sailing matches of the Yacht and Sailing-boat Clubs of the Solent and neighbourhood.

The *Sakuntala* proved by far the most successful of the fleet, winning first prizes in most of the matches she sailed, though she found very formidable rivals in *Polynia*, *Doris*, and *Endrick*, the latter of which made a great reputation the previous year, and she has, too, a somewhat fuller section than either of the new boats.

VARIETIES OF TYPE OF SMALL YACHTS.

THE fluctuations that have taken place in the form and design of small yachts, particularly in those of the racing classes, have been many and remarkable during the last fifty or sixty years.

From time to time designers have come forward with a new type of vessel,

Profile (old type of racing-yacht).

destined, in the designer's mind, to eclipse all others in speed and sea-going qualities; in some cases successful, in others disappointing. Designs, too, varying in size from the 50-ton cutter of the R.Y.S. to the tiny model, or insect class, seen on the Serpentine in Hyde Park on a bright summer's day.

The aim of the designer is, and apparently always will be, so far as the racing-fleet is concerned, to design a boat that shall outsail all others that compete with her. Apart from those of some distinctive class, are many possessing features of interest if not always of special merit. As to such of these of which the Author has been enabled to obtain sketches and other particulars, descriptions and illustrations are given in the following pages.

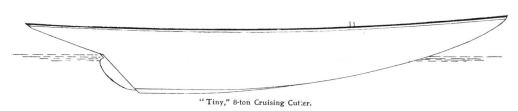

"Tiny," 8-ton Cruising Cutter.

THE TINY, an 8-ton cruising cutter, built in 1897, designed by Mr. H. White, and built by Messrs. White Bros., of Itchen Ferry.

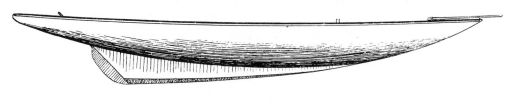

"Yseult."

THE YSEULT, 10-rater, built in 1892 by Messrs. Fife and Son, from a design by Mr. W. Fife, junr., is a boat of great power and exquisite design, the winner in the first year of her career of sixteen prizes, fifteen of which were firsts; and her subsequent record shows that she retained her reputation as a very successful prize-winner.

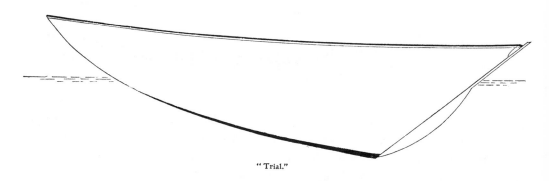

"Trial."

THE TRIAL, 21 feet L.W.L. (three tons), is a boat of remarkable type; she was built by McAlister in 1889, from a design by Mr. W. Scott Hayward. This boat has considerable breadth of beam and very deep keel and aft gripe, with heavy metal ballast attached to the under part of the keel.

The *Trial* was a highly successful competitor in the sailing matches of the Southport Corinthian Yacht Club and the Lytham Yacht Club in the earlier seasons of her career.

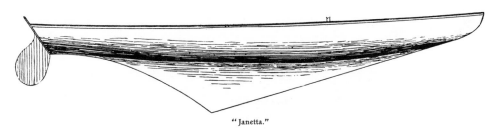

"Janetta."

THE JANETTA, a $2\frac{1}{2}$-rater (or 6-ton boat), designed by Mr. A. E. Payne, and built in 1890, is a capable looking model, though somewhat peculiar in type, with her triangular keel and deep form of rudder.

THE COCK-A-WHOOP, by the same designer, built in 1889, is a boat of similar type.

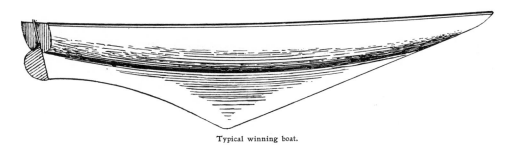

Typical winning boat.

Another boat also of similar type, termed a '*typical winning boat*' (a 5-rater), designed in 1890 by Captain J. Orr-Ewing, shewn by the profile above, is of fuller body than the *Janetta*, but with a considerably extended form of triangular fixed fin-keel, and has the appearance of a powerful sail-carrying boat.

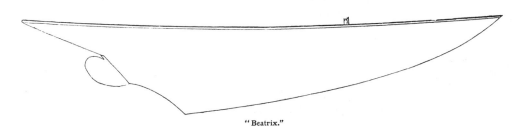

"Beatrix."

THE BEATRIX, $5\frac{1}{2}$ tons, designed and built by Sibbick & Co., of Cowes, in the year 1892, for the Hon. W. Ruthven, is a boat of peculiar type as will be seen by the contour sketch. The dimensions are :—Length over all, 34 ft. ; L.W.L., 24 ft. ; beam, 7 ft. ; draft, 5 ft. 9 ins. ; sail area, 620 sq. ft.

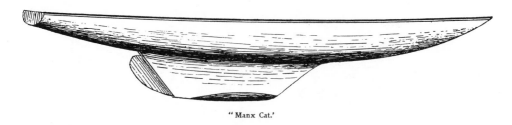

"Manx Cat.'

THE MANX CAT, 2½-rater, 1893 (formerly known as the *Polynia*), is a boat of graceful proportions, fine bow and clean run; she has good beam and powerful bearings, and was always considered a capable boat under sail. She was, however, subsequently converted into a steam launch by the Liquid Fuel Engineering Company.

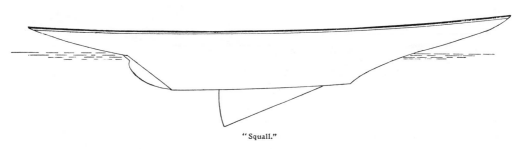

"Squall."

THE SQUALL, described as a 2-rater, was built in 1893 from a design by Mr. A. E. Payne for the Earl of Erne, of the L.E.Y.C., and is a powerful and beautiful boat. It will be observed from the profile that this boat has considerable overhang both fore aft, that she has a long-shaped keel, which is heavily weighted at the lower part, and is in addition provided with a revolving keel; in these respects bearing a striking (though diminutive) resemblance to the famous American yacht *Vigilant*.

The *Squall* is, however, not so flat in the under part of the bilge as the *Vigilant*, and she has more rise at bow and stern and more dip amidships than the American boat. Besides, too, the *Vigilant* carries her fulness well up to her bows, whilst the *Squall* has a longer and more slender-proportioned bow.

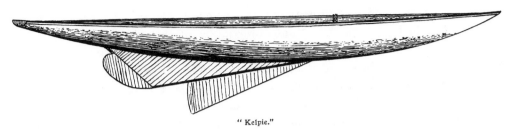

" Kelpie."

THE KELPIE, also described as a 2-rater, and as belonging to a Member of the L.E.Y.C., is a boat of powerful and beautiful design, the very *beau-ideal* of a racing-yacht, broad and full amidships, with a sharp, graceful bow and clean run; she has a long triangular-shaped fin to which her rudder is attached; besides which she has a centre-plate revolving-keel, as shown in the illustration above.

" Helen" (Lord Brassey).

THE HELEN (one of Lord Brassey's yachts) is a boat of remarkable type with triangular fin, and revolving-keel besides, and has the appearance of a boat possessing all the qualities of a racer. She was taken over to Australia in 1896, with a view to sailing in some of the small class matches of the Royal Yacht Club of Victoria.

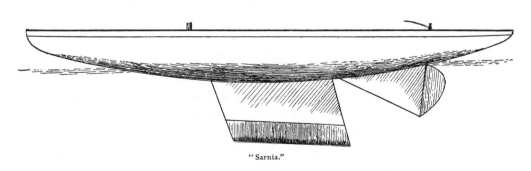

" Sarnia."

THE SARNIA, described as a modern 6-rater, 1897, is a model yacht from a design by Mr. Richard Hartwell, late of Guernsey, and a Member of long practical experience of the Guernsey Model Yacht Club.

The Sailing-Boat.

The yacht is named *Sarnia* after the ancient name of that Island.

It will be observed from the profile illustration of the *Sarnia*, that her form of hull is that of a boat on the best and most approved lines, with a flattish floor, rounded bilge, strong bow and long graduated run, all which are considered the best points for speed and sail-carrying power : that the arrangement of her fin and bulb-keel differs in several respects from all other fin-keeled boats, and is the result of many experiments by the designer, with a variety of keels, the centre bulb-fin-plate of the *Sarnia* giving sufficient stability and lateral resistance, and the smaller, or aft fin, giving steadiness and fine steering qualities, the space between the fins freeing the water without friction or impediment.

Mr. Hartwell has designed, besides models, several sailing-boats which have proved successful prize-winners.

And in the Guille-Allés Public Library and Museum, Island of Guernsey, may be seen a handsome Model Yacht, 'upon the most improved modern principles of nautical construction,' from a design by Mr. Richard Hartwell, which is an object of considerable attraction to nautical men visiting the Museum.

THE WEE-WINN, described as a 10-rater model yacht, designed and built by Mr. W. M. Paxton, 1897. This is a model yacht with fin and bulb-keel of novel and ingenious contrivance, as may be seen on reference to the illustration. The bulb, which in shape resembles a marlinspike—biggest at the fore-end and gradually tapering to a point at the aft-end—is affixed to two steel fin-plates, as shewn in the illustration, leaving a wide open space between them ; the rudder is swung on the aft-end of the stern-fin. (See illustration on next page.)

Whether or not the contrivance is conducive to fast sailing may be doubtful ; but it should be mentioned that the famous yacht *Corolla*, a $2\frac{1}{2}$ linear-rater, had at first a somewhat similar arrangement for her bulb-keel, but as it did not prove satisfactory it was discarded, and in her altered form the *Corolla* was a great success.[1]

There is in the Badminton series, 'Yachting,' Vol. II., p. 26, a skeleton drawing of Lord Dufferin's 4-ton yacht and sails, the *Lady Hermione*, the sails being all workable single-handed. The yacht is apparently of beautiful construction, yawl-rigged, and a lifeboat in principle. The description of the sails, rigging, &c., as given in the volume referred to, is very minute, and well worthy the study of those desirous of fitting and rigging a small yacht, or a sailing-boat, upon the principle of having every rope and sail entirely under the immediate control of the steersman ; in fact, manageable single-handed.

[1] *Supra*, pp. 197–8.

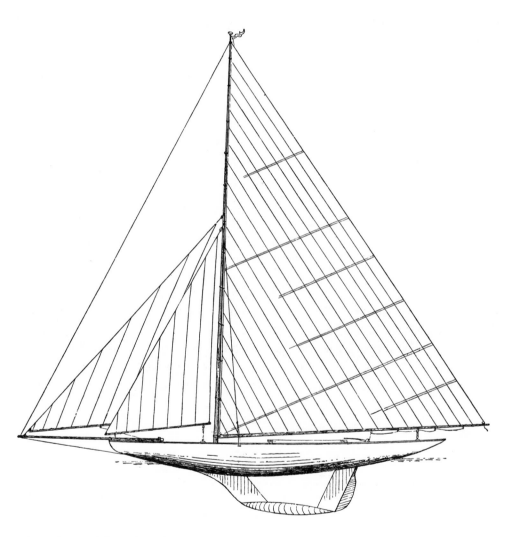

Wee-Win, model yacht with novel arrangement of fin and bulb-keel. (See observations, page 220.)

The Sailing-Boat.

CURIOSITIES OF TYPE AND RIG.

WE are, too, continually adding yachts and boats to our pleasure fleet in the shape of strange things; so that, in fact, some of the curiosities of type of British craft are peculiar and even grotesque.

The majority of these are, perhaps, to be found among the smaller class; there are, however, many eccentric departures among the larger class, and it may be stated generally that some of them are very fast under sail, but the majority are more or less failures in that respect.

And so we have yachts of every conceivable shape—long and narrow, broad and shallow, deep and short, medium and extreme; some with fixed keels, others with revolving keels, centre-boards, centre-plates, fin keels, bulb keels, loaded keels, and many other varieties and peculiarities, instructive to yachting men, designers and others, who take interest in novelty of form and curiosity of type.

But it is by the study and close observance of the forms of hull from time to time emanating from the hands of the most eminent designers, and the principles upon which boats of such infinite variety are designed and constructed, that much useful guidance may be obtained and knowledge acquired as to the form best adapted for fast sailing. And, in the Author's view, the scope of inquiry and investigation should not be limited to models from the hands of British designers, since much is to be learned from a study of the models of other nations.

THE HEATHEN CHINEE has several peculiarities, not only in form of hull but also in its Anglo-Chinese rig; she is a boat of the canoe type, being alike at stem and stern, and about four tons burthen; she has a moderate displacement, beam and draft, easy lines,

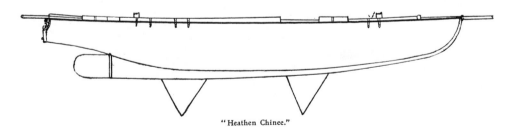

"Heathen Chinee."

small immersed surface, and a sufficient sail-area, so contrived as to be easily handled, and with little weight or bulk of gear aloft. The *Heathen Chinee* was designed by Mr. Landseer MacKenzie, and built at Erith by J. McWharter in 1877, and has been the winner of many cups in the course of her career.

The success of the boat is probably largely due to her rig, which possesses several advantages that fit it specially for a boat of limited stability. A comparatively large area of sail is carried on very light spars and with little gear. The battened sails are in canoe-form and fitted with reefing-gear, which permits of one or two reefs being hauled down with facile expedition, in fact, in less time than the outer earing alone of a cutter's mainsail of the same size could be secured. The battens are of bamboo, from one inch to an inch-and-a-quarter in diameter. The *Heathen Chinee*, both in hull and rig, contains many features that are worthy of a careful study ; and, though a novelty, there is much to commend her to those who desire a safe and handy boat of light draft of water.

THE FAN TAN, which is a boat of similar type and design to the *Heathen Chinee*, but

From a photo by   "Fan Tan."   *West & Son, Southsea.*

about twelve feet longer on L.W.L., and proportionally larger, was also designed by Mr. Landseer MacKenzie. She was built by Mr. J. A. Poole in the year 1888-9, for

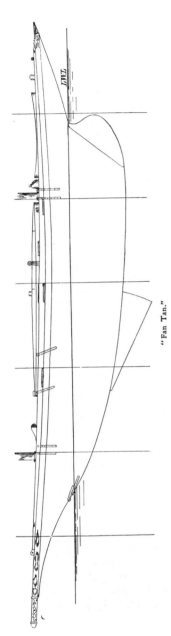

"Fan Tan."

cruising purposes, but her owner allowed her to compete in several sailing matches in the season of 1890, when, out of nine starts, she won eight prizes, open and handicaps.

The *Fan Tan*, as originally designed, had two centre-plates (similar to those of the *Heathen Chinee*); but during the winter of 1889, Mr. MacKenzie had one of the centre-plates (the aft one) removed, her balance rudder was discarded, and an ordinary rudder substituted with raking stern post and dead wood, as shewn by the profile sketch at side; the alterations thus made proved great improvements to the boat for all practical purposes.

The dimensions of *Fan Tan* are:—Length on L.W.L., 36 feet; beam, 9 ft. 6 in.; draft, 6 ft. (with centre-plate down 8 ft.); displacement, 11 tons; sail-area, 1,200 sq. ft.; weight of ballast on keel (all lead), 4 tons 17 cwt.

The rig of the *Fan Tan* is similar to that of the *Heathen Chinee*, viz.: two masts and bat's-wing lug-sails fitted with bamboo cross battens, from one inch to an inch-and-a-quarter in diameter, which serve to keep the sails distinctly flat and enable the boat to hang very close to the wind. The sails are quickly set and may be readily lowered, there being no gaff halliards to manipulate, but only one halliard to each sail, and lifts which snug the sail as it comes down.

The designer states that he finds the rig handy for cruising, good for getting under way, coming to anchor, going in and out of a crowded harbour, and always reliable; that he can readily vary the extent of sail by dispensing with the main-lug, or by setting a smaller, with either of which the boat is under perfect control, as she is also either with or without a jib. Moreover, the rig is decidedly economical as regards the number of hands required on board, as also of sails and gear.

Curiosities of Type and Rig.

DEMPSTER'S TRIANGULAR YACHT "PROBLEM."

SOME thirty or forty years ago a remarkably curious boat, called the *Problem*, was exhibited by the inventor, Mr. Henry Dempster, who called upon the Author several times respecting it. The hull was of triangular shape; the stern-post being made to rake at the same angle as the stem, so that both met and terminated in a triangular point under water, and thus formed simply an angular keel. The yacht was twenty

Dempster's Triangular-Keel Yacht "Problem."

feet in length, and six feet beam; was iron built, and ballasted with lead. It was rigged with three masts, the main-mast being placed exactly in the centre, and in an upright position; the fore-mast had considerable rake forward, and the mizzen-mast the same proportion of rake aft. It was rigged with two square sails, which were set on the main-mast, one above the other, and a triangular sail on each of the other masts.

The Sailing-Boat.

These triangular sails were on a revolving principle, the booms being each secured at the centre of gravity, one to a pivot on the stem and the other to a similar pivot on the top of the stern-post, by which means they would turn round and round, clear of the masts, and could be trimmed to any degree upon a circle. The sails thus possessed a double advantage, and, with the help of the triangular hull, could perform many rapid revolving evolutions, which no other boat could so quickly accomplish.

Among other experiments by the inventor was a very remarkable one, tested at Newcastle-upon-Tyne, by driving two posts into the bed of the river at low water mark, one on each side the channel, across which a strong iron bar was lashed horizontally, in

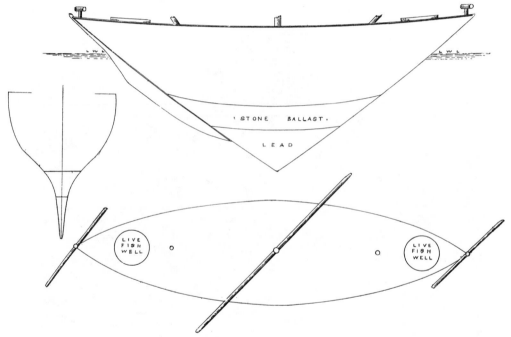

Plans of Hull, Deck and Midship Section.

a similar manner to a leaping-bar. A pole or gauge was then erected alongside the posts, marked to feet and inches, to indicate the depth of water. When the tide had risen sufficiently high to show that there was one foot and a half less water than the *Problem* required to sail clear of the obstruction (consequently that the vessel would strike it with her angular keel), she was sailed *stem on* at the bar, a stiff breeze blowing at the time; she then went over it by *rise* and *fall,* similar to a horse jumping a gate. The performance was repeated several times in the presence of a large assemblage of spectators.

The advantages of a triangular hull (as stated by the inventor) are, that a vessel might be made particularly useful for narrow rivers, where much turning in a small compass is often necessary ; but it will only answer in deep water, and the vessel must always be kept afloat—in fact, such a vessel could not lie aground. It has also been suggested that the invention is well adapted for trawling and fishing boats, and indeed, for any vessel where much turning is required.

The invention of a triangular hull has not, as far as at present known, been carried out in any other vessel than the inventor's *Problem*. The inventor often expressed to the Author his wish to build and equip a trawling and fishing boat upon the same principle, with a large well for live fish ; and he was sanguine as to the ultimate success of such a vessel in the fishing trade, but from unavoidable circumstances he was not able to carry out his wishes.

Models and plans of Mr. Dempster's invention of this ingenious kind of boat, with well, &c., and curious mode of rigging, are exhibited in the Model-room for Nautical Inventions at the Kensington Museum.[1]

The illustrations of the *Problem* (body and deck plans) are from drawings by the Author ; that of the vessel under sail is from a proof impression of a wood-cut drawn by Weedon and engraved by Smythe, which Mr. Dempster brought to the Author for the purpose of illustration in the pages of this work. It is also published in the *brochure* referred to in the note below.

SWAN BOATS.

Swan Boats.

SAILING-BOATS in imitation of a large swan with its wings extended, though a

[1] See also an amusing little work by Mr. Dempster, entitled ' The Decked-welled Fishing Boat,' &c., 1868.

The Sailing-Boat.

curiosity even at the present day, are of great antiquity, and have been already alluded to in the early part of this work, under the head, "Boats of the Ancients."[1]

In shape, the body of the swan forms the hull of the boat, the neck the mast upon which the sails are hoisted, and in some instances, the rudder is made in imitation of the foot of the swan. The sails are also made to resemble the extended wings of the swan. They consist of a single latine, or rather a settee-shaped sail, when sailing with a side wind, and of two such sails when running before the wind.

The chief object to be attained in these boats is to make them resemble as closely as possible a large white swan; and with a little ingenuity on the part of both boat-builder and sail-maker, this may be accomplished.

In the first place, if in building the boat the body of the swan be kept strictly in view, a very broad-beamed, safe, and roomy boat will be the result; the fore part should be covered over so as to represent the shoulder or lower part of the neck of the bird, and yet to form a fore-cabin, and the aft part should also be covered over, so as to represent the rump of the swan, and to form an aft-cabin or sail-room.

The central or main part of the boat should form the principal cabin, the roof of which, though partly uncovered when the boat is in use, when the hatches are closed resembles the back of the bird.

The sails should be made to look like the extended wings of the swan, and if properly cut and well-made, will have precisely that appearance when viewed at a distance; and this whether sailing with a side wind, in which one sail only is used, or scudding, when both sails are set. After the sails are made, they may be painted at the aft-leeches in imitation of the outer feathers of the swan's wings; a few dexterous touches with a paint brush and dark paint will suffice to render the imitation a striking one.

Both sails are hoisted by means of halliards rove through small brass blocks at the top part of the neck of the swan, separate halliards being used for each sail.

These boats, when ingeniously constructed, and the sails and tackle properly arranged, have the appearance when viewed at a distance, of veritable swans. Even when at anchor, with sails furled and lying along the back, the resemblance when seen at a distance of a hundred yards or more is very remarkable.

Boats of this kind have occasionally been built, though more for curiosity's sake than otherwise. There is, or was until recently, an ingeniously contrived Swan boat at Starcross, in Devonshire. It used to be an object of considerable attraction to visitors as also to railway passengers, on the train stopping at Starcross, between Exeter and Dawlish, who could see from the carriage windows of the train, the Swan boat and its little auxiliary the *Cygnet*, either lying at anchor or under sail on the Exe.

---

[1] *Supra*, page 3.

Curiosities of Type and Rig.

THERE can be no doubt as to the invention of twin sailing-boats having originated with the native islanders of the Western Pacific. Our earliest voyagers speak of the double canoes they met with in the Indian Archipelago, and of boats of a narrow form of construction furnished with outriggers for the purpose of enabling them to carry sail safely. Some of the twin canoes of those islanders are ingeniously contrived in this respect; some as small open boats, and others with considerable capacity for carrying cargo.

The idea of placing two boats of a narrow form side by side, at a few feet apart, and securing them in that position by means of a platform placed over both, whereby the stability of the one is preserved by the counterpoise of the other, is perhaps ingenious, but it has never been but a temporary success in European countries.

Several attempts at twin boats, and boats with outriggers, have, from time to time, been made in this country and in America upon the principle of those of the Indian Islanders, but the designers have generally been disappointed in the results, for the reason probably that their mode of joining the boats together was too stiff and unyielding as compared with the matchless contrivances of such twin boats as the flying proa of the Ladrone Islands, the double canoes of the Fiji Islanders and the sailing canoes of Ceylon.[1]

SIR WILLIAM SYMONDS' DOUBLE BOAT.

IT is more than a century ago since one Sir William Symonds, of the Royal Navy, contrived a double boat and sailed it with an ordinary lug sail, which he suspended between two masts, one of which was stepped in each boat, the masts being placed so that each leaned towards the other over the sides of the boats; the masts were then joined together at the top, where a double-sheaved block was hung just beneath the apex, and by means of which the sail was hoisted and the yard suspended between the masts.

The boats were placed side by side, in fact held close together by two wooden bars lashed across the gunwales, one at the bows and the other near the stern.

Double boats, or boats with parallel keels, only answer when placed wide apart, as in the double canoes of the Fiji and Friendly Islands.[2]

The objections to their general use in frequented waters are—the space they occupy

---

[1] Most of these are described and illustrated in subsequent pages of this work.—*Vide infra*, ' Foreign Boats.'

[2] *Infra*, ' Foreign Boats.'

and the wide spread they make on the surface of the water : added to which the separate motion of each is apt to wrench away the one from the other in rough water, and to break the platform, unless very substantially united. Mr. Herreshoff, the eminent yacht-builder of America, actually patented a duplex boat with flexible connections, in or about the year 1876, but little was ever heard of it afterwards.

The most recent production of the kind was in the year 1898, when a Canadian double boat of shallow type, named the *Dominion*, was built to sail a match against an American boat for the Seawanaka Challenge Cup. The *Dominion* proved the faster of the two, and the cup was awarded to her ; but on objection being afterwards raised that she was not a *bonâ fide* boat but a raft of catamaran type, the Canadians immediately gave up the cup.

THE UMBRELLA BOAT-RIG.

Umbrella Boat.

In the season of 1896 a sailing-boat appeared on the Solent with a singular kind of rig, the sail resembling a large Umbrella. It was the invention of Mr. W. G. Wilson and the late Mr. Percy S. Pilcher, who were then experimenting with the boat with a view to improving upon it.

Curiosities of Type and Rig.

The sail, when spread, had precisely the appearance of a large open umbrella; the mast of the boat forming the stick; and it was understood that most of the contrivances in connection with it had been patented by the inventors.

So far as sailing with a free wind, the boat would go ahead fairly well; the lower part of the mast was contrived so that it could be tilted on one side to an angle of ten or fifteen degrees, whilst the boat itself remained on an even keel. With the mast so leaning, the sail could be tipped up a little on one side and the boat would then go ahead with a wind on the weather quarter; but sailing to windward was, obviously, an impracticable performance with the Umbrella-rig. It is claimed for the rig, as its chief advantage, that twice as much canvas can be carried as by any other mode of rig, and that the sail has no tendency whatever to heel the boat over. In fact, under any and every condition of wind and weather, the boat maintains a perfectly upright position, sailing always on an even keel.

The Umbrella sail is of oval shape, 30 feet in diameter, and when furled to the mast, measures 16 feet.

The boat on which the sail was experimented with, measured about 17 feet on the load-water line: it was an old boat of ordinary type.

THE NAUTILUS-RIG.

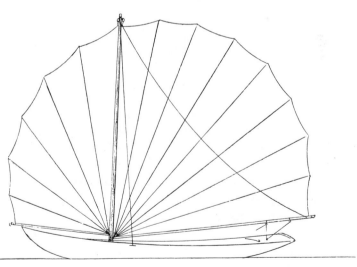

"Nautilus" rig.

THE profile illustration is merely a suggestion by the Author; so far as he is aware, no boat of such a rig has ever been constructed. He has named it the Nautilus-rig from its resemblance, when the sail is *spread*, to a *Nautilus*.

The Sailing-Boat.

The advantages contemplated by the rig are, that it will ensure an absolutely flat surface of sail when close-hauled, for going to windward, thereby enabling the boat to sail closer to the wind than by other ordinary modes; and a large area of sail can be carried in a more compact form than by any other mode of rig.

And as regards safety, the whole of the sail stands low down; lofty peaks are entirely dispensed with. Sail may be shortened with great facility as the battens enable each section to be folded up in fan-like form; and this applies to the fore-sail as well as the main-sail. But as regards the foresail, it will be found more convenient to invert the apex when it is required to reef that sail.

Although, when set, the sails have the appearance of being all in one, they are in

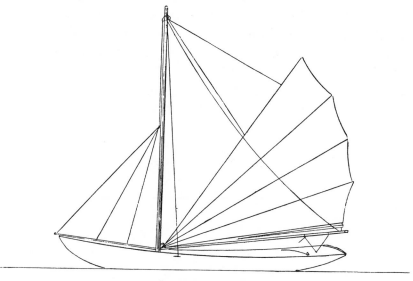

"Nautilus" close-reefed.

fact, in two sails, the division being in line with the mast; and for scudding and running before the wind, a powerful and extensive spread of sail is carried in a compact and low position, enabling the boat to maintain a steadier motion in a sea-way than if rigged with lofty top-hamper.

The Author's design contemplates that the fore-leech of the main-sail be laced to a yard, so that it can be readily hoisted and held close to the mast by the main-halliards. Also that the aft-leech of the fore-sail be laced to a yard, so as to be capable of being hoisted in the same manner as the main-sail, but as an independent sail.

END OF PART IV.

PART V.

———

THE ONE-DESIGN AND RESTRICTED CLASSES.

BY a 'One Class One Design' is meant a Class of Sailing-boats or small Yachts all of the same size and design: a form of boat chosen and adopted by the Club which institutes the Class, the object being that one and all competitors in the sailing-matches of the Class shall meet on fair and equitable terms.

From a photo by   *Beken & Son, Cowes, I of W.*

Start of the Solent One-Design Class at Cowes.

And, accordingly, every boat intending to compete in the sailing-matches of the Class must be not only of the same length, breadth, depth, and internal capacity, but of the same form and design; one and all built from the same moulds, and (usually) the sails cut from the same pattern, so that no one of the fleet shall be either longer, broader, narrower, deeper, shallower, or of a different model or design, or with a larger spread of sail than either of the others.

The Sailing-Boat.

The introduction of a one-design class is the result of the uncertainty and dissatisfaction occasioned by the rules of measurement and rating of the Yacht Racing Association as applied to small racing-yachts, the frequent alteration of those rules, and the facilities afforded for evasion, whereby unfair advantages have been gained, coupled with the expense attendant on the short career of a racing-boat under such rules, involving the building of a new boat nearly every year.

A 'One Class One Design' fixes the dimensions of the boat and the sail-area, and ensures a similarity of type in all other respects, so that *premier* places in sailing-matches between boats of a one-design class can only be secured by skilful handling and superior seamanship.

From a photo by

Solent O.D. Boats Racing.

Beken & Son, Cowes, I. of W

At the time when the proposal was first brought forward (1893) to institute a one-design class there was considerable opposition, and it was asked, ' *cui bono ?* ' Some said that the proposal if adopted would be detrimental to the best interests of yacht-racing, as it would damp the ardour of the yacht-racing fraternity, and be prejudicial to the development of high-class yacht-racing.

Such were naturally the first impressions of those who were opposed to the conception of a ' One Class One Design ' form of boat. But a more mature consideration of the proposal brought about a different conclusion, for it was abundantly clear that the one-design class of boats was not intended to interfere with owners who could afford to build year after year a new racing-boat. This was apparent from the very opening sentences of the written proposal put before the members of the Solent Sailing Club at its first introduction :—

'This Meeting views with the greatest concern the ever-increasing expenditure attendant on small-class racing in the Solent. It is strongly of opinion that the sport should be conducted in a manner suitable to the means of the majority, and not merely with a view to the encouragement of the few who can afford year after year to build a new boat.'

The proposal of a One-Design Class was, after further deliberation, adopted by the Solent Sailing Club, and followed shortly after by other Yacht and Boat-Sailing Clubs throughout the United Kingdom.

From a photo by   *Beken & Son, Cowes, I. of W.*

The chief recommendation of a One-Design Class is the opportunity it gives to small-class yacht-owners of avoiding the heavy expenditure involved in the building of a new boat every year or two, and of enabling a man who has a taste for boat-racing to keep a racing-boat with a certainty of knowing that it will not immediately be outclassed nor become out-of-date as regards type and measurement. And the fact that the boats of the class are all of one design enables a boat-wright with an order to build a fleet of from six to ten or more, to do so at a much lower price per boat than if each was built to a different design. And, further, it encourages men with limited means to indulge in the sport of boat-racing without fear of meeting in their next year's contests some dark stranger of the 'sailing-machine' type, or some boat designed and built in evasion of the rules of measurement with a view to defeating the champion boat of the previous year.

Another advantage of the 'one-design' is that the boats are enabled to compete in most of the sailing-matches of the various Yacht Clubs without the Yacht Racing Association Certificates of measurement and rating. Being all of one class and one design, and, usually, all constructed by the same builder, from one and the same moulds, upon the same lines, and the sails all cut from the same plans, and made by the same sailmaker, their class, measurement, and rating are all identical.

The One-Design Classes are not intended for those whose ambition is that of possessing the fastest yacht or the fastest sailing-boat or the most successful prize-winner of the day. The owner whose ambition carries him so far must, under the precarious rules of measurement prevailing at the present day, have the means at command to design and build, year after year, a new boat to meet the continual fluctuations of the rules and the cunning evasions attendant upon them.

Nor are they intended for the owner who can afford to build from his own designs and adapt them from time to time to the current rules of rating, regardless too of the inutility of his boat when her winning career is past. And, indeed, he must be a courageous owner who, under existing rules, is willing to incur the risk of finding his boat, after one or two successful seasons, overpowered by a craft designed expressly to evade the rules to a greater extent than that of the designer of his own, and thus leave him no alternative but to plunge into the costly expenditure of *another* new boat, and so on, from time to time, *ad infinitum.*

From a yacht-designer's point of view there is not very much that is commendable in the one-design scheme, as it leaves but little, if any, room for immediate improvement or advancement in the science of boat-designing, where the object is to build boats of different designs to compete for supremacy.

The One-Design Class is not applicable to any but a small type of yacht and sailing-boat, and its chief recommendation is that it provides a cheap class of sailing-boat for those whose means do not permit of their indulging in a larger or more expensive kind of boat. Most of the adopted designs combine the requirements of a cruising boat with that of a racing yacht, with ample cabin-room and other comforts seldom found at the present day on board of our small racing-yachts. The career of a one-designer, though of longer duration than the ephemeral racer of the season, is perhaps less interesting. A sailing match year after year between the same fleet of one-designers may in time become monotonous, and shorn of that excitement and interest attending a keen contest between boats of new designs. No such symptoms have, however, at present appeared.

The One-Design Classes are patronised and supported by those for whom they were intended, and the sport of yacht and boat-racing still flourishes, notwithstanding the misgivings of those who were opposed to their introduction at the outset.

And the adoption of a One-Design Class by so many Yacht and Boat-sailing Clubs in various parts of the United Kingdom proves the firm hold it has already taken upon the minds of the boat-sailing fraternity.

From a photo by   *Mr. Harold Fraser, Glasgow.*

Before adopting a One-Design Class of boat it will be well to consider the nature of the locality and other circumstances, such as depth of water, facilities for embarking and landing, lying afloat at anchor, extent of cruising ground, and whether the boats are intended for open sea-sailing, or for confined or narrow waters, or where there is considerable length and breadth of open water, and how affected by tides, etc., etc., all which are matters that cannot prudently be put aside, but should be taken into careful consideration before deciding on a suitable size and type of boat for a One-Design Class.

The Sailing-Boat.

SUGGESTIONS ON THE FORMATION OF A ONE-DESIGN CLASS.[1]

THE boats of a class should in all cases be built by the same firm, and, if possible, at the one time, and a complete set of templets should be made for each boat from the working drawings; some builders have a slovenly habit of shifting one set of templets from boat to boat as the work goes on, with the result that they get hammered or pressed out of shape, and consequently vary the hulls in outline and in weight, as when the outside planking is planed, less is taken off a mean spot, than where showing full in another boat.

The hulls should all be as far advanced as possible before the draw to determine ownership takes place, as some owners are much better acquainted with the actual building operations than others, and consequently if such a one is allotted a boat in its skeleton stage, he, by personally supervising the rest of the work, might possibly influence the workmen to effect a trifling improvement over the others, whereas if he is unaware which will fall to his lot, the superior knowledge he possesses will benefit all alike. The best time to ballot for boats is just before the painting is begun.

Each boat should be painted a distinctive colour, and have a distinguishing number in the peak of the main-sail. The best form for this is to have the figures on small squares of bunting, attachable to the sail by eyelets set in their proper place, so that when fixed on the sail the figures will be upright. This allows of the ready removal of numbers in case the owner objects to them when cruising.

The numbers on sails facilitate committees starting the races; without them indeed it is almost impossible to obtain accuracy if the fleet be numerous.

Owing to the cosmopolitan character of the classes, it has been found possible to arrange much better programmes of regattas and club matches throughout the season. The committees of the clubs are more inclined to reciprocate in the matter of prizes when members of their club are owners in the classes. If a class be dependent on one club only for races and prizes, the strain is too much probably to be kept up the whole season through, and a repetition of the same course—Saturday after Saturday—becomes monotonous, and the class unlikely to hang together so long as if a constant change of venue can be managed.

It is a great advantage to prepare a calendar of fixtures at the beginning of each season, stating definitely, time of start, amount of prize-money, whether the race counts for points in connection with special prizes, if such be given; and, by adding also the time of high-water at the place, much convenience is afforded, especially in a locality where tidal streams play an important part; having all these details at hand, enables owners to make arrangements far ahead, to select the time of year they wish to take their holidays, and to invite a substitute to take their place in the event of their not being able to attend any particular race.

It is very interesting to follow the influence of these fleets on modern yacht racing; unrecognised by any special rules of the Yacht Racing Association, and yet not running counter to that Institution in any material manner; their popularity increases from year to year.

They make their own rules, some of them necessitated by special local conditions: they bind their members hard and fast, and the members having had a voice in framing them, keep them loyally in the spirit, to the benefit of the sport at large.

[1] These suggestions are from the pen of Mr. James Craig, Junr., Associate of the I.N.A.; Hon. Sec. to the Belfast Lough One-Design Classes; and a Member of the Y.R.A., whose courtesy and kindness in assisting the author with drawings and photographs of the Belfast Lough One-Design Classes he desires to acknowledge.

The One-Design Classes.

THE Solent One-Design Class was one of the earliest of the O.D. Classes that were formed after the discussions which took place on the subject in 1893 and subsequent

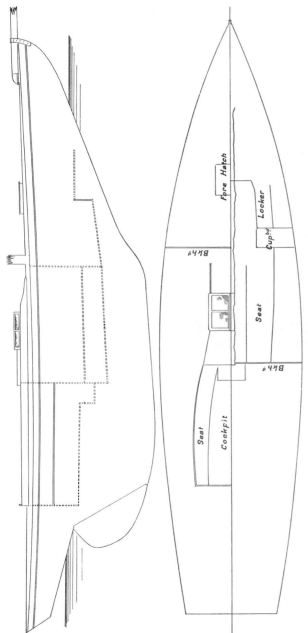

Solent One-Design Class—body and deck plans.

years. It quickly became popular, and was patronised by some of the most energetic and best known yacht owners in the neighbourhood of the Solent and the Portsmouth and Southampton Waters.

The Solent One-Design Class, though formed under the auspices of the Solent Sailing Club, is open to any member of a recognised Solent Yacht Club.

The dimensions of the boats are :—Length over all, 33 ft. 3 in. ; length on load water-line, about 25 ft. ; beam, 7 ft. 9 in. ; draft, 5 ft. ; sail area, 750 sq. ft.; displacement about 5 tons, with 2 tons 13 cwt. of lead on the keel. Rig, cutter, with a bowsprit 6 ft. outboard. As to inside fittings, there is a stipulation that an owner is at liberty to fit his boat internally as he pleases, and may have certain specified extras; but the ground gear (200 lbs. in weight) with stores and fittings, common to the boats, must be carried in a race.

The boats of the Solent One-Design Class are from a design by Mr. H. W. White. Ten of them were built in 1895-6 by Messrs. White Brothers, of Itchen Ferry, Southampton, who kindly sent the Author drawings and general arrangement plan, from which the preceding illustrations have been made. Several other boats have since been built from the same design and moulds by the Messrs. White, and the fleet now (A.D. 1900) numbers more than twenty.

The yachts, which are all keel boats, are of a cruising and sea-worthy type, and compare favourably with the old 2·5 raters ; and they have besides more room on board, better accommodation, and are in other respects more comfortable boats.

From a photo by   *Beken & Son, Cowes, I. of W.*

" Eilun," Solent One-Design Class.

They were raced in 1896 and in every subsequent year, and have usually kept in close company throughout their contests ; they have proved remarkably handy under sail, and quite equal to the rough waters which, in strong winds, agitate the Solent. They were put to a somewhat trying ordeal at the R. Y. S. Regatta on Aug. 5th, 1898, in a match organised by H.R.H. the Prince of Wales, when they sailed a memorable race for a Commodore's Cup, presented by His Royal Highness, for competition by ' yachts belonging to the Solent One-Design Class.' It so happened that the match was sailed in ' half a gale of wind,' and a heavy sea was running all the time, thus putting these able little racing-yachts to a very severe test. One of the conditions of the race for the cup was that owners should steer. Some of the yachts started with double-reefed main-sails, all the others were close-reefed; but notwithstanding, they fought their way to windward in a thoroughly courageous manner, with an over-abundance of wind and sea for such small craft; with coaming sometimes awash, and all on deck well dusted with the dash of spindrift. The boats were ably handled, and sailed a most exciting and meritorious race. The Royal trophy was won by the *Tangerine;* the other boats of the class being in close attendance upon the winner; the tenth (or last) boat was less than ten minutes astern; and this over a long course (twice round) marked out for them.

From a photo by   Beken & Son, Cowes, I. of W.

" Philippine," Solent O.D. Class.

In 1896, the first year of the sailing matches of this One-Design Class, the *Philippine* headed the list of winners of the class. Her name has since been changed, which is also the case with several other boats of the class.

The yachts of the Solent One-Design Class have increased in number and interest every year since their first introduction; and some of the most popular and spirited sailing matches, of recent years, on the waters of the Solent, have been sailed by these boats.

In the early part of the season of 1899, in consequence of the large increase in the number of yachts in this O.D. Class, it was found necessary to divide the class into two divisions, and to award a separate set of prizes for each division; and the same course was followed in the season of 1900.

The Sailing-Boat.

THE REDWINGS.

From a photo by

"Paroquet" and "Jeanie," Redwing Class.

Beken & Son, Cowes, I. of W.

THE Redwing Sailing Club, which was established on the Solent in the year 1896, has a One-Design Small Boat Class, called 'The Redwings'; each boat of the class being the private property of a member of the Redwing Club; and any one who is elected a member of that Club is at liberty to have a Redwing Boat, and to take part in

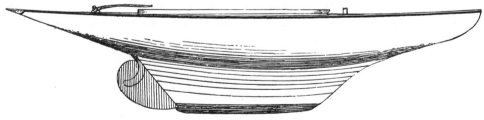

"Redwing" Class—body plan.

the sailing matches of the Club. The boats are termed 'Redwings' because the sails of each boat are, by the rules of the Club, required to be made of a uniform material of red cotton, which has been selected for the purpose by the Committee of the Club.

The object of the Redwing Sailing Club is that of affording inexpensive class racing, and giving the owner of a boat an opportunity of exercising his skill in designing her sails and rig. The form of rig is therefore optional, and in this respect the Redwing Class differs from other one-design classes, in which the sails and rig of each boat are required to be identical.

No spinnakers are allowed in the class-racing of this club as separate sails, but jibs may be boomed out.

Besides the periodical sailing-matches of the Redwing Club, the 'Redwings' are sometimes competitors in other matches for prizes offered by other clubs in the Solent and neighbouring waters, in which they effect a pretty contrast, with their bright red sails intermingling with the white canvas of the yachts of other Clubs.

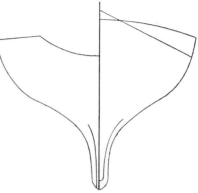

"Redwing" Class—section.

The design of the Redwing Boats is by Mr. C. E. Nicholson, and they are built by the firm of Camper and Nicholson, of Gosport. Their dimensions are as under, viz.: Length over all, 22 feet 1 inch ; length on load

water-line, 16 feet; beam (extreme), 5 feet 5 inches; ditto at L. W. L., 4 feet 7 inches; draft, 3 feet. The sail area is limited to 200 square feet, but the form of rig is optional. These boats have an iron keel, the weight of which must not exceed 10 cwt.

There being no restriction as to the form of rig, the Redwings are rigged some with gaff-mainsail, others with peaked lug (or Solent rig), some with sprit-sail and fore-sail, and one with a kind of split-lug,[1] but preference seems to be given to the gaff-mainsail, as the majority of the boats sporting the Redwing colours are so rigged.

The Captain of the Class and Hon. Sec., Mr. B. O. Cochrane, of Ryde, courteously furnished the author with a copy of the rules of the Redwing Club, and with line drawings and other particulars from which the above description has been written and illustrations made.

THE SOLENT 'SEA BIRDS.'

THE Solent 'Sea Birds' are a recent One-Design Class which came into existence in the early part of the year 1900. The Class was formed by the Solent Yacht Club, whose head-quarters are at Yarmouth in the Isle of Wight. Sir Charles Seely, Bart., is the Commodore of the Club.

The 'Sea Birds' were designed and built by Mr. H. Gale, of Cowes.

Each boat has to be named after a sea bird, as the Class implies.

Their dimensions are:—Length over all, 18 feet; length on L. W. L. 17 feet, 7 inches; beam (extreme) 6 feet; beam at L. W. L., 5 feet, 9 inches; depth (midships) 2 feet, 9 inches; sail area, 200 square feet.

The boats are each ballasted with 7 cwt. of inside iron ballast, and they have a wooden bowsprit extending about 3 feet from the stem.

The 'Sea Birds' are a buoyant and powerful-looking class of boats, sloop-rigged, having gaff-mainsail and foresail; the mainsail is fitted with a boom in the usual way, and the foresail has a roller attached to the forestay, so that the spread of that sail may be readily controlled single-handed.

The 'Sea Birds' have wooden keels, and are fitted with a revolving centre-plate of steel, weighing half cwt. The boats are half-decked and are required to have a bulk-head as shown by the illustration. It is also imperative that they be absolutely identical in every respect, and no deviation from the original design is permitted.

---

[1] *Supra,* p. 51.

The One-Design Classes.

The boats are owned exclusively by members of the Solent Yacht Club. Six of them were built in the first instance, and two or three subsequently: they have given great satisfaction; are good sea-boats, safe and suitable for single-handed sailing on the Solent waters and neighbouring seas, as originally intended.

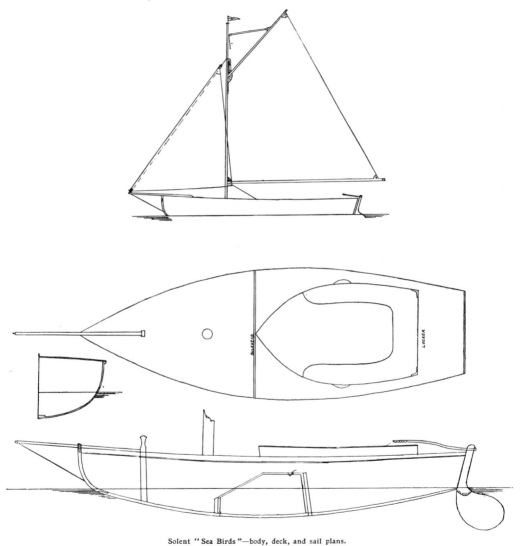

Solent "Sea Birds"—body, deck, and sail plans.

Weekly sailing matches are to be held throughout the season.

The first sailing match of the 'Sea Birds' came off on Saturday, the 16th June, when, after a spirited contest, the *Sea Lark*, Mr. Ramsay Saunders, was the winner; the *Dotterel*, Major Wingfield Stratford, being second.

The Sailing-Boat.

Through the courtesy of the Commodore and the Hon. Secretary of the Solent Yacht Club, the author is enabled to give illustrations and details of this interesting One-Design Class.

THE WEST OF ENGLAND CONFERENCE AND ONE-DESIGN CLASSES.

THE West of England Yacht and Boat-sailing Conference is an Institution that was established in the year 1890, at the suggestion of Mr. A. H Bridson, of Dartmouth, Vice-Commodore of the Dart Boat-Sailing Club. The object of the Institution was that of holding a Conference in the month of February in every year, at which Delegates from every Yacht and Boat-sailing Club in the south-west of England, between Portland Bill and the Land's End, should be invited to attend, for the purpose of adopting Rules as to Challenge Cup matches, establishing uniformity of classification in small Yachts and Sailing-boats, of arranging the dates for holding the several Regattas of the various representative Clubs within the District of the Conference, and for promoting, generally, the welfare of Yacht and Boat-sailing in the south-west of England.

There are now no less than twenty different Yacht and Boat-Sailing Clubs that are represented at the West of England Conferences.[1]

At the Conference held in February, 1899, it was unanimously resolved that there be *three* classes for One-Design Boats; viz., of large, medium, and small draft; one to be known as 'The Western 25 feet L. R. Class,' the boats of which are to be built according to the design of Mr. A. F. G. Brown, submitted by the Torbay and Dart Sailing Clubs, and approved and adopted by the members of the Conference.

At present this is the only class of the three that has been finally adopted and brought out.

---

[1] See the 'W. E. C. Handbook, 1899,' by A. H. Bridson, Esq.

The One-Design Classes.

THE WESTERN 25 FEET L. R. ONE-DESIGN CLASS.

THIS One-Design Class was originated and adopted at the Conference of the W. E. C., in the year 1899, as already stated.

At a meeting held at Paignton, Devon, in the early part of that year (at which Col. R. W. Studdy, Vice-Commodore of the Torbay Sailing Club, presided) several designs were submitted, among which that of Mr. A. F. G. Brown was chosen and adopted, and the Secretary was directed to call for estimates from local builders.

The dimensions and other general particulars of the boats for this One-Design Class are as under :—Length, over all, 28 feet; length at load-water line, 20 feet; beam, 8 feet; draft (centre-plate up) 3 feet; draft (centre-plate down) 4 feet, 10 inches; displacement, 2 tons, 7 cwt.; sail area, 443 square feet.

The boats to be sloop-rigged, and fitted with a drop-centre plate, working in an iron keel, and dropping about 2 feet below it; a roomy cabin with about 4 feet, 9 inches of head-room; and a self-emptying cockpit; the internal fittings of the boats to be optional. Colonel Studdy was appointed Captain of the Class, and Mr. A. F. G. Brown, Hon. Secretary.

It will be seen from the illustrations of the body and midship sections that the boats of this Class are of a very powerful type, and well-suited for the bays and open sea of the south-western coast.

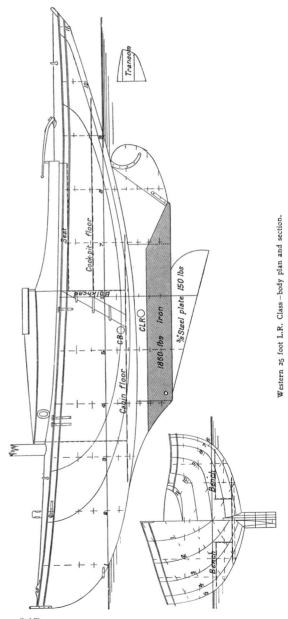

Western 25 foot L.R. Class—body plan and section.

247

The Sailing-Boat.

The illustration[1] of the sail plan shows the rig and how the sail area is distributed over the boat: the area of main-sail being 289 square feet; topsail, 63 feet; head-sail, 90 feet.

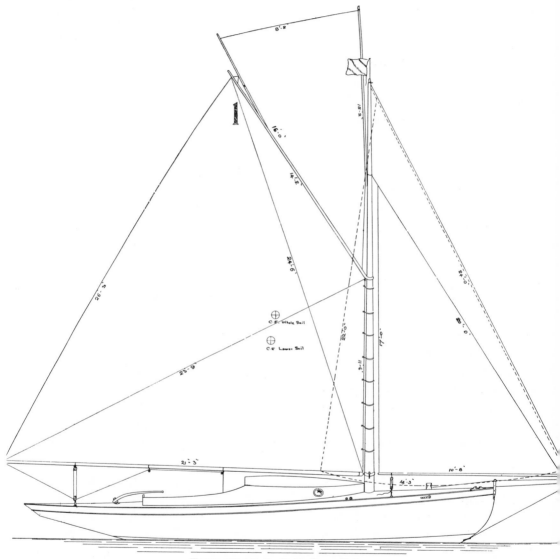

Western 25 ft. L.R. One-Design Class—sail plan.

The three first of these boats, built at Dartmouth, made their appearance on the 1st August, 1899, when they sailed their first race over the Dart Boat-Sailing Club's course.

[1] These illustrations are from drawings obtained by the Author through the courtesy of Colonel Studdy and Mr. A. F. G. Brown.

The One-Design Classes.

In the season 1900 (the second of their career) seven boats of the Western 25 feet L. R. Class made their appearance; two of them, however, took no part in the racing.

In the sailing matches of the five at Dartmouth on the 1st September *Jal Mänä* was first. In that of the Royal Western Yacht Club, *Mystery* (Mr. J. R. Benson) was the winner, *Argonaut* (Messrs Stevens), 2nd, *Jal Mänä* (Col. Studdy) 3rd, and *Narua* (Major Dean and Mr. Longmore) last of the four; but at Plymouth on the 8th September, in the Minima Yacht Club Match for boats of this O. D. Class, *Argonaut* was first, *Narua* 2nd, and *Jal Mänä*, 3rd.

One of the most interesting matches of the season sailed by these boats was a Channel race from Dartmouth to Plymouth on the 3rd September, which was won by *Jal Mänä*, *Narua* being second.

As to the final results of the racing between the boats of this O. D. Class, during the season of the year 1900, it appears that they sailed in all no less than 39 matches; of which *Mystery* heads the list with 114 points, having won 28 prizes; of which 19 were firsts, 5 seconds, and 4 thirds. *Argonaut* comes next with 94 points, having won 29 prizes, 10 of which were firsts, 11 seconds, and 8 thirds. *Jal Mänä* 79 points, having won 25 prizes, 8 of which were firsts, 11 seconds, and 6 thirds. *Narua* 49 points, having won 23 prizes, 2 of which were firsts, 9 seconds, and 12 thirds.

THE RALEIGH CLASS.

THE 'Raleigh Class' was started in the year 1897, under the auspices of the Dart Boat Sailing Club, as a One-Design Class, but not being generally adopted by Members of the Club, was discontinued in the following year, and is now non-existent as a One-Design Class. The author was, however, favoured with a Drawing and other particulars of the design from which the illustration on next page was made.

The Design is by Mr. G. Nowell Philip, of the firm 'Philip & Son,' Yacht and Boat-builders, Dartmouth.

The dimensions are:—Length over all, 18 ft.; length on load water-line, 16 ft.; beam, 6 ft.; depth, 2 ft. 8 in.

The boats were designed to carry a centre-plate of an area of 6 sq. ft., and of the weight of 112 lb.—the displacement being 18 cwt.

There were no restrictions as to the form of the rig, but the total sail area was not to exceed 200 sq. ft.

The Sailing-Boat.

The revolving centre-plate, which is of dagger-like shape, is of $\frac{3}{16}$ in. cold-rolled brass, of the weight above stated; besides which the boats were required to carry 7 cwt. of lead-pig inside.

"Lassie"—Raleigh Class—sail and body plan and section.

The rig of the 'Lassie' is that known as the 'Sliding-gunter,' hoisted in the usual way: all the halliards being fitted with purchases and set up below deck; and the entire control of sheets, halliards, etc., is thus readily at hand in the well of the boat.

The 'Lassie' proved a good sea-boat and was handy and fast under sail, whether

The One-Design and Restricted Classes.

in smooth water or a lumpy sea; and although not now classed as a 'One-Designer,' has been very successful as an 18-footer in many a keenly contested sailing-match, and she has won a good number of prizes; and so recently as the season of 1900 was again victorious in matches she sailed, whether over the sea course or the harbour course of the Dart Boat Sailing Club.

DARTMOUTH ONE-RATER RESTRICTED CLASS.

A NEW One-Rater Restricted Class for Dartmouth was decided on by the W. E. C. Conference at the close of the season 1900, for boats restricted to the following dimensions and requirements:—Length over all not to exceed 22 ft. The least displacement one ton. The boats to be clench-built and half-decked. It is anticipated that several of the Class will be built and ready to take part in some Class sailing-matches to be appointed for next season. Lord Rothes has already built to them.

THE DINGHY CLASS OF THE W.E.C.

THIS is a Class of small open Sailing-boats recognised and adopted by the West of England Yacht and Boat Sailing Conference.

The Boats of this Class are defined as 0·3 rating, old Y.R.A. rule. The stipulations are: that they shall be open Boats not exceeding in length 14 ft., the measurement to be taken over all, instead of on the water-line, in determining the rating. The Boats to be unsinkable. Draft not to exceed 12 in., with centre-boards housed and crew on board. Centre-boards, when housed, not to come above a batten placed across the boat from gunwale to gunwale. No bulb on centre-boards, and no outside ballast allowed.

THE TEIGNMOUTH DINGHY (RESTRICTED CLASS).

THE entrance to the Harbour of Teignmouth, on the Coast of South Devon, is very narrow and intricate of navigation; and the Harbour inside is beset with shoals and sand banks, leaving only a narrow channel for deep craft navigation, and thereby precluding the use, within the Harbour at certain times of tide, of sailing-boats other than those of shallow draft; but outside the Harbour there is always good depth of water and ample sea room.

The Sailing-Boat.

The Harbour itself and the River Teign, are however, a favourite locality for boat-sailing; and the Teign and Shaldon Corinthian Sailing Clubs are located in the neighbourhood.

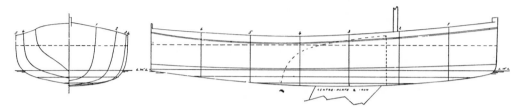

Teignmouth Dinghy—body plan and section.

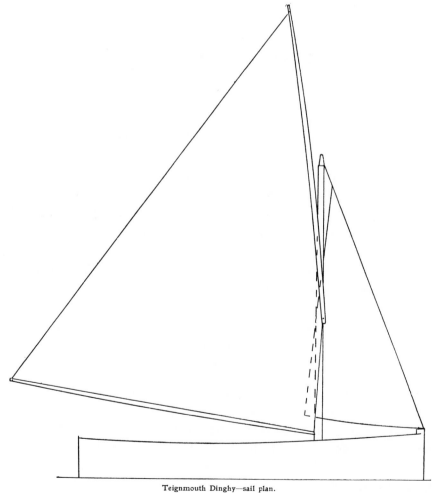

Teignmouth Dinghy—sail plan.

The One-Design and Restricted Classes.

The Sailing-Boats of the Teignmouth Dinghy Restricted Class are well adapted for the locality, and have become very popular with the members of the boat-sailing Clubs before mentioned. The restrictions are as follows :—

1. The Boats must be open boats (*i.e.* not decked in any part).

2. The Rating must not exceed 0·3 under the old length and sail area rule of the Y.R.A.; the length for rating being taken over-all instead of on the water-line.

3. No ballast is allowed below the garboards; the centre-plate excepted.

4. The centre-plate must not, when housed, project below the keel.

5. The centre-plate casing must not stand above the level of the gunwales.

6. No bulbed or ballasted plates are allowed.

The profile illustrations are from drawings of the boat *Century*, built by the Teignmouth Ship and Yacht Building Company, Limited, for Mr. T. Limbery; which, with the particulars as to the restrictions attached to the Class, were kindly forwarded to the Author on application, at the request of the Commodore of the Teign Corinthian Sailing Club.

BRISTOL CHANNEL ONE-DESIGN CLASS.

THIS is an entirely new class which made its first appearance in the season of 1900. It was initiated and adopted in the latter part of the year 1899 as

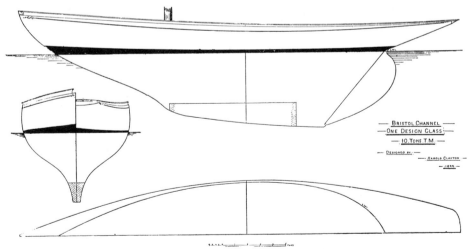

Bristol Channel O.D. Class—body plans and section.

a ten-ton One-Design Class for small yachts owned by members of recognised Yacht Clubs in the Bristol Channel.

The Boats are from a design by Mr. Harold Clayton of Penarth.

The Sailing-Boat.

Their dimensions are:—Length over all, 35 ft. ; length on load water-line, 26 ft. beam, 8 ft. 6 in. ; draft, 6 ft. ; displacement, 8·5 (tons); sail area, 794 sq. ft.; iron keel outside, 2 tons 7 cwt. 56 lbs.

Bristol Channel O.D. Class—sail plan.

The Bristol Channel O.D. Class is one of the largest of the One-Design Classes in the West of England. It will be seen by the illustrations of body plan and midship section on page 253, that the boats are of a sturdy sea-going form, with very moderate overhang fore and aft, being intended chiefly for cruising purposes ; and all yachtsmen who know the Bristol Channel are aware that boats intended for cruising in those waters must be good sea-boats. These Yachts have excellent cabin accommodation, and are, apparently, a very desirable type of sea-going boats.

The yachts of the Class are built, and building by the Penarth Yacht and Boat-Building Company for members of the Penarth Yacht Club.

THE TRENT VALLEY SAILING CLUB ONE-DESIGN CLASS.

THE Trent Valley Sailing Club was formed in the year 1886, with the object of instituting and encouraging competitive sailing among the Owners of sailing-boats on the River Trent in the vicinity of Nottingham. The Club has every year since

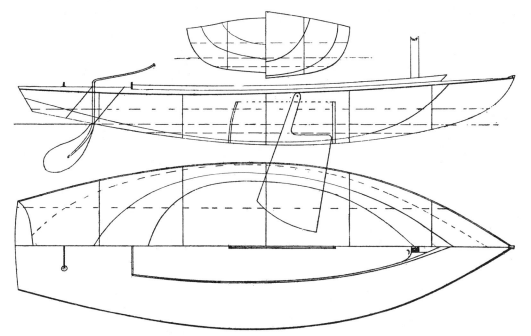

Trent Valley One-Design Class—body plans and section.

had its principal sailing-matches on a broad sheet of water some fifty acres in extent, known as the ' Trent Lake,' at which the sport has been both spirited and attractive.

The Commodore, Mr. W. P. Paget, a gentleman well-known to yachting fame, has been a generous patron of the Club, presenting it in the first and every subsequent year of its existence, with a handsome Silver Cup for competition among the Members of the Club.   In addition to which, special prizes have sometimes been given, including a Cup presented by the Mayor and Sheriff of Nottingham.

The Trent Valley Sailing Club has been a flourishing and successful one.   At the close of the season of 1887, the second year of its existence, it had enrolled no less than fifty-three Members, with a fleet of twenty sailing-boats; and among its members are some enterprising boat-sailers, who, in the course of the season, extend their cruises far beyond the home waters of the Club; and sometimes enter the lists of competitors at Regattas on other inland waters than those of the Trent, from which they have occasionally brought home trophies of success.

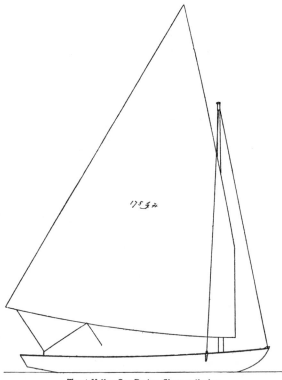

Trent Valley One-Design Class—sail plan.

The boats of the Members of the Trent Valley Sailing Club have been divided into two Classes, known as the A and B Classes respectively.   But it was not until the year 1897 that the Club decided on a One-Design Class; when, at the suggestion of their Commodore, who generously supported his proposal by offering to present one Boat to the Club, as a Club-boat for the use of its Members, and to build another for himself, the proposal was unanimously accepted.

Designs and estimates were applied for and considered, and finally the design of Mr. C. Bathurst, of Tewkesbury, was chosen and adopted; and seven boats were ordered to be built in the first season of the Class, which at once ensured its success: Mr. Bathurst being the builder of them all.

The dimensions of the boats are:—Length over all, 16 ft. 6 in.; length on L. W. L., 12 ft.; beam, 5 ft. 6 in.; draft with centre-plate down, 3 ft. 6 in.; draft with centre-plate up, 9 in.; sail area, 175 sq. ft.

It will be seen from the profile illustrations and dimensions, that the boats are of a modern type, with a fair extent of overhang fore and aft; and that, although somewhat shallow, they have good breadth of beam and powerful aft-bearings.

The boats of this One-Design Class made their first appearance in the season of 1898, when, after preliminary trial, it was decided that they should be allowed to carry a certain weight of inside ballast, whereby their stability was greatly improved; and they were then found to be a handy, safe, and comfortable class of boat for the purpose for which they were intended.[1]

THE ORFORD WHITE WINGS.

THE Orford White Wings are a One-Design Class, established in the year 1898, through the instrumentality of Mr. A. H. E. Wood, of Sudbourn Hall, Suffolk, a gentleman well-known in yacht-racing circles as the owner of the famous little racing-boat *Viva*, of the half-rater class, the winner in the seasons 1895 and 1896 of no less than 85 prizes.

The Orford White Wings were designed and built by Sibbick and Co., of Cowes, Isle of Wight. Seven of the boats were constructed at the close of the year 1898 and in the Spring of that of 1899, since when several others have been added to the fleet.

Their dimensions are: Length over all, 23 feet; length on load-water line, 16 feet 8 inches; beam, 6 feet; draft, 3 feet; sail area, 226 square feet. It will be seen on reference to the illustrations of general *contour* and midship section that the White Wings are boats of exquisite model, well adapted for the locality to which they belong, and combine the qualities of good sea-boats with weatherly powers and sturdy bearings, and they are each required to have a lead keel of the weight of 14 cwt. The rig of the White Wings is simply that of a gaff-mainsail and foresail, the mainsail being fitted with boom and goose-neck in the usual way. The headquarters of the class are at Orford, on the banks of the River Alde, whose course runs at the back of a tongue of shingle at Orford Ness, near Aldeburgh, on the east coast of Suffolk. The Alde, after running inland some few miles, and

---

[1] Through the courtesy of the Commodore and Rear Commodore of the Trent Valley Sailing Club, the Author is enabled to give illustrations of the form and design, with other particulars of the One-Design Boats of this Club.

leaving Aldeburgh on the right, flows over a broad extent of ooze, which, when covered by the flowing tide, forms a wide sheet of water, admirably adapted for small boat-sailing.

The mouth of the Alde at Orford Ness is in near proximity to the River Deben, and within about 12 miles of Harwich Harbour, the estuary of the Rivers Stour and Orwell. The locality of the White Wings is, therefore, favourably situated for yachting and boat-sailing, both on sea and river.

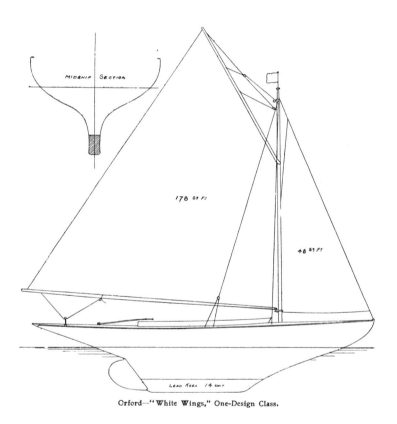

Orford—"White Wings," One-Design Class.

The first match of the White Wings was sailed on the 29th of April, 1899, in a strong, squally, south-westerly wind, when there were seven competitors. It was a trying ordeal for the fleet, but they one and all proved to be good sea-boats, and capable and able little craft. The *Viva (Viva II.)*, Mr. A. H. E. Wood, the Captain of the Class, was the winning boat on that occasion.

The Class has since become so popular that sailing-matches among them are held weekly during the season, at the close of which (in 1899) it was found that every boat in the Class was a prize-winner.

The One-Design and Restricted Classes.

The result of the sailing-matches of the White Wings in the season of 1900 shows that *Viva* heads the list with a total of 28 wins, comprising 16 firsts, 8 seconds, and 4 thirds; and the Challenge Cup, presented by Mrs. Fraser, having been again won by this boat now becomes the property of Mr. Wood as owner of the *Viva*. The *Kipper* comes next with a total of 24 wins, 11 of which are firsts, seven second, and six third prizes. *Emerald* is next with 26 wins, but of these five only were first, 11 second, and ten third prizes. It appears that the White Wings sailed no fewer than 47 matches in the season of 1900.

The Orford White Wings are a smart, handy, and interesting class. The boats are usually well handled, and they always present a clean, snow-white, and capable appearance, worthy of their name—'White Wings.' And at the regattas on the East Coast they are objects of considerable attraction, particularly in the minor sailing-matches, some of which are specially arranged that they may take part in them in competition with other sailing-boats of similar dimensions.

THE YORKSHIRE ONE-DESIGN CLASS.

THIS One-Design Class came into existence in the year 1898 for Hull, Bridlington, and neighbouring yachting and boating stations. The Class was originated by

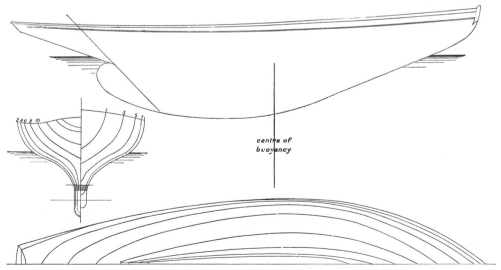

Yorkshire and Hull One-Design Class—body plans and section.

Mr. J. M. Storry, and successfully formed by his efforts, aided by the co-operation of members of the various yacht clubs in the district. The boats are from designs by Mr. J. S. Helyar, and were built by Messrs. Field and Co., yacht and boat builders, of

The Sailing-Boat.

Itchen Ferry, Southampton. Their dimensions are: Length, 25 feet; beam, 6 feet 10 inches; draft 3 feet 4 inches; sail area, 320 square feet, of which the mainsail has 240 feet and the foresail 80 feet.

Yorkshire and Hull One-Design Class—sail plan.

These boats, as a One-Design Class, have given great satisfaction, and are recognised as smart, handy little craft, excellent sea-boats, and fast sailers, and they nearly always carry all sail, except in a heavy sea. They are all fitted with roller fore-sails, which enable them to regulate the spread of that sail according to circumstances as regards wind and sea.

The boats of this Class are of a thorough sea-going type, and their sailing-matches are mostly on the open sea off the coast of Yorkshire, and so well matched are they that there is seldom but a small margin of difference at the finish of their contests, as in the match off Bridlington Bay on June 30th, 1900, when, among five starters on a 15-knot course, at the finish there were only three minutes between the arrival of the first and last boats.

THE ORWELL CORINTHIAN ONE-DESIGN CLASS.

THIS is a small One-Design Class, having its headquarters at Ipswich, Suffolk, on the banks of the River Orwell. The Author has no particulars of them. He applied for the loan of drawings for the purpose of having illustrations made of the design, &c., but his request was not complied with.

THE SOUTHPORT CORINTHIAN YACHT CLUB ONE-DESIGN CLASS—0·75 RATING.

THIS Class of Sailing Boat was originated during the year 1894, when the Southport Corinthian Yacht Club offered a prize for competition by designers of small racing boats, for the best design for a 0·75 rater, limited in cost to a specified amount: the

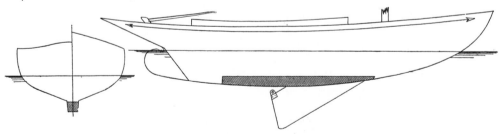

0·75 Rating, One-Model Class—W.L.Y.C. and S.C.Y.C.

design to be for a good sound cruising boat, comfortable, fast, and safe as a sea-boat; of light draught, and suitable in other respects to the requirements of the district.

The prize was awarded to a well-known amateur designer of great repute, Mr. W. Scott Hayward, who is the Commodore of the West Lancashire Yacht Club, as he is also of the Rhyl Yacht Club. The following are the dimensions:—Length over all, 23 feet 5 inches; length on L. W. L., 17 feet 8 inches; beam at deck, 6 feet

7 inches; beam at L. W. L., 6 feet 2 inches; draft, 2 feet $2\frac{1}{2}$ inches; draft with centre-board down, 4 feet $8\frac{1}{2}$ inches; centre-board drop, 2 feet 6 inches; centre-board weight, $1\frac{1}{4}$ cwt.; sail area, 130 feet; iron ballast on keel outside, $7\frac{1}{2}$ cwt.; inside, $6\frac{1}{2}$ cwt. of lead. The two first boats of this Class that were built were the *Queer Girl* and *Imp*, both of which proved very successful in most of the matches they sailed in their first year. Two other boats were then built from the design, and the season 1895 then opened with four of them; and in the following year six more were added, thus making a fleet of ten in 1896, which has since been further augmented by the addition of several others.

The members of the West Lancashire Yacht Club seeing in these boats the very requirements they sought, obtained permission of the Southport Corinthian Yacht Club to build from the design and adopt it as a Class.

WEST LANCASHIRE YACHT CLUB ONE-DESIGN CLASSES.

CLASS I., 0·75 rating. These boats were designed by Mr. W. Scott Hayward, and, as already stated, are of the same model and design as those of the Southport Corinthian Yacht Club. The requirements submitted for the design were, first, a good

"Imp"—West Lancashire Y.C. O.D. Class.

knockabout sea-boat capable of making a passage in bad weather with comfort and safety, and, secondly, as a class racer; all which requirements have been undoubtedly fulfilled, and the boats have given great satisfaction, and become the popular class

The One-Design and Restricted Classes.

of the West Lancashire seaboard, and in their first season—that of 1896—kept all their engagements in the sailing matches at Fleetwood, Lytham, Southport, Hoylake, Rhyl, Llandudno, Beaumaris, Bangor, Menai, Port Dinorwic, and Carnarvon, covering an extent of upwards of 100 miles of open sea-coast, beset in parts with outlying sand-banks, strong currents, and sometimes a rough and heavy sea. These boats, in fact, made so good a reputation all along the coast that the Rhyl Yacht Club, as also the Hoylake Sailing Club, decided on adopting them as a One-Design Class.

The dimensions and sail area, etc., are already stated, *supra*, pp. 261—2.

The illustration (p. 262) of the *Imp*, one of the Class, is owned and sailed by Mr. J. Hatton Hall, Vice-Com. of the West Lancashire Yacht Club. The *Imp* is the champion boat of the class. Her record is, for 127 starts, 97 prizes—viz., 56 firsts, 29 seconds, and 12 thirds. Number of boats in the Class, 13; average number of starters, 7. The *Imp* was also winner of the Pilkington Champion Cup, 1896 and 1898; the W. L. Y. C. Challenge Cup, 1896 and 1898; the Hoylake Challenge Cup, 1896 and 1898; and the Rhyl Challenge Cup, 1896.

At the close of the season of the year 1900, it was found that among the boats of this class the *Wenonah* (Mr. J. Actor) had made the best record. This boat also took the Helmsman's Prize, presented for competition by Mr. W. Scott Hayward to the boat which made the highest score in Club sailing-matches. The *Wenonah* was steered during the racing season by Mr. E. L. Baddeley.

The *Pixie* was awarded the Champion Cup, presented by Sir G. Pilkington, to the boat which made the highest score of the season, including outside sailing matches as well as Club matches.

WEST LANCASHIRE YACHT CLUB ONE-DESIGN CLASSES (CLASS II.).

CLASS II.—*The Seabird Class*, 0·5 rating.—These boats are a new class, eight of which were built by Mr. R. Latham, of Cressens, Lancashire, each of them being named after a sea bird, and designed, jointly, by Mr. W. Scott Hayward and Mr. H. Baggs. Their dimensions are :—Length over all, 20 ft. ; length on load water-line, 16 ft. 4 in. ; beam at deck, 6 ft. ; beam at L. W. L., 5 ft. 6 in. ; draft, 1 ft. 3 in. ; iron centre plate, $\frac{3}{8}$-in. thickness ; sail area, 182·2 sq. ft. The boats of this class have no *outside* ballast, but 6 cwt. of iron inside.

This is another O.D. boat of the strong cruiser type, designed to encounter the heavy seas and rough weather of the Lancashire seaboard, and is, in fact, of similar

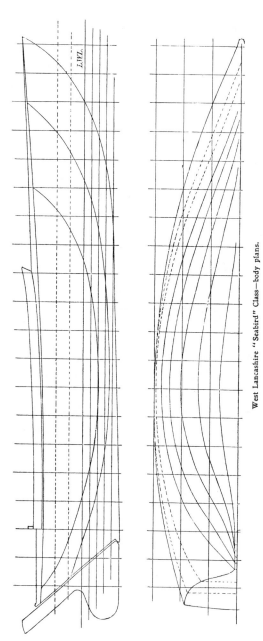

West Lancashire "Seabird" Class—body plans.

design to the 0·75-rater class, but upon a smaller scale, with one or two improvements. They are intended to take part in the sailing matches of their class at the same places on the coast as those of the larger class, going to and fro along the coast to all the matches on their own bottoms.

In the season of 1899 the *Goshawk* came out at the top of this class, and was throughout sailed by her owner, Mr. Dudley Coddington.

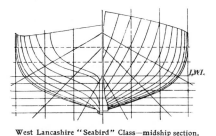

West Lancashire "Seabird" Class—midship section.

And in the season of 1900 the *Goshawk* again heads the list with the best record. This boat is also winner of the Owners' Champion Cup, as also of the Helmsman's Cup of her Class.

The Donaghadee Sailing Club, Ireland, have recently adopted this class, and have already built five boats to the W. L. Y. C. design; but they are calling them 'The Sea Shell Class,' each boat being named after a shell-fish. The new Class has been started under favourable auspices, and promises well.

West Lancashire "Sea-bird," One-Design Class—sail plan.

The Sailing-Boat.

CLASS III.—*The 12-ft. Centre-board Class.*—These are from a design by Mr. G. H. Wilmer, of Liverpool. Their dimensions are:—Length over all, 12 ft.; length on L. W. L., 11 ft. 9 in.; beam (widest), 4 ft. 5 in.; beam at L. W. L., 3 ft. 9 in.; no ballast.

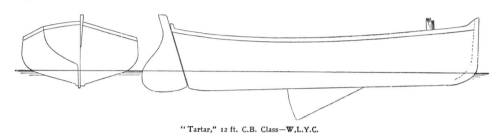

"Tartar," 12 ft. C.B. Class—W.L.Y.C.

This is a new class of open sailing-boat fitted with a centre-board, and destined to take part in the numerous sailing matches for such boats of the various boat-sailing Clubs on the coast.

The *Tartar*, of which a profile illustration is given, was in 1898 the champion of the Class. The *Tartar* is owned and sailed by Mr. E. L. Baddeley, Hon. Sec. to the W. L. Y. C., and Mr. A. Campbell. The sail plan of the boats of this class is the same as that of the *Slut*, illustrated *infra* at page 268.

SOUTHPORT CORINTHIAN YACHT CLUB ONE-DESIGN CLASSES.

The 12-*ft. Centre-board Class.*—These boats were designed by Mr. G. H. Wilmer, of Liverpool. Their dimensions are:—Length over all, 12 ft.; length on L. W. L., 11 ft. 9 in.; beam at widest, 4 ft. 5 in.; ditto at L. W. L., 3 ft. 8 in.; no ballast.

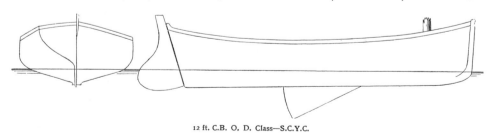

12 ft. C.B. O. D. Class—S.C.Y.C.

They were originally designed as yacht's tenders, but were afterwards formed into a racing class by Mr. W. Scott Hayward, Commodore of the W. L. Y. C. They are besides excellent knockabout boats, and in experienced hands have proved equal to those of any other class of the same size on the coast.

"Ma Mie," Southport Corinthian Yacht Club.

The *Ma Mie*, an illustration from a photograph of which is shown, is the Champion of the Class, and was sailed and owned by Mr. W. Scott Hayward.

THE HOYLAKE SAILING CLUB RESTRICTED CLASS.

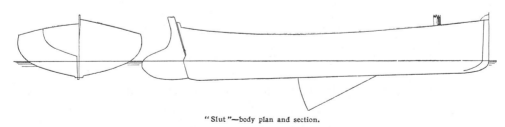

"Slut"—body plan and section.

This is a 12-foot restricted centre-board class of the above-named Club. Dimensions:—Length over all, 12 ft.; length on L. W. L., 11 ft. 6 in.; beam at widest part, 4 ft. 6 in.: ditto at L. W. L., 3 ft. 10 in.; no ballast.

The Sailing-Boat.

The design for this class of small sailing-boats is by Mr. G. H. Wilmer, of Liverpool; there are fourteen boats in the class. The champion boat of the class, the *Slut*, owned and sailed by Mr. W. Scott Hayward (Commodore of the W. L. Y. C.), was built in 1892 by Crook and Sons, and has a remarkably successful record covering a period of seven years, during which she has won no less than 165 prizes, besides seven Champion and Challenge Cups—viz., 100 first prizes, 46 second, and 19 third. She was also the winner of the Hoylake Sailing Club Champion Cup, 1892, 1893, 1894, and 1895; also of the Rhyl Yacht Club Champion Cup, 1896; the West Lancashire Yacht Club Champion Cup, 1896; and the West Lancashire Crews Champion Cup, 1898. Fifty of these matches were open to all comers, for boats of any design, so long as they did not exceed 12 ft. in length over all.

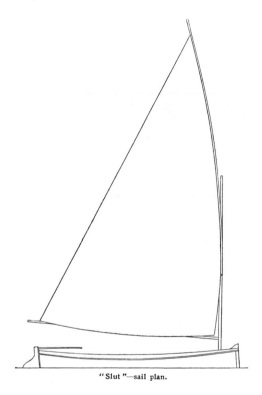

"Slut"—sail plan.

This famous little boat, although in appearance a fine-weather craft, is an excellent sea-boat, and is well known at Lytham, Southport, Mersey, Hoylake, Rhyl, Llandudno, Beaumaris, Bangor, Menai, Port Dinorwic, and Carnarvon, at all of which places she attends the Regattas, going to them on her own bottom, and being sailed in the matches of her own class, always under the able handling of her owner, Mr. W. Scott Hayward, assisted by Mr. A. H. Mitchel as crew.

The One-Design and Restricted Classes.

A beautiful model, by Mr. Willie Crook, of this widely-renowned little boat was exhibited (with a record appended of her career) at the Yachting and Fisheries Exhibition at the Imperial Institute, at Kensington, in 1897. The model was exquisitely finished, and proved an object of considerable attraction to all interested in the delightful pastime of boat-sailing.

THE NEW BRIGHTON SAILING CLUB 18-FOOT CENTRE-BOARD RESTRICTED CLASS.

THE New Brighton Sailing Club is one of the oldest in the United Kingdom, having been established in the year 1869, and appears to have been the first to introduce a girth dimension in its rule of measurement. One of the principal objects of this Club was, from its earliest inception, that of encouraging and promoting open boat sailing.

The 18-foot restricted class was formed in the year 1888, and is still the popular one on the Mersey. By the rule of measurement of this Club boats of the class nominally measured 40 ft. by the N. B. S. C. rule of measurement, viz. :—Maximum girth in feet × $1\frac{7}{12}$ × extreme length in feet, girth being ascertained by straining a tape completely round the boat.

Practically, however, it is a restricted dimension class: —Length over all, 18 ft.; girth, 13 ft. $10\frac{3}{4}$ in.; exposed area of centre plate, 4 sq. ft.; drop of centre plate, 2 ft.; area of mainsail, 160 sq. ft. (exclusive of rounds in head, foot, and leach); area of fore sail, 40 sq. ft.; area of spinnaker, 80 sq. ft. Cloths of mainsail not to be less than 15 inches in width.

No evasion of measurement is permitted, such as cambered keels, elbowed stern-posts, &c.

Rudders not to drop below the keel. No ballast allowed except a crew of four hands.

The centre-plate not to exceed $\frac{1}{4}$ in. in thickness, if of metal.

The planking to be $\frac{3}{8}$ in. thick, and of ordinary clincher build.

The timbers 1 in. by $\frac{1}{2}$ in., spaced 9 in. centres.

THE *MISCHIEF*—NEW BRIGHTON RESTRICTED CLASS.

THIS celebrated boat, one of the New Brighton Sailing Club Restricted Class, was designed by Mr. M. Treleaven Reade, of Blundellsands, and built in the year 1891, and is now owned by Messrs. F. H. Dent and T. H. Wood.

The model and design of this boat are of exact wave form, and so constructed that her under-water body retains the wave form as regards longitudinal displacement up to 20 degrees of heel. To obtain this result in a boat with flared-out sides, it was found necessary to design her so that she tripped gradually by the head as she heeled over; the difference in trim of bow and stern at 20 degrees heel working out to about 3 in.

The *Mischief*, in her first year, won the Champion Record Cup of the N. B. S. C., though having to compete with several other new boats by well-known designers,

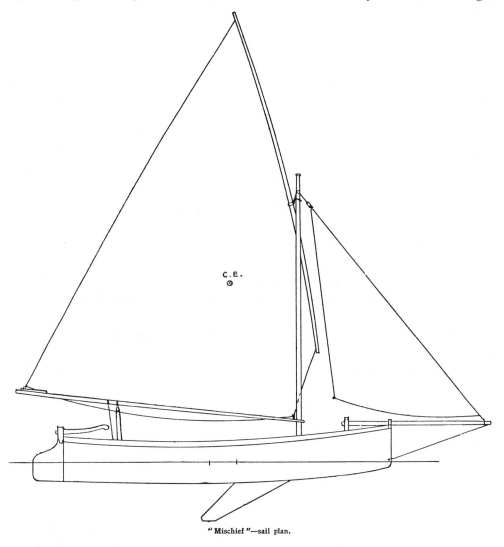

" Mischief "—sail plan.

and she has maintained her reputation, having raced successfully in her class ever since, showing how difficult it is in a properly restricted Class to entirely outbuild a successful boat, yet allowing of scope for modern improvements in model, sails, &c.

The One-Design and Restricted Classes.

The dimensions of *Mischief* are :—

Length over all, 18 ft. ; beam (extreme), 5 ft. 9½ in. ; draft (with centre-plate up), 1 ft. 1½ in. ; draft (with centre-plate down), 3 ft. 1½ in. ; maximum girth, 13 ft. 10¾ in. ; total displacement, 1,475 lbs. ; freeboard (lowest), 1 ft. 2 in. ; freeboard (bow) 2 ft. 1 in. ; freeboard (stern), 1 ft. 6 in.

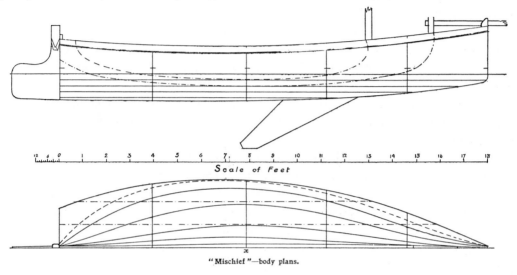

Scale of Feet

"Mischief"—body plans.

In the closing match of the season of 1900, which was sailed on the 22nd September, for prizes presented by Mr. W. B. Anderson, there were six competitors. In the spirited match which ensued the *Mischief* led from start to finish, and was declared winner of the first prize.

This boat, although built, as already stated, in the year 1891, is still one of the best of her class, having won during the season of 1900 (besides other prizes)

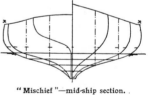

"Mischief"—mid-ship section.

both the N. B. S. C. Challenge Shield and the Record Cup for races sailed under the flags of the N. B. S. C. and M. S. C.

OTHER RESTRICTED CLASSES.

BESIDES the One-Design and Restricted Classes already described, there are some others. One such Class was set on foot in December 1896 by the members of the London Sailing Club, which then had its head-quarters at Hammersmith. The boats of this Class 'were not to exceed 18 feet Y. R. A. measurement and rating;' and the further restrictions were, a minimum displacement of 17 cwt. (ex crew), and a minimum thickness of planking and deck of three-eighths of an inch.

A somewhat larger 'Restricted Class' was afterwards formed in which the boats were not to exceed 24 feet Y. R. A. rating; the other restrictions being the same as in the 18 ft. Class.

Restricted Classes upon those lines were then adopted by the Royal Corinthian Yacht Club, the London Sailing Club, and the Orwell Corinthian Yacht Club. And at a meeting held in October 1898 a resolution was passed 'that the Restricted 24 ft. Class be renewed unaltered for a further period of three years from 1899, subject to any Y. R. A. change of measurement.'

It will be observed that these Classes adopted the Y. R. A. rules of rating and measurement. The consequence was that at the close of the season of 1898 no less than six of the alleged prize-winners out of a fleet of ten had to give up the prizes they were supposed to have won, objections being taken mainly on the ground that they were immersed above their proper load-water line—in some cases said to be owing to soakage; but from whatever cause they were found to be over the Y. R. A. measurement, to the rules of which they had restricted themselves.

The same objection seems to have been taken to other small yachts of the 'Restricted Classes' which sailed under the Y. R. A. rules of measurement.

It is obvious that small yachts, if measured on their load-water-line in dry weather, and when light and buoyant, will, after wet weather and long immersion, be found immersed above that line, thus showing how unreliable and unsatisfactory such rules must be.

Among the 18-footers Restricted Class of the London Sailing Club the boat named *My Lady Dainty* (Mr. S. N. Griffiths) again heads the list for the season of 1900, as the most successful prize-winner of her Class, this being the third year in succession in which she has done so.

And in the 24 ft. Restricted Class the *Vineta* heads the list and takes the Muriel Challenge Cup.

The One-Design and Restricted Classes.

WINDERMERE YACHTS.

THE picturesque surroundings of the Lake Windermere add to the pleasures of yacht and boat-sailing on the surface of its waters ; and the sailing-boats give life and spirit to the picture which, without them, would be cheerless and unattractive.

The head-quarters of the Royal Windermere Yacht Club are at Bowness, which is situated about midway on the east side of the Lake.

From a photo by   *Brunskill & Co., Windermere.*

Yachts becalmed on Lake Windermere.

Although boat-sailing on this beautiful Lake has its charms, it has also its disadvantages and its terrors—the one in the shape of too frequent calms ; the other in the perils which surround its waters, caused by the natural formation of the hills which encircle it and trend far inland behind the lake, forming here and there perhaps beautiful valleys and deep intersecting gullies, which, however, serve to shelter squalls and gusts of wind, and to assist such in gathering power as they rush along the valleys and find an outlet on the surface of the lake ; when woe betide the fragile craft and the inattentive helmsman and his crew, should one of those powerful gusts overtake him in an unguarded moment !

The Sailing-Boat.

The danger is increased considerably by the wonted suddenness with which such squalls almost invariably come, often when the surface of the lake is scarcely ruffled by the softest zephyr, and when all on board are bright and cheery with the joys and pleasures of a sail in company with those whose society adds charms to the cruise and whose gay spirits lend life to the scene.

From a photo by　　　　　　　　　　　　　　　　　　　*Brunskill & Co., Windermere.*

In no part of the British Islands where boat-sailing is practised is there greater necessity for precaution by those having charge of a sailing-boat than on the Lake Windermere. The helmsman and crew must always be on their guard against the sudden gusts of wind which come sweeping along the valleys, often with irresistible force, giving vent to their fury on the tall slender sails of some hapless craft, perhaps nearly becalmed at the previous moment.

The Lake is deep and its waters are cold, and in years gone by, when precautions were less observed than now, and when experiences were fewer, many a bright and joyous boating-party have found a watery grave beneath its glittering surface.

The boats intended for sailing on Lake Windermere must therefore be of good stability, and those who control them must be prepared for sudden squalls and stormy gusts, as well as for calms and gentle breezes, all which are characteristic of the land-locked waters of that delightful locality.

There are, besides the ordinary pleasure-boats of the Lake, two principal classes of yachts and sailing-boats that are recognised as racing craft by the Royal Windermere Yacht Club. The larger class are the yachts belonging to members of the Club, which are rigged as sloops ; and the other, a smaller class of sailing-boats of the *Una* type, also belonging to members of the Club. The latter, although not actually decked all over, have very wide water-ways and high coamings round the well.

The present form of yacht of the larger class differs considerably from the previous or older type inaugurated about twelve years ago, which had full bows, deep fore-gripe, and straight stem.

From a photo by   *Brunskill & Co., Windermere.*

The modern yacht of the R. W. Y. C. is a great improvement upon the older class, and is built in conformity with the new rules and regulations adopted by the Club in the year 1897 for governing the size of yachts and their spars, which compete in the sailing matches of the Club.

[The illustration is that of the *Sirius*, leading in a sailing match on Lake Windermere.]
The new measurements and requirements are, briefly, as under :—

Length of yacht on L. W. L., 22 ft. ; length over all, 32 ft. ; overhang forward not to exceed 4 ft., the angle of which shall not be less than 23 deg. with the water-line ; the contour of the curve of the stem at and about the water-line shall be a fair curve ; the counter, or so much thereof as shall extend aft of the load water-line, shall not intersect a triangle or the produced perpendicular thereof.

Freeboard.—No yacht, when on her load water-line, shall have less than 2 ft. 6 in. freeboard at the stem, and the deck of the yacht shall be carried aft from that point in a fair and reasonable line or sheer.

Beam (extreme outside measurement), not less than 6 ft. 6 in. without beading or moulding.

Draft not to exceed 5 ft. 6 in. when the yacht is on her load water-line.

Spars.—Length of mast from deck to truck not to exceed 26 ft. 8 in. ; bowsprit, from fore side of mast to extreme end, not to exceed 15 ft. in length ; boom, not to exceed 22 ft. in length ; gaff (measured parallel to boom), not to exceed 16 ft. 6 in. in length ; topsail yard not to exceed 18 ft. in length.

Hoist.—Hoist of mainsail not to exceed 16 ft. ; jib, from deck to pin of jib halyard sheave, when hanging parallel to mast, not to exceed 23 ft. 9 in.: topsail sheave, from deck to pin of sheave on mast, not to exceed 25 ft. 9 in.

Ballast.—No yacht to have less than 32 cwt. of ballast, and no ballast to be carried inside of the yacht.

Bulb-keels.—In case of bulb-keels, the keel above the bulb (whether of lead or wood) not to be less than 6 in. in thickness; and the bulb must not project, either fore or aft, beyond the wood keel; and in neither the wood nor lead shall there be a return curve.

Rudder to be affixed to the stern-post in the usual manner.

The above measurements, which came into operation on January 1st, 1897, are not to be altered before January 1st, 1902.

Fore and aft sails—viz., mainsail, jib and topsail only. No square sails are to be used, and no foot-sticks or jack-yards shall be allowed to the gaff-topsails, and no booming out of the sails permitted.

No yachts constructed with shifting keels, steel keels, or plates fitted with lead in bulb, cigar, or other shapes, attached to such plates, are allowed.

From a photo by   *Brunskill & Co., Windermere.*

[The illustration shows the *Turtle* (Mr. A. R. Sladen) a long way ahead of her opponents, and winning in easy, graceful style.]

The most striking alteration between the new and the old class which the

ordinary observer will notice is the disappearance of the straight stem and the sub-
stitution of the modern curved bow. The new boats are also 6 ft. 6 in. longer than
those of the old class; the jibs are 4 ft. shorter on the foot; and the mainsail booms
are lengthened, but the total sail area remains nearly the same.

It will be observed that the yachts have great depth of draft, good beam, and the
weight of ballast they are required to carry low down on their keels, with the limited
spread of sail, make them practically uncapsizable—a very important and necessary precaution in yachts destined to navigate the land-locked waters of the Lake Windermere.

Another precaution is that two life-buoys, 'ready for immediate use,' are required
to be carried on board every yacht.

The Windermere Regattas, at which the sailing-matches of the R. W. Y. C. take
place, are held annually in the month of July. There is generally a good entry, as
the competing yachts, which comprise two classes, are a numerous fleet; and when
favoured with a good breeze the races are most spiritedly contested.

From a photo by

A close finish.

Brunskill & Co., Windermere.

The illustration above is from a photograph by Brunskill, showing the closing scene, in a fine breeze, of one of the closest races ever sailed on the Lake Windermere. The two leading yachts are *Mimosa* (Mr. W. T. Crossley) and *Cachalot* (Mr. J. W. Scott).

THE CLYDE SAILING BOATS AND YACHTS.

YACHT and boat-sailing have for many years past been actively pursued on the waters of the Firth of Clyde, more particularly at Rothesay, the home of the Royal Northern Yacht Club.

The great estuary of the Clyde affords fine sea-room for cruising, and extensive courses for yacht sailing-matches.

The head-quarters of the Royal Clyde Yacht Club are at Hunter's Quay, Holy Loch. The new Club House is beautifully situated, surrounded by lovely scenery and commanding extensive views of the neighbourhood.

The old Club House was burnt down in the year 1888, and a new one erected on the same spot at a cost of upwards of £18,000. Such an expenditure speaks more eloquently than words of the flourishing condition of yachting in those parts.

The Firth of Clyde, in respect of extent of sheltered sailing waters and variety and beauty of scenery, has no rival amongst the yachting centres of the British Islands.

The lower Firth, owing to its great expanse and exposure to southerly winds, and consequent heavy seas, as also to its distance from the headquarters of yachting, is not convenient for racing courses. The cruiser, however, has here greater freedom than in the more confined waters of the upper Firth, with access to the fine scenery of the Island of Arran and the Cantyre coast; and should stress of weather render shelter necessary there are many harbours, natural and artificial, on both sides of the Firth.

Loch Fyne, which in extent and charm of scenery is little inferior to the upper Firth, also provides an ideal stretch of cruising water, open to even the smallest yacht from the upper reaches, through the sheltered channel of the Kyles of Bute.

But the home of Clyde yachting is the upper Firth, which, protected from the full run of the sea in southerly winds by the islands of Bute and the Cumbraes, provides a long and broad expanse of sheltered water, flanked by hills of varying height, some bare and rugged, others wooded from sea to summit. From this inland sea branch off in all directions into the heart of the mountains salt-water lochs of varying length, but one and all of beauty surpassing even that of the Firth itself.

Except in a few narrows, giving access to the less-frequented waters, there is little or no strength of tide, and the yachtsman is therefore free from the necessity of making his arrangements conform with tide-tables.

Nor is he hampered by shoals or the need of entering harbours, for good depth of water is to be found almost everywhere to within a short distance of the shore; and the

The Sailing-Boat.

shelter and holding ground are such that yachts are moored all along the coast, and if reasonable care has been taken to have moorings of proper strength, no uneasiness need be felt in any weather likely to occur during the summer months.

* * * * * * *

The great distance between the Clyde and the other principal yachting centres makes it impossible for the smaller boats to compete in other than home waters, and this, in conjunction with the type of boat produced by recent Y. R. A. measurement rules, has resulted in the practical neglect of the Y. R. A. classes, and the development of a type of craft better suited to the physical features of the Clyde.

From a photo by   *Mr. W. Harold Fraser, Glasgow.*

The principal characteristics of these boats, both cruisers and racers, are considerable proportion of beam and draft to length, and high freeboard, with consequent great sail-carrying power. As overhangs are generally restricted, the boats present a somewhat over-sparred appearance.

The absence of shoal water makes it unnecessary to curtail draft, so that in the case of the 23-foot water-line Class a draft of over seven feet is usual. An almost equally great proportion of draft to length is found among the cruising craft; and the Clyde boats are, as a rule, very capable performers to windward.

* * * * * * *

With the natural advantages possessed by the Clyde, and the frequent and fast communication by rail and steamer provided between Glasgow and the coast towns, it is not surprising that the sport of yachting has attained to its present popularity.

The event of the Clyde season is, of course, the well-known ' Fortnight,' when continuous racing for over two weeks is provided for all classes, from the first-class yachts to the smallest local boats, many representatives from other yachting waters swelling the number of entries in the larger classes.

Racing, however, is not confined to this period of the season, as the numerous Clubs, with yearly increasing funds available for prize-giving, now provide matches for every Saturday in the season, and the number of races offered is growing to such an extent as to make it impossible to avoid clashing of fixtures.

The pastime as pursued in Clyde waters could not be in a healthier state than at present, and the demand for boats is such that no craft of merit need wait long to find a purchaser.

Clyde boat " Alruda."

The Sailing-Boat.

THIS, the most sporting of the Clyde classes, originated in the building in 1890 by the Royal Clyde Yacht Club, to designs by Mr. G. L. Watson, of two cutter-

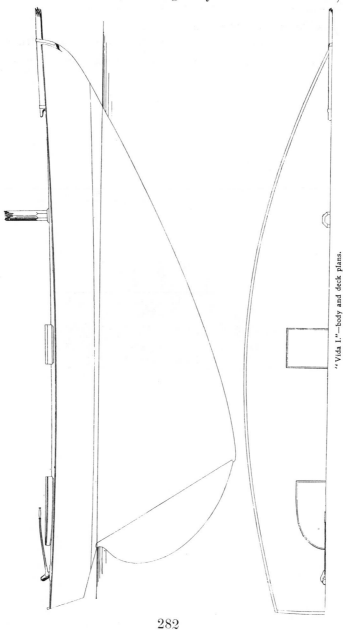

"Vida I."—body and deck plans.

rigged, square-sterned boats, 23 ft. over all in length. These were and are still kept moored off the club-house at Hunter's Quay, and are at the disposal of members of the Club at a moderate rate of hire. These boats, with another built to the same lines, but privately owned, were raced together, and gave such good sport that a third boat joined them, but, being of greater power, proved too fast for the pioneers.

In 1891, *Verve*, built for Mr. Robert Wylie to designs by Mr. G. L. Watson, in her turn took the lead.

The season of 1892 saw other boats taking part in the racing, and interest being awakened in the class, representatives of the leading yacht clubs met together in the autumn of that year, and drew up conditions for the formation of a class as follows :—Dimensions not to exceed : length over all, 30 ft. ; length,

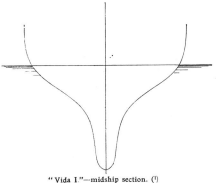

" Vida I."—midship section. ([1])

water-line, 23 ft.; sail area, 750 sq. ft., whereof mainsail not to exceed four-fifths of total. No centre-boards, fin, or bulb-keels allowed.

In 1893, six new boats built to these conditions appeared in the class—three, *Vida*, *Pike*, and *Shuna*, to designs by Mr. G. L. Watson ; the others, *Thaber*, *Lala*, and *Norka*, from the board of Mr. Wm. Fife, jun. *Vida* (Messrs. Wylie) showed the best record at the end of the season, having no less than 19 first, 7 second, and 1 third prizes out of 29 starts. *Thaber* (Mr. P. M. Coats) took second place.

The season 1894 produced one new boat, which, however, proved unequal to *Vida* and *Thaber*, the first-named again heading the prize list with 18 first and 6 second flags for 30 starts.

The year 1895 saw the advent of *Klysma*, and, when the season was somewhat advanced, of *Vida II.*, built for Mr. Wm. A. Wylie from designs by Mr. G. L. Watson, to replace the first boat of that name, which was now laid up. *Klysma* was fairly successful, but did not exhibit the qualities latent in her, and which were destined to place her at the head of the class two years later. *Vida II.* finished her first season with 15 first and 3 minor prizes out of 22 starts, her owner having also 3 firsts out of 6 starts credited to him by *Vida I.* before she was laid up.

In 1896 the leadership of the class was again taken by *Vida II.* with a record of 12 first and 5 second flags for 26 starts.

In 1897, however, Mr. Wylie's monopoly of the championship of the class was interrupted by Mr. Robert Donaldson's *Klysma*, built, as already stated, in

[1] The illustrations of plans of the yacht *Vida* are from drawings furnished to the Author by the designer, Mr. G. L. Watson of Glasgow.

The Sailing-Boat.

1895, she taking first place with 16 first, 6 second, and 1 third prizes out of 27 starts; *Vida II.* following with 7 firsts, 6 seconds, and 1 third for 19 starts.

Possibly owing to this proof that competition with *Vida II.* was not hopeless,

"Vida I."—sail-plan.

a great increase of interest in the class was evidenced in 1898, when eight new boats were built, bringing the strength of the class up to 15. The Royal Western Yacht Club, acting on behalf of a member who preferred to remain anonymous, presented a cup to be awarded to the boat having the best average for the season,

284

calculated by points according to a system laid down. This trophy was carried off by *Vida II.*, which thus resumed her accustomed place at the head of the class

From a photo by   *Mr. W. Harold Fraser, Glasgow.*

"Vida II."

with a record of 13 firsts, 6 seconds, and 4 thirds, out of 33 starts. *Espada* and *Mavis*, both new boats, designed by Mr. Wm. Fife, jun., took second and third places respectively. *Klysma* changed hands before the beginning of the season,

From a photo by   *Mr. W. Harold Fraser, Glasgow.*

"Klysma."

and occupied a less prominent position on the prize list than that to which she had attained in the previous season.

Only one new boat, by name *Lola*, was added to the class in 1899, designed by Mr. Alfred Mylne, to the order of Mr. M. H. Paterson. The *Lola* did not show to any advantage until the season was well advanced, when a new suit of sails

Clyde Class—"Lola" and others racing.

brought out her latent capabilities, but too late to enable her to take more than a modest place in the season's averages.

Though the total of boats belonging to the class was somewhat less than in the previous season, yet the average number of starters was practically the same, and the racing was every whit as keen. The donor of the aggregate cup presented in 1898 repeated his gift, the handsome trophy again falling to *Vida II.*

The championship of the class has thus been held by Mr. Wylie for six out of the seven seasons which have elapsed since the organisation of the class on its present basis. During these seasons Mr. Wylie has had but two boats, *Vida I.* and *Vida II.*, the latter having carried his flag since 1895, and during this period she has had to meet a constant succession of new boats.

The original boats of the class, such as *Vida I.* and *Pike*, were roomy enough for conversion into cruisers, and are still to the fore in that capacity, while racing more or less regularly in the handicap classes. The development of the type has, however, proceeded in the direction of decreased displacement, with consequent shallowing of the underwater body and lower freeboard, thereby reducing the head-room to such an extent that the modern boats are useless for cruising purposes.

The class has not been so strong in competitors during the season just closed (1900) as in the two previous years, the average number of starters not exceeding eight. *Vida II.* was withdrawn from the class very early in the season, and her absence did much to damp the interest taken in the racing between the boats of this class.

The *Mavis* seems to have made the best average, *Psyche II.* coming next: the latter is one of the two new 23-footers which joined the class at the commencement of the season.

THE CLYDE 17-FOOT WATER-LINE CLASS.

THIS class was re-organized by the Committee which, in 1892, arranged the constitution of the 23-foot class; the following restrictions being agreed to:—
Length over all, 19 ft.; length, water line, 17 ft.; total sail area 470 sq. ft.,

From a photo by   *Mr. W. Harold Fraser, Glasgow.*
" Hatasoo."

of which not more than three-fourths might be mainsail. No centre-boards, fin, or bulb-keels.

The class attained to some popularity, the most successful boats up to 1894 being *Harlequin, Celia,* and *Rosalind.*

A number of new boats appeared in that year, some from designs by Mr. G. L.

The Sailing-Boat.

Watson, and one by Mr. William Fife, jun. The latter boat, owned by Mr. James Bain, and named *Hatasoo*, differed considerably in design from the other boats of the class, and proved so fast that in any but very strong winds the destination of the first prize was practically a foregone conclusion.

The great success of *Hatasoo* did much to kill the class; and though racing continued till the end of the season of 1897, it attracted but little attention. Two new boats by the same designer were built to meet *Hatasoo*, but were unable to deprive her of first place, and she finished her career, which was terminated by the expiry of the class at the end of 1897, with a record of one hundred prizes.

THE CLYDE 19-FOOT WATER-LINE CLASS.

The rules governing the 17-foot Class having resulted in the development of an undesirable type of boat, a general desire was expressed that the class should be allowed to lapse. A Conference of representatives of the Clyde Yacht Clubs,

From a photo by　　　　　*Mr. W. Harold Fraser, Glasgow.*
"Ceres."

assisted by the leading designers, was therefore held at the close of the season 1896, with the object of framing a rule whereby a more wholesome type of boat might be produced, and the following restrictions were agreed upon:—

Dimensions.—Length on L.W.L. 19 ft., to be measured without crew, but with ordinary spars, sails, and gear (including anchor and chain) on board; length over all 24 ft.—no part of the boat to project abaft the stern-post, which must be a straight line; beam not to be less than 6 ft. 6 in. at the L.W.L. on a section taken at ·6 of L.W.L. from bow.

Tax on Small Displacement.—In addition to a minimum beam the following further condition shall be imposed, viz. :—

To a section of the boat, taken at ·6 of L.W.L. from bow, a straight line shall be applied in the method shown in the diagram by the line AB. The point B

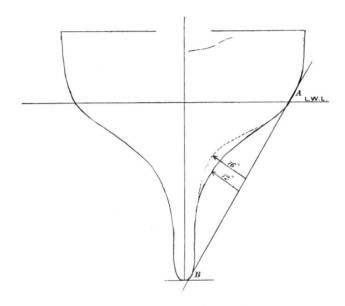

shall be taken at the extreme draft of the boat at the above section, if such draft is or exceeds 5 feet. If the draft at that point is less than 5 feet, the measurement shall be taken to an assumed draft of 5 feet.

If the *sagitta*, or distance from the line AB to the side of the boat at the deepest part of hollow, exceeds 12 inches, the excess in inches over 12 shall be applied in reduction of the sail to be carried by the boat, according to the following formula :—

$$S = (\sqrt{ M S - E^2})^2$$

In this formula :—

    S = Actual sail area to be carried by the boat.

  MS = Maximum sail area allowed for the class.

    E = Excess *sagitta* in inches over the untaxed *sagitta* allowed.

For example, taking two boats, one with 12 inches of hollow, and the other with

The Sailing-Boat.

16 inches, the former would carry the full sail area of 500 feet, while the sail area (S) of the latter would be fixed as follows :—

$$S = (\sqrt{500} - 4^2)^2$$
$$= (22 \cdot 36 - 16'')^2$$
$$= (22 \cdot 36 - 1 \cdot 33')^2$$
$$= 21 \cdot 03^2$$
$$= 442 \text{ square feet.}$$

The effect would thus be that for 4 inches' extra hollow the boat would require to sacrifice about 58 ft. of sail.

Keel—No bulbs, fin-keels, or centre-boards to be allowed.

Rig—To be a gaff mainsail and jib. The angle of the gaff not to be more than 65° from the horizontal, and the gaff not to be less than half the length of the boom.

Sail Area—Total sail area not to exceed 500 square feet, whereof the mainsail shall not exceed the proportion of ·80—spinnakers allowed, the base of the fore triangle to be measured from the goose-neck of mainboom.

Crew—To be limited to five.

The Conference agreed that the period of duration of the new class should be coincident with that of the 23-footers, viz., five years from the close of season 1897; but that it should be recognised for the season 1897 should any boats be built in time to compete.

Several boats, mostly built to the rule, took advantage of the provision as to recognition for the season 1897, and some interesting racing was the result. The honours of the class were carried off by *Verenia*, designed and built at Fairlie; second place falling to *Trebor*, designed and built by McLean, of Roseneath.

The season of 1898 brought additions to the class, the prize-list being headed by Mr. R. Clark's *Vashti*, a new boat designed by Mr. Alfred Mylne, with a record of 29 prizes out of 40 starts. *Verenia* took second place from *Zitella* by a narrow margin.

Two new boats joined the class in 1899—*Tringa*, designed by Mr. W. Fife, jun., and *Jean*, from the board of Mr. Alfred Mylne. An aggregate cup was presented to the class, to be raced for on a basis similar to that of the 23-footers, and was carried off by *Tringa*, which earned 90 points out of a possible 108. *Zitella* and *Ceres* took second and third places respectively.

The class has perhaps not become quite so popular as was expected by its promoters, although the restrictions have to a certain extent had the desired result of evolving a more capable type of boat than the superseded 17-footers. It is regrettable that the rules were not framed to allow of the boats being built with counters, as their appearance would have been much improved thereby, while they would have also benefited in speed. The objectionable box-counter might have been avoided by a simple restriction.

When the season of 1900 opened, it was found that the class had been considerably augmented, no fewer than five new boats having been built to the new restrictions, one of these, the *Valmai* (Mr. Robt. Clark), making the best record for the season's racing, *Tringa*, the previous year's champion, occupying a comparatively obscure position in this year's results.

The *Valmai*, which heads the list with 31 prizes, is also the winner of the points competition of her class, and her prizes include the Clyde Corinthian (No. 2) Tarbet Cup. The *Valmai* was from a design by Mr. Alfred Mylne. *Memsahib*, which ranks second in the class, with 24 wins, is also a Mylne boat.

THE CLYDE 20-TON ONE-DESIGN CLASS.

THIS is a new class (1899); it was the outcome of a desire on the part of several owners to have a boat of medium size, speedy, strongly built, and with good cruising accommodation. This combination being unattainable under the Y.R.A. rules, it was necessary to build to other restrictions, and the principle of a one-design class was adopted. Plans submitted to the intending owners by Mr. Alfred Mylne were accepted, and commissions at once issued for the building of five boats to those lines. The dimensions are—Length over all, 50 ft.; length on L.W.L., 35 ft.; beam, 11 ft.; draught, 8 ft.; and ballast, 10 tons of lead on the keel. They are fine, roomy, cruising boats, with six feet headroom in the saloon amidships. They are rigged as pole-masted cutters, and they carry 1,700 sq. ft.

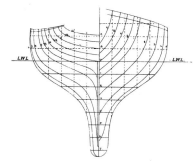

Clyde 20-ton Class (mid-section).

of canvas, of which the mainsail takes 900 sq. ft., the fore-triangle 575 sq. ft., and the topsail 225 sq. ft.

The illustrations are from drawings kindly furnished by the designer, Mr. Alfred Mylne.

When the yachts made their appearance at the opening matches of the season of 1899 their attractive appearance, symmetrical outline, and internal accommodation were the subject of general approbation, while their performances in these their first races showed that they also possessed an excellent turn of speed. The sailing

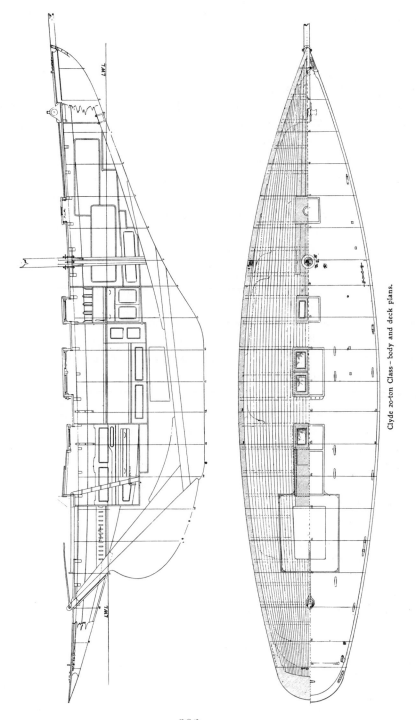

Clyde 20-ton Class – body and deck plans.

The One-Design and Restricted Classes.

matches throughout the season were very keenly contested, with the results appearing by the following table, which gives the class-racing only:—

	Name.	Owner.	Starts.	Prizes.		Total.
				First.	Second.	
1	*Noyra*	Mr. M. Greenlees.....................	36	10	8	18
2	*Tigris*.....................	Mr. T. Wotherspoon	31	8	10	18
3	*Avalon*	Mr. C. MacIver	36	8	8	16
4	*Snarleyyow*....................	Mr. A. F. MacLaren	29	6	3	9
5	*Vagrant* [1]	Mr. Gubbins.....................	16	6	2	8

[1] *Vagrant* was an absentee from the Clyde during a considerable part of the season.

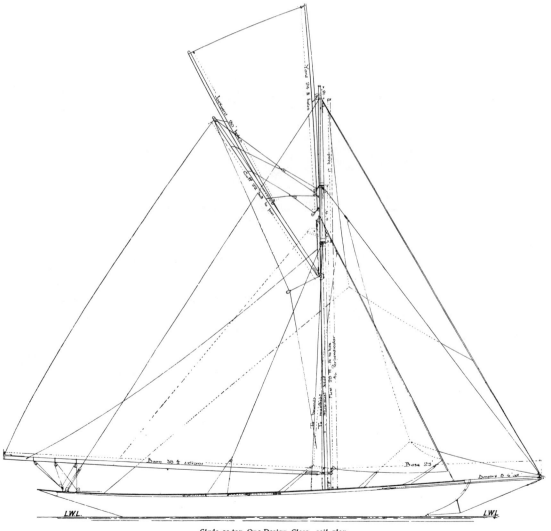

Clyde 20-ton One-Design Class—sail plan.

The Sailing-Boat.

The class, though primarily a local one, did not confine its racing to home waters, but at the close of the 'Clyde Fortnight' proceeded to Belfast Lough and Dublin Bay, and there took part in the regattas of the local clubs. The yachts have given great satisfaction, and have amply fulfilled their owners' expectations.

In the season of 1900, yacht-racing on the Clyde during the 'Clyde Fortnight' fell flat owing to the absence of most of the larger class of racing-yachts. It was,

From a photo by   **"Noyra."**   *Mr. W. Harold Fraser, Glasgow.*

therefore, left to those of the smaller classes to fill the gaps in the programme, and of these the One-Design 20-ton boats of the new class provided some of the most interesting and keenly contested matches of the season; and in the result it was found that *Avalon* was foremost in points of competition, *Noyra* being second and *Vagrant* third. *Rosemary*, a new boat built at Dumbarton, was, at the close of the racing, found at the bottom of the list. Although *Avalon* takes the aggregate points cup, *Noyra* heads the list of the class in prizes, and *Snarleyyow* is a good second in that respect.

The One-Design and Restricted Classes.

CLYDE ONE-DESIGN BOATS OF THE INNELLAN CORINTHIAN YACHT CLUB.

THIS Club was started in the winter of 1895 with the object of forming a class of small boats at a moderate cost. It was at first intended that all the boats should

From a photo by   *Mr. W. Harold Fraser, Glasgow.*
Start of "Innellan"—O.D. Class.

be of one design, but there being some dissension as to type, a division took place, with the result that a number of the boats were built to plans by Messrs. J. & H. M. Paterson, of Greenock, and almost as many to a different model by Ninian, of Largs.

From a photo by   *Mr. W. Harold Fraser, Glasgow.*
"Lola" (Innellan Class).

The Sailing-Boat.

There were thus two types of One-Design boats carrying the burgee of the Club, in all numbering twenty. Very keen racing ensued, the records of the seasons showing Mr. Herbert Brown's *Lola* to have the best average with 19 first, 6 second, and 1 third prizes for 34 starts. *Lola* is one of the Largs-built boats, which have proved fast and able little ships. They are clincher built, and of the following dimensions :—Length over all, 17 ft. ; length water-line, 15 ft. ; beam, 6 ft. 4 in. ; draft, 3 ft.

The other type was from a design by Messrs. J. and H. M. Paterson, of Greenock, who in preparing the design were required to keep in view the essential conditions that the boats were to be cheap, fast, and safe.

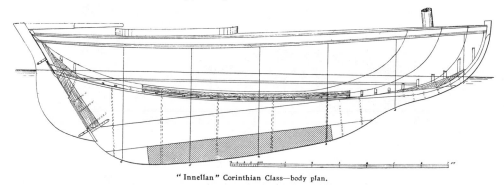

"Innellan" Corinthian Class—body plan.

The original dimensions were, after their first season, slightly extended, they were fitted with bowsprits, their keels lowered, and the sail area increased from 150 to 200 sq. ft. The following are, therefore, the amended dimensions :—Length over all, 17 ft. ; length on load water-line, 15 ft. 4 in. ; beam, 5 ft. 3 in. ; draft, 3 ft. 6 in. ; sail area, 200 sq. ft. ; lead on keel, $10\frac{1}{4}$ cwt. They are decked all over with the exception of the cockpit, the narrowest part of the deck being $10\frac{1}{2}$ in. The boats are clincher built, of larch and yellow pine on elm frames, and are copper-fastened throughout.

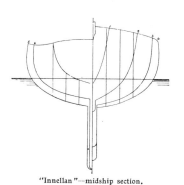

"Innellan"—midship section.

The combined fleet of the class became so numerous that it was found necessary to constitute two sections in order to avoid crowding at the sailing-matches—No. 1, or the Largs section, comprising 12 boats ; No. 2, or the Gourock section, comprising 14.

The illustrations are from drawings kindly sent by Messrs. Paterson, and show the form of hull, with midship section and sail plan.

"Innellan" Corinthian One-Design Class—sail plan.

THE TAY "SEABIRD," 18 ft. L. R. ONE-DESIGN CLASS.

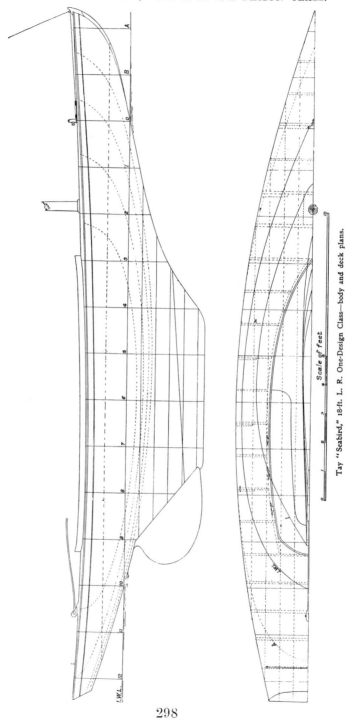

Tay "Seabird," 18-ft. L. R. One-Design Class—body and deck plans.

Scale of feet

The One-Design and Restricted Classes.

At the half-yearly meeting of the members of the Royal Tay Yacht Club, held on the 31st March, 1898, it was decided to form a One-Design Class of 18 ft. linear raters, from a design by Mr. Alfred Mylne, of Glasgow, the boats to be known as the 'Seabird Class.' These boats were all built by Messrs. Gourlay Bros. & Co., Ltd., at Dundee, and are sloop rigged, the gaff-mainsail having Turner's patent boom-reefing gear.

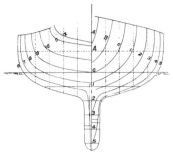

Tay Class, 18-ft. Linear Rater—midship section.

They have proved to be capital little boats, fast, weatherly, and comfortable, and have afforded excellent sport. The racing has been very close, *Osprey* having the best record over the two seasons they have been in commission, with 7 first and 6 second prizes out of

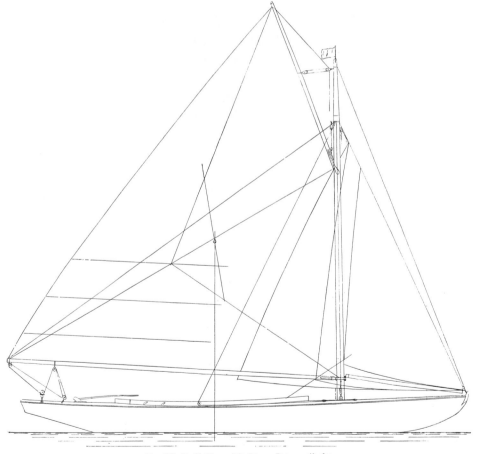

Tay "Seabird" Class, 18-ft. Linear Rater—sail plan.

15 starts. The illustrations on pages 298–9 are from drawings kindly furnished by Mr. Alfred Mylne, the designer, from which it will be seen that they are boats of great stability and powerful capacity.

Tay O. D. Class.

THE HOLY LOCH SAILING CLUB ONE-DESIGN CLASS.

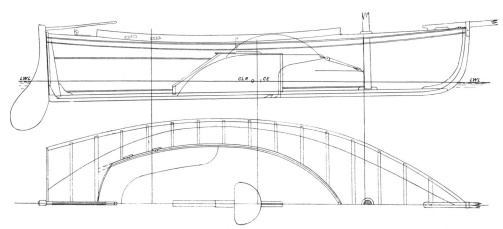

Holy Loch O. D. Class—body and deck plans.

The One-Design and Restricted Classes.

THE Holy Loch O. D. Class was founded in the early part of the year 1898, when, at the Spring Meeting of the Sailing Club, it was arranged that a special class of centre-board sailing-boats, from a design by Mr. Alfred Mylne, should be built, and adopted by the Club as a One-Design Class. The following are the dimensions:—Length over all, 16 ft. 6 in.; length on L.W.L., 16 ft.; beam, 6 ft. 6 in.; beam at L.W.L., 6 ft.;

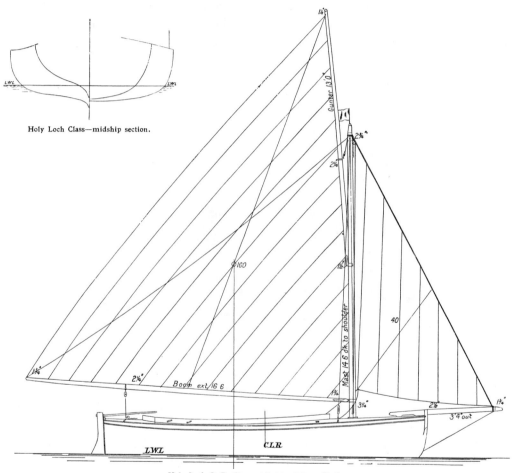

Holy Loch Class—midship section.

Holy Loch O. D. Class, 16 ft. 6 in. C.B.—sail plan.

freeboard, 1 ft. 6 in.; lead ballast, 2 cwt. (inside); sail area, 200 sq. ft., of which main-sail, 160 sq. ft., foresail, 40 sq. ft.; the centre-board to be of steel. All the boats to be built from the same design and frames, and the crews to be limited to three hands for each boat.

The Sailing-Boat.

BELFAST LOUGH, the northern yachting centre of Ireland, the home of the Royal Ulster Yacht Club, of which the Marquis of Dufferin and Ava is Commodore, is admirably adapted for boat-sailing and yacht-racing; a fine open sheet of water with comparative freedom from currents inside the 'Heads' and Orlock Point.

From a photo by   *Mr. R. E. Workman, Belfast.*

Start of Class I.

The Harbour of Carrickfergus affords the safest anchorage inside the Lough, but its entrance shallows at low water to only a few feet, hence limiting the draft of vessels navigating its waters to 6 ft. 3 ins.

At a recent meeting of the members of the Royal Ulster Yacht Club, the noble Commodore observed that 'thirty years ago there was scarcely a pleasure-sail upon their lovely Lough, but now every form of maritime diversion is represented by canoeing, single-handed boat sailing, by yacht-racing and cruising.'

The noble Marquis has all his lifetime been a staunch supporter of yachting and boat-sailing, always his favourite recreation, and it was a happy reminiscence, after many years' absence abroad on his diplomatic duties, to find him again presiding at the annual gathering of the Royal Ulster Yacht Club and taking a keen and lively interest in the sailing-matches of the One-Design Classes.

The One-Design and Restricted Classes.

The new Club House of the Royal Ulster Yacht Club at Bangor, which was formally opened by the Commodore in April, 1899, is a fine substantial building, a worthy memorial of the popularity to which yachting and boat-sailing have attained in those parts, and of the success and prosperity of the Club under the presidency of the noble Commodore.

During the last few years great strides have been made in yacht-racing under the auspices of the members of the various Yacht and Sailing Clubs in the neighbourhood of the Belfast Lough, mainly due to the formation of the One-Design Classes.

From a photo by   Mr. R. E. Workman, Belfast.
"Flamingo" and "Widgeon" Racing.

Prior to the year 1897 the idea of a One-Design Class had been acted upon by the Bangor Corinthian Sailing Club (co. Down), which had four $2\frac{1}{2}$ raters (*Shibbeal I.* type), by Fife, in 1889; four 18-footers L.W.L. (*Ulah* type), by Fife, in 1891; five 18-footers L.W.L. (*Uarda* type), by G. L. Watson, in 1893; and six 15-foot C.B. 'Tadpoles' (*Fidget* type), by Vincent Craig, in 1896.

These were all in their way successful boats, and fine racing among themselves was enjoyed during the years they were in commission.

The present Belfast Lough One-Design Classes were started with the utmost care and forethought, all the experience gained in former years being applied to ensure that the cost of the boats should meet the purse of the majority; their build combine as far as possible the qualities of a racer with the comforts of a cruiser; and, in the junior classes, special safety of construction for the passages between the local yachting centres such as Larne, Donaghadee, Ballywalter, Ardglass, Strangford

The Sailing-Boat.

Lough, &c., a stretch of very forbidding coast-line, where the easterly winds and the strong currents of the tides, with the attendant choppy seas, necessitate an extra streak of freeboard.

There being six clubs in the Lough, it was determined that owners should be members of at least one of them, and that Committees should be formed of all the

" Merle" (Class I.).

owners in each class, thus ensuring that every boat received equal representation as regards the formation of the sailing bye-laws, whilst the general rules were to be similar for and to strictly govern all classes irrespectively that might be formed.

This enabled one secretary to undertake the complete management and control of plans, specifications, &c., and educated, as it were, owners in the smaller classes to a method of harmonious working which would be in every respect similar in the event of their becoming possessed of one of the larger class boats at a future date.

CLASS I. OF THE BELFAST LOUGH ONE-DESIGN CLASSES.

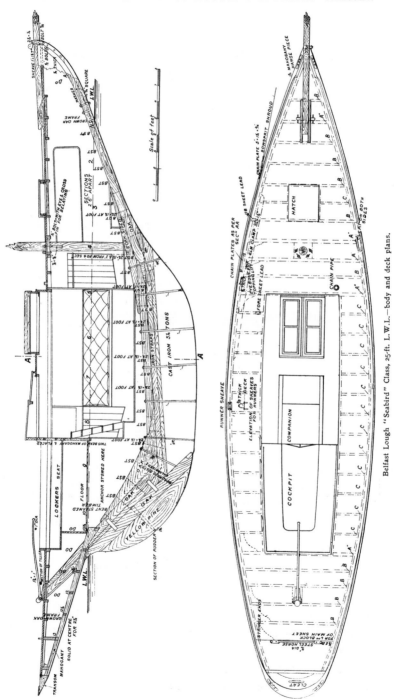

Belfast Lough "Seabird" Class, 25-ft. L.W.L.—body and deck plans.

The Sailing-Boat.

Class I. The boats of this class were designed by Mr. W. Fife, jun., of Fairlie, and are known as the 'Sea-bird Class,' each boat being named after a sea-bird, as *Flamingo, Halcyon, Merle, Tern, Whimbrel,* and *Widgeon.*

The dimensions and other particulars of the boats of this class are :—Length

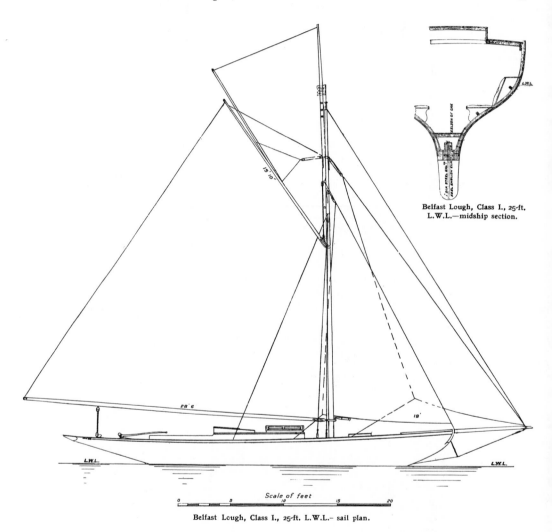

Belfast Lough, Class I., 25-ft.
L.W.L.—midship section.

Belfast Lough, Class I., 25-ft. L.W.L.– sail plan.

over all, 37 ft. 3 in. ; length on L.W.L., 25 ft. ; beam, 8 ft. 8 in. ; draft, 6 ft. 3 in. ; head-room under beam of coach roof, 5 ft. 9 in. ; sail area, 848 sq. ft. ; tonnage, Thames measurement, 9 tons ; registered tonnage, 5·80 ; weight of cast-iron keel, 3 tons 5 cwt. ; coach roof, skylight, full counter, flat keel ; all deck fittings of teak.

Cutter-rig, Sails—main-sail (laced foot 3 battens), top-sail, foresail, 1st jib, 2nd jib, spitfire jib, balloon-jib, balloon-foresail, spinnaker, and trysail.   Builder, J. Hilditch, Carrickfergus.

Nine boats were built to Class I.   The guiding principle in the design and construction of the boats of this class was comfort, not speed ; for the fact had been grasped at the outset that a class of boats all of the same design would race only among themselves, and that therefore the chance of one or more being a few minutes slower than other boats in making a course mattered little when the offset was 5 ft. 9 in. head-room under beams of coach roof, plenty of freeboard, and generally an all-round comfortable craft that made such passages as crossing to the Clyde or English waters a pleasant cruise.

CLASS II. BELFAST LOUGH ONE-DESIGN CLASSES.

Class II. of the Belfast Lough O. D. Classes are also from a design by Mr. W. Fife, jun.   These are beautifully constructed boats, and were, in fact, designed before Class I., which is of similar model ; they have therefore much the same appearance in hull ; but the Class II. boats are a trifle finer in the lines, and not so full-bodied

From a photo by   *Mr. R. E. Workman, Belfast.*

proportionately.   Their dimensions and other particulars are as under :—Length over all, 24 ft. ; length L.W.L., 15 ft. ; beam, 6 ft. 2 in. ; draft, 3 ft. 6 in. ; cast-iron keel, weight 15½ cwt.; sail area, 354·51 sq. ft. ; rig as per drawing, p. 309, main-sail (laced foot 3 battens), 1st jib, 2nd jib, balloon jib, and spinnaker ; decked, cockpit 8 ft.

by 4 ft. 6 in., full counter, flat keel; all fittings teak. Builders of five, A. Hutchinson & Co.; of two, John Hilditch; of two, P. McKeown.

To those who might desire to follow such a type of boat it is suggested that a little more length on the water-line—say, 2 ft.—and less of a cut-away at the forestep,

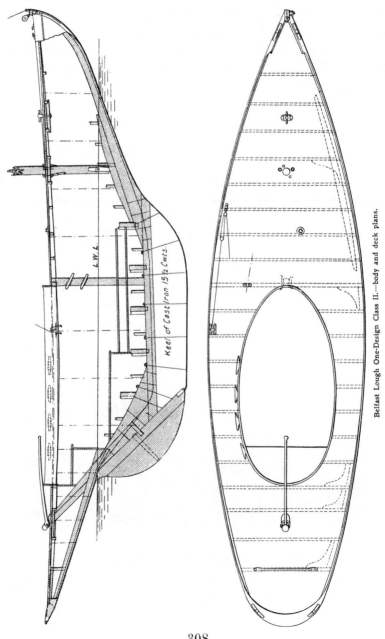

Belfast Lough One-Design Class II.—body and deck plans.

would insure their being less fidgety to handle ; they are too quick in stays, do not carry on enough when going about in bad weather, consequently, unless handled with great care, they are apt to heel over rather too much when meeting the wind on a new tack, the result of having lost way on coming about. The illustration on page 149, of the boat *Sheelah* in a squall is one of the Belfast Lough One-Design Class II.

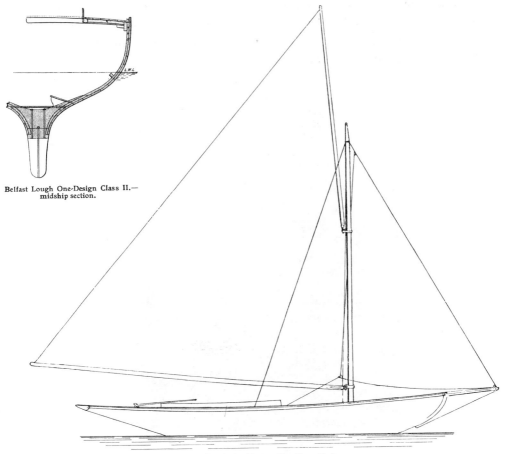

Belfast Lough One-Design Class II.—
midship section.

Belfast Lough One-Design Class II.—sail plan.

CLASS III. BELFAST LOUGH ONE-DESIGN CLASSES.

Class III. of the Belfast Lough O. D. Classes. These are centre-board boats, designed by Mr. Linton Hope, and are termed 'Jewels,' each of the boats being named after some precious stone. Thus they have *Amethyst, Beryl, Coral, Emerald, Iolite, Opal, Ruby, Sapphire, Pearl, and Peridot.*

The Sailing-Boat.

The dimensions, &c., of the boats of this class are:—Length over all, 24 ft.; length on L.W.L., 17 ft.; beam, 6 ft. 6 in.; draft, centre board up, 18 in.; draft, centre board down, 5 ft. 6 in.; weight of centre board, 3 cwt.; inside ballast, 15 cwt.; sail area, 276 square feet. Decked, cockpit, full counter. Builder, Wm. Roberts, Chester.

Owing to the fact that nearly all the owners in Class III. use Cultra as an anchorage, where the tide ebbs far out on a shallow beach, these boats were fitted with centre-boards dropping through a dead-wood keel, iron shod, making it convenient for hauling them up. They are a very popular class, inexpensive, and therefore within the reach of most amateur boat-owners.

From a photo by   Mr. J. McCleery.
"Opal," Belfast Lough "Jewel" Class.

With regard to the three classes above described of the Belfast Lough One-Design Boats, nine were in the first instance built to Class I., nine to Class II., and ten to Class III.; and thus an immediate increase of twenty-eight boats of modern design were classed and arranged in suitable groups, thereby ensuring a well-filled race at every regatta and club-match in the Lough and neighbouring waters throughout the season. And every year since, new boats have been built in each class, so that the Belfast Lough One-Design Classes now form a somewhat numerous fleet.

Belfast Lough, Class III., 17-ft. L.W.L., "Jewel" Class.

311

BELFAST LOUGH NEW ONE-DESIGN CLASS.

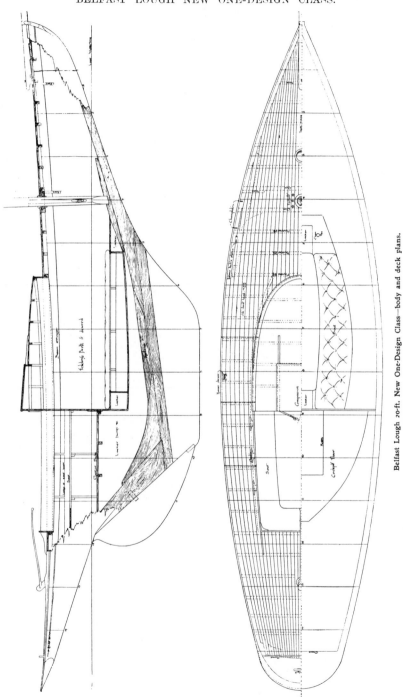

Belfast Lough 20-ft. New One-Design Class—body and deck plans.

The One-Design and Restricted Classes.

A NEW and additional class has recently (1899) been added to the Belfast Lough One-Design Classes. The boats for the new class are from a design by Mr. Alfred Mylne, of Glasgow, and are 30 ft. over all; 20 feet on the L.W.L.; 7 ft. 6 ins. beam, and 5 ft. draft, with iron keels $1\frac{3}{4}$ tons; sail area, 550 sq. ft.

They are therefore a middle class, coming between Classes I. and II., above described.

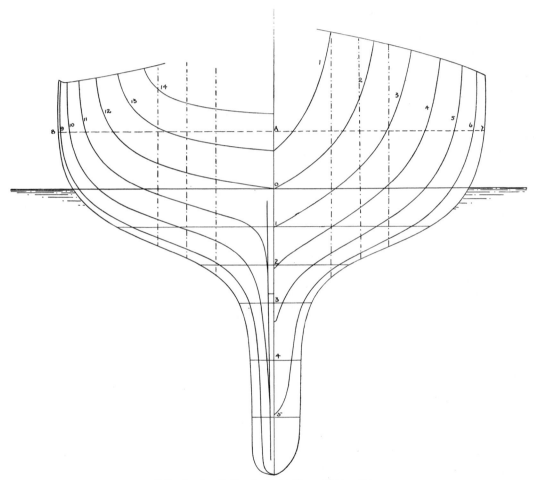

Belfast Lough 20 ft. New One-Design Class—midship section.

The boats are decked all over, with the exception of the cock-pit, the fore part of which is 'coach-roofed,' with good cabin accommodation for two.

This makes five classes of the Belfast Lough One-Design Boats, ranging from the 25-footers before mentioned down to the diminutive but interesting little boats termed the *Insect* Class.

The Sailing-Boat.

The boats of the New Class are, according to the old rating, what would be termed 2·5 raters.

The rig is mainsail and foresail only.

It will be seen from the particulars stated and plans of the design that they are a

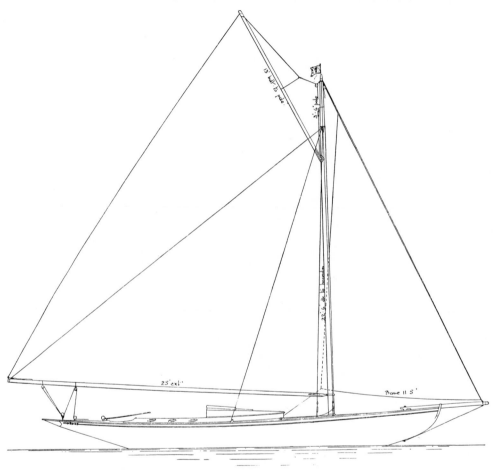

Belfast Lough 20 ft. New One-Design Class—sail plan.

deep-bodied powerful type of boat, with cabin accommodation aboard such as is not usually found (in these days of fin and bulb-keelers) aboard yachts of such a tonnage, except in some of the most approved of the One-Design Classes, as Class I. of the Belfast Lough One-Design boats.

The One-Design and Restricted Classes.

THE ULSTER SAILING CLUB "INSECT" CLASS.

THIS is a class of small open sailing-boats, each named after an insect. These are centre-board boats, with a dagger plate drop-keel, from a design by Mr. W. M. Inglis of the Ulster Sailing Club.

From a photo by   *Mr. R. E. Workman, Belfast.*

Ulster "Insect" Class—"Moth" and "Hornet."

There are 12 boats in this class. Their dimensions are 14 ft. by 5 ft., with a sail area of 117 sq. ft. all in one sail, as shown in the illustration above.

THE DUBLIN BAY 25-FOOTERS.

THE DUBLIN BAY "A Class" (or 25-footers) are a One-Design Class established at Kingstown in the year 1898 by the Dublin Bay Sailing Club. The boats are from designs by Mr. W. Fife, jun., and their principal dimensions are—Length over all, 38 ft. 6 ins.; length (load water-line), 25 ft.; beam, 8 ft. 6 ins.; draft, 6 ft. 3 ins.; sail area, 800 sq. ft.; lead on keel, 3 tons 5 cwts.

They are practically similar to the Belfast Lough One-Design Boats, Class I., but so far only as regards the particulars above stated. The Belfast Lough Boats were undoubtedly also designed by Mr. W. Fife, junr.; but the Dublin Bay boats differ from them in several very important features. In the first place, the new Dublin Bay Class have lead ballast on their keels, whilst those of Belfast Lough have iron; in the next place, the Dublin Bay boats have less displacement, consequently less interior accommodation; the Dublin Bay boats have a somewhat finer midship section, the result of less displacement; and further, the Dublin Bay boats were far more costly to build than the Belfast Lough boats.

THE WATER WAGS.

KINGSTOWN HARBOUR, the home of the Water Wags, is also the headquarters of the Royal Alfred Yacht Club, the Royal St. George's, the Royal Irish, and some other minor boat-sailing clubs. The Harbour is well adapted for boat-sailing and yachting, affording a safe anchorage, with good depth of water; and is accessible at all times of tide, even at low-water the depth being 14 or 15 ft.

The Water Wags are the earliest of the One-Design Classes, dating as far back as the year 1878. The origin of the design is somewhat interesting. Tradition says that a youthful boat-sailor of Shankill, Co. Dublin, having become possessed of a Norway Praäm, conceived the idea of converting his frail but strongly-built little craft into a centre-board sailing-boat; and having obtained a piece of old iron boiler-plate, he contrived to make out of it a small revolving keel, which, by way of experiment, he fitted to the bottom of his Praäm amidships, contriving it so that on beaching his boat on the sands at Shankill, the plate (which weighed nearly a cwt.) could be lifted and taken out of the boat, which was then hauled up on the beach as before. The experiment proved a remarkable success, and he named his boat the *Cemiostama*. He rigged her generously with a good-sized sail of lug-like shape, very much the same as the present rig of the succeeding generation of Water Wags. The *Cemiostama* sailed splendidly, and could lay a course close to the wind, carrying her sail in a stiff breeze right gallantly, to the surprise and admiration of the boat-sailing fraternity of would-be Water Wags. It was found that the boiler-plate keel answered the purpose of ballast as well as that of enabling the boat to hold her course and be worked to windward without making leeway, and when put about she responded to her helm as faithfully as if turning on a pivot; and on beaching her the revolving keel was raised, and she rode over the surf and ran in on to the beach in a few inches of surf water, which, on receding, left her stranded on the beach on her flat, round-shaped bottom in a perfectly upright position.

The success of the *Cemiostama* as an experimental sailing-boat immediately led to the building of several other centre-board boats (not Praäms), but all open sailing-boats 13 ft. in length, with 4 ft. 10 in. beam, each carrying the same extent of sail. The boats proved such excellent little sea-boats, and so well adapted to the purpose of cruising along the coast and beaching, that in 1887 an association was formed, and the droll name given to it of the 'Water Wag Association,' the members consisting chiefly of youths (amateur boat sailors); but gradually the Association grew in importance, match-sailing became general among them, and the Water Wags migrated to Kingstown Harbour. In their new quarters the Association has flourished beyond all anticipation; and sailing matches have been got up for them at all the local regattas in the neighbourhood, the popularity of which is abundantly testified by the number of special prizes that are offered for competition as an inducement to the Water Wags to come and sail for them.

The Water Wags of this, the old type, had a fleet of upwards of 20 boats, all of the same design and sail-spread; and the skill with which they were managed, the closeness of the contests, and the excitement and amusement they have afforded from time to time have been much appreciated by the throngs of spectators who come to see the sports of the Water Wags.

The limitations of a Water Wag boat of the old class are—that her length over all shall not exceed 13 ft., with beam 4 ft. 10 ins., and that she shall be built according to the drawings and specifications of the Water Wag Club. Among which are the stipulations that the mast, from top of keel to truck, shall not exceed 13 ft., and shall not be placed farther aft than 21 ins. from the outer side of the stem. That the pivot of the centre-plate shall be permanently fixed in position in the keel, and no portion of the plate when fully hauled up shall project below the keel-band. The centre-plate to be of steel or galvanised iron $\frac{3}{16}$ in. thick; the exposed area cut exactly to the Club model, which contains $2\frac{1}{2}$ superficial ft.; the front edge of the plate, when fully lowered, shall be vertical, and be 5 ft. 3 ins. from the outside of stem.

It will thus be seen that every precaution was taken to have all the boats identical in every respect, so that their success in match-sailing depended mainly on the skill with which they were handled.

The New Class of Water Wags.—For several years past a project has been on foot amongst the Water Wags for the introduction of a larger type of boat, but it was not until the latter part of the year 1899 that the proposal was carried; it was then resolved that a new type of boat be adopted for the Water Wag Club, from a design by Mr. J. E. Doyle, of Kingstown (the designer of the Colleens), the new boats to be 14 ft. 3 ins. in length (the extra 3 ins. to be utilised in giving the boats a raked transom) by 5 ft. 6 ins. beam; and the sail area 110 sq. ft.; the rig a lugsail and foresail.

Through the courtesy of Mr. J. B. Stephens the author is enabled to give illustrations of the form and design of the new class of Water Wags, together with sail plan,

The Sailing-Boat.

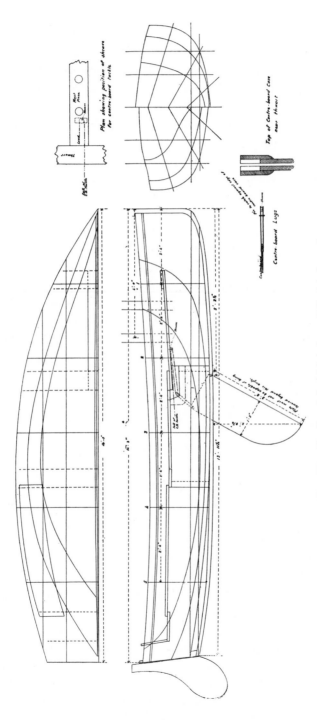

Water Wags: New Class—body and deck plans, midship and other sections.

dimensions, and other particulars, as approved at a general meeting of the Water Wags held on the 31st January, 1900. It will be seen from the dimensions stated that the boats of the new class, whilst retaining all the characteristics of the old class, are larger, being longer and broader than the others, and enabled to carry larger sails, and at the same time have greater power as sea-boats.

The requirements with regard to the sails for the new design are—That the mainsail (lugsail) be loose-footed of 11-in. cloths, material to weigh $5\frac{3}{4}$ ozs. per square yard,

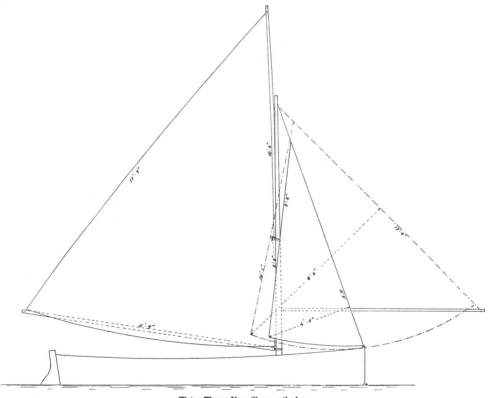

Water Wags : New Class—sail plan.

and be of quality as per sample deposited with Hon. Secretary. Round in foot not to exceed 12 ins. No battens allowed.

The foresail to be of same material as the lugsail.

The spinnaker to be of 34-in. cloths and of material weighing $3\frac{1}{2}$ ozs. per square yard, and of quality as per sample deposited with Hon. Secretary. Round in foot not to exceed 15 ins.

Dimensions shown on sail plan for luff, head and foot of lugsail are the maximum lengths to which the sail can be pulled out on the spars.

319

The dimensions shown for foresail and spinnaker are those which the sails are to hold when new.

Twelve boats were built in the early part of the year 1900 by McKeown, of Belfast, from Mr. J. E. Doyle's new design, for members of the Water Wag Club, and were afterwards rigged in accordance with the requirements above stated. The new boats appear to have given great satisfaction to the owners. Several matches were sailed by them during the season, and the competition among them was keen and spirited, and the excitement and interest taken in the contests were as full and complete as in the merry matches of the past.

At the close of the season it was found that *Kelpie* headed the list with six wins, *San Toy* being a good second with five wins.

THE MERMAIDS.

ANOTHER class of boat was adopted by the Dublin Bay Sailing Club of similar design to that of the Water Wags, but larger, being 18 ft. in length with 6-ft. beam, entirely open boats with centre-board, and sailed without ballast, but allowed to carry a crew of three or four persons, who act the part of 'live ballast,' shifting themselves to windward on every tack.

But as the 'Mermaids' are now an extinct class, being superseded by a new class, called 'Colleens,' it will be needless to add any further particulars regarding them.

THE "DRÒLEEN" ONE-DESIGN CLASS.

THE 'Dròleens' are a One-Design Dinghy Class of boats of the Bray Sailing Club, adopted as such in the year 1897, the fleet then consisting of seven boats. Their class-name 'Dròleens' is derived from the Irish *Dròlin*—a Wren.

The boats were designed by Mr. W. Ogilvy, of Dublin and Bray, who is also a member of the Bray Sailing Club, and kindly sent the author the drawing and photo from which the illustrations have been made.

Their dimensions are:—Length over all, 12 ft.; beam, 6 ft. They are fitted with a metal centre-board (or rather revolving-keel) of $\frac{3}{16}$-in. steel.

The boats are well and strongly built, according to specifications, by Foley, of Ringsand.

The rig of the 'Dròleens' is a single lug-sail containing 100 sq. ft. of yacht cotton, the sail being cut so as to stand almost perpendicular at the head when fairly set. They also carry a spinnaker, containing 46 sq. ft. of double warp calico, for running before the wind, as shown in the illustration below.

As to the centre-plate revolving-keel, it is fitted so as to work in a slot 2 ft. 3 in.

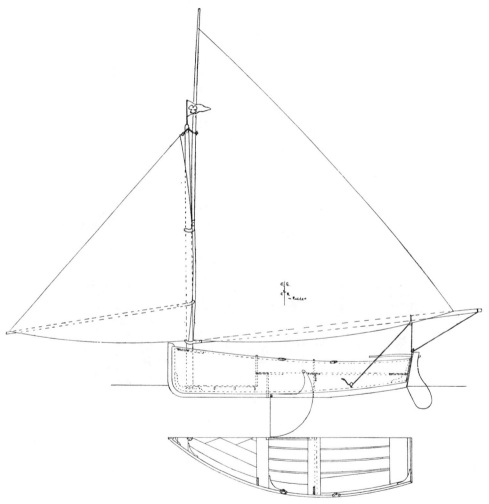

"Dröleen" Class—body and sail plans.

in length, which allows the plate an exposed area, when let down, of 3·67 sq. ft. The pin on which it works is fitted to the keel on the outside of the planking. The plate becomes locked and cannot unship when lowered out of the horizontal position: it rises readily to every obstruction on touching the ground under water, and can be unshipped and lifted out when required; and may then be stowed away conveniently on the bow sheets.

The *Dròleens* are not fitted with purchases of any kind.

From a photo by   "Dròleen" Class Boat.   *Mr. A. L. Doran, Bray.*

The sail is hoisted by aid of a double halliard, which has a block and single fall in the bight, which is forward.

These boats are sometimes exposed to very rough usage; but although strongly built can be lifted, when ashore, by two men.

When racing, the crew is limited to two persons; but they are capable of carrying five safely. They are a very handy class of small sailing-boat for single-handed management; and are of so safe and sturdy a form that they can carry their whole sail, without reefing, in almost any weather that an open boat can be out in. Their best point of sailing is tacking to windward with plenty of wind and sea, which they not infrequently encounter off the coast of Bray and neighbouring waters.

The One-Design and Restricted Classes.

THE CORK HARBOUR ONE-DESIGN CLASS.

THIS is a class of One-Design Boats originating with members of the Royal Munster Yacht Club. The design is by Mr. W. Fife, jun., of Fairlee. The class was adopted at the close of the season 1895, and at the opening of that of 1896 six of the boats were ready and put in an appearance at the sailing matches

Cork Harbour One-Design Class—sail-plan.

of the Club; several boats have since been added to the class, which now comprises a somewhat numerous fleet. The boats of the class are described as one-raters, and all are cutter rigged. The illustration of sail-plan is from a tracing sent by

The Sailing-Boat.

the Honorary Secretary of the Royal Munster Yacht Club, who also sent the photo from which the reproduction has been made; but the author regrets that he has no particulars as to the dimensions and other details, nor any drawings of the body-plan and midship section. The description is therefore incomplete in those respects. The boats are all strongly built and are capable sea-boats, besides which

Cork Harbour One-Design Class.

they are, undoubtedly, very fast in a breeze. This has been clearly demonstrated when they were started on a 20-mile course, exactly half-an-hour after a fleet of five-raters had been sent off on the same course in a strong wind and open sea, when the O.-D. boats covered the distance in less than five minutes under the time of the larger class. The boat named *Little Devil* (Mr. J. H. Gubbins) has perhaps the best claim to the title of champion of the fleet, but *Maureen*, *Minx*, *Querida* and *Elsie* are close rivals.

The class appears to have been very successful from the first, and has become exceedingly popular, there being races among them in Cork Harbour and neighbourhood nearly every week in the season ; and at the close of their first season (1896) each boat was enabled to display her string of winning flags ; and it appears that nowhere in any of the centres where One-Design Classes have been established are honours more equally distributed than in the O.-D. Class of Cork Harbour. In many of the matches they sailed, although over lengthy courses, there was rarely (except in calms) at the finish more than two or three minutes between the first and last of the fleet.

In the matches sailed by these boats in the season of 1900, for prizes given by the Royal Cork Yacht Club, *Little Devil* was the winner ; *Elsie* (Mr. A. N. S. Crawford) taking second prize. The competition between the boats of this class in the numerous matches they sailed in the past season appears to have been as keen and spirited as ever, and the popularity of the class is in nowise diminished.

THE HOWTH SAILING CLUB ONE-DESIGN CLASS.

THE members of the Howth Sailing Club, following the example set them in the season of 1897 by the Belfast Lough Sailing Clubs, have instituted a One-Design Class of boats of similar proportions to those of Class II. of the Belfast Lough ; the intention being that the class should take the place of the Half-Rater Class now abandoned. The dimensions of the Howth One-Design Class are :—Length over all, 22 ft. 8 in. ; length on water-line, 17 ft. ; beam, 6 ft. ; draft, 3 ft. 3 in. The boats are sloop rigged ; the sails consisting of main-sail, fore-sail and top-sail ; and although the boats are each fitted with a bowsprit extending 2 ft. 10 in. beyond the stem (being sloop-rigged) they do not carry a jib. The boats of this class are decked over and have bows similar in form to those of the local craft, but they are built without counters, or rather they have what are termed " box counters," which give them a somewhat ungainly appearance ; but, notwithstanding, they are very capable little craft, fairly good sea-boats, and smart and handy in " coming-about."

The trial match of this One-Design Class was sailed on the 4th of May, 1898, in a steady north-westerly breeze, over a triangular course, thrice round ; the course thus comprising a total distance of 6 knots. An excellent start was effected, and a spirited race ensued throughout the entire contest, but the boat *Leila*

(C. A. V. Yeo) having obtained the lead on the second round maintained it to the finish, and was declared the winner in a fair and keenly contested race.

END OF PART V.

PART VI.

———

FISHING AND SHOOTING BOATS.

SINCE the great International Fisheries Exhibition at Kensington in the year 1883, sea-fishing as a craft has made enormous strides. The bringing together and exhibition of the arts and devices employed for the capture of the various kinds of food fish in different parts of the world gave an impetus to the craft of sea-fishing such as never before occurred.

The Exhibition was a mutual revelation to the general fraternity of fishermen of the secrets of their craft, the various kinds of boats, nets, tackle, trawls, hooks, baits, and other appliances in use in different seas and at different fishing localities not only within the British Dominions, but in many other parts of the world. The appliances exhibited were as numerous and remarkable as they were various and ingenious, including many that were new and unknown to the generality of fishermen ; and among those that were known, some of a vastly improved and modernised type.

It would, therefore, be strange indeed if among the throngs of practical fishermen from every part of the British Islands who visited that Exhibition and viewed and examined those various appliances, there were not many craftsmen who carried away with them some useful wrinkles from among the numerous and ingenious devices there displayed as to the capture of the finny occupants of the seas by fishermen in places remote as well as near to our own fishing industries.

Boats and tackle of the most ancient and primitive type figured side by side with those of the most modern and improved ; and the result has been an all-round advancement in the craft of sea and river fishing, as well as in the design and construction of fishing-boats and fishing-gear of every kind.

Since that great Industrial Exhibition the various arts of sea-fishing have been greatly simplified and extended, with the result that the toils of the fishermen have been considerably lightened, and their successes steadily but surely increased. But of paramount importance is, besides, the improved type, design, and rig of the fishing-boats

The Sailing-Boat.

in various parts of the British Dominions. And although sea-fishing boats of whatever form and rig inevitably encounter perils in heavy weather and gales at sea, the modern type and rig of many of the fishing craft are safer and handier than the older ones; and as a consequence fewer lives are lost than formerly in the pursuit of their (sometimes) perilous calling.

The sea-fishing boats of fifty years ago were much smaller than now, the largest seldom exceeding the burthen of 30 or 40 tons; but owing to modern facilities afforded by steamboat and railway carriage to inland parts of the country, the time of transit of fresh fish is considerably diminished, and the demand steadily increased.

Sailing fishing-boats of a larger and improved class have been constructed on many parts of the coasts of the British Islands, some of them ranging from 70 to 80 tons or more. They are, moreover, fitted with modern appliances that lighten their toils considerably, more particularly such as small steam-engines for hauling the trawl, working the windlass, and performing other laborious work on board the vessel. This, however, applies more particularly to the larger class of fishing vessels sailing under the ketch rig, and to the steam-boat fishing trawlers which are now becoming numerous all around the coast.

THE FISHING SMACK.

On many parts of the coast around the British Islands where there are tidal harbours or river facilities for the entrance of fishing vessels at any time of tide without beaching them, the Smack was formerly the adopted type of the larger of those vessels.

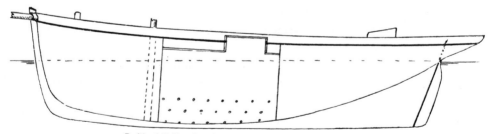

Profile of Fishing Smack, showing perforated Well for Live Fish.

The Smack rig consists of one mast, with gaff-mainsail and boom, fore-stay-sail, jib and gaff top-sail—the same, in fact, as the old cutter rig.

It was found, however, that in heavy weather the larger class of smack-rigged fishing-boats were, with the limited crew they carried, unhandy, chiefly on account of the large main-sail and stout heavy boom; and, as the sea-fishing industry has

328

greatly increased of late years, larger boats were required, and accordingly, the Smack-rig has now been almost entirely superseded by the handier and more comfortable Ketch-rig, which is now the general type of rig for the larger class of the fishing fleet.

The fishing smacks of the class before alluded to were employed chiefly in the North or deep-sea fishing, termed the "cod and ling fisheries." These vessels were built with deep perforated wells formed in the hull amidships, so as to ensure a constant ingress and egress of the sea-water in which the vessel floated. The fish immediately on being caught were put into the well, and so kept alive and fresh for the market.

Some of these vessels were of a capacity of from 50 to 60 tons, but more usually of 10, 15, 20 and 30 tons, and were constructed with a view to fast sailing, the object being to carry the catch of live fish to the nearest market with all possible expedition. But the large increase in steam trawlers during the last twenty or thirty years has considerably damaged the occupations of the fishermen who manned the sailing smacks.

At the present day there are close upon four hundred steam-trawlers hailing from the ports of Grimsby and Hull alone; consequently such a fleet of swift carrying vessels have materially depreciated the value of the sailing smacks, so that many of the latter have been disposed of, to the great loss of the owners, at less than half their original cost.

Stone-Dredging Boats.—The fishing smacks, open boats, and small vessels employed in dredging for cement-stone and other treasures of the sea, are a numerous fleet. They are rigged, some as cutters others as sloops; but the form and build of these vessels has undergone considerable improvement of late years—and although there are among them, here and there, many an old warrior yacht, still the best and finest boats of the class are built expressly for the purpose. The seamen who man these vessels have constantly the very best experience: being out at all seasons of the year, they are frequently exposed to gales and bad weather, when they are some-times compelled to heave part of their hard-earned cargo overboard to lighten their vessels, on which occasions the lesser craft and open boats have to run for safety to the nearest port.

These vessels assemble almost daily in large fleets at favourite spots for stone-dredging in the English Channel off the south-eastern coast: they leave the harbour in the morning and return at night, sometimes in so large a fleet as to produce a very pretty effect. When seen at a distance actively engaged in their pursuits in a lively breeze, they have the appearance of being all huddled together; but seldom do they run foul of each other, although they have many hair-breadth escapes. They are usually short, beamy vessels, and can be turned and put about with great readiness and precision—a very essential qualification in a dredging boat, as well as in a fishing smack.

Some of the finest and best class of dredging boats are those which hail from Harwich Harbour, Brightlingsea, Wivenhoe, and other parts of the coasts of Essex and Suffolk.

SOUTH COAST FISHING BOATS.

The coasting and Channel fishing luggers are a very numerous class. With the majority there is great similarity, particularly in those of the south coast of

South Coast Fishing Boat.

England, which are rigged as luggers, carrying main-lug, mizzen-lug, fore-sail, and mizzen-topsail. The main-mast is stepped as far forward as possible, so that the fishermen have a clear space amidships for working their nets, trawl, and other gear.

The sails of these and of most other fishermen's boats are of a dark colour, being steeped in liquid curriers' tan, for the purpose of preserving them from mildew and otherwise adding to their durability.

Fishing Boats.

CORNISH FISHING LUGGERS.

THESE boats, which are better known as "Mount's Bay fishing luggers," the majority of which hail from St. Ives and Penzance, have been much improved of late years, both in type and rig, and now rank among the handiest and best fishing luggers on the south coast of England.   They are capacious and powerful

Cornish Fishing Lugger.

sea-boats, well adapted in form and rig to the purposes for which they are chiefly employed, viz., in mackerel, pilchard, and herring fishing, with drift-nets.   They have great breadth of beam in proportion to length; and those of the larger class are fitted with a steam capstan.   They are rigged with two masts, one of which (the main-mast) is stepped "chock for'ard," in the bows of the boat, and the mizzen-mast well aft;   the sails used are main-lug, mizzen-lug, and mizzen lug-topsail, all of which are tanned for preservation.   The masts are large and lofty, unsupported by shrouds, the main halliards serving the purpose of back-stay to the main mast.

The hardy race of Cornish men who man these boats make voyages of many hundreds of miles, in the course of the year, in pursuit of their calling.   If a gale over-takes them at sea, unless a very heavy one, they disdain the idea of running for a harbour, and contrive to ride it out at sea by keeping their boats head to the wind by the use of a drogue, or, in the absence of such, by lashing spars and wooden gear together, in the form of a raft, and riding the vessel by it, whereby the force of the waves is broken and the danger of swamping the lugger is considerably lessened.

These boats, navigating as they do the most exposed parts of the coast, are invariably excellent sea-boats; and the able manner in which they are managed in the hour of peril has often been the subject of admiration by those who appreciate good seamanship.

Yorkshire Fishing Coble.

Fishing Boats.

BRIXHAM TRAWLERS.

THE Brixham trawlers have also of late years been considerably improved, and now rank among the best of the fishing fleet of the Devonshire coast. They are a large and powerful form of boat, fitted with the modern appliances of steam-capstan for the heavier work of hauling up the trawl, &c.

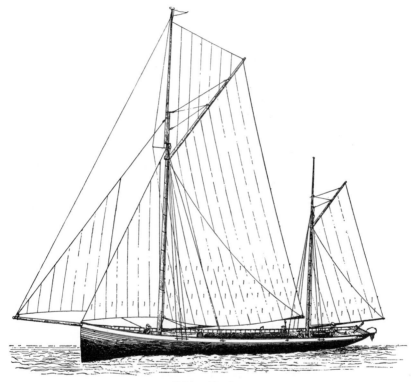

Brixham Trawler.

The Brixham trawlers, as also the fishing vessels of some other parts of the south coast, are mostly ketch-rigged. The ketch-rig has, in fact, been very generally adopted of late years, in preference to the smack and cutter rigs, by the larger class of British sea-fishing vessels. The rig (which has been already described, *supra*, p. 40) consists of two masts with gaff-sails, foresail, jib and top-sails, the larger or main-mast being forward, and the smaller or mizzen-mast aft.

The Sailing-Boat.

In Scotland the chief centres of the herring fishing fleet are Fraserburgh, Peterhead, and Wick; but the fishermen who man the boats comprising the fleet make

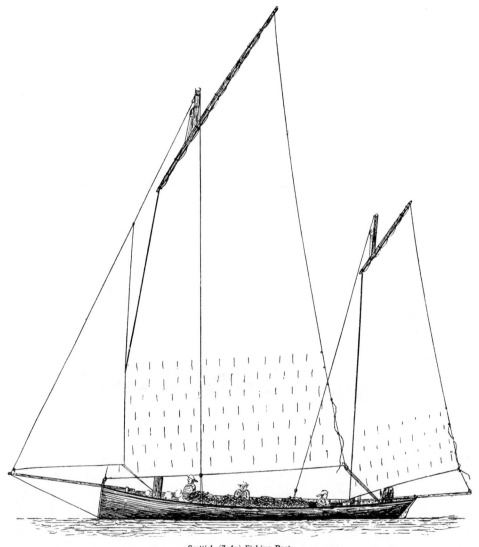

Scottish (Zulu) Fishing Boat.

voyages in pursuit of their calling all along the coast as far north as the Shetland Isles, and frequently far out in the stormy North Sea, their usual field of operations.

334

Fishing Boats.

The fishing boats of the north-east coast of Scotland are employed in the Spring and Summer seasons chiefly in the herring fishery, which is pursued with drift-nets; and in the Autumn and Winter seasons in the "great line" fishing.

These boats are now of a greatly improved type and rig, and are splendid sea-boats. They are called "Zulu" fishing-boats, simply from the fact that the new type of boat was designed and built at Fraserburgh during the time of the Zulu War in 1879 and 1880. They are considered a great improvement upon the fishing-boats previously in use on the coast: the novelty and chief difference being, that in the place of the heavy square (or transom) stern, they have a sharp, raking stern, similar to a Norway yawl or a whale-boat, the advantages of which are, that they are better sea-boats; and when riding by their nets at sea, or with their tackle out at line-fishing, heavy seas which strike them hard astern divide and pass on with less effect upon such a type of boat than on one with a full or square stern; besides which there is the greater immunity from being pooped when running before a gale in a heavy sea; and they are upon the whole a safer, handier, and more comfortable type of craft for sea-going purposes than the transom-sterned vessels of former days. It is essential that fishing-boats of this class should be fast sailers, as directly they have made a good haul and are filled up, they proceed as fast as they can to the nearest port and deliver their catch of fish in as fresh a condition as possible.

If there is little or no wind, or an adverse wind, there are always steam-tugs on the look out to tow them into port.

The modern Scottish Zulu fishing-boat is decked all over, and has a capacious hold for fish, and a good cabin abaft the mizzen-mast: they are boats of a broad and powerful form, with fine, sharp bow and stern; they vary in size from 15 to 25 tons or more, and are usually manned by a crew of six or seven men.

The rig of the Scottish Zulu fishing-boat consists of two masts and three sails, viz.: main-sail, foresail and mizzen; top-sails are not used on these boats; the main-sail and mizzen are both lug-sails. The main-mast, which is of enormous size and height in proportion to the tonnage of the boat, stands well forward in the bows; the extra size of the mast is accounted for in the fact that it is not supported by shrouds, stays, or any kind of standing rigging, as such would be in the way of the crew when working their fishing gear, and the extra height of the mast is essential for the hoist of the main-sail. They never use top-sails (as the South Coast fishing-boats do); the main-sail is therefore a large and lofty form of lug-sail, narrow at the head, and with considerable hoist; the mizzen is also of shapely form; a lug-sail with great hoist in proportion to width. The tack of the main-sail is made fast at the stem of the boat, and the clew to an iron hawse at the stern. Both sails are narrow at the head, and each is laced to a comparatively short yard. The fore-sail is run out on a bow-sprit standing about 8 ft. (more or less, according to the tonnage of the boat) beyond the stem ; and the clew of the mizzen is hauled out on an outrigger extending about 4 ft. (more or less) abaft the stern. There are usually seven rows of reef points in the main-sail and four in the mizzen.

FISHING-BOATS OF THE ORKNEY AND SHETLAND ISLES.

THE position of these Islands, extending far out in the North Sea, their perilous surroundings, intricate navigation, and dangerous cross-currents, render boat-sailing

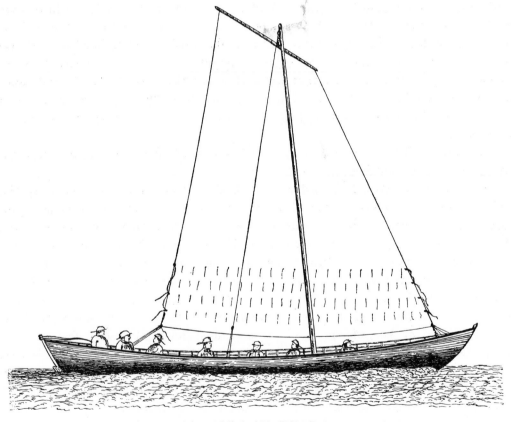

Orkney and Shetland Isles Fishing Boat.

in their neighbourhood exceptionally risky and difficult. A considerable extent of the Island coasts is bounded by precipitous cliffs and jagged rocks, with rare

Fishing Boats.

intervals of a small bay (locally 'voe') or landing place, where boats can be run ashore and hauled up above high-water mark to a place of safety: for it is never practicable to leave them at anchor anywhere off the coasts of these Islands.

The Fisheries of the Orkneys and Shetlands are therefore pursued under risks and difficulties of no ordinary kind, mainly attributable to the natural formation of the surrounding rocks and under-currents, and consequent dangerous character of the sea and frequent bad weather. But native fishermen, conscious of the perils surrounding them, are a daring and enterprising class, possessing a skill in the art of open boat-sailing on stormy seas that is second to no others of the fisher class within the range of the British Islands.

The Orkney Boats of the larger class are now decked, rigged and equipped after the manner of the Scottish fishing luggers. But for the line-fishing, open boats of a smaller class are employed.

The Shetlands, which form the northernmost limit of what is termed the 'Home fisheries of the British Islands,' are the most exposed to the difficulties before referred to, arising chiefly from a combination of circumstances, such as deep water close in shore, cross-currents, very rapid tides, frequent stormy weather and heavy seas, such as would daunt the courage of some of the most experienced sea-fishermen of more southern parts.

The great line-fishing of the Shetlands is carried on mainly from open boats of a type nearly identical with the Norway Yawl; and in the hands of a crew of experienced Shetland boatmen seem to possess sea-worthy qualities such as few boats of any other type would be capable of displaying.

The usual dimensions of these open Shetland Yawls are:—Length over all, 28 ft.; length at load water-line, about 22 ft.; and beam, 8 ft.

The ordinary rig of the Shetland Yawl is one large lug-sail cut narrow at the head and broad at the foot, with four or more reefs, so that when close reefed, nearly half the sail is dispensed with. Some of the larger of these Yawls carry two masts and two separate lugs, and in fine weather they sometimes set a jib as well.

The Sixern Fishing Yawls.—These are a smaller class of the Shetland fishing-boats. The 'Sixerns,' so called, because of six oars being used for their propulsion, are employed chiefly in line-fishing in the North Sea. They are open boats of similar type to the Shetland Yawls above described, but of smaller dimensions, being about 19 ft. in length by 5 ft. 8 or 10 ins. in breadth, and 4 ft. in depth. These boats, like the larger Yawls have high bows and stern, with more or less spring, so that when afloat (particularly when heavily laden) they have the appearance of being low amidships: they are however excellent sea-boats; the hardy Shetland fishermen who man them, proceed under sail far out of sight of

The Sailing-Boat.

land to the fishing grounds in the North Sea, where the 'haaf' or deep sea-fishing is pursued, and there they lay down hundreds of fathoms of baited line, which has to be watched, sometimes for several hours before being hauled up again.

The Sixerns are rigged with one sail only, a lug-sail of similar shape to that of the larger boats; and the mast can be readily 'struck' (*i.e.* taken down), when necessary, which is usually the case when nearing the Islands, or as soon as they arrive in the locality of the swirl, termed locally 'roosts' or 'strings,' which sometimes twist, toss, and twirl the boat about as if a mere cork in a whirlpool: then it is that the six oars have to be plied with all the vigour and muscular power of the crew, in order to keep way on the boat and prevent her being dashed against the rocks and wrecked. These 'roosts' and 'strings' are caused by the meeting in opposition of the strong tides forcing their way between the under-water rocks, causing such sudden rising and lifting of the sea as to make navigation very difficult and perilous. The Somburgh Roost is known as one of the most dangerous of all; causing, with a certain direction of wind, a fearfully rough, broken sea, extending several miles out beyond the coast.

The Shetland fishermen who pursue their calling in the Shetland Yawls and Sixerns have great confidence in their boats, notwithstanding the terrible disaster which befell them a few years since, in the terrific gale which suddenly overtook them when far out in the North Sea, and wrecked a large portion of the fleet.

IRISH FISHING-BOATS.

The Greencastle Yawls.—These are a small class of fishing-boats of a design and construction adopted and used for many years past by the fishermen resident at Greencastle. They were employed chiefly off the Coast of Donegal; but were also largely used by the Co. Galway and North Mayo fishermen. They usually carried a crew of from five to eight men, according to the size and capacity of the boat. But since the Congested District Board for Ireland has been in power, the Zulu type of fishing-boat has been introduced into the Counties Donegal, Mayo and Galway; and under the tuition of Scotch fishermen, who are brought over and deputed to instruct the local fishermen in those parts, in the use of the 'great lines,' they have taken much larger quantities of fish than they used to do with their native boats and gear.

Fishing Boats.

THE PETER-BOAT.

Hark! I hear a gentle splash, there's life upon the stream—
Yes! yes! a whisper too methinks, or is't Dame Fancy's dream?
Then slowly drifting with the tide, a boat appears in sight;
' Good luck t'ye wily fishermen, this is a " catching " night! '
The peter-boat moves silently, the mullet net is spread;
No coarse nor bungling snare is that, but soft and fine as thread.
The fishermen may crafty be, their scaly prize to get,
But craftier still the mullet is, that gaily leaps the net.

THE AUTHOR.[1]

THE Peter-boat, so called from St. Peter the Apostle, is of very ancient origin—indeed, it is said to be precisely the Roman Amphiprora. Peter-boats are much in favour with the fishermen of the English tidal rivers. There are a few peculiarities in their construction worthy of notice. In the first place, a properly built peter-boat has neither gunwale nor top rim, and therefore presents a very unfinished appearance ; the top strake runs in a horizontal line from stem to stern, leaving no graceful fall amidships, nor any other improved lines to strike an admiring eye, but is simply what a fishing boat ought to be—*safe and serviceable.* The object of their being built without gunwale or top rim, is that the nets and cork lines may meet with no obstruction on being run out quickly from the boat. And therefore, although some modern peter-boats are built with gunwale and rim for the purpose of adding to the durability of the boat, they are objectionable to experienced fishermen for the reasons above stated.

[1] The illustration, coupled with the lines immediately beneath it, represents and explains the manner in which the art of Grey Mullet fishing is pursued on the River Stour, in Essex, with peter-boat and fine thread nets. The fish on striking the net cannot escape capture, as the material of which the net is composed is so soft and yielding that on struggling to free themselves they become more and more entangled in its meshes. It is, however, no uncommon occurrence, in this mode of fishing, if the water be clear and there is sufficient daylight or moonlight for the fish to see the net, for a whole shoal of them to leap the obstruction, one after another, like a flock of sheep, and so to elude the snare.

The Sailing-Boat.

Stem and stern of the peter-boat are alike, after the form of a whale boat, but not so sharp, and not curved or elevated. The object of both ends being thus formed is, that in working the peter-net the boat is as frequently propelled backwards as forwards, particularly whilst hauling in the net. Having no keel, the boat can be turned quickly, and in narrow compass. A Well for live fish is built into the boat amidships, and divides it into two compartments, the fore part being where the rower sits, the other for the fisherman and his nets. The Well is generally about two feet wide at the base, and gradually tapering to one foot at the top, extending the whole width of the boat; the depth of the well is just sufficient to bring it upon a level with the thwarts, and, being covered over, forms a seat in the boat. The bottom of the Well is perforated with a number of holes, to admit a constant ingress and egress of water. Fish may be kept alive many days, or even weeks, in these Wells, if the boat remains constantly afloat, and deep enough in the water. The stern sheets of the peter-boat are laid higher than in other boats, on account of the quantity of water which drains from the nets as they are hauled in; but the division caused by the Well prevents the water from getting into the fore-part of the boat, where the rower sits. A small raised bench is placed in the extreme end of the boat at the stern, on which the fisherman stands erect when shooting the net. This elevated position enables him to lift the cork-line high, that the net may run out freely.

THE DOBLE (OR DOVAL).

Used chiefly for amateur fishing up river, is flat-bottomed, has stem and stern similar to a skiff, and, when afloat, has more the appearance of the latter than a flat-bottomed boat. The easy draft of water renders this kind of boat serviceable for shallow waters, where boats of deeper draft would be nearly useless; it is especially convenient for approaching shallow shores, and in tidal rivers where there is an extent of flat soil or ooze; and for up river-fishing the doble is peculiarly adapted. It is also very convenient for the navigation of narrow creeks, and for approaching the brink of rivers, where other boats of deeper draft of water could not go. The doble is a safe and useful kind of boat whilst used for rowing purposes, but is unsuitable for sailing.

340

Boats for Wild-fowl Shooting.

BOATS FOR WILD-FOWL SHOOTING.

THE illustration is from a drawing of the Author's Shooting-Yacht *Wild-fowler*, in which, in years gone by, he had very successful sport in hard winters, chiefly among

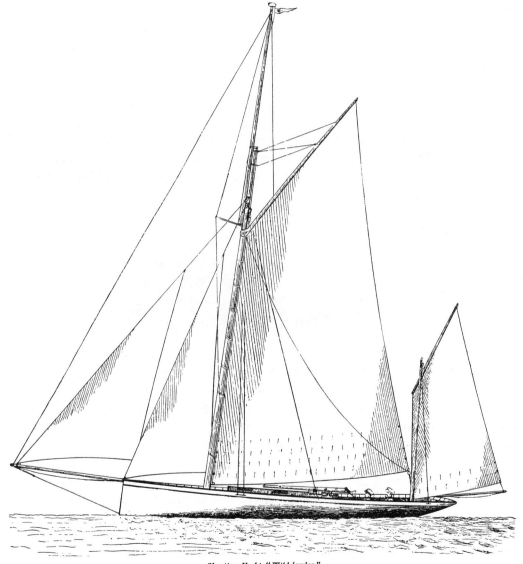

Shooting Yacht " Wild-fowler."

the Brent geese, which used to congregate in large gaggles off the Eastern Coast of England, in the Channel, North Sea, and estuaries, and in the broader parts of the chief rivers of that coast.

The Sailing-Boat.

The *Wild-fowler* was yawl-rigged, and carried a Stanchion, with *pederero*, or swivel-gun, capable of scattering a couple of pounds of shot at a charge. The gun was mounted over the cabin roof, and fitted with recoil spring, swivel, and other apparatus enabling it to be manipulated with the facility of a large shoulder gun.

In a work [1] by the Author, a record of some of his adventures as a wild-fowl shooter may be read by those interested in that captivating and healthful recreation.

THE GUNNING-PUNT.

THE engraving represents a round-bottomed gunning-boat of special type, after the Author's invention, suitable both for sailing and paddling in pursuit of wild-fowl.

A wild-fowling gunning-punt for the purpose of carrying one individual sportsman

Gunning Punt.

with a punt-gun, ammunition-box, shoulder-gun, and other requisites, should be just large enough to be safe and serviceable, but nothing more. The smaller the boat is made to appear on the water the greater will be the punter's chance of success, the more convenient it will be to manage, the quicker he can make up to birds, and the less will be the exertion necessary to propel it.

The size of a wild-fowling punt, however, must be in proportion to the size of the gun intended to be used, and also in proportion to the height and weight of the punter himself. It is a mistake to use a large double-handed punt requiring two persons to propel it, with a gun carrying from a pound and a-half to two pounds of shot.

The most useful sized punt-gun for general purposes is that carrying about half a pound of shot at a charge; and as there are more punt-guns of that size in use on the coast by practical wild-fowl shooters than of any other, the recommendation would seem to be confirmed.

---

[1] The 'Wild-fowler, a Treatise on Ancient and Modern Wild-fowling, Historical and Practical.' By H. C. Folkard. 4th Edition. 1897.

Boats for Wild-fowl Shooting.

A punt to carry a gun of the size stated, with a man of ten or eleven stone weight, should not exceed the following dimensions :—Length over all, 16 ft. 6 ins. ; breadth, amidships, 2 ft. 10 ins. ; ditto, ditto, at bottom, 2 ft. 8 in. ; depth at bows, 4 ins. ; ditto at stern, 8 ins.

A boat of this description may be built either with a flat bottom or a flat floor : the distinction being that one is perfectly flat, as the bottom of a box, which is termed 'flat-bottomed' ; the other, though said to be 'flat-floored,' has a slightly rounded bottom, and the sides do not commence from an angle, as in a flat-bottomed boat, but are round, as a whale-boat, though it is a great desideratum to maintain the floor throughout as flat as it consistently can be with due regard to shape ; and such is by far the best form of punt that can be used for wild-fowl shooting.

The late Colonel Hawker, in his work on guns and shooting, condemns all round-bottomed punts, such as were used in the Colonel's time at Southampton and Itchen Ferry, as on a bad construction; and gives as a reason that they have unsteady bearings.

Now, without disputing the Colonel's assertion as to the Southampton and Itchen Ferry gunning-punts, it is insisted that the reason of round-bottomed punts having unsteady bearings is, because they are *too* round at the bottom. If they be constructed with a long flat floor they will be safer, and even steadier, than a flat-bottomed punt.

The fore part of the punt, from stem to cross-piece, should be covered over with a very thin scantling, adding no more to the weight forward than absolutely necessary, because of the heavy gun which has to be placed there.

The cross-piece alluded to is placed just abaft the scantling, and marks the balance for tipping the gun.

The covered part of the punt may be slightly cambered, and the aft end, where the breech of the gun lies, should then be completed with a neat semi-circular screen piece, rising an inch and a-half or two inches above the scantling-deck, which will afford a sufficient screen to the punter when lying flat on the floor and making up to birds.

Another cross-piece of light wood should be placed athwart the gunwale, about $2\frac{1}{2}$ or 3 ft. from the stem, before the scantling is put on ; this is for the purpose of fixing the rest for the outer end of the barrel. The rest should be a simple copper screw, with a small semi-circular crutch in which to receive the barrel. It should be made in connection with a female screw, attached to the fore cross-piece ; and the male screw should be of sufficient length to raise or lower the elevation of the gun from one to two inches.

As to the position of the chock, or strong-piece, to which is attached the necessary apparatus for checking the force of the recoil, it must depend entirely on the means intended to be employed. If the patent spiral recoil-spring is to be used, the interior of the punt must be fitted accordingly. But if the strain is to be thrown upon the stem-piece, the builder must take care to fix the same strong enough to receive it.

343

The Sailing-Boat.

The gunning-punt may be built entirely of pine, or the upper strakes which are above water may be of pine and the lower ones of elm; if all fir, the boat will be so much the lighter, and more buoyant. A gunning-punt should never be built of oak; it is too heavy for the purpose. Practical punters have expressed their surprise that the late Colonel Hawker should have recommended such a material. During the latter part of the Colonel's sporting career, however, he appears to have given preference to elm and pine.

THE SAILING-PUNT.

The sailing-punt enables the wild-fowl shooter to obviate a good deal of the hard work which he must necessarily encounter in a rowing-punt; and it is, besides, the most eligible kind of boat for approaching wild-fowl in shallow-water by daylight.

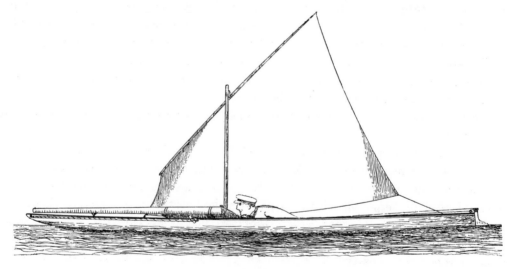

Sailing Punt.

It should be observed, however, that it is not every gunning-punt that can be sailed: a boat of special construction (such as that above described) is required for the purpose: for, so surely as an inexperienced hand attempts sailing an ordinary sculling-punt, such as is used for wild-fowling, so surely will he capsize himself. Of all the forms of gunning-boats, the punt is the least safe under sail, and the least manageable.

A punt intended for carrying sail must be built specially for the purpose, and must have a depth of about four inches of false keel at the stern, gradually tapering to one inch amidships: and it may be so constructed as to be capable of being used either as a sailing or rowing-punt, and so that a strong man may propel it with hand paddles nearly as fast as an ordinary rowing-punt. And such is precisely the description of boat recommended, which, after trying several different forms, the Author finally used for many years, and found it not only a most comfortable, but serviceable boat for the purpose; and it looked no larger on the water than an ordinary sculling-punt.

Neither water-decks nor wash-streaks are required for the sailing-punt, because no reasonable man would venture to set sail in so frail a bark in rough water.

The mast should be so fitted that it may be readily shipped and unshipped at pleasure—a small stick of pine spar, about the size of a mop-handle, and from four to five feet in height. The mast may be stepped either through the scantling in front of the screen-piece, or just abaft it, and a little towards the left side, so as to be clear of the balance-rest on which the punt-gun lies. Neither shrouds nor stays are required: either would incur danger; because should a squall strike the sail, it is better for the little mast to 'go by the board,' carrying all sail along with it, than to capsize the boat, which would be the result under such circumstances if the mast were confined. It is preferable, therefore to select a slender mast that has not sufficient substance to overturn the punt. Never mind it bending in a breeze; the carrying away of a small mast is far less to be regarded than the upsetting of the punt. The sail should be a low standing settee, and made of very light duck or white calico. It is unnecessary to give the exact dimensions of the sail, as they must be in suitable proportion to the stability of the punt.

The rudder-bands should be of sufficient length to enable the punter to steer his craft when lying at full length on the floor of the punt.

No other ballast will be required than that of the punter himself (who is virtually *the ballast*), the punt-gun, ammunition-box, and other accoutrements; all of which must be placed in exact position, so as to trim the boat to a nicety. If the sail be not too large, but fairly proportioned according to the stability of the punt, it will be quite safe in smooth water in experienced hands.

The rapidity with which a little boat of this kind skims along on a reach in smooth water is astonishing, and the wild-fowl shooter will often be agreeably surprised at the easy and unsuspecting manner in which it may be run up within range of wild-fowl in a steady breeze; and if a shot cannot always be obtained before they take wing, by luffing the punt whilst they are rising, in the same manner as with a yacht or sailing-boat (as explained in the author's work on wild-fowl shooting) an excellent flying shot may frequently be made.

It is not the strength of the wind, but the roughness of the water, that causes the risk of sailing so fragile a craft; for if the water be smooth, sail may be

The Sailing-Boat.

carried safely in an ordinary, and even a stiff breeze. But the inexperienced are warned against the peril of carrying sail on a punt in any but smooth water. The effect of venturing into rough water with a long low craft, whilst pressing her ahead under sail, would be to drive her bows under water; and the weight of the gun on the head of the punt must tend to increase the danger. Therefore, the young wild-fowler is cautioned *not to venture into rough water with the sailing-punt,* for a sportsman's life is supposed to be of more value than that of a duck.

THE SLOOP-RIGGED SHOOTING-BOAT.

THE illustration is from a drawing of the author's sloop-rigged shooting-boat named the *Hooper* which he used for wild-fowl shooting in shallow water and over tidal flats.

The sloop-rigged shooting-boat is used chiefly for wild-fowl shooting in large

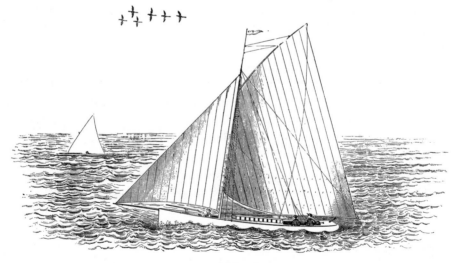

" Hooper " (Sloop-rigged shooting-boat).

rivers and shallow bays, where the shooting-yacht is precluded from proceeding because of drawing too much water. Thus the shooting-yacht and stanchion-gun are used for sea-going purposes, and the open sailing boat, with gun of similar proportions, for inland waters and shallows.

A boat for this purpose should be about twenty feet in length by seven feet beam; a shallow craft with powerful bearings.

Boats for Wild-fowl Shooting.

Stability being a great desideratum in a boat for this diversion, it is not desirable that the craft should list on her side too much when under sail, as it interferes with the management of the stanchion-gun. A narrow deck-way of twelve inches or more may be formed on each side of the boat, but the deck-way should be upon a level with the gunwales. The fore and aft part of the boat may also be partly covered in by a flush-deck, but in other respects it should be entirely open.

A boat of this description will require several cwt. of lead or iron ballast, which must be deposited with careful discretion beneath the platform, so that the proper trim of the boat is preserved.

The stanchion-gun should be fitted with chock and necessary recoiling apparatus upon the flush-deck, in such a position as to give room for the shooter to manipulate it clear of mast and rigging in the most advantageous position for shooting.

Probably no better form of boat could be invented for traversing the shallow waters of inland bays and rivers, the resort of wild-fowl, than a sloop-rigged revolving centre-plate boat, the keel of which can be raised or lowered at pleasure; whilst the shallow form of the boat would enable the wild-fowl shooter to go over almost any ooze or sand-bank with facility where there might be a depth of only one or two feet of water.

The Sailing-Boat.

THE BEACON-LIGHT. [1]

The Beacon-light.

THERE'S a signal well known to the mariner brave,
His guide o'er the waters from perils to save;
'Tis hailed with a welcome wherever in sight,
And the mariner calls it 'the Beacon-light.'

A true friend in distress, ever brilliant and gay,
Whether fixed or revolving will ne'er lead astray;
Tho' many brave hearts, on a thick foggy night,
Have quaked at th' eclipse of 'the Beacon-light.'

[1] This poem was written by the Author in the year 1852, on his return from a long sea voyage.   It was first published in a local newspaper in the same year.   It has since been published in several editions of this work.

The Beacon Light.

Tho' far from the land, should a beacon appear
'Tis the mariner's warning that danger is near;
Then he warily steers, whilst he still keeps in sight
Of his monitor dumb, ' the Beacon-light.'

And tho' mermaids lie slumb'ring 'neath white-crested waves,
And rovers who woo'd them met watery graves;
Now onward he steers, his ship staunch and tight,
For high on the rock stands ' the Beacon-light.'

When darkness fast creeps o'er the wide-ranging sea,
And the grim shark is lurking close under his lee,
Tho' gloomy the prospect and dismal the night,
His fears are dispelled by ' the Beacon-light.'

Should a gale overtake him and danger appal,
The mariner skilful may weather the squall;
But how gladly he looks thro' the darkness of night
On his guide and director, ' the Beacon-light!'

The gale may increase, spreading terror around,
And 'neath the blue waves gaping sands may abound;
Yet fearless he steers, his guide full in sight,
'Midst the bright gleams that fall from ' the Beacon-light.'

When far out at sea on the perilous deep,
And the high-swelling waves appear lull'd into sleep;
There's the compass to steer by, and stars shining bright,
But he's sad at the loss of ' the Beacon-light.'

Long parted from friends and dear ones at home;
Long time he's been toss'd on the white surgy foam;
Then how cheer'd is his heart when welcomed at night,
With a happy return—by ' the Beacon-light.'

END OF PART VI.

PART VII.

___

SAILING CHARIOTS AND ICE YACHTS.

SAILING CHARIOTS

'But who is this, what thing of sea or land?
Female of sex it seems,
That so bedeckt, ornate, and gay,
Comes this way, sailing
Like a stately ship
Of Tarsus, bound for th' Isles
Of Javan or Gadier,
With all her bravery on, and tackle trim,
Sails filled and streamers waving,
Courted by all the winds that hold them play.'

MILTON.

IT appears, from many authorities, that sailing chariots are a very early invention, though there is but little trace of their use in this country; and for reasons which it is not difficult to imagine, for nothing can be more likely to frighten horses, and thereby to cause accidents on public thoroughfares than a sailing chariot.

Sailing chariots have long been known and used in Holland. In 'A Description of Holland,' published A.D. 1743, are contained a few remarks on one belonging to the then Prince Maurice, which he kept at Scheveling, a village in the neighbourhood of the Hague. This chariot is said to have been made by Stephinus, a great mathematician. The form of it is stated to be plain and simple, but resembling a boat moved upon four wheels of an equal size, and steered by a rudder placed between the two hind wheels. It had two sails. The mode of stopping the chariot was either by luffing or lowering the sails. It is also stated that in the space of two hours it would pass from Scheveling to Putten, a distance of forty-two miles. But it is obvious that this could only have been accomplished with a favourable wind.

Walchius[1] also speaks of the Scheveling sailing chariot, and affirms it to be of such prodigious swiftness in its motion, and yet of so great a capacity as to its

___

[1] Fabularum Decas. Fab. 9.

burthen, that it far exceeded in swiftness any ship under sail, with ever so fair a wind ; that in the space of a few hours it would convey six or ten persons twenty or thirty German miles, and that with little labour to him who sits at the helm, who may easily guide the course of it as he pleases.

Milton, in his 'Paradise Lost,' thus speaks of sailing chariots being employed on the barren plains of China :—

> ' But in his way lights on the barren plains
> Of Sericana, where Chineses drive
> With sails, and wind their canie waggons light.'

Bishop Wilkins[1] gives a chapter on sailing chariots, in which he says they are commonly used on the Champion plains of China. He also speaks of the Scheveling chariot.

Sailing chariots are also mentioned by Grotius in several of his epigrams.[2] And Hondius, in one of his large maps of Asia, gives a conjectural description of such as are used in China.

Bishop Wilkins gives two illustrations of sailing chariots, neither of which can be commended at the present day as of any practical use ; one of them, containing seven persons, is a cumbersome boat-like contrivance, placed upon four wheels, all of the same size ; it is fitted with two masts and square-sails, the larger one being placed aft and the smaller one in front. This chariot appears to be provided with a rudder which terminates at the lower end in a point or spike, and which, it is presumed, was intended to be raised or lowered at pleasure.

Wilkins's second illustration is a suggestive one, which he thought might be more conveniently framed with moveable or revolving sails, shaped after the manner of a volute propeller, so as to impel the chariot with a force proportionably equivalent to that of a windmill. The fore-wheels in this are much smaller than the hind ones. But the revolving sails are apparently so contrived as to catch the wind from any quarter, and set the volute in motion ; and consequently (by mechanical contrivance) the wheels of the carriage.

It is possible that these volute sails might be used with effect upon a sailing-chariot, but it is highly improbable.[3]

Sailing Barrows.—It is stated in the Journal of Van Braam Houckgeest, in his ' Embassy to China,' that sailing barrows are used in China, but the sailing apparatus is

---

[1] ' Mathematical Magic,' by Bishop Wilkins, 1680. Book ii. cap. ii.

[2] Gro. Eps. v. xix. xx. and xxi.

[3] Since the publication in previous editions of ' The Sailing-Boat ' of the Author's notes and references as to the impracticable contrivances above referred to, the illustrations from Bishop Wilkins's ' Mathematical Magic ' (A.D. 1680) have been reproduced in a modern work on Yachts and Boats.

merely an additional contrivance to relieve the toils of the barrow-men when the wind is fair. These sailing barrows are described as having a little mast, very neatly inserted in a hole or step, cut in the fore part of the barrow. To this mast is attached a sail, made of matting, or more commonly of canvas, five or six feet high, and three or four wide, with reef-tackle, yards, and braces, like those of the Chinese river-boats. The braces lead to the shafts of the barrow, and by means of them the conductor trims his sail.

Van Braam says he could not help admiring the contrivance, and felt real pleasure in seeing a score of them rolling along one after another.[1]

The Shuldham Land-Sailing-Boats.

THE SHULDHAM LAND-SAILING-BOATS.

THESE are an invention by the late Captain Molyneux Shuldham, R.N., the author of many useful and valuable nautical contrivances. It is one which afforded considerable amusement to himself and friends, when prisoners of war at Verdun in 1809; they having been desired by General Wirion (the commandant of the English prisoners) to discontinue the use of their sailing and rowing-boats on the river Meuse, because of a complaint and petition of the fishermen that ' the sailing boats of the English prisoners frightened all the fish away!' But Capt. Shuldham determined that he would not be

---

[1] 'Je ne pouvais m'empêcher d'admirer cette combinaison, et je goûtais un plaisir réel en voyant une vingtaine de ces brouettes voilières cinglant l'une à la suite de l'autre' (tome i. p. 150).

deprived of the pleasures of a sail; and accordingly he invented a land-sailing-boat. The first he made was with one mast, the other a schooner—both being represented in the engraving, which is made from drawings kindly sent to the Author by the late Capt. Shuldham.

In the previous editions of this work a description was given of a steering apparatus, with full details, as furnished to the Author by the late Capt. Shuldham, but as such a mode of steering would, at the present day, be treated as out of date (since the more modern and effective mode, as applied to motor cars and tricycles, which could of course be readily applied to a land-sailing-boat) the Author has not reproduced Capt. Shuldham's steering apparatus in this edition.

There is no doubt that wind power can be used with advantage in various ways and on many occasions; and land-sailing-boats may afford a good deal of sport and amusement on plains, commons, and hard sands by the sea-side and elsewhere; but there are many and obvious objections to their use on public highways.

SAILING CYCLES.

ALTHOUGH bicycles and tricycles propelled by pedal or other manual exertion are now almost universal, a Sailing Cycle is a novelty nowhere to be met with in any European country. Yet the contrivance of one would not in these days involve any very special ingenuity. Its utility might be doubtful, or, at all events, very limited.

It is not by any means improbable that, sooner or later, some enterprising individual may give attention to the subject with a view to the production of a modern Sailing Chariot, or Sailing Cycle, for crossing, under sail, extensive plains, if not within the limited area of the British Islands, perhaps in more remote countries where other modes of conveyance would be impracticable, or perhaps attended with such difficulties as to render them so.

The use of Sailing Cycles in any shape could not be permitted upon public highways. The objections to their use are many and obvious; but on a wide open country, with a tolerably level surface, a Sailing Cycle might be utilised as a pleasant and expeditious mode of travelling; and with a favourable wind it would be found a swift and economical means of journeying over long distances, where neither the costly railway and steam-engine nor the motor car have yet, in the absence of level roads, bridges and viaducts, been able to run their iron wheels and rattling machinery.

A Sailing Chariot of the kind suggested would require four wheels, and perhaps a fifth, or front wheel, for the purpose of steering. It would have to be constructed so that the body of the chariot, under pressure of sail in a side wind, did not lift the windward wheels off the ground. This could be contrived by the body of the chariot being suspended upon a rounded iron bar, resting in sockets supported at each end upon the axle of the wheels, the bottom of the chariot being ballasted at the under part with a bar of lead of the same length as the body of the cycle, and of a weight proportioned to the extent of sail spread. In other respects the body of the chariot might be fitted up like the interior of a modern four-wheeled private carriage, more or less luxuriously, according to fancy.

A Sailing Cycle of smaller size might readily be contrived for amusement and recreation upon private roads, as in the case of an owner of an extensive private park, with good level roads and other facilities for the enjoyment of a novel kind of sailing, or cycle travelling under sail; all that is requisite to enliven the scene being a fair wind, a side wind, or indeed any wind that is not directly adverse to the course of the cycle.

Ice Sailing-Yachts.

ICE SAILING-YACHTS (OR RAFTS).

SAILING over ice is a pastime indulged in with considerable spirit and enthusiasm in those countries where there is, every winter, long enduring frost with considerable extent of frozen water, as in Russia, Finland, Holland, and on the lakes and broad rivers of North America and Canada, where in winter there are long, broad and expansive stretches of frozen surface on which to enjoy to the full extent the cold but healthful pastime of sailing upon the ice.

Ice-yachts, when ingeniously constructed, sail at a flying pace, and on smooth ice the slightest wind suffices to move them along.

Ice-boats have long been common in Holland, where they are found useful in winter for conveying goods and passengers many miles along the dykes and lowlands of that country.

Wilkins[1] also mentions that in Holland small ice-boats are used, having sledges instead of wheels, and being driven with a sail. But the bodies he describes as being like little boats, so that if the ice should break they might still hold the occupant safely upon the water.

The winter season of 1895 was the most recent in which ice yachting has been available as a recreation in England. In that season the Lake Windermere was frozen over, and for a short time ice-yacht sailing was indulged in on that broad and beautiful expanse of water.

In a few other places within the British Islands, where there was a sufficient extent of frozen surface, ice-yachting on a small scale was practised by some of the few English people who possess ice-yachts; but the duration of the frost was so short that the sport soon came to an end, and a succession since of mild winters has prohibited the use of ice-yachts within the sphere of the British Islands.

---

[1] 'Mathematical Magic.' By Bishop Wilkins.

The Sailing-Boat.

THE SHULDHAM ICE-BOAT.

THIS boat, the invention of the late Captain Molyneux Shuldham, R.N., is constructed with a strong frame-work of wood (in the form appearing in the illustration),[1] resting upon four large skates, two of which are affixed under the fore part of the frame, and two under the aft part; so that there are two on each side in line one with the other. Under the centre line of the frame are also two cutting-skates, one in the fore part, and one in the hind part; the foremost serving as rudder, the hindmost as keel. The foremost, or rudder-skate, is also fitted

The Shuldham Ice-boat.

with a long tiller, by means of which the boat is steered by the helmsman as he sits amidships, just in front of the mast.

There are, therefore, six skates in all, which are placed on three parallel lines. The front middle skate and the rudder one are affixed to the midship line, and those are the only two that are allowed to cut into the ice, in order to prevent lee-way, and should be ground as sharp as hatchets. All the others (four in number) are curved, so as to offer the least possible resistance; these are fixed two to each of the side rails, which form the breadth of the boat: the midship ones only are a little deeper, just sufficient to raise the weather skates clear of the ice, and also

[1] The engraving is from a drawing by the late Captain Shuldham, R.N.

to prevent the cutting-skates from penetrating too deeply into it, merely enough to prevent lee-way. Thus the boat is moved upon four smooth curved skates and two cutting ones. The inventor found this arrangement answered admirably. The chief resistance to the propelling power was in the longitudinal line, amidships, as it should be.

As to the rig of the Shuldham ice-boat, it is fitted with a mast, bowsprit and outrigger; the latter for the shrouds; and rigged with two sails only (main-sail and fore-sail) as shewn in the illustration; an arrangement which admits the carrying of very low canvas, as the main-sail boom almost sweeps the surface of the ice in a strong wind. The sails are also laced to booms, the jib-boom being shortened just sufficiently to clear the helmsman's knees.

The seat for the helmsman is a strongly constructed one bolted securely to the frame, and placed close to and in front of the mast, to which it serves as a material support, as it also is to the outrigger, both being firmly held to it. To the back of the seat are also affixed the cleats for the main and jib halliards.

The main and fore sheets are rove through small single-sheaved blocks, and secured to the midship rail. In turning to windward, the sails work themselves without any trimming of the sheets, which is almost indispensable, because of the quickness with which the boat performs all her evolutions.

The manner in which the ice-boat is stopped under full sail and brought to anchor, is by a very simple contrivance. The performance is effected by merely turning a conical screw, pointed downwards, which is fitted amidships, the handle being placed within reach so that it can be turned with the right hand whilst steering with the left. The point scrapes the ice when screwed downwards, and clears it when screwed upwards; thus giving the power to stop the boat as gradually as possible and eventually to anchor without the necessity of shortening sail.

The arrangement of an ice-boat of this kind would answer on a larger scale by employing larger skates in proportion to the greater weight of the boat; but as the climate of the British Islands is not conducive to the sport of ice-sailing, ice-boats could only be used for amusement, and it would be convenient to construct them as lightly as possible, and only large enough to contain one or two persons.

The Sailing-Boat.

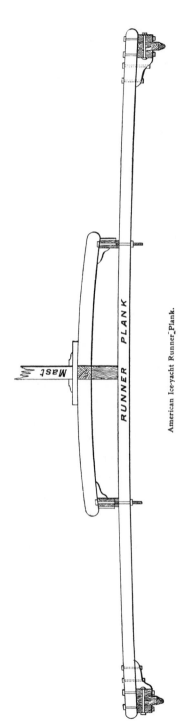

American Ice-yacht Runner-Plank.

AMERICAN ICE-YACHTS.[1]

A WINTER in the Northern States of America is, to the residents, a highly enjoyable season, particularly to those who are robust in health and full of life and vigour. Unlike a winter in the ever changeable climate of the British Islands, where, if we happen to be favoured with a week or ten days of seasonable hard frost, it is suddenly supplanted by a succession of half-mild, half-wet, or foggy, damp, unhealthy weather; so that in England we rarely can rely, even in depth of winter, on more than a week or ten days in succession of ice-bearing frost. But in the Northern States of America, after the winter once sets in, there is usually a continuous hard frost for two or three months or more, with bright exhilarating and thoroughly enjoyable weather: then is the time for active out-door sports and exercises in great variety on the hard-frozen Lakes and Rivers of that extensive continent.

And, as a recreation much appreciated, is that which is afforded by the ice-boat (or more properly ice-rafts), which are made to skid along the frozen surface of the ice at flying speed in a good wind.

Amongst the best and most scientifically constructed ice-yachts to be found in any part of the world are some of those belonging to members of the Ice-Yacht Sailing Clubs on the Hudson, in America.

Ice-yacht sailing matches are held every winter on the Hudson, and a very picturesque and exciting scene it is to witness a numerous fleet of those snow-winged craft skidding along the ice at flying speed in a keenly contested race.

The sloop rig is that generally used, but occasionally the cat rig. The latine rig has also been introduced on the Hudson in some of the most recent of the ice-yachts.

[1] For details as to construction of Ice-yachts, with scale drawings &c., see 'The Scientific American' Supplements, No. 63, p. 996, and No. 624; also 'Scribner's Monthly Magazine,' 1881, p. 658.

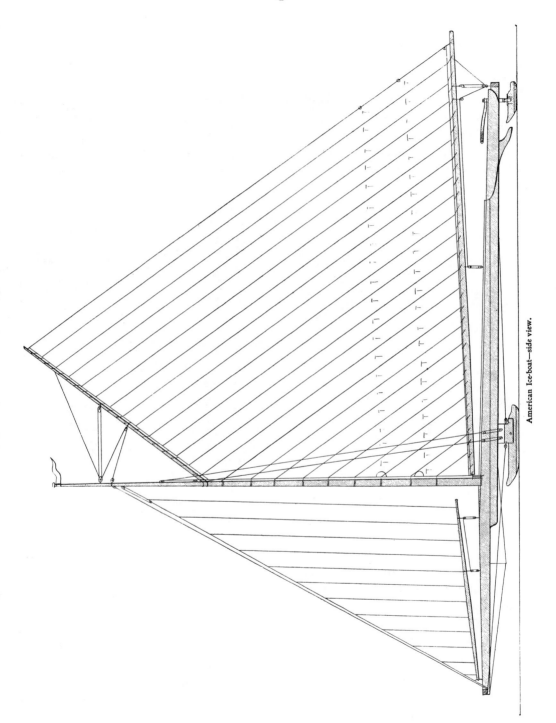

American Ice-boat—side view.

The Sailing-Boat.

At a point thirty miles above New York, the Hudson River is by the 1st of January, in every year, almost invariably frozen, presenting a long stretch of solid ice extending northward to a distance of 100 miles or more, and of a breadth varying from one to two miles.

The New York Central and Hudson River Railroad skirt the easterly bank of the river, and the ice-boats sometimes go racing along for many miles side by side with the railway trains, to the delight and amusement of the passengers—as the ice-boats, in a good breeze, easily outstrip the trains—amidst the waving of handkerchiefs and the lusty cheers of the railway passengers. The speed of the trains on this line rarely

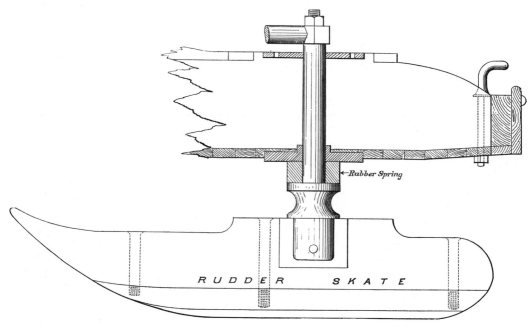

←*Rubber Spring*

RUDDER SKATE

American Ice-yacht Rudder Skate.

exceeds 35 miles an hour, but the ice-yachts, in a good breeze, with a free wind, travel at the rate of from 40 to 60 miles an hour, and they have been known to go (under exceptionally favourable conditions) at a much faster rate of speed, averaging above 100 miles an hour.

Poughkeepsie, a beautiful city on the high sloping banks of the River Hudson, is the home of the Hudson River Ice-Yacht Club. The yachting station is Hyde Park, Dutchess County, New York; the Club Houses and anchorage are at Roosevelt's Point and Crum Elbow. The Club have a Commodore, Vice-Commodore, Secretary, Treasurer, Measurer, and Regatta Committee, the duties of each of whom are prescribed by the Articles of Constitution.

Ice Sailing-Yachts.

They have also a Code of Signals, Bye-laws, and Sailing Rules and Regulations.

They have also a Challenge Pennant, which is sailed for every year, and is open to competition by any organised Ice-Yachting Club in America, or in Europe. The flag is a silk pennant 30 ft. long, with the words " Ice-Yacht Challenge Pennant of America " in gold letters on a blue ground.

There are several other Ice-Yacht Clubs on the Hudson, and in other parts of the Northern States of America; and many sailing-matches are held every year for other Challenge trophies and Club prizes, given for competition by the four different classes of ice-yachts—the first class measuring 600 square feet of sail area and over; the second class measuring 450 and under 600 square feet; the third class measuring 300 and under 450 square feet; and the fourth class measuring less than 300 square feet.[1]

RUSSIAN ICE-YACHTS.

THE sport of ice-yachting is, every winter, freely indulged in on the Neva and the broad expanse of frozen waters in the neighbourhood of Cronstadt, where ice-yachting is recognised as one of the most popular pastimes of the season. The 'Boier,' or Ice Yacht, is the attraction when the ice is not too deeply covered with snow, and when the surface is tolerably free from fissures and yawning gulfs of open water.

It would appear that considerable pains are taken in the construction and fitting out of the Russian ice-yachts. One of the largest is described as measuring 58 ft. in length by 28 ft. beam, or space between the runners. This yacht, named the *Yolka*, is the property of Mr. Olsufieff, and was built by Mr. G. W. Esch, of St. Petersburg, in whose name a recent work on 'Yachting in Russia' has been published, one portion of which deals largely with ice-yachts, and contains full details as to their form and construction, rigging, mode of sailing, &c., &c.

Ice-Yachting in China.—On the Pei-ho river, in China, the sport of Ice-Yacht Sailing is also freely indulged in by Europeans in the winter season, the Pei-ho being usually frozen over from about the middle of December to the middle of March, and thereby affording a very extensive frozen surface. The ice-yachts employed are of similar type to those of America, and are chiefly sloop-rigged.

[1] The Author takes the opportunity of acknowledging the courtesy of Mr. John A. Roosevelt, of Poughkeepsie, in sending him a copy of the Club Book of Rules, &c., and other information as to American Ice-yachts.

END OF PART VII.

PART VIII.

———◆———

FOREIGN AND COLONIAL BOATS.

CANOES.

THE term 'canoe' has in modern times acquired a much wider significance than formerly: as originally understood it implied a primitive form of boat constructed out of the trunk of a tree by hollowing it out with sharp cutting tools and by burning with gum or other resinous substance; and such was the original mode of construction of the canoe, not only by the ancient Britons but by the native savages and uncivilised inhabitants of remote islands and distant countries.

Of late years, however, the term 'canoe' has become of more general adoption, and is applied to special forms of boats of British, as also of American and Colonial construction; some of which are of admirable model and exquisite workmanship, designed as pleasure boats for cruising and voyaging: others of smaller size, from those known as Rob Roy Canoes, propelled by the double-bladed sweep, to the larger type of sailing and cruising canoe; but all professing to take the form, at bow and stern, of what has always been recognised as the canoe type.

In most books of voyages and travels, canoes are mentioned. Various nations have different methods of constructing them. The wild savages of remote islands form boats out of solid timber, with no other tools than sharp stones and shells, which they select from the shingle on the coast. With some the process is first to make a fire round the bottom part of a growing tree suitable for the purpose, whereby they burn it down. When fallen, the trunk is stripped of its branches, and hollowed out with flints and shells.

With others, the tardy operation of hollowing is accelerated by burning resinous gums on the part they wish to clear away. Some islanders, having iron at hand and larger tools than others, proceed as follows:—They cut down a large, long tree, and square the uppermost side; then, turning it upon the flat side, they shape the bottom, the outside, the head, and stern. Three holes are then bored in the bottom—one in the middle, and one at each end—down to the thickness they wish to leave it; for without some such gauging they would cut away the inside, and leave the bottom thinner than intended. The tree is turned, after the gauging-holes are bored; and being propped or fixed with the flat side uppermost, the tedious process of hollowing is commenced. It is usual, in a middle-sized canoe, to leave the bottom three inches thick, and the sides two inches at the lower part and one and a-half at the top. The ends are afterwards shaped and finished off to a point. With some islanders, after the tree is hollowed out, the sides are raised by wooden boards sewn on to the other part of the canoe with tough thongs and fibrous material; a primitive but secure mode of fastening. The famous sailing canoes of Ceylon[1] are instances of this mode of construction.

It is very remarkable that dug-out canoes should be so much in use at the present day; but another instance is found in Liu-Kiu, one of the islands of the Malay Archipelago, more especially as the materials necessary for their construction cannot there be too plentiful. They are in this part of the world almost purely characteristic of the Malayan race, and would be more likely to be the last relics of a bygone people than later introductions to a much further advanced civilisation.[2] And the same author observes:—'The only species of boat used in the interior of the country (Kamschatka) is the dug-out canoe,—a clumsily shaped craft made from the trunk of the *topyina* or poplar tree. They are generally about 25 or 30 ft. long by 2 ft. in beam and depth, and are made to a great extent by burning out the interior of the tree trunk selected, the finishing only being done by means of axes.[3]

Considerable time and labour are sometimes expended in carving figures on the stem and stern of native canoes, which in some countries are ornamented with carved ivory, shells, &c.

The canoes belonging to Hudson Straits and Greenland are flat-bottomed and flat-sided, and do not represent much of a sea-going quality; still it is surprising the sea they go through when under the expert management of the natives. The sails of these are made of skins and intestines of the walrus.

The canoes of the South Sea Islanders are larger, stronger, and better constructed than those of most other islanders. These will be the subject of a fuller description in subsequent pages.

A small-sized light canoe of peculiar construction is used on the coast of Labrador, capable of accommodating one person only, being entirely covered in fore and aft, leaving a round open space sufficient only to admit the body of its occupant on a low seat placed amidships. The length of these canoes, which are flat-bottomed, is from 16 ft. to 20 ft.—the depth about 14 in.; the breadth at the middle part (where it forms

[1] *Infra*, p. 454.
[2] 'The Cruise of the *Marchesa* to Kamschatka and New Guinea'; by F. H. H. Guillemard, 1886.
[3] *Ibid*, p. 136.

two angles) is about 2 ft. : from these angles it gradually inclines to a point at each end. In construction they are composed of a very light frame-work of wood, covered with walrus skins, and they are so light that they may be swept along at a rapid rate with the double paddle, and may be carried on the head many miles by one person only.

Models of many of these canoes may be seen at the United Service Museum, Whitehall; and will well repay inspection by those interested in such curiosities.

There are also many other kinds of canoes, some of which will form the subject of a more lengthened description in the subsequent pages of this work.

BOATS OF THE ANCIENT EGYPTIANS.

It appears that among the ancient Egyptians there were two classes of boat-builders—carpenters and wicker-workers. The boats built by the latter were used chiefly for fowling and fishing; they were made of osiers, and bound together with bands taken from the stalks of the papyrus or cyperus.[1]

Boats made from the papyrus are frequently mentioned by ancient writers. Isis is described by Plutarch, as going in search of the body of Osiris, 'through the fenny country, in a bark made of the papyrus.'[2] But they were so small and light, as to be easily carried from place to place on a man's shoulders.[3]

They are also described by Strabo,[4] at the cataracts of Syene, passing the falls in perfect safety, to the astonishment of the beholders; and Celsius affirms, that they were made of the papyrus.

Theophrastus mentions boats made of papyrus, and their sails and ropes of the rind of the same.[5]

Pliny also speaks of boats woven of the papyrus,[6] the rind being made into sails, curtains, matting, and ropes; and he elsewhere observes, that the papyrus, the rush, and the reed, were all used for making boats in Egypt.[7]

Vessels made of bulrushes, are mentioned in the Old Testament.[8]

The mode of binding and sewing boats with bands of the papyrus, are also alluded to by Lucan : 'Conseritur bibula Memphitis cymba papyro.'[9]

With these evidences before us, and those of the sculptures of Thebes and Memphis, there can be no doubt that boats were anciently made of the material

---

[1] *Vide* 'Champollion's Monuments de l'Egypte.' Also 'Manners and Customs of the Ancient Egyptians,' by Sir Gardner Wilkinson, F.R.S., M.R.S.L., &c. Third Edition. Vol. iii. A.D 1847.

[2] Plut. de Is. s. 18.   [3] Achilles Tatius, lib. iv. Plin. v. 9.

[4] Strabo, xvii. p. 562.   [5] Theophr. iv. 9.

[6] 'Ex ipso quidem papyro navigia texunt.' Plin. xiii. 11.   [7] Plin. vi. 22, vii. 16.

[8] Exod. ii. 3. Isaiah xviii. 2.   [9] Lucan iv. 136.

papyrus; and employed in various parts of Egypt, for fowling and fishing. Punts and canoes, made of osiers and papyrus, are still used on the Nile, and the lakes of Egypt.

The Egyptian 'boats of burden' were called *baris;* they are described by Herodotus as made of a thornwood, very similar to the lotus of Cyrene, from which a tear exudes, called gum. Of this tree they cut planks measuring about two cubits, and having arranged them like bricks, they built the boat in the following manner:—They fastened the planks around firmly with long pegs; and after this, they stretched over the surface a series of girths, but without any ribs, and the whole was bound within by bands of papyrus. A single rudder was then put through the keel; and a mast of thorn wood, and sails of the papyrus (rind) completed the rigging.

Pliny speaks of papyrus vessels crossing the sea, and visiting the island of Taprobane (Ceylon).—'Quia papyraceis navibus armamentisque Nili peteretur (Taprobane).'[1] It may be, however, that he merely alludes to the sails of the vessels being made of the papyrus; for there is abundant evidence that the ancient Egyptians had large boats of burthen, made of wooden planks.

Sir Gardner Wilkinson observes:—'We may be certain that the Egyptians had strong and well-built vessels for the purpose of trade, by sea; and for carrying merchandize, corn, and other heavy commodities, on the Nile; and that, even if they had been very bold and skilful navigators, they would not have ventured to India, nor have defeated the fleets of Phœnicia, in their paper vessels.'[2]

MODE OF NAVIGATION OF THE VESSELS OF THE NILE.

NEITHER sails nor rudders were used with the canoes and punts of the ancient Egyptians; they were propelled with paddles, in deep water, and pushed ahead with a pole, in shallow water. But the absence of a sail in the canoes did not always depend on the size of the vessel; for it appears that many of their fishing canoes, some of which were very small, were provided with a mast and sail.

The pleasure boats of the ancient Egyptians were usually provided with two rudders, one on each side of the stern; the rudder consisted of a long broad paddle, of great size and strength; and the tiller, which formed part of the paddle, or rudder, was supported by pillars. The steersmen moved the rudder by means of a rope fastened to the tiller head.

Other boats, though of large size, appear to have had but one rudder, and this was usually placed in a groove, or notch, in the centre of the stern.

[1] Plin. vi. 22. [2] 'Manners and Customs of the Ancient Egyptians,' vol. iii. p. 189.

The Sailing-Boat.

The only kind of sail used by the ancient Egyptians appears to have been a sort of square-sail, with a yard both at the top and bottom.

The prow of the ancient Egyptian boats was generally decorated with a painted eye on each side of the stem; a peculiarity that has been kept up by the Chinese through centuries past, to the present day. The head and stern of the Egyptian pleasure boats were generally ornamented with a painting, or carving of a richly coloured flower.

Most of the ancient Egyptian boats are shown with a man standing at the prow

Boat of the Ancient Egyptians.

with a pole in his hand, wherewith to sound the depth of the water and signal to the helmsman when near a shoal, or sand-bank. The precaution of the sounding-pole is still adopted in all the Nile boats, wherever the pilot is doubtful about the depth of water.

The war-galleys of the ancient Egyptians were also provided with a square-sail, but it differed from the rig of the pleasure boats, inasmuch as it had no lower yard; the sail was therefore the more readily furled, by means of four separate furling-ropes, or brails, which, on being pulled, frapped the sail close to the upper yard in four or five folds.

The square-sails were always guided by braces, or guy-ropes, called *pedes*; these were attached to the extreme ends of the upper yard of the sails. Some of the boats were rigged with a sort of shear-mast, which consisted of two separate spars, placed wide apart below, but closing at the top, so as to leave sufficient space for the yard of the sail to be hoisted between them. The mast was secured by one fore stay and several back stays. None of the boats of the ancient Egyptians appear to have been fitted with more than one sail to each mast. When a single mast was used, it was very firmly fixed, the foot of it being secured to a strong beam, which extended across the whole breadth of the floor; it was also supported by strong knees and lashings, and finally secured by stout stays and shrouds, leading from the mast head to the sides and stern of the boat; and it appears, that all these were necessary to compensate for the heavy yards and sail that were carried on the boat; and which, when hoisted and fairly set, were so considerably elevated, that the lower yard was fully 6 ft. above the gunwales.

When they wished to lower this sail, the upper yard was let down, whilst the lower one continued stationary; and in this position the sail was stowed, and remained so until again required.

The yards consisted of two separate pieces, scarped and joined in the middle.

The sails of the grand pleasure-boats of the ancient Egyptians were sometimes painted with gaudy colours, and embroidered with fanciful devices; but these sails were made of linen, woven expressly for sails; the leeches of which were strengthened with borders, and sometimes with a small rope.[1]

BOATS OF THE MODERN EGYPTIANS.

NILE BOATS.

' Like a young Nile-bird, turn'd my boat
To the fair island, on whose shores,
Through leafy palms and sycamores,
Already shone the moving lights
Of pilgrims, hastening to the rites '

T. MOORE.

THE native Nile boats, though of a somewhat antiquated appearance as regards their form of hull, are well adapted for the navigation of that grand and interesting river.

The various classes of native boats of the Nile are:—

The *Djèrm* (Germ): the *Maádil, Aggub* (Akkub): *Maash*, or *Rahleh, Dahabéëh, Cangia* (Kangeh): *Kyás* (Kyáseh): *Sándal, Seféence, Garib* (Kárib): and *Maadéëh*.[2]

Of these, the largest are the *Germs*, which are only employed on the Nile during the inundation, when the water is deep; or between Alexandria, Rosetta, and other ports on the Mediterranean. During the summer they are laid up and covered with matting, to protect them from the sun. The *Germs* have capacity for carrying a large cargo of corn; in the transport of which they are chiefly engaged: they are rigged with two masts, large latine sails and a foresail.

---

[1] *Vide* 'Manners and Customs of the Ancient Egyptians,' by Sir Gardner Wilkinson, F.R.S., &c., 1847. 3rd edit. cap. IX.

[2] *Vide* 'Modern Egypt and Thebes,' by Sir Gardner Wilkinson, F.R.S., M.R.S.L., F.R.G.S., &c., &c. Vol. i. A.D. 1843.

The Sailing-Boat.

The *Maádil*, or as it is sometimes called, kyás, is a similar kind of vessel, but much smaller.

The *Aggub* is used almost exclusively for carrying stone, and is remarkable among the boats of the Nile for its peculiarity of rig; for, whilst all the other sailing boats are rigged with latine sails, the *Aggub* carries a square sail.

The remaining five are small open boats.

Sándal implies a small sort of *Cangia* or ship's boat.

The *Garib* is a fishing boat.

The *Maadéëh* is a ferry boat.

The *Maash*, *Dahabéëh*, and *Cangia*, are all passenger boats, and employed chiefly as such on the Nile; all three are furnished with cabins.

Of these, the *Maash* or *Rahleh* is the largest, and has the most lofty and commodious cabins.

The *Dahabéëh* and the *Cangia* are the favourite boats of English tourists, and in some respects they are similar in appearance, but the arrangement of the masts and sails is different. The *Dahabéëh* is, however, the larger and more commodious of the two, and is furnished with a gangway on each side of the cabin, extending to the steerage. The modern *Dahabéëh* has also a rounded stern, which the *Cangia* has not. Both kinds are rigged with two masts and latine sails, with lofty peaks to catch the wind above the high banks of the river when the water is low.

In the *Dahabéëh*, the foresail is much the larger sail of the two, and is attached to a

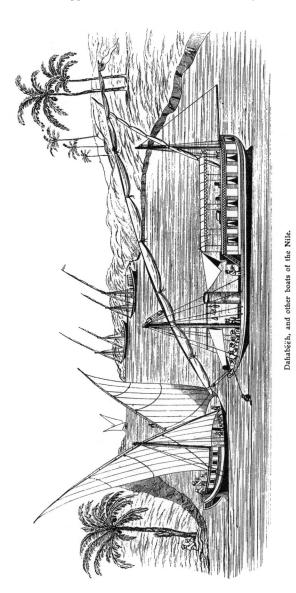

Dahabéëh, and other boats of the Nile.

very long tapering yard; in some of the boats upwards of 100 ft. in length, thick at the lower end, but gradually diminishing to a slender substance at the peak; at the extreme point of which the flag or pennant is hoisted. The main-mast which is short and thick, is stepped in the fore part of the vessel, and the mizzen-mast at the stern, abaft the cabin and quarter-deck. The mizzen-sail is also a latine, but not nearly so large and lofty as the mainsail. The boatmen set both sails on going up the Nile against the current, when the wind is suitable; but on coming down, they stow away the mainsail and shift the mizzen-sail to the main-mast, and so drift steadily down with the current.

A large water filter, encased in a wooden frame, usually occupies the centre of the main-deck, and forms a prominent feature in that part of the boat.

The bulwarks are very low, scarcely 6 in. in height above the level of the deck.

The stern, or aft part, of all the native Nile boats is much higher out of water than the fore part, and the rudders are, of necessity, very large and powerful.

The keel of the Nile boats is of concave form, being deepest at the stem and stern, whilst there is scarcely any keel at all amidships; the advantage of which is, that when they get aground forward, by putting the helm to port or starboard, the hollow part clears the bank, and enables the boat to get off immediately.

There is, among the naval collection of models in the Kensington Museum, a beautiful model upon a large scale of a *Dahabëeh* with sails, rigging, &c., complete; it is, in fact, a model of a Nile boat that was built some years since for His Highness the then Viceroy of Egypt. It has a sharp hollow bow, but is broad in the aft part, with a flat floor and shallow form of hull; and, like other Nile boats, is low at the bows and high at the stern, with cabin and gallery, after the manner represented in the illustration.

It will be seen that the main-mast in the *Dahabëeh* is placed in the forepart of the boat, thereby enabling the mainsail to be manipulated without interference with the promenade deck and saloon: the mizzen-mast and sail standing at the extreme end of the boat; and being very small in comparison with the main-mast and sail, cause no inconvenience to the passengers.

The best of the modern *Dahabëehs* are now built on the Clyde, and taken out to the Nile; these, needless to say, are of superior construction to the native-built boats, particularly in regard to saloon, cabin, and other accommodation; and they are more comfortable and convenient, as well as safer under sail than the old style of native boat: but the mast, spars, sails and rigging are all of the native form and design; long experience proving that such are best suited to the navigation of the Nile. The dimensions of a modern *Dahabëeh* of the newest type, built on the Clyde, are—length over all 108 ft., beam 17 ft. 6 in., draft 2 ft., with spacious saloon and cabins, all with good head room, and promenade deck over.

The Sailing-Boat.

A modern native *Dahabéëh* is fully and minutely described in a work of great merit and interest,[1] as 97 ft. in length from bow to stern, and 14 ft. 2 in. in width.

The *Cangia* is about 30 ft. long, with two masts and latine sails, the larger of which is set amidships, and the smaller one in the bows. The sails require constant attention and nice management, or there is sometimes great risk of capsizing, by the sudden squalls which come down from the hills in some parts of the regions intersected by the Nile.

The aft part of the *Cangia* is occupied by a double cabin, with a narrow space between; the principal one opening on to the deck, and prolonged as it were, by means of an open verandah, under which it is pleasant to sit during the great heat of the day. There is also a bench on each side of the main cabin, which has windows with green blinds, that can be opened and shut at pleasure.[2]

The *Sandal*, which is a small kind of *Cangia*, is rigged with one mast only, and a latine sail.

When they row the larger class of native Nile boats, they lift alternate planks from the deck, which are made to shift for the purpose; these they place on such as remain, and sit upon them, dropping their feet through the openings, and in such position they are enabled to ply their long oars with considerable effect. When the wind is fair, the sails only are used; when it is foul they are furled; but if the rowers do not use the oars, they commence 'tracking,' or towing the vessel by means of a hawser, to which smaller ropes are attached and passed over the shoulders of the trackers on the banks of the river, one to each man. The progress is exceedingly slow, five miles a day being about the average. The boatmen never use the sails for tacking as we do ; they are too large and unwieldy for that purpose, and are somewhat dangerous if sudden gusts of wind catch them.[3]

The Nile boatmen are careless sailors, and much in the habit of making the main-sheet (*shoghóol*) fast : and to this, and the disproportionate size of the sails, may be attributed many of the accidents which occur to the smaller Nile boats.

When a squall is observed approaching, the Egyptian pilot directs the attention of his crew to the halliards and brails, by the signal ' *Arless! arless !* ' which means, ' take care ' or ' be ready ; ' it is then surprising to witness the alacrity of the boatmen, who are otherwise often lazy and inactive, but when aroused by warning of danger just the reverse.

Nevertheless, they make not the least objection to jumping into the water with their clothes on (they are not over-burdened with such) on any emergency, and swimming to the shore or to neighbouring boats.

[1] 'Four Months in a Dahabéëh,' by M. L. Carey, 1863, pp. 80 and 81.
[2] 'The Nile Boat,' by W. H. Bartlett, 5th ed. 1862, p. 125.
[3] 'Up the Nile,' &c., by F. H. Fairholt, F.S.A., 1862, p. 81

Nile Boats.

The mode of furling the sails of the larger Nile boats is interesting. Whilst peaked up high in the air, and swaying to and fro in the wind, the crew run up the mast and climb along the lofty yard with the agility of ancient *funambuli* ;[1] distributing themselves at equal distances apart from each other; and in such positions, clinging to or sitting astride of the yard, they furl the sail with the smartness of English man-of-war sailors. In the large boats, sometimes as many as eight at a time are upon the main-yard furling the sail. The lightest youth goes first and highest up, to the

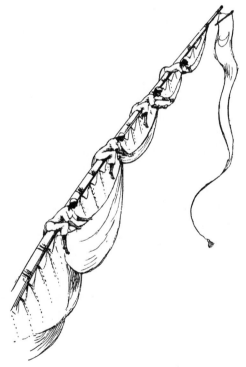

Egyptian Funambuli, furling the sail.

slender part of the yard; the next lightest follow behind him, and so on, leaving the heaviest below, at the thick end of the yard and broadest part of the sail.

Catamarans, or Log-Boats of the Nile.—The primitive notion of crossing rivers on logs of buoyant wood is one that still prevails, even in countries where arts and sciences are liberally cultivated and broadly extended; and notwithstanding that boats and vessels of superior form and construction are daily before the eyes of those who are in the habit of using such rustic contrivances.

[1] *Supra*, p. 8.

The Sailing-Boat.

The Nile catamarans are simply thick logs of wood, about 4 ft. or 5 ft. in length, cut from the date tree, the fore end being trimmed and pointed with a view to diminishing the resistance to the water; sometimes two or three of the logs are lashed together, so as to form a more burdensome raft, for the purpose of carrying passengers and cargo across the river.

When a single log is used, the weight of the occupant is sometimes alone sufficient to sink it below the surface, although still maintaining buoyancy enough to keep the adventurer above water.

The manner of sitting and using the native catamarans on the Nile is remarkable, and requires considerable practice. Some of the Nubian boys are very skilful in the management of them, and afford great amusement to the Nile-boat voyagers; they sit and lie upon their catamarans in various positions; sometimes at full length, on their stomachs, and yet propelling the log with undiminished speed, paddling across the bows of the passenger Nile boats, as if to mock their tardy progress; and all the while using nothing but their hands and legs to propel the log ahead. Sometimes they bind their bundles on the top of their heads and seat themselves astride the log-raft on crossing the river or shooting the rapids. Others sit upright, with their legs stretched out straight before them along the sides of the log; and then, with a balance-sweep or double-bladed oar, they propel the raft ahead, by alternate strokes to right and left. In this way the Nubian inhabitants of Assouan, to this day, ferry themselves across the Nile to feed and look after their sheep and goats on the opposite shore; sometimes carrying bundles of fodder, in the shape of Indian corn leaves, and other provender, lashed to the catamaran with cords made from the fibres of the same date tree of which the floating log itself forms part. The Nubian boys perform very venturesome feats with these catamarans; riding upon them apparently without fear, as they shoot over the most perilous and roaring cataracts, choosing, as they do, for the sake of daring, the fiercest and most rapid parts of the torrent, to the astonishment and amusement of the Nile-boat voyagers; and all the while guiding their rolling barks and retaining their positions upon them with admirable skill.[1] Sometimes they appear totally submerged, log and all, and apparently half drowned; but they never fail to come up again, and, with smiling faces, ask for that undying gratification, 'backsheesh.'[2]

[1] See 'The Nile Boat,' by W. H. Bartlett, 1862, p. 208 (5th ed.).
[2] See 'The Nile and its Banks,' by Rev. Alfred Charles Smith, 1868. Vol. ii., p. 11.

American Boats.

AMERICAN BOATS.

TIME flies, but records of great victories are preserved. It is now just fifty years since one of the most sensational matches ever sailed in British waters came off under the auspices of the Royal Yacht Squadron, in a stiff breeze, on a fine course from off Cowes harbour round the Isle of Wight to the eastward, and home by the Needles to the west, which resulted in a yacht of American design and construction carrying off the palm of victory from the shores of our Island, immediately beneath the spotless ensign of the Royal Yacht Squadron.

It is matter of history that, in the year 1851, a famous schooner yacht, named the

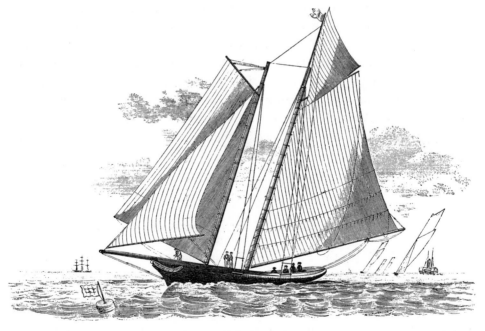

American Yacht " America."

America, owned by Mr. J. C. Stevens, then Commodore of the New York Yacht Club, was sent across the Atlantic and arrived at Cowes on July 31st in that year, to compete at our regattas on the Solent and elsewhere with the fastest yachts of the British pleasure fleet; and, in fact, she brought with her a challenge to sail a match with any yacht that might be chosen to compete with her.

The Sailing-Boat.

The *America* shortly afterwards was entered among a fleet of seventeen English yachts; and on August 23rd in that year sailed in the memorable match of the Royal Yacht Squadron, when no less than fifteen started, seven of which were schooners of large tonnage and eight were cutters; and among the fleet were some of the most celebrated of the British racing yachts of the period. In this, her first race in English waters, the *America* proved victorious, and carried off, with great triumph, the prize Cup of the Royal Yacht Squadron.

In several subsequent matches with chosen yachts of our pleasure fleet she was also eminently successful, and proved an invincible clipper.

The yacht *America* was in fact the wonder of her day, and was frankly admitted to be without a rival in British waters. The sensation created at the time in yachting circles by her marvellous powers ' on a wind ' and repeated victories will not soon be forgotten.

Since the period alluded to, several remarkable contests have taken place in American waters, between American and British yachts of the larger class, which it is not the Author's intention in these pages to enter upon in detail; this volume being devoted mainly to yachts of the smaller class; some of which, however, have come from America to compete with those of British construction; and in many cases the American boats have been victorious. The performances of several of these have already been referred to in previous pages;[1] it would therefore be superfluous to repeat them here, where the Author's purpose is chiefly that of the descriptive, as regards the different types of boats and small yachts, and of their varieties of rig and other distinguishing features.

AMERICAN CENTRE-BOARD (OR REVOLVING-KEEL) SAILING BOATS.

THE Continent of North America with its numerous outlying islands, deeply indented coast line, extensive lakes, bays, and inlets, affords advantages for yachting and boat-sailing unequalled in extent by those of any other nation.

In the immediate vicinity of New York the waters are, however, too crowded with shipping and commercial traffic to allow of a free indulgence in those pastimes. But off the shores of Maine and the eastern sea-board of North America, for more than a thousand miles in extent, no more advantageous coast can be found for enjoyment of the delightful recreation of yachting and boat-sailing. And as many parts of the coast are sandy and shallow, the native boats are constructed of a form and rig to suit the surroundings.

[1] *Vide* pp. 93, 183, 198-9, 201.

American Boats.

In the United States of America the use of the revolving centre-board for small yachts and sailing-boats is almost universal. But the form of the yacht or boat, the size and sometimes the position of the centre-board, are somewhat different to those of English construction.

When the revolving ' centre-board ' first came into use in America, it was, usually, made of oak, though occasionally of pitch pine ; but the foot of it was always bolted and clamped with iron.[1]

It is claimed for the American revolving ' centre-board ' sailing-boat, that she will stand up to her canvas by means of her shape, without the aid of ballast, and that she will ride over a sea that would put the decks of an English cutter, of the same tonnage, under water. An important feature in the rig of an American centre-boarder is, that the sails be made so as to stand as flat as possible, and the mainsail laced to the boom.

The American revolving centre-board sailing-boat is usually of broader construction than those built in England. The broad beam of the American boat is said to give her great stability and buoyancy, enabling the boat to carry a large spread of canvas, with but little list to leeward. And standing up so well to her canvas enables her to carry the centre-board in its most favourable position for resisting lee-way.

The light draft of the American boat is also of considerable advantage in those parts of the coast where they are employed; such being chiefly in tidal harbours obstructed by shoals and sand banks ; as by raising the centre-board, the boat may be sailed in shallow water, and so run over such obstacles and got into port, whilst the deep-keel boat has to bring-up at anchor and await the flow of the tide.

It is also said to be a mistake to suppose that the American revolving centre-board boat is fit only for smooth water ; it is claimed for them that they are excellent sea-boats. Being of so buoyant a form, they ride over the waves ; and having but little water to displace, and answering readily to the helm, their movements are very quick. And in fine weather their light draft and great spread of sail naturally enable them to move very briskly ; and it will be found that even under double reefs, in a strong wind and heavy sea, they labour far less than a keel boat of narrow form and deep draft. Under a double-reefed mainsail these boats do not require a foresail when on a wind ; but when off the wind, with a following sea, a head sail of some kind is requisite to make them steer well and avoid the possibility of broaching-to. All centre-board boats steer very hard with the wind abaft the beam.

Another advantage boats of this type possess is that, in taking the ground the revolving centre-board is forced up, whereby the boat is enabled to sit upon the bottom in an upright position.

[1] An illustration of the famous boat *Truant*, an American revolving centre-board boat, has already been given, *supra*, page 92.

The Sailing-Boat.

THE NEWPORT OR CAT RIG.

THE Newport (or Cat rig as it is now generally called) is known in England as 'the *Una* rig.' It is in very general use in the United States of America, and is in fact more widely distributed there than any other form of rig. It is found on all parts of the coast from Maine to Florida; and is distinctly American.

Cat-rigged boats are usually very broad and shallow, with a deep revolving centre-

The Cat Rig.

board ; their single mast is 'chock for'ard' in the extreme bows of the boat ; and although the gaff is short and the sail narrow at the upper part, it is very broad at the foot, and requires a long boom to spread it, extending several feet over the stern.

The American Cat boats of the Una type, with only one sail, are remarkably handy in tacking and turning to windward, being quick and certain in stays—in fact no boat of any rig is more so.

The larger of the Cat-boats are rigged, some as sloops and some as yawls ; but the smaller, or those of less than 25 ft. in length, are of the Cat rig, with one sail only.

The Double Cat Rig.—The American 'double cat,' or that known as the rig of the Makinaw Boats, is a simple, convenient, and handy kind of rig of the yawl type. It is in use also on some of the larger lakes, and in the vicinity of Detroit, Michigan.

THE SHARPEY.

THE American Sharpey is usually from about 32 ft. to 35 ft. in length, and from 6 ft. to 7 ft. beam ; it is therefore a narrow type of boat. The Sharpey has an upright stem and flat-shaped sides, with a raking stern ; it is also flat-bottomed, but with considerable spring at both ends, so that as the Sharpey sits afloat upon the surface,

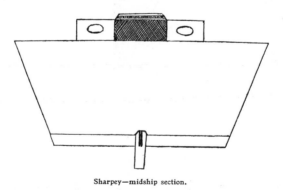

Sharpey—midship section.

the stem is about 6 in. and the stern about 4 in. out of the water. Her draft amidships is from 8 in. to 12 in.

The rig of the Sharpey is peculiar, and is confined to two sails, which are set on tall tapering masts, without either shrouds or stays. The sails are of jib-like shape, as shown in the illustration. The tack of each sail is bowsed down to the lower part of the mast ; from the tack the sail rises gradually to the outer end aft, where it is seized to the boom ; the inner end of the boom is set in an eyelet made to receive it at about

3 ft. or 4 ft. above the tack; and on the clew of the sail being hauled out taut at the outer end of the boom, the sail is made to stand very flat. This mode of fitting the boom to the sail is similar to that of the native Bermudian rig.

The Sharpey is also fitted with a revolving centre-board at about midships, which is let down when working to windward, but has to be hauled up when the boat is

Sharpey—two masted.

navigated in shallow water. The rudder is of iron, and of the form indicated by the illustration; the post of the rudder is worked through an iron pipe, which serves as a case for it, the rudder itself hanging in a drooping position at the aft end so as to obtain a better grip of the water. The Sharpey is decked all over with the exception of a cockpit abaft the mainmast, and has good cabin accommodation. Drawing so little water, the Sharpey sails fast in light airs, but requires careful handling, being narrow and flat-bottomed; it is nevertheless said to do well in a sea-way.

When working to windward in shallow water in a breeze, with the centre-plate up,

American Boats.

the crew sit to leeward, or list the boat with some weight (usually bags of sand), so that the straight side may take hold of the water. They are built of 1 in. stuff, are

Sharpey—single masted.

an inexpensive kind of boat, used mostly at Fair Haven and New Haven in Long Island Sound for oystering; and they have the reputation of being fairly good sea boats under experienced handling.

The Sailing-Boat.

THE DORY.

THE American Dory is a boat of small dimensions, employed chiefly along the New England coast. Being easy to build and cheap, it is in common use everywhere, chiefly by fishermen, to the exclusion of other more costly boats.

The Dory is usually 16 ft. to 18 ft. in length, with raking stem and stern, both pretty high; very sloping sides, and consequently narrow bottom. The sides consist of two wide planks, and there is a good deal of spring in the floor. These boats are light and buoyant; and in the hands of those accustomed to their use are said to be far better in a heavy sea than any other craft.

To a stranger they appear very ticklish, but although they heel very readily, are not easily capsized. They run smoothly, but turn with a slight movement of the oar. Drawing but little water, the Dory is very handy in landing on a beach, and may be readily hauled up and easily launched. Occasionally they are fitted with a small revolving centre-board, placed well forward. Their rig consists of one small triangular sail. They are steered with an oar over the aft side.

The thwarts of the Dory are movable; and it is usual for the larger class of fishing vessels from the coast towns to take six or eight of them aboard, packing them one inside the other; and on arrival at the fishing grounds they are unshipped and the thwarts replaced. Each Dory is then manned by two fisherman, with tackle, gear, and other requisites.

THE RIVERSIDE DORY CLASS.

THE members of the Riverside Yacht Club, New York, have recently established a Dory Class, with a view to the encouragement of single-handed boat-sailing. Boats of the class are to be 17 ft. in length over all, and 13 ft. on the keel, with a beam of 4 ft.; they are to be fitted with a centre-board, and the rig to comprise mainsail and foresail only. The boats are all to be painted white, and each named after a salt-water fish; they will be very inexpensive to build, and it is expected that much good racing and amusement will be derived from them.

Canadian Boats.

CANADIAN YACHTS AND BOATS.

THE main hydrographical feature of British North America is the extensive chain of lakes, containing an area of 150,000 square miles, connected with and contributing to the great river system of the St. Lawrence. The upper area, which comprises nearly two-thirds of the Dominion, is a region of water-ways and great river systems.

By the British North America Act of 1867, the Provinces of Upper and Lower Canada (Ontario and Quebec), Nova Scotia, and New Brunswick, were united under the title of 'Dominion of Canada.'

Canada is rich in timber and beautiful varieties of woods of every degree of hardness, toughness, and flexibility. The Dominion is therefore highly favoured with facilities for the production of yachts and boats of a superior class, and its beautiful lakes and rivers afford a ready means of indulging in aquatic sports and pastimes to the very heart's content of the residents.

THE "GLENCAIRN" CANADIAN RACING-BOAT.

THE illustration shows the profile of the Canadian representative yacht *Glencairn*, the winner of the 'International' Yacht Race for the Seawanhaka Corinthian Challenge

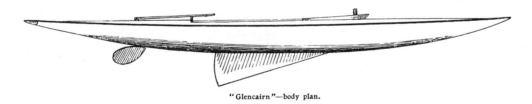

"Glencairn"—body plan.

Cup. The match was sailed in Oyster Bay, Long Island Sound, in 1896. The *Glencairn* was designed by Mr. G. H. Duggan, of Montreal. Her dimensions are: length over all, 23 ft.; length on L.W.L., 12 ft. 6 in.; beam, 6 ft. 3 in.; draft, 6 in.

It will be seen from these dimensions that this boat has very extensive overhang fore and aft, and that her load-water-line length is little more than half her actual length over all; she therefore represents a very extreme type of overhang, the angle of the load-water-line being scarcely perceptible as the boat sits upon the surface of the water; and when pressed upon her side by a strong breeze her load-water-line becomes a myth.

The Sailing-Boat.

The *Glencairn* is a very shallow boat, broad and flat at the bottom, with a steel centre-plate having its apex at about equal distance from point to point of stem and stern.

It will also be seen from the illustration of the sail-plan that for a boat of such dimensions and small displacement her sails are very large, the area of the mainsail being 246 square feet, and that of her racing foresail 52 square feet. Through the courtesy of the Commodore of the Royal St. Lawrence Yacht Club, and of the designer, Mr. G. H. Duggan, the Author is enabled to give the illustration of sail plan and dimensions.

A model of the hull of the *Glencairn* was exhibited at the Yachting Exhibition at the Imperial Institute in the summer of 1897, from which, aided by the drawings sent by Mr. Duggan, the Author has been enabled to have a profile illustration made of the hull of this boat.

It should be mentioned that the *Glencairn* had been launched only about two weeks previous to the time when she was shipped to Oyster Bay to take part in the International match above referred to.

In the following year (1897) the Seawanhaka Corinthian Yacht Club matches were sailed on Lake St. Louis, Montreal, when the race for the International Challenge Cup for boats of a larger class than in the previous year was contested between *Glencairn II.* (Canadian boat) and the *Momo* (American). The *Glencairn II.* was a boat of similar type to *Glencairn I.*, but somewhat modified on account of the difference in size of the boats of 1897 and those of 1896, and the restrictions that were agreed upon, making it desirable to have proportionately less beam than in the boat of the previous year; but the revolving centre-board (which was of steel) was of the same shape as that of *Glencairn I.* The rig was, however, quite different, *Glencairn II.* being rigged with a gaff-mainsail, and her principal dimensions were : L.O.A., 32 ft.; L.W.L., 17 ft. 6 in.; beam, 8 ft.; sail area, 500 sq. ft. The overhang fore and aft, therefore, though rather less in proportion to the previous year's boat, was nevertheless very extensive.

In the first of the series the race was won by the *Momo*, but the second, third, and fourth races were all won by the *Glencairn II.* The Canadian boat thus retained the trophy, which was wrested from the Americans in the previous year by *Glencairn I.* in Oyster Bay.

In 1898 the Seawanhaka Corinthian Challenge Cup was again the object of keen competition, two new boats being built for the American Yacht Club to take part in trial races, and two others by private individuals; also a new boat for Lord Strathcona from the board of Mr. G. H. Duggan, who designed the two famous Glencairn boats.

The boat selected for the American Yacht Club was named the *Challenger*, and that for the Canadians the *Dominion*. The race, which was sailed on Lake St. Louis, was again won by the Canadian boat; but owing to objection by the New York Yacht

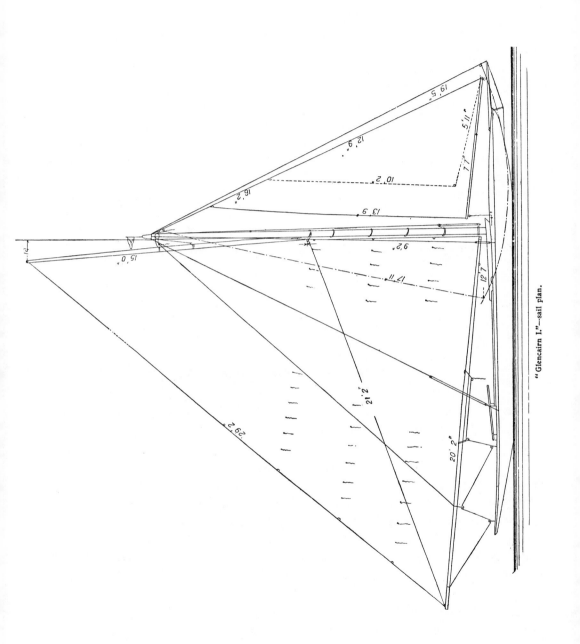

"Glencairn I."—sail plan.

Club, after the match was sailed, that the *Dominion* was a 'freak' sort of boat, the winner handed back the trophy to the Americans.

Full explanations, not a fitting subject for these pages, may be seen in *Forest and Stream* of the date referred to.

In July and August, 1899, a series of races for the Seawanhaka Challenge Cup were again sailed on Lake St. Louis, the competing boats being the Canadian boat *Glencairn* and the challenging yacht *Constance*. In these contests the two first of the matches were won by *Constance*, and the two next by *Glencairn*. In the final match the *Constance* unfortunately took the ground before the starting-gun was fired, and afterwards refused to proceed, thus leaving the *Glencairn* to sail over the course alone. The trophy is therefore still held by the Canadian yacht *Glencairn* of the Royal St. Lawrence Yacht Club of Montreal.

The Royal St. Lawrence Yacht Club has now adopted a One-Design Class, particulars of which were published in *Forest and Stream* of April 29th, 1899.

BIRCH-BARK CANOES.

'He hollow'd a boat of the birchen bark,
  Which carried him off from shore;
The wind was high and the clouds were dark,
  And the boat returned no more.'

T. MOORE.

THE Iroquois Indians are the most expert makers of the birch-bark canoes. The largest are called 'North Canoes,' some of which are thirty-six feet in length by about six in breadth. These are propelled with paddles by a crew of sixteen men (besides a bowman and steersman), who by the short quick stroke drive the canoe along at the rate of eight miles an hour when going with the stream.

The bowman is the chief navigator; he 'fends off' at the bow with his pole when running rapids, and directs the crew as to the paddling of the canoe. These canoes are sometimes sailed when the wind is free, but not otherwise. Small sails only are used, for the canoes are tender under sail, and require very careful management.

The birch-bark canoes are used for travelling through the wild and unsettled parts of North America; voyages of nearly one hundred miles per day are sometimes performed in them. In a canoe of this kind the Governor of the Hudson's Bay Company used to perform his annual trip to the Red River settlement. They were also formerly used by the old 'North-West Company' for the purpose of conveying the peltrie (*i.e.* furs) from inland parts, and as far north as Hudson's Bay to Montreal.

The smallest of the birch-bark canoes are about twelve feet long; these may be carried by one man, and are what are termed 'light hunting canoes.' They are also used as postage canoes. But even the largest of the birch-bark canoes are so light that they are often carried on the shoulders several miles by four men.

In building the birch-bark canoe, a skeleton is first made of light wood; the casing or planking of bark is then put on—not lengthwise, like the streaks of an ordinary boat, but transversely, passing under the boat and ending at the gunwales—the broadest strips being placed amidships. The bark is sewn together with the fibrous roots of the fir-tree, and the seams are well dressed with the gum of the balsam-tree. When they become leaky, the place is stopped by warming the gum, and plastering over it a thin piece of birch-bark.

The bark of which these canoes are made is stripped from the birch-tree in winter, the largest trees affording the most useful bark. The canoes are also sometimes trimmed and strengthened with wicker wreaths, and ribs or timbers of cedar, which are almost as light as cork. The wicker wreaths are about as thick in substance as a silver crown-piece, but the birch-bark is as thick as two crown-pieces, and the cedar ribs as thick as three or four. On the inside of the boat a rim or gunwale of tough wood is fitted, and the top ends of the cedar ribs are enclosed in it.[1]

Canadian Birch-Bark Canoe.

Canadian Birch-Bark Canoes.—The Canadian birch-bark canoes are ingeniously and beautifully constructed, and are a credit to the industry and skill of the inhabitants of the country which produces them. They are also remarkable for the material of which they are composed, and for their extreme lightness and buoyancy, matters of great importance in the navigation of rivers abounding with rapids, cataracts, and other obstructions. The whole of the outside, or planking, consists of the bark of the American birch-tree—a material tough enough in its nature, if carefully employed, but easily ripped or injured when coming in contact with hard substances.

[1] For a minute description as to the mode of building these canoes, see Peter Kalm's 'Travels in North America.'

The Sailing-Boat.

The lightness and easy transport of these boats overland, is a great advantage in Canada, where the navigation of the rivers is continually interrupted by cataracts, waterfalls, and shallows.

A full-sized Montreal bark canoe, from which the above illustration was drawn, was exhibited in the International Exhibition of 1851. It is described as made from the bark of the white birch, and as one of the largest class of canoes used in the north-west country. Prior to its being forwarded to England, it made a voyage in the spring of the previous year of upwards of 3,000 miles, with a crew of twenty men and their stock of necessaries and provisions.

Being exceedingly light, part of the crew are enabled to carry one of these canoes, when it is essential to avoid the falls and rapids; and, for months together, the birch-bark canoe forms the home by night and by day of the hardy voyagers during their transit to and from the Far West.[1]

'Soon as the woods on shore look dim,
We'll sing at St. Ann's our parting hymn,
Row, brothers, row, the stream runs fast,
The rapids are near and the daylight's past.' [2]

Birch-bark canoes are also used by the Sioux (who purchase them of the Chippeways) in gathering wild rice, which grows about the rivers and lakes of the north country. The manner of gathering it is curious. One woman paddles the canoe, whilst another, with a stick in each hand, bends the rice over the canoe with one, and strikes it with the other, and so shells it into the canoe, which is constantly moving along until it is filled.[3]

They are also used for wild-fowl shooting; wild-fowl of all kinds being abundant in those parts; and as they feed and fatten on the rice, they are plump and fleshy and well worth the shooting, at certain seasons of the year.

[1] 'Exhibition Catalogue, 1851,' vol. ii.
[2] T. Moore, 'Canadian Boat Song.'
[3] 'Letters and Notes of the Manners, Customs, and Condition of the North American Indians,' by George Catlin (1841).

Birch-Bark Canoes.

LIGHT CANOES OF OTTAWA

'Where the wave, as clear as dew,
Sleeps beneath the light canoe,
Which, reflected, floating there,
Looks as if it hung in air.'

T. MOORE.

THE light canoes of the river Ottawa are also made of birch-bark, and are of the very frailest description, notwithstanding the heavy burthens they have to carry. They are about 36 ft. in length, sharp at each end, and about six feet in width at the broadest or middle part. The sheets of birch-bark of which they are constructed are sewn together with vegetable fibre, and the seams gummed up close. The sides are strengthened and steadied by four or six cross-bars of wood, lashed to the rim of the canoe; and the inside is also protected by slender ribs of a light wood, but the bottom by only a few loose poles. They are called 'light canoes,' or *canots légers*, because intended to go swiftly, and to carry only provisions and personal baggage. The usual complement of a 'light canoe' is nineteen, that is, fifteen paddle-men and four passengers, the latter sitting each on his rolled-up bed in the middle compartment of the canoe.[1]

BIRCH-BARK CANOES OF SOUTH AMERICA.

THE bark canoes of South America are formed of the whole unbroken bark of a tree, called *yga-ywera*. The natives take off the bark in one piece; then, keeping the middle straight and stretched by means of thwarts, they curve and contract the two ends by fire, and the boat is made. The bark is about an inch in thickness, and the canoe is commonly about four feet wide by forty in length. Some of them are capable of carrying forty persons, but the natives seldom proceed farther in them than half a league from the coast. In bad weather they land, and carry the canoe on their shoulders to a place of safety.[2]

[1] 'The Shoe and Canoe,' by J. J. Bigsby, M.D., &c., &c. (1850).
[2] Southey's 'History of Brazil.'

The Sailing-Boat.

BIRCH-BARK CANOES OF PRINCE EDWARD ISLAND.

THE birch-bark canoes of Prince Edward Island are exceedingly well made. The interior, or skeleton, is formed of flat ribs of wood, a quarter of an inch in thickness, and an inch or more in breadth. These are placed nearly close together throughout the whole structure, and the bark is then put on outside, and laced or sewn together, the seams being well dressed with gum. There are no thwarts, but five or six cross-pieces, like stretchers, at the top, as if to keep the canoe in shape. The top rim, or gunwale, is neatly worked with wicker. The paddles are small and short.

Birch-Bark Canoes of Nova Scotia.

BIRCH-BARK CANOES OF NOVA SCOTIA.

THE birch-bark canoes of Nova Scotia are also made of the same light material as the various other kinds of birch-bark canoes already described; but the form of them is different, as may be seen by the illustration.

Each side of the Nova Scotia canoe is made of one broad piece of birch-bark, and so also is the bottom; the whole being strengthened on the inside with light strips of wood.

The interior of the canoe is bulged out amidships, but the ends of the two sides meet both at stem and stern, where they are sewn together. The outer sides are curiously wrought with fancy work, woven in a variety of colours and fantastic designs.

Canadian Canoes.

The birch-bark used in the workmanship of them on the outside very much resembles wicker, and appears to be worked in a similar manner. These canoes are no heavier than large wicker baskets; light weight being an important consideration, as they have frequently to be taken out of the water and carried on the shoulders past rapids and other obstructions.

Those of New Brunswick are precisely similar to these.

CEDAR BOATS OF THE WILLAMETTE.

THE cedar boats of the Willamette are built at Okonagan, and are somewhat after the model of a whale-boat, but much larger. They are constructed chiefly of the native cedar-wood, and are remarkable for their lightness and capacity, although capable of carrying three tons of merchandise, with a crew of eight men and a padroon. They may be carried easily on the shoulders by three or four of the crew, which is often necessary on passing over the portages.

These boats are clincher-built, and are strong and buoyant. The usual length is 30 ft., by $5\frac{1}{2}$ ft. in breadth, with a sharp bow and stern. The planks and gunwale are of cedar, and extend the whole length of the boat. They have no knees, but flat oak timbers are bolted to a flat keel, at distances each about 1 ft. apart. The rowlocks are made of birch.

One very remarkable peculiarity in the construction of the cedar boats is, that they are merely riveted at each end; and the seams being well dressed with gum of the pine-tree, they require no nailing or other kind of fastening. In case of accident, they are easily repaired, a supply of gum being always carried in the boat.

The crews who man these boats are chiefly Canadians, with the exception of about one-fourth, who are Iroquois Indians. When the wind is fair, they set a small square-sail, but they rely chiefly on their oars.

AMERICAN BATTOES.

BATTOES [1] are a kind of flat-bottomed boat, much employed in Albany. They are used chiefly for carrying goods up and down the rivers, where the birch-bark canoes would be unfit, by reason of their slender and delicate construction.

[1] From the French *bateaux*.

Battoes are constructed of boards of white pine. The bottom is flat, in order to enable them to go with facility into shallow water. In form they are sharp at both ends, and somewhat lower amidships than fore and aft. The sides are almost perpendicular. They are of various sizes, from 3 to 4 fathoms in length, about 3 ft. 6 ins. in breadth, and from 1 ft. 8 ins. to two ft. in depth.[1]

Canoe of Oregon Indians.

CANOES OF OREGON INDIANS.

The native canoes of the Oregon Indians, although made from the single trunk of a tree, are really of elegant form, with gracefully peering bows and stem, full midship section, and rather tapering stern, with a spring both fore and aft.

The interior is so carefully hollowed that the sides are only three-fourths of an inch in thickness, and the thwarts are ingeniously fitted to the interior, so as to prevent the sides from warping or getting out of shape.

These canoes are preserved with great care, and when not in use are never allowed to lie exposed to the sun, for fear of injury. But where cracks and rents occur, they are repaired with much ingenuity. After boring holes on each side of the crack, small withes are passed, crossed, and pegged in such a manner as to draw the crack close. When the tying is completed, the whole is well dressed with gum of the pine-tree, and the damage is thus neatly and effectually repaired.

VANCOUVER ISLAND CANOES.

It appears that the canoes which Captain Cook met with at Nootka in his 'Voyage to the Pacific' (now upwards of a century ago), and which he describes as 'well calculated for every useful purpose,' is a description which tallies with the native canoe of the present day. Many of them are 40 ft. long, 7 ft. broad, and about 3 ft. deep; capable of carrying 20 persons or more, and formed of the trunk of a single tree.

[1] Kalm's 'Travels in North America.'

Bermudian Sailing-Boats.

From the middle, towards each end, they become gradually narrower, the stern post ending perpendicularly, with a small knob on the top; the stem having a protuberance stretching upwards, and ending in a notched point or prow, considerably higher than the sides of the canoe, which run nearly in a straight line. For the most part, they are without any ornament; but some have a little carving, and are decorated with seals' teeth, set on the surface like studs, as is the practice on their masks and weapons. A few have likewise a kind of additional head-piece in shape resembling a large cut-water, which is painted with the figure of some animal. They have no thwarts nor any other supports to the insides than several round sticks, little thicker than a cane, placed across at mid-depth. They are very light, and their breadth and flatness enable them to float firmly without an outrigger, which none of them have—a remarkable distinction between the boats of all the American nations and those of the southern parts of the East Indies, and the islands of the Pacific. Their paddles are small and light, the shape in some measure resembling that of a large leaf, pointed at the bottom, broadest in the middle, and gradually losing itself in the shaft, the whole being about 5 ft. long. The natives have acquired considerable dexterity in the management of these boats, and in the use of the paddles, sails forming no part of their art of navigation.

BERMUDIAN SAILING-BOATS.

'Where the remote Bermudas ride,
In the ocean's bosom unespied.'
A. MARVELL.

THE Bermudas, or Somers Islands, mere specks on the map of the wide Atlantic Ocean, are a salubrious cluster.

'Those leafy islets on the ocean thrown,
Like studs of emerald on a silver zone.'

They comprise numerous small islands, about fifteen of which are inhabited, the remainder being mere rocks. The chief town is Hamilton, which is situated on the coast of the Long Island. The climate of the Bermudas is very salubrious in winter, the thermometer ranging between 60° and 70°, and as there are now some large and excellent hotels these islands have become a favourite winter resort of visitors from Canada and the neighbouring States of America.

It was at Bermuda, the poet Moore wrote some of his most charming verses,

The Sailing-Boat.

during the time he there held a Government appointment. The poet describes his arrival in the harbour at Bermuda in the following expressive lines—

'The morn was lovely, every wave was still,
When the first perfume of a cedar hill
Sweetly awak'd us, and with smiling charms
The fairy harbour woo'd us to its arms.'

'Nothing can be more romantic than the little harbour of St. George's. The number of beautiful islets, the singular clearness of the water, and the animated

Bermudian Sailing-Boats.

play of the graceful little boats—gliding for ever between the islands, and seeming to sail from one cedar grove into another—formed altogether as lovely a miniature of Nature's beauties as can well be imagined.'[1]

The Bermudas are surrounded on three sides (east, west and north) by coral reefs extending to seaward on the north and west sides, about seven miles from the coast. These reefs, which lie in patches, are intersected in various directions by narrow channels of deep transparent water, the navigation of which is intricate and perilous to any but the native boatmen, who, with their keen eyesight, aided by the transparency of the water, pilot their sailing-boats with confidence and safety, though many of the reefs lie hidden beneath the surface.

[1] T. Moore, in note to a poem written at Bermuda.

Bermudian Sailing-Boats.

It is therefore obvious that, for the purpose of navigating such intricate waters, the sailing-boats must be short, handy, and quick in stays.

The Bermudian boats are built chiefly of the native cedar, which is hard and tough, and very suitable for the purpose.

The history of these boats is somewhat interesting. Many years ago the prevailing rig of the Bermudian boats was schooner-like, with two masts, but even then no gaffs were used; the form of sail being triangular as now. The present rig is said to have been introduced to the islanders in the early part of the nineteenth century by an experienced boat-sailor, the Hon. H. G. Hunt, who, having lost a schooner boat-race in the native waters, had an impression that the one mast would have an advantage over the schooner-rig, and accordingly he challenged his antagonist to another race; meanwhile he secretly proved the superiority of the single main-sail by a private race with a schooner at midnight, and on the following day was eminently victorious in a public sailing-match.

Previous to this the schooner-rig had been the popular one in the islands, but from that period the chosen rig has been that with one mast only.

Boat racing had always been a favourite amusement with the islanders, and afterwards became more so than ever. A yacht club was established and yacht racing became general. Boats were constructed regardless of every consideration but that of speed. Their cedar bottoms were polished, so as to present the smoothest possible surface to the water, and they had neither gunwale nor cabin, not even bulk-heads. They were built with camber decks of light wood, just strong enough to bear the weight of one or two of the crew. Such consummate skill was displayed in the construction of the hull and other details that, combined with the exquisite seamanship of a well-disciplined racing crew, a boat of only 13 ft. in length on the keel, upon the then improved plan, would beat one of the old-fashioned form of 25 ft. in fair ordinary weather.

The mast of the Bermudian boat is a tall tapering spar of white spruce, placed forward in the bows of the boat close to the stem-piece, with considerable aft rake, so that the drop of a plumb-line suspended from the truck of the mast would fall at about amidships on deck.

The mast has no shrouds; the jib halliards are rove through a tackle within a few feet of the mast-head.

The rig of these boats consists, ordinarily, of two sails—mainsail and foresail. The mainsail is triangular or nearly so, and is extended by a boom several feet abaft the stern, and there being no gaff to sway the sail to leeward, and only one other sail before the mast, the great spread of canvas abaft enables the boat, when judiciously handled, to go within three points of the wind in ordinary trim; and when well equipped and ballasted will work within the seven points.

The Sailing-Boat.

The boom is necessarily of considerable length in proportion to that of the boat. The fittings and rig of the boom are peculiar. Instead of being goose-necked to the mast the inner end is set in an eyelet in the luff of the mainsail, and projects in front of the mast to the extent (in a boat of about 5 or 6 tons) of 3 ft. or more, and the boom itself is held close to the mast by a grommet. The boom stands about 4 ft. above deck at the fore end in front of the mast. The tack of the mainsail is secured to the lower part of the mast, and the clew is then hauled aft to the outer end by means of a tackle and tail-block attached to the fore part of the boom. The mainsail is thus made to stand very flat. The deep rounded

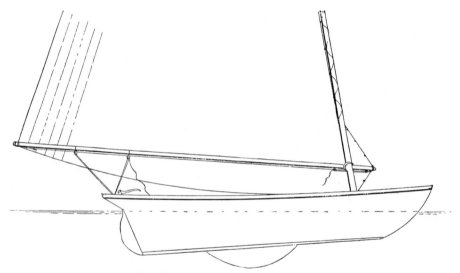

Bermudian rig, showing boom fittings and fin-keel.

foot of the mainsail which hangs below the boom is fitted with lanyards, which the crew hold in their hands when the boat is close hauled, and, assisted by the main sheet, the lower part of the sail is thus also made to stand as flat as the upper part. These boats carry a large foresail and bowsprit of considerable length, which is rigged with a wire rope bobstay and forestay. The foresail is hoisted by halliards rove through a standing block about 4 ft. below the mast-head.

A topsail is occasionally used when going free in very fine weather; it is of different shape, and set in a different manner to anything of the kind used for other boats. A large square-sail or a spinnaker is also used when running before the wind in a race.

A model of the Bermudian yacht *Undine* was exhibited by Lieut. Taylor, of the 39th Regt., in the International Exhibition of 1862.

There is also in the United Service Museum, London, a model of a celebrated

Bermudian Sailing-Boats.

Bermudian boat, the *Lady Ussher*, of 15 tons, presented by the late Mr. Triscott, of Plymouth.

The rig is well adapted to the enclosed waters and narrow channels of the islands and coral reefs of Bermuda, amongst which the sea is smooth, and during a considerable part of the year there is generally a fresh breeze. The rig, however, is not suited to the open sea, nor, indeed, to any but their own waters.

The Bermudian rig was introduced at Plymouth about fifty years ago by Mr. Triscott, the gentleman above mentioned, who was thoroughly familiar with it, having previously resided many years at Bermuda. The rig has ever since been more or less popular with some members of the Royal Western Yacht Club who have yachts of the Bermudian rig.

At the Royal Clyde Yacht Club Regatta, July 6, 1895, the *Mimine*, Bermudian rigged boat (Mr. D. F. D. Neill), was the winner of the first prize, beating six other yachts, all described as of 'lug rig.' Also on the 8th, at the same Regatta, the *Mimine* was again victorious, beating nine or ten other yachts, all of the 'lug rig.'

The Bermudian rig ought not to be extended to vessels above 18 tons, because any mast fit to carry a proportionate area of canvas would be too ponderous, and would imperil the safety of the boat.

The best point of the Bermudian rig is the facility with which a boat, so rigged, may be worked to windward in narrow channels and smooth water; but in a seaway the rig is not nearly so effective.

The following dimensions of a Bermuda yacht, with racing gear, are taken from a pamphlet on Bermuda by Surgeon-General Ogilvy :—

Tonnage ... ... $4\frac{3}{4}$ tons	keel	16	ft.[1]
	beam	8	,,
	depth	4	,,
Length of mast		44	,,
,, ,, boom		$33\frac{1}{2}$	,,
,, ,, bowsprit		19	,,
,, ,, spinnaker boom		25	,,

It will thus be seen that the beam of these boats is just half their length on the keel. This great breadth is, it appears, required to enable them to carry so lofty a mast and sail and to facilitate their quickness of turning or tacking in the narrow channels of the coral reefs.

[1] Although only 16 ft. in length on the keel, the length over all is usually from 20 to 25 ft.

The Sailing-Boat.

Instead of a revolving centre-board, the modern Bermudian racing boat is fitted with a fixed half-moon shaped fin, which is bolted to the keel on the outside. This undoubtedly adds to the weatherly qualities of the boat in working a course to windward.

The sailing skiffs and dingies of Bermuda are rigged in a similar manner to that of the larger boats.

When Lord and Lady Brassey visited Hamilton in 1883, in their yacht the *Sunbeam*, they each presented a challenge cup for competition by Bermudian yachts.

Amateur sailing matches are held annually at certain seasons of the year under the auspices of the Royal Bermuda Yacht Club, the contesting yachts being steered and manned by amateurs.

Portuguese Boats.

PORTUGUESE SAILING-BOATS.

The Portuguese pleasure-boats, or cahiques, employed at Lisbon and other places on the coast of Portugal, are fine, fast-sailing boats. They are rigged with two latine sails and a mizzen, the latter being set in a similar manner to a Bermudian sail, the yard serving the purpose of mizzen-mast. Sometimes a jib is used besides; but either with or without the jib, the rig is an exceedingly light and graceful one, and well adapted to boats of a long or shallow form of hull. The sails are set on

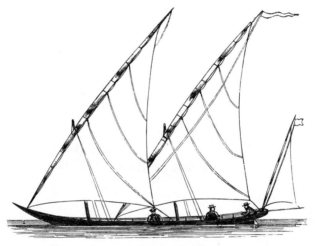

Portuguese Sailing Boat.

bamboo yards, which, though looking large are very light and stiff; each yard being generally composed of several pieces of bamboo at the ends, so as to give them a pointed and graceful appearance. These boats are high both at bows and stern, but low amidships: and although intended for sailing in fine weather, under skilful management, they may be safely handled even in strong winds; but on such occasions one or more of the sails is dispensed with. Each sail is fitted with brails and brail-ropes, so as to be capable of being frapped close to the yard with facility.

The Sailing-Boat.

BOATS OF THE ISLAND OF MADEIRA.

THE native cargo boats of the Island of Madeira are of a very antiquated form, as will be seen by the illustration below. They have large elevated stem and

Madeira Boat.

stern-posts of great strength, and are, upon the whole, somewhat crudely constructed; but they are wide and roomy inside, and capable of carrying a good-sized sail and a heavy cargo.

THE CATRIA.

THE Catria is a fine open sea-boat, employed by the fishermen and pilots of the Douro. These boats are 30 ft. long, by about 6 ft. in breadth amidships, and 3 ft. deep; they have also considerable sheer. When under oars, they are pulled by twelve or more, the rowers sitting double-banked. Being often exposed to heavy seas and broken water, they are provided with a large rudder, extending deeply below the bottom of the boat.

The Catria is rigged with a large latine, or rather settee-sail, the tack of which is hooked to the inside of the bows of the boat, and the clew sheeted astern.

Boats of the Mediterranean.

BOATS OF THE MEDITERRANEAN.

MALTESE GALLEY.

THE Galleys of the Island of Malta were, in the 15th and 16th centuries, important vessels of war in the Mediterranean Sea. They relate back to the same

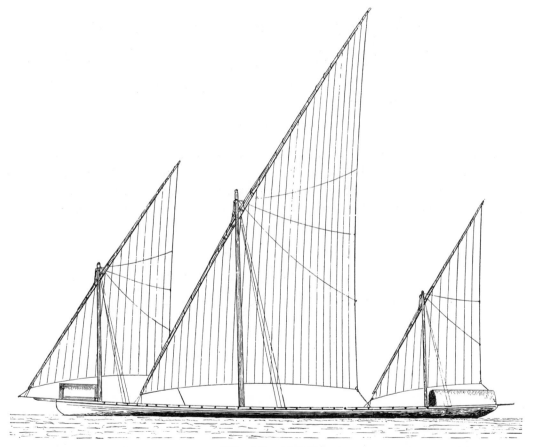

Maltese Galley under sail.

age as the Venetian galleys. The Felucca was a boat of similar type, but smaller; and in the three there was always a strong resemblance. In fact, the galley of Malta may stand as the representative of the whole class.

The Sailing-Boat.

The Maltese galley was a long, low vessel drawing but little water; and had usually three masts, with lofty tapering latine sails; the middle one, or main-sail, being the largest, the foresail the next in size, and the mizzen the smallest.

The deck of the galley was fitted on each side with rowing-benches, from which a numerous crew worked the long powerful oars. The 'Celeustes' (Coxswain) in an elevated position at the stern of the galley, directed and regulated the stroke of the oarsmen by blowing a whistle for that purpose; and thus a regular stroke of the oars was maintained.

Some of these galleys were upwards of 150 ft. in length, and the deck 30 ft. in

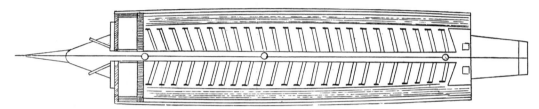

Maltese Galley—deck plan.

width; and, in addition to the sails, were propelled by above 100 oars, each oar being of great length and balancing in the rowlock, which enabled it to be used with greater effect and regularity. When about to board an enemy, the fighting members of the crew assembled on the 'rambade,' or platform, erected across the prow.

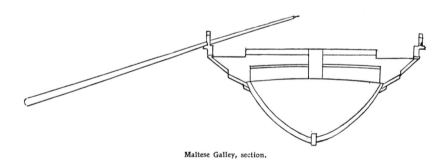

Maltese Galley, section.

In sultry weather, a striped awning was spread above the deck over the whole length of the galley.

The Maltese Galley is in many respects a very interesting and remarkable vessel, of a type differing from every other class of boat and vessel then in existence: it was, as already stated, of great length and shallow form, with a broad deck and flanging sides, but the underpart of the galley was of a somewhat crank form (as may be seen on reference to the section), and, notwithstanding that the galley

Boats of the Mediterranean.

was rigged with three masts and lofty latine sails, was also provided with a great number of long, powerful oars (seldom less than 60), 30 on each side; so that when pursued by an enemy, if the wind failed, and it was found that the sails alone could not be relied on to save the galley and crew from capture, resort was had to the oars, which were then plied with great vigour and effect; thus propelling the craft at a tremendous speed; and it was very rarely that the chase ended in the capture of the galley. And on the other hand, when the galley was itself the pursuer, it required a vessel of unusual speed to escape it.

The long tapering yards of the Maltese Galley were contrived of two or more spars, fished at the central part where the joining was effected: the yards were thus much stronger and less liable to fracture than if of one entire long spar. This somewhat ancient mode of rigging the long tapering yards of the latine sail is the same as that in use in all parts of the Mediterranean to this day.

There is in the United Service Museum, at Whitehall, a beautiful model of a Maltese Galley of the 18th century, from which sketches were made by the author for the reproductions here given.

The model is that of *La Capitana*, and is stated to have been built under the galley arches, at Malta, in the 18th century, and presented to the Museum by Rear-Admiral Sir Wm. Symonds, R.N.: it appears therefore to be a very reliable representative model.

There is also a model of a Maltese Galley in the Kensington Museum.

The modern sailing-boats and small yachts of the English residents at Malta, at the present day, are of various sizes up to about 20 tons: they are rigged chiefly as Cutters, but there are a few of the Bermudian rig.

THE FELUCCA.

THE Felucca is an ancient type of boat of the Mediterranean, of great similarity to the Maltese Galley, but smaller; it is similarly rigged with three masts and latine sails. In addition to the sails, the Felucca (like the Maltese Galley) is provided with long powerful oars, which are of great assistance in the frequent calms of the Mediterranean.

Feluccas were formerly the favourite craft of the Greek pirates, on account chiefly of their great swiftness under sails and oars.

The yards used to spread the sails of the Felucca are each sometimes in two, three and four parts, the stoutest part being put in the middle, and the smaller parts neatly fished to the larger, and tapering at the outer ends in a similar manner to those of the Maltese Galley; and thus the much admired bend of the latine yard is greatly assisted, and upon the whole a lighter yard is formed than if it were all in one spar; besides which, when a breakage occurs to the yard it is seldom that more than one part is injured at a time, which may then be promptly repaired.

The Felucca sails fastest on an even keel, down wind, with sails goose-winged. The long yards of the Felucca are seldom lowered to the deck, except in very heavy winds, when one of the larger sails is usually dispensed with. Each sail can be brailed up close to the yard by means of brail-ropes attached to the throat of the sail; but the sails are more frequently frapped by the crew, who are very nimble in that performance, and climb up and along the yards of the sails with remarkable agility.

VENETIAN GALLEYS.

VERY similar to the Felucca and the Maltese Galley, not only in form and size, but historically, were the Venetian Galleys.

So early as the 9th century, the galleys of Venice were reputed to have excelled those of any other nation—indeed, they were then the most beautiful, as well as most useful, vessels of the age. But that was the period of ancient greatness of the Venetians—an age which has long since passed away; and the beautiful galleys of Venice are now superseded by the more sombre, but graceful and interesting gondolas.

Boats of the Mediterranean.

Modern Sailing Boats of the Mediterranean.

MODERN SAILING-BOATS OF THE MEDITERRANEAN.

The prevailing rig of the modern pleasure-boats of the Mediterranean is the Latine; a form of sail that has been in use at most of the principal sea-side resorts of the sunny shores of that sea, on the European Coast, for centuries past; and although the type and build of the boats varies somewhat at different localities, the form of rig remains the same as in the days of the Maltese Galley and the Felucca.

Some of the local sailing-boats are rigged with one latine sail only, and some with three, but the majority have two.

At Nice, Cannes, San Remo, Genoa, and other places where there are numerous

403

The Sailing-Boat.

English residents, English yachts and sailing-boats of the cutter, schooner, and sloop rig are very prevalent; but the native sailing-boats are, for the most part, latine rigged.

VENETIAN GONDOLAS.

"There is a glorious city in the sea,
　The sea is in the broad, the flowing streets,
Ebbing and flowing; and the salt sea-weed
Clings to the marble of her palaces,
No track of men, no footsteps to and fro,
Lead to her gates, the path lies o'er the sea."

ROGERS.

AMONG the objects of attraction to the visitor at Venice, none are more worthy of observation than the pleasure-boats, or Gondolas and Gondolettes which grace the lagoons and water-ways of that interesting city.

The streets being principally canals, the gondola is the chief means of conveyance to and from all parts of the city. It is, in fact, as much in request on the Venetian canals as the horse and carriage in an English city; and for a similar purpose of transit from one part of the city to another.

The only equipage of the noble and wealthy Venetian is his elegant gondola, in which he, his lady, family, and *suite*, are conducted to all places of amusement, visits to friends, and other excursions. Coachmen and grooms are supplanted by liveried gondoliers; the rattling sound of carriage-wheels is never heard; and nothing, save the leisurely plying of the oar and musical cry of the gondolier, denote the movement of the lifeless craft—

'Gliding up her streets as in a dream,
So smoothly, silently,—by many a dome.'

The annual procession of the brides of Venice is thus poetically alluded to in an old legend:—

'And through the city, in a stately barge
Of gold, were borne, with song and symphonies,
Twelve ladies, young and noble. Clad they were
In bridal white, with bridal ornaments,
Each in her glittering veil; and on the deck,
As on a burnished throne, they glided by.'

There was formerly so much rivalry in the magnificent manner in which these boats were painted and gilded, that it was considered expedient to establish a law (still in force) prohibiting any other colour than black being used on the exterior of all passenger - vessels plying within the waters of Venice, the gondolas of State alone being allowed gay colours; and the heads and sterns of these are, in some instances, gilded and richly ornamented, and the interiors fitted up in a very costly manner.

The gondolas belonging to certain Venetian corporations or societies, such as those of Chiozza, are also of more elegant and attractive proportions than those which are commonly let for hire, and are generally decorated in an antique style.

The smaller gondolas, large enough for one or two persons only, are called *gondolettes*; these are as light and buoyant as the little wherries of the Upper Thames, and are moved about very swiftly and with little exertion, but are rowed differently to boats of other European nations. The rowers in these sit facing the prow, and with a light pair of sculls, by a reverse motion, force the handle *from* the chest, instead of drawing it towards it.

The gondola is usually

Venetian Gondola.

about thirty feet long and five broad, of light and elegant form; and elaborate workmanship is sometimes displayed in the carving and finish of the prow. A closed compartment is constructed in the centre for the occupants, and is fitted with windows, cushions, carpet and curtain. The gondola has no keel.

Mode of Propulsion.—The gondola is propelled by the gondolier, who stands on the decked-aft-part of the gondola; those of the upper classes have two or more gondoliers for greater speed and magnificence. The long-bladed oar, by which the gondola is propelled, rests on a 'fórcola,' a sort of crooked rowlock rising about a foot from the boat's quarter for greater leverage. The 'fórcola' is of different forms according to the size and uses of the boat, and it is always somewhat complicated in its parts and curvature, allowing the oar various kinds of rests and catches on both its sides, but perfectly free play in all cases; as the management of the boat depends on the gondolier being able in an instant to place his oar in any position for controlling the movement of the boat, the fórcola is set on the right-hand side of the gondola some six feet from the stern; the gondolier stands on a small sloping platform, behind the fórcola, and throws nearly the entire weight of his body upon the forward stroke, using the oar with dexterous but graceful motion to impel and guide the boat. Propelling a gondola at speed is hard and breathless work, though it appears easy and graceful to the onlooker.[1]

On approaching cross canals and corners, the gondoliers, by a musical cry, signal their approach and warn those unseen as to which direction to take in order to avoid collision, which would otherwise frequently be inevitable.

The gondolier's cry 'premi' is the warning from the one gondolier to the other to send his boat's head round *to the left*, whilst the cry 'stali' warns him to go *to the right*. The warning cry 'sciar' signals the gondolier to stop the boat as suddenly as possible to avoid collision; this is done by slipping the blade of the oar in the water in front of the fórcola. The cry 'sciar' is never heard except when the boatman finds himself unexpectedly in risk of a collision.[2]

The remarkable grace displayed by the native boatmen in the conduct of their charge, the nicety with which they measure distances, and the quiet progressive movement by which the gondola is made to glide through narrow canals, round sharp corners, among crowds of gondolas, and other craft, without touching an obstruction of any kind is remarkable, and affords to strangers agreeable sensations of pleasure and safety in their transit from place to place on the Venetian lagoons.

So many poets have sung of picturesque scenes on the Grand Canal at Venice, and of the fair and lovely occupants of the gondolas and gondolettes, which at all hours of

---

[1] *See* Ruskin's 'Stones of Venice,' p. 189.
[2] *Ibid.*

Venetian Gondolas.

day and night are moving to and fro upon the still waters of that once magnificent city, that no apology is made for the following extract :—

> ' When the gondola is laden
> With its light and lovely burthen,
> There, with sturdy arm, the boatman
> Rows Bettina o'er the billows
> To a light and joyous measure,
> Thus he warbles to Bettina,
> While his cheek is flush'd with pleasure,
> " Non v' è rosa senza spina." '

The Grand Canal is the fashionable parade of the Venetians, and in fact what the Champs-Élysées and the Bois de Boulogne at Paris are to the French, or Rotten Row and Hyde Park, in London, to the English. Gondolas are the Venetian equipages, the sombre colour of which shows off to advantage the gay dresses of the fair occupants and the smart liveries of the gondoliers.

The highways of Venice being principally canals, the gondola has for centuries past been, as already observed, the chief means of transit for residents, visitors, and tourists to and fro in all parts of the city and for navigating the water-ways intersecting its numerous island homes and public buildings.

Of late years, however, the calm waters of the Grand Canal have been invaded by the modern Steam Launch, with its accompanying smoke, steam, puffing, machine-rattle, and shrill whistle, and thus the tranquillity of the neighbourhood of the Piazza of St. Mark, the Doge's Palace, the Bridge of Sighs, and other historical places of interest are each in turn greeted with the awakening echoes of harsh screaming sounds as the ubiquitous tourist, with rush and scrimmage, dashes along from lagoon to lagoon in hot haste by the steaming launch; and thus one of the most attractive features of the silent city, the gondolas, are in peril of being supplanted and the gondoliers thrown out of employment by the competition thereby engendered.

But the better taste of the majority of visitors to the Island City still clings to the native craft. Venice without its gondolas would be to most travellers and visitors a city shorn of one of its most distinctive features. Let us hope that the day is far distant ere the shriek of the steam whistle on the picturesque canals of the famous old city shall have driven the gondola from its waters and the gondoliers from their industrious and time-honoured occupation.

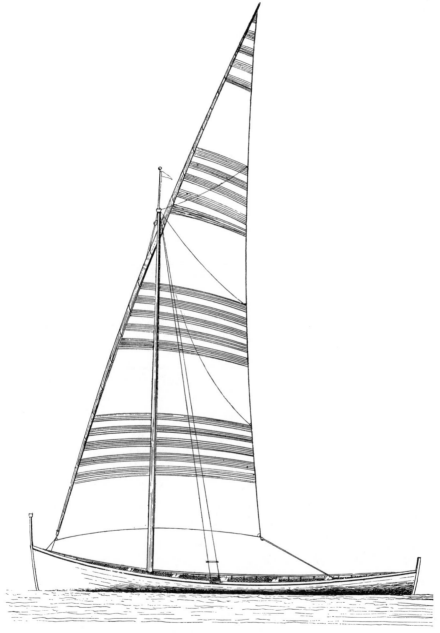

Boat of the Italian Riviera.

Boats of the Lakes of Switzerland.

BOATS OF THE ITALIAN RIVIERA.

'The sun is warm, the sky is clear,
  The waves are dancing fast and bright;
Blue isles and snowy mountains wear
  The purple noon's transparent light.'
                                        SHELLEY.

THERE is great similarity in the native sailing-boats of the Italian Riviera, more particularly in the rig. Most of the pleasure boats at the coasting towns along the Italian frontier are rigged with tall, tapering, latine sails; some with one mast and sail, others with two and occasionally with three. And the sails are sometimes ornamented with bright-coloured stripes, which have a pretty effect as they glide along the coast beneath a warm sun and bright azure sky.

SWITZERLAND.

BOATS OF THE LAKE OF GENEVA.

SAILING-BOATS appear to the prettiest advantage on the beautiful blue, transparent lake of Geneva, surrounded as it is by the most enchanting scenery and frowning upon its banks are some of the grandest mountains in the world.

The lake itself is upwards of 50 miles in length; in the widest part it is over 9 miles in breadth; and near Chillon which is its deepest part, it is 600 feet in depth.

One of the greatest peculiarities of this lake is the deep blue colour of its water; and in this respect it differs from the other Swiss lakes, which are all more or less of a light green tint.

At the south end of the lake, which is narrow, the water becomes much contracted, and consequently rushes through the town of Geneva with torrential rapidity. Indeed, boats are prohibited from approaching the *Pont des Bergues*, on account of the dangerous rapidity of the current; and so, too, in some other parts of the lake, the currents caused by the rising of subaqueous springs are sometimes so strong and rapid that no oar can resist them.

Yachting and boat-sailing are vigorously pursued on the Lake of Geneva.

The Sailing-Boat.

'The Société Nautique de Genève' has its club-house on the banks of the lake. Among the numerous yachts and sailing-boats which spangle the waters of the lake are many of British type, some by the most eminent of European yacht builders, others by native Swiss boat-builders,—admirable productions, well-built and of approved British model, having all the characteristics of modern racing craft, with their fin-bulb-keels and graceful overhang fore and aft. Some, however, of native construction, have in recent years proved the champions of the fleet at the aquatic contests of the Société.

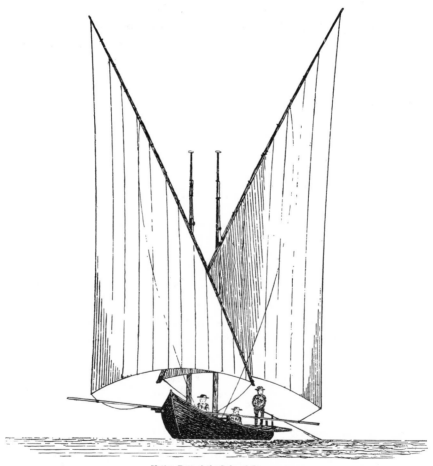

Native Boat of the Lake of Geneva.

The prevailing native rig is the latine; most of the trading or cargo-boats being so rigged. There is a peculiarity about the hull of these native cargo-boats such as is never seen in the boats or barges of other nations, in this—that they have flanging sides, or wings, extending outwards beyond the gunwale of the boat itself, but so constructed as not only to provide additional space for stowage and conveyance of light goods, but also to hold the vessel up under sail, in case of any sudden lurch caused by undue pressure of the wind; they have also very high bows, which stand considerably above the water. They are rigged with two masts and lofty, pointed latine sails, which the crew shift into various positions with considerable tact, acccrding to the quarter from which the wind blows, or the course they wish to steer. These native boats are very pretty objects under sail, from whatever quarter of the lake they are viewed.

The latine sails are not reefed, even in the large boats; sail is shortened by the brails, more or less as occasion may require; or one of the sails is dispensed with, according to the weather and strength of the wind.

On encountering a storm or heavy wind, they are enabled to make for a harbour of refuge in a very short time, as both sides of the lake afford frequent places of shelter.

One of the greatest disagreeables encountered in the neighbourhood of the Swiss lakes is the heavy rain, which sometimes half fills an open boat in the course of ten or twelve hours; and for this reason, when it is wished to keep the sails white, and to preserve them from mildew, they are not left about in the boat, but rolled up and deposited in a sail loft.

BOATS OF LAKE ZURICH.

This beautiful lake is also studded with many boats of English and American rig, the broad and shallow form of hull being, apparently, the favourite; for the lake itself is very shallow about the town of Zurich, and on various parts of its shores.

The native pleasure-boats are mostly rigged as latines, like those of the Lake of Geneva. Some of them have a wooden covering similar to that of a Chinese sampan; others have a canopy or awning over the middle and aft part.

The cargo-boats of Lake Zurich are a useful and burthensome sort of craft, of barge-like structure, flat at the bottom, but very broad amidships, and with flanging sides, like those of the lake of Geneva, and high-peering sloping bows and stern—the latter not pointed at the extreme ends, but broad--and the stern is generally higher than the bows. Steps are formed in the slope of the bows, from the top to the floor of the vessel; and the same at the stern. The steps are of the greatest convenience in carrying goods in and out of the boat from the quay or wharf; and a further advantage is, that instead of occupying a space to the extent of their whole length, when lying alongside a wharf, they lay stem or stern on, and thereby only occupy their *width* of space, instead of length; and in that position they are laden and unladen from the banks of the lake with great facility.

The Sailing-Boat.

These cargo-boats are fitted with a tall, slender mast, placed nearly amidships, upon which is hoisted an elongated square-sail, but only when the wind is fair. In calms and adverse winds, they are propelled by the crew with long oars or sweeps.

Cargo Boat of Lake Zurich.

The rudder is at the extreme end of the stern; and when its services are not required, it is hoisted up out of the water, in the manner represented by the illustration.

BOATS OF THE LAKES LUCERNE, THUN, AND BRIENZ.

THERE is a great similarity between the pleasure and passenger-boats of the lakes Lucerne, Thun, and Brienz. They are mostly of a broad and shallow form, with high

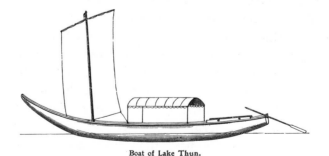

Boat of Lake Thun.

peering bows; but the stern in some of them is scarcely higher than the midship section of the boat, and is broad and flat on the outside. These boats are provided in summer with a canopy or tilt amidships, under which the passengers sit, so that the

412

boatmen have both ends of the boat to themselves for the management and navigation.

In the fore part, near the bows, they place the mast, upon which they hoist a small lug-sail when there is a fair wind; in the absence of which they strike sail and ply their oars.

These boats are carvel-built of pine-planking, about an inch in thickness, fastened to stout timbers and knees. They are about 22 ft. long by 5 ft. beam; but at the load-water line the length is only about 16 ft.

On Lake Constance similar boats are employed; also large cargo-boats or barges, rigged with tall masts and large square-sails; and some are rigged with a gaff-mainsail and fore-sail.

BOATS OF THE ITALIAN LAKES.

THE native boats of the Italian Lakes, like those of the Swiss lakes, have considerable rake both fore and aft. Thus a boat 23 feet long, by seven feet beam, has five feet rake at the bows, and three at the stern; the bottom being flat and only three feet wide, but flaring out to the width of seven feet at the gunwale; the bow rising slightly, and the stern a good deal. A canopy is erected in the middle, over the thwarts destined for the passengers; this is supported by broad half-hoops, in the form of arches.

In the boats of the Lago Maggiore the lower part of the canopy-frame forms an outrigger, in which thowls are fitted for the oars; and in the boats of this lake the canopy is in the fore part, supported by a light frame; but in the boats of the Lago Lugano and Lago di Como the canopy is in the aft part of the boat, supported by a stout framework of broad wooden hoops.

The boats of the Italian lakes have large rudders, and when sailed are rigged with a small square-sail, made of thin home-spun flax or hemp. The mast, in some of the boats, is without either block or sheave-hole, but has a fork at the top, over which the halliards go, and are belayed in the aft part of the boat, in the most primitive fashion.

The sheet is usually hitched to one or other of the hoops forming the arc of the canopy. The sail is sometimes ornamented with coloured stripes or checks, and not unfrequently is bent to the yard with strips of its own material.

Many gentlemen who have villas on the banks of these lakes are provided with boats of British form and rig; these are not however copied by the natives.

The Sailing-Boat.

ITALIAN BOAT-SAILING ON LAKE MAGGIORE.

THE boat-sailing matches which are held twice a year (in June and August), on the beautiful Lake Maggiore, are sailed under the auspices of the Royal Verbano Yacht Club. There are two classes of the contesting boats; one of which comprises those of a size not exceeding one ton; and the other, those over one ton but not exceeding two tons. In the August matches, however, there is an additional class, for yachts of any tonnage. The conditions usually are, as regards the boats of the smaller class, that they be sailed single-handed.

The Regio Verbano Yacht Club and Regio Regate Club, Lariano, have started a One-Design Class, to last for five years from 1899, for a small class of Sailing Yachts.

NORWEGIAN BOATS.

NORWAY YAWLS.

'For now in our trim boats of Noroway deal,
We must dance on the waves with the porpoise and seal;
The breeze it shall pipe, so it pipe not too high,
And the gull be our songstress whene'er she flits by.'
Claud Halcro's Norse Ditty.—' PIRATE.'

AMONG foreign European boats possessing qualities best adapted to sea-going purposes, few can compare with the open sailing-boats of the Norwegians—a people who display great ingenuity in the type and rig of their sailing-boats.

The sailing boats of the Norwegians have a great reputation as safe and fast sailing sea-boats; and they are of a type such as is not found among the people of any other nation, save only in the sister countries of Sweden and Denmark; but the type of their yawl-rigged boats has been adopted by the fisher-boatmen of the Shetland Isles.

There are two general classes of Norwegian boats—Yawls and Praäms (or Prahams); the form of the one class being totally different in type and construction to that of the other; the Yawls are clinch-built and wedge-like, the Praäms carvel-built with rounded bottoms; but both classes are constructed entirely without nails; the planking being fastened throughout with hard wooden pegs.

The form of the Yawls is crescent-like at the upper part and wedge-like at the under part; with high-pointed stem and stern, both alike; whilst the form of the Praäms is entirely the reverse, being so rounded at the bottom as to be nearly flat; and the stern end is wide and square, but the bow is spoon-shaped, and peering high above the water. In fact, the Praäm is, in miniature shape, like an ordinary wooden boat-scoop with the handle sawn off.

The usual form of rig of a Norway Yawl is a single lug-sail, but of a very

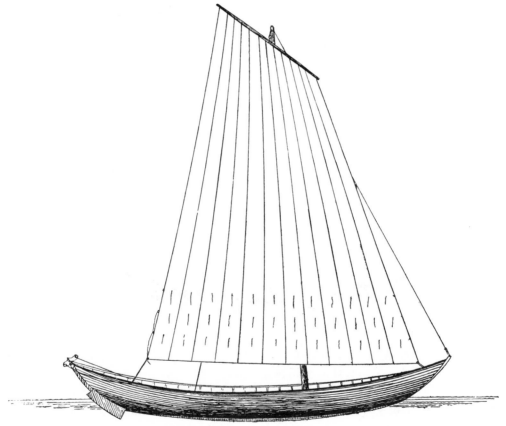

Norway Yawl.

different cut to an English lug. The Norwegian lug-sail is narrow at the top, the lower part being more than twice the width of the upper; the tack is made fast at the inner part of the weather bow, the clew being sheeted in the boat's aft quarter. Although the mast is stepped amidships, and the short little yard at the top of the sail is slung nearly in the middle, still the greater part of the sail stands in front of the mast; this is effected by hooking the tack of the sail in the weather bow of the boat, near to the stem.

The Sailing-Boat.

THE beautiful open fishing-boats of Sondmore, on the west coast of Norway, are of the Norway yawl type; long, shallow, and of graceful proportions, stem and stern alike, and high at both ends. In common with all properly constructed boats in which fishing-nets have to be shot out and hauled in, these boats have neither gunwale nor top rim.

They have a rather deep keel, extending from bow to stern, and are fitted with

Sondmore Yawl.

a powerful rudder, which is broadest at the under part, and extends along the stern-post below the keel; the rudder is controlled by a long elbow-tiller fitted to the rudder's head, and reaching several feet from the stern of the boat; the object being to enable the steersman to sit in the body of the boat (near the clew of the sail), and so to assist in preserving its stability. In fact, when under way none of the crew are permitted to seat themselves in either end of the boat, as such would enhance the risk of a heavy sea breaking over and into the boat; one of the first principles of boat-sailing in a heavy sea being to keep the ends of the boat as light and buoyant as possible, which are matters of considerable importance in open boats when under sail in a sea-way.

The rig of the Sondmore Yawls is an excellent one. It consists of an ingeniously contrived lug-sail, very narrow at the top, but broad at the bottom (see engraving); and notwithstanding such peculiarity of shape, there are the same number of cloths in the head of the sail as in the foot; the canvas being worked gradually narrower all the way up. The mast is stepped with a slight aft rake, and is supported by several shrouds or stays, leading from the mast-head above the short little yard; the shrouds are made fast *in* the boat (not to gunwales or rim, for the boat is destitute of both) by means of little wooden fids or thumb-cleats, and the fore-stay is made fast to the upper part of the stem. The bulk of the sail stands in the fore-part of the boat, and the tack is made fast to the inner part of the stem inside the boat. The reef-tackle forms an important part of the rigging, and is very complete; two reefs reduce the sail considerably, it being so much wider at the foot than at the head. The sail is also fitted with down-haulers, one on each side.

The lower part of the boat is divided into several compartments by bulk-heads, which run up to the level of the thwarts. The divisions so formed are convenient for holding the fish when caught; they also facilitate the baling out of water if a sea is shipped. The ballast (which consists of a few large stones) is placed amidships, just abaft the mast.

These boats are also provided with long powerful oars, for use in emergency, and in calm weather; they are worked, not between thowls, but in straps, with a fixed thowl-pin for leverage; the loom of the oar, where it chafes, is squared.

A very complete and beautiful model of one of these boats was exhibited in the International Exhibition of 1862, from which the drawing was made by the Author for the preceding engraving.

NORDLAND FISHING BOATS.

The fishing boats of Nordland (north of Norway) are similar in form, though not in rig, to those of the western coast, but not quite so raking at the bows. They are rigged with a lofty mast and lug-sail, though not nearly so ingenious in shape and design as the Sondmore boat-sail; it is, in fact, an elongated lug-sail, without a peak, but a little broader below than at the top. These boats also have bulk-heads, similar to those of the Sondmore boats.

THE NORWAY PRAÄM.

The Praäm (or Praham) is also a boat of Norwegian contrivance, and of peculiar form. The Praäms, like the yawls, are built of 'Noroway deal,' but without nails, the planks being fastened to the keelson and timbers with hard wooden pegs;

notwithstanding which they are very tight and secure, as well as strong and durable.

The shape of the Praäm is similar to a wooden boat-scoop without a handle, having a broad, round shaped bottom; the greatest breadth of beam is at the stern, the head and bows gradually rising forward, and sometimes finishing with a carved figure-head. Small-sized Praäms are used generally as rowing boats; it is only the larger size that are sailed.

The Sailing-Praäm requires a good depth of false keel, on account of its very

Norway Praäm.

flat floor, and the buoyancy with which it sits upon the water. Some of the largest of these boats sail remarkably well, when judiciously rigged and ballasted.

The engraving represents a large Sailing-Praäm, adapted and rigged in British waters with two masts and lug-sails, running before the wind, with the fore-sail hauled aweather—a common method of steadying a boat in a sea-way.

The boats employed on the coast of Denmark are very similar to the Norway boats, especially the Praäms, some of which are longer and narrower than the Norway Praäms, and have, besides, a long tapering bow.

FINMARKEN FISHING-BOATS.

THE open fishing-boats of Finmark are similar to those of the west coast of Norway, as regards the type of the boat and being *minus* both rim and gunwale; the stem, however, is by no means raking, but rather inclining inwards at the top, and therefore presenting a full or prominent fore-gripe. They are rigged with a square-shaped lug-sail.

Faroë Islands Fishing-Boats.

The fishing-boats of Drontheim are nearly identical with the Finmarken boats, both in form and rig.

The larger or decked fishing-boats of Finmark are of stronger build than the others, and have square sterns; they are rigged as cutters, but not very gracefully; and they have a cabin-house amidships, which occupies the entire breadth of the boat.

FAROË ISLANDS FISHING-BOATS.

THE fishing-boats of the North Faroë Islanders are much like the yawls and boats of the western coast of Norway. They are of crescent-like form, and are high at stem and stern; they have a deep keel and deep rudder, broadest at the under-part. These boats are rigged with a lug-sail, widest at the bottom; in form resembling that of the Norwegian Yawls.

The Faroë Islands Fishing-Boats sail remarkably well; the large-sized ones in particular, which are fine-looking craft, and good sea-boats.

LAPLAND BOATS.

THE native inland boats of the Laplanders (even the large ones) are very light; they are made of thin planks of fir secured to a keel and ribs, the planks being sewn together with sinews of the reindeer, which resemble English catgut. This light form of boat is rendered necessary by reason of the number of cataracts that intersect the rivers and lakes of Lapland.

In some parts of that country, where the natives are enabled to procure cord or twine, they use it in boat-building, instead of the sinews of the reindeer; but before doing so, they generally dress it with a kind of glue, which they prepare from the skins and scales of fish.[1] The cord, on being dressed with glue is rendered more durable and is then impervious to air and water.

The small fibrous roots of the fir tree are also sometimes used by the natives in boat-building, when neither cord nor sinews can be procured.[2]

The skiffs of the Laplanders are of fragile and peculiar construction. The keel is about one fathom in length at the bottom, but extending to two fathoms upwards,

[1] Regnard's 'Journey to Lapland.'
[2] Ehrenmalm's 'Travels in Lapland.'

being equally high and pointed at each end. The floor is rather flat in form. The ribs or timbers on each side are only three or four in number, and very small; these are covered and doubled with thin fir planks, that are joined with the sinews or other cordage before mentioned. When completed in the most approved manner they are, nevertheless, very fragile; a strong man might crush them between his arms; and on stepping in and out, care is required to be taken to tread only on the bottom, as any hard pressure on the sides would injure them.

FINLAND BOATS.

THE native inland boats of Finland are also very light, being built in a similar manner to those of the Laplanders.

They are made of thin strips of fir, sewn together with the sinews of the reindeer, or dressed cord, and fastened to a skeleton composed of a keel and ribs; and so constructed, they are buoyant and flexible. But, notwithstanding the lightness and flexibility of the materials of which they are composed, these boats are very strong; and when borne by the violence of the torrent, and exposed to rough usage, such as striking against stones and rocks which abound in the rivers of that country, they appear to bear such shocks without injury; and for such usage the mode in which the planks are joined together is better than if secured with clenched nails; since a boat of elastic construction is more capable of sustaining, without injury, a bump against hard rocks than one of firm and unyielding mould.

Many a stranger would be struck with alarm on first witnessing the perils to which these boats and their occupants are exposed when borne rapidly down a torrent of waves, foam, and stones, in the midst of a cataract; the noise of which is so deafening that it is useless for any one of the crew to attempt speaking to the other—all must be done by signs, and the boat controlled by individual skill and courage. The Finland boatmen are particularly bold and skilful in the management of their boats in cataracts, and are everywhere else ingenious in steering small vessels. One dauntless Fin stands at the stern, and steers with an oar, whilst two others row as hard as they can, in order to escape the danger of quick-following waves, which threaten to overwhelm them. The perils encountered on passing through some of these cataracts are many: the boats are driven along with great rapidity, apparently diving into waves and raging torrents of foam, as if never to rise out of them, and then re-appearing on the crest of a lofty wave, with keel exposed to view, and disappearing again as if going down endwise;

and during these perils there are others around, in the shape of rocks, stones, and other obstructions, which, by judicious steering, the pilot has to avoid.[1]

In the travelling-boats of Finland, the Fins insist on the passengers landing when they come to a dangerous cataract; and in this they consult their own interest, as well as the safety of the passengers; for the lighter and more buoyant the boat, the less is the danger incurred.

Most of the larger boats are furnished with a lug-sail, and a mast that can be raised and lowered at pleasure. Sails are found of great service to the boats of this country, in those parts where smooth waters and lakes abound, though often intercepted by dangerous cataracts; and it is in passing through these that the calmness, courage, and skill of the Fins are particularly conspicuous.[2]

BOATS OF HOLLAND.

THE BOËYER RIG.

THE Dutch pleasure-boats have many peculiarities, both as regards the form of hull and the rig and cut of their sails; and notwithstanding the fact that they are neat and trim-looking boats, they have a somewhat antiquated appearance—at least in British waters and from a British point of view. They are very strongly built, with round sides, broad beam, and flat floor. They have a good deal of dead wood, both at the fore-gripe and stern, but no false keel amidships; so that, when run aground, they sit perfectly upright. There are no upper projections as regards stem or stern; but the rudder is very large, and forms a conspicuous object outside the stern and sternpost of the vessel. They are also provided with lee-boards, which supply the place of false keel. These are suspended, one on each side of the vessel, to an iron bolt or pivot, so that, by means of a small tackle, they may be let down or hauled up, as required, when the vessel is under sail. The lee-board on the lee-side is lowered when reaching or working to windward; but if the wind be free the services of the lee-boards are not required, and they are then hauled up.

The hull of Dutch pleasure-boats, externally, is seldom painted, a decided preference being given to bright varnish, which gives the wood a rich brown polished appearance, the upper or bulwark-strake only being coated with paint, usually a bright

---

[1] Pinkerton's 'Voyages and Travels,' vol. i. 'Journey of Maupertuis.'
[2] 'Journal of a Voyage to the North,' by M. Outhier. (Trans.)

green picked out fancifully with white and red. Much labour is sometimes expended on the stern and aft body of Dutch pleasure-vessels, the carved workmanship of which is beautifully polished, and ornamented with gilding. The lee-boards of the Dutch yachts are also of finely polished oak, sometimes carved, and the outer edges bound with brass. A number of carved and polished wooden fend-offs are usually hung over the bows on each side of the yacht; which, whilst useful in saving the sides from scratches and bruises by other craft coming alongside, are also fanciful and ornamental to the vessel.

Dutch yachts and sailing-boats are almost invariably rigged with either the

Boëyer Rig.

Boëyer or the Spiegel rig. The Boëyer rig is the one used for small yachts, and the Spiegel for large ones. The gaff-main-sail of the former is lofty, but very narrow at the head, consequently requiring only a very short gaff. The mast, a tall one, is placed in an upright position, and the lower part of the sail does not extend beyond the outer end of the stern, so that the main-sail looks tall and narrow. The fore-sail which has also considerable hoist, is a tall narrow-shaped sail, attached to the fore-stay. No jib is used, the Boëyer rig consisting of two sails only, neither of which extends beyond the deck of the vessel fore and aft.

A Dutch Boëyer yacht, twenty-four feet in length, is usually about seven feet in breadth.

Boats of Holland.

THE SPIEGEL RIG.

THE Spiegel rig differs slightly from the Boëyer, but in two respects only. In the first place, the main-sail of the Spiegel rig is a little wider at the head than in the other; and, in the next place, the rig consists of three sails, instead of two—a bow-sprit and small jib forming part of the Spiegel rig, but not of the Boëyer. The mast is very lofty, in proportion to the length of the boat; for instance, a yacht forty feet in length by thirteen in breadth, and drawing only four feet of water aft, by three and a half forward, carries a mast fifty-six feet above the deck! All the sail, with the exception

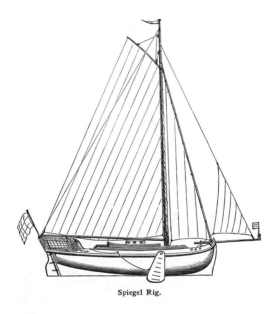

Spiegel Rig.

of the jib, is in-board, the boom of the main-sail not extending beyond the extreme end of the stern.

The hull of the Spiegel-rigged yacht externally is similar to that of the Boëyer; but the stern and aft quarters have a carved and ornamented poop, and there is besides, excellent cabin accommodation.

When full-rigged, they carry a large flag-staff and flag at the stern, and a very tiny one at the tip of the bowsprit, as shown in the engraving.

A peculiarity applicable to both rigs, and indeed to Dutch vessels generally is, that the lower end of the fore-stay is secured to the stem at the bows of the vessel by means of a lanyard rove through a number of eyelet-holes in a large dead-eye; the lanyard thus forming a dozen or more separate parts, thereby facilitating the operation of tightening or loosening the stay on setting up or adjusting the same as occasion may require.

The Sailing-Boat.

THE Dutch fishing Schuyts are of a similar form of hull to the Dutch vessels already described, but of heavier and broader construction, and less graceful proportions; and they are very flat-floored.

The illustration is from a drawing of one of the fishing Schuyts hailing from

Dutch Fishing Schuyt.

Scheveningen employed in the herring fishery. This class of boat is also known as the Pink or Bom.

The Dutch fishing Schuyts are rigged with less canvas, in proportion to the size of the hull, and have shorter masts and heavier spars than the pleasure-vessels; but all have lee-boards, which they use when sailing *on* a wind, to prevent lee-way. These fishing Schuyts come on voyages from different parts of Holland to the north and east coasts of the British Islands, with the east winds of March, to fish in the Channel and North Sea, in company with the British and French fishing boats.

424

Boats of the Bosphorus.

Having once arrived at the fishing-ground, be the weather ever so rough, they seldom make for a harbour, but either contrive to ride out the gales or drive about at sea, laid-to, with fore-sail hauled aweather.

When provisions are wanted the Schuyts are usually run ashore on the open beach, under shelter of some bay or inlet, where they remain until the crew have made all necessary purchases and replenished the stores of the vessel.

The floor of these vessels is of so flat a construction that, when aground, they sit perfectly upright; and such appears to be a very important consideration in the construction of Dutch sailing vessels.

BOATS OF THE BOSPHORUS.

TURKISH CAÏQUES.

AMONG the Caïques of Constantinople and other cities on the Bosphorus are some of very attractive appearance and of as light and elegant construction as any boats in the world. These are very flat-floored, and swim buoyantly on the water, though often heavily laden with a crew of eight or nine, besides two or three passengers. They are lined throughout with thin polished wood, and fitted up with exquisite taste—soft cushions to sit upon and a carpet for the feet.

The prow and stern are graceful and picturesque, exhibiting elaborate carving, with the figure-head of a peacock, pheasant, or other beautiful bird, as an ornament to the prow. The upper sides are also finely carved and gilded, so also are the stern, rudder, back-board, and cross-rail at the bows. Even the stretcher-boards for the feet of the crew are beautiful and delicate pieces of carved work, which yield with a springing elasticity to the muscular efforts of the rowers. The oars are peculiar, the loom being full and heavy, but the blade is apparently light and slender, and of a scientific and beautiful form; they are worked in brass rowlocks, neatly covered with leather.

Some of the State Caïques, and those belonging to persons of dignity, are larger than those in ordinary use on the Bosphorus, and are generally propelled by a numerous crew, who sit doubled-banked and row the Caïque at great speed.

There is a tastefully formed canopy in the aft part of the Caïque, supported by light ornamental pillars, and hung with richly embroidered curtains and drapery, enclosing an elaborate cushion or wool-sack in a gorgeous silk covering, on which the ladies and other distinguished occupants of the Caïque sit or recline at their ease.

Among the many graceful Caïques, with their long, sharp prows and gilded carvings, are several varieties. Some are seen freighted with a bearded and turbaned Turk, squatted upon his carpet beneath the canopy, hookah in hand, and muffled closely in his furred pelisse, the very personification of luxurious idleness.[1]

Some are broad and powerfully-formed boats, others so narrow and ticklish

Turkish State Caïque.

that it is safest to sit on cushions in the bottom of the Caïque. They shoot along very swiftly under oars, when manned by a stalwart crew. Some are occasionally sailed under one or more latine sails.

There are also Caïques of slender and exquisite mould, made of carved and polished walnut-wood; their minute gilded ornaments glittering in the sunlight as they glide to and fro.

'From the gilded barges of the Sultan to the common passage-boat that plies within the port, the Caïques are all beauty; and as they fly past you, their long and lofty prows dipping downwards towards the current at every stroke of the oars, you are involuntarily reminded of some aquatic bird moistening the plumage of its glistening breast in the clear ripple.'[2]

'The long, dark, crescent-shaped Caïque, immediately in the wake of the Sultan, with its three gauze-clad rowers and its flashing ornaments, carries a pasha of the Imperial suite. He is hidden beneath the red umbrella which the attendant, who is squatted upon the raised stern of the boat, is holding carefully over him.'[3]

'You may see a third bark just creeping along under the land—a light buoyant, glittering thing, with a crimson drapery, fringed with gold, flung over its side, and almost dipping into the water. A negress is seated behind her mistress, with a collection of yellow slippers strewn about her; and at the bottom of the

[1] 'The City of the Sultan,' by Miss Pardoe.
[2] Ibid. p. 228 (4th ed.). [3] Ibid. p. 229.

426

boat, reclining against a pile of cushions, and attended by two young slaves, you may distinguish the closely-veiled Fatma or Leyla, whose dark eyes are seen flashing out beneath her pure white *yashmac*, and whose small, fair, delicately-rounded, and gloveless hand draws yet closer together the heavy folds of her *feridjhe*, as she remarks the approach of another Caïque to her own. She is the wife of some pasha- -the favourite wife, it may be—musing, as she darts along the water, with what new toy her next smile shall be bought.' [1]

Lady Brassey,[2] with reference to the Sultan's visit to the Mosque at Fundukli, says—' About twelve o'clock five Caïques glided alongside the steps of Dolmabagtcheh : the Sultan entered the first, which was white, lined with red velvet and gold, and having a gold canopy. The cushions were embroidered in gold and precious stones, and facing those on which the Sultan sat, knelt two of the chief ministers, their heads bowed down and their hands folded across their breasts, in the most abject attitude. Behind stood the steersman, gorgeous in green and gold. The front Caïque was manned by twenty-four oarsmen, dressed in very full white shirts and trousers, purple and gold jackets, and scarlet fezzes, who, prior to every stroke, knelt down and touched the bottom of the boat with their foreheads, then rose to a standing posture, and sent the oars in with a tremendous sweep. The pace is terrific (they beat easily the fastest steam launch afloat), and the exertion is equally so ; for though picked strong men, the rowers generally break down at the end of two years. The whole effect is one of the prettiest imaginable, and the boat looks almost too good for the use of mortal man.'

The caïquejhes (native boatmen) are, generally speaking, a very fine race of men ; and they take a pride and delight in the cleanliness of their boats, keeping sponges and brushes for wiping and cleaning them, and soft leathers for rubbing the brass and ornamental work, and they always take off their shoes before stepping in, and never suffer any one to get in with dirty boots.

No one is allowed to sit in the raised parts of the graceful bows and stern of the Caïque, for fear of disturbing the trim of the boat, besides disfiguring the elegant carving and fancy-work. Strangers are assisted into the Caïques with the greatest care, and luggage is removed with nice caution and quiet management. On landing their passengers, the Caïque crew always turn the boat, and back ashore stern foremost.

[1] 'The City of the Sultan,' p. 229.
[2] In ' Sunshine and Storm in the East,' 1888, p. 92.

The Sailing-Boat.

FRUIT CAIQUES OF THE BOSPHORUS.

'And this slowly-moving bark, rather dropping down with the current than impelled by the efforts of its two Greek rowers, and which looks so cool and so pretty, with all that pile of green leaves heaped upon its stern, is one of the fruit Caïques for the supply of the houses overhanging the Bosphorus. The wild, shrill cry of the fruiterers, announcing the nature of their merchandise swells upon the air; and as you pass close beside the boat, the wind, sporting among the fresh branches that are strewn over the baskets, blows aside the leaves and the tempting fruit is revealed to you in all its cool ripe beauty.'[1]

THE MISTICO,

Or Mystaco, of the Greek Archipelago, is a decked vessel, with a long, low hull, used formerly by the Greek pirates; it was rigged with two short stumpy masts and tall latine sails, much resembling those of the felucca of the Mediterranean.

ARABIA.

ARAB BATELLE.

Arab Batelles were the boats principally used by the Joaseme pirates of the Persian Gulf, who, in years gone by, were a terror to the native mariners, until exterminated by the united efforts of the King's ships and the Honourable East India Company's vessels-of-war. They were very destructive to trade, because no vessel could escape them; and their weatherly qualities prevented square-rigged ships from capturing them except in strong breezes. But their fame has now passed away by the introduction of steam vessels, previous to which it is said, 'there was no vessel ever built that could sail so close to the wind.'[2]

[1] 'The City of the Sultan,' p. 229.
[2] *Vide* Official Catalogue, International Exhibition, 1851.

Boats of Arabia.

It is also stated that when the pirates on board were supposed to be on the point of surrendering, they used to make off with the Batelle in gallant style, within gun-shot of the ship, and were chased and pursued in vain.

Batelles have considerable overhang fore and aft in the form of raking bows and stern, the latter inclining upwards in a most peculiar manner from the keel; and the rudder consequently, when the vessel is under way, is let down to the level of the keel; but when at anchor the rudder is hoisted above the surface of the water, as shown in the engraving.

To the aft part of the rudder on the outside is affixed the tiller, which has a

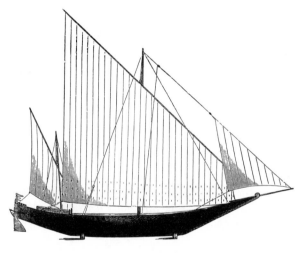

Arab Batelle.

curve pointing upwards. The yoke-lines attached to it are led inboard by means of an outrigger at the side; and with these the helmsman steers the Batelle. The rudder so formed requires very little head, as it is confined to a certain point by spreaders fastened to the stern-posts.

These vessels are exceedingly well built, upon scientific lines; they have good beam, a sharp and hollow floor, clean run, and a perfectly wedge-like entrance, which offers little or no resistance to the water.

The rig of the Batelle is the latine; and they usually have three suits of sails, all made of very fine cotton canvas, woven by hand at Bahrein. In calms, they are propelled by long sweeping oars.

Batelles of the largest size are about 150 tons burden; these are now used only by the Arab chiefs of the Persian Gulf on state occasions and visits of ceremony.

The Sailing-Boat.

The main-yard of the Batelle is longer than the vessel itself, the main-sail is therefore of large and powerful proportions.

The latine sails of the Batelle are so made that they are not what may be termed true latines, because they have the fore angle cut off, the advantages of which are, that the sails so cut may be reefed at the foot, which is not generally the case with ordinary latine sails.

The same kind of latine sail (with the fore angle cut off) is sometimes used for the pleasure-boats and other vessels in various parts of India, by reason of the facility it affords for reefing. When close-reefed the sail presents a true latine appearance.

A beautiful model of one of these remarkable vessels was exhibited in the International Exhibition of 1851, from which a drawing was made by the author for the purpose of illustration in this work. The model, which is now in the Indian Museum, is considered perfect in every respect, as a whole; and as to the details, the making of it is said to have been superintended by an Arab from the Persian Gulf.

ARAB PIRATE BOATS.

Another and more ancient kind of craft of the class of armed pirate boats that formerly infested the Persian Gulf, is that shown by the subjoined illustration.

It will be observed that the type of the Arab Dhow may be traced in the

Arab Pirate Boat.

form of its hull; and the rig savours of the Malayan form. The boat has a square transom, with raised deck astern; it has no rudder, but is steered by the primitive contrivance of two ponderous oars, one on each side of the transom stern.

The rig of this craft is, too, as ancient and curious as its type of hull: the main-sail being supported by a tripod mast similar to that of the Malays in the Celebes. Other details of the rig may be best explained by reference to the illustration.

THE BUGALA.

THE Bugala (also termed Bugla), though of remarkable type, is a useful class of boat known as a trading vessel on the coast of Cutch; employed chiefly between Bombay and the Persian Gulf.

It will be observed on reference to the illustration, that the form of hull, as

The Bugala.

also the rig, are distinctly those of the Arab Dhow type. The term 'Dhow' is not, however, strictly correct, Bugala being the original and proper name by which they are best known. These boats, which vary in size from small craft up to vessels of 150 tons or more, are built at several places in the Persian Gulf, but chiefly in the neighbourhood of Muscat. They have high sterns, with gallery, and are rigged with two masts and latine-shaped sails, the mizzen-sail being very much the smaller of the two.

A smaller class of Bugalas are also employed on the Indus.

THE MATAPA.

THE Matapa is a native boat of the Northern Rivers of East Africa, and is one of very primitive and fragile construction, being built of strips of the tree-bark sewn together with thongs of hide; the seams being caulked with cotton stuff and warmed gum. The Matapa boats are a purely native craft, built and used only by the negroes for the purpose, mainly, of conveying the inland produce of the country, such as ivory, gum and other goods, down to the coast. They are sailed only with a fair wind; and the sail is as primitive as the boat itself, consisting merely of a square of rush matting, hoisted up the mast by a rope of the same material.

The Matapa boats are a very leaky kind of craft, and when on a voyage, either up or down river, one or more of the crew are kept constantly employed in baling them out.

BOATS OF THE TIGRIS.

MR. CLIVE BIGHAM, in his interesting work descriptive of his travels through Western Asia,[1] speaks of the different kinds of boats he met with on his journey up the flooded valley of the Tigris. Mr. Bigham says :—' The four kinds of boats used are : Mehalas or Feluccas, with one large sail; Kalatches, or pig-skin rafts; Bellums, a sort of small Gondola; and Gophers.'

The Gophers, of which a photographic illustration of a cluster of several is given at p. 170 of the work referred to, are of a primitive and curious kind of construction, quite circular in form, and bulging all around the outer part like a monster bird's-nest : they are apparently of wicker or basket-like contrivance,

---

[1] 'A Ride through Western Asia, 1897,' by Clive Bigham.

with a strong circular rim, and an outside covering of skins or tarpauling of some kind. It would appear, by the photographic illustration alluded to, that they are propelled by a hand-paddle; or, when in shallow water by a setting-pole or sweep, as there are no thole-pins or other provision for propulsion or steering.

Coracles of the Gopher type are mentioned by Herodotus. Sidonian and Phœnician Coracles were of circular form.[1]

The Dhoneys or Ferry boats of the Cavery, in Mysore, are apparently of identical form and construction to the Gophers mentioned by Mr. Clive Bigham.[2]

GELVES.

THESE remarkable vessels are of a very ancient type; they are used chiefly on the Red Sea; and are built entirely of the wood of the cocoa-tree, which, on being sawn into planks, are sewn together with a kind of twine, spun out of the bark of the same tree and twisted into ropes and cables. The Gelve, thus built, is tough and flexible; and if it chance to strike against a rock or run aground, it receives comparatively little or no injury, by reason of its peculiar construction enabling it to yield to the blow.

The sails of the Gelve are made of the broad leaves of the cocoa-tree stitched together.

It is a curious fact, that out of the cocoa-tree alone a vessel of the Red Sea may be built, rigged, and fitted with mast, sails, cordage, and ropes; and victualled with bread, water, wine, sugar, vinegar, and oil.

[1] *Supra*, page 10.   [2] *Infra*, page 453.

The Sailing-Boat.

BOATS OF HINDUSTAN.

Boats of every size, and as numerous in variety as those of any nation under the sun, are met with on the noble rivers and shores of Hindustan. The chief traffic of the country was, prior to the introduction of railways, carried on in covered boats, some of which are of symmetrical and graceful form and very capable sailing vessels in smooth water. Those employed on the Ganges have high stems and sterns, and are well adapted to the intricate navigation of that locality. The boats of the Ganges have necessarily a large rudder, and even that is often rendered powerless by the rapidity of the currents. Great presence of mind is sometimes necessary in the navigation of boats on the Ganges, particularly by the man at the prow, who, with surprising agility, has to dart his long bamboo pole to the opposite bank, and turn the boat, or fend off in the midst of rapid currents, to avoid disaster. The boats employed between the Gulf of Cutch and the Sinde, or Indus, are chiefly bugaloes, naodees, muchoos, coteyahs, and gungos.

Almost all Indian boats have considerable rake at the bows. The fastest have long, sharp, and generally hollow bows, and the stern is often as sharp and tapering as the bow; but those used for the purposes of trade have less graceful proportions.

The Indian method of construction differs from the European in many respects. Instead of nailing and clinching the planks, they are carefully rabbeted together in a neat and durable manner, and although such a method occupies a vast amount of time and labour, the vessels so constructed seldom require caulking; all the seams and interstices being filled with cotton stuff, and the whole exterior served over with gum or other resinous substance. The wood used by the Indians in boat and ship-building is chiefly teak, which is well known as a hard, tough, and durable material.

INDIAN SAILING BOATS.

Indian sailing-boats of the class illustrated sail very fast with a free wind, but, generally speaking, are too long for turning to windward with effect on any but broad, open waters. They are usually flat and full amidships, but drawn out to extremes at each end, with a fine, sharp, hollow bow and tapering stern.

Boats of India.

The common mode of rig of Indian sailing-boats is that known as the latine. But many of the trading and passage boats are rigged with a kind of lug-sail.

The style of rigging the latines of India differs from that of the Mediterranean. The Indian latines have seldom more than two masts, of which the hinder one is much the smaller; though some of the light, modern pleasure-boats have three, and a small

Indian Pleasure-Boat.

jib besides. The sails of the Indian latine, instead of being right-angled triangles like true latines, have the foremost angle cut off, so that they are nearer the principle of the old settee sail. A great advantage, however, is, that latine sails so cut may be reefed at the foot with every facility, which is not generally the case with latine rigged boats.

BOATS OF THE PUNJAUB.

The pleasure-boats of the Punjaub are of a long and graceful form, but broad amidships, and they have a good cabin. They are, however, very shallow, and drawn out to great length at the bows, but are decked all over, and have a railing along each side of the deck. Some of these boats belonging to Chiefs and natives of distinction are gilded, painted, and ornamented with considerable taste.

The Sailing-Boat.

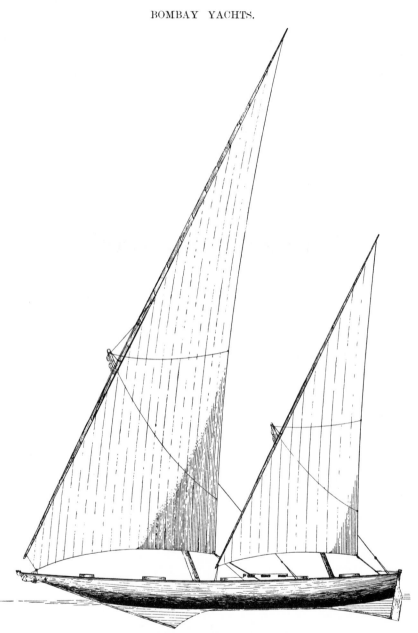

A Famous Yacht of the Royal Bombay Yacht Club.

THE illustration is from a drawing of a famous yacht belonging to a member of the Royal Bombay Yacht Club; and, although there are members of that Club who possess yachts of European type and rig, it is the *native* type and rig which the author is here desirous of illustrating and describing.

The yacht depicted is an excellent representative of the native Indian type, which it will be seen shows a comparatively flat-shaped floor, hollow entrance, sharp flat run and rather shallow draft. It will be observed that the most striking feature of the hull, and that in which it differs most from the yachts and boats of European construction, is in its false keel, which is of crescent-like form, the fore and aft ends extending several feet below the keelson, whilst the midship portion of the hull would seem to be devoid of any false keel at all; and such are the chief peculiarities of the Indian type of vessel of almost every kind.

One of the advantages of such a form of keel is said to be that, if the vessel runs aground, she is the more readily got off than if she had a straight keel; but this and other alleged advantages are not so manifest to the minds of European yacht-builders as they are, apparently, to the Indians. That the deep-projecting fore and aft portions of the keel have their advantages in enabling the yacht to hold a good weatherly course on a wind is undoubted, but modern British and American yacht-builders do not place a deep keel so far forward in the hull of the vessel—on the contrary, the latest development is to dispense with fore-gripe and to place deep keels farther aft.

It is a fact, however, that the crescent-like form of keel has for centuries past taken a firm hold on the minds of Indian boat-builders as possessing advantages not to be obtained by any other form. And this would seem to be verified by the success which frequently attends the native boats in sailing matches in Bombay waters in competition with yachts of other nations—a success which may not perhaps be attributable solely to the crescent-shaped keel. The rig is peculiar, with its lofty tapering sails and tall slender peaks, which in light winds and smooth waters are very effective, particularly when sailing under high cliffs and in land-locked waters.

The native yacht, the subject of illustration, is rigged with two masts and latine sails; the masts, as usual in vessels so rigged, are placed in leaning position, the rake being towards the stem; the foresail, which is much the larger sail of the two, is laced to a long yard tapering at each end, and considerably longer than the boat itself, but the mizzen-sail has a yard of similar shape though much smaller, and of about the same length as the yacht itself.

The sails of the yachts so rigged are usually made of native cotton drill, sewn in narrow cloths.

The native yachts of this type and rig are quick in stays; and on 'coming about' the sail and yard are readily shifted to the other side of the mast without being lowered, and in 'waring,' sheet and tack are both eased off; and under the manipulation of a native crew, the yacht is managed with a dexterity equal to that of a European yacht with European crew.

The Sailing-Boat.

There are models of Indian yachts in the Museum at Kensington; one of which was exhibited so long ago as the International Exhibition of 1851, the dimensions of which were given as under:—Length over all 46 ft., extreme breadth 12 ft., depth amidships 3 ft. 8 ins.; length of spars:—Main-mast, 36 ft.; main-yard, 65 ft.; mizzen-mast, 22 ft.; mizzen-yard, 40 ft.

It will thus be seen that the main-yard of the latine main-sail was 19 ft. more than the entire length of the yacht.

BOMBAY FISHING BOATS.

THE Bombay fishing boats rank among the fastest of the trading class in India, and are worthy of imitation in many respects. Some of them are splendid sea-boats, but not so quick in staying, nor so convenient for turning to windward in narrow channels, as the boats of some other nations. Their greatest draft of water is forward—which is the reverse of the European and American systems. They have also a sharp and hollow bow, and the breadth of beam is carried well aft, finishing with an over-hanging stern. The rig consists of two latine sails; but no bowsprit, nor is a sail of any kind set beyond the stem. Both masts are short and rake forward; the mizzen-mast is generally a trifle more than half the length of the main-mast, and the yards in the same proportion. Some of these boats are of the burden of 20 or 30 tons; the main-yard for the latter is nearly a hundred feet in length. The fore-leech of the sail is usually of about the same dimensions as the aft-leech. Neither shrouds nor rigging are used in these boats, the main-halliards being the only stay to the mast. The tack of the main-sail is managed with a luff-tackle purchase at the stem, in the same manner as the clew by the main-sheet; the double block being seized into the tack, and the single block strapped to the mast. In 'waring,' both sheet and tack are eased off; but in tacking, the sail and yard are shifted to either side of the mast, as may be required, without being lowered.[1]

BOMBAY COTTON BOATS.

THESE boats belong to the port of Bombay. They are called cotton-boats because they are employed chiefly in conveying cotton from the shore to ships bound for China and Great Britain, loading with that commodity. They are, in fact, the only boats made use of in loading and unloading the numerous kinds of outward and inward cargoes of ships visiting the port.

This method is also adopted in the latine-rigged boats of the Mediterranean.

Boats of India.

They measure in length from 25 ft. to 35 ft., and in breadth from 10 ft. to 13 ft., and 3½ ft. to 4 ft. in depth. They are roughly but strongly built, and the largest of them will carry 15 tons of dead-weight. They are also employed in bringing the produce of the Island of Salsette—such as grain, grass, vegetables, &c.— to Bombay; and for the conveyance of troops, with their baggage, to and from Panwell.

The inside of the cotton-boat is lined with bamboo matting, to protect the cargo from bilge water. These boats are generally navigated each by a crew of six men and a *tindal*—principally Mohammedans—who live in the boat.

On one side of the mast is a fireplace, and on the opposite side a cask or tank containing fresh water. The bottom of the boat outside is annually, or oftener, paid over with a mixture of chunam, or lime and vegetable oil, which hardens and is a good protection against worms. They have one mast, stepped so as to rake forward, and a yard of about the same length as the boat, on which a latine sail is spread.

BOMBAY DINGHY.

Bombay Dinghy.

THE dinghy, dingee, or bum-boat, of Bombay, is from 12 ft. to 20 ft. in length, 5 ft. to 7 ft. in breadth, and 18 ins. to 2 ft. in depth. It is similar in form to the cotton-boat before described, but smaller. These boats are rigged with a raking mast, latine

439

sail, and a yard of about the same length as the boat. They are navigated by a crew of three or four, who, not infrequently, are joint-owners of the boat.

They are employed in carrying persons to and from vessels in the harbour; also in carrying persons desirous of visiting the islands of Elephanta, Caranjah, and others in the harbour of Bombay.

BATELLES OF BOMBAY AND SURAT.

THESE vessels belong principally to merchants, and are decidedly the best constructed and best found in fittings and stores of any kind of boat of Western India. They are built entirely of teak-wood, well planked and fastened with iron nails and bolts; they have a great rise of sheer forward, and a regular stem, with madows, abaft. Some are fitted with a cabin under the poop, but the majority of them carry bamboo decks, over beams fitted for the purpose.[1]

They are from 35 ft. to 50 ft. in length, 15 ft. to 20 ft. in breadth, and 5 ft. to 7 ft. in depth, and from 25 to 100 tons burthen.

They are rigged with latine sails, of similar shape to those already described; and with main and mizzen-masts, both raking forward. The main-yard is a little longer than the extreme length of the boat. They are also provided with a bowsprit on which a jib is set. These vessels have a break in the top sides, from the fore part of the poop to the luff of the bow, nearly level with the beams, for the facility of shipping and unshipping heavy cargoes. At sea this break is stopped up with bamboo mats on the inside, and with soft mud or puddle on the outside, which renders it as water-tight as any other part of the hull.

It is a remarkable fact, that no one ever hears of damage being done to the cargo from any defect in this part of the vessel, although when the boat is fully laden, the break is only about 12 or 18 ins. above water. These boats import cotton from Surat, Broach, Cambay, and other cotton-growing districts, to Bombay; and teak timber from the northern forests, which is extensively used in shipbuilding at Bombay.

THE BUDJEROW.

BUDJEROWS (sometimes called Bengalee boats) are a good deal used by Europeans for travelling on the Ganges, and in various other parts of India. They have high sterns, full bulging form amidships, and rounded bottoms. They are of various

[1] *Vide* Official Catalogue of the International Exhibition, 1851.

sizes, from 25 ft. up to 60 ft. in length. Some of the longest are rowed by as many as 20 oars, and are steered with a sweep (or large oar) extending nearly 10 ft. abaft the stern. They are sailed with a square-sail, and square-topsail in fine weather.

The budjerow is decked all over, throughout its whole length, with bamboo. On the deck is erected a low, light fabric of bamboo and matting, like a small cottage without a chimney. This is the cabin and baggage-room, and also the sitting and sleeping apartment for passengers; and if intended for a cooking-boat, there are one or two small ranges of brick-work, like European hot-hearths, but

Ganges Sailing-Boat.

not rising more than a few inches above the deck, with small round sugar-loaf holes, like those in a lime-kiln, adapted for dressing victuals with charcoal.

The roof of the cabin being far too fragile for men to stand upon—and as the apartment itself takes up nearly two-thirds of the vessel—upright bamboos are fixed by its side, which support a platform of the same material immediately above the roof, on which, at the height of about six or eight feet above the surface of the water, the boatmen sit or stand to work the vessel. They have for oars long bamboos with disc-shaped blades, a longer one of the same sort being used to steer with; a long rough bamboo for a mast; and one, or sometimes two, sails of a square form (or rather broader above than below) of coarse and flimsy canvas, which is set on a bamboo yard.[1] Some of the fastest of these boats are of a

[1] *Vide* Bishop Heber's 'Narrative,' vol. i. p. 84. Also Forrest's 'Tour of the Ganges.'

somewhat superior form and construction, and have three square-sails, one above another.

With a fair wind, these vessels sail merrily over the water, though they make but slow progress with a foul wind. The Europeans at Bengal and elsewhere have made great improvements of late years in the native budjerows, by introducing a broad flat floor, square stern, and full bow; and in that form they are safer and faster, and enabled to carry more sail; and being of less draft of water, they do not so often run aground. Some of them have cabins six or seven feet in height, and very commodious.[1]

A gentleman in his budjerow is usually attended by a *pulwah*, or large open boat, for the accommodation of the kitchen, and a smaller boat, called a *panchway*, for taking him ashore.

THE PANCHWAY.

THE larger-sized Panchway, or passage-boat, used on the Ganges is a very characteristic and interesting kind of vessel, large, broad, and shaped like a snuffer-tray. It is also decked fore and aft, and the middle part is covered with a roof of palm branches, over which is lashed an awning, forming an excellent shade from the sun.

The *serang*, or master, stands on the little aft-deck, and steers with a long oar, the loom of which is lashed to a stanchion standing above the deck on the port side of the stern; another of the crew has a similar oar on the starboard-quarter. There are also six rowers, who sit cross-legged on the deck upon the tilt, and ply their short paddles with much effect, resting them on bamboos, which are fixed to the sides, instead of rowlocks or thowls.

When the wind is fair, they use an elongated square-sail of thin transparent sackcloth, in three pieces, very loosely laced together, and secured to a bamboo yard, and hoisted on a mast of bamboo. These singular-looking boats are sometimes taken on very long voyages, plying from various places on the Ganges to and from Calcutta.

[1] 'Voyage to the East Indies,' by J. S. Stavorinus, Esq.

Boats of India.

THE BHAULEA.

The Bhaulea, or Ganges boat, is very much like the budjerow. A peculiarity among many of the different forms of boats of the Ganges is the gallery, upon

Ganges Rowing-Boat.

which light goods are carried; and the *manjee*, or steersman, also sits there to steer and guide the boat.

CUTCH COTIYAHS.

These boats belong to the ports of Cutch, Mandivee, Poar Bunder, and some to Kurrachee, in the territory of Sinde. They trade between Bombay and those ports. They are very well built, with a square tuck, and many of them have a regular built stern, with ports, and are handsomely carved. Some have a deck fore and aft, but more commonly they have frame-work between the beams—to ship and unship, for the facility of stowage—and a bamboo deck. Their general length is from 30 ft. to 50 ft., by 12 ft. to 23 ft. in breadth, and 7 ft. to 10 ft. deep.

They are navigated by a crew of 15 to 20 men and a *tindal*. They are latine-rigged, with main and mizzen sails, both masts raking forward, as usual with the native latine-rigged boats.

THE PATTAMAR.

The Pattamar (or pattamach) is a trading sailing boat of Hindustan, employed by the natives of the Deccan and at Bombay for the conveyance of rice and other articles of merchandise. The Pattamar, like most of the native sailing vessels of that country, is remarkable for its peculiar-shaped keel, which forms part of a circle, the hollow being directly under the midship section, where there is much less keel

443

than at the extremities. The extent of curvature varies according to the form of the boat; those with very flat floors have the greatest curve, but in narrow and

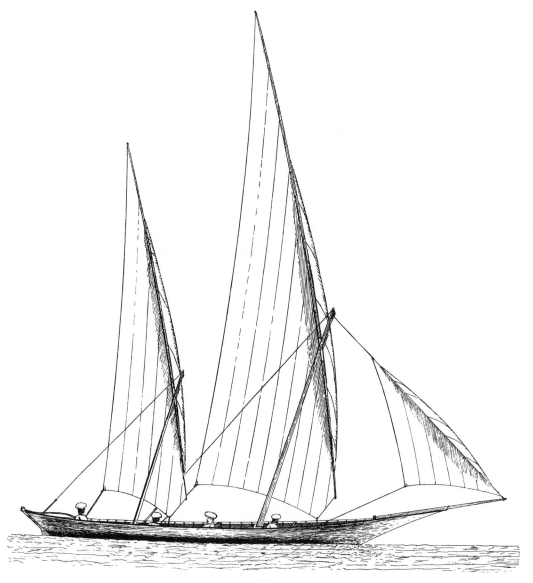

Pattamar, sailing with a free wind.

sharp-bottomed boats the curve is less. The chief advantages of a keel so formed are that it gives additional weatherly qualities under sail; and also that when they get aground (as they are very liable to do in the Deccan), they may be got off again without difficulty. The pattamar has a hollow bow with raking stem; is rigged with two masts, which rake forwards, the fore-mast being the larger, as customary with Indian boats; and the main-yard is considerably longer than the boat. The pattamar is sailed under latine sails, and is a stiff and fast-sailing boat off wind, but not so well adapted for tacking or turning to windward.

THE MUCHOO,

or Muchwa, is a fishing-boat of the Deccan, bearing strong resemblance to the pattamar, but much smaller. The muchoo sails remarkably fast, even when close-hauled, but from its small size is better suited to smooth water.

BUNDER BOAT.

THIS is a stout and strongly built type of native boat, used in and about the Indian harbours—hence the name, from *bundur*, a harbour. It is generally rigged with two masts, and sailed under two latine sails.

THE BHOLCO.

THE Bholco is a small light boat, employed in the Upper Provinces of India for the conveyance of passengers to short distances.

CHEEP BOATS AND PARINDA BOATS.

THESE are Bengal river boats—long, narrow, and shallow—with a hood or cabin roof abaft, and latticed deck, or raised grating, made of bamboo.

MOHR PUNKEE.

THE Mohr Punkee, or peacock-boat, so called from its being built to resemble a peacock, and having at its prow a carved figure-head of that bird, with its tail extending the whole length of the boat; the plumage on each side is beautifully

445

portrayed in imitation of the gaudy feathers of the peacock, and the stern is usually ornamented with the head of some ferocious animal. The extreme length of some of these boats is 80 ft. and upwards, and the extreme breadth, which is towards the front, is about 9 ft.; from which they gradually diminish towards the stern, which terminates in a point. Over the broadest part a canopy is erected, and covered with crimson velvet richly embroidered with gold, as are also the curtains which hang on each side, the whole being supported by several gilded pillars, the lower part of which are surrounded by a light rail. A narrow balcony, extending beyond the sides of the pavilion, serves as a receptacle for confectionery, fruit, sherbet, and other refreshments.

The floor of the pavilion is carpeted and cushioned, the occupants sitting upon it with their feet doubled under their bodies. The throne, or seat of eminence, is in front of the pavilion, where the Nabob, or person of highest distinction, sits.

Mohr Punkee.

The boat is propelled by a crew of thirty or forty, who sit double-banked behind the pavilion, with faces fronting the direction in which the boat is to go. The paddles are each furnished with two brass rings on their handles, which, clashing and rattling together, serve to keep the rowers in time.

The Mohr Punkee draws but very little water and glides along with great velocity under the paddles. It is steered by a long oar, fastened on the larboard side near the stern. At the head and stern a flag-staff is set up, on which streamers of crimson silk are displayed.

The crew are directed by a pilot, who stands at the prow, and generally makes use of the branch of some plant to regulate their rowing, using much gesticulation, and telling his story to excite alternately laughter and exertion. These boats belong alone to the princes and nabobs of the country. They are an expensive luxury owing to their great length, and the carving and costly decorations with which they are fitted.

Boats of India.

THE Massoolah boats (sometimes spelt Mussulah, also Masuli) are a remarkable and curious kind of surf boat, employed on the coast of Madras for beaching and putting off in the surf to ships when at anchor in the roads there. The exposed nature of the coast at Madras, the entire absence of any harbour or shelter, and the heavy broken seas which constantly prevail there, render it difficult, and sometimes impossible, to effect a safe landing of either passengers or goods in any boat of ordinary construction. Under these circumstances, the ingenuity of the native beachmen has been turned to the subject, and the result is that they have succeeded in contriving a boat which, though of grotesque appearance and curious construction, is peculiarly adapted to meet those difficulties, so that passengers and

Massoolah Surf Boat.

goods may now be safely put off or landed through the heavy surf and broken water on that perilous coast.

Neither nails, pegs, nor bolts are used in any part of the structure of a Massoolah boat, but the planks and other parts are sewn and laced together with the strong fibres of the cocoanut-tree, layers of cotton being placed between the planks. Over the seams, inside, a flat narrow strip of tough fibrous wood is laid, the whole being then drawn tightly together with cordage; and the planks are joined to stout stem and stern-posts in the same manner. The object in so building them is to avoid the effect of the severe thumping and bumping they have to encounter on the shore when being beached or launched through the heavy surfs at Madras, which it is impossible to avoid; so that, if fastened with iron nails or bolts, such kind of rough usage would very quickly loosen the planks, the boat would become leaky, and in the course of a very few trips would be a perfect wreck.

The Massoolah boat, however, remains for a long time almost as uninjured from the thumping and bumping as if made of leather. The wood of which it is composed being tough and flexible, the fastenings of an elastic nature, and the material that is interwoven between the planks being soft, all tend to resist with

447

yielding effect the force and power of the surf by which the boat is dashed and thumped upon the beach.

In course of time the fibrous lashings and fastenings of the planks decay and become loose; the seams are then re-sewn with new material of the same kind, and fresh layers of soft cotton are introduced between the planks; and when all is completed, the boat is as tight and secure as when new.

In shape, the Massoolah boat resembles no other. It is flat-bottomed, but has very high flaring sides, so that the top of the boat is considerably broader and longer than the bottom; in fact the upper part of the boat is more than twice the length of the lower part.

The Massoolah boat varies in size, though not in form. It is always very high at the sides and deep inside, very broad at the top in proportion to its length and the small size of the bottom; and as regards the external appearance of the boat, that is, upon the whole, its greatest peculiarity.

A strong rowlock is fixed to the top of the stern-post, with the object of giving a powerful leverage for twisting the boat with a long oar on any sudden emergency. The steersman stands in an elevated position at the stern, and guides the Massoolah boat with the long oar, which has a circular blade at the lower end, about a foot or foot and half in diameter. A good deal of courage and nerve are requisite in the steersman of a Massoolah boat in a heavy sea. It is rowed by six oarsmen, who sit facing the prow, and row double-banked, *i.e.*, two on a thwart. The passengers sit aft, on a bench not so elevated as the thwarts of the rowers.

Notwithstanding all these precautions, there is sometimes a good deal of risk in landing on the beach at Madras; but the Massoolah boats are considered the safest form of vessel that can be used for the purpose. There is also the same risk when putting off from the beach; indeed, the launching of the Massoolah boat is an art only to be acquired by local practice. The semi-naked, hardy native boatmen who effect it cannot always, with all their expertness, prevent the water from breaking over the boat and drenching the passengers to the skin.[1]

Massoolah boats are never sailed; and they are all required to carry their numbers distinctly painted on each bow.

MADRAS CATAMARANS.

STRANGERS, on visiting the coast of Coromandel, are generally much interested in these remarkable and fragile-looking rafts, and the manner in which they

---

[1] Colonel Napier's 'Wild Sports of Asia' (1844). Hall's 'Fragments of Voyages and Travels,' &c.

Boats of India.

breast the heavy breakers off the coast at Madras. The breakers, though nothing very formidable to look at, are irresistible in their force.

The Catamarans of Madras are formed of three logs of the cocoa-tree—not rounded logs, but shaped and roughly levelled on the upper side. The length of the raft is from 20 ft. to 25 ft., and the breadth $2\frac{1}{2}$ ft. to $3\frac{1}{2}$ ft.; the logs are secured together by being lashed to three spreaders or cross-pieces. The centre log of the three is much the largest, and is fitted with a stem-piece, having a curved surface at the fore end, which turns upwards to a point. The two side logs are similar in form, but smaller, having their sides straight and fitted to the centre log.

They are generally navigated each by two men, though sometimes by one only, but with the greatest skill and dexterity, as they think nothing of passing through the heaviest surfs, when the boats of the country could not live on the waves.[1]

These Catamarans are used chiefly for conveying letters, messages, &c., to and from ships in the roads at Madras; and when seen at a distance, the men appear as if they were treading or kneeling upon the water, performing evolutions with a racket, and bobbing about in the surf.[2] They carry letters in their conical-shaped skull-caps, which are of waterproof material, and tied as well as waxed to their heads. The caps ease the force of the heavy breakers, under which they are often obliged to dive their heads. Sometimes they appear completely buried in the surf, which is constantly breaking over them; notwithstanding which, they are seldom known to be lost or swept from the raft, although they frequently venture out to sea many miles from the shore. But if they chance to be washed off by a heavy sea, woe betide them! for sharks abound on that coast.

Even then, however, the case is not quite hopeless, since the shark can only attack from an undermost position, after turning on his back; a rapid dive therefore by the agile native, if not in very deep water, will sometimes save his life. If the catamaran-man be lucky enough to escape the voracious jaws of the shark, he quickly regains his position on the raft, and, generally, without losing his paddle, an instrument these catamaran-men use with singular dexterity. When they come ashore the raft is untied and the logs left on the beach to dry.[3]

[1] 'Exhibition Catalogue, 1851,' vol. ii. p. 909.
[2] In the log-book of one of the early Indian voyagers is the following droll entry, made whilst 'lying off' in the roads at Madras:—'This morning, six a.m., saw distinctly two black devils playing at single-stick. We watched those infernal imps above an hour, when they were lost in the distance. Surely this doth portend some great tempest!'
[3] 'Letters from Madras,' by a Lady (1846). 'Voyages and Travels,' &c.

The Sailing-Boat.

THE Fishing Catamarans employed on the coast of Coromandel are complete skimming-dishes, but of superior and ingenious contrivance, as may be seen by the illustration. They are larger than those last described, but possess the same buoyant and life-boat qualities, being composed of four logs of wood, flattened on the top and rounded at the bottom. The two central logs are the longest, the whole being neatly shaped, and when fastened together forming an unsinkable Catamaran of buoyant capacity, useful contrivance, and powerful bearings. The outer edges of the side logs are higher than the insides, so that a gradual slope is formed from the sides to the central surface. There is a gradual rise at the

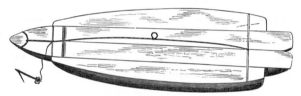

Madras Fishing Catamaran.

fore part of the raft, and the same at the aft part, and the logs are shaped so as to be light at the fore ends, but heavier and thicker at the aft ends.

A rope is looped to the stem of the Catamaran, and fastened down at the bows and stern, but left slack up the middle of the raft, so that it may be used by the crew for holding on by in a heavy sea, and for securing the fish, fishing-tackle, and other gear on board the Catamaran, and to prevent the same being washed off by the sea.

A wooden anchor, with a heavy stone for the shank, is still, as it has always been, the primitive contrivance used for anchoring the Catamaran.

On these shallow-looking rafts the native fishermen of the coast put to sea, and pursue their daily avocations with every confidence in their craft; beaching and putting off in broken water and heavy breakers without fear or danger, so long as they can retain a hold upon the surface of the Catamaran.

Boats of India.

CEYLON CATAMARANS

THE Catamarans of Ceylon are similar to those of Madras; but the middle log of the Ceylon Catamaran inclines upwards at the fore end and forms a sort of stem. The side logs, too, are rather wider and more substantial than those of the Madras raft. The Ceylon Catamaran is employed in the same kind of service and answers the same purpose as a Madras Catamaran.

MADRAS SAILING-CATAMARANS.

THE Madras Sailing-Catamarans are of a superior kind, composed of three carefully-shaped solid logs of wood turning up at each end with considerable sheer. Each log is cut flat on the upper side, and rounded at the bottom; the fore ends forming the bows are also rounded, but the stern ends are squared. The middle log, which is much the largest, is placed lower than those at the sides, and hangs down like a round-shaped keelson (see the engraving and section); the two other

Madras Sailing-Catamaran and section.

logs, therefore, form sides and seats for the crew of the raft, and the lower one a sort of well or interior, and place for the feet of the crew. The three logs are held together by three cross-pieces, firmly secured upon the upper surface of the logs, besides which they are bolted together at the sides, and upon the whole form a very useful sort of raft, but of narrow form, apparently much too narrow to carry sail without some artificial contrivance; and therefore an outrigger is attached to the Sailing-Catamaran on one side, with a heavy solid log, neatly shaped and smoothed in the form of a long narrow boat.

These Catamarans sail well, and in smooth water will hold a course to windward equal to that of a vessel with a deep keel. The natives fearlessly venture out to sea upon them many miles from the coast, and seem to regard strong winds as ordinary weather; their Catamaran being a life-boat in principle, they have no fear of its foundering.

THE LANGADY.

THE Langady, or native ferry-boat of Nursapore, is somewhat curious; it is a sort of twin canoe, made from the trunks of palmyra trees. Both trunks are quite hollow inside, and have an opening at the top for passengers and goods. The stern ends are fitted with circular pieces, like the head of a cask. Two or three poles are lashed across the head part, to hold them at a proper distance apart; but at the stern they are merely held together by a rope. The ferryman stands on the aft part of one of the pontoons, and conducts and propels the Langady with a setting pole.

THE DHONEY.

THE Dhoney, or Yatrawe, is one of the largest kind of native trading vessels of Ceylon; and is employed in the conveyance of merchandise to various parts of

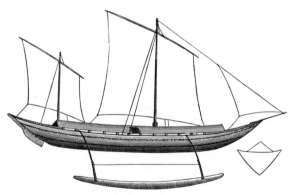

The Dhoney and section.

the Indian Archipelago. No nails or pegs are used in the construction of these vessels; but the planking is neatly and mechanically joined and secured with lacings, made of a strong fibrous material called coir yarn. A caulking of soft matting stuff is also ingeniously laid over and interwoven between the seams, so as to make them water-tight. The hull of the Dhoney is wide at the top and sharp below, somewhat resembling a Norway Yawl, only with rather less curve amidships, and less rise at bow and stern; but they have considerable rake both fore and aft, and are sharper at the stern than at the stem. The roof of the cabin extends almost the whole length of the vessel, and is formed of bamboo canes, but the deck is wood. Several cross-beams are placed across the vessel under the gunwale and deck, fore and aft, to the projecting ends of which the shrouds, sheets, and tacks of the sails are made fast. These Dhoneys are fast-sailing vessels, and are usually fitted with shifting outriggers, suspended over the side in the same manner as the outriggers of other Ceylon boats.[1]

The Dhoney is rigged with two masts and three sails—mainsail, foresail, and mizzen; the main and mizzen sails are in shape like lug-sails, the mizzen being much the smaller of the two. The masts are fitted at the heel with a pin, so that they may be struck when required. The bowsprit is short, and points upwards in line with the rise of the bow. They have wooden anchors like the Malays, and are upon the whole a curious and primitive-looking craft.

The Dhoneys of Jafnapatam are differently constructed to those of Ceylon, being fastened with nails and iron bolts; they have no outrigger, and therefore carry smaller sails.

DHONEYS OF THE CAVERY, IN MYSORE.

THE Ferry-boats of the Cavery, in Mysore are called 'Dhoneys.' They are merely wicker-baskets of a circular form, from 8 ft. to 10 ft. in diameter, and covered on the outside with leather. In fact, they are virtually Coracles as regards the materials of which they are composed, but differing in shape to the Coracles of Great Britain.[2]

In these fragile ferry-boats men and women, goods and merchandise are transported with tolerable safety.

Mr. Clive Bigham, in his recent travels through Western Asia, seems to have met with some boats called 'Gophers' on the Tigris, which were almost identical with the Dhoneys above described.[3]

---

[1] Sir J. Emerson Tennent, in his work on Ceylon, says:—'The Singhalese Dhoney, south of Colombo, is but an enlargement of the Galle canoe, with its outrigger so clumsily constructed that the gunwale is frequently topped by a line of wicker-work smeared with clay to protect the deck from the wash of the sea.'

[2] *Vide supra*, p. 9.

[3] *Vide supra*, p. 432, 'Boats of the Tigris.'

The Sailing-Boat.

THE BALHAM.

THE Balham (or Ballam) is a kind of canoe belonging to the estuaries and shallow lakes around the northern coast of Ceylon. It is made by carving and hollowing out the trunk of a single tree of enormous size, and is the largest description of boat so constructed. The Balham has a deck or covered compartment fore and aft, and is chiefly employed in carrying rice to different parts of Ceylon. It is rigged with a single square-shaped sail.

SAILING-CANOES OF CEYLON.

'Sometimes swiftly as swallow blithe
    Skimming the ocean's breast,
Sometimes sleeping with folded sail
    In calm and dreamy rest;
Their cordage fine, in the white moonshine,
    All "beauteously confest."'

CAPTAIN G. P. THOMAS.

THE Ceylonese (also called Cingalese) or Point de Galle canoes are very remarkable, not only for their curious form of hull, but also as regards the manner in which they are rigged and sailed. They are sometimes called double canoes, though one portion is merely a balance-log, carried at the extremity of two outriggers, each about 18 ft. in length. They have always been constructed without nails; and although such was the practice in the remotest period it is retained at the present day.[1]

These extraordinary little vessels are life-boats in principle. They carry no ballast, but their peculiarly buoyant nature and ingenious form enable them, under the skilful handling of the natives, to be as safe a kind of boat as any in which to venture out to sea in those parts.

The Ceylonese canoes are of various sizes, their dimensions being from 18 ft. to 30 ft. in length, by only 2½ ft. in breadth, and from 2 ft. to 3 ft. deep, exclusive of the wash-boards, which are from 10 in. to 18 in. deep, and sewn to the gunwale with coir yarns, loose coir padding being bound over the seams or joinings.

The hull of the Ceylonese canoe is formed from the trunk of the doop-wood or

---

[1] Sir J. Emerson Tennent's 'Ceylon,' vol. ii.; *Vide* also 'Picturesque Ceylon,' by Henry W. Cave, 1893.

Boats of Ceylon.

pine-varnish tree, hollowed and smoothed in the usual way, but not left so open at the top as in other canoes, the hollowed trunk being more like a cylinder, with a narrow strip about eight or ten inches wide cut out of it on the inside from end to end. The leeward side of some of these canoes is bow-shaped in the longi-

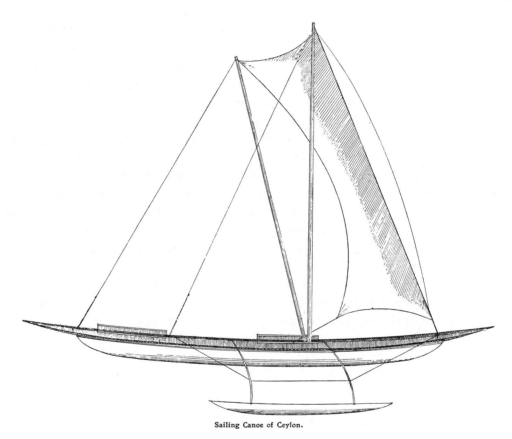

Sailing Canoe of Ceylon.

tudinal form, though inclining to flatness; but the weather side is fuller and rounder, and in this respect they are something like the flying proa of the Ladrone Islands.[1] Upon the cylindrical or bottom part of the Ceylonese canoe they build a sort of trough, extending from one end to the other. The cylindrical part of the canoe turns up at each end, so also the trough-like or top part. The latter also projects two or three feet beyond the cylinder at each end, and the stem and stern of the canoe stand high above the water. The flat sides of the top part standing up above the cylinder, considerably add to the ticklish nature of the whole fabric; but in order to prevent

[1] *Infra*, page 463.

455

The Sailing-Boat.

the canoe from over-setting, and to preserve its stability on the water, an outrigger is fitted on one side of the canoe in the following manner:—Two spars, curved downwards at the outer ends, are fixed across the top part of the trough of the canoe, at right angles to its length, and projecting from the weather side some twelve, fifteen, or twenty feet (according to the size and capacity of the canoe), where the outer ends of the spars are secured to a log of buoyant wood, about half the length of the canoe, and placed parallel with it, the log being shaped as a boat, and sharpened and turned up at each end. The outrigger, thus fitted, acts as a powerful counter-poise to the canoe, and preserves its stability under great pressure of sail.

The rig of the Ceylonese canoe is peculiar; the sail is of primitive form, a sort of elongated square-sail, secured only at the four corners, the two upper ones being made fast, one to the top of the tall slender mast, the other to the top of the yard, which is within a foot or two of the same length as the mast, the heel of the yard forming an apex at the foot of the mast; the luff of the sail is secured to a rope which, when the sail is set, forms the fore-stay; and the remaining corner of the sail forms the clew, to which the main-sheet is attached. The mast is sup-ported by a back-stay extending from the top of the mast to the aft part of the canoe, and the yard is supported by a similar back-stay, also extending from its top part to the aft part of the canoe.

In a strong breeze, one or more of the crew climb out to the extremity of the outrigger, keeping their footing on the spars, and holding on by a man-rope attached to the mast; and in this manner the extra pressure of the wind is counterpoised.

Flanging thwarts, resting upon cross-pieces, are fastened to the top-sides aft of the canoe, so that the crew sit out beyond the gunwale, and facing each other, their legs hanging down in the trough, or interior, of the canoe.

These narrow and fragile-looking craft are managed with much skill and dexterity by half-clad natives, who venture out to sea with them distances of twenty miles or more from land—for it is said that a Cingalese canoe will live at sea in any weather—and they skim along among the shipping at Point de Galle with fear-less velocity, bringing up now and then to offer for sale delicious cooling fruits, and beautiful but unfamiliar fishes of extraordinary colours and fantastic forms.[1]

Vessels passing the southern coast of Ceylon are generally boarded by some of the crews of these canoes, even at the distance of twenty-five miles from the shore.

When they land, the Ceylonese canoe is run ashore at full sail on to the beach, suffering no damage by the force with which it strikes the shore, owing to the peculiarity of its construction in being laced with coir instead of fastened with rivets.[2]

MALDIVE AND LACCADIVE BOATS.

The native sea-boats of the Maldive and Laccadive Islanders (in the Indian Ocean) have a very grotesque and antiquated appearance. Cocoa-nut is the wood chiefly used in their construction, there being no other in those islands suitable for the purpose. The planks are fastened together with hard wooden pegs: the larger boats are thus made very strong. The form of the Maldive boats is not much adapted for fast sailing, but they are broad and safe-looking vessels, rigged with two sails—lug-mainsail and large triangular fore-sail. The main-sail stands nicely flat, and is spread at the lower part with a boom, the fore end of which works in a rest or cross-piece a few inches before the mast; the fore-sail is large, and set out on a bow-sprit. The stem of the Maldive boat is aquiline and curious.

BOATS OF BURMA.

The native Burmese war-boats were of primitive construction, formed out of the solid trunk of a single teak-tree, hollowed partly by fire and partly by cutting. They were formerly of considerable notoriety; the largest were from eighty to one hundred feet in length; but the breadth seldom exceeded eight feet, and even that width was only produced by extending the sides after the trunk had been hollowed.

[1] *Vide* Sir J. Emerson Tennent's ' Ceylon,' vol. ii.
[2] ' Picturesque Ceylon,' by Henry W. Cave, 1893.

The Sailing-Boat.

The stern of the native Burmese boat is high and shaped like the lashing tail of a fish; in fact, the whole fabric of the native war-boats was in imitation of the body of a long fish, the broad flanges of the fish-tail serving as steps to the top of their high-peering sterns.

The Burmese war-boats were usually manned by a crew of fifty or sixty rowers, the oars used being short ones, each worked on a spindle. The steersman of a Burmese boat is called the 'Leedegee.'

The native boat-building was always and is still an important industry among the Burmese; the whole process, from the felling of the tree to the carving and finish of the boats, is fully described and illustrated from photographic reproductions, in a beautiful and interesting modern work on Burma, by two residents.[1]

The wood of which the native boats are built is the *Thingán*, which is tough and durable, steams well, and grows near the water. A boat built of thingán wood lasts from 20 to 30 years.

The ancient type is still preserved in the modern boats of Burma, particularly the high poop and prow, which in those of the superior class of pleasure-boats are sometimes carved and ornamented with much fanciful taste.

The two principal classes of the Burmese boats are the *Laung-gô* and the *Laung-zát*.

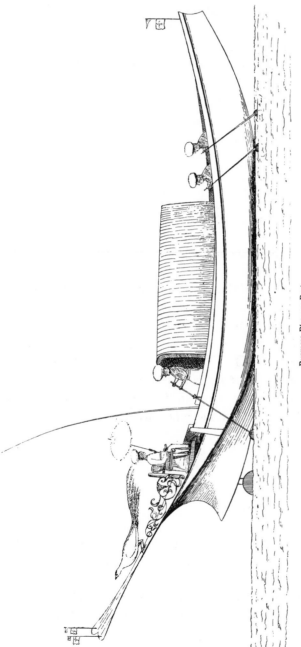

Burmese Pleasure-Boat.

[1] 'Burma,' by Max and Bertha Ferrars, 1900.

Boats of Burma and Bangkok.

They only sail with a free wind, and then carry a great expanse of sail, which, it appears, is necessary to stem the current of the Irawadi.[1]

In the superior class of modern pleasure-boats of Burma the fish fan-tail at the stern (already referred to) is one of its most striking peculiarities. Some of these boats are of light, buoyant and even elegant proportions; beautifully carved and ornamented, with Chair of State for the steersman, little flags, weather-cocks, carved peacock, pheasant or other gay plumaged bird, flowers and other ornamental carvings, but no gay colours; the latter being reserved for the garments and head-gear of the occupants, which are thus in attractive contrast with the quiet natural colours of the thingán and other woods of which the pleasure-boats of the native Burmese are constructed.

BANGKOK (SIAM) BOAT-SAILING.

A BOAT-SAILING Club has recently (1894) been established among Europeans and Americans at Bangkok. There are two classes of sailing-boats attached to the Club, both of British or American design; the larger class being of the canoe-yawl type, measuring about 20 ft. on the water-line, 22 ft. over all, 6 ft. beam, and 2 ft. 3 ins. draft; the ballast consists of 13 cwt. of lead. The boats are half-decked, and have a steerage-well of circular form, about 9 ft. diameter, which is fitted with hatches, so that it can be closed when necessary.

The other, or smaller class, comprises open boats of about 15 ft. in length.

The members of the Boat-sailing Club use their boats for cruising, when at leisure, up and down the picturesque coasts of the Gulf, and for navigating the shallow waters of its upper end, together with the river itself at Bangkok, which, however, is usually much crowded with shipping; it is, therefore, essential that the boats should be handy and quick in stays, besides being good sea-boats, capable of navigating with safety the Meinham bar, in the rough waters which encircle it (more particularly during the south-west monsoon), and also be able to withstand the strong breezes of the north-east monsoon.

The larger-sized boats of the club are rigged, some as canoe-yawls, with battened sails, and some as sloops; but the smaller class (which were all built at Hong-Kong) are rigged with Chinese lug-sail and mizzen.

---

[1] *Vide* 'Burma,' by Max and Bertha Ferrars.

The Sailing-Boat.

CANOE OF THE ANDAMAN ISLANDERS.

'This happy bark is from Eastern isles,
  Where the loving sun doth shed
Warm kissing glances, where they lie,
  Beauties on ocean's bed.'

CAPTAIN G. P. THOMAS.

THE Andaman Archipelago is a group of small islands in the eastern part of the Bay of Bengal, the largest of which is the Great Andaman. The surrounding waters are studded with numerous small islets, many of them exceedingly pretty and picturesque in appearance, rising as they do like beautiful oases in the wild waste of ocean that lashes their rocky shores.[1]

The inhabitants of the Andamans have always been considered one of the most

Canoe of Andaman Islanders.

savage races on the face of the earth, whom civilisation has as yet found it impossible to tame, or, as it appears, even to approach.[2] Port Blair with its safe and spacious harbour on South Andaman, constitutes the civilised portion of the Andamans.

But notwithstanding their uncivilised nature, the Mincopie, or natives of the Andaman Islands, possess very ingeniously constructed canoes, scooped out of the solid trunk of a single large tree. In shape the native canoes are long and narrow; and they are fitted with an outrigger, the utility of which is that of steadying them and preserving their stability when at sea.

The buoyancy of the Andaman canoes is such that they float lightly on the top of the waves; and unless they have received some injury causing them to leak, it is considered almost impossible to sink them. The outrigger attached to these canoes in some respects resembles that which the Cingalese fishermen attach to their boats. The use of this outrigger must be a thing of comparatively recent practice among the Mincopie, for no former writers have ever alluded to them. Dr. Mouat suggests the

[1] 'The Andaman Islanders,' by F. J. Mouat, M.D., &c., &c. (1863).
[2] Ibid.

460

probability that during one of the monsoons a Cingalese outrigger may have drifted on to the beach of one of the Andaman Islands, and the natives thereby acquired the notion.[1]

These outriggers enable the crew to proceed in safety to sea to more distant fishing grounds.

The paddles are extremely well made of a hard-grained wood, the smallest about 3 ft. long, the middle-sized 3½ ft., and the largest 4 ft. The work of making them is entrusted solely to the native women and children.

With the assistance of such simple, but well-shaped paddles, these canoes are propelled at such a rate that, in a fair race with an English ship's boat (the captain's gig), rowed by a prize crew of Chinese and others, the gig was completely distanced by the canoe, and all attempts to recover a fair position in the race were found to be entirely unavailing. The gig and crew appeared to have no chance with the Mincopie.

' Our first cutter also had a trial with the Mincopie boat, but her desperate efforts to win back our character for unsurpassed speed were hopeless. The Mincopie were superior, and had it all their own way.' [2]

[1] 'The Andaman Islanders,' p. 317 *et seq.*
[2] Ibid. p. 320.

The Sailing-Boat.

POLYNESIA AND THE MALAY ARCHIPELAGO.

THE Boats and Canoes of the islands and groups of islands of Polynesia, and of the Malay Archipelago, are a numerous and remarkable class, varying in size from the smallest canoe hollowed out of the trunk of a tree, to vessels of the burthen of 40 or 50 tons, which navigate their native group from one extremity to the other.

Many of these vessels are ingeniously contrived, particularly the sailing-vessels, some of which possess very striking peculiarities; those of each island or group of islands, having generally some distinct feature in type or rig and sometimes in both. But the most remarkable circumstances with regard to the building of these outlandish boats and vessels are, that in some of the islands the natives construct them with the most homely kind of tools; often without a single iron or metal instrument of any kind, but entirely with those of their own contrivance, made of flints, bones, and shells, and yet with such primitive tools they display labour and ingenuity worthy of a civilised community. The peculiarities of many of these will form the subject of description and explanation in the following pages.

It should be observed however, that of late years, probably owing to more frequent intercourse with voyagers and traders from civilised nations, and the acquisition of suitable tools and implements, considerable advances have been made in the arts and industries of the natives; and that a community of canoe and boat-builders now exists in some of the most important islands, who have acquired a skill and ingenuity in the art of canoe architecture in no wise inferior to that of the artisans of European countries.

FLYING PROAS OF THE LADRONE ISLANDS.

THE Flying Proas (or Prahus) of the Ladrone Islands are among the most ingenious as well as the most remarkable sailing-boats in the world. Through ages past they have been the principal sailing-vessels used by the natives of those islands.

The invention of the Flying Proa is one which would do honour to the most educated and ingenious of mankind, and yet it appears to have originated entirely with an unlettered people, the inhabitants of a few small and remote islands; and the natives are no less dexterous in the management of the Proa than in the building of it.

The Flying Proa is admirably adapted to the peculiar navigation of the Ladrones, lying as they do, all of them, nearly under the same meridian, and within the limits of

Boats of the Ladrone Islands.

the trade-winds; and therefore vessels employed in the navigation of those islands, and in passing from one to the other, require to be specially and peculiarly well fitted for sailing with a side wind; and when we examine the uncommon simplicity (yet ingenuity) of the construction and contrivance of the Flying Proa, and consider the extraordinary speed at which it sails, we shall in each of these particulars 'find it worthy of our admiration, and meriting a place amongst the mechanical productions of civilised nations where arts and sciences have most eminently flourished.'[1]

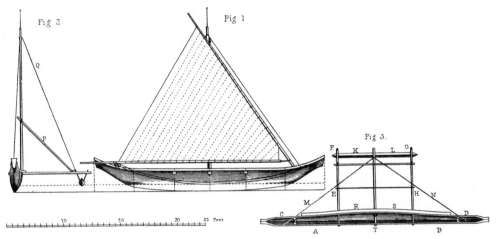

Flying Proa of the Ladrones.

Explanation of the Plate.

Fig. 1 represents the Flying Proa with her sail set, as she appears when viewed from the leeward.

Fig. 2. is a view of the Flying Proa from the head (or stem on), with the outrigger to windward.

Fig. 3 is a plan of the whole, where A B is the lee side of the proa; C D the windward side; E F G H the outrigger, or frame, laid out to windward; K L the boat at the end of it; M N two braces from the head and stern, to steady the frame; R S a thin plank placed to windward, to prevent the Proa from shipping water, and for a seat for the man who bales out the water; and sometimes goods are placed on it. T is the part of the middle outrigger on which the mast is fixed. The mast itself is supported (fig. 2) by the shore P, and by the shroud Q, and by two stays, one of which may be seen in figs. 1 and 2; the other is hidden by the sail.

The Flying Proa, besides being an object of curiosity, may well furnish both the

[1] Lord Anson's 'Voyage Round the World.'

The Sailing-Boat.

shipwright and sailing-master with wrinkles of no mean or contemptible character. The Rev. Richard Walter, M.A., [1] observes, with reference to the swiftness with which these Proas sail : 'From some rude estimations made by our people of the velocity with which they crossed the horizon at a distance, when we lay at Tinian, I cannot help believing that, with a brisk trade-wind, they will run near twenty miles an hour.'

The form and construction of the Flying Proa is in direct opposition to the principles of boat-building as adopted in European countries, and indeed in almost every country in the world. For, as the rest of the world make the two sides of the vessel as exactly alike as possible, those of the Flying Proa are totally different; one side being round, or bilge-shaped, whilst the other is flat and perpendicular as a wall; but the head and stern of the Proa are as exactly alike as possible, and the vessel may be sailed with either end foremost, but always with the rounded side to windward, and the flat one to leeward; therefore, on the return voyage, the *boat* is not turned round, but the *sail*. Indeed, the boat never need be turned round but twice a year, and that only when the trade-winds shift, which they do once a year only, blowing six months in one direction, and six in the opposite.

Being therefore, always enabled to know for a certainty the quarter from whence the wind will blow, and that wind being always a side one throughout the whole range of the Ladrones, the islanders have been acute in turning such knowledge to useful advantage; finding it unnecessary that their boats should possess the power of tacking and working to windward, or of sailing before the wind, but exclusively that of reaching or sailing with a side wind. Therefore the Ladrone inventor places a very large sail on a very narrow form of hull—indeed, such a sail as would inevitably upset the Proa in a breeze, unless it were counterpoised against the force of the wind by some artificial contrivance.

It has been already stated that the lee side of the Proa is flat, or, in other words, the shape of the hull is something like one-half of a boat severed longitudinally, and then the whole open side boarded up from stem to stern with straight planking; all which materially contributes to render it the more ticklish, and easy to capsize. But in order to prevent such a catastrophe, the Proa is fitted with an outrigger, which forms a most important feature in the boat, and one of its greatest peculiarities.

The outrigger consists of a frame made of bamboo poles, affixed to the Proa, and standing out to windward. At the extreme end of the frame is fastened a log of wood, slightly hollowed, and fashioned into the shape of a small boat. The weight of the frame and log is intended to counterpoise the Proa against the force of the wind acting upon the sail, and to prevent the vessel from being capsized.

The hull of the Proa is very neatly made and put together. The bottom is of one

[1] The Chaplain of His Majesty's Ship *Centurion*, in Lord Anson's expedition.

piece, made like the bottom of a canoe, very neatly dug and left of a good substance. This bottom part is instead of a keel, 26 ft. or 28 ft. long. The under part of the bottom is made round, but inclining to a wedge, and smooth, and the upper part is almost flat, having a very gentle hollow, and is about a foot broad. From this bottom, or keel, both sides of the boat are carried up to about 5 ft. high, with narrow planking of about the breadth of 4 in. or 5 in.; and the Proa is so formed that it has a considerable rise both at bow and stern.

The breadth of the Proa depends in a measure upon the length; but it seldom exceeds 4 ft. or 5 ft. amidships, and is much less at the bow and stern.

The mast, it should be observed, although placed amidships longitudinally, is not so latitudinally, but stands in the bilge of the Proa, close to the weather-gunwale, and is fixed to the middle beam or bamboo of the outrigger.

The sail is triangular, or latine-shaped, but much wider at the foot, and less lofty than the latines of other nations; and although it looks not a large sail in the illustration, yet when it is considered how long and narrow the hull of the Proa is, it will be found to be a very large sail, in proportion to the stability of the boat, when viewed independently of the outrigger.

The fore end of the yard is secured in a socket made purposely to receive it, either at bow or stern. The sail is also fitted with a boom, so that it stands nearly as flat as a board; and the boom is also used for furling the sail, and rolling up a portion of it when the wind is heavy; and such is the mode of reefing the sail of the Proa.

The material of which the sail is made is Indian matting stuff; and the mast, yard, boom, and outrigger are all of bamboo.

When the Proa alters her tack for the return voyage, her crew bear her away a little to bring her stern up to the wind; then by easing the halyard, raising the yard, and carrying the heel of it along the lee-side of the Proa, they transfix it in the opposite socket, whilst the boom, at the same time, by easing off one part of the sheet, and hauling on the other, shifts into the contrary or required position; with the result that what was the stern then becomes the prow, and the Proa is trimmed on the other tack.

The Flying Proa generally carries a crew of six or seven, two of whom are stationed, one at the bow and the other at the stern. These steer the vessel alternately, with a paddle, according to the tack on which she goes. The duties of others of the crew are to bale out the water when she leaks or accidentally ships any, and to trim, adjust, and attend to the sail.

From the description given of these extraordinary vessels, it will be seen how admirably they are adapted for the range of the Ladrone Islands; and from the great power they possess in the sail, the flatness of their lee-side, and their narrow form of hull, assisted by the outrigger, they are enabled to fore-reach with immense power, and without any apparent lee-way. [1]

Vessels bearing some resemblance to the Flying Proa are often met with in various parts of the Archipelago, but none of them appear to have any pretensions equal to those of the Ladrone Islanders, either in the ingenuity of form and construction, or in the speed at which they sail. Voyagers have, therefore, asserted their belief that the Flying Proa was the original invention of some genius of the Ladrones, and was afterwards imperfectly copied by neighbouring islanders.

It is mentioned by Pliny, eighteen hundred years ago, that vessels navigating the seas to the west of Taprobane (Ceylon) had prows at either end, to avoid the necessity of tacking. [2]   And the same fact is also mentioned by Strabo, who says they were built with prows at each end, but without holds or keels. [3]   Still, this mention by Pliny and Strabo does not appear to clash with the general impression of the early voyagers, that the original notion was derived from the Ladrone Islanders.

Even at the present day, with all our modern European improvements in marine architecture, it may be fairly questioned whether the Flying Proa of the Ladrones is not incomparable as a vessel for swift sailing, close to the wind.   And what other vessel makes so little leeway ?   Besides, too, the flatness of the sail, combined with the flat lee-side of the vessel, would seem to be the most scientific combination of weatherly qualities ever invented.

Modern attempts at the art of constructing a Flying Proa, to sail in English waters, have occasionally been made ; one of the latest was in the year 1860, by a member of the Royal Mersey Yacht Club, who, assisted by the ingenuity of an able mechanic and boat-builder on the Mersey, appears to have been, in a measure, successful in turning out a veritable Flying Proa, which was for a short time a great attraction, as one of the most remarkable novelties ever seen on that river. This Anglo-Ladrone Proa was fully described in the columns of 'Bell's Life' during the month of June, 1860.

BOATS OF BORNEO.

SOME of the boats of Borneo and Celebes are exceedingly well made.   The sailing-boats have high and very broad sterns and long raking bows.   They have

---

[1] The illustration (p. 463) and explanation above given have been taken chiefly from a description of one of these remarkable vessels which fell into the hands of the crew of His Majesty's ship *Centurion*, when on an expedition to the South Seas, under the command of Lord Anson, in the year 1744.

[2] ' Ob id navibus utrinque proræ ne per angustias alvei circumagi sit necesse ' (Pliny, Hist. Nat. vi. 24).

[3] Strabo, lib. xv. c. 15.

a double or shear mast, and long-shaped square-sail; they have also a stage or gallery, and other peculiarities, which will be better understood by reference to the illustration.

Some of the canoes which Captain Mundy[1] met with in the Gulf of Boni he

Sailing-Boat of Borneo and Celebes.

describes as of very long shape, propelled by fifteen paddles, and ornamented both at prow and stern with carved wood.

The small sailing-boats he describes as fitted with wooden outriggers, which, weighted with men, enabled them to carry a sail of enormous size. On the inland waters, some of the canoes are forty or fifty feet long, by only two and a-half wide, and covered with a small kajang or mat. Others are so small as scarcely to float a child of five years of age—in fact but a hollowed log.[2]

BOATS OF BRUNI.

ONE of the greatest novelties at Bruni is the floating bazaar. There being no shops in the city, the market is held every day in covered canoes. These are moored in tiers, forming lanes on the river, up which the purchasers ply in paddling canoes, look on, and make their purchases.

The trading boats come in every morning at sunrise, from all parts of the river, laden with fresh fruit and every other commodity produced in the vicinity.[3]

[1] 'Borneo and Celebes,' by Captain Mundy, R.N. (1848).
[2] 'Life in the Forests of the Far East,' by Spencer St. John, F.R.G.S., &c. (1862).
[3] 'Borneo and the Indian Archipelago,' by F. S. Marryat (1848).

The Sailing-Boat.

The floating market is thus alluded to by Mr. Spencer St. John, in his interesting work on Borneo:—

'Several hundred canoes, each containing one or two women covered over with mat hats a yard in diameter, floated up and down about the town, pulling through the water lanes, and resting for a while in the slack at the back of the houses.'

PROAS (OR PRAHUS) OF BORNEO.

THE Proas—Praus or Prahus[1]—of Borneo are swift-sailing vessels, though made of the trunk of a tree, hollowed and fashioned at both ends; they have neither keel nor rudder, but are steered over the quarter with a long paddle, thirty feet in length, and about twelve or fourteen inches wide in the blade. The thwarts are placed across the boat above the gunwale. As a precaution against the danger of capsizing under sail, these boats are fitted with 'outlagers'—a framework consisting of two long poles which are run out on each side, one across the fore part and one across the aft part of the Proa, the outer ends of the poles being secured to a large bamboo. When the wind is heavy, part of the crew run out on the windward outlager to keep the boat upright. These Proas are fitted and sailed with a large latine-shaped sail made of matting.[2]

BAJU AND BALIGNINI PIRATE PRAHUS.

THE Balignini, which are of the Bajow or sea-gipsy tribe, have large Prahus, with crews of seventy or eighty men, who sometimes row double-banked; and to each Prahu a long and fleet small boat is attached, which will hold from ten to fifteen men.

The Balignini and Baju pirates were formerly the terror of the Indian seas. Mengkabong was the headquarters of those lawless people.

The Baju Prahus are rigged with tripod-masts, which consist of three tall bamboos, the two foremost being fitted on a cross-beam, the other loose; so that when a heavy squall threatens, the masts can be immediately struck.[3]

The arrangement of the tripod-mast fitted to the Tartar galley (and described at

---

[1] Different voyagers and authors spell this word in different ways, but 'proa' seems to be the most general.
[2] 'Voyage to and from the Island of Borneo,' by Captain Daniel Beeckman.
[3] Spencer St. John's 'Borneo.'

page 471) is somewhat different to that of the Baju boats, the *fore-leg* of the mast being the one by which the tripod of the Tartar galley can be struck; whereas the *aft-leg* in the Baju Prahu is the loose one.

CANOES OF THE SOOLOO ISLANDS.

THE canoes of the Sooloo (or Sulu) Archipelago are curiously and ingeniously contrived. They differ from those of the other islands, not only in shape, but also in the outrigger. A Sooloo canoe is made of a single log of wood hollowed out, but it

Sooloo Canoe.

Sooloo Canoe—Section.

is seldom large enough to carry more than two persons at a time. The outrigger is a double one, *i.e.* it extends on both sides of the canoe, so as to give it extra stability. A railing is also placed above the sides of the canoe with supports, which rest upon the bearers of the outrigger.

Small canoes of this kind are never sailed. They are sometimes built upon and enlarged with wash-boards or upper strakes secured to the trunk.[1]

THE SOOLOO OR ILLANAN PRAHUS.

' Woe to the craft, however fleet,
These sea-hawks in their course shall meet!

For not more sure, when owlets flee
O'er the dark crags of Pendelee,
Doth the night-falcon mark his prey,
Or pounce on it more fleet than they.'

T. MOORE.

THE Sooloo or Illanan Prahus are the largest kind of Prahus in the Indian Archipelago; formerly they were employed by the pirates of the Sooloo Islands, who went

---

[1] See Wilkes' 'United States Exploring Expedition,' vol. v. p. 332: also 'The Cruise of the *Marchesa*,' vol. ii. pp. 53, 54.

by the name of 'Lanans.' These Prahus were from twenty to thirty tons burthen, nearly a hundred feet in length, and of considerable breadth of beam, with a sharp hollow bow; the lower part of the hull was strongly built of timber; but the bulwarks, decks, and internal fittings were chiefly of bamboo, ingeniously fastened together. The crew was generally a very numerous one, sometimes from forty to fifty. A raised platform was constructed on both sides of the Prahu, for the convenience of the pirates in their lawless pursuits, and as a fighting stage. These boats were propelled both by sails and oars; sometimes fifty oars being used at a time. They drew but little water, were fast under sail, and well adapted for navigating the seas of the Archipelago. They were rigged with two separate shear-masts, each consisting of two spars lashed together at the top. The heels of the foremost were set in a base, which partly revolved, and the shear-mast could thus be raised and lowered at pleasure; so that, when attacking a vessel, the sail could be let down, and the shear-mast directed in such a manner as to fall on the side or bulwarks of the attacked vessel; it then formed a ladder for the pirates to climb from the Prahus to the deck of the vessel. The shear-mast could also be dropped on the bank of a river, so as to form a bridge; it might also be used for scaling walls, and other marauding practices. The sails of these Prahus were made of matting and bamboo canes, and were of large size; they also generally carried a square red flag at their foremast head. They used to assemble in a numerous fleet when on their piratical adventures.

The Sooloo were said to be the boldest and most cold-blooded pirates in the Archipelago. They infested the Straits of Macassar, the Sea of Celebes, and the Sooloo Sea; but piracy in those waters has long since been put down.

TARTAR GALLEY.

THE vessel used by Capt. Forrest in his voyage along the coast of New Guinea was a Tartar galley, in fact a Sooloo boat of about ten tons burthen. This boat had a kind of gallery built on each side, from stem to stern, projecting about thirty inches over each gunwale, upon which the rowers sat, sometimes twenty in number.

Although the Tartar galley was but 25 ft. long on the keel, she overhung so much forward and abaft that her length over-all was 40 ft., and her draft of water about $3\frac{1}{2}$ ft.

This boat had a tripod-mast, made of three stout bamboos. The feet of the two which stood abreast were bored at the lower end, across, with holes about 3 in. in diameter for the purpose of receiving a spindle, which, like a main-shaft,

Boats of the Malay Archipelago.

was placed across the boat from side to side, so that the two spars could be turned as on a pivot.

The fore-spar of the tripod-mast was fixed forward to a knee amidships, with a forelock, by unlocking which the mast could be struck with ease by three men.[1]

The main-sail was a large four-cornered one, called by the Malays *lyre tanjong* (pointed sail). The boat also carried a fore-mast, on which a latine sail was set; also a mizzen-mast, on which another latine could be used. When the wind was heavy, the lyre tanjong was lowered, and a smaller sail (a latine) was set, and the vessel then resembled the rig of the Mediterranean galleys.

The advantages of the lyre tanjong appear to be that it is a very powerful

Tartar Galley.

sail in a breeze, and may be quickly reduced or reefed by luffing into the wind, easing off the sheet and then rolling and winding up the sail, by the simple means of turning the winch or cross-bar that is fixed to the inner end of the boom.[2] By this contrivance the sail may be entirely rolled up (so that the boom and yard meet, and lay side by side together) and so furled. In the same manner, by turning the winch the other way, the sail may be unfurled, and as quickly set, or half set, according to the weather.

[1] Captain Forrest's 'Voyages.'
[2] The Kolay, Malay Jellore, and other boats, are also reefed in the same manner.

The Sailing-Boat.

The cabin, or covered part of the Tartar galley, was thatched with the leaves of a palm-tree, called *nipa*, being the same material as that used by the natives for covering their houses on the south-west coast of Sumatra, and in most of the Malay countries. The small apartment abaft was covered with boards, and was called by the Malays *koran*.

The Molucca Proas and vessels of burthen are all fitted with the tripod-mast and lyre tanjong.

PADUAKANS OF CELEBES.

THESE singular-looking boats of the island of Celebes are called ' Bugis Paduakans.' [1] They are built at Bera, at which place were formerly the chief building-yards of the Macassars. The Paduakans are remarkably well-built boats.

They are made very tight by the system of dowelling the planks together, as

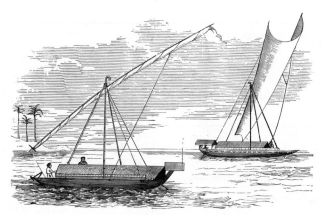

Paduakans of Celebes.

coopers do the parts which form the head of a cask; and they put the bark of a certain tree between the planks, in the place of oakum, which, when wet, swells and keeps the craft tight.

Their system of boat-building is the very reverse of the British in this—that they put the outside planks together first and then the inside timbers (or ribs); whereas we set up the timbers first and then secure the planks to them.

The natives adhere to their old models, and seldom venture on new designs. One remarkable peculiarity in these vessels is that the bow is lower than the stern, and in that respect they are rather unsightly to European eyes; besides,

[1] Forrest's ' Voyage to Mergui.'

too, when under sail in rough winds, the bow is often driven under water; but in order to keep off the spray at the bows, a bulk-head is raised a few feet abaft the stem. In other respects they are not decked, but have a light roof or covering extending all over the vessel from the bows.

The Paduakan is rigged with a tripod-mast and *lyre tanjong*. The tripod-mast is formed of three stout bamboos, and fitted in a similar manner to that of the Tartar galley before mentioned.

The illustration represents two of these curious vessels—one with its sail furled, the other under full sail.

The Catamarans of Discovery Bay, in New Guinea, are made of three or more cocoa-nut trees lashed together and sharpened at the ends. Some have a small platform about a foot high, in the centre, on which to carry the goods dry; but most of them are without this, and then the sea washes freely over them. Their beautiful native canoe-paddles are shaped like the long narrow leaves of some water plants, with a spine running down the centre.[1]

BUGIS OR MACASSAR PRAUS.

THE author of a most interesting work[2] on the Malay Archipelago made a voyage from Macassar to the Aru (or Aroo) Islands, a distance of 1,000 miles, in a native Prau. These islands, which are quite out of the track of European trade, are inhabited only by black mop-headed savages, who nevertheless contribute to the luxurious tastes of the most civilised races. Pearls, mother-of-pearl, and tortoise-shell find their way to Europe; while edible birds'-nests and 'tripang,' or sea-slug, are obtained by shiploads for the gastronomic enjoyment of the Chinese.

It is from these islands that birds of Paradise, of the two kinds known to Linnæus, were first brought to Europe. The native vessels can only make the voyage once a year, owing to the monsoons. They leave Macassar in December or January, at the beginning of the west monsoon, and return in July or August, with the full strength of the east monsoon. Even by the Macassar people themselves a voyage to the Aru Islands is looked upon as a rather wild and romantic expedition, full of novel sights and strange adventures.[3]

To this 'Ultima Thule' of the East the author went, having the courage and

---

[1] 'New Guinea and Polynesia,' by Captain John Moresby, R.N., 1876, pp. 216, 217.
[2] The 'Malay Archipelago,' by A. R. Wallace (1869).
[3] *Ibid.*, vol. ii. pp. 158, 159.

daring to trust himself on a voyage of 1,000 miles in a Bugis Prau, and for six or seven months among lawless traders and ferocious savages.

The Prau is described by the author as a vessel of about 70 tons burthen, and shaped something like a Chinese junk. The deck sloped considerably downward to the bows, which are thus the lowest part of the ship. There were two large rudders; but instead of being placed astern, they were hung on the quarters from strong cross-beams, which projected out two or three feet on each side, and to which extent the deck overhung the sides of the vessel amidships. The rudders were not hinged, but hung with slings of rattan, the friction of which keeps them in any position in which they are placed, and thus perhaps facilitates steering. The tillers were not on deck, but entered the vessel through two openings, each about a yard square, into a lower or half deck about three feet high, in which sit the two steersmen. Should a heavy sea break over the vessel, there is nothing to prevent the water from having free access to the interior, and there are no water-tight bulk-heads.

In the aft part of the vessel was a low poop, about three and a half feet high, which formed the captain's cabin, its furniture consisting of boxes, mats, and pillows. In front of the poop and main-mast was a little thatched house, on deck, about four feet high to the ridge; one compartment of which, forming a cabin six and a half feet long by five and a half wide, the author had all to himself; and he says it was the snuggest and most comfortable little place he ever enjoyed at sea. It was entered by a low sliding-door of thatch on one side, and had a very small window on the other. The floor was of split bamboo, pleasantly elastic, raised six inches above the deck, so as to be quite dry. It was covered with fine cane mats, for the manufacture of which Macassar is celebrated. Against the further wall were arranged his gun-case, insect-boxes, clothes, and books; his mattress occupied the middle; and next the door were his canteen, lamp and little store of luxuries for the voyage; while guns, revolver, and hunting-knife hung conveniently from the roof.

The vessel was rigged with two tripod-masts, similar to those of the Tartar galley already described and illustrated.[1] The main-yard was formed of many pieces of wood and bamboo, bound together with rattans in an ingenious manner. The sail carried by this was of an oblong shape, and was hung out of the centre, so that, when the short end was hauled down on deck, the long end mounted high in the air, making up for the lowness of the mast itself. The fore-sail was of the same shape, but smaller. Both these were of matting, and, with two jibs, and a fore-and-aft sail of cotton canvas astern, completed the rig.[2]

[1] *Supra*, p. 471.
[2] The 'Malay Archipelago,' vol. ii. pp. 160—2.

Boats of the Malay Archipelago.

The crew consisted of about thirty men, natives of Macassar and the adjacent coasts and islands. Their dress generally, when at work, was a pair of trousers only and a handkerchief twisted round the head; to which in the evening they would add a thin cotton jacket. Four of the elder men were 'jurumudis,' or steersmen, who had to squat two at a time in the little steerage before described, changing every six hours. Then there was an old man called the 'juragan,' or captain, but whom we should call the first mate; he occupied the other half of the little house on deck.

The great mat sails are very awkward things to manage in rough weather, the only way to furl them being to roll up the sail on the boom. It is dangerous to have them standing when overtaken by a squall.[1]

The large sails cannot be shifted round so as to go on the other tack without first hauling down the jibs; and the booms of the fore and aft sails have to be lowered and completely detached to perform the same operation.[2]

THE COROCORA (OR KORA-KORA).

A Corocora (or Kora-Kora) is an ancient and curious-looking boat or vessel, used chiefly by the inhabitants of the Molucca Islands; and the Dutch have fleets of them at Amboyna, which they employ as *guarda costas.*

The Corocora.

[1] The 'Malay Archipelago,' vol. ii. p. 168.
[2] *Ibid.,* p. 173.

The Sailing-Boat.

The Corocora has high-peering stem and stern, and is generally fitted with outriggers, in the manner explained by the engraving. They vary in size from small boats to vessels above 10 tons burthen. On the cross-pieces which support the outriggers are often put, fore and aft, planks, on which part of the crew sit and ply the paddles when there is no wind; besides which, others who sit in the vessel use long oars. In smooth water the Corocora is propelled in this manner sometimes by a good number of hands and is steered with two *commoodies* (broad paddles).

The author of the 'Malay Archipelago' describes a boat of the kind called 'Kora-Kora,' belonging to the Island of Batchian, as being quite open, very low, and of about four tons burthen. 'It had outriggers of bamboo about five feet off on each side, which supported a bamboo platform extending the whole length of the vessel. On the extreme outside of this sit the twenty rowers, while within was a convenient passage, fore and aft. The middle portion of the boat was covered with a thatch house, in which baggage and passengers are stowed. The gunwale was not more than a foot above water; and from the great top and side weight and general clumsiness these boats are dangerous in heavy weather, and are not unfrequently lost.' [1] They are rigged with a triangle-mast and mat sail, similar to some other vessels of the Indian Archipelago, already described.

In the Kora-Kora described by Mr. Wallace there was a little cook-house in the bows, where the passengers could boil their rice and make their coffee. And he adds :—' The passage would have been agreeable enough but for the dreadful "tom-toms," or wooden drums, which are beaten incessantly while the men are rowing. Two men were engaged constantly at them, making a fearful din the whole voyage.' [2]

---

[1] The 'Malay Archipelago,' by A. R. Wallace, vol. ii. p. 69.
[2] *Ibid.*

Boats of the Malay Archipelago.

BOATS AND CANOES OF THE KEI ISLANDS.

The native Canoe-builders of the Kei Islands are the most expert of any in the whole region of the Malay Archipelago. The Canoes and Proas of many of the neighbouring islanders are built in the Kei Islands, by that ingenious class of boat-builders, whose models, designs, and workmanship are far in advance of any other race of native Canoe-builders.

The Canoes of these islands are not all of one type ; they are various in design as they are in size ; but those that are built by the native Canoe-builders are of superior form and construction. The beautiful crescent-shaped canoes, so much admired by modern voyagers, when seen at a distance, have a very striking appearance, sitting upon the surface of the water with a buoyancy and grace that never fail to win the admiration of Europeans whose good fortune enables them to navigate the interesting seas and islands of the Malay Archipelago.

Some of the native Canoes of the Kei Islands have a roofed platform of excellent construction, broad, smooth, and strongly yet lightly made, the roof serving the purpose of protection from the scorching rays of the sun, and the platform the receptacle of fruits and vegetables, the produce by industry of the natives, and fish, the result of their dexterity and skill in spearing and hooking.

The canoes which Mr. Wallace[1] saw at the Kei Islands, on his voyage from Macassar to the Aru or (Aroo) Islands, he describes as

[1] The 'Malay Archipelago,' by A. R. Wallace, vol. ii. p. 176.

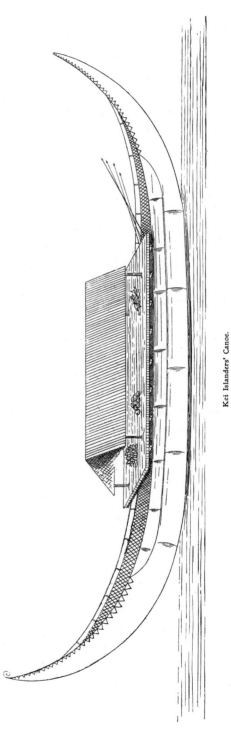

Kei Islanders' Canoe.

long canoes, with the bow and stern rising up into a beak, six or eight feet high, decorated with shells and waving plumes of cassowaries' hair. He also gives an admirable description of the whole process of their construction.

The natives of Kei excel in the art of boat-building. Their small canoes are beautifully formed, broad and low in the centre, but rising at each end, where they terminate in high-pointed beaks, more or less carved, and ornamented with a plume of feathers. They are not hollowed out of a tree, but are regularly built of planks, running from end to end, and so accurately fitted that it is often difficult to find a place where a knife-blade could be inserted between the joints. The larger ones are from twenty to thirty tons burthen, and are finished ready for sea without a nail or particle of iron about them, with the aid of no other tools than axe, adze, and auger. 'These vessels are handsome to look at, good sailers, and admirable sea-boats, and will make long voyages with perfect safety, traversing the whole archipelago from New Guinea to Singapore, in seas which, as every one who has sailed much in them can testify, are not so smooth and tempest-free as word-painting travellers love to represent them.'[1]

The forests of Kei produce abundance of magnificent timber, tall, straight and durable, some of which is said to be superior to the best Indian teak. To make each pair of planks used in the construction of the larger boats an entire tree is consumed. It is felled often miles away from the shore, cut across to the proper length, and then hewn longitudinally into two equal portions. Each of these forms a plank, by paring down with the axe to a uniform thickness of three or four inches, leaving at first a solid block at each end, to prevent splitting. Along the centre of each plank a series of projecting pieces are left, standing up three or four inches, about the same width and a foot long; these are of great importance in the construction of the vessel. The planks, when cut, are dragged to the beach. A foundation-piece, broad in the middle and rising considerably at each end, is first laid on blocks and properly shored up. The edges of this are worked true and smooth with the adze, and a plank, properly curved and tapering at each end, is held firmly up against it, while a line is struck along it, which allows it to be cut so as to fit exactly. A series of auger-holes about as large as one's finger are then bored along the opposite edges, and pins of very hard wood are fitted to these, so that the two planks are held firmly, and can be driven into the closest contact; and difficult as this seems to be—without any other aid than rude practical skill in forming each edge to the true corresponding curves, and in boring the holes so as exactly to match both in position and direction—yet so well is it done that the best European shipwright could not produce sounder or closer-fitting joints.

[1] The 'Malay Archipelago,' vol. ii. p. 176.

Boats of the Malay Archipelago.

The boat is built up in this way by fitting plank to plank till the proper height and width are obtained. We have now a skin held together entirely by the hard-wood pins connecting the edges of the plank, very strong and elastic, but having nothing but the adhesion of these pins to prevent the planks gaping. In the smaller boats, seats, in the larger ones, cross-beams are now fixed. They are sprung into slight notches cut to receive them, and are further secured to the projecting pieces of the plank below by a strong lashing of rattan. Ribs are now formed of single pieces of tough wood, chosen and trimmed so as exactly to fit on to the projections from each plank, being slightly notched to receive them, and securely bound to them by rattans passed through a hole in each projecting piece, close to the surface of the plank. The ends are closed against the vertical prow and stern-posts, and further secured with pegs and rattans. The boat is then complete; and when fitted with rudder, masts and thatch covering, is ready to do battle with the waves. 'A careful consideration of the principle of this mode of construction, and allowing for the strength and binding qualities of rattan (which resembles in these respects wire rather than cordage), makes me believe that a vessel carefully built in this manner is actually stronger and safer than one fastened in the ordinary way with nails.[1]

DYAK WAR-BOATS.

THESE are long-shaped canoes, of more substantial construction than the Malay prahus, and are, besides, sufficiently capacious to hold from seventy to eighty men.

They are made with a flat keel, having a curve or sheer of hard wood. A long keel does not exceed six fathoms, and upon such they build a boat of eleven fathoms over all. The extra length is brought up with a sheer. The seams are caulked with a bark that is plentiful in the jungle. No other fastenings but rattans are used.

These boats are painted red and white. When they have no ochre for the red they use a red seed, pounded; the white is simply a lime made from sea-shells.

The bark they employ for caulking is very tough; when beaten out it serves to make useful and comfortable coverlets, as well as waist-cloths and head-dresses.[2]

The Dyak War-boat has also a roof or gallery to fight upon; and the stern is ornamented with feathers.

Notwithstanding the heavy top-weight of gallery and fighting men, these boats, as well as the Malay prahus, are remarkably swift under numerous oars.[3]

[1] Wallace, the 'Malay Archipelago,' vol. ii. p. 186.
[2] 'Life in the Forests of the Far East,' by Spencer St. John, F.R.G.S., F.R.S., &c. (1862).
[3] Marryat's 'Borneo,' &c.

The Sailing-Boat.

MALAY PIRATE PRAHUS.

THESE are of much smaller size than those of the Sooloo pirates, being only from ten to twelve tons burthen, but, in proportion, better manned, and the crew ply with more efficiency their oars and paddles.

These Prahus formerly infested the Straits of Malacca, Cape Romania, the Carimon Islands, and neighbouring straits, sometimes visiting the Straits of Rhio.

They have a long, low hull, and are provided with several guns, though not very large ones. They seldom attacked unless the sea was calm, when they could be more certain of success. They were generally found in small flotillas of from six to twenty.

The rig of the Malay pirate Prahus consists of two masts, with sails of matting. A platform is erected over the bows of the Prahu, and extending some distance beyond; this platform is as wide or wider than any other part of the boat, and was the rendezvous of the pirates when attacking a vessel.

BOATS OF SUMATRA—JELLORES AND BALLELLANGS.

THESE curious boats of the island of Sumatra are of a long and narrow form, and are fitted with double outriggers, which stand out a considerable distance from

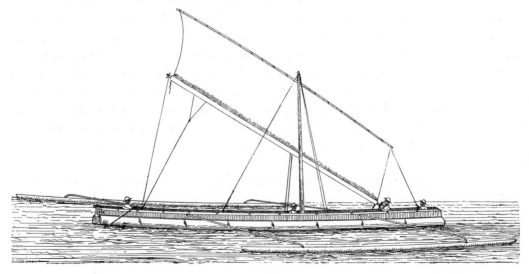

the sides. They are usually rigged with two masts and *lyre tanjong* sails, though sometimes with lug-sails. The Ballellang is rather broader than the Jellore, but still comparatively narrow; yet they are capable of mounting two small swivel guns, with a native crew of twenty or thirty. They sail well in light winds, and in strong winds too, if the water be smooth. The illustration represents a Jellore with the sail partly rolled up, after the manner of reefing adopted in those parts. The wide-spreading outrigger enables these vessels to carry a large sail in smooth water. Jellores have sometimes only one outrigger, which is then alternately to windward and leeward; when to leeward it buoys up the boat, and when to windward counterpoises the power of the sail.

Panchallangs are vessels with one mast and the lyre tanjong.

The *bantang* has two masts, is tolerably large and broad, and has no outrigger.[1]

ACHĒN FISHER-BOATS.—THE KOLAY.

THESE boats, called by the natives *Kolay*, are rigged with one mast and a square-sail, which is slung and set after the manner of a lug-sail, but with a boom and bridle below. To the fore end of the yard a rope is made fast, for the purpose of hauling it down and peaking the aft part. When it blows hard the sail is reefed, in the same manner as the lyre tanjong above described, *i.e.* with a cross-stick or pin, which passes through the inner end of the boom, whereby the sail may be rolled up as occasion requires. This seems to be a very simple and expeditious mode of reefing a small sail. Captain Forrest says he never saw anything so convenient in any European boat.

In putting about, the sail is dipped in the same way as an English lug-sail.[2]

The Kolay is steered with an oar, which is passed through a lashing on the aft-quarter of the boat.

PRAUS OF CERAM AND THE MATABELLO ISLANDS.

THE native praus of Ceram and the Matabello Islands are peculiar. In a description of one of about four tons burthen, it is said that there was not an ounce of iron or a foot of rope in any part of its construction, nor a morsel of pitch or paint in its decoration. The planks were fastened in the usual ingenious way, with pegs

[1] See Forrest's 'Voyage from Calcutta.'
[2] *Supra*, "Dipping the Lug," p. 48.

and rattans. The mast was a bamboo triangle, requiring no shrouds, and carrying a long mat sail; two rudders were hung on the quarters by rattans; the anchor was of wood; and a long thick rattan served as a cable. 'Our crew consisted of four men, whose sole accommodation was about three feet by four in the bows and stern, with the sloping thatch roof to stretch themselves upon for a change.'[1]

In this little craft the author of the 'Malay Archipelago' travelled nearly a hundred miles, 'fully exposed to the swell of the Banda Sea, which is sometimes very considerable'; but he luckily had it calm and smooth, so that he made the voyage in comparative comfort.

It appears that the praus of the Ceram and Matabello Islands are all made by that wonderful race of boat-builders, the Kei Islanders, who, it is said, annually turn out some hundreds of boats, large and small, which can hardly be surpassed for beauty of form and excellence of workmanship.[2]

THE LEPER-LEPER OF THE ISLAND OF AMBOINA.

THE common boats or canoes of the Island of Amboina are called *Leper-lepers.* They are made from the trunk of a large tree, hollowed out and then built upon with strips of plank, to raise them to the proper height. Both ends are sharp and curve upward. About four feet from the bow a pole is laid across, and another the same distance from the stern. These project outward from one side of the boat six or eight feet, and to them is fastened a bamboo outrigger. The canoes themselves are so narrow that without an external support of the kind they would be very crank, and liable to be upset; and the whole fabric is, besides, very shallow.[3]

BOATS OF THE PHILIPPINE ISLANDS.

THE Indians at Manilla are very skilful in the art of boat-building. The native boats have some peculiarities, but they are nevertheless well built and of considerable variety.

On the river and along the shore may be seen a number of prettily-built boats, with sharp bows, and furnished with bamboo outlagers,[4] or poles, like the yard of

---

[1] The 'Malay Archipelago,' by A. R. Wallace, vol. ii. pp. 92, 93.
[2] *Ibid.*, p. 107.
[3] *Vide* 'Travels in the East Indian Archipelago,' by Albert S. Bickmore, M.A. (1868), p. 165.
[4] These must not be confounded with the *outriggers* of the canoes of some other islands; there is no outrigger to these canoes, but merely an *outlager*, or pole, laid across the vessel amidships, and extending several feet beyond the sides.

a square-rigged vessel, laid across the boat and jutting out beyond the sides. When it blows hard, one, two, or more of the crew are put out on the windward end of the outlager, to counterpoise the effect of the wind upon the sail. This contrivance, however, does not always ensure safety, for at times the bamboo yards which form the outlager break; in which case the boat is seldom saved from capsizing, and the whole crew are sometimes lost.

PANGUES.

THESE are small native ferry-boats, used chiefly for crossing the rivers; they are made of the hollow trunk of a tree. Those usually employed are large enough for two or three persons only, though some of larger size are occasionally met with in some parts of the islands. They are generally propelled by oars, assisted sometimes with a small sail.

MINDANAO PLEASURE-PROA.

DAMPIER describes a pleasure-proa he met with at Mindanao, belonging to the Sultan of that island. It was large enough to carry fifty or sixty persons, or more. The hull was neatly built, with a round head and stern; and over the hull was a small house slightly built with bamboos, about four feet high, with neat little windows of the same material to open and shut at pleasure. The roof was almost flat, but neatly thatched with palmetto leaves. The house was divided into two or three small partitions or chambers, one in particular for the Sultan himself, which was matted underneath and round the sides and furnished with a carpet and pillows. The second was the ladies' room, or that for the Sultan's wives, and was much like the former. The third for servants, who attend the ladies with tobacco and betel-nut. The fore and aft part of the vessel was for the crew; but the outlager was the place for them when navigating the vessel.

The proa was fitted with outlagers on each side, but very different from the flying proas of the Ladrone Islands. The Mindanao proa has no flat side; both sides are rounded, or bilge-shaped, and there is no outrigger-boat. Beams are placed across the protruding bamboos, but they do not touch the water on either side, as the Ladrone proas do, but are two, three or four feet above the surface, and serve for the boatmen or paddlers to sit upon and row or paddle from.

The Sailing-Boat.

MANILLA BANCAS.

THE passage-boats of Manilla are termed Bancas; they are much used on the canals, and although made of the single trunk of a tree, are prettily formed and are a very useful kind of boat. The trunk is carefully hollowed, so that the boat is very light and rows easily. The bottom is narrow and round-shaped; therefore the banca is easily upset under careless or awkward management.

The thwarts for the passengers are placed very low, so as to keep the weight

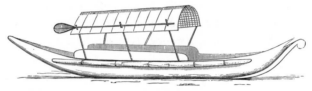

Manilla Banca.

of the occupants as close to the bottom as possible, and preserve the stability of the vessel. A stout bamboo is attached to the top rim of the banca, outside, which serves the purpose of a fender on going alongside, and also renders the vessel more buoyant when heavily laden or when lurching on one side. The banca is also fitted with a light top or awning (as shown in the engraving), to protect the passengers from the heat of the sun.

These vessels are steered with a large shovel-like paddle, which when not in use they lay up on the top of the awning.

THE MANILLA SARABOA.

THE Saraboa is a fishing raft employed by the natives; it is composed of two or more layers of bamboos, or light wood, laid transversely one above the other, with a little Gothic hut at one end.

The native fishing is chiefly performed on rafts of this kind. They take fish at the mouth of the river in nets suspended by the four corners from hoops attached to a crane, by which they are lowered into the water.

The Paroa is a larger kind of trading or passage-boat used at Manilla.

Boats of the Philippine Islands.

THE TAMBANGAN.

THE Tambangan, or Sourabaya passage-boat, of the Island of Java is curiously rigged. The boat itself is very broad and shallow, but uncommonly roomy, convenient, and useful for its purpose. It is *partly* flat-bottomed, that is to say, it has in part a flat floor without a keel, but is flanged and rounded at the lower sides, like an English doble.

As to the rig, the sail is a very light one, of triangular shape, and is set with the apex downwards on a mast raking forward, and is fitted with yard and boom, both of which are in two parts.

Tambangan.

A light canvas awning is set up in the aft part of the boat, in the manner represented by the engraving.

BOATS OF MADURA.

ON the north coast of Java, at Madura, they have boats with outriggers, each boat having one such float on the leeward side; while, on a kind of rack on the windward side, they sometimes place a canoe and everything on board that is movable. Each boat carries two triangular sails, made of narrow white cloths, with occasionally a red or black one in the middle or on the margins, by way of ornament.[1]

'Travels in the East Indian Archipelago,' by Albert S. Bickmore, M.A., p. 56.

The Sailing-Boat.

THE Sandwich Islands constitute a solitary group in the North Pacific Ocean, far north of the main range of islands in the Western Pacific.

The Canoes of the native islanders, though of primitive construction, are well made, considering that they are formed entirely by hollowing out the trunk of a tree. They are however, very ticklish on the water, and easily upset. Those which are used singly are fitted with a small log of wood for an outrigger which is armed with a cut-water at the fore end, the whole standing out several feet beyond the canoe, in the form represented by the engraving.

Sandwich Islands Canoes.

The double canoes of these islands consist merely of two ordinary canoes held together, at the space apart of from four to six feet, by strong beams, which are arched and stand up above the canoes. They are sometimes assisted with a small sail of very primitive form, the mast for which is stepped in one of the canoes, and the sail sheeted in the other.

The bow and stern of the Sandwich Islands canoes are ingeniously shaped, and are different to those of any other islanders.

Sailing Canoes of the Fiji Islands.

FIJI ISLANDS CANOES.

THE Fiji are a group of more than 200 islands in the South Pacific Ocean, extending about 300 miles from east to west, and lying about 1,100 miles to the north of New Zealand, the largest of which are Viti Levu (Great Fiji) and Vanua Levu (Great Land); and the island of Rotumah was annexed in the year 1881.

The Sailing Canoes of the Fiji Islanders are of a very superior class. The largest size are as much as a hundred feet in length, and of the double or twin form, consisting of two canoes of different sizes united by cross-beams, on which a platform is constructed. But although these are called 'double canoes' by Europeans, the second or attached canoe is sometimes merely an outrigger, the bottom part of which is composed of a tree hollowed out for the sake of buoyancy, like the canoe itself. The mast and sail are fitted to the larger of the two canoes; the smaller one, as above stated, serving as an outrigger to the other.

These canoes are generally built of a native wood known as the vas-wood.

The bottom of each of the canoes is formed of the trunk of a single tree, hollowed out and built upon with considerable ingenuity. The sides and coamings are fitted and secured to the canoe by dovetailing the planks, which are also drawn closely together with lashings of cocoa-nut plait, passed through flanges left for the purpose on each of the planks. The joinings and crevices are filled and closed with gum taken from the breadfruit-tree, which is also used as an outer dressing in the place of tar or paint. The planks are secured to small ribs or timbers, which are placed at regular intervals, similar to the European mode of boat-building.

The fore and aft ends of the two vessels forming the double canoe are decked over; the larger one to the extent of about twenty feet at each end, and the smaller one somewhat less. This is done to prevent the shipping of seas in rough water.

The platform is firmly secured over the top of the open part of the canoes, resting on the cross-beams and raised sides (or coamings), and extending, on the outer sides, two or three feet beyond them. The depth of hold under the platform is about seven feet.

On the platform, nearly amidships, between the two parts of the canoe, there is a stage, about eight feet square by four or five high, with a railing on each side. On the stage there is space for several persons to stand or sit, more particularly for those who give directions as to the steering and management of the canoe. Beneath the stage is a small thatched house or cuddy, for the crew when seeking protection from the weather.

The covered fore and aft part of the canoes belonging to the chiefs of the Fiji

The Sailing-Boat.

Islands are prettily ornamented with shells, and the sails with white flags and streamers.

The sail of the Fiji canoes is of triangular shape, and so large as to appear quite out of proportion to the vessel. It is made of tough yet pliable matting, and is set with the apex downwards.

The mast is about half the length of the longer of the two vessels composing the canoe. It is stepped into and secured by a chock on the platform, at an equal distance

Fiji Islands Sailing Canoe.

from each end of the larger canoe. The yard is nearly twice as long as the mast, and the boom somewhat less than the yard.

The halliards are passed over a crescent at the top of the mast. They are bent on to the yard nearly in the middle, so that, when the sail is hoisted with the fore end of the yard secured on deck, the seizing on the yard comes nearly upon a level with the top of the mast.

The mast is supported to windward by two ropes or shrouds, fastened to a rail fixed to two posts and fitted to the platform, so that the heels of the posts are secured to the outer side of the coamings of the smaller of the two vessels.

The Fiji Islanders are very expert in the management of these vessels; both ends of which being alike, they are sailed either end foremost; but when under sail, it is necessary that the smaller canoe or outrigger should always be on the weather side, therefore the canoe itself is never tacked, but the sail. The process of tacking will be better understood if given in the words of one who has seen it performed :—' The operation of tacking was effected by luffing into the wind, when the rake of the mast, which is stepped on a kind of hinge, and always inclines forward, was reversed, and at the same time a number of men, clapping on the tack of the sail, or the point where the yard and boom meet, hauled it aft. The yard, being nicely poised in the slings, and hoisted over a fork at the mast-head, then swung round, and the "unwilling tack" was dragged to the loop, or becket, into which it was inserted at the other end of the vessel. The business was conducted apparently with very little order, and the process occupied a much longer time than that of tacking ship would have done with us.' [1]

Under the skilful handling of the natives, these canoes are enabled to carry sail in heavy winds and to travel fast, preserving an almost upright position. This is maintained by several of the crew squatting on the windward side of the platform, or in the hold of the outrigger, and thus, by the extra weight, counterbalancing the pressure upon the sail.

It is customary for the chief to hold the end of the sheet, and it is therefore his task to prevent the upsetting of the canoe or the carrying away of the mast. The canoe is steered with a large-bladed oar of stout proportions.

In smooth water these vessels sail very swiftly ; but when any extra pressure of sail is put upon them, it is found that their hulls are scarcely equal to the strain, and they become leaky, and require one or two hands to be constantly baling out the water. They nevertheless make long voyages of hundreds of miles—to Tonga, Kotuma, and the Samoan Islands.

The building of one of these double canoes, by the natives, frequently occupies several years. Even a small one is never built under three or four months. The tools employed are of the simplest kind, consisting chiefly of axe, gimlet, chisel, and knife ; and a few nails, obtained by barter with Europeans, have been used of late years.

The carving is performed with tools made of the teeth of small animals, set in hard wood ; and yet the workmanship is excellent.

DIMENSIONS OF A FIJI DOUBLE CANOE OF THE MOST COMMON SIZE :—[2]

	feet.		feet.
Length of larger canoe	70	Breadth of cuddy	6
,, smaller canoe	55	Height of platform above water line . .	10
Distance of the canoes apart	7	Draught of water	2 to 3
Length of platform	30	Length of mast	35
Breadth of do.	15	Length of yard	60
Length of cuddy	15	Booms	15 & 35

A canoe of this description will carry conveniently forty or fifty persons.

[1] Erskine's 'Western Pacific Islands,' p. 139.   [2] Wilkes' 'United States Exploring Expedition.'

The Sailing-Boat.

CANOES OF THE FRIENDLY ISLANDS.

THERE is much similarity between the canoes of the Friendly Islands and those of the Fijis; and there can be no better evidence as to the ingenuity of the natives than in the art displayed by them in the construction of those vessels, which, in point of neatness and workmanship, are stated by Captain Cook [1] to exceed anything of the kind he met with in the Western Pacific. The planks, or pieces of which they are composed, are sewn together in so neat a manner that on the outside it is difficult to see how they are joined, all the fastenings being on the inside, and passing through cants or ridges, which are wrought on the edges and ends of the several boards which compose the vessel.

All those which are called single canoes have outriggers, and are sometimes navigated with sails, but more generally with paddles, the blades of which are short and broadest in the middle. The single canoes are from 20 ft. to 30 ft. in length, and about 20 in. or 22 in. in width amidships. The stern terminates in a point, and the head in a wedge-like form. The fore and aft parts of the canoe are covered over, or decked, to the extent of one-third part of the whole length of the vessel, and open in the centre part. In some of these canoes the middle part of the deck is ornamented with white shells, stuck in a row on little pegs, wrought out of the wood of which it is composed.

The double canoes of these islands are composed of two vessels, each about 60 ft. or 70 ft. long, and 4 ft. or 5 ft. broad amidships, and each end terminates nearly in a point, similar to the single canoe; but those which compose the double canoe have sides or coamings round the middle or open part, in the form of a long trough, composed of boards closely fitted together, and well secured to the body of the vessel. The double canoe is formed of two of the last-described vessels fastened together, parallel one with the other, about 6 ft. or 7 ft. apart. The joining together is effected by means of strong cross-beams, supported by stanchions fixed to the canoes, and secured by bandages and lashings of sennit, made of cocoanut bass. Upon these beams a boarded platform is laid and fixed, extending from side to side, and a little beyond the outer side of each canoe, the width from outside to outside being 13 ft. 9 in.; thus the double canoe is made very strong and burthensome, but light and buoyant as the nature of the work will admit, and so it becomes a vessel of burthen fit for distant navigation. The double canoe is rigged with one mast, the heel of which is stepped and secured through the platform into the fore part of the larger of the two canoes,

[1] See Cook's 'Voyage towards the South Pole.'

and can be raised or lowered at pleasure. The sail is made of matting, and of triangular shape, with the apex downwards. It is fitted to a long yard and boom. On the platform of the double canoe a cabin or hut is erected, which generally contains a movable fireplace, or trough of wood filled with stones. There are hatchways leading through the platform into each hold of the canoes.[1]

Friendly Islands Double Canoe

Captain Cook observes that the only tools used by the natives of the Friendly Isles in constructing their boats are: hatchets, or rather thick adzes, made out of a smooth black stone which abounds at Toofoa; augers made of sharks' teeth fixed on small handles; and rasps of the rough skin of a fish fastened on flat pieces of wood. With tools such as these they contrive to build these curious vessels; and they make them not only neatly, but strong and durable.

SAILING AND MANAGEMENT OF THE DOUBLE CANOES OF THE FRIENDLY ISLES.

THESE twin canoes are rigged with one sail only. The slings by which it is hoisted are attached to the yard nearly in the middle. When the natives change tacks, they do not turn the canoe, but luff it up into the wind, ease off the sheet (just as the Ladrone Islanders do), and bring the heel or tack-end of the yard to the other end of the boat, and the sheet in like manner. There are notches or

[1] Captain Cook's 'Second Voyage.'

sockets at each extremity of the vessel, in which the end of the yard fixes. When they sail before the wind, the yard is taken out of the socket, and the sail is squared.

All the sailing-vessels of these islanders are *not* rigged to sail in the same manner; some of them, of the largest size, being rigged so as to tack about. These have a short but stout mast, which is stepped on a kind of roller that is fixed to the deck near the fore part. It (the mast) is made to lean or incline very much forward; the head is forked on the two points of which the yard rests as on two pivots, by means of two strong wooden cleats secured to each side of the yard, at about one-third its length from the tack or heel, which, when under sail, is confined down between the two canoes by means of two strong ropes passing through a hole at the head of each canoe; for it must be observed that all the sailing-vessels of this sort are double. The tack being thus fixed, it is plain that in changing tacks the vessels must be put about. The sail and boom on the one tack will be clear of the mast, and on the other will lie just as a whole mizzen.[1]

'The outriggers, and ropes used for shrouds, &c., are all stout and strong. Indeed, sail, yard and boom are altogether of such an enormous weight that strength is required.'[2]

In order to form some idea as to the rate of sailing of these canoes, Captain Cook tried experiments on board one of them with the log-line, and found the rate to be about seven knots an hour, the canoe being close-hauled, and the wind very strong.

TONGA ISLANDS CANOES.

THE Tonga Islands are a group lying in the Southern Pacific, E. S. E. of the Fiji, and rather less than 400 miles from the latter. The Tonga is composed of three smaller groups—Tongatabu, Haapai, and Vavau.

The canoes of Tongatabu are very similar to those of the Fijis—indeed, the larger of them are generally built in the Fiji Islands, as Tonga produces no timber fit for the purpose; but the Fijians are said to have acquired the art of building their large double canoes from the Tongans.[3] In all these canoes, whether double or single, there are small hatchways at both ends, with high coamings; and it would appear as if they constantly leaked, for whenever they are seen under way there is always some one in each of the end-hatchways baling out the water.

---

[1] Cook's 'Voyage towards the South Pole,' vol. ii. p. 17.
[2] *Ibid.* p. 17.
[3] Erskine's 'Western Pacific Islands,' p. 439.

Canoes of the Tonga and Salômon Islands.

The double canoes, or those with a heavy outrigger, sail much faster on a wind than before one; and it is obvious that these vessels require a special kind of seamanship, in which the Tongese are particularly expert. When there is no wind, they propel the canoe by a mode of sculling that is peculiar to the Tongese and Fijians. The sculler, instead of using the oar in the regular way, stands behind it, holding it perpendicularly, in a manner so as to throw the whole weight of his body upon the oar, and so assist his strength in using it. The oar is thrust through a hole in the platform, and so confined whilst being employed; these oars are ten feet long, and have broad blades. There is generally one oar at each end. When several oars are used, the Tongese scullers are kept in strict time by a tune or song, in which they all join; this custom, however, does not appear to be practised among the Fijians.

These apparently fragile vessels are navigated, in the face of trade-winds, voyages of hundreds of miles to and fro between the Fiji, Samoan, and Tonga Islands.

Wilkes (in his 'U.S. Exploring Expedition,' vol. iii.) speaks of a canoe he saw off the Island of Ovolau, belonging to Tanoa, the King of Anibau, which was under the management of a crew of forty Tongese. He says:—'It had a magnificent appearance, with its immense sail of white mats; the pennants streaming from its yard denoted it at once as belonging to some great chief. It was a fit accompaniment to the magnificent scenery around, and advanced rapidly and gracefully along. It was a single canoe, 100 ft. in length, with an outrigger of large size; the canoe was ornamented with a great number (2,500) of the Cyprœa ovula shells. Its velocity was considerable, and every one was struck with the adroitness with which it was managed and landed on the beach.'

The platform is the general resort of those aboard the double canoes of the Tongans; the hull, even of the main canoe, is seldom occupied by any one except those employed in baling out the water at sea.

These canoes, as also those of the Fiji Islands, are carefully protected when not in use, and placed under cover of the lofty canoe-sheds which are erected on the beach.[1]

The smaller canoes of the Tongese are similar to those of the Samoan Islanders.[2]

CANOES OF THE SALÔMON ISLANDS.

AMONG the many objects of interest and attraction to voyagers visiting the Salômon (or Solomon) Islands, are the canoes and the canoe-sheds in which the natives keep

[1] Erskine's 'Western Pacific.' Wilkes' 'Voyages.'
[2] *Infra*, page 497.

their large canoes, which it appears belong to certain tribes. Some of the sheds are remarkable for the elaborate manner in which they are constructed; the roof is supported by a number of carved wooden pillars, each pillar representing a human figure, about half life-size, standing on a pedestal.[1]

Among the canoes of the Salômon Islands are some of the best to be met with in

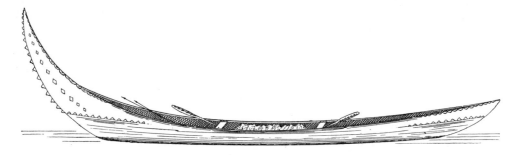

Canoe of Salômon Islands.

any of the Pacific groups, being well built and ingeniously carved, and ornamented with white Cyprœa ovula shells and mother-of-pearl, neatly and tastefully inlaid about the bows and stern of the canoe.

It appears that the native islanders go in their canoes to the Tonga Islands, where they get the Cyprœa ovula for the purpose of the decoration of their canoes. They do not buy the ovula of the Tongans, but they themselves fish for it on the outlying reefs of those islands.

Some of the canoes of the Salômon Islands have been described as 'perfect gems of beauty,'[2] displaying excellent workmanship, mould and design, and considerable good taste in the manner in which they are carved and ornamented.

FULANGESE CANOES.

The Island of Fulanga is one which produces fine timber; and it is, therefore, much resorted to by the Vavau and Tonga Islanders, as the depôt for canoe-building.

Commander Wilkes, who visited this island about the year 1840, makes mention of three large canoes he saw in the process of construction under a long shed. One of these vessels, on measurement, was found to be 102 ft. long, 7 ft. wide, and 5 ft. deep; and he speaks of it as 'a beautiful model.' The other two were somewhat smaller.

[1] See 'A Yachting Cruise in the South Seas,' by C. F. Wood (1875).
[2] *Ibid.*

Canoes of the Western Pacific.

The builders informed him they were intended for a Vavau Chief, and the work was being performed under a contract, the price agreed on to be paid in whales' teeth, axes, guns, &c.

SAVAGE ISLAND CANOES.

THE main parts of these canoes are made from a single tree, wash-streaks being afterwards fastened to the sides, which are low. The fore and aft parts are covered over, and handsomely carved. They are from 20 ft. to 24 ft. long, and furnished with an outrigger, composed of a log of wood, which floats in the water parallel with the

Savage Island Canoe.

canoe, and is kept in that position by three small spars placed across the gunwales of the canoe. The outer ends of the spars are fastened to the log, but raised to the level of the sides of the canoe by means of small props affixed to the log; the spars so fixed also form a sort of platform on which the crew place their spears and other implements.

The contrivance of the outrigger is absolutely necessary to enable them to maintain their equilibrium in the smoothest water; but the outrigger must not be confounded with that of an outlager, or spar projecting to windward when under sail, to enable the canoe to be ballasted or counterpoised by some of the crew going out and sitting upon it,[1] as described under the head 'Samoan Canoes' and others.

The paddles employed in these canoes are very prettily shaped, like a plantain leaf; they are short and concave in the blade, and handsomely carved.

CANOES OF THE PENRHYN ISLANDS.

THE Canoes of the Penrhyn group of islands in the Western Pacific are of interesting and remarkable construction. The author of 'Wild Life Among the Pacific Islanders,' whilst voyaging in the Omuka territory, says that—he saw for the first time a Penrhyn canoe under sail; its mode of propulsion, he should think, was the most

[1] Erskine's 'Western Pacific Islands.'

original to be seen in any part of the world. The sail is as simple in construction as it is primitive in appearance. For the purpose three long palm boughs are cut from the nearest tree, and after a few strips of bark have been torn from them they are conveyed to the canoe. The lower or thick end of a bough is placed at the bottom of the canoe, with its long slender leaves standing perpendicularly to the height of about 10 ft., and made fast to the cross-bar of the outrigger, which runs across the little vessel. A bough is then placed on either side of this, attached to it at the bottom, but inclined outward, and also fastened to the cross-bar. At the top the slender ends of the latter are bowed over to the centre, the mingling leaves of all being inter-laced a little to present further resistance to the wind. This, when completed, forms a broad sail. Strips of bark are fastened to the most extended part of the outer boughs, which are again secured to the stern outrigger ; and thus the cocoa-nut tree supplies sails, masts, spars, and rigging, all being constructed in a few minutes from its boughs.[1]

NEW CALEDONIA AND LOYALTY ISLAND SAILING-CANOES.

CAPTAIN ERSKINE[2] alludes to some large canoes he met with in these islands, rigged with two sharp-headed sails of matting, laced to long flexible yards, and having somewhat the appearance, when set, of the sprit-sails in common use among the Thames barges. They appeared to be fitted for long voyages, and had earthen fireplaces constructed on deck. They were each apparently capable of accommodating thirty persons on board.

SAMOAN CANOES.

SAMOA, the native name of the group of Islands called by Captain Cook the 'Navigator's Islands,' are a group in the Southern Pacific from 400 to 500 miles north of the Tonga, or Friendly Islands. The largest of the Samoan group are Upolu, Savaii, and Tutuila. Apia, the principal town, is situated in the Bay of Apia on the coast of Upolu.

The natives of these Islands display considerable ingenuity in the construction of their canoes.

The largest of the Samoan canoes are from 30 ft. to 60 ft. in length, and capable

[1] *Vide* ' Wild Life among the Pacific Islanders,' by E. H. Lamont (1867), p. 242.
[2] Erskine's ' Western Pacific Islands.'

of carrying from ten to fourteen paddlers, besides a sitter. They are formed of planks, fastened together with sennit. There is no regularity in the length or breadth of the planks. On one of the edges of each plank a ledge or projection is formed, which serves to attach the sennit, and to connect and bind it closely to the adjoining one. The labour bestowed in joining so many small pieces of plank is surprising. Before the pieces are joined, gum from the bark of the breadfruit-tree is used to stick them close, and prevent leakage. On the outside, the pieces are so neatly joined as to require a close examination before the seams can be detected; and this perfection of workmanship is the more astonishing, when it is considered that the only tools they use are a gimlet or piercer, and a piece of iron tied to a staff, thus forming a sort of adze.

The Samoan canoes are long and narrow, and their shape approaches even to

Samoan Canoe.

elegance. They are decked fore and aft, and provided with an outrigger, as shown in the engraving.

When propelled with paddles the natives sit two abreast, and the canoe is guided by a steersman. The seat of honour is on the forward deck, in the centre of which is a row of pegs, which are covered with the large white ovula shell by way of ornament. The striking peculiarity of these canoes (and in which they differ from those of other islanders) is that they have both prow and stern, and therefore the sail cannot be shifted without tacking the boat; consequently, the outrigger that constitutes their safety under sail is alternately to windward and leeward; when to leeward it is not half the protection to the canoe in preserving its stability that it is when to windward. These canoes, however, carry less sail than those of other islands of Polynesia; and in order to guard against the danger of upsetting when the outrigger is to leeward, the precaution is taken of rigging a *suati* (*i.e.* a sprit or boom), in fact an outlager,[1] which projects from the windward gunwale; when the wind is heavy, one or two of the crew go out upon the *suati*, and so counterpoise the canoe against the force of the wind.

The sail is made of matting, in the manufacture of which considerable labour is sometimes bestowed. It is of triangular shape, and set with the apex downwards, the sail standing about 10 ft. high. The mast is stepped at about one-third from the bows. The matting used for the sails is made entirely by hand, by interlacing the

---

[1] *Vide supra*, p. 482, note 4, as to the distinction between an outrigger and an outlager.

fibres. Some of the finest textures are as soft and pliable as cotton canvas. These canoes are not calculated for long voyages.

The Samoans have no large double canoes, such as those of the Tongans and Fijians, except those which they procure, by barter, from those islanders.[1]

The usual Samoan fishing-canoe is made of a single tree, with a small outrigger to balance it.

UNION GROUP ISLANDS CANOES.

THE canoes of the Union Group, Western Pacific Islands, are single canoes, with outriggers, resembling those of the Samoan group, being made of pieces of wood sewed together, and partly decked over the fore and aft parts; they are also ornamented, at

Union Group Islands Canoe.

each end, with ovula shells, in the same manner as the Samoan canoes. 'No sails were observed, but a small model of a canoe, purchased among the curiosities, had the usual triangular sail.'[2]

The blades of their paddles also resemble those of the Samoans, being oblong and slender.

CANOES OF THE ISLAND OF MITIARO.

THE island of Mitiaro, one of the Hervey group, is famous for its tomano wood, which grows in abundance in that island. This wood, which in colour resembles mahogany, is most beautifully waved and capable of a high polish, but very hard and difficult to work with such tools as the native islanders possess; they are nevertheless justly celebrated for their canoes, which are made of the tomano wood, and are light, buoyant and graceful in form. These canoes are also an article of trade and barter with the natives of other islands.[3]

---

[1] Erskine's 'Western Pacific.' Wilkes' 'Exploring Expedition.' And see also 'The South Sea Islanders,' by W. T. Wawn, 1893.

[2] Wilkes' 'United States Exploring Expedition,' vol. v. p. 11.

[3] *Vide* 'Wild Life among the Pacific Islanders,' by E. H. Lamont, 1867.

Canoes of the Pacific Islands.

KINGSMILL ISLAND CANOES.

THE canoes of the Kingsmill and Ellice Group, Western Pacific Islands, have many interesting peculiarities. They are commonly from 12 ft. to 15 ft. in length, from 2 ft. to 3 ft. in depth, varying from 15 ins. to 2 ft. in width; those in the northern islands being much larger—some of them 60 ft. in length.

These canoes are very well modelled, and, in some respects, better built than those of many of the other islanders in the Pacific; they have considerable sheer, and are built in frames, each canoe having six or eight ribs or timbers. The sides are in irregular pieces of cocoa-nut plank, varying in length from a few inches to 6 ft. or 8 ft., and from 5 ins. to 7 ins. in width. They are joined very neatly and sewn with sennit; and in order to make them water-tight, slips of the pandanus leaf are inserted under and between the planking, in the same way as brown paper is used in British boat-building.

The manner in which the uprights are attached to the flat timbers displays consider-

Kingsmill Island Canoe.

able ingenuity. They are so secured as to possess all the virtue of a double joint, making them easy in a sea-way, and capable of withstanding the force of the waves. One side of the canoe is nearly flat, and in this respect they bear some resemblance to the proa of the Ladrone Islands. They are provided with an outrigger, but of smaller proportions to those of other islands, and the stage or platform covers less space.

These canoes are tacked and sailed in the same manner as those of the Fiji Islanders, the outrigger being always kept to windward, so that they sail with either end foremost.

Wood being an exceedingly scarce article with the natives, the masts and yards are of several pieces neatly joined together. Some of the canoes are built entirely of wreckage-wood, which is always a great prize to them. But notwithstanding the odds and ends of which the canoes are composed, they are strong and durable, and even elegant in appearance. One of them, of a suitable size for ten persons, occupies five or six months in building.[1]

The shape of the sail is triangular, and very similar to that of the Fiji canoes; the mast is stepped in a fore-raking position, and the boom is considerably elevated.

[1] Wilkes, vol. v.

The Sailing-Boat.

The natives are very expert in the sailing and management of these canoes, and always avoid using the paddles as much as possible.

Their paddles are sometimes made of a piece of cocoa-nut board; others have a tortoiseshell blade, about 6 ins. square, secured to a round stick for a handle.

BOATS OF TAHITI.

TAHITI (or Otaheite) is the principal island of the Society group in the Pacific Ocean, and is also one of the most beautiful. The canoes of Tahiti and the neighbouring islands may be divided into two general classes—Ivahahs and Pahies.

The Ivahah, in shape, is wall-sided and flat-bottomed; it is used for short excursions to sea. The Pahie is bow-sided and sharp-bottomed, and is used for longer voyages.

The Ivahahs vary in length from 10 ft. up to 70 ft. or more. The breadth is in no way proportionate; those of 10 ft. long are about 1 ft. wide, whilst those of 70 ft. long are scarcely 2 ft. wide.

Ivahahs may be classified as war Ivahahs, fishing Ivahahs, and travelling Ivahahs; the war-boat being by far the largest, with the head and stern peering in a crescent-like form to the height of 17 ft. or 18 ft. in some of the boats, though the body be only 3 ft. deep. These Ivahahs never go to sea singly, but two are lashed together side by side, and kept at a distance of about 3 ft. apart by strong poles laid athwart the gun-wales; and upon these, in the fore part, what is called the 'fighting-stage' is a raised platform on pillars about the height of 6 ft., the stage being about 10 ft. or 12 ft. long and somewhat wider than the boats.

The fishing Ivahahs vary in length from 10 ft. to about 40 ft.; all those of the length of 25 ft. and upwards occasionally carry sail. Two of these boats are sometimes joined together by means of a platform, on board of which a small hut is erected; but this is not common.

The travelling Ivahahs are always double, and fitted with a small neat hut, about 5 ft. or 6 ft. broad, and 6 ft. or 7 ft. long, which is erected on the aft part of the platform, for the convenience of the principal occupants of the boat, who sit in it by day and sleep there at night.

All these Ivahahs have high-peering sterns; in those 25 ft. long the stern rises about 4 ft., and so in proportion. The bows and stem are covered with a board, which projects forward about 4 ft., and forms a sort of fore-deck, the chief advantage of which appears to be the convenience it offers for stepping in and out from the beach.

The Pahie also varies in length from 30 ft. up to 60 ft.; and, like the Ivahah, is very narrow. The sectional form of the Pahie is rather full, as shown by the section, which also illustrates their form. The first stage, or kelson, *below* the dotted line *a a*, is formed of a tree, hollowed out like a trough; this part sometimes consists of three trees, as one could not be had of sufficient length. The next stage, or that between the dotted lines *a a* and *b b*, is formed of straight planks, about 4 ft. long, 15 ins. broad, and 2 ins. thick. The third stage, or that between the dotted lines *b b* and *c c*, is, like the bottom, formed out of the trunks of long trees, hollowed into its bilging form. The upper part, *c c*, or *coamings*, as they are termed in boats of British build, is formed of straight planking.

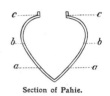

Section of Pahie.

To form all these parts separately, without saw, plane, chisel or any other iron tool, may well be thought no easy task—still less so to join them together; but the natives do so with considerable ingenuity, by sewing, clamping, and lacing them with strong thongs of plaiting; and the nicety with which this is done may be inferred from the fact of their being sufficiently water-tight for use without caulking. As the plaiting soon rots in the water, it is renewed at least once a year; in order to do which, the vessel is taken entirely to pieces.

Those that are used for sailing are generally double, and the middle-sized are said

Tahiti Sailing Canoes.

to be the best sea-boats. The natives are sometimes a fortnight or more at sea in these boats, and could go longer voyages if they had more stowage for provisions and water.

Those that are sailed singly are fitted with a log of wood or outrigger, which is fastened to the end of two poles that are placed across the canoe and project over to windward from 6 ft. to 10 ft. beyond the sides, according to the size of the Pahie. The outrigger is essentially necessary to preserve the stability of these vessels when the wind is heavy.

Some of them are rigged with one mast, and some with two. When the length of the Pahie is 30 ft., that of the mast is somewhat less than 25 ft. It is stepped through the frame that is placed across the canoe.

The sail, which is made of matting, stands about one-third higher than the mast, and very much peaked at the top, square at the bottom, and curved at the side. The outer leech of the sail is completely framed with wood, and there is no contrivance either for reefing or furling it. At the top of the mast and peak of the sail are placed a bunch and streamer of feathers. They have no other contrivance for steering than the paddles, which two or more of the crew use at the aft part of the canoe.

The Pahies are kept with great care in boat-houses, built specially for their reception. These are constructed of poles set in rows in the ground, the tops being drawn together and fastened so as to form a sort of Gothic arch, which is then thatched from the arch to the ground, the ends only of the arch being left open. Some of these canoe-sheds are 50 or 60 yards long.

When on their long voyages, the natives steer by the sun during the day, and by the stars at night, many of which they distinguish by names.[1]

Common Tahitian Canoe.

The common canoes of the Island of Tahiti are of better form and construction than those of the Disappointment Islands.

The outrigger in some of these canoes is neatly secured on one side of the canoe, by inserting the supports through small round holes in the upper strake of the canoe, instead of over the top. The common Tahitian canoe is also provided with a similar landing-stage to that of the Ivahahs and Pahies, except that it is placed at the stern,[2] instead of the bows.

The trading canoes of Tahiti are somewhat different to the last described, inasmuch as the outrigger of the trading canoe is attached in the more usual way, the bearers being lashed across the top of the gunwales.

[1] Hawkesworth's 'Voyages,' vol. ii.   [2] Wilkes, vol. ii.

Canoes of the Pacific Islands.

DOUBLE CANOE OF THE PAUMOTU GROUP.

THE Paumotu Group is a range of coral islands in the Low (or 'Dangerous') Archipelago, extending E.S.E. from the Society Islands.

The double canoes of the Paumotu Islands are remarkably curious. They are composed of two canoes, each 35 ft. in length by 4 ft. 6 in. in width, which are joined side by side by means of a strong framework of wood, and a platform which extends nearly over the whole surface of the two vessels. When long voyages are undertaken in the double canoe, a temporary hut is erected on the platform.

Every part of these canoes is neatly put together, and secured with twine and

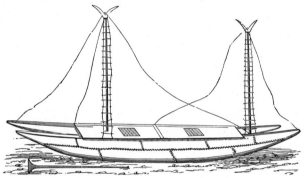

Double Canoe of the Paumotu Group.

sennit, made of cocoa-nut fibres. No iron or metal of any kind is used in their construction, nor hempen nor manilla rope for the sails and rigging. They are fitted with two masts, the shrouds and rigging of which are merely tough branches of the vine plant, and these supply the place of ropes and cordage. Each mast has a forked top-piece, in shape resembling the extended wings of a bird at the moment of alighting. Over the forked top-piece other vine ropes are placed, and by these the sails are hoisted and lowered.

The sails are made of matting and cocoa-nut fibres, and the canoe is steered with a large oar, the shape of which resembles the flat section of a straight trumpet. In these canoes the islanders undertake voyages of many miles to neighbouring islands, steering by the sun in the daytime, and by the stars at night, when out of sight of the coast.

The natives thus carry on a small trade; but these are principally the Chain Islanders, who supply themselves at Tahiti with various small articles, in exchange for their cocoa-nut oil and dried fish.[1]

[1] Wilkes, vol. 1.

The Sailing-Boat.

THE canoes of Wytoohee (one of the islands of the Paumotu group) are very small, being only from 12 ft. to 15 ft. in length. They are built of strips of cocoa-nut wood sewn together; and when completed are so light that two persons may carry them on their shoulders.

These canoes have projecting stem and stern-pieces, as shown in the engraving; and

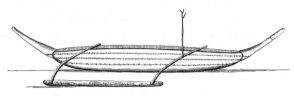

Wytoohee Canoe.

it is by aid of these projections that the natives are enabled to get into them from the water without upsetting them.

They are also provided with an outrigger of a very simple kind, but which gives additional stability to the vessel. The paddles by which they are propelled are curved backwards.[1]

[1] Wilkes, vol. i.

504

South American Sailing Rafts.

SOUTH AMERICAN SAILING BALZA.

THE South American sailing Balza is in reality a sailing raft, composed of five, seven, or nine logs of wood, or trunks of trees, called ‘Balza.’   The natives of Darien call the tree ‘Puero.’   The balza is a soft, whitish wood, and very buoyant.

Balzas of this type are not only used on the rivers of Ecuador, but short sea-voyages are made in them.

They are of various kinds and sizes.   Some are fishing balzas; some are used for

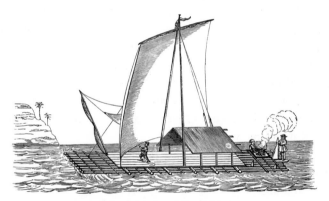

South American Sailing Balza.

carrying goods from the custom-house to Guayaquil, and from thence to Puna, the Saltode, Tumbez, and Paita; and others, of a more curious and elegant construction, are employed in removing native families to their estates and country houses.

Some of these sailing-rafts are formed of the trunks of large trees, 2 ft. or 2 ft. 6 ins. in diameter, and from 60 ft. to 70 ft. in length.   The trunks are lashed together with *bejucos* (withes), and so securely that, with the cross logs, which are also fastened together in a similar manner, they are enabled to resist the rapidity of the currents and heavy seas in their voyages to the coast of Tumbez and Paita.   The width of the raft varies from 15 ft. to 30 ft. and upwards, according to the size of the logs.

A platform is placed over the upper logs, which forms a broad and extensive deck for carrying cargo, working fishing-nets, and generally for the use of the crew in the navigation of the raft.

Over the aft part of the platform, abaft the mast, a strong tilt or hut is erected, the roof of which is formed of reeds.

The Sailing-Boat.

The raft so constructed is rigged with a double or shear-mast, composed of two poles of mangrove-wood, the lower ends of which span the platform from right to left, and the upper ends are firmly fastened together. From the shear-mast so erected a main or square-sail is suspended. Those which carry a fore-sail have an extra shear-mast, composed of two smaller poles, which are set up in the fore part of the raft, in the same manner as the main-mast.

Abaft the platform, and near the stern end of the raft, a broad flagstone is placed; and upon this the crew make a fire and cook their food, as occasion and convenience require.

The larger of these rafts are capable of carrying between 400 and 500 quintals (equal to 25 tons) of merchandise, without damage by proximity to the water, for the waves of the sea never sweep over the platform; neither does the water splash up between the beams, and the raft always follows the motion of the water.

But the greatest singularity of this floating contrivance is, that it is sailed, tacked, and worked in contrary winds with the facility of a vessel with a keel, and it makes but little lee-way. This advantage it derives from an antiquated and original method of steering other than by a rudder, *viz.*, by *guaras*, which are boards shaped like a rudder, and of a size corresponding with the capacity of the raft. These are placed vertically, both fore and aft, between the main logs; and the crew, by thrusting some of them deep down in the water and raising others, bear away, luff, tack, lie-to, and perform all the other tactics of a sailing vessel.

A *guara* being thrust downwards in the fore part of the balza causes it to luff or keep nearer the wind; and by lifting or taking it out and dropping one astern, the balza bears away or falls off.

Such is the method used by the South Americans in steering their rafts; sometimes they use five or six *guaras* at a time to prevent lee-way.

These *guaras* are probably the origin of sliding keels and centre boards, described *supra*, page 90.

The method of steering by *guaras* is so primitive and simple that, when once the balza is put on her proper course, one or two only are made use of, which are then raised or lowered as occasion requires; and thus the sailing raft is always kept to her course without making lee-way, and can be tacked and wore by means of these *guaras* with a degree of precision truly wonderful. Perpendicular slits are cut in certain parts of the raft between the main trunks, through which the two principal *guaras* are worked up and down as required.

When it blows hard and the balza is sailing with a side wind, several *guaras* are kept down to leeward to enable the raft to hold a better wind.[1]

---

[1] *Vide* 'Relacion Historica del Viage á la América Meridional hecho del órden de S. Mag.,' &c., Impresa del órden del Rey en Madrid (1748). Ulloa's 'Voyage to South America.' Hall's 'Fragments of Voyages and Travels,' &c., &c.

Peruvian and Brazilian Boats.

PERUVIAN BALSAS.

THE Balsas employed on the south coast of Peru are famed for their excellent capabilities as surf boats. They are, however, of a totally different construction to the sailing balsas last described. The Peruvian balsa is of twin tubular construction, and is used for crossing the surf off the cost of Mollendo. Captain Hall[1] describes them as being made of two entire seal-skins inflated, placed side by side, and connected by cross planks of wood and strong lashings of thongs; over all, a platform of cane mats forms a sort of deck, about 4 ft. wide and 6 ft. or 8 ft. long, upon which the person who manages the balsa kneels, and by means of a double-bladed paddle (which he holds by the middle, and strikes the water alternately on each side) sweeps it along through the heavy breakers and surf on the coast. The passengers and goods are placed on the platform behind him.

The buoyancy and twin form of construction of these balsas enable them to cross the surf in safety and without wetting the passengers at times when an ordinary boat would be swamped in the attempt. All sea-borne goods destined inland at this part of the coast are landed in this manner. The great bars of silver, and the bags of dollars also, which are shipped in return for the merchandise landed, pass through the surf on these tender though secure conveyances, which are sometimes laden with a cargo of a ton or more in weight.

They can keep the sea in any swell or surf, in the hands of the natives, but are slow in their progress through the water, on account of their spare length.[2]

A similar kind of balsa is also used at Coquimbo, and other places off the coast of Chili.

THE MONTARIA OF BRAZIL.

FOR short excursions and for fishing in still waters, a small boat, called a Montaria, is commonly used on the rivers and inland waters of Brazil. It is made of five planks: a broad one for the bottom, bent into the proper shape by the action of heat, two narrow ones for the sides, and two small triangular pieces for stem and stern. It has no rudder; the paddle serves both for steering and propelling.

The montaria, in some parts of Brazil (where the natives lead a semi-aquatic life, as on the creeks and canoe-paths of the rivers Amazon and Para), takes the place of horse, mule, or camel of other regions.

Mr. Bates says[3]:—'It was interesting to see the natives in their little heavily-

---

[1] 'Journal written on the coasts of Chili, Peru and Mexico,' by Captain Basil Hall (1824).
[2] 'Travels in Peru and Mexico,' by S. S. Hill (1860).
[3] 'The Naturalist on the River Amazon,' by H. W. Bates (1863), vol. i. p. 74.

laden montarias. Sometimes they were managed by handsome, healthy young lads, loosely clad in straw hat, white shirt, and dark blue trousers turned up to the knee. They steered, paddled and managed the *varejão* (the boating-pole) with much grace and dexterity.'

THE IGARITÉ OF BRAZIL.

BESIDES one or more montarias, almost every family has a larger canoe, called Igarité. This is fitted with two masts and sails, a rudder and keel, and has an arched awning and cabin near the stern made of a framework of tough lianas thatched with palm leaves. In the Igarité they cross stormy rivers fifteen or twenty miles broad. The natives are all boat-builders. It is often remarked by white residents that an Indian is a carpenter and shipwright by intuition.[1]

THE CUBERTA OF BRAZIL.

ANOTHER kind of canoe used on the Amazon is called Cuberta. This vessel is of about six tons burthen, of a square structure, with the floor above the water-line, and an arched covering over the hold. It is also fitted with two masts and sails; and there is considerable room aboard for stowage of goods, sleeping-places, &c.[2]

CANOES OF THE TOCANTĪINS AND RIVER MOJŪ.

THESE canoes are roughly made, but in some respects convenient, having a tolda— or palm-thatched roof like a gipsy's tent—over the stern which forms the cabin; and in the fore part, a similar one, but lower, under which the provisions and baggage are usually stowed. Over this is a rough deck of cedar boards, called the jangada, where the men work at the oars and travellers take their meals and smoke when the sun is not too hot. These canoes have two masts and fore and aft sails, and are about 24 ft. long by 8 ft. wide.[3]

Some of them must be well made and seaworthy, for Mr. Wallace says:—A little above Barra the river is from six to ten miles wide; 'and when there is much wind, a heavy sea arises which is very dangerous for small canoes.' In parts, it appears, and indeed 'for several hundreds of miles, the two banks of the river can never be seen at once; they are probably from ten to twenty-five miles apart.'[4]

[1] 'The Naturalist on the River Amazon,' by H. W. Bates (1863), vol. i. p. 76.
[2] *Ibid*, vol. ii. p. 72.
[3] 'Travels on the Amazon and Rio Negro,' by A. R. Wallace (1853).   [4] *Ibid.*

Brazilian Boats.

BAHIA MARKET-BOAT.

BAHIA (or San Salvador), a city and seaport of Brazil, is delightfully situated on the east side of the entrance to All Saints Bay, on the high cliffs and steep banks within Cape San Antonio, on which stands a revolving beacon-light 140 ft. above sea-level. The city consists of an upper (*alta*) and lower (*baixa*) town, which are connected by very steep streets, and of late years by a powerful hydraulic elevator for pedestrians.

Bahia Market-Boat.

The harbour is one of the best on the coast, and the shipping and trade carried on in fruits, sugar, tobacco and other productions of the country are considerable. The illustration shows the type and peculiarities of rig of the Bahia market-boat, with its tall mast standing in a very sloping position, and supporting its narrow-headed main-sail; the fore-sail in shape resembles an ordinary lug-sail, but is set on a fore-mast which leans slightly forward towards the stem of the boat, and therefore in a contrary direction to the slope of the main-mast. These boats also carry a third mast of shorter length than either of the others, which is stepped in the extreme front part of the bows and leaning over the stem; on this they set, in fine weather, a third sail of similar shape to the second, but smaller. The rig is local and peculiar, but not by any means modern, having been in use at Bahia, it is believed, for centuries past.

BAHIA FRUIT-BOAT.

THE Bahia fruit and sugar boat is also of peculiar rig, but very different to that of the market-boat. The Bahia fruit-boat is rigged with two masts; the fore or main-mast is stepped well forward in the bows, and carries a large square sail, with yard, but no boom. The chief peculiarity of the rig is in the mizzen, a long low standing sail

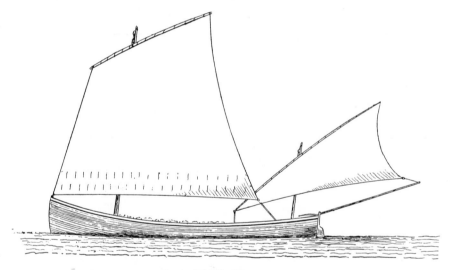

Bahia Fruit-Boat.

in shape like a jib-sail with the fore-leech laced to a long slender yard, by which it is slung and hoisted on the low-standing mizzen-mast, with the apex of the sail pointing downwards in the boat several feet in front of the mizzen-mast; and the clew of the sail is sheeted to a jigger or stern-outrigger, extending several feet over the taffrail beyond the stern of the boat, in the manner represented by the illustration.

The rig is apparently of local origin and ancient contrivance, and is peculiar to the locality.

Brazilian Catamarans.

THE sailing-rafts of Brazil, South America, are of a peculiarly interesting, simple, but ingenious type, and they are among the most useful craft of the Brazils. These rafts are various in size as they are also in construction. Some are called Zangadas,

Zangada of Pernambuco.

others Catamarans. Some are used by the Brazilian fishermen, others take the place of ordinary ferry and passenger boats; whilst those of a larger class are employed for trading purposes in carrying goods from place to place, and a smaller class take the place of small open sailing-boats.

The Sailing-Boat.

The navigation of these rafts is not confined to the rivers of Brazil, short sea-voyages being sometimes made in them. They are in many respects of similar construction to the South American sailing balza of Ecuador (already described, *supra*, page 505), but the rig is different.

The zangada is rigged with one mast and sail, the latter of triangular shape, which is kept flat by the boom on sailing to windward; the fore-end of the boom being set in an eyelet in the fore-leech of the sail, in the manner represented by the illustration, and on the clew of the sail being hauled taut at the aft end of the boom, a very flat surface is presented to the wind, which facilitates the working of the raft on its course to windward.

The seat of honour for the sailing-master, who directs the course of the raft and attends to the main-sheet, is at the aft-end of the platform, on the highest of the elevated thwarts; from which position he is enabled to see over the roof of the hut and to shape his course clear of obstructions.

There is always a numerous fleet of zangadas and catamarans at Pernambuco, where those of the smaller class appear to supply the place of ordinary open sailing-boats. The zangada is as simple, primitive, and inexpensive a kind of sailing-raft as could well be contrived.

The Brazilian fishermen of Pernambuco use them constantly, and have every confidence in their safety and capabilities as sea-going craft. When close-hauled in a fresh breeze, they sail at the rate of five or six knots an hour, and much faster when going free.

The zangada anchor is a most primitive contrivance, composed of pieces of wood forming a sort of frame-work encasing a large stone.

A complete model of a zangada, with sail, anchor and other fittings, may be seen at the United Service Museum, from which model the illustration below was made by the Author.

Fuegian Canoes.

FUEGIAN CANOES.

THE native canoes of Terra del Fuego are curious. They are constructed of bark, sewn together with shreds of whalebone, seal-skin, and twigs.

The top rim, or gunwale, is formed by binding canes or small poles to the sides. The canoe is kept in shape by stretchers lashed across from one gunwale to the other; the two longest and strongest being placed amidships, across the top of the canoe.

Fuegian Canoe.

They have no thwarts; the occupants squat on dried grass strewn about the floor on the inside.

Frail as the Fuegian canoe is, a fire is generally carried in the bottom on a stone in the deepest part of the canoe, which always contains water surrounding the fire. One person is generally employed in baling out the water and attending to the fire.

The Fuegians 'seldom venture outside the kelp,' and their paddles are so small as to be of little use in propelling their canoes, unless the weather is calm.[1]

[1] Wilkes' 'American Exploring Expedition,' vol. i.

The Sailing-Boat.

CHINESE BOATS.

' I saw their boats, with many a light,
Floating the live-long yesternight.'

THERE is no other nation in the world where so great a variety and so many thousands of boats are met with, as on the rivers and at the sea-port towns of China. But it is very remarkable that although there has been considerable advancement and improvement for many years past in the art of boat-building by the Chinese—some of their most modern boats being as perfect in model and as elegant in form as those of any

Chinese Boats.

other nation—-yet the advancement of the Chinese in naval architecture in no way keeps pace with the sister art of boat-building. The same type of Chinese junk and lorcha which furrowed the deep centuries ago, with their high towering sterns and lofty mat sails, still navigate the seas in that same antiquated form.

At Canton the crowd of boats of all sizes, shapes and colours, passing to and fro— with the 'hubbub and clamour of ten thousand different sounds coming from every quarter, and with every variety of intonation'—make an impression almost similar to that of awe upon the first visit of the stranger.[1]

There are few more extraordinary places than the Canton River, supporting as it does a vast population which inhabits the numberless boats of all forms and all sizes.[2]

On the great Yang-tse River, at Nanking, Chin-Kiang, Soochow and other large towns, the surface of the waters absolutely teems with boats, junks, and vessels of every size, shape and design; those which bring down the produce of the country from the interior range in size from the ordinary sampan to the cargo junk of 100 tons.

Soochow has been described as the Venice of China, with its net-work of canals, lakes and navigable rivers, which largely play the part of streets. Let the European traveller go where he will on the rivers and waters of China, the same throngs and tiers of boats, with their full complement of human life on board, meet his eye.[3]

Besides the sampans, or common covered boats, there are many palatial craft, with elaborately-carved and gilded fronts, which in the evening show a blaze of light, with busy waiters moving about among the feasting Celestials, and painted Chinese women mixing with the crowd—not unfrequently gambling-houses, or places of licentiousness and debauch. It is altogether a scene not to be forgotten; and as night advances, the streets of boats are extended by the crowds of sampans which have been plying during the day, but which at sunset take up their stations side by side in the canals, within which they are secured by a boom, just as the gates of the city are kept closed during the night.[4]

As evening comes on, also, numerous large house-boats, two storeys high, richly decorated and ornamented, return from their various picnic excursions, a number of half-clad Chinamen poling them slowly and laboriously along. Meantime groups of the better class stand at the doors, enjoying the scene; and others may be seen through the windows, seated in the saloon, drinking tea and smoking; while the upper windows disclose many fair ladies in their boudoirs, adorning themselves for the delectation of their lords.[5]

At Canton every boat is registered, whatever its size. So long ago as the year 1833, the whole number on the river adjacent the city of Canton was 84,000, a large majority of which were tankeä (*i.e.* egg-house) boats.[6] Many thousands of the Canton boats are sometimes swept away and destroyed by the terrible typhoons which occasionally occur in those parts. Such was the case in August, 1862, when upwards of 40,000 persons perished in that memorable disaster.

[1] 'The Fan-qui in China,' by C. T. Downing, 1838; 'Recollections of a Three Years' Residence in China,' by W. T. Power, D.A.C.G. (1853).
[2] 'Rambles of a Naturalist on the Shores and Waters of the China Sea,' by C. Collingwood, M.A. &c. (1868), p. 333.
[3] 'Narrative of a Journey from the Arctic Ocean to the Yellow Sea,' by Julius M. Price, F.R.G.S. (1892).
[4] 'Rambles of a Naturalist on the Shores and Waters of the China Sea,' p. 333.
[5] *Ibid.* p. 333.　　　　　　　　　　　　[6] 'Chinese Repository,' vol. i.

The Sailing-Boat.

THE SAMPAN.

The smaller boats of the Chinese are a numerous class, and are called "sampans," which signifies 'three boards,' such boats being constructed, originally, of three or four planks only. They are very shallow, have no keels, and therefore draw but very little water.

The sampan is the general type of small boat employed in the various occupations of the Chinese in all parts of the rivers and bays of China, and is in great variety as

Sampan.

regards size. Some of the pleasure-sampans are of superior type and finish; the fishing sampan is the largest. Those used as ferry-boats, pilot-boats, egg-boats, fruit-boats, &c., are smaller, and these are seldom sailed.

Children of both sexes are taught the management of the sampan as soon as their strength enables them to pull an oar, hoist a sail, or trim a sheet; and it is no uncommon thing to see a woman sculling a sampan with an infant tied to her back, or a fishing sampan sailed and navigated entirely by a crew of females.

The ordinary sampan is from 12 ft. to 15 ft. in length; those used as ferry-boats are frequently navigated by women, who seek a maintenance by carrying passengers to and fro in different parts of the Chinese inland waters.[1] The sampan and indeed most Chinese boats are propelled by a scull which rests on a pivot at the stern.

[1] For a description of many other boats of the sampan class, see Archdeacon Gray's 'China,' vol. ii. p. 278.

Chinese Boats.

CHINESE RIVER JUNKS.

ALTHOUGH tens of thousands of boats be assembled together on the Chinese rivers, yet good order and decorum is kept to a certain extent. All boats with the same kind of goods are moored together in tiers at a certain place on the river allotted to them by the local magistrates; and watchers and other officials are appointed and set over them, both by night and day,[1] to enforce regularity and conformity to the orders of the authorities. Fairs and markets are also held on the river; and trades of all kinds are

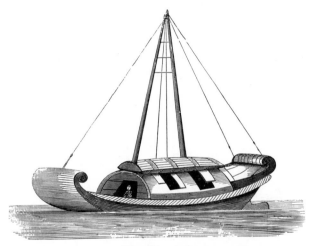

Chinese River Junk.

carried on in the boats by the people who form the aquatic population of the Chinese rivers.

All the Chinese *sea-going* craft have a great goggle-eye painted on each side of the bows; the river craft alone are without that ornament. They also have very large rudders; and instead of iron they use generally *wooden* anchors, which, though clumsy and inelegant in appearance, are tolerably efficient.

For caulking purposes, instead of pitch, the Chinese use a cement like putty, which Europeans call 'chinan.'[2]

[1] Nieuhoff's 'China.'   [2] Osbech's 'China.'

The Sailing-Boat.

CHINESE FAMILY BOATS.

On entering a Chinese port, a stranger would think half the population lived in boats, and indeed there are thousands of families living throughout the summer entirely in boats. These family boats are constantly cruising up and down the river in pairs. When at anchor they are arranged in regular tiers, forming liquid streets for small craft to move up and down among them, and broad channels for the larger vessels.

The lesser craft are managed with remarkable dexterity by the men and girls, who scull and pole them about, threading their way through the maze among the never-ceasing noise and jabber of thousands of voices. Screaming and helpless little children are also crawling about the decks, with hollow gourds or bladders tied at the back of their necks as life-buoys,[1] to keep their heads above water when they tumble overboard; and with the same they are taught, in infancy, to swim.

The family boats all have wooden or bamboo cabins of a size in proportion to that of the boat.

CHINESE SAILING BOATS.

Some of the sailing pleasure-boats of the Chinese are admirable models, though original and peculiar in appearance, with their broad and high sterns and low-pointed prows, and they sail splendidly, when rigged in the most approved style, and fitted with

[1] Power's 'China'; Downing's 'Fan-qui.'

518

bamboo and mat sails of a superior make and texture. When caught in a breeze the lofty sails bear them along at great speed. In some of these boats the stern, prow and other parts are decorated in a very costly manner with elaborate carving and gilding.

The mat sails are preferred by Chinamen to those of any other material, because they are said to hold a better wind, and may be kept flat and stiff. When first turned out from the sail-maker's hands, these bamboo and mat sails really look very neat and pretty, particularly those made of the superior sort of matting.

Occasionally a sailing-boat may be seen with sails made of blue nankeen, but it is not generally liked by the Chinamen, as it soon gets out of shape, and is not so durable as the mat material.

Some of the mandarin pleasure-boats are lined with crimson silk, and the canopy edged with gilded carving; the outside is also neatly painted, the edges being adorned with vermilion and gold-leaf, and fringed with scallops of prepared leather. The seats and couches are covered with blue and scarlet velvet.

CHINESE FAST-BOATS.

The Chinese " Fast-boats " (so called) are a superior class of boat; and prior to the introduction of steam launches were used chiefly by business-men, on short expeditions in which time was of importance.

The hull of a Chinese Fast-boat is about 30 ft. in length, by 8 ft. or 9 ft. in breadth, much higher out of the water abaft than forward, and provided with a large flat-roofed cabin in the centre, arranged into compartments with cupboards, kitchens, &c. The cabin is usually very comfortably fitted and furnished. When there is little or no wind as many as eight or ten men work the boat ahead with a single large broad-bladed scull placed over the stern.

In hot weather a temporary awning is erected overhead as a protection from the sun. This is taken down when a breeze springs up, and the sails are again hoisted.

These boats are rigged with two masts and sails, the masts being supported by shrouds and stays in the usual way. The sails consist of squares of matting sewn together, and spread with a bamboo yard at the top (as lug-sails); also with battens, or cross-pieces of lighter bamboo below, at the distance of two or three feet asunder, all the way down the sail, for the purpose of stretching and keeping it flat.

The halliards are rove through a block at the mast-head, and the yard is slung in the usual way as for a lug-sail. The sail is also fitted with parrels, which keep it close to the mast from top to bottom, but yet allowing it to traverse freely up and down the mast.

The Sailing-Boat.

The sail is controlled by numerous guys of small rope and ratline, fastened to the yard end or peak of the sail and the extremities of the battens and aft-leech of the sail. These are all collected as a bridle, and after passing through small wooden blocks, ultimately terminate in a single rope or main-sheet, which is belayed upon deck. The rudder is large and capable of being raised or lowered, so as not to exceed the draft of the vessel in shallow water.

Although these Fast-boats are by no means strongly built, they are so light and buoyant as to be able to live at sea in the roughest weather, when strong, heavy vessels of the same size would probably be wrecked.

CHINESE FLOWER-BOATS.

'The barge she sat in, like a burnish'd throne
Burn'd on the water. The poop was beaten gold;
Purple the sails, and so perfumed that
The winds were love-sick with them. The oars were silver;
Which to the tune of flutes kept stroke, and made
The water, which they beat, to follow faster,
As amorous of their strokes.'

SHAKESPEARE.

THE 'Hwa-chow,' or Chinese Flower-boat, is one of the greatest ornaments to be seen on the waters of that country. On the Canton River they are called by the Chinese 'Wang Lau' or 'Fa-Shun'; and by foreigners 'Flower-boats': they are in reality floating Cafés, often richly decorated, and having stained-glass windows. They are illuminated at night by chandeliers of crystal and variegated lamps, and present a very gay and attractive appearance.[1]

The Chinese Flower-boats are the resort of citizens of the upper and middle classes; and when lighted up at night are visited by Chinese fast men and wealthy rakes of the city, who shape their course to them under covered sampans, by the great highway of the river. When once aboard they are secure from public intrusion, and there, in company with the pretty women who inhabit them, indulge in the luxuries of fragrant tea, tobacco, opium, choice wines and *liqueurs*—music, song, dance and mirth all lending their aid to influence the imagination.

On the roof of the Flower-boat vases and pots of choice and fragrant plants and flowers are tastefully arranged; and round and about them are pretty balconies communicating by flights of steps with the luxuriously fitted interior.

[1] *Vide* 'China,' by Archdeacon Gray, 1878, vol. ii. pp. 77, 78 and 272.

Chinese Boats.

At night, when lighted up with coloured lanterns, they are even more picturesque than by day—

> ' At the helm
> A seeming mermaid steers; the silken tackles
> Swell with the touches of those flower-soft hands,
> That yarely frame the office. From the barge
> A strange invisible perfume hits the sense
> Of the adjacent wharfs.' [1]

None but Chinese are admitted aboard these mysterious boats. On several occasions, when Europeans have attempted to obtain admittance they have been maltreated by the men aboard them.[2]

Tan-Poo Boats.—The boats called ' Tan-Poo ' or Bed-boats, are of a similar class to the Flower-boats, but smaller and less gorgeous; they have carved wooden window-shutters or venetians, which are painted a bright green and give a gay-looking appearance to the exterior.

MANDARIN BOATS.

THE Chinese mandarin boats are among the prettiest of all the river craft—very light, elegantly proportioned, fitted and ornamented with neat carving and fancy-work, and painted with exquisite taste—and the masts, sails, and rigging are quite in character with the hull.

On board each of these boats a mandarin is stationed, with about sixty or seventy soldiers under his charge, who, with the mandarin, live aboard the boat; and their office is to cruise about the river, and seize all the smugglers they can catch, as well as others who commit offences against the laws. These boats are well provided with weapons of war, and have, besides, several small swivel-guns.

The manner in which they are usually painted is as follows :—The upper part, outside, bright blue, and all the lower part snowy white. In the blue strake are oval port-holes for the oars; the latter are white, and the interior of the port-holes red. Sometimes as many as thirty oars are employed on each side of the boat.

The Mandarin boat is decked with a brown hard wood, which is kept bright and polished. The crew squat on the deck, but the mandarin sits at the stern on a handsome mat.

A light and elegant wooden roof, of Gothic form, is supported several feet above

---

[1] Shakespeare.

[2] *Vide* Dr. Downing's ' Fan-qui.' Also Power's ' China.' Mr. Power says :—' Mr. Thom, late Consul at Ningpo, trusting to his knowledge of the language, attempted to gratify his curiosity, and introduced himself in a Chinese garb; but he was detected and captured. He was stripped, and carried on a pole through the suburbs of Canton, exposed to all the insults of the crowd. The ill-usage he met with nearly cost him his life, and quite cured him of any desire to peer too closely into the ways of his neighbours.'

the deck by tall round pillars at each of the four corners. The interior of the roof is painted and ornamented with good taste. During the hottest weather in summer and the coldest in winter, the roof is covered with mats of paddy straw, neatly and regularly placed over the top, thereby giving it the appearance of a newly-thatched cottage roof.

The mandarin boat is fitted with two masts, and long tapering topmasts, ornamented with little flags, pennants, and golden balls. The sails are made of a very fine sort of matting, neatly sewn together, 'and are somewhat of the shape of an acute-angled triangle.'

From the ensign staff at the stern hangs a beautiful white flag, marked in the centre with bright scarlet devices.

At the stern there is a rail, somewhat similar to the tail-board of a hay-cart, projecting upwards in a slanting direction from the deck; which not only lengthens the vessel, but also serves as a cool reclining place.

These gay-looking boats are exceedingly pretty objects on the Chinese waters; and, as they pass swiftly up and down the rivers, are much admired by strangers.[1]

CLERK'S BOATS.

THESE, with the exception of the Flower boats, are the most ornamental of the Chinese boats. They are fair specimens of the floating houses of the upper classes of the Chinese people. A good deal of taste is displayed about them in lattice-work, carving and painting; the roof is ornamented with pots of choice flowers, and a coloured flag is hoisted at the stern. These boats are moved about with a pair of large oars, and sometimes a small sail is set above the roof of the building.[2]

[1] Downing's 'Fan-qui.' Power's 'Three Years' Residence in China,' &c.

[2] For a full and more detailed description of these remarkable floating residences, see the 'Fan-qui,' by Dr. Downing, vol. i. p. 160.

Chinese Boats.

HOPPO'S BOAT.

Hoppo's Boat.

THE engraving above will more clearly illustrate the superior kind of house-boat used by the middle class of Chinese people.

The Hoppo's boats are, in fact, a kind of wooden house raised upon the floor of the boat, having the entrance at the bows. This entrance is, in some of the boats, carved in a most superb style, forming a prelude to what may be seen within. At night numerous lanterns are suspended from the roof of the cabins; looking-glasses, pictures, and poetry adorn their sides, and the peculiarities of this singular people may be discovered in these their floating palaces.[1]

FISHER-BOATS.

SOME of the Chinese fishing-boats are remarkably fine and powerful boats, and, in point of form and sailing qualities, are infinitely superior to the junks and larger craft. It is usual for each fisher-boat, or pair of boats, to be the only home and habitation of a whole family, who rely for support entirely on their own exertions and success in fishing.

Clumsy, slow and ugly as are the junks and larger vessels, there is nowhere to be seen finer fishing boats, or river craft better adapted for work, or of greater variety of build.[2]

Fishing is a calling that is exercised by the Chinese with great industry, and on a scale almost unexampled. The pursuit is conducted not so much on the open sea, amid tempest and peril; but by numerous individuals in the lower ranks, whose boats are their only abode, and who spend their lives and find their support upon the waters.[3]

[1] See Fortune's 'China,' vol. i. p. 121 (3rd ed.).   [2] Power's 'China.'
[3] Crawfurd and Murray's 'China.'   Barrow's 'Travels.

They do not venture very far upon dangerous seas, but pursue their avocations chiefly on the lakes, rivers, and sheltered bays of the empire—forming as it were, a nation by themselves.

They are, however, often exposed to great risk; and after all their hardihood and enterprise, they have much difficulty in providing themselves with the actual necessaries of life, and most of what they do obtain is by barter.

DRAGON-BOATS.[1]

THE Chinese Dragon-boats are so called from their resemblance to a dragon. The prow of a dragon-boat is in the form of a dragon's head and neck, and the stern is made to represent the tail. These boats are of a very long and narrow form, some of them from 60 ft. to 70 ft., and only 4 ft. or 5 ft. in width. The prow, stern, and gunwales are hung around with gold and silver fringe; and they are among the lightest, longest, and gayest-looking of any of the Chinese boats.

The festival of Dragon-boats is observed during the fifth moon, in honour of Kieuh-yuen, a virtuous statesman, who is said to have drowned himself during the dynasty of Chau (about 2,300 years since), to avoid the displeasure of his Sovereign. The festival, which lasts several days, is kept on all the rivers of the empire. On the occasion of the celebration, each boat is manned by sixty to eighty men with paddles in their hands, who stand in a double row in the boat. The steersman—surrounded by several others whose duty it is to assist him when any difficulty in the navigation arises—is conspicuous in the stern, grasping a long scull that projects far out over the stern. Any ordinary rudder would be of little service with a boat of this kind, when manned by so numerous a crew.

At the festival (which is observed with great rejoicings throughout the eighteen provinces of China) the Dragon-boats assemble at a particular place on the river. When the sports begin, the men in each boat stand with the paddles in their hands poised in the air, ready for immediate action. At a given signal every man's paddle is instantly brought down into the water; and the excitement becomes intense. The rhythmic motion of the men is the more conspicuous because of their standing to their work; and the regularity with which they stoop when they dip their paddles to propel the boat ahead, makes these Dragon-boats look like gigantic centipedes, which under the influence of terror, are using their numerous legs to escape from some imminent peril. The spectators gaze with absorbed attention upon the competitors as they lash

---

[1] Nieuhoff's 'China.' Du Halde's 'China.'

the water into foam, and incite each other by shouts to the exertion of all their powers.[1] After the races, the boats are buried in mud or sand, to prevent their becoming warped and spoiled, where they remain until the following year.

The festival is principally kept up by the different public officers, who frequently stake considerable sums of money on their boats.[2]

CENTIPEDES, OR SMUG-BOATS.

THESE are the boats of the Chinese smugglers. They are called 'centipedes' from the great number of oars employed in calm weather, each of which is looped to a bamboo thowl-pin; and so silently do they creep about at night, that they seem, as it were, to walk the waters with their oars as if upon so many legs. They are also termed by the mandarins 'fast crabs' and 'scrambling dragons,'[3] terms by no means inappropriate, for it is seldom the mandarins are able to overtake and capture them.[4]

But these boats are not always propelled by oars; some of them are rigged with two masts and mat sails, similar in shape to those of the mandarin boats, but of a coarser material. They are large, flat-looking, decked boats, with considerable breadth of beam, and very smooth bottoms; they have also high bulwarks, with weapons of war lashed inside—and all are provided with a house or covering, made of common bamboo-tiles and matting. They have high sterns, and a tail-board similar to a mandarin's boat; which, without the elegancies, they resemble. No bright-coloured paint is bestowed upon them; on the contrary, they present a dull brown-coloured appearance. They are strongly built, and whether under sail or oars are very fast. The fellows who man them are usually a desperate set; and as to mandarins, customs' officers and others, they sometimes set them all at defiance. A small fleet of these boats has been known to frighten and drive off all the Government boats, and then attack and pillage Canton itself.[5]

[1] See an interesting account, with a photographic illustration of the festival of the Dragon boats, in 'Pictures of Southern China,' by Rev. J. Macgowan, (1897), p. 288; see also Gray's 'China,' vol. i. p. 259.
[2] 'Chinese Repository,' vol. xx. p. 89 (1851).
[3] A new class are called 'Muscle-shell boats' (*vide* 'Chinese Repository,' vol. i. p. 159).
[4] Downing's 'Fan-qui.' Power's 'China,' &c.
[5] Power's 'China.'

The Sailing-Boat.

DUCK BOATS.

THE duck boats must be ranked among the curiosities of Chinese craft. They are large flat-bottomed boats, with low sides, and a house erected upon them. They have a broad deck, or duck-walk, covered with lattice-work, extending the whole length of the vessel on each side of the covered parts.

The aft, or best part of the house is given up to the accommodation of the ducks; whilst the proprietor, with his wife and family, content themselves with a less com-

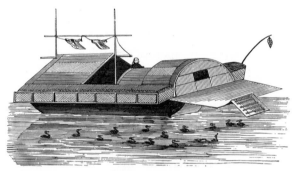

Chinese Duck Boat.

modious apartment at the fore part. In the morning, at sunrise, the doors of these floating duckeries are thrown open, and the feathered occupants are then permitted to waddle around the premises at their pleasure.

Stepping-boards are also let down at the sides, and at the fore part of the boat, towards the water on one side, and towards the land on the other. Up and down these the ducks waddle to and fro, as inclination dictates, or their watchful owner directs. At roost time, they are called aboard the boat by a whistle, to the sound of which they are taught to return home; and when they are all on board, the stepping-boards are drawn up, and the birds are then made secure for the night.

TANKEA BOATS.

THE tankeä, or egg-house boats, are probably more numerous than those of any other class. They are generally not more than 12 ft. or 15 ft. long, and about 6 ft. broad— some of them much smaller. They are the oddest things of the kind ever seen, being flat-bottomed, wall-sided, and very shallow, the gunwale standing only about 6 in. above the surface.

526

Chinese Boats.

In the middle of the boat is a little house or covered cabin, consisting merely of matting spread over half-hoops, or lattice-work, forming a sort of archway; the interior is also lined with matting.[1] They are kept very clean, and are each managed by two Chinese girls.

BARBERS' BOATS.

These are among the very smallest of all Chinese boats. They are about 8 ft. to 10 ft. long, and just wide enough at the stern to admit the body of the Chinese barber, whilst his legs are stretched forward towards the bows; and in order to trim the little craft, a large stone is placed in the bows to keep the proper bearings.

The barber propels his little boat with a wooden paddle, shaped like a spade, with this he moves among the shipping, digging his way and attracting the attention of his customers by every now and then striking a flat piece of metal with a small steel instrument like a musical fork, with the notes of which all who have visited Chinese ports are familiar.

Dr. Downing, in the 'Fan-qui,' says of these curious little boats :—' In leaning over the side of the poop, on a clear fine day, protected from the burning heat of the sun by the awning spread above you, you will frequently hear a sound like that of a large grasshopper, or the striking of a musical fork, proceeding from the water. On looking about to discover the cause, you see a Chinaman dressed in a blue frock, with one of the great umbrella-hats on his head, directly under your eye. This is the barber in his boat, who, at the same time, turns up his head to see if he has attracted any customers.'

WASH BOATS.

These remarkable boats, which are in great numbers at Whampoa and other places, are each under the control and occupation of three or four Chinese girls, who scarcely ever leave them to go ashore throughout the whole year, unless to attend the ghosh-house. They are about 20 ft. in length, and of proportionate breadth, with square or cropped ends, and flat bottoms. They are managed by two oars, one at the side and one at the stern ; the inside of the boat is decked, or covered over with boards, many of which are removable at pleasure, so as to form extensive cupboards between the deck and flat bottom of the boat. In addition to the deck, there is also a house or roof, raised above

[1] 'Chinese Repository,' vol. i.

the gunwales, and supported by wooden pillars. The roof or covering is composed of a rough kind of matting, formed of thin pieces of bamboo woven together and arched, and supported on ribs of stiffer portious of the bamboo. Two or three of these coverings are placed upon the framework, one portion overlapping the other, and the whole forming a very good protection from the sun and weather. During cold or wet weather, the interior of this remarkable domicile is hung with a lining of rough cloth; and every night, or whenever the inmates seek privacy, the open front of the house is closed with a curtain of matting or cloth. The interior is also provided with a square of matting and a wooden pillow for each inmate. The author of the 'Fan-qui' says: 'The meanest beggar in England would shrink from being confined to such a place, yet these girls seem not only content, but even cheerful and happy; their red, good-natured faces are to be seen peeping out of the matting, and always with a smile or a laugh at your service.'

They apparently get their living by washing clothes for the sailors and petty-officers of ships; they also undertake needlework and mending for any of the crew, always remaining with their boat fast to the ship until the articles are returned.

CANAL CARGO BOATS.

THE 'Tsaou-chuen,' or Canal cargo boat, is much employed for the conveyance of grain on the coast and up the canals as far as Pekin. The Chinese government is said to possess many thousands of them. Their average burthen is about 2,000 peculs (or above 100 tons); they are flat-bottomed, high out of the water, and have the appearance of a much greater capacity than they possess. They chiefly sail up from the southern provinces during the fourth moon, or about June, when the monsoon is favourable; and return in the ninth moon, or November.

When the wind is foul, the canal boats are propelled by a class of men called 'trackers,' who, for a trifling remuneration, are compelled by poverty to perform the part which horses act in other countries—that of towing the vessel ahead by means of a rope, which is laid across the shoulders of the men. The work they have to perform is very laborious; besides which, they are frequently obliged to wade across small rivulets and delfs of mud whilst towing the vessels against a rapid current and foul wind.

Japanese Boats.

BOATS OF THE KWEIKONG.

THE boats of the Kweikong, or Cassia River, in China, are of a different form and construction to those seen at Canton. They have flat bottoms, and curve up high at the bow and stern, the object apparently being that the helmsman and the man on look-out forward may be placed in elevated positions, so as to see some distance ahead and avoid the rocks in the course of their navigation of the boat down river with the rapid current.[1]

The Cassia River abounds in rapids and shallows, so that, on ascending it, the crew have constantly to be dragging the boat over obstructions, notwithstanding that it draws only about five or six inches of water.

JAPANESE BOATS.

THE sailing-vessels of Japan are curious and different in some respects to those of any other nation. First among their peculiarities is the high stem-post, which peers above the deck, and higher than the level of the roof of the cabin, or rather range of cabins, which extend nearly from end to end over the whole vessel. The

Japanese Cargo Boat.

form of the hull is tapering from the middle towards the stem. The stern is the most peculiar part about them, being broad and flat, and provided with a wide opening, extending in some boats more than half-way down to the water's edge and laying open to view the inside of the vessel. It is supposed that this opening was originally intended for the management of the rudder, but was afterwards forced upon the people by a penal law of the State.[2] But whether or not this law be still in force, it is a fact that the aperture at the stern remains in most Japanese vessels, and is used to considerable advantage for the landing of goods, and as a

[1] See 'Sketch of a Journey from Canton to Hankow,' by Albert S. Bickmore, 1868.
[2] Kæmpfer's 'History of Japan,' translated by Scheuchzer; vide also Belcher's 'Voyages.'

means of access for the crew to and from the vessel—the rudder being unshipped and employed as a bridge over the space between the wharf and the vessel. When lying in port, the rudder is triced up, in the manner represented in the engraving.

The mast is stepped abaft the middle of the vessel, and in a slightly aft-raking position. It depends for security almost entirely on a powerful stay, and is fitted so as to be raised and lowered with pulleys : when lowered, it is stowed away above the cabin roof, on bearers provided for the purpose, as shown in the engraving.

The deck-way consists simply of boards, laid loosely over the bearers, without any fastening ; but it is almost entirely covered with the cabin-roof, which stands nearly six feet high. The fore part of the deck is clear, for the anchor and cable. In wet weather, and at night, the mast is lowered, and the sail is spread over it, from end to end, as a shelter. The watermen's benches, for rowing, are towards the stern. The stem is usually adorned with a knot of fringes, black strings, or hair.

In the common mode of rigging, parts of the sails are made to lace and unlace, so that they are reduced instead of being reefed, by unlacing and removing some of the lower strips of canvas. In the larger vessels the sails are divided into many parts in this manner ; and, as the outer cords are securely attached to their bolt-ropes, the middle cloths must be those that are removed by reefing. The Japanese vessels are not wanting in sailing qualities, if properly fitted with light spars and canvas, but they are crippled by the enormous mast that is put into them.

JAPANESE PLEASURE BOATS.

THE pleasure-boats of Japan are a very numerous class, exhibiting a variety almost equal to those of China. The size, shape, and finish of these boats depend on the taste,

Japanese Pleasure Boat.

wealth and dignity of the owners. They are, however, generally contrived for rowing rather than sailing.

Japanese Boats.

The class of large boats have upper and lower decks and cabins. The upper one is the principal, being of lofty dimensions with handsome decorations, windows and folding screens, and so divided into several partitions; the under cabin is low and is the one used by the crew.

The prow of the principal boats is generally ornamented with a tassel of long black strings; and when persons of distinction are on board them, the cabin is hung about with cloths on which their armorial bearings are embroidered.

Japanese boats are kept scrupulously clean, though unpainted, and they are generally gaily decorated with flags of various shades and colours; even the coast-guard boats being so adorned. The crews of the latter are usually all dressed alike; and the boats are propelled with sculls, which they use as oars, the rowers keeping time to a monotonous song.

JAPANESE FISHING BOATS.

THE fishing boats of Japan are also curious, though very well built. They have sharp bows, a large projecting stem-piece, or cut-water, in shape like the blade of a large knife, very broad open sterns, and large rudder, which hangs below the keel or

Japanese Fishing Boat.

bottom of the vessel, and can be shipped and unshipped at pleasure. The rudder is placed in a cramped position, and can only be turned to a limited extent on either side. These boats have flat upper sides, and flat bottoms, but rounded lower sides, and broad sterns.

The mast is a lofty one, and, as in other vessels of Japan, is stepped, not in the fore part of the boat but in the aft part, about a third or more from the stern. The thwarts are fitted across the boat, resting upon the top of the gunwales; the ends of the thwarts project beyond the sides, and a thowl-pin is fixed upon and near the extremities. The oars they employ are peculiar, being composed of two separate pieces—one a long straight blade, of the same width throughout; the other, the handle, which is about two or three feet in length, and bends or inclines inwards, for the apparent purpose of obtaining extra leverage in rowing.

The Sailing-Boat.

JAPANESE PASSAGE-BOATS.

THESE boats have a similar kind of stem-piece, or cut-water, to that of the fishing boats above described. They have, besides, a prettily-formed wooden canopy, erected on four small pillars, and extending over the fore and centre parts of the boat.

The stern of the Japanese passage-boat is open, like the other vessels. Their mode of propulsion is by a very long oar or sculling-sweep at the stern.

There are good models of Japanese fishing and passage-boats of the class above described in the United Service Museum.

The sails of Japanese boats are very singular, and somewhat picturesque, consisting generally of three cloths of sail canvas or matting, united by a kind of lace-work, and thus forming one whole sail. It has a pretty effect, and the connected parts can be unlaced, and so one or more taken in when necessary.[1]

The Japanese junks, though strange looking vessels, are by no means so heavy as those of the Chinese.

Their plain wooden sides, with the exception of a narrow band of black or red, about half-way down, are entirely innocent of paint.[2]

ARCTIC REGIONS.

GREENLAND BOATS—THE OOMIAK.

THE boats chiefly used by the Greenlanders are of two sorts—the Oomiak (or umiak), which is the women's boat; and the other, the Kaiak, or kajak (also sometimes spelt 'kayak'), which is the men's boat. The lightest and smallest kajaks are those they use in their seal-hunting, fowling and fishing pursuits.

The Oomiak, or women's boat, is considerably the larger of the two, and is commonly from 14 ft. to 20 ft. in length, and of a proportionate breadth and depth, varying from 4 ft. to 6 ft. in width, and from $2\frac{1}{2}$ ft. to 4 ft. in depth. Oomiaks are all flat-bottomed; the prows and sterns of some of them being sharp and pointing upwards; others are bluff, or even square, and have two projecting arms at each end, like a bier.

The form and construction of the Oomiak are remarkable; the bottom consists of three main beams; the principal one forming the middle part of the boat—as a keelson,

---

[1] 'A Lady's Visit to Manilla and Japan,' by Anna D'A. (1863).
[2] *Ibid.*, p. 223.

and the others, one on each side, are bent so as to meet at each end ; upon these beams thin cross-pieces are morticed; stout ribs are then affixed to the outer beams, and secured at the top to the gunwale, and also to a second or lower beam, to which the rowing-benches are attached; and in this manner a good strong framework is got up, though all are secured with wooden rivets and whalebone bands. When the skeleton of the boat is completed, the men's work is done, and the women commence theirs, by covering the whole with newly-dressed seal skins, which are as soft and pliable as chamois leather ; and they caulk the seams with grease, and finish off their work neatly, making the boat perfectly water-tight. In fact, with careful handling, they are not so liable to leak as wooden ones.

They take them out of the water when not in use; and when in the water the stitches swell as soon as wetted and fill up any slight leakage which when dry might exist. If they accidentally rip a hole in the boat, they directly do it up by patching a piece of soft seal skin over the place; but they handle their boats with so much care that they are seldom injured ; and almost every year they renew the outer covering of the boat.

Lieutenant Hooper, in his ' Arctic Boat Expedition in Search of Sir John Franklin,' mentions having often made use of these oomiaks ; and with reference to one which he purchased, he observes :—' We purchased an oomiak (woman's or family boat), made of two walrus skins sewed together, and stretched tightly over a light wooden frame, with paddles complete. Its price was a large butcher's knife, a looking-glass, and a quantity of tobacco and beads.' * * * * * ' Workmanship was displayed in the manufacture of her frame which would not have disgraced a skilful carpenter ; it was particularly neat and well fitted, which made it much stronger than its lightness would lead one to suppose.'

These boats (oomiaks) are rowed and managed entirely by women, generally five to each boat, four of whom ply the oars or paddles, and one steers. The men never interfere in the management of the oomiak, except in case of danger, as in heavy seas.

The oars they use are short, but broad in the blade, and of a shovel-like shape ; they are secured to their place on the gunwale by straps of skin. In fair winds they use a small square-sail, which they hoist from a mast they set up in the fore part of the boat ; the sail is generally made of skins from the intestines of fish and animals. Some boats of the more wealthy or trading Greenlanders, have sails made of white linen striped with red.

In these oomiaks the Greenland women sometimes perform voyages of many miles along the coast, carrying with them their tents, goods, family and whole substance ; but on these long voyages the men keep with them near at hand in their kajaks ; and in heavy seas they attend the oomiak very cautiously, sheltering it from the heaviest waves, and holding the gunwales to keep it upon a balance. They frequently travel as many as twelve leagues a day in these boats; and every evening, when they halt they go ashore, unload their boats and draw them to land, turn them upside down, and load the beams fore and aft with stones, that the wind may not blow them away. When they come to any difficult or impassable part of the coast, they carry the boat on their heads overland to more navigable water.

THE KAIAK, KAJAK, OR KYAK.

THE kaiak, which is a marvel of the toil, ingenuity and enterprise of an outlandish and illiterate people, is used by the native Greenlanders chiefly for seal hunting and fish spearing. It would be difficult, if not impossible, for the most ingenious and scientific of European boat-builders, with twenty years or more experience in their art, to make a boat so admirably adapted to the purpose as the native kaiak. Buoyancy, lightness, safety, speed, and adaptability to the seas and purposes for which it is required, are the chief characteristics of the Greenlander's kaiak.

The kaiak is formed of a light framework of wood, covered externally with skins; as a rule with the skin of the saddleback seal, or of the bladder-nose or hood seal. The latter is not so durable or so water-tight as the former. Those who can afford it use the skin of the bearded seal, which is the best and strongest.[1]

The kaiak has no keel, but its underpart at both ends is generally fitted with bone flanges, designed to save the skin outer-covering from being ripped or damaged by contact with floating ice. When completed the kaiak is so light that it may be carried by the kaiaker on his head, or even under his arm.

In the centre of the kaiak, on the top of the covering, is a circular hole formed with a rim or hoop of wood, through which the Greenlander slips his legs and body when about to proceed on his aquatic excursions. Having stretched his legs out under the covering, he finds a seat on a small board covered with soft skin; and in that position the rim reaches just above his hips. He then draws down the lower part of his water-pelt or seal-skin coat over the rim of the hole so that no spray or water can get inside the kaiak, though the spray should fly over him and well souse both boat and outer garment of its occupant; as it frequently does.

The coat is, at the same time, very closely folded and buttoned about his face, shoulders and arms, with bone buttons.

A kaiak for a Greenlander of average size measures, in the neighbourhood of Godthaab, about six yards in length. The greatest breadth of the kaiak at the front

---

[1] 'Eskimo Life,' by Fridtjof Nansen (trans. by Wm. Archer), 1893.

part of the circular hole is about 18 ins. or a little more, but it narrows considerably in the under part, towards the bottom; the depth is generally from 5 ins. to 6½ ins.[1]

In this fragile little craft the Greenlander passes the greater part of his daily life, and performs most of his ordinary and extraordinary sporting adventures, whereby he obtains food, sustenance and clothing for himself and family throughout the year.

On each side of the top of the kaiak he places his lances (consisting of an anguvigak and harpoons, bird arrows and shafts), and secures them under straps of leather, affixed for the purpose. In front of him lies the lance-line for seal-hunting, coiled on a small circular platform purposely fixed for it, and behind him he places the bladder, to which the extreme end of the lance-line is secured. The bladder

Greenlander's Kaiak.

floating upon the surface enables the Greenlander to follow the stricken seal and capture it.

His pautik, or double-bladed oar, is made of solid red pine, bound at each end of the blades with a thin plate, 2 ins. or 3 ins. in width; and it is further protected from the ice by the edges of the blades being inlaid with bone. So equipped, he is enabled to propel his little boat at great speed. He fears neither storms nor heavy seas; his kaiak is as light and buoyant as a cork. When a wave strikes it abroadside, he balances himself and his fragile craft with the pautik. And if he happens to be capsized (which is not a very uncommon occurrence), by a peculiar and difficult muscular exertion, to which the Greenland lads are trained from their youth, he swings his body by aid of the pautik, and rights himself and his kaiak in a moment, though he be turned over with boat bottom upwards. He keeps fast hold of the pautik, for if he loses or breaks it in a strong wind or heavy sea, his chance is almost hopeless, if far from shore or assistance.[2]

It is not by any means a simple and easy matter to sit a kaiak without capsizing; a good deal of practice is necessary before a firm seat can be obtained.

Altogether it is, beyond comparison, the best and most ingenious form of boat

[1] Dr. Nansen, 'Eskimo Life.'
[2] *Vide* Scheffer, 'De Militia Navali Veterum.' M. Hassæus, 'D. Leviathan Jobi.' Crantz, 'Greenland.' 'Ten Months among the Tents of the Tuski,' by Lieut. Hooper, R.N.

for the locality in which it is used, and for the purposes required, that could possibly be devised.[1]

Kajaks were employed by Sir Leopold M'Clintock and his party, for the purposes of shooting and fishing, when in the Arctic regions; and it appears they are used by pilots, as well as fishermen and seal-hunters. It is stated in M'Clintock's narrative that, when passing Godhaven, the pilot was launched off the deck of the *Fox* in his little kayak, without stopping the ship, and without the addition of a capsize—a feat which it would be difficult for an Englishman to perform in any boat of English construction.

ESQUIMAUX CANOES.

THESE very fragile boats are similar in many respects to the kajaks of the Greenlanders. They are made of seal and walrus skins stretched over a light framework of

Esquimaux Canoe, and section.

wood, and they are entirely covered over at the top, with the exception of a circular hole, higher at the back than in front, to admit the body of the occupant.

It would appear to be almost impossible for any kind of boat to be of lighter form, and they are propelled with ease and rapidity by the native Esquimaux, who use for the purpose a double-bladed oar, like the Greenlander's pautik.

LABRADOR CANOES.

THERE is a great similarity between these canoes and those of the Esquimaux, with the exception that they have not such high-peering ends at stem and stern as the latter have. In other respects they are nearly identical, being built in the same way, and with the same sort of materials. Some of them are large enough to carry two or three persons, a separate hole being formed in the top for each occupant.

[1] In Dr. Nansen's 'Eskimo Life,' p. 44, are illustrations of the frame-work and deck-plan of the Kaiak; with a description of the mode of building, the manner of seal hunting, harpooning, &c., and illustrations of the pursuit.

Boats of the Arctic Regions.

TCHUKTCHI SKIN CANOES.

THESE primitive canoes are, in fact, the counterpart of the Greenland 'Oomiak.' The natives of Tchuktchi have no wood wherewith to build either huts or boats. Their tents, as well as their boats, are composed chiefly of a framework of the large bones of whales and walrus, covered over with skins of the walrus, seal, and reindeer, and yet both tents and boats are admirably constructed.

On each side of the skin canoe they usually fasten a seal-skin, blown out full of

Tchuktchi Skin Canoe.

air, with the ends firmly secured. These serve as floats, or safety-buoys, when the canoe heels over.

Some of these skin boats are of large size, fitted with rudder, mast, and large square-sail, and capable of carrying two tons or more of merchandise. Even an ordinary-sized skin canoe will carry five persons, with tent, blankets, cooking utensils, provisions, &c.[2]

In the cold, icy regions in which these canoes are employed, it is often absolutely necessary for one of the crew to stand at the bows with a pole, shod with iron, to push aside the masses of drift-ice and tangle of driftage which intercept the navigation. But withal a skin boat has its advantages. The tough, flexible skin will *give* for several inches without necessarily tearing, and will stand more wear and tear than the cedar canoes of British Columbia.

Skin canoes, quite open, capable of containing twenty or more persons with their effects, and hoisting several masts and sails, are now frequently to be observed among both the sea-coast Tchuktchis and the inhabitants of Northern Alaska, and occasionally

[1] 'Travel and Adventure in Alaska,' by F. Whymper (1868), p. 89.
[2] *Ibid.*, p. 196.

<
<

others which might be called 'full-rigged' canoes, carrying main, gaff, and sprit-sails; but these are probably recent and foreign innovations.[1]

A smaller-sized skin boat is used for the purposes of the chase, such as seal and walrus hunting, and also for capturing the reindeer when driven or hunted into the water. These are light but very tough, being composed of walrus skins, which are beautifully prepared and sewn over a light frame-work of bone or wood. They are flat-bottomed, and nearly wall-sided, about 3 ft. 6 ins. in breadth at the widest part of the gunwales, and about 2 ft. 6 ins. below, decreasing in width at the ends, which are just wide enough to admit a man's body. The top rim is neatly worked over with strips of hide or whalebone. They are propelled with great speed by hand-paddles, which are also used in bow and stern to direct their course. The smooth surface of the walrus skin offers little resistance to their passage through the water; and they are carefully preserved from any incrustation, being carried on shore when not in use, turned over, and beaten with stout sticks, to drive off the moisture and keep the skin in shape, as it would otherwise be liable to bag.[2]

BOATS OF KAMTSCHATKA.

THE Kamtschatkans have two sorts of boats—one is called *koaihtahta* and the other *tahta*. The former is very similar to an English Peter-boat, except that the prow and stern are higher, and the sides lower.[3]

The tahta has the prow and stern of an equal height; the sides are not rounded outwards, as in most boats, but rather incline inwards at the midships; consequently they are very unsafe, and soon fill and swamp in rough water.

The Kamtschatka boats are built chiefly of poplar-wood.

BAIDARS.

THE boats of the Kurilski Islands and Lopatka are called *baidars*. These are built with a keel similar to an English boat, with the exception that the planks are sewn

---

[1] 'Travel and Adventure in Alaska,' p. 249.
[2] 'Ten Months among the Tents of the Tuski, with Incidents of an Arctic Boat Expedition in Search of Sir J. Franklin,' by Lieut. W. H. Hooper, R.N.
[3] 'History of Kamtschatka.' Translated by Dr. Grieve (1764).

together, and the seams caulked with moss. The Kuriles have no proper wood for boat-building, except that derived from wreckage drifted ashore by the sea. In transporting their goods to and from these islands, they usually lash two Baidars together, and form a sort of platform across them, on which they carry the goods safer and drier. The northern inhabitants of Kamtschatka—the settled Koreki and Tchuktcha—for want of proper timber and plank, make their Baidars of the skins of sea-animals stretched on poles.

END OF PART VIII.

PART IX.

———

NAUTICAL VOCABULARY.

Aft, Abaft, or **Astern.**—Towards the stern of a vessel.

A-lee.—The side opposite to the wind; the situation of the helm when in an opposite direction to that from which the wind blows.

Amidships.—Any part of the middle of a vessel with regard to her length and breadth.

Athwart-hawse.—Across the direction of a vessel's head, under the bow-sprit.

Athwart-ships.—Across a vessel from side to side.

A-weather.—On the weather side, or towards the wind; the situation of the helm when in the same direction as that from which the wind blows—opposed to *A-lee*.

Back-stays.—Ropes or stays extending from the mast-head to the sides of the vessel, abaft the mast.

Beam.—The width of a vessel at the widest part.

Bear.—To *bear-up* is to turn a vessel from the wind, by putting the helm up, or towards the quarter from which the wind blows. To *bear-down* is to pursue a vessel from a windward quarter.

Bearings.—The lower part of a vessel, or that which is below the water line when in proper trim.

Becket.—A short piece of rope, with a loop at one end and a knot at the other, used for confining a spar or rope in a convenient place.

Belay.—To make a rope fast to a cleat by two or more turns without hitching it.

Bend.—To make fast: to *bend a sail* is to attach it to the mast or yard by lashings or otherwise.

Berth.—A sleeping apartment aboard a vessel. A safe anchorage is termed a good berth.

Bight.—A noose or folded part of a rope: any part may be called the bight, excepting the ends.

Bilge.—The protuberant part of a cask: the breadth of a vessel's bottom, or that part on which a vessel rests when lying aground on her side.

Binnacle.—A box containing a mariner's compass.

Bitts.—Perpendicular pieces passing through the deck on each side the heel of the bowsprit: the cable is generally made fast to the bitts, if there is no windlass.

Board.—The distance a vessel goes upon any one tack when beating to windward. The mast of a vessel is said to go by *the board* when it snaps off and falls over the bulwarks. To *make a good board* is to sail a long distance in a straight line when close-hauled. To *make short boards* is to tack frequently.

Bobstay.—A small chain or rope attached to the lower part of the stem of the boat to keep the outer end of the bowsprit down.

Bolsters.—Pieces of soft wood tacked on each side of the mast above the cheeks, on which the eyes of the shrouds rest.

Boom.—A spar used to spread the foot of the main-sail.

Nautical Vocabulary.

Boomkin.—A small iron bowsprit to which the tack of the fore-sail is hooked in a small boat.

Boom-rest.—A shifting iron of the same shape as an iron rowlock, in which the outer end of the boom is laid when the sails are furled.

Bowline.—A rope used in square-rigged vessels for holding out the leech when sailing close-hauled. Sailing on a bowline is when the wind is on the quarter and the sheet is not close-hauled.

Bowse.—To pull or haul on a rope or a tackle.

Bowsprit-shrouds.—Ropes on each side for protecting the bowsprit.

Brails.—Ropes connected with the throat of a sail, by which the canvas is drawn up close to the mast or yard.

Breakers.—Waves of white spray denoting shallow water ; also a small cask containing water.

Bridle.—A rope is called a bridle when the two ends are made fast to the leeches or yard ends of a sail.

Broadside.—The side of a vessel lengthwise.

Bulk-head.—A temporary partition separating different parts of a vessel.

Bull's-eye.—A piece of wood the shape of a block, but with a hole in the centre for a rope to reeve through, and without a sheave ; also a thick piece of glass for a cabin light.

Bulwarks.—The boarding round the sides of a vessel above the deck.

Bumkin.—(*See* **Boomkin**).

Bum-boats.—Boats which attend alongside vessels with provisions, fruit, &c.

Bunting.—Woollen stuff for making flags.

Cable.—A large rope for holding a vessel at anchor. A ship's cable is usually 120 fathoms, or 720 feet, in length.

Camber-deck.—A slightly arched deck, which facilitates the running off of water coming on deck.

Carry away.—To break a spar or rope.

Carvel-built.—A vessel is carvel-built when the planks are laid in smoothly, and not lapped over, as in clench, or clincher-built vessels.

Cat-heads.—Strong timbers projecting from the bows of vessels, to which the anchor is secured when heaved up.

Cat's-paw.—A very light current of air occasionally felt during a calm.

Caulk.—To fill the seams of a vessel with oakum.

Channels.—Strong pieces of wood attached to a vessel's side, to which the shrouds or rigging are secured.

Cheeks.—Small carved projections on each side the mast, upon which the tressel-trees rest.

Chinse.—To fill the deck seams with oakum, and serve them over with melted resin.

Clamp.—A mast-clamp is an iron for securing a boat's mast to the thwart.

Cleat.—A small iron or wooden pin for belaying ropes to.

Clench or Clincher-built.—When the planking of a vessel is lapped over, similar to weather-boarding.

Clew.—The lower corner of a square-sail, and the after or outer corner of a fore-and-aft sail. To *clew-up* is to haul up the clew.

Clew-garnet.—A rope used in square-rigged vessels for hauling up the clew of a sail.

Close-hauled.—When the sheets are hauled in close, and the sail set as flat as possible.

Comb-cleat.—A comb-shaped cleat fitted to the outer end of the boom, one on each side, through which the reef-pendant is passed on hauling down a reef in the main-sail.

Companion-way.—The staircase leading to and from the cabin.

Crank, or Cranky.—Not stiff. A vessel is said to be crank when inclined to roll on her side, or when unable to carry much canvas.

Cringle.—A short piece of rope worked grommet-fashion into the bolt-rope of a sail, and containing a metal ring or thimble.

Cross-trees.—Iron or wooden pieces secured to the mast above the cheeks, for steadying and spreading the topmast-shrouds.

The Sailing-Boat.

Crown.—To crown a knot is to pass the strands over and under, so as to form a crown above the knot.

Cuddy.—A small cabin in the fore part of a boat.

Cutwater.—A sharp projection forward of the vessel's bows.

Davit.—A projection of wood or iron over a vessel's side with a sheave in the end, used for hoisting up boats. A *fish-davit* is a short spar, with a sheave in the end, used for fishing the anchor.

Dead-eye.—A small solid circular block, with three holes through it for the lanyards of rigging to reeve through ; they are used instead of blocks.

Dead-water.—The eddy under a vessel's counter.

Doubled-banked.—When two rowers sit upon the same thwart.

Douse.—To lower a sail suddenly.

Down-haul, or **Down-hauler.**—A rope attached to the peak-end, or other top part of the sails, for hauling down.

Draft.—The depth of water required for a vessel to float in.

Drive.—To drift down a tideway or scud before the wind.

Drum-head.—The top of a capstan.

Earing.—A rope attached to the aft-leech-thimble of a sail, for bending the sail to the boom-end, or for reefing purposes.

Eye.—A loop in the end of a rope or stay.

Fender, or **Fend-off.**—A soft substance of rope or tow covered with canvas, used for hanging over the side of a vessel, to protect it from striking or chafing when alongside.

Fid.—A sort of thumb-cleat attached to a loop of cord or ratline ; it is used for expedition in reeving through the thimbles of ropes and sails, as for holding the fore-sheets to the clew of the sail.

Fish-Davit.—(*See* **Davit.**)

Flukes.—That part of an anchor which holds in the ground, forming the arms and flat triangular tips.

Flying-Jib.—The sail set above and beyond the jib.

Fore-and-Aft.—From stem to stern. A fore-and-aft rigged vessel has no square-sails.

Forecastle (pronounced 'foaks'l').—A small cabin before the mast, in the bows of a vessel ; called in yachts, the galley.

Fore-gripe.—An additional piece secured to the lower part of a vessel's stem.

Fore-reach.—To pass a vessel when close-hauled and on the same tack.

Fore-sail.—The sail next before the main-sail.

Fore-stay.—A rope leading from the top of the mast and secured to the stem of the boat.

Founder.—To fill with water and sink.

Frap.—To pass a lashing round a sail to prevent it from blowing about.

Full-and-by.—Sailing close to the wind without shaking any part of the sails.

Furl.—To roll up a sail close to the yard and secure it with lashings.

Gaff.—The top spar of a cutter's main-sail.

Galley.—A long-shaped boat ; also the forecastle aboard a yacht.

Gammon.—An iron hoop or ring by the side of a vessel's stem, through which the bowsprit is run out.

Gangway.—An opening in a vessel's bulwarks, for convenience of getting from the vessel to a boat.

Garboard-strake.—The strake or planking of a vessel nearest the keel on each side.

Gaskets.—Pieces of plaited yarn, used for lashings when the sail is furled.

Nautical Vocabulary.

Goose-neck.—An iron joint connecting the boom with the mast.

Goose-winged.—A term applied to schooners or vessels with two masts, when running before the wind with sails boomed out on each side.

Gores.—Angles at one or both ends of such cloths as increase the width of the sail ; goring-cloths are sometimes added when a sail is required with a narrow head and wide foot.

Grapnel.—A kind of anchor, with four or more claws or barbs, used for securing the earings of fishing nets when spread in the water.

Grommet.—A rope ring, much used in boats and ships ; it is formed by laying round a single strand of rope.

Ground-tackle.—Consists of anchors, cables, &c. : anything used for anchoring and securing a vessel at anchor.

Guntackle-purchase.—A rope working through two single-blocks.

Gunwale, or Gunnel.—The inside rim leading from stem to stern on each side the boat, and to which the top strake is nailed.

Guy.—A rope for steadying a spar or boom, and for keeping it in its place.

Halliards, Halyards, or Haulyards.—Ropes or tackles used for hoisting and lowering sails.

Hatchway.—The opening in a vessel's deck, leading to the cabin or hold.

Hatches.—Shifting boards fitting over the hold of a vessel.

Hawse.—An iron rail fixed across the deck at the stern for securing the main-sheet to its berth.

Hawser.—A large rope for securing a vessel either at anchor or otherwise.

Head-sails.—Sails used before the mast, as fore-sail and jib.

Heave-short.—To heave the vessel close up to or over the anchor, by drawing in the cable.

Heave-to (*also* **Lay-to**).—To haul the fore-sail to windward, so that the vessel makes little or no headway.

Helm.—The tiller or wheel by which a vessel is steered.

Hold.—The interior of a vessel, where the cargo is placed.

Horns (also called **Jaws**).—That part of the gaff to which the trucks are attached, and which fits close to the mast.

Hounds.—The shoulders at the mast-head, where the tressel-trees rest.

Housed.—The top-mast is housed when lowered down and secured at the heel by a lashing.

Housing-line.—A small cord used for seizings.

Hull.—The body of a vessel.

Jaws (*see also* **Horns**).—Gaff-ends hollowed out to fit the masts.

Jib.—A triangular sail set out on the bowsprit in front of the fore-sail.

Jib-boom.—A spar rigged out beyond the bowsprit.

Jigger.—A small tackle for hoisting or hauling.

Jumper-stay.—An iron bar used in vessels with two masts, connecting one with the other at the top.

Jury-rig.—A temporary rig when a mast is carried away.   A temporary mast is called a jury-mast.

Jybe.—To shift a boom sail from one side of a vessel to the other.

Kedge-anchor.—An anchor with a shifting stock.

Kelson, or Keelson.—A strong piece running the whole length of the vessel's bottom, and to which the keel is attached ; it is in fact the back-bone of the hull.

Kevel-head, or Kevel.—A strong piece bolted to some part of the bulwarks, for belaying ropes to.

Knees.—Bent pieces used in boat-building for holding the planks together.

Knight-heads.—Strong timbers near the stem, on each side the bowsprit

Knot.—A mile as marked on the log-line.

The Sailing-Boat.

Lanyard.—A small rope, one end of which is made fast, whilst the other is used for securing anything to its place.

Lapstrake.—Signifies clench-built (vulgarly, clinker-built).

Larboard (now obsolete, *Port* being the term applied).—The left side of a vessel, looking forward.

Lay-to.—(*See* **Heave-to.**)

Lay-aloft.—An order for some part of the crew to go up the rigging.

Lead-line, or **Sounding-line.**—A small cord, with a lump of lead attached, for testing the depth of water; termed by the Anglo-Saxons *Sund-gyrd.*

Leading-wind.—A free wind : when the wind is abeam, or nearly right aft.

Lee.—The opposite side to that from which the wind blows.

Lee-board.—A board which turns on a pivot and is attached to the side of flat-bottomed vessels; it is lowered to prevent lee-way when the vessel is going to windward.

Leeches.—The outer edges of sails, fore and aft.

Lee-way.—The distance lost by a vessel drifting from the wind.

Leeward.—From the wind, the opposite to windward.

List.—To lay on one side by the pressure of the wind upon the sails.

Log-book.—A journal kept aboard ship, as to working the vessel, winds, weather, distances, &c.

Log, Log-line, and **Log-ship.**—Used for regulating and ascertaining the rate at which the ship sails.

Loggerhead.—A block with a small neck and larger head, for making ropes fast to.

Luff.—To bring the ship near to the wind by putting the helm *down*; the fore-leech of sails.

Luff-tackle.—A purchase comprising a double and a single-block.

Main sheet-hawse.—An iron rail secured to the deck at the stern for holding the main-sheet to its berth.

Marline.—A kind of spunyarn; small soft stuff used for lashings.

Marlinspike.—A wooden or iron pin gradually tapering to a sharp point : used for splicing ropes, and various other purposes.

Midships.—The middle or broadest part of a vessel.

Miss-stays.—When the helm is put down, and the vessel fails to come about to the other tack.

Mizzen.—A mizzen-mast or mizzen-sail is a small mast or sail abaft the main-mast.

Mooring.—Securing by two anchors placed in different directions.

Mouse.—To tie a small spunyarn round the hollow of a hook, to prevent it from slipping off.

Neap-tides.—Small or low tides, occurring at the middle of the moon's second and fourth quarters.

Nock.—The upper end forward of a boom sail.

Oakum.—A sort of tow, made by picking old rope to pieces.

Offing.—Distance from shore.

Outhauler.—A rope used for hauling out the tack of a jib or the clew of a boom sail.

Outrigger.—A spar for spreading an extra sail beyond the hull of the vessel. A boat with projecting rowlocks. Also a weight suspended over a vessel's side.

Overhaul.—To examine : to slack a rope through a tackle, by letting go the fall, and pulling on the leading parts.

Painter.—A rope secured in the bows of a boat, and used for making fast to a ship or otherwise.

Palm.—A sailmaker's thimble.

Parcelling.—Winding tarred canvas round a rope, to prevent its chafing.

Nautical Vocabulary.

Parral, or **Parrel.**—A band of rope, or collar, for securing a yard to a vessel's mast at its centre.

Pawl.—An iron bar for securing the windlass or capstan from turning back.

Pay-off.—To haul the jib or fore-sail aweather, for the purpose of turning the vessel's head from the wind. To *Pay-over*: to cover with pitch or tar. To *Pay-out*: to slack out a cable from the vessel.

Pazaree.—A rope secured to the clew of a fore-sail, and leading through a block on the boom; used for guyingout when scudding.

Peak.—The upper aft corner of a main-sail.

Pendant, or **Pennant.**—A long narrow streamer carried at the mast-head. A *Swallow-tailed Pennant* is called a *broad pennant*, and is only hoisted by the commodore of a club or fleet.

Pintle.—An iron bolt belonging to a rudder.

Port.—To port the helm is to put it to the left, or contrary way to starboard.

Port-hole.—A small opening in the bulwarks for pointing cannon.

Purchase.—A mechanical power applied to ropes rove through blocks, where extra power is required.

Quarter.—A term applied to that part of a vessel's sides which extends from the main channels to the stern.

Quarter-deck.—Applied to large vessels; that part of a vessel's upper deck abaft the main-mast.

Ratline.—A kind of rope ladder formed across the shrouds by means of a small line, called ratline.

Reaching.—Sailing on a side wind.

Reef.—To reduce a sail by tying up the reef-points.

Reef-earings.—Ropes attached to the reef-thimbles of a sail.

Reeve.—To pass a rope through a block or sheave-hole.

Rigging.—A general term applied to shrouds, stays, and other ropes of a vessel.
Running-rigging applies to such ropes as lead through blocks, and can be altered at pleasure.
Standing-rigging applies to shrouds and stays which seldom require hauling down or slacking.

Ring-Tail.—A light studding-sail set abaft the main-sail by a yard slung from the gaff-end.

Roach.—The fore-leech of a sail which appears to draw by the pressure of the wind.

Rolling-tackle.—An extra tackle for steadying sails in a heavy sea.

Rowlocks.—A rest for the oars of a boat to work in.

Run.—The hollow or narrow part of a vessel's stern.

Scantelise (erroneously *Scandalise*).—To scantelise the sail is to cause it to shiver in the wind: to take the power out of it.

Scud.—To run before the wind in a gale with little or no sail.

Scull.—To propel a boat by means of a single oar at the stern. A *Scull*: a small oar.

Scuppers.—Openings in the lower part of a vessel's bulwarks for the water to run off the deck.

Scuttle.—A small hatchway. To *Scuttle*: to bore holes in a vessel's bottom for the purpose of sinking her.

Scuttle-butt.—A cask kept on deck from which the water is taken for daily use.

Seize.—To secure by means of small stuff called seizings.

Selvagee.—A strong neat strap made by marling several rope yarns together.

Serve.—To wind small marline or spunyarn round ropes to prevent chafing.

Serving-board.—A small board or mallet for winding taut and putting on the service stuff.

Shackle.—An iron link, with a shifting pin, for connecting chains together.

Sheave.—The roller or wheel in a block on which the rope runs.

Sheave-hole.—A hole in a spar or block for a rope to reeve through.

Sheer.—The line of plank under a vessel's gunwale.

The Sailing-Boat.

Sheet.—A rope attached to the aft-clew of a sail, by which it is worked from one side to the other.

Sheet-anchor.—The largest anchor a vessel carries.

Shrouds.—Ropes for protecting the mast, leading from the mast-head to the sides of the vessel.

Skeet.—A scoop with a long handle, used for wetting sails.

Sky-scraper.—A light triangular sail used in large ships, properly called a sky-sail; it is set above the royal.

Snatch-block.—A single-block, with a hole in its side, for the bight of a rope to reeve through.

Snorter.—A small rope strop, into which the heel of a spreet is set.

Spencer.—A sail used in schooners, set on the fore-mast, with gaff, but no boom.

Splice.—To join the ends of two ropes by interweaving the strands.

Spreet.—A light spar for setting a sprit-sail.

Spring-a-leak.—To commence leaking.

Spring-a-luff.—To force a vessel closer to the wind.

Standing-rigging.—Shrouds and other ropes made fast and not very often requiring alteration.

Starboard.—The right-hand side of a vessel, looking forward.

Stay.—A rope for protecting the mast. To *Stay*: to tack a vessel, or put about. In *Stays*: the situation of a vessel at the instant of tacking, when all sail is shaking in the wind's eye.

Stay-sail.—Implies a sail set upon a stay.

Steerage.—That part of the vessel (between decks) forward of the cabin.

Stem.—The fore piece of a vessel, and to which the two sides are united.

Stern-board.—The back motion of a vessel moving stern foremost.

Stern-post.—That to which the rudder is fixed; the extreme end aft of a vessel.

Stern-sheets.—The aft part of a boat, abaft the rowers, intended for passengers.

Steve.—The angle of a bowsprit when raised more or less from the horizontal.

Stiff.—An essential quality in the hull of a sailing-vessel which enables large sails to be used in safety or without causing the vessel to list on one side.

Strand.—A yarn, or number of yarns, twisted together.

Strike.—To strike the mast is to lower it down into the boat.

Sweep.—A long oar of extra size, used in small sailing-vessels when becalmed or requiring to be forced ahead.

Tacking.—Turning, or beating, to windward. To *Tack* is to put a vessel about by putting the helm a-lee, thereby bringing it round on another tack. The tack of a main-sail is the corner nearest the goose-neck.

Tackle.—A purchase formed by a rope rove through a block or blocks.

Taffrail.—The rail, or top-piece, leading round a vessel's stern, level with the side rail above the bulwarks.

Tail-block.—A block with a rope spliced into, and hanging from, the end.

Tarpaulin.—Canvas rendered waterproof by being dressed with tar.

Taut.—To haul tight.

Tell-tale.—A compass suspended from the beams of a cabin.

Thimble.—A metal ring, with concave surface, used in sail-making and for splicing into rope-ends when required.

Throat.—That part of a sail where the brails catch and draw it close to the mast; the inner end of a gaff, near the jaws.

Thwarts (properly *Athwart*).—All seats across a boat are so called.

Tiller.—The lever by which the rudder is moved.

Topping-lift.—A rope leading from the upper part of the mast to the outer end of the boom, and by which the boom is topped up, or raised.

Nautical Vocabulary.

Traveller.—An iron or metal ring, with a hook below and an eye at top. A *Traveller* leads up and down the mast or along a bowsprit, for keeping the sail close to the spar.

Tressel-trees.—Strong pieces placed horizontally, and fore and aft of the mast-head, to support the cross-trees and top.

Trice-rope.—A rope used for hauling up the main-tack.

Trice-up.—To haul up the main-tack by means of the trice-line.

Trim.—To arrange the ballast, or cargo, in the most advantageous manner.

To *Trim* a sail is to set it in the best and most effective position with regard to the wind.

Truck.—The flat circular piece, on the very top of the topmast-head, through which signal-halliards are rove.

Trysail.—A fore-and-aft sail, set with boom and gaff at the main-mast of a brig ; also a small extra-stout gaff-sail used for cutters in a gale.

Tye.—A rope belonging to a boat's yard, with a hoisting tackle at one end.

Unbend.—To untie, to cast off.

Under way.—A vessel is under way when moving through the water by the action of the wind upon the sails.

Unship.—To take out of a vessel ; to remove out of its place.

Veer.—To turn a vessel from the wind and bring her round on another tack.

Waist.—The middle part of a vessel's deck, between the quarter-deck and forecastle.

Wake.—The track of a vessel in the water.

Wales.—Strong planks in the upper part of a vessel's sides running the whole length fore and aft.

Warp.—A strong rope for securing a vessel.

Wash-boards.—Shifting boards attached to the gunwales of boats for preventing the water from washing into the boat in a rough sea.

Weather-board.—That side of a ship which is to windward.

Weather-helm.—A vessel carries a weather-helm when the tiller requires to be slightly inclined towards the windward, to keep the vessel on her course and prevent her from flying into the wind.

Weigh anchor.—To draw the anchor up from the bottom.

Whip-purchase.—A purchase formed by a rope rove through a single-block.

To *Whip*, to secure the end of the rope from unravelling by winding twine round it.

Worming.—Winding cord, or marline, spirally between the strands of a rope, to give it a neat appearance.

Yard.—A spar, tapering at each end, for spreading a sail.

Yoke.—A top-piece, fitting on a boat's rudder, with lines attached for steering ; it is used chiefly for rowing-boats, instead of a tiller.

END OF PART IX.

INDEX.

	PAGE
A CHĒN Fisher-boats 481	
Amboina, Leper-lepers of . . . 482	
'America,' famous schooner-yacht . . 373	
American Boats 373 379	
Ancient Pleasure-boat 4	
Ancients, Boats of the 1	
Andaman Islanders' canoes 460	
Anglo-Bermudian rig 25	
Anglo-Chinese rig 222	
Anglo-Saxons, Boats of the 7	
Angulated jib 117	
Arab Batelle 428	
„ Pirate boats 430	
Arctic Regions, Boats of 532	

B AHIA Fruit-boat 510	
„ Market boat 509	
Baju and Balignini Pirate Prahus . . 468	
Balance-lug rig 48	
Balance-reef 158	
Balham (or Ballam) of Ceylon . . . 454	
Ballasting, Importance of 108	
„ improperly secured, Danger of . 154	
„ outside 107	
„ trimming, Unfair practice of . . 143	
(And see Trimming and Ballasting).	
Ballellangs of Sumatra 481	
Balsa (Peruvian) 507	
Balza (South American) 505	
Banca of Manilla 484	
Bangkok (Siam) Boat-sailing . . . 459	
Bangor Corinthian Sailing Club . . . 303	
Bantang of Sumatra 481	
Batelle, Arab 428	
Batelles of Bombay and Surat . . . 440	
Battens to sail, use of 119	
Battoes, American 389	
Baidars of the Kurilski Islands . . . 538	

	PAGE
Beacon-light, The 348	
Beeching, James (Prize Life-boat) . . . 55	
Belfast Lough (Yachting centre) . . . 302	
„ „ O.-D. Classes . . 302—314	
Bembridge Club boats 71	
Bermudian Sailing-boats 391	
Bhaulea (or Ganges boat) 443	
Bholco, The (of India) 445	
Birch-bark Canoes 384	
Bireme (of ancient Greece) 2	
'Blanketing' in yacht-racing . . . 144	
Blocks, Tackles and Purchases . . . 100	
Boat-racing . . . . . 139—147	
Boat-sailing . . . . . 102—161	
Boats of the Ancients 1	
„ „ different varieties of . 5	
Boëyer rig (Dutch) 421	
Bombay, Batelles of 440	
„ Cotton-boats 438	
„ Dinghy 439	
„ Fishing-boats 438	
„ Yachts 436	
Borneo and Celebes, Boats of . . . 466	
„ Proas (or Prahus) of . . . 468	
Bosphorus, Boats of the 425	
Brazilian Boats . . . . 507—512	
Bristol Channel O.-D. Class 253	
Britons, Ancient, Canoes of the . . . 8	
„ „ Coracles . . . 9	
Brixham Trawlers 333	
Bruni, Boats of 467	
Budjerows (or Bengalese Boats) . . . 440	
Bugala (or Bugla) 431	
Bugis (or Macassar Praus) 473	
Bulb-keels . . . . . 111—115	
Bunder Boat of India 445	
Burma, Boats of 457	
„ Pleasure-boats 458	
„ War-boats . . . . . ib.	

Index.

PAGE

CAIQUES, Turkish 425
  Canadian Birch-bark Canoes . . 385
    ,,   Yachts 381
Canoe Cruising Yawl 77
   ,,   rig (Rushton's) . . . 75
   ,,   Yachts 44, 79
Canoes of the Ancient Britons . . . 8
   ,,   Andaman Islanders . . . 460
   ,,   Birch-bark 384
   ,,   Brazilian 508
   ,,   Canadian Birch-bark . . 385
   ,,   Ceylon Sailing . . . 454
   ,,   Cruising 74
   ,,   Esquimaux 536
   ,,   Fiji Islands 487
   ,,   Friendly Islands . . . 490
   ,,   Fuegian 513
   ,,   Fulangese 494
   ,,   Kingsmill Island . . . 499
   ,,   Labrador 536
   ,,   Mitiaro 498
   ,,   New Caledonia . . . 496
   ,,   Nova Scotia 388
   ,,   Oregon Indians . . . 390
   ,,   Ottawa 387
   ,,   Paumotu Group . . . 503
   ,,   Penrhyn Islands . . . 495
   ,,   Prince Edward Island . . 388
   ,,   Salômon (or Solomon) Islands . . 493
   ,,   Samoa 496
   ,,   Sandwich Islands . . . 486
   ,,   Savage Island . . . 495
   ,,   Sooloo Islands . . . 469
   ,,   South American . . . 387
   ,,   Tahiti . . . 500—502
   ,,   Tonga Islands . . . 492
   ,,   Union Group . . . 498
   ,,   Vancouver Island . . 390
   ,,   Wytoohee . . . 504
Capsizing of Boats, causes of . . 150—154
Cat rig 376
Catamarans, Ceylon 451
   ,,   Madras 448
   ,,   Pernambuco . . . 511
Cedar Boats of the Willamette . . 389
Celebes, Boats of . . . 466
   ,,   Paduakans of . . . 472
Centre-board keels 90
Ceram, Praus of 481

PAGE

Ceylon Catamarans 451
   ,,   Sailing Canoes . . 454
Chariots, Sailing 350
Cheep Boats (of Bengal) . . . 445
China, Ice-yachting in . . . 361
Chinese Boats . . . 514—528
   ,,   Sailing-barrows . . . 351
Clyde, Firth of (yachting centre) . . 279
   ,,   Restricted Classes . 282—297
Cobles, Yorkshire . . . 55
Como, Lake, Boats of . . . 413
Coracles (early British) . . . 9
   ,,   of Ireland . . . 12
   ,,   of South Wales . . 11
   ,,   propulsion, mode of . . 12
Cork Harbour O.-D. Class . . 323
Cornish Fishing Luggers . . . 331
Corocora (or Kora-kora) . . . 475
Cruiser (30-rating) . . . 202
Cuberta of Brazil . . . 508
Curiosities of type and rig . . 222
Curragh, modern Irish . . . 12
Cutch Cotiyahs 443
Cutter rig 33

DAHABÉÉH (Nile boat) . . 368
  Dandy rig 43
Dempster's Triangular keel Yacht . 225
Dhoney (or Yatrawe) of Ceylon . . 452
Dhoneys of the Cavery (Mysore) . . 453
Dhow (see Bugala).
Dipping the lug 48
Doble (or Doval) . . . 340
Dory (American Boat) . . . 380
   ,,   (Riverside N.Y.) Class . . ib.
Double or twin Boats . . . 229
Dragon Boats of the Chinese . . 524
Drogue, The 156
Dröleens (Bray Sailing Club O.-D. Class) . 320
Dublin Bay 'A Class' (or 25-footers) . 315
Duck Boats (Chinese) . . . 526
Dutch Fishing Schuyts . . . 424
Dyak War-boats . . . 479

ECUADOR, Sailing-balzas of . . 505
  Egyptian Funambuli . . . 371
Egyptians (Ancient), Boats of the . . 364

	PAGE
Egyptians (Modern), Boats of the	367
Ellice Group Islands, Canoes of	499
Esquimaux Canoes	536

	PAGE
Faroë Islands Fishing-boats	419
Felucca, The	401
Fiji Islands Canoes	487
Fin-and-bulb keels	112
Finland Boats	420
Finmarken Fishing-boats	418
Fisheries, International Exhibition, 1883, advantages of	327
Fishing Boats (British)	327
,,　　Brixham Trawlers	333
,,　　Cornish Luggers	331
,,　　Doble (or Doval)	340
,,　　Irish (Greencastle)	338
,,　　Irish, Tory Island	14
,,　　Orkney and Shetland Isles	336
,,　　Peter-boat	339
,,　　Scotch (Zulu)	334
,,　　Sixern Yawls	337
,,　　Smack	328
,,　　South Coast	330
,,　　Yorkshire Fishing Coble	332
Flower Boats (Chinese)	520
Flying Proas of Ladrone Islands	462
Foreign and Colonial Boats and Canoes	362
Friendly Islands Canoes	490
Fruit Caïques of the Bosphorus	428
Fuegian Canoes	513
Fulangese Canoes	494
Furling the sails	138

	PAGE
Gale, Management of Sailing-boats in a	157
,,　Precautions in anticipation of a	158
,,　at sea, to ride out in safety	160
Galleys, Ancient	2
,,　of the Mediterranean	399
Ganges Rowing-boat	443
,,　Sailing-boat	441
Gelves (Red Sea Boats)	433
Geneva, Boats of Lake of	409
Gondolas of Venice	404
Gophers (Asiatic Boats)	432
Greeks, Boats of the early	2
Greencastle Yawls (Irish)	338

	PAGE
Greenland Boats	532
,,　the Kaiak (or Kyak)	534
,,　the Oomiak	532
Guaras (their use in steering rafts)	506
Gunning-punts	342
Gunter-rig	29

	PAGE
Half-decked Boats	17
Half-raters	177, *et seq.*
Hindustan, Boats of	434—454
Holland, Boats of	421—425
Holy Loch O.-D. Class	300
Howth Sailing Club O.-D. Class	325
Hoylake S.-C. Restricted Class	267
Hudson River Ice-Yacht Club	360
Humber Yawl Club, Sailing-boats	76
,,　　,,　　,,　Cruising Yawls	77

	PAGE
Ice-sailing Boats (Shuldham's)	356
,,　　,,　　,,　(American)	358
,,　　,,　Yachts (or rafts)	355
,,　　,,　　,,　(Russian)	361
Igarité of Brazil	508
Indian Sailing-boats	434
,,　Yachts	435
'Innellan' Corinthian O.-D. Class	295
'Insect' Class (Ulster)	315
Iroquois Indians' Canoes	384
Italian Lakes, Boats of	413
,,　Riviera, Boats of	408
Ivahahs of Tahiti	500

	PAGE
Japanese Boats	529—532
Java, Boats of	485
Jellores of Sumatra	480
'Jewel' Class (Belfast Lough O.-D.)	309

	PAGE
Kaiak (or Kyak)	534
Kalatches (pig-skin rafts)	432
Kamtschatka, Boats of	538
Keels, Centre-board	90
,,　Drop oldin	95
,,　Fin-and-bulb	111
,,　Revolving	90

Index.

	PAGE
Keels, Sliding	90
Kei Islands Canoes	477
Ketch rig	40
Kingsmill Island Canoes	499
Kolay, The (of Achēn)	481
Kurilski Islands, Boats of	538
Kweikong (China), Boats of	529

	PAGE
LABRADOR Canoes	536
Laccadive Islands, Boats of	457
Ladrone Islands, Flying Proas of	462
Langady, The (of Nursapore)	452
Latine rig	60
,, Indian	435
,, Mediterranean	399—403
,, Norfolk	63
,, Strangford	65
Lead ballast, Advantages of	111
Leper-lepers of Amboina	482
Liburnian Galleys	2
Liftable bulb-keels	116
Lucerne, Boats of Lake	412
Lugger-rig, The	47
,, Balance	48
,, Three-masted	49
,, Split	50
Lyre tanjong (Malay rig)	471

	PAGE
MACASSAR Praus	473
Madeira, Boats of the Island of	398
Madras Catamarans	448
,, Fishing Catamarans	450
,, Sailing Catamarans	451
Madura, Boats of	485
Maggiore, Italian Lake, Boat-sailing on	414
Malay Archipelago, Boats of the	462
,, Pirate Prahus	480
Maldive and Laccadive Boats	457
Maltese Galley	399
Management of Sailing Boats	102
,, setting sail	122
,, reefing	123
,, sailing to windward	126
,, reaching and sailing on a bow-line	131

	PAGE
Management (continued)—	
,, running before the wind	132
,, boat in stays	135
,, bringing up at moorings	136
,, furling the sails	138
,, in squalls	148
,, causes of boats capsizing	150
,, in a gale	157
,, precautions in anticipation	158
,, riding out a gale at sea	160
,, of rowing boats in heavy seas	155
Mandarins' Boats (Chinese)	521
Manilla Bancas	484
,, Saraboas	ib.
Massoolah Surf Boats	447
Matabello Islands, Praus of	481
Matapa (of East Africa)	432
Match sailing	139
Measurement, effect of modern rules as to	163
Mediterranean, Boats of the	399—409
Mindanao Pleasure Proa	483
Mistico (or Mystaco)	428
Mitiaro, Canoes of Island of	498
Model Yachts and Clubs	106
Mohican rig	76
Mohr Punkee (or Peacock Boat)	445
Montaria of Brazil	507
Moorings, Bringing up at	136
Muchoo (or Muchwa)	445

	PAGE
NAUTICAL Vocabulary	540—547
Nautilus rig	231
New Brighton S. C. Restricted Class	269
New Caledonia and Loyalty Island Sailing Canoes	496
Newport (or Cat) rig	376
Nile boatmen	370
Nile Boats, various classes of	367
Nordland Fishing-boats	417
Norfolk Latine rig	63
,, Wherries	66
Norway Praäm	417
,, Yawls	414
Nova Scotia, Birch-bark Canoes of	388
Nursapore, Native Ferry-boat of	452

Index.

		PAGE
ONE-DESIGN Class, Suggestions on the formation of a	. . . .	238
One-Design and Restricted Classes .	. .	233
,, Belfast Lough	. . . .	302
,, Bristol Channel	. . .	253
,, Clyde .	. . . .	282
,, Cork Harbour	. . .	323
,, Dròleen	. . . .	320
,, Dublin Bay	. . . .	315
,, Holy Loch	. . . .	300
,, Howth Sailing Club	. . .	325
,, Hoylake	. . . .	267
,, Innellan Corinthian	. . .	295
,, New Brighton	. . . .	269
,, Orford White Wings	. . .	257
,, Redwings (I. of W.)	. . .	242
,, Solent	. . . .	239
,, Solent Sea Birds .	. . .	244
,, Southport Corinthian	. . .	261
,, Tay	. . . .	298
,, Trent Valley .	. . . .	255
,, Water Wags	. . .	316
,, West Lancashire	. . . .	262
,, Western (25 ft.) .	. . .	247
,, Yorkshire.	. . . .	259
One-raters (Yarafts) .	. . .	188 *et seq.*
Oomiak (of Greenland) .	. . .	532
Oregon Indians, Canoes of .	. . .	390
Orford White Wings O.-D. Class	. . .	257
Orkney and Shetland Isles, Fishing Boats	.	336
Osiers, boats made of	. . . .	10
Otaheite (see Tahiti)		
Outlagers and Outriggers	. . .	468
,, ,, distinction as to, note (4)	482
Outriggers .	. . 451, 456, 460, 464, 486
,, double	. . . .	469, 480
PACIFIC Islands (see Canoes).		
Paduakans of Celebes	. . .	472
Pahies of Tahiti .	. . . .	500
Panchallangs of Sumatra	. . .	481
Panchway (of the Ganges)	. . .	442
Pangues (of the Philippines)	. . .	483
Papyrus, Boats made of	. . .	364
Parinda Boats	. . . .	445
Pattamar (of Hindustan)	. . .	443
Paumotu Group, Double Canoe of the	. .	503
Peacock Boat	. . . .	445

		PAGE
Penrhyn Islands Canoes .	. . . .	495
Pernambuco, Catamarans of	. . .	511
Peruvian Balsas	. . . .	507
Peter Boat, The .	. . . .	339
Philippine Islands, Boats of	. .	482—484
Pilot Luggers	. . . .	16, 20, 47
Pole-masted Rig	. . . .	35
Polynesia and the Malay Archipelago, Boats of	462
Portuguese Sailing-Boats	. . .	397
Praäms, Norwegian	. . . .	417
Prahus of Borneo	. . . .	468
Prince Edward Island, Birch-bark Canoes of.	388
Proas, Flying (Ladrone Islands)	. . .	462
Problem (Dempster's triangular keel-yacht) .	225
Punjaub, Boats of the .	. . . .	435
Punts for Wild-fowl Shooting .	. . .	342
,, Sailing	. . . .	344
QUANT, Norfolk	. . .	67
RACING (small Yachts and Yarafts)	.	140
,, Cutter	. . . .	141
,, old type (1850)	. . .	143
(And see ' *Boat-racing*,' also ' *Match-sailing*.')		
Radix folding centre-plate	. . .	73, 95
Rating (see Rules of)		
Reaching and sailing on a bowline	. .	131
Redwing O.-D. Class	. . . .	242
Reefing the sails .	. . .	123
Restricted Classes (see One-Design Classes)		
Revolving keel .	. . . .	91
Revolving rig .	. . . . .	82
,, rigged boats, management of	.	87
Rig, varieties of—		
,, Anglo-Bermudian	. . .	25
,, Anglo-Chinese	. . .	222
,, Bermudian .	. . .	393
,, Boëyer (Dutch)	. . .	421
,, Cat (American)	. . .	376
,, Cutter .	. . .	33
,, Dandy .	. . .	43
,, Ketch .	. . .	40
,, Latine .	. . .	60
,, Lugger .	. . .	46
,, Mohican .	. . .	76
,, Nautilus .	. . . .	231

Index.

		PAGE
Rig, varieties of (*continued*)—		
„ Newport, or Cat rig	. .	376
„ Revolving	. . .	81
„ Schooner	. . .	36
„ Settee	. . .	27
„ Sliding-gunter	. .	28
„ Sloop	. . .	32
„ Solent	. .	68, 69
„ Spiegel (Dutch)	. .	423
„ Sprit-sail and foresail	. .	21
„ Umbrella	. . .	230
„ Una	. .	30, 376
„ Yawl	. . .	41
Rigging	. .	98, 120
„ screws	. . .	121
Roller boom	. . .	126
„ fore-sail	. . .	125
Rolling the sails, reefing by	. .	ib.
Roman Galley	. . .	7
Romans, Boats of the	. .	2
Ropes (in rigging)	. . .	98
„ precautions as to	. .	153
Row and Sail Boat (combined)	.	17
Rowing, ancient practice of	. .	3
„ boats, management of in a heavy sea		155
Rudder, revolving or drop	. .	95
Rules of rating and measurement	.	164
„ „ „ effect of		165
„ „ „ (International)		166
Running before the wind	. .	133
Russian Ice Yachts.	. .	361
SAFETY and Seaworthiness, essentials of	.	167
Sailing Chariots	. .	350
Sailing Cycles	. . .	353
Sailing terms explained	. .	98
Sailing to windward	. .	126
Sails and sail-fitting	. .	116
Salômon (or Solomon) Islands Canoes	.	493
Samoan Canoes	. . .	496
Sampan (Chinese)	. .	516
Sandwich Islands' Canoes	. .	486
Saraboa of Manilla	. .	484
Savage Island Canoes	. .	495
Schooner rig	. . .	36
Schuyt, Dutch Fishing-	. .	424
Scottish (Zulu) Fishing-boats	. .	334
Scudding	. . .	132

		PAGE
Sea Birds, Solent O.-D. Class	. .	244
Sea Bird Class, Belfast Lough	. .	306
„ (Royal Tay Y. C.)	. .	299
„ (West Lancashire Y. C.)	.	263
Settee rig	. . .	27
Setting sail	. . .	122
Shallow type of Sailing-boats	. .	168
Sharpey (American type of boat)	.	377
Shooting Yachts and Boats	. .	341
Shuldham's Land-sailing boats	.	352
„ Ice-sailing boats	. .	356
„ Revolving rig	.	81—89
Sioux Indians, Canoes for rice gathering	.	386
Sixern Fishing Yawls	. .	337
Skin Boats of Peru	. .	507
„ of the Tchuktchi	.	537
Sliding gunter rig	. .	28
Sliding keels	. . .	90
Sloop rig	. . .	32
Small Racing-yachts and Yarafts	.	162
Small raters and their dangers	.	173
„ different classes of	.	176
Solent Classes Racing Association	.	176
Solent O.-D. Class	. .	239
Solent rig	. .	68, 69
Solent Sea (an ideal yachting locality)	.	175
Solent Sea Birds (O.-D. Class)	.	244
Sondmore Yawls	. .	416
South American Birch-bark Canoes	.	387
„ Sailing Balzas	.	505
Sooloo (or Sulu) Islands Canoes	.	469
South Coast Fishing Boats	. .	330
Southport Corinthian O.-D. Class	.	261
Spiegel rig (Dutch)	. .	423
Split-lug rig	. . .	50
Sprit-sail and fore-sail rig	. .	21
Squalls, management of sailing-boats in	.	148
„ preparations for	.	149
Square-rigged schooner	. .	38
Stability of Sailing-boats	. .	106
Start, the (in match-sailing)	.	139
Stays, boat in	. . .	135
„ missing	. . .	ib.
Stone-dredging Boats	. .	329
Strangford Latine rig	. .	65
Sumatra, Boats of	. .	480
Swan Boats	. . .	227
Swiss Lakes, Boats of	.	409—413

Index.

	PAGE
TACKLES, Purchases and Blocks	100
Tahiti, Boats of	500
Tambangan (or Sourabaya passage-boat)	485
Tartar Galley	470
Tay O.-D. Classes	298
Tchuktchi Skin Canoes	537
Teignmouth Dinghy Class	251
Thun, Lake, Boat of	412
Tigris, Boats of the	432
Tocantiins and River Mojū Canoes	508
Tonga Islands Canoes	492
Tonnage as a basis for rating	168
Tory Island Fishing Canoe	14
Trent Valley O.-D. Class	255
Triangular Keel Boat	225
Trim of Sailing-boat, its importance	108
Trimming and Ballasting	108
Tripod Mast of Tartar Galley	470
Trireme (ancient Greek boat)	2
Truant (famous American Sailing-boat)	93
Turkish Caïques	425
Twin Sailing Boats	229
ULSTER Sailing Club 'Insect' Class	315
Ulysses' Boat	1
Umbrella Boat	230
Una rig	31
Union Group Islands Canoes	498

	PAGE
VANCOUVER Island Canoes	390
Venetian Gondolas	404
WATER WAGS (O.-D. Class)	316
West Lancashire O.-D. Classes	262
West Lancashire 'Seabird' Class	263
West of England Conference	246
Western, 25 ft. O.-D. Class	247
Wild Fowl Shooting Boats	341—346
„ Sailing Punt	344
Willamette Cedar Boats	389
Windermere Lake and Yachts	273
Windward, sailing to	126
Wytoohee Canoes	504
YACHT and Boat-racing	139
Yarafts	163—164
Yarmouth Beach Boats	54
„ Salvage Yawls	52
Yatrawe (or Dhoney) of Ceylon	452
Yawl rig	41
Yawls, South Coast	43
Yorkshire Coble	55
Yorkshire O.-D. Class	259
ZANGADA of Pernambuco	511
Zurich Lake, Boats of	411

THE END.

(continued from front flap)

SHIPWRECKS IN THE AMERICAS, Robert F. Marx. (25514-X) $12.95

AMERICAN MERCHANT SHIPS, 1850–1900, Frederick C. Matthews. (25538-7) $11.95

THE PIRATES OWN BOOK: AUTHENTIC NARRATIVES OF THE MOST CELEBRATED SEA ROBBERS, Marine Research Society. (27607-4) $10.95

DONALD MCKAY AND HIS FAMOUS SAILING SHIPS, Richard C. McKay. (28820-X) $13.95

THE FABULOUS INTERIORS OF THE GREAT OCEAN LINERS IN HISTORIC PHOTOGRAPHS, William H. Miller, Jr. (24756-2) $13.95

THE FIRST GREAT OCEAN LINERS IN PHOTOGRAPHS, 1897–1927, William H. Miller, Jr. (24574-8) $14.95

GREAT CRUISE SHIPS AND OCEAN LINERS FROM 1954 TO 1986: A PHOTOGRAPHIC SURVEY, William H. Miller, Jr. (25540-9) $12.95

THE GREAT LUXURY LINERS, 1927–1952, William H. Miller, Jr. (24056-8) $14.95

MODERN CRUISE SHIPS, 1965–1990: A PHOTOGRAPHIC RECORD, William H. Miller, Jr. (26753-9) $13.95

PICTORIAL ENCYCLOPEDIA OF OCEAN LINERS, 1860–1993, William H. Miller, Jr. (28137-X) $16.95

PICTURE HISTORY OF THE ITALIAN LINE, 1932–1977, William H. Miller, Jr. (40489-7) $16.95

STEAMBOATING ON THE UPPER MISSISSIPPI, William J. Petersen. (28844-7) $15.95

AROUND THE WORLD SINGLE-HANDED: THE CRUISE OF THE "ISLANDER," Harry Pidgeon. (25946-3) $8.95

SAILING ALONE AROUND THE WORLD, Joshua Slocum. (20326-3) $6.95

VOYAGE OF THE LIBERDADE, Joshua Slocum. (40022-0) $5.95

THE ARTS OF THE SAILOR: KNOTTING, SPLICING AND ROPEWORK, Hervey Garrett Smith. (26440-8) $8.95

ADVENTURES AT SEA IN THE GREAT AGE OF SAIL, Elliot Snow (ed.). (25177-2) $11.95

Paperbound unless otherwise indicated. Prices subject to change without notice. Available at your book dealer or write for free catalogues to Dept. 23, Dover Publications, Inc., 31 East 2nd Street, Mineola, N.Y. 11501. Please indicate field of interest. Each year Dover publishes over 200 books on fine art, music, crafts and needlework, antiques, languages, literature, children's books, chess, cookery, nature, anthropology, science, mathematics, and other areas.

Manufactured in the U.S.A.

HENRY COLEMAN FOLKARD
SAILING BOATS
FROM AROUND THE WORLD
THE CLASSIC 1906 TREATISE

This comprehensive, profusely illustrated volume by a noted British authority documents the state of the sailing arts at the beginning of the 20th century. In these pages readers will find a detailed, informative instructional manual for both beginning and experienced sailors, a review of the great variety of small vessels then in popular use, an overview of the history of boats and sailing, a survey of the remarkable diversity of boat types from around the world, and a nautical vocabulary.

Nearly 100 pages are devoted to classes of racing boats of the period, followed by a section on work boats. Of particular interest is the section in Part IV ("Small Racing Yachts"), *Curiosities of Type and Rig,* which describes odd and experimental vessels from a hundred years ago, ranging from the triangular-keel yacht *Problem* to boats shaped like swans with winglike sails.

Complete with line drawings, photographs, and a wealth of body, deck, and sail plans, this definitive sixth edition of a classic treatise will be of special interest to small-boat builders and ship modelers. However, its vast amount of information and detailed pictorial documentation are certain to delight any maritime enthusiast.

Unabridged Dover (2000) republication of *The Sailing Boat* as published by Chapman and Hall, Ltd., London, 1906 (6th edition). Nautical vocabulary. Index. Over 380 black-and-white illustrations and photographs. xx+556pp. 6½ x 9¼. Paperbound.

ALSO AVAILABLE

THE BOOK OF OLD SHIPS: FROM EGYPTIAN GALLEYS TO CLIPPER SHIPS, Henry B. Culver. 256pp. 5⅜ x 8½. 27332-6 Pa. $8.95

THE SEAMAN'S FRIEND: A TREATISE ON PRACTICAL SEAMANSHIP, Richard Henry Dana, Jr. 240pp. 5⅜ x 8. 29918-X Pa. $8.95

Free Dover Complete Catalog (59069-0) available upon request.

ISBN 0-486-41099-4

90000

9 780486 410999

$19.95 IN USA